T0293765

A THIRD PATH

HISTORIES OF ECONOMIC LIFE

Jeremy Adelman, Sunil Amrith, Emma Rothschild,
and Francesca Trivellato, Series Editors

A Third Path: Corporatism in Brazil and Portugal by Melissa Teixeira

Power and Possession in the Russian Revolution by Anne O'Donnell

Toward a Free Economy: Swatantra and Opposition Politics in Democratic India
by Aditya Balasubramanian

No Return: Jews, Christian Usurers, and the Spread of Mass Expulsion in
Medieval Europe by Rowan Dorin

Desert Edens: Colonial Climate Engineering in the Age of Anxiety
by Philipp Lehmann

Distant Shores: Colonial Encounters on China's Maritime Frontier
by Melissa Macauley

A Velvet Empire: French Informal Imperialism in the Nineteenth Century
by David Todd

Making It Count: Statistics and Statecraft in the Early People's Republic of China
by Arunabh Ghosh

Empires of Vice: The Rise of Opium Prohibition across Southeast Asia by Diana S. Kim

Pirates and Publishers: A Social History of Copyright in Modern China
by Fei-Hsien Wang

Sorting Out the Mixed Economy: The Rise and Fall of Welfare and Developmental
States in the Americas by Amy C. Offner

Red Meat Republic: A Hoof-to-Table History of How Beef Changed America
by Joshua Specht

The Promise and Peril of Credit: What a Forgotten Legend about Jews and Finance
Tells Us about the Making of European Commercial Society by Francesca
Trivellato

A People's Constitution: The Everyday Life of Law in the Indian Republic by Rohit De

A Local History of Global Capital: Jute and Peasant Life in the Bengal Delta by
Tariq Omar Ali

A Third Path

CORPORATISM IN BRAZIL
AND PORTUGAL

MELISSA TEIXEIRA

PRINCETON UNIVERSITY PRESS
PRINCETON & OXFORD

Published by Princeton University Press
41 William Street, Princeton, New Jersey 08540
99 Banbury Road, Oxford OX2 6JX

press.princeton.edu

All Rights Reserved

Library of Congress Cataloging-in-Publication Data

Names: Teixeira, Melissa, 1986– author
Title: A third path: corporatism in Brazil and Portugal / Melissa Teixeira.
Description: Princeton: Princeton University Press, 2024 | Series: Histories
    of economic life | Includes bibliographical references and index.
Identifiers: LCCN 2023023931 (print) | LCCN 2023023932 (ebook) |
    ISBN 9780691191027 (hardback) | ISBN 9780691258157 (ebook)
Subjects: BISAC: HISTORY / Latin America / South America |
    POLITICAL SCIENCE / Political Ideologies / Capitalism
Classification: LCC HC187.T428 2024 (print) | LCC HC187 (ebook) |
    DDC 330.98—dc23/eng/20230823
LC record available at https://lccn.loc.gov/2023023931
LC ebook record available at https://lccn.loc.gov/2023023932

British Library Cataloging-in-Publication Data is available

Editorial: Priya Nelson, Morgan Spehar, and Emma Wagh
Production Editorial: Theresa Liu
Jacket/Cover Design: Katie Osborne
Production: Lauren Reese
Publicity: William Pagdatoon
Copyeditor: Cindy Milstein

Jacket image: Center for Research and Documentation of the Contemporary History of Brazil, Fundação Getúlio Vargas, Rio de Janeiro

This book has been composed in Classic Arno

10 9 8 7 6 5 4 3 2 1

CONTENTS

Acknowledgments vii

List of Abbreviations xiii

Introduction   1

PART I

1 Crisis   25

2 Experiments in Corporatist Constitutions   59

PART II

3 Corporatist Economics and the Third Path   97

4 Just Price and Production   130

5 Popular and Political Economy   164

PART III

6 Wartime Economics   191

7 Corporatism to Planning   226

Conclusion   257

Notes 265

Bibliography 321

Index 357

ACKNOWLEDGMENTS

THE WRITING OF THIS BOOK—much like the project itself—has unfolded across many cities and countries. I begin with a few words of gratitude for the individuals and institutions that have supported me along the way.

First, thanks go to three mentors who have each been a constant source of encouragement and model of how to be a scholar-teacher. Jeremy Adelman has been beyond generous in seeing the full potential of this project. He has time and again guided me in thinking globally and boldly about the ideas discussed in this book, while always encouraging me to stay true to my instincts and priorities as a historian. He has also been my champion in all areas of my professional growth, with his optimism assuring me along the way that I was on the right track, even when I was not so sure myself. Emma Rothschild is the reason I became a historian, thanks to her unfailing support of me as a scholar, teacher, and person over the past fifteen years. She is the sharpest reader of my work and model for how to continuously expand the nature of economic history. Barbara Weinstein has given me a singular model for how to combine intellectual rigor with warmth and compassion. She has always been generous with her time and feedback, and discussing Brazil—past and present—with her has directly informed so many of my own research commitments.

At the University of Pennsylvania, I am grateful to work alongside a supportive group of scholars and teachers. Department of History chairs Antonio Feros, Sophia Rosenfeld, and Beth Wenger have consistently gone above and beyond with their support of junior faculty. My colleagues have been my closest interlocuters as I finished this book, and also provided many welcome diversions with happy hour drinks and by watching soccer games. I particularly thank Oscar Aguirre-Mandujano, Eiichiro Azuma, Cheikh Babou, Mia Bay, Anne Berg, Warren Breckman, Kathleen Brown, Lee Cassanelli, Brent Cebul, Roger Chartier, Frederick Dickinson, Jared Farmer, Siyen Fei, Roquinaldo Ferreira, Marc Flandreau, Sarah Barringer Gordon, Sarah Gronningsater, Emma Hart, Peter Holquist, Firoozeh Kashani-Sabet, Ada Kuskowski, Walter Licht, Ann Moyer, Benjamin Nathans, Marcy Norton, Kathy Peiss, Eve Troutt Powell, Ramya Sreenivasan, Karen Tani, Josh Teplitsky, and Secil Yilmaz. I am especially grateful to Ann Farnsworth-Alvear for her continued mentorship—and offering to read and comment on the manuscript, providing vital feedback at key stages of the writing process. Amy Offner read and offered feedback on the entire manuscript too, and I remain beyond grateful for her moral and practical advice. In the history department, Octavia Carr, Yvonne Fabella, Angela Faranda, Joan Plonski, and Chris Sabella make the research and teaching we do possible.

At Penn, I have also benefited from conversations with colleagues in other departments and fields. Annette Lareau and Emily Steiner have been exceptional mentors to junior scholars like myself. A special thanks to the Wolf Humanities Center and 2020–21 fellows who provided much-needed intellectual connection (over Zoom) during the pandemic. I am especially fortunate to be a member of the Center for Latin American and Latinx Studies. Thank you to Catherine Bartch and Tulia Falleti for inviting me to be part of so many wonderful events as well as their support of my teaching and research. Thanks, too, to Michael Hanchard and Zita Nunes for the continued research collaborations and their friendship. At Penn Libraries, I am indebted to all the librarians who have tracked down books for me, especially to Joseph Holub and Nicholas Okrent.

The Joint Center for History and Economics at Cambridge University and Harvard University has been my second intellectual home. From my studies at the University of Cambridge to the Prize Fellowship in Economics, History, and Politics at Harvard University, the center has been the space where I have workshopped chapters, organized conferences, and made deeply supportive friendships. Emily Gauthier, Inga Huld Markan, and Jennifer Nickerson make all of these collaborations and events possible. Thanks to the wider center network for reading and engaging with my work over the years, including Sunil Amrith, Aditya Balasubramanian, Abhijit Banerjee, Elsa Génard, Namrata Kala, Diana Kim, Ian Kumekawa, Jonathan Levy, Jacob Moscona, Kalyani Ramnath, Pedro Ramos Pinto, Pernille Røge, Amartya Sen, David Todd, Francesca Trivellato, Richard Tuck, and Lola Zappi. I am especially grateful for the writing group formed with prize fellows Shane Bobrycki, Paige Glotzer, and Anne Ruderman; thank you for workshopping several chapters in this book.

I began research for this project as a graduate student at Princeton University and remain indebted to its faculty, staff, and vibrant graduate community. Daniel Rodgers agreed, from early on, to invest in a project both thematically and geographically quite removed from his own area of research. For this, I remain immensely grateful. For their comments, questions, reading suggestions, and encouragement, I am grateful to have studied and worked with Vera Candiani, Mariana Candido, Bruno Carvalho, Hendrik Hartog, Harold James, Steven Kotkin, Pedro Meira Monteiro, and Philip Nord. Rob Karl has been a mentor and friend throughout this process. His commitment to teaching and his students is an inspiration, and he has provided essential feedback on both the dissertation and book, not least with help in designing the two maps featured. My graduate school experience was marked by camaraderie and intellectual exchange thanks to Diana Andrade, Teresa Davis, Rohit De, Catherine Evans, Margarita Fajardo, Cristina Florea, Christopher Florio, Sergio Galaz García, Evan Hepler-Smith, Molly Lester, Jessica Mack, Martin Marimón, Iwa Narwocki, Padraic Scanlan, Marcia Schenck, Humberto Schwarzbeck Aguirre, Fidel Tavarez, Paula Vedoveli, and Alden Young. From Princeton to Philadelphia, Alex Chase-Levenson and Meg Leja have been true and trusted friends, offering words of encouragement and pragmatic advice. Special thanks is owed to Valeria López Fadul for her unwavering friendship and generous readings of many chapters in this book. And from Princeton to Rio de Janeiro, Lisbon, and Cambridge, Carolina Sá Carvalho and Nathaniel Wolfson have become family.

I am particularly grateful to belong to a community of Brazil and Latin America scholars who have commented on conference papers, read chapters, and discussed the book's ideas and methods with me. Special thanks to Celso Castilho, Sidney Chalhoub, Amy Chazkel, Marshall Eakin, Federico Finchelstein, Brodwyn Fischer, John French, Casey Lurtz, Gillian McGillivray, Elena Schneider, and Christy Thornton. Researching this book in archives in Brazil and Portugal, moreover, was a far more rewarding process (and far less lonely than one might expect) thanks to Genevieve Dempsey, Rosanna Dent, Aiala Levy, Alexander Ponsen, Gabriel Rocha, and Marcio Siwi.

The transnational scope of this project would not be possible without generous support from several research institutions. At Penn, both the university and School of Arts and Sciences has offered generous research support and sabbatical leave that made it possible for me to complete this book. I am especially thankful to the Fulbright Commission, which sponsored a yearlong research trip to Brazil in 2014. The History Project (supported by the Joint Center for History and Economics and Institute for New Economic Thinking), Fundação Calouste Gulbenkian, and Fundação Luso-Americana made possible several research trips to Portugal. At Princeton, the Department of History alongside Princeton Latin American Studies and Princeton International and Regional Studies made possible research trips to Portugal and Brazil at the earliest stages of this project. Additional grants like the Whiting Fellowship in the Humanities and Bassi Scholarship have supported me at different stages. Finally, my path to becoming a historian began with the Thouron Award, which made it possible for me to study at the University of Cambridge from 2008 to 2009. A special thanks is owed to the Thouron family—Jan, Rachel, and Rupert—and ever-expanding network of Thouron alums for their continued support.

In Brazil and Portugal, I benefited from the generosity of many colleagues and friends who invited me to partake in the academic life of their universities as well as helped me find my way in local archives and historiographical debates. In Lisbon, I remain especially grateful to António Costa Pinto, who supported me as a visiting scholar at the Instituto de Ciências Sociais, and invited me to be part of his ever-expanding and multinational network of scholars working on corporatism. Thank you for the invitations to workshops, many books sent my way, and invaluable feedback offered on the manuscript. In Lisbon and Coimbra, Pedro Cardim, José Luís Cardoso, Rita Almeida de Carvalho, Dulce Freire, and Álvaro Garrido also provided invaluable suggestions on necessary readings and how to navigate archives. In Brazil, Lilia Moritz Schwarcz supported this project in its earliest stages and has been so generous with her suggestions. André Botelho has been a trusted friend and interlocutor since the beginning of this project. I am especially grateful for his invitations to seminars and the many conversations we have shared in seminars and over beers about some of the central intellectuals featured in this book—and the lasting importance of these figures for thinking about Brazilian politics today. Lastly, an enormous debt of gratitude is owed to Luciano Aronne de Abreu, Bruno Biasetto, Nathalia Henrich, Ângela de Castro Gomes, Francisco Palomanes Martinho, Marco Aurélio Vannucchi Leme de Mattos, and Luís Rosenfeld for inviting me to be part of their network of researchers working on corporatism. At workshops, on conference panels, and in informal conversations, I first tested the ideas and arguments presented in this book with them, and the book is stronger thanks to their questions, comments, and critiques.

This book would not be possible without the help of countless librarians and archivists in Rio de Janeiro, Niterói, Brasília, São Paulo, Lisbon, and Coimbra who went above and beyond to help me gain access to documents and books. In particular, Odette Martins at the Arquivo Nacional do Torre do Tombo in Lisbon, Portugal made it possible for me to view documentation not yet cataloged or opened to the public. Similarly, the staff of the Casa Oliveira Vianna in Niterói, Brazil, allowed me to research at this site despite closures, and were so generous and flexible with their schedules.

I am especially grateful to the editors of the History of Economic Life Series at Princeton University Press for their continued support of this project. Editor Priya Nelson has been so encouraging and helpful in shaping the book, and I am thankful to have the support of Emma Wagh and Theresa Liu during the final stages of production. Beyond PUP, thanks also to development editor Pamela Haag, who helped refine my voice and give the book a clearer structure.

I am grateful to my friends and family for forgiving my long absences during research trips, offering words of encouragement, and drawing me away from writing for much-needed diversions. To friends in Rio de Janeiro—especially Clarice—who invited me to stay in their homes during research trips, and made sure that I made room for beer and samba, thank you. Daniella was my first roommate in Rio de Janeiro, and is still one of my truest and oldest friends. To so many longtime and recent friends, in and beyond Philadelphia—especially

Anna, Ashley, Caroline, Elisa, Natalie, Natasha, Rebecca, and Vicky—thank you for asking about the book and also talking about anything but the book. My family—Tia Esmeralda and my late Tio João; Tio Artur and Tia São; and my cousins Andie, John, Logan, Melanie, Sidney, Steven, and Suzy—is my biggest source of constancy and encouragement. In Lisbon, Maria Alice and Tony have always given me a home away from home during research trips, alongside Luca, Luna, Quelia, and Ricardo.

Last and foremost, this book is dedicated to my parents, Carlos and Maria. This book would not be possible without them. They have consistently prioritized my education, even though they never had access to even a fraction of the educational opportunities that I have been afforded. They also never allowed their US-born daughter to forget how to speak Portuguese and took me often to Portugal so that I could develop my own ties to the country. Whether they knew it at the time, these experiences inspired a curiosity in me about the history of the Portuguese-speaking world that has sustained this project. Above all, I thank them for their unconditional love and support.

ABBREVIATIONS

AIB   Ação Integralista Brasileira (Brazilian Integralist Action)

CEPAL   Comisión Económica para América Latina y el Caribe (Economic Commission for Latin America and the Caribbean)

CFCE   Conselho Federal de Comércio Exterior (Federal Council of Foreign Trade)

CME   Coordenação da Mobilização Econômica (Coordination for Economic Mobilization)

DOPS   Departamento de Ordem Política e Social (Department of Political and Social Order)

IBGE   Instituto Brasileiro de Geografia e Estatística (Brazilian Institute of Geography and Statistics)

NST   Tribunal de Segurança Nacional (National Security Tribunal)

MAP 1. Brazil. Created by Girmaye Misgna, mapping and geospatial data librarian, University of Pennsylvania Library.

Atlantic
Ocean
Minho River
Bragança
Viana do
Castelo
Braga
NORTHERN
Douro River
Vila Real
Porto
Douro River
Azores
Aveiro
Viseu
Guarda
Madeira
Coimbra
CENTRAL
Castelo
Branco
Leiria
Spain
Tejo River
Santarém
Portalegre
LISBON
Guadiana River
Lisbon
Setúbal
ALENTEJO
Evora
N
Beja
Lisbon (National capital)
District capital
District boundary
Regional boundary
Guadalquivir River
ALGARVE
Faro
Gulf of
Cadiz
0
42.5
85 Mi
0
35
70
140 Km

MAP 2. Portugal. Created by Girmaye Misgna, mapping and geospatial data librarian, University of Pennsylvania Library.

A THIRD PATH

Introduction

IN AUGUST 1941, Marcello Caetano (1906–80), Portuguese law professor and future dictator, arrived in Rio de Janeiro for a conference to commemorate recent constitutional innovations in Brazil and Portugal. In the 1930s, both nations eschewed liberal and laissez-faire conventions to adopt constitutions that overturned protections for individual liberties and formally installed a corporatist system that emboldened state powers to regulate labor relations and market competition. It was an unusual moment to celebrate constitutional matters: World War II was a struggle between democracy and authoritarianism, and it had become increasing difficult for the dictators in power in Brazil and Portugal to fend off growing opposition that their constitutions were anything but a farce. And yet the intellectuals, jurists, and government officials gathered at this conference redoubled their efforts to celebrate their corporatist path as a "third path"—one neither liberal nor socialist, neither laissez-faire nor state controlled—guiding their societies to political stability, social peace, and economic progress. To them, corporatism remained key to solving pressing challenges, those lingering from the Great Depression and mounting with each country's drive for economic development. Corporatism was not only better suited to these societies than liberalism, so they constructed their argument, but also had nothing to do with Fascist Italy—a necessary disclaimer during the war. "Corporatism is a timeworn principle, one that maintains its relevance," Brazil's *Correio da Manhã* concluded from reporting on Caetano's visit.[1]

A Third Path explores Brazilian and Portuguese efforts to overcome the Great Depression by reinventing, as they saw it, a medieval guild system in order to explain why corporatism proved so enduring in Europe and Latin America. In the 1920s and 1930s, countries as diverse as France, Italy, Spain, Portugal, Austria, Romania, Brazil, Mexico, and Argentina, among others, experimented with corporatist modes of organizing political representation, labor relations, and economic production. Corporatism offered new possibilities for how to harness the powers of expanding government bureaucracies to improve societal welfare, increase domestic food production, and industrialize quickly, and many proponents of this third path advocated for programs similar to those adopted by countries experimenting with other models of the mixed economy. Corporatism is thus key to understanding the rise of new forms of the state's management of economic life in the interwar decades, and yet it has also remained a somewhat vague concept, partly because, as political scientist Philippe Schmitter notes in his iconic essay "Still the Century of Corporatism?," it "can be found everywhere and, hence, is nowhere very distinctive."[2] What made corporatism unique, however, was how this technocratic project got grafted onto older utopian visions of society comprised not of atomized individuals but instead vertically organized social and economic interests. To study corporatism is then to consider some of the forgotten ideological and institutional origins of the midcentury regulatory state.

I explain the emergence and persistence of modern corporatism by looking at its parallel, and connected, rise in Brazil under dictator-turned-populist president Getúlio Vargas (1882–1954) and Portugal under the dictatorship of António de Oliveira Salazar (1889–1970), where each regime took the name of Estado Novo (New State). Vargas took power following the 1930 Revolution that toppled Brazil's First Republic (1889–1930), in which political power rested with regional oligarchs tied to commodity-export sectors. He governed Brazil from 1930 until his ouster from power in 1945—a period largely defined by the authoritarian corporatist Estado Novo regime installed through his self-coup in 1937. A political chameleon, Vargas managed to return to power in 1951 by popular electoral mandate, shedding his associations with interwar dictatorships, and embracing a populist and developmentalist platform.[3] Salazar was a university professor who started his improbable political rise as finance minister in 1928, imposing a severe austerity program to address Portugal's financial crisis. Appointed prime minister from power in 1932, Salazar governed Portugal until 1968. He implemented his own corporatist, authoritarian Estado Novo that survived until 1974 under his successor, Caetano. As committed as Brazilian and Portuguese officials were to their united efforts to reinvent past traditions in order to displace political and economic liberalism, their corporatist experiments to address long-run problems—especially underdevelopment—were hardly straightforward translations of doctrine into practice. On both sides of the South Atlantic, jurists, intellectuals, and political officials debated the meaning of corporatism for the modern world as they stretched the illiberal logic underpinning their ambitions to new programs and policies in order to fix economic problems. The Vargas and Salazar dictatorships show the durability of corporatism, and the historical as well as continued relevance of this conservative, hierarchical, and statist worldview.

Defining Corporatism

Corporatism itself is not easy or obvious to define, and indeed its mutable definitions and different uses are a key theme throughout this book. This ism had no founder, canonical text, or country of origin. It was an inherently transnational phenomenon, with multiple intellectual genealogies that, at times, appeared at odds.[4] The jurists, intellectuals, bureaucrats, industrialists, landowners, and workers who supported corporatism held a variety of opinions and ideological leanings. They also themselves struggled with definitions, frequently united more by their opposition to other ideologies than by their own policies.

In broadest and simplest terms, corporatism is a system that sets out to organize society according to economic and social interests, and vertically integrate these groups into the state so that it can intervene in labor relations and economic production. While committed to private property and individual initiative, corporatists wanted these impulses subordinated to the greater needs and interests of the nation. Corporatism mirrored other mixed economy experiments in the 1930s in which the state regulated economic activities. Distinctively, however, it disavowed individual freedoms and emphasized the preservation of existing social hierarchies. Corporatists instead stressed the importance of social rights and representation through sectoral interest groups that were supported and protected according to national imperatives.

Beyond this simple definition, corporatism contains multitudes and paradoxes. Corporatists were nationalists who supported increased state powers over national life, but did not envision a state that directly controlled the mode of production. Corporatism was a strategy for political legitimacy and survival too. Sometimes, corporatism is lumped with fascism or allied with nebulous intellectual tendencies on the Right.[5] Still others see corporatism as a general orientation, neither Left nor Right, but conservative and Catholic, or they treat it as a narrow and well-defined set of institutions to organize industrial relations.[6] Sometimes it is defined with a school of economic thought that promoted state-led coordination of the economy with special attention to the collective rights of labor and capital, and sometimes it is a political system in which both democratic participation and governments are organized around profession and class. Others see corporatism as a corrupted system of regulations and controls that has benefited certain industries and groups above others, viewing it as synonymous with categories like state capitalism, crony capitalism, or regulatory capture.[7]

Despite or because of corporatism's categorical ambiguity, this book contends that its proponents attempted to assert the originality of their experiment by mounting powerful critiques of the failures of democratic political institutions, laissez-faire capitalism, and liberal internationalism in the 1920s and 1930s. Its history is as essential to understanding the breakdown of liberal governance as it is to explaining the lure of dictatorships in these crucial decades. Historian Eric Hobsbawm famously suggests in *The Age of Extremes* that the history of the twentieth century was not as simple as a contest between the two "binary opposites" of capitalism and socialism.[8] For Brazil and Portugal, this book shows the complexity that lay between or, better, outside two extremes.

This struggle for a third path was global. Corporatism was transnational in its application as well as its theoretical evolution. Comparison and translation were at its core.[9] As a point of departure, this book builds on the richly established field of transnational history to consider how debates within and across national contexts shaped the meaning and practice of corporatism.[10] It features a loose network of jurists, intellectuals, economists, and public officials between Brazil and Portugal, while also recognizing the asymmetrical nature of this exchange as well as how these networks stretched into other contexts such as Fascist Italy or the New Deal United States. Brazil and Portugal are often cast as passive recipients of ideas and models from the industrial North Atlantic. By turning the gaze southward and utilizing this multicentered and transnational approach in the South Atlantic, this book positions a region not often studied for its legal or economic creativity as a major hub of policy experimentation.[11]

In combining methodologies of transnational history, intellectual history, and political economy, this book is ultimately a history of economic life that captures the rise of state-led development in Brazil and other contexts. It demonstrates how the economies of the South Atlantic embarked on a global project to carve out an alternative to liberal or laissez-faire capitalism. With a few notable exceptions, corporatism has been left out of recent histories of capitalism in the twentieth century because scholars characterize it as a deviation from so-called proper stages of development, conflate it with fascism, or dismiss it as the window dressing of nationalist dictatorships. While corporatism has been a vibrant area of research among historians in Brazil and Portugal, it is less familiar for English-language audiences.[12] This book expands that scholarship by asking new questions: How did corporatist experiments inform new ideas of economic development and social peace? How did these ideas shape how national governments intervened in economic life in the 1930s and 1940s? How did corporatism survive into the postwar period to shape the rise of bolder state-led projects for modernization, industrialization, and development?

These questions are especially salient because increased state intervention in labor relations, economic production, and commerce is not exclusive to corporatist regimes. Over the past few years, historians have explored the ways that states tinkered with the economy during the interwar decades to understand how the state emerged as a primary actor for economic development in the twentieth century.[13] Sociologist Johanna Bockman and others have questioned or upended older dichotomies between "capitalist" and "command" in twentieth-century histories of development, either by exploring the connections or parallels between capitalist and socialist contexts, or debunking prior assumptions of ideological purity.[14] Corporatism is missing in this conversation about the emergence of new economic regimes in the twentieth century. Corporatist experiments were neither ephemeral nor reducible to the dictators who first introduced them, and persisted through democratic and authoritarian governments.

Corporatism is so difficult to pin down in part because it is not exclusively a law, institution, or government but rather a framework, logic, and worldview concerning state-society relations with long-lasting legacies. Brazil and Portugal stitched corporatist ideas into their legal and constitutional fabric, which is one of the features that distinguished their corporatist experiments from other forms of the mixed economy. Corporatism codified the notion that rights should be unequally distributed according to economic function and the greater national interest, thereby transforming a de facto feature of most liberal regimes from an institutional failure into a necessary ingredient for social peace and economic development. Consequently, I argue that corporatism was not an interwar exception to liberal governance; its institutions and logic survived World War II to shape how the state intervenes in labor and market relations to the present day.

A History of Corporatism

When Vargas and Salazar used corporatism, they were not inventing a new concept but instead refashioning an ancient one to modern uses. Corporatism derives from the Latin word *corpus*, or *body*, and when applied to society suggests a singular organism in which each part has a designated role, in contrast to a collection of atomized individuals. This ideal of society as more than the sum of its parts is one unifying thread among the many corporatisms that evolved over centuries. Corporatist antecedents existed in Roman law, for example, with the corporation a "legal fiction" representing a collective of people in a lasting entity that would survive any individual person, but the concept is generally associated with the Middle Ages.[15] By the fourteenth century, Roman conceptions of the corporation were applied to self-governing city-states and guilds in Europe, granting legal personality to these governing units. Corporate personhood was defined hierarchically as well as by economic and social function, whether granted to guilds, the church, or the military. Laws issued by these legal entities regulated local economic conditions. Merchants and artisans formed guilds to control entry into their industry, and regulate the price and quality of goods. The Spanish and Portuguese Empires extended this system to their overseas colonies, assigning rights and privileges to corporate institutions, and in effect legalizing social and racial hierarchies. In Brazil and the Spanish Americas, distant monarchs sent bureaucrats and magistrates to preside over diverse colonial populations and dispense justice in ways that afforded distinct legal protections to each corporate group, but always in accordance with the goals of the Crown.[16] This system of variegated justice epitomized, for instance, with the *fueros* in the Spanish Empire in which different classes, communities, or regions were governed according to distinct legal codes was predicated on a logic of inclusivity but not equality.[17] Centuries later, modern corporatist dictatorships would take inspiration from earlier monarchical and imperial models.[18]

The French Revolution, independence wars in the Americas, and liberal revolts during the nineteenth and early twentieth centuries shattered this system of controls and privileges, giving rise to constitutional monarchies and republican governments. Both Brazil and Portugal established constitutional monarchies following Brazil's independence in 1822. Those advocating for liberal reforms wanted protections for individual rights and property, a separation of church and state, the dissolution of trade monopolies, and free trade as engines of growth and progress.[19] But liberalism and its emphasis on individual freedoms was not endorsed by all social groups, and not only because of the persistence of slavery in Brazil and the Portuguese Empire.[20]

Historians call the "long" nineteenth century the century of liberalism, but corporatism as an ideal and economic system never really disappeared. Nineteenth-century French political economist Henri de Saint-Simon, for example, urged technocratic and coordinated political solutions to address the hardships that the working classes endured with industrialization, calling on industrialists to head the effort.[21] His critiques of liberalism and individualism informed positivist thinkers like French philosopher Auguste Comte, who became especially influential to Brazilian military generals and engineers in the late nineteenth century.

After the abolition of slavery in Brazil in 1888, military generals overthrew the monarchy to drive greater modernization. Positivism and corporatism have distinct genealogies, but these ideologies overlapped in that they both described society as a living organism comprised of the sum of its specialized parts—the family, military, and different productive classes. Brazilian historians debate the finer points of positivist influence on the First Republic, but generally agree that it offered a model for "progressive conservatism" or "modernizing conservatism."[22] Scholars trace the origins of modern authoritarianism to positivists like Alberto Torres, who influenced a later generation of corporatists.[23] Insisting on Brazil's lack of preparedness for elections and representative government, positivists promoted technocracy and rule by experts, guided by military personnel and engineers. Positivists also shaped republican projects to address Brazil's stagnation, especially in public health and infrastructure, but always with the goal of progress with order.[24]

The persistence of corporatism can partly be explained as a conservative reaction to the rise of anarchist, socialist, and syndicalist movements. For conservative intellectuals in particular, corporatism aligned closely with anticommunism and rising Catholic social thought, with its emphasis on duties over rights and social peace over class conflict. This is as much the case in Brazil as in Portugal. In 1891, Pope Leo XIII's *Rerum Novarum*, subtitled *Rights and Duties of Capital and Labor*, called on governments and employer classes to respect the dignity of workers and concede collective bargaining solutions to improve their conditions. The encyclical lamented the diminished role of corporate bodies during the nineteenth century, and called for workers and employers alike to organize themselves into associations along vocational lines. In Catholic societies, these intermediary institutions—between the individual and the state—would be responsible for the moral and material well-being of their members.[25] *Rerum Novarum* denounced the inherent greed of capitalism that impoverished the working classes while magnifying the lure of anarchism, socialism, and other anti-Catholic movements.[26]

The interwar resurgence of corporatism was further stoked by alarm over the Bolshevik threat. Historians have largely explained the rise of corporatist dictatorships as responses to fears that social unrest could end with revolution, as in Russia. This "red scare" led Vargas's and Salazar's governments to create secret police and national security laws for political purges that targeted the Communist Party, trade unions, and other leftist groups.[27] Corporatist institutions, especially labor policies, allowed these conservative governments to defuse class conflict by turning it into a legal or technical problem, arbitrated by the state. This book, however, argues that anticommunism does not explain the economic policies implemented in the 1930s. Jurists, economists, and government officials in Brazil as much as in Portugal became far more preoccupied with how to fix the excesses of liberal capitalism. Corporatists turned their critique of the laissez-faire order into a new system designed for economic renewal and development.

Conservative intellectuals in Brazil or Portugal understood the value of crafting corporatism as the refashioning of a medieval or colonial order while updating this system to address contemporary challenges. The corporatist idiom fit comfortably with older Iberian traditions, including the privileged role of the Catholic Church and centralized-decentralized model of governance across Portugal's vast empire. Adherents in Brazil and Portugal argued that liberalism was an imported ideology—one that might work for Britain or France, but not for their societies.[28] Nearly all the books written by interwar corporatist

theorists began with invectives against the French Revolution—with its proc-
lamation of liberty, equality, and fraternity—as the root cause of recent economic and social crisis, targeting especially laws that had abolished guilds in
favor of free enterprise. To be sure, liberalism was itself hardly a consistent or
coherent ideology, with its own distinct national traditions, internal contradictions, and slippery definitions.[29] Corporatists nonetheless relied on superficial
and reductive depictions of liberal doctrine and the failures of past governments. Yet this book carefully interrogates the overwrought arguments made
by Brazilian and Portuguese intellectuals to discredit the core liberal values of
equality and liberty precisely because they used those arguments to build their
own authoritarian, hierarchical, and profoundly unequal political system.[30]

Hence corporatism was hardly a new idea when dictators started seizing on
this model, but rather an attempt to rehabilitate older traditions. Brazilian and
Portuguese intellectuals latched onto their shared language and history to create a political alternative to liberalism.

Corporatism as a Nationalist and Transnational Experiment

Brazilian and Portuguese efforts to mobilize the deep historical roots of corporatism also served a political purpose, allowing its proponents to insist that
their system did not share its origins with fascism. The relationship between
fascism and corporatism—whether these two isms are synonymous or productively distinguished in practice—was a question that interwar intellectuals
could not ignore. And it remains central to the historiography on interwar
corporatism, with scholars often falling into one of two camps. For some, corporatism and fascism were all but synonymous, and any attempt to disaggre-
gate them amounted to an apologia to fascism. For others, corporatism was a
labor and economic system that could be adapted to different political regimes,
while fascism was a mass political movement underpinned by violent, racist
impulses.[31] This camp contends that the two isms should not be confused or
conflated, even if they happened to overlap in some regimes. This book argues
for taking corporatism seriously on its own terms while still insisting that the
two ideologies share a political and intellectual history. This is especially true
for corporatist economics. The rise of corporatism as a new economic system,
as this book shows, cannot be divorced from its Italian influence and the entangled intellectual networks that connected Fascist Italy to dictatorships in
Latin America and Iberian Europe.

Rather than assume corporatism to be a pathology of poor, underdeveloped Latin countries, *A Third Path* reframes it as a political experiment among

other transnational experiments in the interwar decades. As societies world-wide grappled with the outbreak of revolutions, collapse of empires, social unrest, and financial and broader economic crises, they enacted new political programs. The 1920s saw rising experiments with socialism, radical republican-ism, dictatorship, nationalism, self-determination, and fascism. From the ruins of the Ottoman and Austro-Hungarian Empires in eastern and central Europe, a flurry of constitutions ratified in the early 1920s converted territories in the Balkans and along the Baltic Sea into nascent democracies. The drive to create new governing systems was also evident at the constitutional apex of the Mexican Revolution in 1917, and how President Lázaro Cárdenas (1934–40) would later give political expression to its promises for social and economic justice with the corporatist-style system he created.[32] This revolutionary fervor, however, had other expressions too, including the 1917 Russian Revolution along with the rise of Benito Mussolini in Italy in 1922 and Miguel Primo de Rivera in Spain in 1923. New dictatorships promised order, stability, and modernization. Modern corporatism was but one of many possible paths at this global juncture as new—or previously unsavory and marginal—ideas vied for influence.

At first glance, corporatism fits comfortably with the narrative of height-ened nationalism, protectionism, and isolationism in the interwar decades. Corporatist dictators supported policies to grow internal markets and secure national self-sufficiency, while celebrating national greatness and renewal. Yet despite the ferocity with which Vargas and Salazar proclaimed their Estado Novo to be national revolutions against toxic, foreign, liberal ideologies, or exploitative and volatile international markets, their experiments with corpo-ratism crystallized in a deeply transnational and global context. The intellec-tual origins of modern corporatism, as scholars often note, are largely found in French, German, or Italian writings.[33] Yet for Brazilian and Portuguese intel-lectuals, corporatism was not borrowed but instead a by-product of collabora-tion and mutual inspiration. When political and intellectual elites in Brazil and Portugal denounced so-called imported ideas, they rejected a model of diffu-sion from core to peripheral countries, and instead emphasized that they too were active participants in the search for new political and economic orders. One of the challenges, and I hope innovations, is to show how a nation-centric project was constituted through transnational conversation, debate, and ex-change. Ideas circulated in multiple and unpredictable directions, and were translated, appropriated, and misunderstood along the way.[34]

More specifically, I center the production of economic knowledge and practice in the Portuguese-speaking Atlantic to explore how interwar govern-ments approached economic decline and political instability. With the rise of regional and area studies in the latter half of the twentieth century, Brazil's development is frequently compared to that of neighboring Latin American economies while Portugal is often inserted into eurozone histories. Over the past twenty years, historians have made a strong case that we must think beyond the nation-state to understand how new ideological tool kits and policies emerge. Connections between Brazilian and Portuguese intellectuals and bureaucrats not only amplified the diffusion of corporatist ideas abroad but also legitimized this third path at home. Those who supported Vargas's and Salazar's regimes consistently defended corporatism as ideally suited to their societies by mobilizing sociological, cultural, and racial arguments.[35] To anchor this study in Brazil and Portugal is also to contend with the real and imagined afterlives of imperial bonds.[36]

Brazil provides a unique vantage point for examining the rise and fall of corporatism for its connections to several regions—cultural and historical ties with the Portuguese Empire, growing influence from Fascist Italy and the New Deal United States, and increasing ties to other Latin American countries—as well as its impressive economic and social transformations during the twentieth century. Brazil's population was about fourteen million in 1890, doubling to thirty-one million by 1920, and reaching fifty-two million by 1950. In 1920, agriculture accounted for 32 percent of Brazil's GDP and industry 17 percent; by 1960, industry outpaced agriculture, and so Brazil's industrial takeoff cannot be separated from the Vargas era.[37] This trend accelerated in the 1960s with Brazil becoming an industrial powerhouse. Historians have debated whether the 1930 Revolution was more a point of rupture or continuity, yet few deny that Vargas's dictatorship not only intensified all the above processes but shaped their institutional form and political focus too.

In the case of Brazil, Vargas's rule did not initiate processes of industrialization, domestic market diversification, or the rise and organization of the working classes. Rather, Brazil was already undergoing a profound transformation in its economic and social organization when Vargas seized power in 1930s. As historian Steven Topik has argued, the laissez-faire logic was more myth than reality during Brazil's First Republic (1889–1930) as both state and federal governments intervened in markets with valorization schemes to prop up coffee prices and subsidies for railroads.[38] Such forms of state intervention, however, were limited in scope and largely relegated to commodity sectors. More important, they were often defended as exceptional or emergency measures, driven more by necessity than doctrine. Vargas's state-led economic programs were not just more profound, systematic, and large-scale but defended on doctrinal terms as well, formally elevating as norm and obligation the state's role in the economy.[39]

During the Vargas era, intellectuals, industrialists, and government officials used corporatist ideas to design state intervention in labor, price, and production. The corporatist structure of Brazil's development path is especially evident in labor relations. Corporatists seized on the notion of "social peace" that was implicit in legal theory about the social question circulating throughout the civil law world to make their case for the dissolution of preexisting forms of labor activism. Prior to 1930, workers in both rural and urban settings had organized autonomous *sindicatos* (labor unions) to demand better conditions, the right to arbitration, minimum wages, and government measures to stabilize the rising cost of living. Following the 1930 Revolution, Vargas implemented several decree laws to require that all sindicatos, cooperatives, associations, and other collective organizations be recognized by the state.[40] These efforts to manage labor relations, Brazilian historians emphasize, were essential to Vargas's emergent state developmentalist model by generating a vast system of welfare and social rights to support the growth—loyalty—of an industrial labor force.[41]

The corporatist structure of Brazil's economy is most evident in labor relations, but corporatism went beyond this arena. Indeed, corporatism as it persisted and survived became both the ideological and institutional substrate through which the state increased its role in Brazil's economy, and is a missing piece that explains some of the puzzles and paradoxes of its economic development. This was apparent in the rise of technocratic modes of governance, in which economic policy was debated and drafted by special commissions created in the 1930s and 1940s—commissions staffed by not only bureaucrats but industry representatives too, whether agricultural, industrial, or commercial.[42] Corporatist institutions also increasingly shaped how goods were produced, traded, and exported in Brazil. For agricultural staples like coffee, sugar, or maté, Vargas's government created national institutes to discipline producers as well as establish price control and export regulations. But here corporatist ideal and practice frequently diverged, not only because the corporatist system never extended to all sectors or all regions, but also because not all forms of economic planning fit squarely with corporatist doctrine. This is key to the durability of corporatism in Brazil: this system was flexible enough that it could comfortably accommodate, for example, the creation of state-owned steel plants or oil companies. Corporatism was one approach to state-directed economic development, and one way of coordinating private capital, independent producers, and the citizenry in the name of national progress. What made it "corporatist" was that interests were understood according to sector, and rights and privileges were negotiated within sector associations.

The very ambiguity and multivalent meanings of corporatism make the transnational perspective essential for understanding not only how it shaped Brazilian and Portuguese economies but also for why corporatism matters in twentieth-century debates over development and the role of the state in economic life. Salazar oversaw one of the most complete and long-lasting experiments with corporatism. In the case of Portugal, as much as for Brazil, corporatist strategies to organize national production in the 1930s and 1940s created the institutional foundations for postwar development efforts.

Portugal is an ideal counterpart to Brazil not just because the two countries share language, history, and legal systems. Portugal's Estado Novo dictatorship was in place for over forty years, meaning that corporatism could evolve and expand.[43] While Portugal's model would also depart from pure theory, many of Salazar's closest advisers were theorists of corporatism, responsible for its normative and practical elaboration. Portugal's economic transformation in the twentieth century was less dramatic than that of Brazil's, but no less disruptive to social, political, and cultural life. Portugal's population was about 6 million in 1920 and jumped to 8.5 million by 1950, remaining stable at this number for several decades as lower infant mortality rates coincided with high emigration rates. Agriculture remained the base of Portugal's economy throughout the Estado Novo, but industry made important advances too; 56 percent of the active Portuguese population was employed in agriculture and fishing in 1920—a number that decreased to 44 percent by 1960.[44] As in Brazil, the urban working classes were organized into sindicatos recognized by the state, but in Portugal this system was most pronounced among those rural workers and producers who joined grémios, or agricultural guilds. For some sectors, membership in grémios was mandatory; for others, it was voluntary. Grémios were responsible for not only representing members' interests and providing social security benefits but also regulating local market conditions, ensuring that price controls and production quotas were observed by members, and facilitating the acquisition of machinery and other licensing. For export sectors such as wine, cork, or cod, grémios oversaw the warehousing and export of goods, again with the goal of price stability.

When Salazar came to power, Portugal was a small and impoverished country on the edge of the Iberian Peninsula. But it was also an empire stretched across Africa and Asia, and so Estado Novo officials constantly vacillated between a state of resignation about the country's second-rate status in Europe and pompousness about its former imperial greatness. Following Brazil's independence in 1822, Portugal attempted to reconstitute its empire with schemes to build settler colonies in Africa, particularly in Angola and Mozambique, and harness their economic potential. Despite grandiose ambitions, it endured financial failures, territorial losses, and geopolitical embarrassments, which is why Salazar made imperial renewal central to his governing ideology.[45] The Estado Novo extended its corporatist bureaucracy to the empire in order to increase commodity production and supply Portuguese industries with raw materials. While Salazar's corporatist project in the empire remained limited and threadbare, it is not possible to explain the evolving meaning or practice of corporatism in Portugal without accounting for the symbolic and economic importance of efforts to tighten commercial relations between metropole and colonies. The specter of past—and promise of future—imperial glory also animated renewed intellectual and political connections between Brazil and Portugal in the 1930s. Empire became essential to why corporatism held such appeal in both countries.

Brazilian and Portuguese intellectuals looked to each other, although the nations diverged in size, geography, and demography. This book is not an exercise in comparison but instead one in how comparison gets used politically. In Portugal, "scientific pessimism" infused how intellectuals, scientists, and political leaders contended with the alleged social pathologies of the Portuguese people.[46] For the Portuguese, the nineteenth century was a period of decline and stagnation, with the loss of both Brazil in the 1820s and territories in Africa to the British in 1890. Portuguese intellectuals, sociologists, and anthropologists obsessively debated the geographic, economic, or cultural traits that limited the country's development. They made all but unavoidable comparisons with Britain or Germany as competition between nations intensified over colonial possessions. Portuguese intellectuals, however, looked increasingly to Brazil for evidence that it was once a great imperial power.

Brazil also wrestled with the notion of empire in the 1920s, albeit in different ways. Brazilian elites worried not about decline but rather degradation. Brazil had been a slave society for nearly four hundred years, during which slavery had underpinned continued political and social support for monarchy following its independence from Portugal. In 1822, Brazil transformed from colony to empire. Its political and legal institutions continued to support the interests of the landholding classes, with law and violence wielded to enforce a social and racial hierarchy in which enslaved labor constituted the pyramidal base.[47] By the end of the nineteenth century, Brazilian elites embraced Darwinian social theory, positivism, and scientific racism to further assert the supposed innate superiority of some races over others even as Brazilian intellectuals and scientists tried to celebrate their population's unique adaptability to local climates and geographies.[48] The abolition of slavery in 1888 occurred during a period of mass migrations to Brazil from the Middle East, Japan, and especially southern Europe. From the 1870s onward, Brazil's state and federal governments intervened to support European migration in particular in order to "whiten" their multiraced population, turning miscegenation into a civilizing tool.[49] By the 1920s, Brazil was the world's most diverse multiethnic, multiracial society. For political and economic elites, demographic trends became a source of pessimism—a hinderance to Brazil's ability to reach the ranks of wealthy, industrialized nations. In the years following abolition, sociologist

Mara Loveman argues, "the idea of progress itself became racialized."[50] By the 1920 census, Portuguese immigrants in Brazil accounted for nearly 30 percent of the foreign-born population.[51] Brazilian elites emphasized ties with Portugal as a strategy to erase or minimize the country's Afro-Brazilian heritage. As conservative jurist Levi Carneiro later articulated, the growing closeness between the two Portuguese-speaking nations owed not just to their "shared language" and "common past." It was a vehicle for Brazilian intellectuals to stress the nation's "Europeanness."[52]

Across the Luso-Atlantic, Brazilian and Portuguese intellectuals underpinned their corporatist models with an imperial logic, promising modernization while preserving the existing social and racial hierarchy. The corporatist model attempted to formalize, not equalize, social and economic differences across classes and regions. By drawing Brazil and Portugal together, it becomes possible to see the multiple and entangled ways in which ideas broadly labeled *corporatist* circulated across the Atlantic. Ideas and institutions did not flow unilaterally from Brazil to Portugal (or vice versa). Rather, the 1930s and 1940s were years of mutual influence and admiration. There was no "original" or "copy."[53] And with corporatism, theory cannot be emphasized at the expense of implementation because both nations were working simultaneously to fix mounting economic problems.

Corporatism as Law

The working out and fixing of economic problems through corporatism is evident especially in law. In Vargas era Brazil, law became a primary tool for putting the corporatist economic system into practice, and thus I put corporatist legalism under a microscope in this book. The centrality of law is not surprising given Brazil's legal culture, like other civil law contexts in which law is more aspirational than a reflection of social realities.[54] Similar dynamics unfolded in Salazarist Portugal, a regime largely run by jurists and law professors who demonstrated a consistent—and even obsessive—tendency not just to draft constitutions and laws but also to detail new legal theories to defend how these laws departed from normative conventions.

Law, in this book, is useful for what it reveals about the intellectual history of competing economic visions and political stakes. The fact that authoritarian regimes on both sides of the Atlantic obsessed over writing and rewriting laws also reveals something about the ongoing struggle for political and popular legitimacy, evident in the almost compulsive need for both Estado Novo regimes to constantly outline their ambitions to the public. Brazilian political scientist Vanda Maria Ribeiro Costa explains that for corporatist intellectuals, their "utopia" was to believe in law as a corrective instrument and moral force for social change.[55] In the 1930s in particular, the jurists' task was to create legal parameters for the social transformations wrought by Brazil's economic transformations—in other words, to correct the injustices and disequilibriums produced by industrialization. This legal history reveals the competition between liberalism and corporatism as well as among different corporatist visions.

Constitutions are a primary focus. Brazil and Portugal are two of only three corporatist dictatorships that ratified corporatist constitutions in the 1930s. Legal scholars are often quick to dismiss Brazilian and Portuguese corporatist constitutions as shams, or window dressings for dictatorships. Partly this skepticism stems from the fact that corporatist constitutions tended to come and go with new dictators, and derives from the North Atlantic standard that "constitutions have the aspiration to remain stable."[56] Political theorists and legal scholars have long debated whether autocratic rulers can effectively limit the exercise of their powers with institutions of their own making, arguing that "self-binding" is so difficult to enforce in authoritarian contexts because dictators can change or violate their own rules with impunity.[57] While corporatist constitutions might not pass the test of real constitutions—those that guarantee individual rights and limit the powers of government—this does not mean that they were irrelevant. Historians and social scientists are increasingly paying attention to how dictatorships attempt to institutionalize their power, whether to appease elite power-sharing or promote autocratic stability.[58]

In Brazil and Portugal, dictators wrote constitutions (alongside trusted legal advisers) to quell ideological conflict and respond to political and economic crises. With each new constitution, previous models might have been preserved or abandoned, and dictatorship itself constituted a choice. Constitutions, after all, are aspirational documents. This is as much the case for dictatorships as for democracies, even if the aspirations of dictators do not include liberty or equality. Brazilian historians and legal scholars in particular have placed renewed attention on authoritarian constitutions in order to unpack the ideological underpinnings of dictatorship, and explain the continuities between the Estado Novo and the military dictatorship installed in 1964.[59] Vargas and Salazar defended dictatorship as modern and progressive in contrast to the chaos of "too much choice" in liberal democracies.

To the extent that interwar corporatist constitutions have been analyzed in a global context, scholars then—and now—have debated if and how foreign influences might have corrupted national ideals. Brazil's 1937 Constitution, for example, is often discredited because it "copied" the Portuguese and Polish Constitutions as well as the Italian Carta del Lavoro.[60] Its foreignness is frequently taken as the reason why democratic principles were betrayed, but the transnational flow of similar models was precisely what made legal authoritarianism possible. This point is key. As Brazilian historians Luciano Aronne de Abreu and Luis Rosenfield recently argued, the 1937 Constitution was not just Vargas's attempt at legitimacy but rather a legal project to defend authoritarian modes of government.[61]

These constitutions and laws mattered, moreover, because they transformed economic life, even if in unintended and unpredictable ways. I am concerned not only with legal theory and lawmaking but also with laws in action. Where the implementation of labor courts and protections afforded to the working classes are often studied as the pinnacle of the corporatist system, I focus instead on how both the Vargas and Salazar regimes mobilized special police forces and tribunals for economic crimes and enforced laws concerning fair price and just competition. Vargas and Salazar deployed censorship, secret police, special military tribunals, and other legal and extralegal tactics to suppress left-wing movements, labor activism, liberals, and even extreme right-wing opposition forces in order to usurp power as well as legitimize their regime in the name of national security. These dictatorships, however, also wielded these draconian legal tools and policing strategies to intervene in market life and hold accountable merchants who gouged prices or producers who failed to abide by price controls on essential goods. The extension of authoritarian legal tools to the marketplace required a reinvention of the ideologies and institutions that had previously regulated commerce: a liberal emphasis on the primacy of private contracts and private property gave way to a corporatist emphasis on disciplining private interests for national imperatives.[62] Rather than take the legal experiments of the Brazilian and Portuguese dictatorships as failures, this book explores how jurists and lawmakers used law to both imagine and create new powers for the state to intervene in national economic life, and how citizens customized these laws to their own ends.

Across the nineteenth century, law was primarily concerned with the protection of property rights and enforcement of individual contracts. During the first decades of the twentieth century, legal scholar Duncan Kennedy contends, jurists and social reformers questioned this limited scope as the stresses of industrialization along with unbridled competition proved too serious to ignore. Increasingly, law became a tool for achieving social ends and economic development.[63] In the South Atlantic, this trend began to crystallize under interwar corporatist dictatorships. Debates over corporatist law, legislation, and policy were debates over how to structure the relationship between state and market, how to order and organize interests, and how to assert a hierarchy for economic development. Rather than emphasize how the Vargas and Salazar dictatorships deviated from liberal constitutional norms, I ask how their authoritarian legal tool kit was used to build something different: a new economic system.

Corporatism as an Economic System

Ultimately, then, this is a history of economic ideas in action. It shows how intellectuals and technocrats in the South Atlantic attempted to build a new economic system out of the interwar crisis of capitalism.[64] *A Third Path* takes the state as its primary object of analysis, and highlights the voices of low-, mid-, and high-level public officials as they responded to economic problems. Corporatism was not always explicit in their debates or policy designs, but it provided the scaffolding for how they thought about the economy. Without ceding rhetorical or political ground to leftist logics of class conflict as engines for economic transformation, state actors looked beyond individual actions and decision-making in order to organize and integrate economic groups into the state and thereby balance competing interests according to national development objectives. Driving this history of corporatism is the challenge to take seriously the history of the state in relation to the economy.

Corporatist intellectuals in Brazil and Portugal were often technocrats employed by the state who crafted theory in the process of designing policy.[65] Corporatism was ideally suited to address three distinct (but connected) economic problems: underdevelopment, dependency on international markets, and inchoate domestic production. Inside new government ministries, corporatists pushed ideas and policies to discipline prices, production, and commerce. Historians of Brazil in particular have emphasized the importance of looking beyond law as written on paper in order to understand how workers and industrialists alike maneuvered within the political frame to advocate for their rights and interests, and the consequences for those excluded.[66] The jurists and bureaucrats who designed these laws and institutions also had to confront the shortcomings of their planning, as their legal and economic thinking evolved to address new problems. Their concept of the state and how it should function, moreover, was sometimes nebulous, incomplete, or inconsistent.[67] While many chapters probe the limitations and frustrations with these corporatist experiments, the story I tell is not one of failure but rather evolving expectations of the state, and the persistence of broken or inadequate models.

In this light, this book also tells a new history of the Great Depression—one that shifts the intellectual and technical landscape of crisis management to new spaces on the margins of global capitalism. The US New Deal or Nazi Germany are the focus of many global studies.[68] Still, there are lessons to be learned beyond the industrialized world. Brazil and Portugal show how a crisis of capitalism in the center jolted bold programs for government action in the periphery.[69]

By starting with the problems facing agricultural producers in both Brazil and Portugal, I highlight the importance of corporatist ideas and institutions in how governments on both sides of the Atlantic tried to protect and grow the domestic production of agricultural staples not only for export but also increasingly for domestic consumption too.[70] In the economic sphere, corporatist experiments zeroed in on price as a key variable in their theory, models, and policy. To legitimize government actions to control prices for key goods, stakeholders had to combat classical economic models that asserted price as a variable dictated by laws of supply and demand along with liberal legal codes that asserted the primacy of private contracts between individuals.

In the corporatist worldview that emerged in both Brazil and Portugal, price acquired a different meaning. Fair prices became another instrument of economic justice and social peace under corporatist dictatorships. This focus on price was not unique to interwar corporatist dictatorships as evident with the rise of price controls and fair competition regulations in the United States or Chile.[71] But in each country, governments had to justify new pricing policies according to local ideological and institutional traditions. And for Brazil and Portugal, legal and moral definitions of fair pricing depended on corporatist critiques of the free market. Corporatists seized on their efforts to stabilize prices and wages as evidence of how they offered a new type of democracy as they attempted to detach democracy from a liberal emphasis on liberty and representation to instead assert their Estado Novo regimes as guarantors of economic justice. Promise and practice diverge under these dictatorships; nevertheless, the experiment changed public expectations of the role of the state in economic life.

Authoritarian Development

Brazilian and Portuguese intellectuals who embraced corporatism ultimately claimed it as a newer, more progressive model for democracy—one that valued order over liberty and in which rights were defined by economic profession and sector. Forging an alternative economic model to laissez-faire or free market capitalism also became a project to define economic values like prices, wages, and interest, not according to market forces but instead careful negotiations between group interests and the greater economic imperatives of the nation. This project to brand corporatist dictatorships as democratic was not just authoritarian doublespeak, I argue, but an intellectual, legal, political, and institutional project to devise new rules and responsibilities for the state's intervention in economic life, and new channels by which industrialists, agricultural producers, and consumers could stake their claims to economic justice. At the same time, in both Brazil and Portugal, corporatist states were decreed following political coups, and put into practice by regimes that embraced state censorship and police repression as essential tools to remain in power. The history of twentieth-century corporatism is inseparable from the history of authoritarianism, at least in southern Europe and Latin America. Key to understanding this nexus is not just how Vargas and Salazar touted promises for economic justice to vindicate their dictatorships but also how they seized on promises for economic recovery and transformation.

Corporatist ideas were so readily absorbed in Brazil and Portugal in part because of long-standing anxieties over delayed or lagging development. I emphasize the concept underdevelopment, to be clear, not to categorize either country's economic performance. Rather, underdevelopment was an intellectual and discursive project in the twentieth century, as historians Joseph Love and Paul Gootenberg have shown in their works on Brazil and Peru, respectively—one that informed how public officials grappled with economic problems.[72]

The problem of underdevelopment became one of the threads connecting Brazil's corporatist experiment to that of Portugal. It has also been central to debates over the relationship between corporatism and authoritarianism. Social scientists writing on corporatism in the 1960s and 1970s in particular often interpreted it as a deviation from proper capitalist development, dominant in southern Europe and Latin America on account of their cultural-historical traditions.[73] Historian John D. Wirth acknowledged that much was new in Vargas's Estado Novo, but still framed corporatism as an update of "old Iberian traditions of patrimonialism" that Vargas "revamped into the mystique of technocracy."[74] Other scholars turned to corporatism to explain the rise of dictatorships, especially as a new wave of authoritarianism took hold in Latin America.[75] Corporatism seemed to offer a strategy for overcoming "delayed dependent capitalist development" by having the state integrate key groups into the decision-making structure of government to ensure political stability and coordinated developmentalist policies.[76] Latin America and southern Europe—the latter less theorized—were latecomers to the transition from agrarian to industrial societies, which was presumably why strong, centralizing, and authoritarian states guided the modernization process.[77] Some social scientists writing about the resurgence of corporatism across South America in the 1960s and 1970s, moreover, took the examples of Salazarist Portugal and Francoist Spain as archetypes for the rise of institutionalized—and highly bureaucratized—authoritarianism.[78] Portugal's Estado Novo was not a "fossil" still responding to bygone crises of the 1920s and 1930s, Schmitter contends, but a relevant case study in how a dictator and his narrow circle of advisers managed to build a governing system for steering "development without change; participation without freedom; capitalism without capitalists."[79] Corporatism, however, was hardly a static system, nor could its architects ever quite insulate it from change—or fully define it outside of capitalism.

This argument that corporatism offered a variety of capitalism without capitalists nonetheless dominated much of the early scholarship on corporatism. For historians and social scientists writing about Brazil and Portugal as both countries navigated transitions from dictatorship to democracy in the 1970s and 1980s, debates over corporatism turned into debates over the relationship between economic system and democratic possibilities. For Brazil in particular, a group of social scientists, largely from the University of São Paulo, explained the country's repeated turn to authoritarianism in terms of its incomplete transition from an agrarian society to an industrial one, in which no dominant class emerged powerful enough to temper the actions of the state and ground democratic practices.[80] Since the 1980s, historians such as Eli Diniz and Barbara Weinstein have challenged these notions about Brazil, rejecting the premise of Brazil's "missing bourgeoisie" by showing how industrialists maneuvered within Brazil's corporatist apparatus to impose their interests and design the very laws governing this system.[81] As much as powerful interests were able to tilt the corporatist scale to benefit capital over labor and thereby shape Brazil's economic trajectory, the intellectual and political project to carve out a third path did not evaporate but rather evolved into debates over the possibilities of building new models to fix economic problems.

A *Third Path* does not intervene in debates over whether corporatism should be considered its own system or enfolded as a variation of capitalism. Rather, it considers how those who supported corporatism were themselves trapped by this debate. It does so by bringing the history of development back to the interwar period and reframing it as a response to the crisis of capitalism.[82] The history of developmentalism as it has evolved over the past twenty years largely focuses on the post–World War II period, which couples the rise of developmentalism to the advance of liberal democracy and decolonization.[83] At first glance, the dichotomies of the Cold War might suggest that only two options were available to the developing world: capitalism or communism. This study of corporatism, however, illuminates not only the creative efforts to forge an intermediate path between those competing systems but also the importance of looking to alternative spaces to understand how interwar disruptions continued to shape postwar competition between different economic models. Rather than conclude that corporatism failed because it diverged too much in practice from its ideal type, in Brazil and Portugal we see how these interwar experiments generated durable models for public-private collaboration in the drive for economic development. Essential to their corporatist logic, Vargas and Salazar oversaw the design of new administrative channels for policymaking, conflict resolution, and enforcement, all while isolating these channels from public scrutiny and democratic accountability. Corporatism cannot be reduced to an authoritarian model for development, but its history is essential to understanding the enduring appeal of top-down, technocratic, and even undemocratic policy actions in times of economic crisis.

Chapter Summary

Chapter 1 explores how corporatism emerged out of the 1920s' crises that discredited liberalism and laissez-faire capitalism. The Great Depression in 1929 was the culmination of decades-long political, economic, and financial crises impacting Brazil and Portugal, together explaining the rise of corporatism. Chapter 2 argues that the project to replace liberalism began as a legal experiment. This chapter traces the entangled histories of Brazil's experiments with corporatist constitutionalism and Portugal's 1933 Constitution. It excavates the many drafts written and discarded in both nations to examine how liberal democratic institutions were dismantled and replaced with corporatist-inspired ones. Jurists, political leaders, and intellectuals insisted that their aim was not to eliminate democracy but instead to replace liberal democracy with "authoritarian democracy."

Chapter 3 follows a network of economists that encompassed Brazil, Portugal, and Italy working to design "corporatist economics," or an economic model that could replace classical economic theories. One of this network's main theoretical interventions was to rethink price as an economic variable that needed to respond to social and economic interests. To ensure harmony between different economic groups and sectors, corporatist intellectuals emphasized the role of the state in national economic life, presenting the state as the necessary antidote to the failures self-adjusting markets. Chapter 4 shifts from ideas to institutions to show how corporatist economics shaped policymaking. Chapter 5 draws together legal and constitutional ideas with the initiatives to correct the failures of laissez-faire capitalism to consider how Brazil's experiment with corporatism altered the economic lives of merchants, bankers, and bakers. The chapter follows how Vargas and his legal team decreed a law to defend "popular economy," targeting the petty crimes of price gouging in food markets, usury, and other monopolistic activities.

The last two chapters describe the failures of corporatism as well as its survival in the postwar decades. Chapter 6 looks at the economic consequences of World War II in Brazil and Portugal. War disrupted the corporatist experiment inaugurated in the 1930s, but those same state institutions were seamlessly adapted to meet the wartime emergency. The chapter concludes with a paradox: the war strengthened Brazil's and Portugal's commitment to a state-directed economy, even as popular support for such interventions buckled, with citizens blaming inflation, shortages, and black markets on the excess of controls. Finally, Chapter 7 explores the decline of corporatist thinking, but also its paradoxical survival with the rise of economic planning and development-ism from the 1940s to the 1960s. By the war's end, the conviction with which intellectuals and technocrats alike had at one point defended the anti-liberal, top-down, and authoritarian project was tempered on both sides of the Atlantic as they came to terms with the shortcomings of their experiment. This was certainly more the case for Brazil than for Portugal, where competition between ideas was always more dynamic and a formal alliance with the Allied powers drew it into the democratic opening at the war's end. But Salazar had to contend with a groundswell of criticism and opposition too. In 1945, that one regime survived while the other did not was neither evident nor inevitable during the war. In Brazil, *corporatism* disappeared in name, but it survived in institutions well into the postwar period. By contrast, in Portugal, corporatism survived in both name and law, yet was reformulated to fit new postwar economic paradigms. In both countries, corporatist institutions survived to guide economic planning and developmentalism in the postwar decades.

Economic crises create opportunities for bold experimentation. Across seven chapters, *A Third Path* explores corporatism as an intellectual project and as a project in state making in order to recover the ideological and institutional coordinates that guided the process of economic recovery and development in twentieth-century Brazil and Portugal. Corporatism is no relic of interwar dictatorships, but a governing logic that continues to evolve as new economic problems emerge and different collective interests try to influence political power. To revisit earlier experiments with corporatism is to contend with the inherent problems of a system designed to channel (or limit) how citizens exert influence on national economic policies and priorities, but also to be reminded of the allure of new paths when old formulas appear broken.

PART I

1

Crisis

IN MAY 1922, Portuguese journalist and poet António Ferro (1895–1956) arrived in Brazil for a yearlong visit, having been invited to stage his controversial (and later censored) play *Mar Alto* in São Paulo.[1] Brazilian modernism had celebrated its spectacular inauguration in São Paulo in February during Semana de Arte Moderna, or Modern Art Week. The weeklong event featured avant-garde artists, architects, and poets who abandoned the formalism and academicism of previous generations that had looked to European styles in order to inaugurate a distinctly Brazilian art and modernism.[2] Ferro, then in his twenties, was himself a leading figure of Portuguese modernism, respected as a journalist, poet, novelist, and cinematographer. Brazilian poet and diplomat Ronald de Carvalho had read aloud Ferro's poem "Nós" ("We") during Semana de Arte Moderna.[3] This poem—later published in *Klaxon*, the official magazine of Brazilian modernism—was a frenzied dialogue between the *multidão* (the "masses") and *eu* ("me"). A stream-of-consciousness commentary on the modern era, it jumbled personal and political anxieties over the electrification of cities, destruction caused by World War I, rise of revolutionary movements, and recent expansions to "the rights of man."[4] "Nós" caught the attention of Brazilian audiences with its emotional and energetic treatment of growing tensions between the individual and collective, and between elite and popular experiences of politics. Ferro's poetry turned these crises into a connective tissue between Brazil and Portugal.

Ferro (figure 1.1) traveled to Brazil in 1922, excited to reopen artistic and intellectual channels between the two Portuguese-speaking nations.[5] While both nations had long looked to France and England for artistic and intellectual inspiration, Ferro championed Luso-Brazilian exchanges, and a decade later was in a position to turn these ideas into a political reality. In 1933, Portuguese dictator António de Oliveira Salazar would appoint Ferro to be director of the Secretariado da Propaganda Nacional, or Secretariat of National Propaganda, the Estado Novo's propaganda ministry, where he put modernist aesthetics to work to construct a cult of personality around Salazar, elevating the once austere

FIGURE 1.1. Portuguese poet and journalist António Ferro (February 1922).
Image courtesy of the Arquivo Nacional Torre do Tombo. Collection Empresa
Pública do Jornal *O Século*, fotografias de 1921–1925, doc. PT/TT/EPJS/SF/006
/01509.

finance minister into a national savior. Ferro was the inventor of Salazarismo, a political movement grounded in nationalism, imperialism, and corporatism.[6] As propaganda minister, he championed Portugal's imperial past and present—a project that led him to strengthen ties between Brazil and Portugal.[7] His mission was to advocate for a new *cruzada da lusitanidade*; the word *cruzada* was loaded with religious symbolism, and connoted both a religious crusade and crisscrossing.[8]

Whether Ferro knew it at the time, his trip to Brazil was the first step in a multidecade project to devise a new political experiment out of the decay of nineteenth-century liberalism. He was not alone in this project. The year 1922 was a turning point worldwide. From the founding of the Soviet Union and rise of Joseph Stalin to the Fascist Blackshirts' March on Rome that brought Benito Mussolini to power and the final dissolution of the Ottoman Empire, the nineteenth-century world order came to a close.[9] These global events shaped Ferro's political and intellectual trajectory as he bounced from Brazil to Angola to Italy and beyond. Over the next few years, he also visited Spain during the dictatorship of Miguel Primo de Rivera and Turkey under Mustafa Kemal Atatürk, marveling at the autocratic governments taking hold in Europe. His writings on 1920s dictatorships—compiled into *Viagem à volta das ditaduras* (1927)—documented new ways of governing beyond liberal coordinates. While no political theorist, Ferro had a knack for converting political ideas into emotions and experiences. He set out to dislodge the nineteenth-century emphasis on "liberty" as the pillar of political—and economic—life. Instead, "state," "nation," "authority," "church," "discipline," "work," and "family" became his political buzzwords, plus a long-forgotten category given fresh meaning: *corporações económicas*, or "economic corporations."[10]

This chapter is organized according to the succession of crises that Brazil and Portugal endured following World War I, up to and including the Great Depression. This is not to assert that the rise of corporatism was emergency driven, ad hoc, or ephemerally opportunistic.[11] Rather, political instability, social unrest, economic stagnation, and financial distress in the 1920s exposed the failures of liberal political and economic institutions in Brazil and Portugal, thereby emboldening conservatives who had long rejected liberalism and attracting new sympathizers to the antiliberal camp.[12] While interwar crises were hardly uniform across the two nations, they produced parallel anxieties over "backwardness" and a shared rejection of nineteenth-century liberalism that created the conditions for corporatist ideas to take hold.[13] Even in its experimental and early years, corporatism offered an evolving intellectual belief system and organizational logic that therefore would exist beyond times of crisis and long into the twentieth century. Along this Portuguese-speaking corridor, intellectuals, economists, and political officials looked to each other for political inspiration—a gesture that required a reckoning with their shared colonial past and entangled efforts to aggrandize Luso-Brazilian "civilization," a catchall and ubiquitous category couched in racial and cultural terms. Brazil and Portugal's joint turn to corporatism had as much to do with the political and economic dislocations that both nations endured throughout the 1920s as with the cultural narratives woven by people like Ferro to explain why corporatism was the only suitable path.

Crisis of War and Peace

Both Brazil and Portugal joined the Allied powers in World War I, but were marginal to the main theaters of war. Neither nation endured much physical destruction or many military casualties. As part of the Allied coalition, neither was burdened by reparation payments. Nor did either experience the revolutionary fervor or demoralizing postwar slumps such as occurred in Weimar Germany. Rather than a catastrophic break, World War I accelerated chronic social and economic problems in Brazil and Portugal, namely those related to their agrarian economies. The war also shattered the cultural and political hegemony of western European powerhouses, which created room for Brazil and Portugal to start looking to each other.

During the war, Portugal suffered far greater casualties on the home front than the war front. Only 8,000 soldiers were lost in combat, but nearly 140,000 civilians died from the great influenza epidemic and thousands more from malnutrition.[14] These statistics are staggering for a country of about 6 million people. Portugal's fledging First Republic, founded in 1910 following the overthrow of its monarchy, could not withstand the internal pressures. Successions of republican governments failed to galvanize public support for the war owing to the predominantly rural and illiterate populations that bore the brunt of inflation and food scarcity. Portugal was largely dependent on imports for essential goods, especially wheat and coal. The war disrupted international trade, both because essential goods were needed for the war effort and due to Germany's submarine offensive. The domestic production of essential goods also fell, and basic staples such as codfish practically disappeared from the internal market. With Portugal's war expenses estimated at seventy million British pounds, the Banco de Portugal was forced to print money and thus inflation became another hardship. From 1914 to 1918, price levels in Portugal increased by nearly 200 percent.[15] According to economic historian Nuno Valério, banknotes in circulation increased by nearly 200 percent as well during the war.[16]

With no battlefield victories to celebrate or heroes to canonize when the Allies won in 1918, most Portuguese contemporaries saw the war as politically and economically catastrophic.[17] It did not help that Portugal benefited little from the spoils of victory. Portugal's experience parallels—albeit less dramatically— Italy's, where peace proved disappointing in terms of new territories acquired.[18]

Portugal had joined forces with its longtime ally Great Britain partly on the promise of picking up Germany's colonies in Africa. This calculation was misguided. Portugal acquired only the Kionga Triangle on the coastal northern tip of Mozambique.[19] The impoverished Iberian nation also received little in the way of reparations and was denied any major role in the League of Nations.[20] If anything, the war confirmed Portugal's status as a second-rate nation, excluded from the inner circle of international powers trying to govern the world.

Across the Atlantic, Brazil joined the Allied powers in October 1917. Brazil's wartime experiences were not as destructive or demoralizing as Portugal's or other belligerent nations. Brazil made important gains on the world stage, playing an active role during peace negotiations at Versailles. But the war exposed cracks in the economic and social foundation of Brazil's First Republic. It disrupted the free circulation of people, goods, and capital that had sustained Brazil's export-led economy for decades. Throughout the nineteenth century Brazil's economic growth relied on the export of rubber, sugar, cotton, and especially coffee. As the world's largest supplier of coffee, Brazil depended on access to consumer markets in the United States and Europe. To expand coffee production, Brazil required consistent flows of immigrant workers, especially from southern Europe, and foreign loans to finance valorization programs, railroad construction, and other infrastructure.[21] These flows halted in 1914.

Shipping costs soared while trade blockades disrupted supply chains. The war might have been a boon to some sectors, stimulating demand for rubber, sugar, and beef, but it devastated other sectors, especially coffee. Overall, Brazilian exports (in British pound sterling) fell by 16 percent during the war, while imports decreased by 24 percent.[22] Just before the outbreak of war, food accounted for about 25 percent of Brazil's total imports, with manufactured goods about 50 percent. Wheat, largely imported from the United States and Argentina, represented nearly 10 percent of Brazil's total imports by 1912, or about as much as iron and steel or machinery.[23] With the war, Brazil also struggled to import fuel and machinery, while the cost of textiles jumped nearly fourfold between 1913 and 1918.[24]

Brazil's dependency on foreign markets for foodstuffs and manufactures not only wreaked havoc on its current accounts but became a political vulnerability too. The war brought economic dislocation and social unrest. Inflation soared while food and other essential goods were scarce.[25] Internal prices doubled during the war, in part because Brazil abandoned gold convertibility and increased emissions in paper currency.[26] To protest the rising cost of living in major urban centers, thousands of workers, consumers, and urban poor mobilized against the government, demanding fair prices and stable supplies of bread.[27] Popular protests against food scarcity, unaffordable rents, and depreciating wages culminated in the 1917 general strike, a remarkable feat of collective action.[28] In the capital Rio de Janeiro, the government responded with police raids to disband protests. During the First Republic, the market—as with other touchstones of social conflict such as public health or labor conditions—was treated as a *caso de polícia*, or police matter.

Inflation and food scarcity in Brazilian urban centers had deep structural causes: the predominance of export-oriented monoculture, poor transportation between rural producers and cities, and inefficient agricultural practices. Major cities were hit hardest, as local, state, and federal governments scrambled to respond. In Rio de Janeiro, for example, the government issued price ceilings for essential goods as a stopgap measure to control runaway inflation. Wartime price controls to some extent harked back to colonial market controls sanctioned by the Portuguese Crown to stabilize the food supply in major cities—measures repealed with the advent of liberal economic ideas in the early nineteenth century. Following independence, Brazilian municipal governments largely embraced liberal policies to guarantee free exchange while also not hesitating to briefly reinstate price and supply controls in moments of acute shortages.[29] The severe economic crisis during World War I required an unprecedented mobilization of government resources to regulate economic life. Brazil's federal government was slow to respond, however, and wartime planning remained largely uncoordinated between cities and regions.[30] The public protested and ridiculed measures such as price controls and antihoarding laws as ineffective. Political cartoons and popular protests frequently blamed economic problems on corrupt interests and greedy intermediaries.[31] The *Revista do Brasil*, for example, a prominent literary and political magazine, caricatured the *açambarcador*, or hoarder, who selfishly withheld foodstuffs from consumer markets to send prices soaring, profiting from scarcity (figures 1.2 and 1.3).[32]

Government efforts to root out speculative practices could hardly be called a success. Its price tables failed to protect vulnerable citizens. Food crises became a political liability. Strikes organized by workers in major cities like Rio de Janeiro built on earlier labor organizing practices by attempting to impose or enforce price tables on local venders and manufacturers. Price became a site of social conflict as industrial elites petitioned the government to step in and impose economic order.[33] The war gave new urgency to questions of economic justice as shortages and inflation exposed the failures of free and self-correcting markets to efficiently meet basic consumer needs.

Crisis of Politics

In Brazil, unlike other belligerent nations, war did not immediately trigger government collapse. Still, political tensions simmered in the 1920s as popular classes, intellectuals, a rising industrial elite, and certain factions of the military pushed for modernization and development. These voices—for different

O AÇAMBARCADOR

— De que serve agora a tabella? De que serve tambem a discurseira do José Bezerra? Podem agir contra ou a favor, já tenho a barriga cheia.

(Raul — *Jornal do Brasil*, Rio).

FIGURE 1.2. Political cartoon "O açambarcador," or "The hoarder" (1918). Translation of the caption: "What use is the price table now? And what use are José Bezerra's (minister of agriculture, industry, and commerce) speeches? You can be for or against it, my belly is already full." Printed in *Revista do Brasil* (September 1918). Image courtesy of Harvard University Library.

reasons and with different arguments—clamored against the liberal oligarchic politics of the late nineteenth century. In 1922, the Brazilian Communist Party (Partido Comunista Brasileiro) was founded—the culmination of years of general strikes and collective action among the popular classes and working poor seeking social rights and political recognition.[34] During the 1920s, the party grew modestly as it attempted to build support among organized labor, and became the target of police repression and censorship.[35] In the 1930s, Getúlio Vargas would seize on anticommunist sentiment to transform the Communist Party along with other labor and left-wing movements into internal threats to national security in order to legitimize his usurpation of power.

The year 1922 brought another political movement as well: the First Tenente Revolt in which young army officers seized Fort Copacabana in Rio de Janeiro. This revolt began with officers protesting the imprisonment of one of their own,

O AÇAMBARCAMENTO DOS GENEROS

Os varejistas — A freguezia tem que pagar as migalhas a peso de ouro ;
nós é que não vamos no prejuizo.

(*Storni* — ''D. Quixote''. Rio de Janeiro)

FIGURE 1.3. Political cartoon "O açambarcador dos gêneros," or "The hoarder of foodstuff" (1917). Translation of the caption: "The retailers—the customers will have to pay for crumbs in their weight in gold; we won't be the ones to suffer loss." Printed in *Revista do Brasil* (August 1917). Image courtesy of Harvard University Library.

but eventually became a radical political movement calling for economic modernization, agrarian reform, cooperatives to organize agricultural production, and the nationalization of mineral wealth. The largely lower-middle-class *tenentes* were military engineers by training and saw the army as the necessary agent for national progress. As John D. Wirth argues, the tenentes were primarily concerned with Brazil's "backwardness" given that many of them witnessed firsthand the poverty-stricken hinterlands. While Wirth notes that the tenentes were "ideologically unsophisticated," they did take inspiration from late nineteenth-century positivist writers like Alberto Torres and their own contemporary, sociologist Francisco José de Oliveira Vianna, whose writings already circulated widely.[36] The officers wanted to seize power and impart change as they called into question old ideas and institutions on a political platform of aggressive nationalism and modernizing ambitions. Tenentes were anticommunist but also antiliberal and had an authoritarian leaning. They would take center stage immediately following Vargas's 1930 Revolution, but their program fused with other ideas and interests to give rise to Brazil's corporatist experiment.

Meanwhile, as the Tenete Revolt unfolded, an avant-garde group of experimental painters, writers, and poets grappled with Brazil's past and futures. Those gathering in São Paulo in February 1922 were hardly united in their aesthetic or political convictions.[37] Brazil's modernist movement drew intellectuals and artists as much from the Left—those with revolutionary politics and sympathies for working-class struggles—as from the Right. Several protonationalist groups emerged out of Semana de Arte Moderna, including verde-amarelismo, or the green-yellow movement, a nationalist group that included poet, writer, and political ideologue Plínio Salgado, future founder of the Ação Integralista Brasileira (AIB), Brazil's homegrown fascist movement. In the 1920s, the verde-amarelismo movement assailed universalizing ideals, and mobilized art and literature to construct idealized Brazilian traditions—a project that depended on abstract, reductive discourses on the country's Indigenous origins. By the late 1920s, Salgado had shifted from literature to politics as his nationalist project took on an increasingly illiberal and conservative orientation. In 1930, Salgado traveled to Italy, where he met with Mussolini, thereby cementing his admiration for Italian Fascism.[38] On his return from Italy, Salgado created the AIB. In Brazil, the AIB expressed overt antisemitism as well as explicit sympathies with Italian Fascism and German Nazism. Strongest in São Paulo, this militarized movement inspired thousands of "green shirts" and "green blouses" to march in the streets.[39]

Integralism is a largely forgotten ism, but it was powerful in Catholic societies during the first decades of the twentieth century.[40] Following in the spirit of French political philosopher Charles Maurras and the Action Française, integralists were profoundly antiliberal, Catholic, and traditionalist.[41] A counter-revolutionary movement that emerged across Europe and in Latin America, integralism aimed to reverse the social and political movements that followed the French Revolution. Integralists advanced the ideal of the "integral nation," in which the family, church, and professional corporations became the cellular units of society. Like corporatism, integralism positioned itself as a third path of sorts. A Offensiva, Brazil's integralist newspaper, declared that "while socialism fights and liberalism sleeps, integralism builds."[42]

Whereas integralism remained a spiritual, Catholic, and nationalist movement, corporatism became a system of governing and creating—quite literally—new states with a bureaucratic system built in the 1930s to organize labor and production. Ultimately these two ideologies would fiercely clash. Despite affinities between the two isms, integralist movements were targeted as internal enemies in the 1930s, as both Vargas's and Salazar's dictatorships used censorship, military tribunals, and state violence to purge integralists in order to solidify their grasp on power.

Portuguese journalist Ferro was in Brazil as these nationalist political movements started to take form. Ferro and Salgado ran in similar circles, and it is
possible that they met during his visit.[43] It is challenging to piece together
these transnational networks—connections were episodic, and the interwar
decades saw constant ideological shifts and conflicts. Nationalist movements
needed to strike a balance between finding inspiration in foreign movements
and asserting homegrown, authentic qualities. Ferro would spend much of
his career working for Salazar's conservative, nationalist, and corporatist dictatorship in Portugal. To many, Ferro is a paradox: he celebrated modern art and
modern political expressions—from mass politics to mass communication—
but also became the steward of a political movement that emphasized Catholicism, traditionalism, and agrarianism.[44] The parades and posters he oversaw
as Secretariado da Propaganda Nacional director idealized the Portuguese as
farmers—pious, modest, and obedient—unperturbed by the social upheavals
and class conflicts of economic modernization. His enthusiasm for Brazilian
modernism might be dismissed as a youthful dalliance. But Ferro's impulse to
overturn the cultural status quo found broader expression in the illiberal
political movements of the 1920s.

In 1923, just a year after traveling to Brazil, Ferro went to Italy as a reporter
for *Diário de Notícias* (figure 1.4). He wrote about El Duce with awe and admiration, reinforcing Mussolini's image as an uncompromising "force of nature."[45] Ferro made two trips to Italy in the 1920s, interviewing Mussolini
alongside key figures in the Fascist Party—and a handful of antifascist opponents—to explain to Portuguese audiences how fascism worked. Ferro celebrated dictatorship as a modern form of government.[46] In Italy, he found not
just a political leader but a spiritual movement too. He called Mussolini the
"dictator of Italy, dictator of his own self, dictator of his body and soul!"[47]

Mussolini began his rise to power after Italy's embittered victory in World
War I. While on the winning side, Italy faced embarrassment at the terms of its
victory and disappointment with its lack of territorial gains. At home, the war
brought destruction and deprivation. Wartime expenditures had commanded
as much as one-third of Italy's national income from 1916 to 1918. The country
faced extreme food scarcity and a 164 percent increase in price levels during the
conflict. After the war, inflation worsened and Italy's currency, the lira, steeply
depreciated. Farm and industrial workers unionized and labor strikes proliferated. Workers occupied farms and factories during the "red two years" (*biennio
rosso*) from 1919 to 1920.[48] Fascist squads transformed from local movements
that attacked striking workers and farmers into a national political party. Violence functioned as both political strategy and ideology. In 1921, the National
Fascist Party took 22 percent of the vote, with Mussolini securing a seat in the
Chamber of Deputies. In October 1922, Fascist blackshirts organized the

FIGURE 1.4. Portuguese poet and journalist António Ferro (*third from the left*) for the newspaper *Diário de Notícias* aboard the *Cap Polonio* (February 1926), standing with journalists representing Portuguese and international newspapers. Image courtesy of the Arquivo Nacional Torre do Tombo. Collection Empresa Pública do Jornal *O Século*, Álbuns Gerais no. 1, doc. PT/TT/EPJS/SF/001-001 /0001/0278A.

infamous March on Rome, which led King Victor Emmanuel III to concede and appoint Mussolini as prime minister.

Long before it became a derogatory epithet to describe a range of autocratic regimes, fascism was Italy's "revolutionary" political system.[49] Mussolini's government ruthlessly suppressed opposition voices, banned political parties, and curtailed free speech and press. Fascism offered a path forward for those unconvinced by liberalism and fearful of socialism. Much has been written about fascist ideology: its rebuke of liberalism, charismatic dictatorship, and cult of violence; its nationalist mass movement, territorial and cultural imperialism, and racialized construction of the nation; its futurist aesthetics, revolutionary appeal, and reactionary social vision; its extreme anticommunism and also its claims to be "the natural child of revolutionary Marxism."[50] Fascists were, from the start, denounced as totalitarian by their opponents—a label that Mussolini appropriated as core to his political philosophy. Italy's dictatorship attempted the total control of society, shaping family planning, labor relations, and commercial life. Liberty became a slur, a sign of decadence and weakness.

Although much has been written on fascism, it is not easy to define.[51] Ferro started his interview with Mussolini by asking if he could "give me, in a few sentences, a summary of fascism?" Mussolini appeared annoyed, saying, "I do not like to repeat myself." Where Mussolini did elaborate at length was on "why fascism?" Fascism was a break with the "old categories" and "old classifications" of liberalism, which did not suit Italy.[52] Mussolini and his followers—and even some future scholars of fascism—believed fascism emerged for reasons endemic to Italy: the inability of liberalism to penetrate its fragmented geography, weak civic culture, apolitical peasantry, and the centuries-old system of local clientage.[53] For Mussolini, however, fascism was not a mark of failure but rather a promise of revival. Fascism was modern, futuristic, and revolutionary, while at the same time it restored "to Italy its lost traditions."[54]

Ferro saw in fascism a model to restore greatness to Portugal. "I think of Portugal and I become sad," he wrote during one of his trips to Italy. "In our country," he lamented, "an experiment of this order is not possible. . . . [I]t is not possible because everyone has their eyes closed, because everyone is sleeping."[55]

From 1917 to 1926, Portugal was governed by more than thirty governments, experienced coups in 1917 and 1926, and saw an attempt to reestablish monarchy in 1918.[56] This decade of perpetual political crisis began when Sidónio Pais seized power.[57] A military officer active in Portuguese politics following the overthrow of the monarchy in 1910, Pais had vehemently opposed Portugal's participation in the war. By December 1917, Portugal's military failures, especially its inability to defend its prized colony, Angola, triggered a crisis of political legitimacy. Pais staged a coup and organized a plebiscite to decree himself president. Salazar and his supporters would later celebrate this move to replace the parliamentary system with a strong presidency.

Ferro watched the coup unfold from Angola, where he was completing military service and working for Governor-General Filomeno da Câmara de Melo Cabral.[58] He fiercely admired and exalted Pais for awakening Portuguese nationalism as well as connecting with the people: "The people adored him, gave themselves to him."[59] Pais enjoyed support from conservative Catholic factions, but also built a popular mass following. His República Nova (New Republic) repressed opposition movements, especially Portugal's incipient labor movements. While the República Nova lacked a refined ideological platform, it explicitly opposed Bolshevism and parliamentary democracy. Pais's collaborators pushed to create a senate composed of professional and economic interests. In Europe, his dictatorship was the first to experiment with corporatist forms of representation in government.[60]

The República Nova was short-lived. In November 1918, as the war came to an end, a general strike erupted across the country—the culmination of years of workers' activism for political recognition, better employment conditions, and enforcement of price controls to mitigate the cost-of-living crisis. In the Alentejo village Vale de Santiago, rural workers occupied landed estates during a four-day standoff. Pais responded with police force and detained thousands of political prisoners.[61] The government eventually suppressed the strike, deporting some workers to Portuguese Africa. A week later, one participant in the Alentejo uprising assassinated Pais in Lisbon's Rossio train station.[62]

In addition to turmoil and crisis at home, the postwar geopolitical order threatened Portugal's empire. The Portuguese government had joined the Allied powers in the hopes of acquiring new territories, but the League of Nations scrutinized human rights abuses in the Portuguese colonies.[63] In 1926, US anthropologist Edward Ross traveled to Angola and was horrified by the persistence of forced labor.[64] His exposé inspired an international scandal as many world powers questioned Portugal's legitimacy as a colonial power. Portuguese officials questioned the motives of these humanitarian campaigns, convinced that foreign powers—whether Germany, Italy, or corporate commercial interests—had their eyes on Portuguese territories.[65]

The Italian government in particular blatantly coveted Angola. Throughout the 1920s and 1930s, Portuguese diplomats anxiously reported on Italian schemes to encourage immigration to Angola and establish Italian agricultural enterprises.[66] During his 1926 visit to Italy, Ferro confronted Mussolini about rumors of Italian plans to develop agricultural colonies in Angola, which Mussolini dismissed as "fantastic and ridiculous!"[67] Nevertheless, foreign threats combined with the empire's own political and financial instability led many in Lisbon to recognize the urgent need to overhaul the relationship between metropole and colony.[68]

Elected officials appeared inept at addressing compounding crises of politics, economics, and imperial decline. Conservative factions increasingly blamed liberal democracy for mounting instability. According to one political manifesto, published ahead of the last free elections prior to the 1926 military coup, "Portugal's Parliament has generated distrust, raised the cost of living, abandoned the working masses, destroyed nascent industry, ruined Angola and opened a crisis whose outcome no one can predict."[69] Salazar would seize on this sentiment to usurp power.

Historian Mark Mazower notes that there was hardly a president or prime minister in Europe who remained in power for more than a year in the 1920s.[70] Exceptions to this rule were dictators. The facile association of authoritarianism with order might well have inspired Ferro to publish his collection of essays *Viagem à volta das ditaduras* (Traveling around dictatorships) in 1927. Together, these essays on Italy, Spain, and Turkey read as an aspirational blueprint for Portugal.

Ferro found in these countries political leaders reckoning with backwardness. Ferro's thoughts on the matter, as was true of his Portuguese contemporaries, often imbued economic and political explanations with cultural, racist, and biological discourses. When in Turkey, Ferro obsessed over the Ottoman tradition of wearing a fez, and asked whether change in dress could change political culture. One might expect that Ferro would identify most with Primo de Rivera's regime in Spain given how the politics of *iberismo* and *hispanismo* inspired his later work as Salazar's propaganda minister. Yet it was Turkey under the leadership of Mustafa Kemal Atatürk that excited Ferro about the modernizing potential of dictatorship. He praised the Turkish National Assembly as the most orderly and disciplined chamber in the world, but also equated "parliaments fabricated by dictators" with "barbarian organs." As Ferro admitted, "I understand Mustafa Kemal, his civilizing urges. He wanted to rid Turkey of the stigma of barbarism."[71] Ferro's obsession with "civilization" versus "barbarism" in Turkey overlaid his lamentations for Portugal and worries that poor nations might never overcome their endowments.

Ferro's travels are a window into the anxieties and aspirations motivating political experimentation in the 1920s. In many ways, Brazil and Portugal were at the margins of European and world politics, but Ferro connected them to each other as well as to events in Italy, Spain, and Turkey. These countries—whether conservative, populist, or fascist—offered answers to the failings of classical liberalism.

Crisis of Liberalism

In Brazil and Portugal, critiques of liberalism took hold in the 1920s, and the nationalist movements that emerged depended on transnational connections. This was no contradiction.[72] As Brazilian integralist Álvaro Pinto later observed during a trip to Portugal, Brazilian and Portuguese intellectuals for too long had "confused *nationalism* with *nativism*."[73] Following Brazil's independence from Portugal, anti-Portuguese sentiments were not uncommon among Brazilian political elites or popular classes.[74] World War I, however, shattered the cultural and economic hegemony of the Great Powers. Brazilians began to look elsewhere for political inspiration. Despite disruptions to international travel during the war, intellectual and political ties between Brazil and Portugal strengthened. Growing Luso-Brazilian connections did not necessarily replace influences from France or England for either country, but they did forge an alternative for these two societies on the margins of global intellectual production.[75]

In 1916, for example, the University of Lisbon created its first endowed chair in Brazilian studies, to be held by a Brazilian national and partially supported by the Brazilian government. The preeminent University of Coimbra, Portugal's oldest university and the academic home of future dictator Salazar, inaugurated its Sala do Brazil (Brazil Classroom) with the collaboration of Brazilian students in 1925.[76] While a short-lived venture, the Sala do Brasil was reinaugurated in 1937 as a joint political initiative under the Vargas and Salazar Estado Novos.[77]

Rapprochement between these two nations formerly bound through empire unfolded at a moment when the world was organized according to racial and cultural categories, and racial discourses about putatively innate political tendencies were inseparable to some extent from critiques of classical liberalism. The rise of eugenics and scientific racism in previous decades did not just inform the reformist social and public health policies that governments implemented to improve their populations, targeting poor, marginalized, and immigrant communities.[78] Racialized theories of degeneracy also affected how nations engaged in geopolitics and legitimized the "scramble" to acquire colonies.[79] This ossified hierarchy of nations, cultures, and races shaped relations between Brazil and Portugal, attempting to shed their reputations as developmental laggards.

The voice of this generation was Brazilian jurist and well-known sociologist Oliveira Vianna (1883–1951). Oliveira Vianna penned one of the introductory essays accompanying the 1920 census to elaborate his thesis on the pace of Brazil's population whitening—research informed by scientific racism to endorse a fixed racial hierarchy.[80] Owing to his intellectual standing, Vargas would appoint him to serve as juridical consultant in the Ministério do Trabalho, Indústria e Comércio, or Ministry of Labor, Industry, and Commerce (hereafter the Ministry of Labor), created following the 1930 Revolution. From that office, Oliveira Vianna became the legal architect of Brazil's corporatist system. His writings on labor and economic questions rarely explicitly discussed race or racial hierarchies, but his early writings on Brazil's racial and social formation undoubtedly informed his political and economic programs to transform Brazil.[81]

Born in 1883 in Saquarema, on the outskirts of then capital Rio de Janeiro, Oliveira Vianna saw his family's fortune erode as the nation's productive center shifted to São Paulo and its expanding coffee sector.[82] A member of the dwindling *fazendeiro*, or landholding, class, he trained in law as a suitable liberal profession and became a well-respected law professor in Niterói.[83] Writing about Brazil's social question in the aftermath of abolition and the inauguration of the First Republic, he wrestled with problems of national disunity following the imperial breakdown.[84] In 1921, he published *Populações meridionais do Brasil I*, stylized as the "first scientific analysis of the nation's formation."[85] He argued that Brazil's vast geography and dispersed early settlement patterns caused a high degree of decentralization. It was difficult for formal political authority to exert control over social and economic life. Filling this vacuum, rural clans monopolized the local exercise of power, a clientelist system in which codes of honor governed in place of the rule of law.

Oliveira Vianna's writings fed conservative critiques of the First Republic and its failed promises. He equated political liberalism with the despotism of individuals, blaming nineteenth-century experiments with federalism and laissez-faire capitalism for national fragmentation and disorganization. Disorganization, specifically, became Oliveira Vianna's buzzword, and connoted the incapacity of key social and economic interests to coordinate themselves to exert influence over public life.[86] In Brazil, he contended, public opinion remained too fragile, electoral politics too clientelistic, class consciousness too inchoate, and populations too dispersed and heterogeneous.[87] For Oliveira Vianna, Brazil's liberal republican experiment had dismantled the progress made under empire. He was nostalgic for Brazil's imperial past because empire was based on hierarchy and unity; empire could integrate vastly different regions and populations because each group understood its privileges and obligations. Oliveira Vianna embraced corporatism because it re-created this imperial mode of governance.[88]

Oliveira Vianna's pessimism about Brazil's trajectory coexisted with his admiration for Anglo-Saxon civilizations. The Brazilian sociologist did not universally reject liberalism but instead insisted that certain preconditions first had to be met. Some scholars see his (occasionally) ambivalent position on liberalism as an example of "instrumental authoritarianism," in which he supported dictatorship as a transitory solution to forge the preconditions for a future liberal democratic society.[89] This ambivalence, though, should not distract from Oliveira Vianna's theoretical and practical role in dismantling liberal institutions in Brazil, or his career-long commitments to building an authoritarian state. Rather, his praise of liberalism in Britain or the United States informed his pessimism about Brazil in his writings to legitimize authoritarian models.

The crisis—and abandonment—of liberalism connected Brazil to Portugal. Growing condemnation of liberalism by leading intellectuals like Oliveira Vianna contributed far more to growing support for corporatism among conservative groups than fears of communism. On both sides of the Atlantic, intellectual and political elites protested how previous generations had indiscriminately imported laws and institutions from northern Europe and North America. In the 1880s, Portuguese novelist José Maria de Eça de Queiroz used his lighthearted protagonist in Os Maias to explain why Portugal remained backward: "Here, we import everything. Laws, ideas, philosophies, theories, subjects of conversation, aesthetics, sciences, style, industries, fashions, mannerisms, jokes, everything comes in boxes on the boat. Civilization is very expensive, what with the customs dues: and it's all secondhand, it wasn't made for us, it's short in the sleeves."[90] Portugal's alleged tendency to look abroad for political, legal, and intellectual inspiration resonated in Brazil. In his 1927 *O idealismo da constituição*, Oliveira Vianna quoted Eça de Queiroz to empower his own critique of Brazil's nineteenth-century institutions: "Eca de Queiroz once said that of the maladies that afflicted Portugal, some were due to the temperament of their own people, but others were 'translated from French.' With our own [problems], we can say the same thing."[91] Oliveira Vianna embodied, but never acknowledged, the paradox that he inveighed against liberalism as a misplaced foreign ideology in Brazil, while still looking to Europe for alternatives.[92] To him, Brazil's problem was straightforward: the First Republic was a sham for its heterogeneous mix of "French democracy, English liberalism, and American federalism."[93] Integralist Plínio Salgado agreed, once remarking, "Brazil improvised its civilization and its progress the only way it could: importation."[94]

These assertions resonated in Portugal, where political and economic instability were unraveling its republican experiment along with promises of liberty and fraternity. Salazar, like many of his contemporaries, harbored a mix of pessimism and skepticism with respect to Portugal's preparedness for representative democracy and capacity for economic modernization. He too sometimes imbued his later political manifestos with cultural and civilization arguments. As Salazar noted in 1930, Portugal had for too long used "political formulas" that were "exotic imported plants."[95]

Born in 1889, Salazar belonged to a family of modest landowners in rural northern Portugal, a region characterized by small plots of land under family cultivation (*minifúndios*) largely engaged in subsistence or local market production. The seminary offered one of the few avenues for those of limited means to access education. Salazar attended the Seminário de Viseu from 1900 to 1908, before studying law at the University of Coimbra. There, he became a professor of law and political economy.[96] During his university days, Salazar collaborated with conservative Catholic think tanks, and here his political education began.[97]

Even as a young scholar and professor, the future dictator harbored few sympathies for liberal republicanism. Absorbing civilizational and eugenic discourses of the early twentieth century, Salazar conceded that Latin peoples lacked the prerequisite initiative and rationality necessary for democracy.[98] According to Portuguese historian Valentim Alexandre, Salazar was influenced by French sociologists Gustave Le Bon and Edmond Demolins, who defended a "natural" hierarchy of races and cultures in which Latin nations were inferior to English, French, or German ones.[99] In April 1914, at a conference on democracy and the Catholic Church, Salazar outlined an argument that later informed his corporatist dictatorship: a nation's political institutions should be chosen according to the "innate tendencies of that race, its way of being and thinking,

its customs and culture, its state of civilization, and even its geographic con-
figuration, climate, and soil."[100] For Portugal, liberal democracy did not work,
and the mismatch explained much of the country's failure to develop.

Crisis of Backwardness

Anxiety over backwardness was thus another thread that connected the rise of
corporatism across southern Europe and Latin America. Luso-Brazilian intellectuals stressed the economic as well as political dimensions of backwardness.
In Brazil and Portugal, the theorization of a new economic model—one called
corporatist—happened in real time and through entangled debates. Whether
in Brazil or Portugal, leading economic thinkers were grappling with their
country's disadvantaged position in the global economy. For these agricultural
societies, contemporaries were keen to point out all the ways that nineteenth-
century economic formulas had failed to bring about progress and development. In Brazil, one São Paulo politician admonished his peers for offering
only "words, words, words." "Brazilian people," he lamented, "remain oblivious
to what is happening in other countries of the world in terms of economic
preparations to increase production."[101] Similar frustrations and defeatism
could be heard in Portugal. Across this South Atlantic corridor, economists,
industrialists, and politicians were dismayed at how their nations lagged
behind more industrialized nations.

Statistical yearbooks were published more frequently in the 1920s, thereby
making national comparisons more commonplace. The gap between the industrialized and agrarian world had widened, not narrowed, in the previous
century.[102] Portugal's GDP per capita was the lowest in western Europe on the
eve of World War I.[103] Whereas in 1820, Portugal's GDP per capita stood at
54 percent of the United Kingdom's, a century later this value had dropped to
only 27 percent.[104] Brazil's economic trend was similar: in 1820, its GDP per
capita was 38 percent of the United Kingdom's—a value that dropped to
21 percent by 1920.[105] Brazilian and Portuguese economic commentators were
pessimistic about their respective country's trajectories due to limited manufacturing, the lack of local market integration, and especially their distressed
agricultural sectors. An integralist writer epitomized Brazil's defeatism: "We
are just a poor and backward people, sick with [our] civilization."[106]

Looking beyond cultural or civilizational explanations for why Brazil and
Portugal had fallen behind, journalists and essayists writing about the economy argued that their nation's precarious position in global markets disadvantaged them in international trade. Decades before Argentinean economist
Raúl Prebisch maintained that the collapse of commodity prices in the early
1920s was symptomatic of structural inequalities in the world economy,

economists in many parts of the world were coming to terms with why the price of raw materials and agricultural goods declined relative to manufactured goods over time.[107] In Brazil and Portugal, university professors, journalists, and trade representatives commenting on economic affairs started to intuitively—even if not theoretically—reckon with how their nation's dependency on primary commodity production might be the cause of their economic stagnation. In the 1920s, they did not use concepts such as terms of trade or "center-periphery" popularized by postwar Latin American economists.[108] Rather, they worried about their trade balances and gold reserves, lamenting that it was both a cause and consequence of underdevelopment that a nation should have to import more than it could export. Ricardian optimism that free trade would benefit all had evaporated and a view of trade as a zero-sum game took its place. In his 1921 study of Portugal's codfish sector, which provided a staple of the Portuguese diet, economist Moses Bensabat Amzalak, renowned for his writings on the history of economic thinking and a leading figure in Lisbon's Jewish community, explained, "Although the economic interdependence of various nations is a given, the fact of the matter is that efforts must be made so that each country, according to its resources, produces the maximum economic value for the satisfaction of its needs, especially in terms of food supply."[109] Amzalak concluded that openness to international trade had led to the dismantling of Portugal's fishing industry, and he recommended subsidies and tariffs to protect national industries and increase codfish production.

Anxieties over backwardness were fueled by international comparisons as well as concerns about national security and well-being. World War I exposed the perils of dependency on international markets for essential goods. The war, one Brazilian journalist wrote, offered the "most flagrant and practical demonstration of how necessary it is for a people to rely on their own resources to guarantee independence and well-being."[110] Tomás Cabreira, who had served as Portugal's finance minister in 1914, agreed. He attributed the country's hardships to long-term patterns in international trade: Portugal did not produce enough to feed its population, and did not export enough to cover food and industrial imports. Cabreira was trained in and remained largely faithful to classic economic models, yet he also started to question the benefits of free trade.[111] Portugal needed to increase its industrial capacity, he argued in 1917, calling for "collaboration between agriculturalists, industrialists, and merchants with public officials." Like Amzalak, Cabreira embraced a neomercantilist logic that if a nation could not produce something at home, it should import from its own colonies before trading with foreign powers. Brazil was part of his imperial imaginary. "Feeding the Portuguese people," he wrote, "will fall to the metropole, the colonies, and Brazil, which is still for all patriots an extension of our homeland."[112] Early whispers of Portuguese economic nationalism comfortably accommodated Brazil as a trading partner as well as a nation facing similar structural disadvantages.

Brazil's role as an exporter of agricultural staples and raw materials factored into debates about how the country had fallen behind. Brazilian economists noted a paradox: despite the country's wealth in natural resources, "we are one of the poorest nations in the world."[113] A growing cohort of public intellectuals held that the country needed to become a great manufacturing power in order to become a world power. Industrialists in particular worried that unless Brazil fixed its trade balance, foreign capital would look for investment opportunities elsewhere. As future finance minister José Maria Whitaker wryly observed in 1927, Brazil would need to jump-start its economic transformation "without a Mussolini to cut imports and increase exports."[114]

The rise of corporatism in the Portuguese-speaking world was fueled by the overlapping and reinforcing crises of war, politics, and empire, and tangled around discourses of race and political tendencies right from the start. Beyond specific policies or programs to be discussed below, the political movements to seize power in Brazil and Portugal readily adopted corporatism because of its theoretical and practical rejection of liberal democracy and economic liberalism. Despite how jurists, economists, industrialists, and producers in both countries blamed foreign ideas and dependency on foreign markets as the cause of national underdevelopment, their embrace of corporatism was paradoxically transnational, conditional on growing connections between Brazilian and Portuguese intellectual networks.

Economic Crisis and the Start of Corporatism

Added to more general concerns about backwardness, Brazil and Portugal were in economic crisis in the 1920s. During World War I, belligerent nations had 30 to 40 percent of their GDP controlled—directly or indirectly—by the state.[115] To varying degrees, wartime governments engaged in economic planning to set price controls, implement rationing to manage especially urgent food shortages, and even directly control certain industries.[116] After the war, government leaders confronted the question of whether they should return to the laissez-faire ways of the previous century, or continue some state interventions to stabilize consumer prices, stimulate industry, and protect domestic producers. Most post–World War I governments eliminated wartime controls, but wartime planning nonetheless left an indelible mark. The wartime emergency had eroded the "distinction between public and private sectors," historian Charles Maier explains, and also generated new citizen expectations.[117] In the 1920s, popular demands for governments to intervene in matters of food security and the cost of living galvanized progressive, socialist, and social democratic groups to experiment with new policies: Weimar Germany implemented rent control and Argentina's largest political party, the Radical Civic Union (Unión Cívica Radical), distributed low-cost *pan radical,* or radical bread, as a form of direct assistance to constituents (even as government commitments to social welfare remained limited so as to not disrupt powerful landowners' interests).[118]

It was in this postwar context that modern corporatist experiments began to take shape. First in Italy and then in Brazil and Portugal, corporatist ideas influenced new government-led efforts to increase national production, stabilize prices, and grow domestic markets. Early economic campaigns targeted wheat and rice production to feed national populations and ensure national self-sufficiency. Conservative, fascist, and corporatist movements understood that they could neither totally retract prior gains in social welfare nor ignore popular economic hardships.

Fascist Italy was the first to experiment with corporatism to overhaul state-market relations. Following World War I, Italy continued experiencing high inflation and currency instability. The economic output suffered, with GDP declining in 1919 by 14.5 percent and in 1920 by 7.6 percent.[119] The value of the lira tumbled. Mussolini rose to power amid this economic turmoil without any sort of economic program, and his first task was the painful process of financial reconstruction.[120] He appointed Alberto de' Stefani, a professor of political economy, as finance minister. Stefani cut expenditures, simplified tax collection, and eliminated wartime economic controls and civil servant jobs to balance the budget.[121] In his autobiography, Mussolini celebrated his austerity program as an illustration of bold action: "I had to give a smashing blow to useless expenditures, and to those who sought tribute from the Treasury. I had to rake up tax-slackers. I had to establish severest economy in every branch of State administration."[122]

At first, Mussolini's economic policy embraced the return to laissez-faire. Stefani was a committed liberal, following an austerity program based in monetary and fiscal orthodoxy. He advocated for the free circulation of people, goods, and capital as essential to postwar prosperity, even as other nations increasingly embraced protectionism.[123] Despite initial international praise for his balanced budget, Stefani's relationship with the Fascist Party soured as Italian industrialists and large landowners protested cuts to subsidies and other protections, and the country's economy deteriorated. In July 1925, Mussolini replaced Stefani with Giuseppe Volpi, an industrial entrepreneur turned public servant. Volpi's business ventures in tobacco, utilities, and infrastructure extended beyond Italy to the Balkans. Appointed governor of Libya from 1921 to 1925, he cultivated close ties between the government and the private sector, arguing for the state's role in tackling credit scarcity.[124] Volpi's administration jettisoned liberal ortho-doxy to embrace corporatism. As finance minister, he emphasized—and even institutionalized—close collaboration between state and industry.[125]

In 1925, Mussolini announced the first of two economic campaigns that would define fascist political economy: the Battaglia per la Lira (Battle for the Lira) and Battaglia del Grano (Battle for Wheat). The Battle for Wheat was the first of Italy's corporatist programs, requiring agriculturalists, business in-termediaries, and labor all to "bend to Fascist authority."[126] The Battle for Wheat aimed to increase the domestic production of wheat to end the dependency on imports. By 1925, Italy's grain imports cost nearly four billion lire, or about 25 percent of imported goods and services.[127] The Battle for Wheat created new government commissions that trained farmers in efficient cultivation methods, offering prizes to producers with the highest output per hectare, facilitating access to machinery and fertilizers, and distributing genet-ically curated seeds for high yields.[128] It also introduced protectionist measures such as tariffs, trade restrictions, and subsidies. By 1931, millers and bakers were legally required to use at least 95 percent Italian wheat in making bread and pasta. Moreover, the regime introduced acreage, supply, and price controls—measures enforced by new state and parastate agencies in corporatist fashion. The Permanent Wheat Committee—headed by Mussolini, and staffed with high-ranking state officials, agricultural scientists, and representatives of farm-ers' syndicates—was responsible for overseeing the battle.[129] State-controlled agricultural cooperatives, farmers' syndicates, and peasant unions represented landowners and rural workers in this new system, but were also tasked with enforcing local compliance with state directives.[130] The Fascist government vertically integrated economic decision-making into the state, using state agencies and farmer associations.

The Quota novanta (ninety quota) supported the Battle for the Lira by fixing the rate of 92.46 lire per British pound sterling—a rate that increased Italy's 1925 currency to its value when Mussolini assumed power in 1922.[131] Comple-menting the protectionist measures in the Battle for Wheat, the Quota novanta symbolized Mussolini's push for economic self-sufficiency. For Italian finan-ciers and industrialists, however, it was an egregious overvaluation that re-quired immense sacrifice from the public because the overvalued currency made imports more expensive, which aggravated the cost of living, and indus-trialists had to pay more for machinery.[132] Scholars tend to agree that this cam-paign was more a political than economic decision. Economist Clara Mattei, for instance, argues that the Battle for the Lira went beyond monetary opera-tions to consolidate "a class system into stable hierarchies under the name of necessary national efforts for economic redemption."[133] Mussolini insisted that a strong nation needed a strong currency.

Over the next ten years, Italy's Fascist government increased state powers over the economy, beyond the grain sector. By the mid-1930s, a range of para-state agencies represented industrial and labor interests. These confederations, consortia, and syndical institutions became tools for extending government controls over wages, imports, exports, prices, the licensing of new industrial plant construction, and labor conditions. Corporatist-style market controls touched all aspects of economic production and commerce. The Battle for Wheat significantly reduced Italy's dependence on imports as grain yields increased by 50 percent between 1924 and 1932.[134] Following the Great Depression, Italy's industrial production quickly rebounded to pre-1929 levels by 1935, offering a performance comparable to that in Great Britain and Germany and better than in France. By 1937, Italy's industrial production had overtaken its agricultural sectors as it ascended to the ranks of modern industrial nations.[135] New economic problems also emerged. Subsidies and price controls benefited wheat producers while penalizing others. Such incentives shifted production to grains and away from fruits, wine, and vegetables. Putting more land under cultivation significantly harmed animal husbandry too. And ultimately, consumers paid higher prices for bread, chiefly to the benefit of medium- and large-sized landowners.[136] Economic performance, however, was secondary; control was the objective. As Mussolini himself said, "Corporatism is the disciplined economy and therefore also the controlled [economy], because one cannot imagine discipline if one does not have control."[137]

By the mid-1920s, Mussolini's economic accomplishments had earned his regime fame abroad. Foreign journalists, academics, and industrialists traveling to Italy also reported on Mussolini's repressive and violent regime, documenting the gaps between propaganda and reality, and Fascism had its skeptics.[138] But Mussolini drew sympathizers across Europe and the Americas, including in the United States as well as in Japan and China. Italian ideas were hardly embraced wholesale; some elements were adopted and others discarded, but the Fascist model nonetheless offered an aspirational vision of illiberal development.[139] In Brazil and Portugal, conservative groups took notice, and Italian events influenced political and popular talk about the economy. Italian legislation circulated worldwide, with parts of its 1927 Carta del Lavoro (Labor Charter) eventually copied into Brazilian and Portuguese laws in the 1930s.[140] Italy's Battle for Wheat would inspire similar campaigns in Brazil and Portugal, and its early experimentation with corporatist organization and labor laws modeled how the state could mobilize both capital and labor toward national economic goals. The Fascist state exemplified why *both* political and economic liberalism had to be discarded.

In July 1926, one provincial Azorean newspaper featured news of Italy's economic reorganization. It celebrated new state programs that implemented controls over production and pricing. Mussolini's actions resonated in Portugal precisely because he turned problems of democracy into those of poverty, and the latter would have to be addressed before the former could be attempted. Liberal democracy, the Italian dictator pronounced, "is a luxury of rich nations, [a path] blocked to poor nations."[141] In public debates, the argument that economic challenges required abandoning liberal democracy and its protections for individual freedoms was becoming ever more persuasive.

In Portugal, Italy also drew attention because the two nations faced similar postwar challenges. Portugal's postwar financial crisis led to the collapse of the First Republic with the 1926 Revolution.[142] In May of that year, two military coups occurred, one in the north and the other in the south, and they ultimately joined forces to form a provisional military dictatorship that enjoyed the support of conservative groups—monarchists, integralists, nationalists, and Catholics fed up with the liberal political and economic orientation of previous governments.[143]

These factions, however, lacked any unified, cohesive program for Portugal's new government or its urgent economic problems, which continued after World War I. Between 1919 and 1927, prices in Portugal had increased sixfold and the escudo, Portugal's currency, depreciated from 8 to 108 escudos per British pound sterling.[144] Portugal's weak currency position was its greatest postwar economic hurdle.[145] Added to all of this, contemporary economists and industrialists pointed to listless economic growth.[146]

Salazar, then a professor of political economy at the University of Coimbra, rose to power during these economic crises to become a quintessential interwar austerity dictator. Leaders of Portugal's military dictatorship, the myth goes, repeatedly begged Salazar to leave his university post to tackle financial reconstruction. Salazar obliged in April 1928, in a move that he consistently framed as an act of self-sacrifice rather than a power grab. Salazar's improbable rise to power began in the Finance Ministry, where he took control of Portugal's budgets and imposed ruthless cuts in order to tame inflation and stabilize the escudo. To achieve balanced budgets, he took control of other ministries, even appointing himself the minister of the colonies in 1930 to extend this program for fiscal discipline to Portugal's empire. After years of chronic budget deficits, Portugal enjoyed budget surpluses for nearly ten years, starting in 1928.[147] Salazar's financial dictatorship not only catapulted him to power in Portugal but became essential to his cult of personality too. Historians continue to debate to what extent Salazar should take credit for Portugal's financial recovery.[148] Yet it is difficult to deny the political advantage of initial successes or the appearance thereof.

Financial restructuring became a tool for building a corporatist regime.[149] By delivering a stable currency and protectionism, Salazar earned the support of industry and agricultural producers, the Estado Novo's loyal social base.[150]

It is not clear whether Salazar himself had written about or advocated for corporatism before his arrival in the Finance Ministry. Much of his academic scholarship had focused on monetary policy. Salazar likely embraced corporatism because conservative factions during the previous ten years had wanted it, and corporatist reforms were already in motion by the military dictatorship. In April 1927, for instance, just a few days before Italy's Carta del Lavoro, the dictatorship decreed the Conselho Superior de Economia Nacional (Superior Council for the National Economy) to foster collaboration between the private sector and the government.[151] This organ was composed of government ministers alongside representatives from leading industries, including major banks, industrial associations, fishing and agricultural associations, mining firms, the transportation sector, and academic experts in law, agronomy, engineering, and economics.[152]

As in Italy, wheat became the first sector reorganized in corporatist fashion in Portugal. Decree No. 17.252 launched the Campanha do Trigo (Wheat Campaign) in August 1929. Increasing grain production was a matter of national security and a financial imperative. By 1928, wheat accounted for 12 percent of Portuguese imports, which aggravated current account balances.[153] Austerity alone could not stabilize prices and strengthen the escudo; Portugal needed to produce more and import less. The Wheat Campaign began with bold objectives to "dignify the agricultural industry as the most noble and most important of all the industries."[154] Decree No. 17.252 created new commissions at every level of government to convene farmers and agronomists to modernize the cereal industry by providing credit, subsidies, seeds, fertilizer, machinery, silos, and transportation. Portugal's government committed to guaranteeing "daily bread" to its citizens—a promise steeped in Catholic imagery and evocative of the social rights later codified in the 1933 Constitution (figure 1.5).

Within a matter of years, a more profound experiment was underway to reorganize the grains sector according to a corporatist logic. The aim was not to collectivize agriculture but instead to organize producers of key commodity sectors to encourage entry into the market.[155] In Portugal, cooperative organizations had already been established from the late nineteenth century onward to organize farmers into autonomous organizations in order to coordinate supply to the market and prevent prices from collapsing.[156] This trend in Portugal parallels how an autonomous cooperative movement rose across Europe and the Americas in these decades. Thus the shift to corporatism was one of scale and form, not function.[157] Portugal's government now required that farmers in certain sectors join grémios da lavoura, or farmers guilds, at the municipal level. In many cases, these grémios replaced existing collective organizations.[158] Grémios were semiautonomous, but ultimately regulated by the Ministry of Agriculture (and after its creation in 1940, the Ministry of the

FIGURE 1.5. Posters on public display in Portugal for the Campanha Nacional do Trigo, or National Wheat Campaign (1929). Image courtesy of the Arquivo Nacional Torre do Tombo. Collection Empresa Pública do Jornal *O Século*, Álbuns Gerais no. 15, doc. PT/TT/EPJS/SF/001-001/0015/1511D.

Economy). This pyramid of corporatist organisms issued directives for price controls and quality standards to discipline production, organize warehouses, and license the purchase of equipment.[159] Grémios were not only responsible for regulating wheat production and commerce but also for administering welfare and social security benefits to members. In other words, grémios had a dual function as both regulatory bodies with public powers over local economic conditions and representative associations to advocate for members. Membership in grémios was mostly mandatory for wheat producers and flour millers (depending on the region), but other sectors were organized through voluntary grémios in which the government incentivized membership so that it could regulate local production. During forty-plus years of Portugal's corporatist dictatorship, the grémio system expanded beyond wheat to other sectors such as codfish and wine. By 1974, 143 mandatory grémios existed to organize various productive sectors, 236 voluntary grémios for agricultural producers, and another 307 grémios for related industries and commercial interests.[160] This system, however, never encompassed all production. Some might see this incomplete implementation as a failure, but few could deny how corporatist regulations impacted the everyday economic activities of citizens, whether or not people belonged to a grémio.[161]

Initially, the Wheat Campaign expanded wheat production enormously. The national production of wheat increased by 180 percent between 1926 and 1934, even surpassing domestic demand. The campaign even alleviated the depletion of foreign reserves to pay for grain imports.[162] Prices also stabilized. Price controls were key to this early success. Rather than focus on one cause for price fluctuations, as in the past, corporatist organs were increasingly responsible for regulating the entire supply chain, from wheat producers to flour millers to bread bakers to consumers, in order to ensure fair prices. Luíz da Cunha Gonçalves, a Goan Portuguese jurist whose legal scholarship influenced corporatist thought in both Brazil and Portugal, announced in 1934 that wheat campaigns had achieved "truly affordable bread, and not the politicized bread of yesteryears."[163]

In Brazil, the early experiments with corporatist organization started with rice. During the post–World War I crisis, some early corporatist strategies were first tested at the state level. These regional experiments later influenced national policy. Vargas's rise to power began in the powerful Rio Grande do Sul, the southernmost state in Brazil with pronounced secessionist traditions. Vargas was born in São Borja, a city bordering Argentina at the center of regional wars and smuggling activities, in 1882. His father, an influential rancher, had fought in the War of the Triple Alliance (1864–70) and then became active in local republican politics. Vargas had tried to establish a career for himself in the military, but eventually studied law in Porto Alegre.[164] Early on, he embraced the rise of positivism, especially political strands that outlined in practical terms a political and administrative action plan.[165] After rising to prominence in the state legislature in the 1920s, Vargas served briefly as minister of finance for the federal government, despite having no fiscal experience—a political bargain to divide cabinet positions among powerful states. Historian Pedro Cezar Dutra Fonseca explains that Vargas was "intimately" acquainted with political power prior to 1930 as a "typical" politician of the oligarchic system dominated by regional elite interests.[166] In 1928, he was elected governor of his home state, replacing someone who had led the state's machine politics for nearly thirty years. Vargas, alongside Rio Grande do Sul interior secretary Oswaldo Aranha, later one of the most important ministers and diplomats of Brazil's Estado Novo, launched several campaigns to organize rice producers into state-sponsored cartels and cooperatives.

Rio Grande do Sul's economic orientation differed from that of other Brazilian regions because it produced for internal, not export, markets. It supplied meat, rice, wheat, maté, and other staple goods for growing urban centers like

São Paulo and Rio de Janeiro.[167] The growth of the *gaúcho*, or Rio Grande do Sul, economy was another consequence of World War I. With Brazil's largest urban centers cut off from imports (especially wheat), domestic production became even more vital to feeding the nation. The postwar economic slump hit Rio Grande do Sul hard. Market protections provided by the war were gone, gaúcho commodities glutted the internal market, and prices dropped. In 1926, a group of rice planters found inspiration in the coffee valorization program—inaugurated in 1906 by the federal government in coordination with state governments to purchase and warehouse coffee in order to prop up prices—and started their own program to stabilize prices.[168] Gaúcho rice planters, millers, and merchants joined together to form a cartel, the Sindicato Arrozeiro do Rio Grande do Sul (Rice Syndicate of Rio Grande do Sul), which purchased and warehoused rice, controlling its sale and export to raise prices and stabilize the market. At first they had limited support from the state government. The sindicato financed its own valorization program, while the state granted tax exemptions and certain export privileges.[169] This collective action proved successful in the short run. Rice prices stabilized, while coordinated private-public measures allowed regional producers to export more rice, thus increasing their market share. In 1923, rice accounted for 8 percent of the state's exports, and by 1927 this figure had jumped to 13 percent.[170] While this cartel initially enjoyed a great degree of autonomy in regulating production and prices, the state government increasingly took greater control. In 1936, Rio Grande do Sul's government created an institute to regulate the rice industry—a "simple transformation," according to historian Joan Bak, of the sindicato into a state-sponsored agency with formal regulatory powers over producers.[171]

In Rio Grande do Sul, the shift away from free trade in rice took the form of a monopoly in which the pursuit of private interests happened to resolve regional economic challenges. It was certainly not the first state to intervene to protect its key commodity sector. Brazil's federal government was hardly as laissez-faire as Vargas's intellectuals would claim in the 1930s.[172] But Brazil's ruling economic class remained quite liberal in its orientation, defending temporary or emergency state interventions as exceptions, driven by necessity, not doctrine. Emergency measures also did not alter or undermine extant legal or institutional frameworks. The programs that Vargas oversaw, first in Rio Grande do Sul and then nationwide, were not just larger than earlier statist interventions. Rather, he defended these programs with a new, albeit inchoate, economic doctrine that formalized the responsibility of the state to stabilize problems of production and pricing. While it is true that these associational experiments were transnational in the late nineteenth and early twentieth centuries, the gaúcho experiment, as historians such as Bak have argued, was distinguished by its ideological underpinnings. Vargas, who was influenced by positivism and also closely followed events in Italy and Portugal, did not hide his disdain for liberal parliamentary mechanisms or his distrust of individual self-interest and free markets to bring about general economic prosperity.[173] This made it possible for Vargas to fold the sindicato into an emerging intellectual project to break with liberal models. The gaúcho rice experiment was not just a policy that predates corporatist policies in the 1930s but also a doctrinal shift in how conservative elites envisioned state action over the economy. Vargas pushed for the organization of producer cooperatives—comprised of farmers and ranchers—to counterbalance powerful cartels in order to afford rural workers some degree of collective bargaining and social insurance. This corporatist structure promised economic organization and social control. Cooperatives, when recognized by the state, managed supply chains in order to discipline competition, control production, and set prices so as to secure social peace and economic order.

As governor, Vargas backed state-supported cartels and cooperatives. In 1928 and 1929, the regional government attempted to expand this system by establishing three state-sponsored cartels for beef jerky, wine, and lard. Vargas created a state bank to finance these measures, arguing forcibly for the importance of centralizing market interventions so that group interests meshed with the needs of the regional economy. Following the 1930 Revolution, and in the midst of the crisis of capitalism that erupted with the Great Depression, Vargas took this experiment to the national level.

Crisis of Capitalism and the
Deepening Corporatist Experiment

In October 1929, a crash in the US stock market triggered a worldwide panic and shocked the global order. A series of bank failures made credit scarce in the United States and beyond. Brazil and Portugal did not suffer the same fall in industrial production and corresponding uptick in unemployment as more industrialized countries. Instead, they were impacted by the collapse of international trade. The volume of global exports fell by 26 percent between 1929 and 1932, while the value of this trade dropped by 61 percent.[174] With steep decline in global demand, nations worldwide suffered severe price deflation, currency devaluations, debt default, bank failures, and industrial and agricultural stockpiles. Protectionist tariffs and import quotas emerged as reflexive responses to the crisis, amplifying the skepticism of the 1920s toward free trade and open borders. The crisis deepened both distrust toward liberalism and support for corporatism.

The pithy statement "O café caíu. O Brasil por sua vez caíu em si mesmo" (Coffee collapsed. And Brazil, in turn, has come to its senses), from the polemical *Brasil errado* (1932), summarized the Great Depression's impact on Brazil.[175] Its political system was one and the same as its economic system. The coffee crisis triggered the collapse of Brazil's hyperfederalized and oligarchic political system. Historians of twentieth-century Brazil have added nuance and dimension to this account of events, but it remains the most straightforward explanation for the fall of the First Republic and rise of Vargas in 1930. This joint political and economic crisis was also a moral crisis because so many aspirations were attached to coffee—aspirations that burst in 1929. During the nineteenth century, many in Brazil had come to see coffee as the nation's gateway to modernity. Noel Rosa and João de Barro captured the irony in their irreverent song "Samba da boa vontade": "Que iremos à Europa / num aterro de café" ("We will get to Europe / on this landfill of coffee").[176]

By 1931, the price of coffee stood at one-third of its 1925–29 level. Stockpiles were impossible to sell. The valorization schemes used in previous economic downturns could not keep pace with the downward spiral of prices. Instead, the Brazilian government created the Departamento Nacional do Café (National Coffee Department) to purchase and destroy seventy-seven million bags of coffee over the next decade—approximately three years of global consumption—by burning them in public or dumping them in the ocean.[177] To be sure, some in Brazil celebrated this as the end of *escravidão caféeira*, or "coffee slavery," seeing the Great Depression as emancipation from the reliance on foreign markets.[178] The irony of this analogy seemed lost on the integralist journalist who called the 1929 crisis "emancipatory": coffee production had spurred the rise of a second slavery in Brazil, delaying abolition until 1888.

Brazil's economic future seemed bleak in the early 1930s. Its GDP fell by more than 8 percent between 1929 and 1931.[179] Economic historians emphasize, however, that Brazil's economy rebounded relatively quickly. Its GDP exceeded pre-1929 levels by 1933 and, due to lower levels of industrialization, unemployment never reached the heights experienced in North Atlantic economies. Economist Carlos Díaz-Alejandro attributes Brazil's swift recovery to Vargas's "reactive" response to the international crisis, but there is more to the story.[180] The crisis required that Brazil reorient its relationship to international markets and also remake its domestic economy.

The Depression had immediate and long-lasting political consequences. The First Republic was governed by the politics of *café com leite*, in which the president was chosen, on an alternating basis, from São Paulo and Minas Gerais, the two strongest states. This system broke down during the March 1930 elections, when Paulista president Washington Luís picked another Paulista, Júlio Prestes, as his successor. Vargas exploited this crisis of succession to form a coalition—the Aliança Liberal (Liberal Alliance)—with political brokers from Rio Grande do Sul, Minas Gerais, and Paraíba, all disgruntled with São

Paulo's power grab. When Prestes won, the opposition claimed fraud. In October, an armed revolt swept Brazil. Vargas assumed power as leader of the provisional government.

The 1930 Revolution, historians emphasize, was an elite power play, not the expression of class conflict or ideological clashes. Vargas's rise to power thus began with a makeshift coalition that offered vague promises. Still, his movement was not aimless. With the 1929 crisis, the question of how to manage the economy became paramount. Coffee planters and foreign creditors waited to see how the new government might address their problems, and unemployment ticked upward. Scholars often refer to the first two years of the provisional dictatorship as the radical phase of Vargas's government, stressing the wave of social legislation.

In November 1930, Vargas's provisional government inaugurated the Ministry of Labor, which would remain a hotbed for corporatist thinking and policy for the next fifteen years. This ministry enforced the first legislative measures to reorganize Brazilian society in corporatist terms under Decree No. 19,770, which stipulated that all employer associations, agricultural cooperatives, and labor sindicatos now had to be recognized by the state, and only a single association could represent class interests for a particular sector in a specific region. The decree codified the difference between corporatist labor relations and the associational pluralism that predated the 1930 Revolution: the state needed to recognize and create the organs representing professional and class interests, and each of these entities had a monopoly over representation in the region where it operated. As historians of Brazil continue to debate the origins and consequences of corporatist labor legislation, recent scholarship explains these legislative feats not as an *outorga*, or gift bestowed by a benevolent dictator, but instead as the culmination of decades of class-based activism, in which industrialists as much as the working classes pressed the government to address economic and social problems. Rather than resolve conflicts between labor and capital, the social and economic legislation promulgated following the 1930 Revolution created new legal spaces and bureaucratic channels by which groups would continue to advocate for their interests and struggle for justice.[181]

As the Depression deepened worldwide, this provisional dictatorship brainstormed strategies for economic recovery. Some bold and unusual proposals from aspiring technocrats and unorthodox economists circulated within government ministries. Economic fixes and solutions were also debated in the public sphere—newspaper editorials, books, and even samba lyrics—and by citizens across regions, professions, and social classes. Ordinary citizens petitioned the government with solutions and a large number of letters reached Vargas's desk with policy proposals. In one such petition, a man in Pará called for the federal government to create an agency dedicated to the purchase of essential goods so as to normalize supply and prices.[182] Another letter, from Belo Horizonte, suggested that Brazil might be able to pay some of its accumulating external debt if it requisitioned gold from churches, estimating that the government could procure well over six hundred kilograms of gold from just a single church in Ouro Preto.[183] These suggestions—as heterodox and impractical as they might seem—signaled a shift in citizens' expectations about government and its role in economic life. The crisis had shattered old economic formulas.

For many in Portugal, the gravity of the 1929 crisis was that it was the latest in a "series of consecutive crises" that had unfolded during the 1920s.[184] Unemployment rose to nearly thirty thousand by 1932, even though national income slipped only slightly and even surpassed pre-1929 values by 1931.[185] Quick recovery was partly due to the fiscal and monetary reforms of the 1920s, which allowed Portugal to return to the gold standard in June 1931, just months before Great Britain abandoned gold parity. Those loyal to the regime argued that Portugal had managed to avoid the worsening of the crisis, thanks partly to early state intervention in key commodity sectors and the "somewhat effective," to quote the governor of the Banco de Portugal, turn to protectionism.[186] Others were not quite so sanguine. Even if unemployment was lower than that experienced in industrialized nations, major sectors such as cork and fishing industries were hit hard by the fall in global demand. Furthermore, organized labor formed regional and national commissions to debate the Depression and propose solutions, yet workers were hardly united by a single political or ideological platform. Anarchists, revolutionary syndicalists, communists, and socialists were often divided on what policies were necessary, or whether to participate in the military dictatorship's reformist agenda at all.[187]

For Portugal, like other nations, the Great Depression triggered social and political conflicts over how the government should respond. The dictatorship attempted to set the terms of this debate by issuing an economic questionnaire to survey industrialists, academics, bankers, and agriculturalists on the causes and consequences of the crisis. The survey was about more than policy—it was ideological. The governor of the Banco de Portugal asked whether the country would fall back on old policies to suffer "economic regression" or would choose a "progressive" path, one that required those in power to "renounce a classical conception of the economy for a strategy that is rational, coherent, and scientific."[188] Many credited the protectionist measures already in place in sectors like cereals for the comparatively light impact of the crisis in Portugal. They called for more protectionism to stimulate national production and self-sufficiency. Others noted that the country had been spared on account of its small industrial sector, but this was not necessarily an advantage. The president of the Centro Comercial do Porto, for example, emphasized the deeper crisis of the "backwardness of some branches of production," lamenting that "we should be able to feed a population ten times greater than ours, but the truth is that we cannot feed, with goods from our land, our six million inhabitants."[189]

Across surveys and letters, whispers of new economic ideas were emerging. An engineer at the University of Porto called for public works projects and even cited US automobile magnate Henry Ford to make his case for higher salaries to stimulate aggregate demand.[190] Bankers and industrialists called for protectionism, measures to drive consumer demand, and state support for key industries to promote economic development. Bankers, academics, and industrialists used words like *rationalization, order,* and *organization* to talk about the economy, distancing themselves from the laissez-faire logic of the previous century.

In July 1930, Salazar, still minister of finance, responded to the unfolding global crisis in a speech to top government officials. Rather than treat politics and economics as two separate spheres, Salazar integrated them into a bold proposal to overhaul the administrative state. "We cannot aspire to build a strong and balanced state," he announced, "without the coordination and development of the national economy, which today, more than ever, has to be integrated into our political organization."[191] He stressed *disorder* as the primary cause of Portugal's successive crises—political, financial, economic, and social.

Opposition mounted to the provisional dictatorship following the 1929 crisis. The military dictatorship responded to protests with violence as well as by accelerating earlier efforts to create a corporatist state that could incorporate pliant and disciplined interests into the state while further delegitimizing those outside the system.[192] Portugal's corporatist experiment—inchoate and imprecise—was quickly taking shape with the creation of new ministries and government organs. In September 1931, Decree No. 20.342 outlined new principles of Portuguese "democracy," understood in terms of how the state would create, organize, and coordinate between representative bodies for professions and the economic interests of major sectors. It created Portugal's corporatist system, establishing the grémio as the cellular unit of economic and social life. The grémio was not autonomous; it was regulated and sometimes even created by the government according to its economic priorities. "State intervention in economic life," this decree outlined, was essential to "compensate for the gaps and failings of private initiative," and "reconcile or resolve the competing interests of various branches of national production."[193] The state became responsible for economic development and citizens' social well-being. Putting these ideas into practice, however, would prove a frustratingly incomplete experiment.

————

In October 1932, Brazilian journalist Alceu Amoroso Lima, known by the pseudonym Tristão de Ataíde, spoke about the enduring connections between Brazilian and Portuguese societies in front of Rio de Janeiro's political and intellectual elites gathered at the Casino Beira Mar in honor of Portuguese ambassador Martinho Nobre de Melo. Tristão de Ataíde was an important figure in Catholic intellectual circles as well as an editor and contributor to several niche publications. This meeting was the result of the project started a decade earlier with Ferro's visit to Brazil to revive Luso-Brazilian connections. Both Brazil and Portugal had experienced drastic political and economic ruptures during the previous ten years. And yet Tristão de Ataíde saw it as more critical than ever that Brazil and Portugal draw closer together. He praised recent works by Portuguese anthropologist António Augusto Mendes Correia and Brazilian sociologist Oliveira Vianna that celebrated Portuguese colonialism as an archetype model for assimilation and ethnic harmony, in sharp contrast to Anglo-Saxon colonialization "via mass elimination."[194] Even before the 1933 publication of Gilberto Freyre's, *Casa grande & senzala*, the trope of racial harmony was already a discursive link between these countries.

Tristão de Ataíde had political motivations for this argument. The celebration quickly shifted from discussions of an idyllic distant colonial past to what was at stake for the present. Both nations were "at the threshold of a new era," he explained, "as the capitalist, decrepit, and pagan world expired." He discarded examples from both "Yankee" and Soviet models to embrace an alternative better suited to Luso-Brazilian realities that would "cultivate a new *homo economicus* and *politicus*."[195] Corporatism offered a way forward.

The next chapter follows how these early moves toward corporatism were codified into law. Even those supporting dictatorship protested the provisional nature of Vargas's and Salazar's rule by decree. New laws and governing principles were necessary to turn revolutionary impulses into national reality. This process converged in the task of writing new constitutions as a site of negotiation over each country's future.

2

Experiments in Corporatist Constitutions

ON THE EVENING of November 10, 1937, as he was staging a coup, Getúlio Vargas addressed the Brazilian public to explain his "exceptional decision" to dissolve Congress (figure 2.1). In this long and somber speech, the president cum dictator outlined why Brazil needed to discard its "institutional frameworks and methods for governing," dramatizing threats of communist subversion to make his case for the failure of democracy.[1] Vargas's usurpation of power capped years of political unrest following the 1930 Revolution. Beginning in 1935, the government had decreed states of emergency to thwart alleged plots to overthrow the government. In September 1937, the army had "discovered" the infamous, but fabricated, Cohen Plan outlining a communist invasion of Brazil.[2] Vargas now used this fabrication to put the coup in motion. Brazilians were gearing up for a presidential election in January 1938. Three presidential candidates campaigned, but the public knew that Vargas—technically ineligible for reelection under the 1934 Constitution—would prevail. As the 1937 samba "A menina presidência" predicted, "Na hora H, quem vai ficar é seu Gegê" or "When the time comes, the one who will stay is Vargas."

Vargas's coup surprised no one, but what did shock the public—even Vargas's closest allies—was that the coup came with a new Constitution, one decreeing a new regime, the Estado Novo. Newspaper headlines focused more on the Constitution than the coup. Some protested the secrecy with which the Constitution had been written or how it was promulgated with military force. Oswaldo Aranha, serving as Brazil's ambassador to the United States, made it clear that he "supported the coup, but not the Constitution."[3] He argued that this charter departed from the spirit of prior constitutions: it did not limit the powers of government, recognize the vote as a vehicle for direct representation, or guarantee fundamental and inviolable rights for citizens. Quite the opposite. Brazil's 1937 Constitution made a deliberate break with liberal democracy. As Vargas explained in his speech, pluralism, political parties, and

FIGURE 2.1. Getúlio Vargas at Catete Palace in Rio de Janeiro addressing the public to decree the 1937 Constitution (November 10, 1937). Image courtesy of the Centro de Pesquisa e Documentação de História Contemporânea do Brasil, Fundação Getúlio Vargas.

even the peaceful transfer of power did not work in Brazil, where politics remained beholden to clientelist arrangements propping up special interests to the detriment of the nation.

In Brazil, corporatism as an idea and set of institutions enabled this shift from democracy to dictatorship. The 1937 Constitution, after all, was the second Constitution promulgated under Vargas's tenure. The first was the 1934 Constitution, written by a popularly elected constitutional assembly to return the country to legal normalcy after the 1930 Revolution. The 1934 Constitution, however, was short-lived, partly because it attempted to hybridize liberal democratic models and newer models that emphasized strong executive power, technocratic governance, and corporatist representation. The 1937 Constitution inherited much from its forerunner, but this new charter also rebranded many of the innovations introduced by its precursor with a corporatist idiom to mark the country's formal break with liberalism. On paper at least, the line between democracy and dictatorship was quite subtle.

Still, why write a constitution in the first place? It seems reasonable to assume that leaders who usurp power through force will govern outside the laws they create, or implement laws in arbitrary ways to amass personal and political power.[4] Yet this chapter looks beyond normative questions of whether constitutions work in authoritarian contexts to argue instead for other ways that constitutions matter. Constitutions articulate the aspirations of a new government. This process of writing constitutions, in any context, is a negotiation between different ideological and political projects.[5] Even dictators need to figure out which voices to elevate and which to eliminate. Constitutions thus reveal priorities for a new regime.

In the 1930s, the economy became Vargas's priority. Brazil was still enduring the consequences of the Great Depression, and it is not surprising that Vargas defended his coup by insisting on the need to "recalibrate the political organism to the economic necessities of the country."[6] These imperatives explain the choice of corporatism as the political and economic system to replace liberalism. While committed to private property and individual initiative, corporatists wanted these impulses subordinated to the greater interests of the nation. Corporatism mirrored other experiments in the 1930s in which the state stepped in to regulate economic activities. What made corporatism distinct was its emphasis on upholding existing social hierarchies through its vertical organization of society.[7]

Vargas was not alone in this project to use the constitution to implement a new economic state. To answer the question of why Vargas and his team of jurists opted for corporatism to replace liberalism, first, in part one, it is necessary to look beyond Brazil. With all the disruptions of the early twentieth century, old regimes fell and new governments needed a social compact. Brazil was influenced by a wave of constitution writing in the 1920s and 1930s as nations across Europe and Latin America (both democracies and dictatorships) experimented with new governing institutions and ideas of citizenship.[8] Brazil, moreover, was not the only nation to put corporatism into constitutional form. Portugal and Austria did as well, and Portugal proved to be the far more relevant example for Brazil.[9] Vargas's new regime in 1937 even took its name from Portugal's Estado Novo, inaugurated in 1933 with its own corporatist constitution.

This chapter analyzes the many drafts of Brazil's 1934 and 1937 Constitutions alongside Portugal's 1933 Constitution to explore in part two the joint questions of why a constitution and why corporatism. Brazil and Portugal were united—and unique—in that they both bothered to write constitutions in the first place.[10] Both Vargas and Salazar flipped the usual calculation: rather than see consensus as a prerequisite for writing constitutions, they saw constitutions as tools for building consensus. Close readings of constitutional proposals and legal opinions reveal the constitution-drafting process as itself a negotiation between different political projects that expressed who was included and excluded from power. Dictatorships are not monoliths; they are forged through contestation and compromise.[11]

The third and final part of this chapter turns to the two institutional innovations that shaped efforts in Brazil and Portugal to build a corporatist state. First, jurists overhauled the legislative branch to introduce corporatist representation while expanding executive powers. The legislative branch was no longer the lawmaking branch of government—a responsibility that now fell squarely to the executive branch. To support the executive branch in its exercise of enhanced powers over the economy, new technical councils and corporatist bodies were created to integrate representatives for leading economic sectors into the governing architecture. Brazil's and Portugal's constitutions fashioned corporatism into a technocratic mode of governance to replace elected representatives with *técnicos*, or experts. Law became a tool for expanding state powers over the economy to jump-start development by intervening in wages, prices, and production. The second major innovation followed from the first: corporatist constitutions decreed social and economic rights.[12] In corporatist contexts, though, the expansion of economic and social rights went hand in hand with the curtailment of civil and political liberties. As Brazilian jurist Francisco José de Oliveira Vianna explained, individual freedoms "come second to the more important reforms, of a social and economic nature, that need to be realized."[13] Corporatist dictatorships turned to constitution writing to legitimize their usurpation of power and invent new categories like "authoritarian democracy" or "economic democracy" that codified their arguments for order and discipline above liberty as prerequisites for economic development.

Few events are more nation-centric than writing a constitution. Brazil's constitution writers, for example, insisted time and again that their constitution should absorb the "smell of Brazilian soil."[14] Even so, the lens of the nation-state can miss and distort how institutional choices in Brazil were inspired by the transnational, global circulation of legal texts and ideas.[15] Constitutions written by dictators in Brazil and Portugal were conditioned by choices made in other nations, both democratic and authoritarian. Corporatist constitutionalism coincided with rising nationalism and extremism, and thus foreign influences were frequently muted to preserve the national character of constitutions. Still, it was easier to borrow from some places than others. This chapter focuses on exchanges between Brazil and Portugal to explain how corporatism became the system of choice. Jurists across these two countries mobilized historical, cultural, and civilizational arguments.[16] The rise of corporatism depended on enduring assertions for why Anglo-American liberal democracy did not work in these societies, as Luso-Brazilian jurists looked to each other to champion corporatism as the path forward.

Global Constitutional Currents and Trends

In June 1932, António de Oliveira Salazar—still finance minister—lent his copy of Boris Mirkine-Guetzévitch's *Les nouvelles tendances du droit constitutionnel* to his longtime mentor Quirino Avelino de Jesus. The two were working on a new constitution, and Quirino de Jesus, a Catholic jurist influential in shaping the

Estado Novo's early ideology, was curious about innovations in other countries.[17] In the 1920s and 1930s, Mirkine-Guetzévitch, as his book title suggests, examined the growing trend of new constitutionalism, including how social rights constituted "new positive obligations of the state."[18] A Russian-born jurist who had immigrated to France after the Russian Revolution, Mirkine-Guetzévitch was one of the founders of the field of comparative constitutional law.[19] He celebrated this rise of social constitutionalism in which the state's role in guaranteeing the economic and social well-being of its citizens became a constitutional question, not solely a legislative matter.

Following World War I, "new" constitutions proliferated with Mexico's 1917 Constitution, the 1919 Weimar Constitution, the 1924 Soviet Constitution, and the constitutions of new nation-states in central and eastern Europe.[20] Mexico's Constitution, while not a case that Mirkine-Guetzévitch considers, was the first to codify labor rights while also limiting property rights via articles on subsoil rights.[21] In terms of both property and social rights, twentieth-century new constitutionalism departed from the negative rights of liberal nineteenth-century constitutions. In Latin America and Iberia, this departure from the nineteenth-century liberal tradition in fact deepened the tendency of law in these regions to hold the public good above concerns for individual rights.[22] New constitutions were now not (just) concerned with individual rights but with social questions and national economic imperatives too.

Newer "new" constitutions proliferated with the Great Depression in Spain (1931), Portugal (1933), Austria (1934), Brazil (1934 and 1937), Colombia (reforms in 1936), Ireland (1937), and Bolivia (1938), to list just a few.[23] The codification of social rights became the rule rather than exception. Brazil's 1934 Constitution exemplified the trend by giving women the vote and codifying labor rights while establishing legal grounds for nationalizing mineral wealth. Portugal's 1933 Constitution codified social rights as well. Like Vargas in Brazil, or even Mussolini in Italy and Franco in Spain, dictators who came to power in the 1930s did not attempt to quash social constitutionalism. Instead, they further institutionalized social rights to diffuse social conflict while expanding state power. This was not only a political calculation to pacify popular sectors. Social rights in corporatist contexts functioned to order and organize society, rejecting liberal traditions in which rights guaranteed individual freedoms and entitlements.[24]

Especially influential in Brazil, Mirkine-Guetzévitch's name was invoked constantly in sessions of Brazil's National Constitutional Assembly, convened to ratify a new constitution after the 1930 Revolution. He was cited so often that his ideas sometimes appeared contradictory. Some Brazilian delegates read Mirkine-Guetzévitch for his expanded conception of citizenship, while others found arguments for "the elimination, in the name of greater social interests, of certain fundamental rights."[25] In 1933, at the height of constitutional deliberations, Brazilian jurist Cândido Mota Filho, a nationalist with integralist leanings, even translated Mirkine-Guetzévitch's book, publishing it with a translation of Spain's Republican Constitution despite his antiliberal views.[26] Transnational exchange in the 1930s was a messy process that defied neat ideological categories.

The task of writing new constitutions largely fell to jurists and legal scholars. While this might seem unremarkable, it turned the crisis of democracy from a social into a technical problem. This is consistent with another trend that Mirkine-Guetzévitch underscored: the outsize role played by "legal sciences" in new constitutionalism, or how "legal theorists have exerted their influence."[27] In Brazil and Portugal, lawyers had always enjoyed a privileged role in political life, but the political coups of the interwar decades amplified jurists' political actions and turned politics itself into a series of legal measures. Brazilian sociologist Luiz Werneck Vianna even coined the term *juristas-políticos* to describe the architects of Vargas's Estado Novo.[28] Brazilian scholars debate in particular the category *cidadania regulada*, or regulated citizenship, which describes how the state created the institutions through which social groups, especially workers, were integrated into the state so that it could centralize citizen demands and expectations.[29] In the 1920s and 1930s, Mirkine-Guetzévitch described this problem differently, viewing social rights as part of a broader push for the "rationalization of power," or efforts to codify legally the modern state's powers. To this end, interwar constitutions made another innovation: they emboldened state powers in the executive branch, to then be put into practice by new ministries, tribunals, and technocratic councils connected to the executive branch. Mirkine-Guetzévitch in fact lamented that the timing of social rights coincided with rising enthusiasm for authoritarian types of government. "It is necessary to protect," he warned, "these new rights against the brutal assault of the idea of dictatorship."[30]

In addition to a new emphasis on the positive obligations of the state, a second shift in legal thinking was specific to the Portuguese-speaking world, and built on shared language, history, and legal traditions.[31] Jurists in Brazil and Portugal shared the conviction that liberalism did not work for their societies; it was an imported ideology, poorly adapted to local realities. To make this argument, Luso-Brazilian jurists mobilized civilizational categories—Latin versus Anglo-Saxon—in constitutional debates.[32]

To many in Brazil and Portugal, the first task in writing new constitutions was to figure out how to dismantle a legal system predicated on equal and universal individual rights for citizens. Corporatism offered an alternative by organizing society like a pyramid according to economic function and social role, where each unit had an inherent value based on how it served the nation. The corporatist model critiqued socialism and liberalism, which both in their own ways claimed citizens' equality before the law. Corporatism, albeit differently in different contexts, followed the tenet that "inequality is a law of nature."[33]

Goan Portuguese jurist Luís da Cunha Gonçalves (1875–1956), in his 1935 *Princípios de direito corporativo*, evoked the metaphor of the body to make his case that the corporatist order was the "natural" way of organizing society, reminiscent of the early modern stress on the *corps politique*. Born in Goa in 1875 to a prominent Indian family, Cunha Gonçalves was one of just a few Indian Portuguese lawyers trained at the University of Coimbra.[34] After Coimbra, he became a law professor at the Instituto Superior de Ciências Económicas e Financeiras, where he taught administrative and civil law. This institution, established in 1930, was a business school, training professionals in management and finance. While it would become one of the preeminent schools for teaching economics in Portugal, the University of Coimbra and University of Lisbon were still at this time bastions of political influence.[35] Cunha Gonçalves was an outsider in intellectual debates over corporatism in Portugal, neither invited into Salazar's inner circle nor given a prominent posting in the Estado Novo. Even so, he was widely read in Portugal and especially abroad, offering some of the clearest and most often-cited arguments for how to design law beyond liberal coordinates. His writings on corporatism elaborated a system of justice defined according to order and hierarchy, not equality.

The corporatist model was imperial. In contrast to liberal republics, empires require a political system that can reinforce hierarchy.[36] Historians of nineteenth-century liberalism have tackled these (apparent) contradictions between liberalism and empire, or how these two systems coexisted even as the former insisted on the universality of political and civil rights while the latter denied those rights to subjugated populations.[37] The corporatist state, however, was not mired in this contradiction, which partly explains why corporatism appealed to dictators.

Like many of his generation, Cunha Gonçavles wrote extensively on Portugal's imperial history, focusing on religious pluralism in India and Indigenous rights in the colonies in addition to works on law. He held several political and administrative positions in Portugal, Mozambique, and Goa, which in turn informed his thinking about law and empire. If empire, as Jane Burbank and Frederick Cooper contend, is an "unequal but incorporative polity," then corporatism seemed perfectly compatible with it.[38] For Cunha Gonçalves, corporatism organized the "natural" inequalities of society: "Unequal are the five fingers of the hand; unequal are . . . vocations and professions, the wise and the ignorant, the healthy man and the invalid, the worker and the indolent. Well! Justice lies in treating unequally those who are unequal."[39]

Cunha Gonçalves was one of many jurists to crisscross the South Atlantic, visiting the law schools of Recife, Rio de Janeiro, and São Paulo. His legal writings also traveled to Brazil, where his textbooks on civil and commercial law became required reading for law students. Even before Vargas and Salazar had come to power, Cunha Gonçalves elaborated critiques of open trade and free markets that would become foundational to corporatist economic policies, bridging intellectual trends in Brazil and Portugal. In the 1920s in Brazil, for instance, he published *Da compra e venda no direito comercial brasileiro*, a book dedicated to the Faculdade de Direito de São Paulo (Law School of São Paulo). This book was a sequel of sorts to his earlier writings on international commercial law to account for World War I as a rupture in international trade.[40] Brazilian and Portuguese editions all begin with commerce—specifically, the need for different groups to trade with one another—as the force that propelled societies from a "state of complete brutality" to "civilization." His musings on the civilizing power of trade did not endorse Ricardian theories of comparative advantage, though, or envision international trade as a vehicle for national progress. Instead, Cunha Gonçalves argued that not all nations benefited equally from international trade as "one can divide the world into agricultural countries and industrial countries." Over the years, he explained this global divergence as not only conditioned by what each nation produced—industrial goods versus "colonial commodities" like coffee, sugar, and cacao—but also by a hierarchy of "civilization": "All peoples of the Anglo-Teutonic race, endowed with special skills, initiative, and energy for the great expansion of industries and transportation, are distinguished in this [civilizing] role and exercise their supremacy throughout the world."[41] Cunha Gonçalves's textbook on commercial law began with digressions on how culture and race shaped economic outcomes, as he typecast nations and their successes according to presumably innate traits. For him, matters of law were inseparable from thoughts about "natural" inequalities, both between and within nations.[42] These questions were as relevant to his analysis of Portugal as Brazil, which is perhaps why his writings became essential reading in Brazilian law schools.

The problem of backwardness permeated constitutional debates in both Brazil and Portugal, as intellectuals and jurists explained why liberalism seemed to work in the United States or Great Britain, but not in the South Atlantic. In Portugal, political and legal elites blamed the 1911 Constitution for decades of economic and political instability. As Salazar maintained in 1932, the defining moment of Portugal's new constitutionalism was the realization that "we do not have the power to choose our blood, our language, or our ethnic and traditional character."[43]

Brazilian and Portuguese intellectuals might have been united in their pessimistic cross-national comparisons, but they differed in how they explained these divergences. For Brazilians, their civilizational anxieties were closely tied to legacies of slavery, which had made Brazil one of the world's most multiracial and multiethnic societies. Intellectuals and jurists explained their nation's backwardness as a direct consequence of its social and racial composition. While collaborating on the 1934 Constitution, for example, future Brazilian labor minister Valdemar Falcão insisted that Brazil's unique "historical and racial formation" mattered for its laws, and contrasted it to "Anglo-Saxon development."[44] Oliveira Vianna wrote successive books to burnish these sensibilities with social scientific objectivity.[45] He contended that Brazil's geographic and racial diversity had fragmented society, dominated by "small clans surrounding smalltime political bosses." To him, this "clanic spirit" had delayed the formation of organized class interests that could anchor political parties and drive policymaking. In Brazil, he concluded, and in contrast to "Germanic" or "the English race," "*there is no sentiment of collective interest.*"[46] Oliveira Vianna worked on the first draft of the 1934 Constitution, equipped with these pessimistic assessments of Brazil's stunted political development. His sociological conclusions about Brazil—underpinned by vestiges of scientific racism as much as he tried to distance himself from biological determinism—were essential to his legal arguments that direct suffrage and other democratic institutions were misplaced in Brazil.

Scholars have explored the consequences of scientific racism, eugenics, and civilizational discourses for the late nineteenth-century expansion of colonialism, or genocide during World War II, where these hierarchies legitimized violence, dispossession, and "ethnic cleansing." Jurists in Brazil and Portugal mobilized racialized discourses in more subtle but still pernicious ways to defend dictatorship and legally codify social inequalities.

Why Write a Constitution? Brazil and Portugal

On May 28, 1932, to celebrate the sixth anniversary of the 1926 Revolution, newspapers across Portugal published a draft of the proposed new Constitution. Pedro Theotónio Pereira, architect of Portugal's corporatist system, provided the preamble: "The modern world finds itself in a phase of wishy-washy transition," he wrote, "marked by disconcerting uncertainty."[47] A constitution, in other words, would end ideological infighting and social unrest. It may seem odd that a government that came to power with a military coup would see a constitution as the means to solidify a revolution.[48] Yet this reasoning prevailed in Brazil and Portugal. Integralists, corporatists, liberals, communists, socialists, and anarchists advanced their political platforms with protests, bloody rebellions, journalism, and petitions. Many of these factions conceded that the tenets of eighteenth- and nineteenth-century constitutionalism—individualism, universal suffrage (in theory at least), the separation of powers, and legislative sovereignty—were inadequate to address the current crises. Some also agreed that a new constitution was the only way to restore order. Others wanted a new constitution to reorganize national space and experiment with new economic systems. The constitution-writing process was enthusiastic and aspirational. The paths not taken—as much as those that triumphed—reveal pressing national or imperial problems along with priorities. How did corporatism prevail and become the path taken?

For four years, during Vargas's provisional dictatorship and while Brazil's 1891 Constitution remained suspended, newspaper editorials, pamphlets, and letters flooded into Rio de Janeiro—from those in distant states as well as those in exile in Paris, Buenos Aires, and Lisbon—to petition key members of the 1930 Revolution on the timeline and structure for Brazil's next constitution. These petitions voiced the opinions of common citizens and regional elites alike. The improvised political theory in these letters and editorials captured changing political vocabularies that enabled the rise of corporatism.

The most contentious question was whether to bother with a new constitution at all. In August 1931, Aranha, serving as finance minister from 1931 to 1934, received a letter from Goiás celebrating how "today, without a constitution, we have fairness, honesty, patriotism, and freedom." Its author proposed that the constitution be delayed at least two years so as to achieve the "goals of the revolution."[49] Another petitioner insisted on extending the period of rule by decree by eight years. This person feared that "those fallen reactionary oligarchs," if granted a quick return to constitutional order, would simply retake the reins of power for personal gain.[50] Others worried that Brazil was not prepared for representative democracy. One Methodist clergy member in São Paulo argued instead for "a semiconstitutional regime" with an eight-year provisional dictatorship. A quick return to representative government would simply allow "new political bosses [to] emerge, lacking ideas and only serving their own interests."[51] Critiques of clientelism had long inspired conservative distrust of liberalism in Brazil. Still, it would be a mistake to overlook how some people mobilized a new political vocabulary in the 1930s to make dictatorship seem rational and even democratic.

Others did want a new constitution, in part because they worried about a revolution without principles. In 1931, a coronel who had participated in the 1920s' tenente uprisings lamented to Vargas, "To date, these statements have not reflected, nor have they disseminated, any great thoughts or grand visions. To date, they have been small, narrow, ridiculous and hateful, unfit for men in charge of rebuilding the country."[52] He outlined six guidelines for the revolution, including measures to deal with the economy, specifically to target problems of overproduction and unemployment. He nevertheless denounced the government's policy of purchasing and warehousing commodities like coffee, calling instead for the immediate sale of all exportable goods at whatever prices necessary to eliminate stocks and restore balance.

What type of government Brazil should adopt became a question inseparable from how to reorganize the economy. As much for Vargas's closest advisers as for those marginal to the official constitution-drafting process, Brazilian jurists wrangled over which economic system best served Brazil's development. In 1934, for example, prominent law professor Luiz F. S. Carpenter argued that Brazil should be divided into two distinct administrative units: "territories" comprised of underpopulated and underutilized lands in the interior, and "states" comprised of industrializing coastal regions that would enjoy full political and economic rights.[53] Territories—carved out of Mato Grosso, Goiás, Amazonas, and Pará—would be organized as large cooperative units in which landownership was communal, whereas private, profit-seeking interests would have free rein in the rest of Brazil. He called his proposal "a capitalist regime for the states and a socialized regime in the territories, without coming into conflict with each other."[54] Carpenter, whose political views were social democratic or socialist, wanted to combine socialist and capitalist systems—an impulse shaped by interwar aspirations for third paths. In his view, the relationship between territories and states should mirror that of colony and metropole in how Brazil's interior regions would exclusively produce foodstuffs and raw materials for its urban centers.

An imperial framework kept creeping into Brazil's legal debates in the 1930s, although Brazil was no longer an empire. Empire was a metaphor—perhaps even an aspiration—for how to manage difference and attain political centralization across diverse racial, ethnic, geographic, and climatic spaces. Prominent jurists like Oliveira Vianna obsessed over Brazil's colonial and imperial past, rehabilitating empire as a force for national unity, unlike the hyperliberal and hyperfederalized First Republic.[55] As Oliveira Vianna explained, Brazil needed a political structure that was "at the same time centralizing and decentralized."[56] Corporatism offered precisely this, because it concentrated political power in a strong executive while consigning administrative powers to corporations organized according to economic sector. The corporatist emphasis on economic hierarchies obscured even as it also reinforced preexisting social and racial inequalities.[57] Corporatism promised transformation while protecting the status quo. The intersection of nostalgic imperial discourses with corporatist theory is key for understanding the lure of corporatism in Brazil but especially in Portugal, as the next section elaborates.

In Portugal, the 1933 Constitution grew out of imperial crises. Its writing, in fact, began with the Acto Colonial ratified in July 1930. It is unsurprising that the Estado Novo Constitution started in the overseas colonies after World War I. Portugal's efforts to exercise more direct control of its overseas possessions was marred by local rebellions and financial mismanagement, while international public opinion had turned against its imperial project owing to the continued practice of forced labor in its colonies.

The 1911 Constitution had only obliquely mentioned empire, using the term *províncias ultramarinas*, or overseas provinces, for the colonies. Just one article discussed the governance of the empire, outlining a "decentralized regime" that granted autonomy to the colonies for their political, economic, and financial management.[58] Few could deny, however, that decentralization was broken from the start. Following World War I, reformers chipped away at the colonies' autonomy. In August 1920, Law 1.022 created the High Commissioner office, reporting directly to Lisbon. Officials appointed to these offices were soon overwhelmed by their own scandals. With Angola on the brink of insolvency, a political conflict erupted between those in Portugal who argued that the colonies were insufficiently developed to govern themselves and local colonial elites pushing for greater autonomy precisely because centralization inhibited colonial growth.[59] As separatist sentiments intensified, many in Portugal worried about once again losing its wealthiest colony, as it had Brazil in 1822.

Hackneyed debates over centralization versus decentralization sputtered along until the 1929 Depression exposed the dismal state of colonial coffers. In early 1930, Salazar, still finance minister, took control of the Ministry of the Colonies. Political leaders, academics, and intellectuals organized conferences and books to advocate for a stronger commercial relationship between metropole and colony in order to improve Portugal's current account balance. Arguments for economic nationalism were in fact arguments for a new type of mercantilism, as economist Moses Bensabat Amzalak observed in his 1929 *O néo-mercantilismo*.[60]

As these debates continued, tensions peaked in Angola. Colonial elites resented the imperial managers sent from Lisbon intervening in local affairs. Among these new imperial officials was High Commissioner Filomeno da Câmara de Melo Cabral, an integralist who supported organic Catholic nationalism and favored a government with strong executive powers. Filomeno da Câmara was a vocal admirer of Benito Mussolini in Italy and Miguel Primo de Rivera in Spain, as he professed in his preface to António Ferro's *Viagem à volta das ditaduras*.[61] His work in Luanda was vexed from the start, with local elites protesting austerity measures. As the political situation destabilized, Filomeno da Camâra fled, leaving his cabinet chief, another integralist from Lisbon, in charge. In March 1930, violence erupted in Luanda and the high commissioner returned to Lisbon in disgrace, prompting the government to find new ways to tame rebellion.[62]

The Acto Colonial, ratified July 1930, was the military dictatorship's response to this political unrest, codifying a new imperial pact designed to ignite Portugal's economic renewal. Little archival evidence exists on how it was written, yet scholars generally agree that the ambitious Salazar spearheaded it, with help from Quirino de Jesus.[63] The Acto Colonial responded to the economic anxieties of the 1920s: the need for fiscal discipline, more trade between colony and metropole, and government support for development. While not expressly corporatist, the Acto Colonial, as Quirino de Jesus explained in 1932 in *Nacionalismo português*, was conceived "under the influence of the same historical, reformist and civilizing ideals that gave origin and form to the new Constitution."[64]

The Acto Colonial reversed the empire's decentralized administration under the First Republic. It reduced colonial authority by substituting the office of high commissioner for governors-general. Colonies could no longer borrow from foreign countries and protectionist measures were introduced to privilege Portuguese goods.[65] Beyond these centralizing impulses, the Acto Colonial codified Portugal's civilizing mission in economic and social terms, echoing the new constitutionalism. Portugal had long been shamed by international public opinion for imperial mismanagement. Coastal trading networks and extractive economic motives may have sufficed in past centuries, but modern colonialism called for engineers and doctors to develop so-called backward territories.[66] True to the aspirational legal culture of the Iberian world, Portugal's first step was to write new laws. The Acto Colonial asserted Portugal's "historical" and "moral" duty to "colonize overseas territories" and "civilize Indigenous populations."[67] Title II guaranteed social assistance for native populations, banned forced labor, and outlined welfare rights. Social and economic protections promised in law, though, did little to eradicate forced labor.[68] In fact, the neomercantilist spirit of this economic project intensified extractive and exploitative practices.

In the years that followed, the Acto Colonial became known as the "first constitutional law of the Estado Novo."[69] Yet the link between the Acto Colonial and the 1933 Constitution was a matter of sequence as well as substance. The Acto Colonial harnessed the neomercantilist and interventionist ethos that underpinned corporatism. It codified the corporatist emphasis on hierarchy, recognizing that diversity and inequality were inherent and unavoidable for modern nation-states and empires alike. Caetano Gonçalves (no relation to Cunha Gonçalves), an imperial magistrate born in Goa, saw in the Acto Colonial precisely what made the corporatist model superior to liberal modes of governance:

> In the formation of a new colonial empire that claims to be unitary and integral we see that it is only this in spirit because the strong centralization of its administration, enacted in 1933, cannot deny the financial and economic diversity among the colonies, populated by different races with different customs, different monetary systems, and diverse capacities for production and consumption.[70]

Debates over how to govern difference laid the groundwork for corporatism as the only suitable alternative to liberalism in Portugal.

The next step was to draft a constitution. Just weeks after the ratification of the Acto Colonial, the provisional dictatorship convened a special commission in Lisbon to bring the nation back to, as one journalist described, "constitutional normality in order to ensure the continuation of work begun on 28 May [1926]."[71] This was a keenly anticipated meeting. In Brazil, the *Correio da Manhã* reported that the dictatorship planned to invite mayors from across Portugal to meet in July to draft the new constitution.[72] These meetings soon disappeared from the official record, however, with no archival trace of a draft in 1930. This is suggestive of the constitution-writing process in Portugal: numerous official channels were created, but in practice, the Constitution was drafted in informal meetings, convened by Salazar along with his handpicked academic and political allies. Accordingly, some scholars have even dubbed the 1933 Constitution "Salazar's Law."[73]

Such a narrow focus on Salazar, though, overlooks the other figures involved in writing the constitution and the process through which they vied for influence. The years between the Acto Colonial and the 1933 Constitution were rattled by political, social, and intellectual agitation that, in hindsight, shaped the Estado Novo's founding principles. The consequences of the Great Depression were starkest in these years, and economic uncertainty led to social unrest. Republicans and socialists in Portugal (and those living in exile since 1926) mounted a counteroffensive against the military dictatorship in summer 1931.[74] Protests, student movements, and general strikes erupted across Portugal and its colonies.[75] Even those loyal to the 1926 Revolution recognized that the provisional dictatorship had failed in its promise to restore order. For example, in March 1931, Theotónio Pereira relayed to Salazar his frustrations over university protests, which he considered a boon to underground communist organizers. The dictatorship had failed to establish new governing principles: "The political problem has not been resolved. Brought to power by a current of rejuvenating antiparliamentary opinions, the dictatorship has not done a thing in the sphere of ideas. It purports a perfect neutrality that is incomprehensible and absurd, not creating principles or opening itself to new horizons."[76] Theotónio Pereira was one of Salazar's closest confidants and a primary architect of Portugal's corporatist system. Born in 1902 to a prominent family of merchants and financiers, he studied mathematics at the University of Lisbon. In his youth, he was active in student integralist movements, but eventually shed these associations. In the 1920s, while working for his family's insurance business, he took a six-month internship with an insurance company in Switzerland to acquire training in actuarial sciences. Salazar would rely on Theotónio Pereira not only for this expertise but also for his links to Catholic and nationalist movements in Portugal—and his distance from Far Right fascist movements.[77] In 1933, Salazar appointed Theotónio Pereira as the subsecretary of state for corporations and social welfare, overseeing efforts to create a social security system, and from 1936 to 1937, minister of commerce and industry. Over the years, Theotónio Pereira became disillusioned with the slow progress of corporatism, candidly voicing his criticisms to Salazar. In frustration, he resigned from his ministerial posts in 1937, but his loyalty to the Estado Novo was rewarded with ambassadorships to Spain in 1937 and Brazil in 1945. Before these official postings, Theotónio Pereira was one of many to insist to Salazar that a return to constitutional normalcy was the only way to diffuse social and political unrest.

Against this backdrop of rebellions and protests, the drafting of Portugal's 1933 Constitution began meekly. While the military dictatorship convened a special commission comprised of top government officials and leading law professors to draft the constitution, this process unfolded from the start on Salazar's terms.[78] In December 1931, Salazar found himself in poor health, too fatigued to read, write, or move from his house.[79] The first round of meetings for the Constitution convened secretly at his private residence on Rua do Funchal in Lisbon. Many scholars and contemporaries alike have credited Quirino de Jesus, Salazar's mentor and rumored ghostwriter for early speeches, as the mastermind behind this first draft, partly to discredit Salazar as more of a narrow-minded bookkeeper than a visionary thinker.[80] Notwithstanding this skepticism, the archival record clearly shows Salazar's involvement in every stage of the constitution-writing process, although this was by no means a solo endeavor. Across more than ten different drafts, Salazar worked with a tight circle of legal advisers (largely from the University of Coimbra) and government ministers. They forwarded drafts to one another, annotating them with margin comments, questions, and amendments. Salazar brought in a few new voices along the way while dismissing some of his allies in the process. This group was close-knit, but there were also important fault lines within this circle that would prove critical to the evolution of corporatism. Military generals controlled the provisional dictatorship yet were largely marginal to this process, unsurprisingly. Salazar's Estado Novo was a hyperlegalistic civilian regime, in which university professors, social scientists, and journalists wielded power until another military coup in 1974 brought down the regime.[81]

The drafting process for the 1933 Constitution had two phases: the first was a deeply conservative draft inspired by Catholic, integralist, and corporatist ideas, while the second introduced several compromises between liberal democracy and corporatism. Many of those involved in the initial drafts were integralists, advocating for a decisive break with liberalism. Their Catholic and organic vision of the nation pushed church and state closer. In addition to

Quirino de Jesus, this group included Domingos Fezas Vital, Coimbra professor of constitutional law and future deputy to the Câmara Corporativa, the
corporatist chamber for professional representation. They were the most
important advisers to Salazar for the Constitution, but others made their mark
as well. Integralist Martinho Nobre de Melo, also educated at the University
of Coimbra before becoming a law professor at the University of Lisbon,
played a notable role in early constitutional drafts but was eventually sidelined,
to such an extent that rumors circulated that his appointment as ambassador
to Brazil in March 1932 was a ploy by Salazar to eliminate his input altogether.[82]
Finally, Marcello Caetano, with his recently minted doctorate in law from the
University of Lisbon, served as secretary to record the drafting process.[83]

   Much of the work on the Constitution occurred in January and February 1932, and involved many ad hoc meetings between Salazar and his team.
This format in and of itself indicates shifting political times: in contrast to
nineteenth-century practice, no constituent assembly was convened. Instead,
well-positioned experts steered the process, which is carefully preserved in
Salazar's archive in many drafts with amendments, revisions, and marginalia.
These multiple drafts document the fall of old political institutions and rise of
new ones as well as the emergence of a new vocabulary for citizenship.

   In remarkable contrast to Portugal, the writing of the 1934 Brazilian Constitution
generated copious transcripts of all official committee meetings and the National
Constitutional Assembly, not to mention a wealth of memoirs documenting
individual perspectives. The abundance of documentation in Brazil's case makes
it daunting to figure out which ideas mattered and how drafters reached a final
consensus, with at least four drafts and extensive amendments proposed throughout the process. For Brazil, it is also necessary to contend with two distinct but
connected constitutions. The 1934 Constitution was short-lived, suspended by
states of emergency in 1935 and then a coup. Brazil's 1937 Constitution, in turn,
became the defining document of Vargas's rule, lasting until 1945. This second
Constitution, however, is riddled with its own enigmas. It was implemented with
a coup and written in secrecy, largely by Francisco Campos, appointed justice
minister on the day before Vargas's 1937 self-coup. Yet it too was constantly debated and amended in the years that followed, albeit barely implemented. Only
by bringing these constitutional moments together do their primary innovations
and motivations become apparent.

   In Brazil, the constitution-writing process unfolded in multiple arenas
through force and deliberation. Rising support for semiconstitutions or
antidemocratic ones did not totally drown out support for liberal democracy.
Liberal opposition to Vargas was strongest in São Paulo and among the burgeoning middle class of other urban centers. Regional elites in São Paulo

worried about their loss of political hegemony to Vargas's centralizing impulses. Such regional anxieties were couched in a platform demanding the immediate return to the rule of law, expansion of civil liberties, and electoral reforms, rallying behind the unfulfilled promises of the 1891 Constitution to push classical liberalism. In 1932, Paulistas staged the Revolução Constitutionalista (Constitutionalist Movement), a three-month armed revolt against Vargas. This uprising against the provisional dictatorship's federal encroachment on regional interests mobilized soldiers and other volunteers across races and classes, claiming hundreds (and even thousands) of lives.[84] To quash rebellion, Vargas finally agreed to convene a National Constitutional Assembly in November 1933.

Before the National Constituent Assembly could convene, Vargas promised a provisional constitution to govern until the new constitution was ready. Rather than reinstate or amend the 1891 Constitution, the 1932 *constituição provisória* included many innovations later codified in the 1934 and 1937 Constitutions: corporatist representation, a rearranged legislative branch, enhanced executive powers, and social and economic rights. This provisional constitution—drafted and ready to go—was never enacted. It is not clear why. Some of Vargas's legal advisers worried that any "provisional" or "small" constitution would simply "feed new doubts about the convening of that assembly."[85] Or perhaps Brazil's constitutional theater amounted to Vargas's strategy to further delay the country's return to the rule of law.

The actual process of drafting the 1934 Constitution began with the Comissão do Itamaraty (Itamaraty Commission) in November 1932. Afrânio de Mello Franco, minister of external relations, gathered this special subcommittee at his private residence to write the first draft. It brought together key figures of the 1930 Revolution: government ministers, regional elites, politicians, a military general, and Oliveira Vianna, the sole academic invited.[86]

Constitutional Innovations

In the South Atlantic, corporatist ideas informed new strategies for organizing the powers of government and increasing the state's ability to intervene in economic and social life. This section underscores two of these innovations. First, it emphasizes efforts to reorganize the legislative branch to make room for professional representation, technical councils, and corporatist chambers. Second, it highlights Brazil and Portugal's codification of social and economic rights, ultimately at the expense of civil and political rights. These innovations become essential to another trend in interwar constitutions: the legalization of dictatorship.

Portugal's 1933 Constitution is often cast as a total sham, a dictator's window dressing.[87] This is at least partially a fair assessment: the forty-plus-year

Estado Novo dictatorship was not governed by on-paper stipulations. Salazar, formally appointed prime minister in 1932 in addition to other ministerial postings, governed beyond constitutionally decreed powers. He turned decree law into the basic legislative mode—a tool that according to the Constitution, should only have been used "in cases of urgent public necessity."[88] Elections, albeit not very competitive ones, were held throughout the Estado Novo for the president, National Assembly, and local offices under the Constitution. Both chambers of the legislative branch—the National Assembly, composed of ninety deputies elected by direct suffrage, and Câmara Corporativa, for corporatist representation according to profession and industry—functioned more as consultative than legislative bodies. They convened to debate and offer feedback on legislation or investigate key issues. Ultimate legislative authority rested squarely with Salazar.

At the same time, governing still required consultation and negotiation through formal and informal channels, and in this respect the 1933 Constitution did inform the functioning of the Portuguese state and even citizens' rights.[89] Moreover, this exercise in constitution writing mattered in other ways. If autocratic rule is defined as the exercise of state powers without restraint, then Portugal's 1933 Constitution shows how Salazar used the Constitution to remove constraints, both ideological and political.

Both of these constraints and negotiations concerning them are imprinted on the many drafts of the 1933 Constitution. Its first draft, prepared in December 1931 or early January 1932, was the longest version, with 294 articles, and was explicitly Catholic and corporatist.[90] Where prior constitutions had treated the individual as the cellular unit of society, this one assigned social bodies—the family, local parishes, municipalities, and professional corporations—with rights, obligations, and political representation. Inspired by Catholic social thought, it codified a pyramidal structure for society with the family as the base connecting individuals to the parish, municipality, corporation, and ultimately the nation.

This organic vision of society informed a new design of the legislative branch. The 1911 Constitution, maligned by Portuguese officials as the "last" of the nineteenth-century constitutions for its decentralized framework and excessive emphasis on individual rights, had established a popularly elected bicameral legislature.[91] Salazar vilified legislative organs as echo chambers for self-interest and factious political parties. He and his legal team found support abroad for their attack on legislative supremacy and direct suffrage, claiming that "the great revolutionary activists of today are all antiparliamentary."[92] Salazar and his collaborators were emboldened by European fascists, radical republicans, and socialists who questioned the legislative branch as the fulcrum of modern democracy.

The 1933 Portuguese Constitution ultimately retained a bicameral structure, but its drafters redesigned the legislative branch, shifting powers to the executive branch and limiting popular sovereignty. Constitutional drafters vested sovereignty in the nation, not the people, placing the nation's well-being above individual or group interests. This priority was especially pronounced in debates over suffrage. The first draft rejected direct voting: Congress still had two chambers, but municipal councils and professional corporations would elect representatives.[93] This vision was not ratified, however. In the draft sent to the Council of Ministers in February 1932, government ministers proposed several amendments, overwhelming the document by pasting over it with bits of paper and handwritten changes. They partially reintroduced direct suffrage, with half the delegates elected by direct vote and half by professional corporations. In further revisions, Salazar and his advisers fully reintroduced direct suffrage (though not universal) for the National Assembly, signifying a return to liberal conventions. With these compromises, the constitution's ideological position shed the Catholic and organic orientation of early drafts. The Catholic Church protested its political losses; not only did Salazar opt for a constitution that affirmed the separation of church and state, but his regime increasingly sidelined existing religious associations as it built corporatist institutions like *casas do povo* to turn social welfare into a statist and secular project.[94] With patchy and incomplete records on these changes, Portuguese historian António de Araújo concludes that Salazar's pragmatism drove the final version.[95]

The most important innovation for the legislative branch was the creation of the Câmara Corporativa, or Corporatist Chamber. In mid-February, Salazar sent the sixth version of the Constitution to Fezas Vital and Nobre de Melo, on the one hand, and Quirino de Jesus, on the other. Quirino de Jesus's revisions were the first to mention that the National Assembly should function alongside a chamber comprised of representatives from the various "corporations" of the nation.[96] Fezas Vital and Nobre de Melo called this corporatist organ the Câmara Corporativa. Scribbled on three pieces of paper, their revisions outlined a chamber composed of representatives from major social, economic, and cultural groups. The word *corporation* signaled a paradigm shift in how this Constitution positioned itself vis-à-vis the antecedent liberal democratic order. The Câmara Corporativa was an original feature of the Portuguese Constitution. It was a deliberative chamber, not a lawmaking body; its sole function was to give *pareceres*, or legal opinions or briefs, on legislation according to standing professional and economic interests. This chamber privileged "expert intervention" and expertise to override the factious political parties of parliamentary democracy.[97]

It might seem ironic that Salazar and his collaborators expended so much energy on drafting and redrafting legislative institutions when in practice,

Portugal's Estado Novo was governed by Salazar, and largely through decree law. Recently, though, Portuguese historians have reevaluated how the Assembleia Nacional and Câmara Corporativa functioned, arguing that these organs should not be dismissed as shams. These organs were not lawmaking bodies, but that was precisely the point. They were designed as deliberative bodies, tasked with research, surveys, and debate.[98] Some of the richest documentary evidence that will be presented in this book, for example, on how corporatism functioned in practice—including evidence of corruption and abuses of power committed by corporatist organs—comes from parliamentary investigations. The Câmara Corporativa, especially in the first decade of the Estado Novo, produced hundreds of parceres on policy and legislation. It was most active with matters related to finance and the economy. Within this chamber, industrialists, academics, agriculturalists, and designated experts debated not just policy but also economic theory. Its delegates took up the task of defining corporatist doctrine as they generated new ideas about how the state should intervene in the economy.

In Brazil, the group working on the first draft of the 1934 Constitution represented the full ideological spectrum, including corporatists like Oliveira Vianna and General Pedro Góis Monteiro; socialists like João Mangabeira, who would later spend fifteen months in prison for his opposition to Vargas; members of the Clube Três de Outubro (Third of October Club), a political organization comprised of tenentes with corporatist leanings and an authoritarian vision; and individuals opposed to the group's centralizing impulses. Their platforms were diverse and oppositional, and to complicate matters, individual voting did not neatly overlay ideological factions. The group debated what type of economic system Brazil should adopt. Socialist? Laissez-faire? Corporatist? The Constitution was a place to deliberate between systems, yet without achieving consensus. This group, as one commentator noted, fluctuated "between indecisive aspirations for social justice and a state model influenced by new dictatorial models in Europe."[99]

It took a year for the Itamaraty Commission to produce a first draft. As in Portugal, the legislative branch became the focus of heated experimentation for both practical and ideological reasons. Vargas suspended Congress with the 1930 Revolution, so the path back to the rule of law demanded the reinstatement of legislative sovereignty. As one jurist explained, "Of the three constitutional powers—one remains suspended—the legislative."[100] This branch had become the target of antiliberal thought, with many pointing to its incompetence in dealing with economic challenges. Oliveira Vianna pushed for a corporatist model that was statist and technocratic, unencumbered by factious political parties. He opposed direct representation, the secret ballot, and plebiscites. Surprisingly, he even rejected the type of professional representation written into Portugal's Constitution on the grounds that organized class interests were still too "embryonic" in Brazil.[101] Oliveira Vianna rehearsed arguments presented in German political theorist Carl Schmitt's 1932 *Legality and Legitimacy*, published on the eve of Adolf Hitler's rise as chancellor in Germany. The Brazilian jurist had a copy of Schmitt's book in his personal library, highlighted and annotated around passages that rationalized the eclipse of liberal, parliamentary democracy. The Weimar Republic had failed, in Schmitt's account, because of Parliament's inability to represent the citizenry's will and act decisively against unrest. In Brazil, as in other contexts, constitutional drafters were keen to build an administrative state of nonelected agencies with powers to implement policies without contentious debate or voting to slow down decision-making. In Brazil, such agencies were already at work in commodity sectors and labor relations. For Oliveira Vianna, Schmitt offered the legal rationale for turning such agencies into a governing system, not just an emergency solution. Schmitt defended the "administrative state" as the "antipode" to the "legislative state," and a superior governing instrument for its "purely practical and objective spirit."[102] Oliveira Vianna underlined this passage and wrote in the margin, "The corporatist State?"[103]

Oliveira Vianna's vision for Brazil rested on the creation of technical councils to write laws and exercise administrative powers. He contended that for too long, Brazilian laws were "written without prior consultation from the interested classes, without . . . advice from 'professionals,' 'experts,' and 'practical experience.'"[104] Oliveira Vianna campaigned for the "constitutional consecration of technical councils."[105] He imagined *conselhos técnicos* as "a system of corporations, of professional character, that represented the grand social, economic and cultural interests of the nation." For him, this model was the only way to implement effective policy, and it had quickly become a transnational trend: "Look at how they legislate today in France. Look at how they legislate today in Italy. Look at how they legislate today in Belgium, Germany, Spain, Russia, Japan and . . . how they will legislate soon in Norway and in Portugal. . . . Look at how they are legislating all over the world."[106] Oliveira Vianna wanted to formalize how private interests lobbied government. As much as he criticized Brazil's progress in implementing new forms of representation, he praised Vargas's early efforts to organize commodity producers and grant them regulatory powers over their own sector. Now he wanted to transpose this corporatist vision into constitutional form.[107]

The National Constitutional Assembly, convened in November 1933, quickly dismissed the Itamaraty draft as too radical and would compile its own draft. This assembly already bore the imprint of corporatist ideas, with delegates elected by direct suffrage and professional groups.[108] Delegates to this assembly produced three more drafts until the National Constitutional Assembly finally compromised to ratify a new Constitution in July 1934. With multiple drafts and many voices present at the National Constituent Assembly, it would be impossible to synthesize all the changes—big and small—that distinguished the 1934 Constitution from its 1891 predecessor. It did centralize and expand federal powers to intervene in economic and social questions, but in many ways it was a hybrid document that left vague or avoided many controversial points. The legislative branch, for example, combined ideas from earlier drafts. It included a lower house, the Câmara dos Deputados (Chamber of Deputies), elected both by direct and professional suffrage. The Constitution also included a Senado Federal, or Senate, comprising two delegates from each state, responsible for authorizing federal interventions at the state level. At first glance, this structure harked back to liberal conventions. But the Senate was unorthodox because it stood outside the legislative branch, imagined as a "fourth power," akin to the *Poder Moderador* (Moderating Power) under the empire that balanced legislative and executive powers.[109] The Senate was responsible for "plans to solve national problems" in collaboration with conselhos técnicos, absorbing arguments by Oliveira Vianna and others for a more technocratic approach to lawmaking, but leaving the details to future legislation.[110]

Emphasis on governing with experts and not politicians permeated debates over the 1934 Constitution in Brazil. These debates were, to be sure, not new to the Vargas period. Following the overthrow of the constitutional monarchy of the Empire of Brazil in 1889, military generals, inspired by positivist ideas, had also pushed for government by expertise and based in scientific reasoning.[111] This earlier tradition now merged with a global trend, thereby garnering legitimacy. Oliveira Vianna highlighted parallel experiments from France, Portugal, and the United States to show how experiments in governing by economic councils and other technocratic chambers had multiplied in recent years.[112] Salazar similarly insisted that the 1933 Constitution allowed expertise to triumph over politics, guided by "great ideas of sociology and social economics."[113] Technical councils and corporatist chambers, however, led inevitably to the question of who would decide who was an expert or what type of expertise should have lawmaking powers.

The word *compromise* cast a shadow over the 1934 Constitution. The National Constitutional Assembly tried to please too many, attempting to reconcile liberals, socialists, and corporatists while also balancing the regional interests of Minas Gerais, São Paulo, and Rio Grande do Sul. In 1977, Caetano, Portuguese law professor and future dictator, commented during his exile in Brazil after the fall of the Portuguese Estado Novo that with all of these efforts by Brazilian drafters to reimagine the different branches of government, they ended up being "excessively disfigured."[114] The 1934 Constitution was ultimately suspended and replaced with the 1937 Constitution, an explicitly corporatist document bearing striking similarities to Portugal's.

In writing the 1933 Constitution, Salazar argued that dismantling liberal democracy amounted to the construction of a new type of democracy, centered on economic and social rights. In 1932, while working on a draft, Salazar said, "The essence of democracy is neither parliament nor elections: it is the democratization of credit, work, hygiene, property."[115] Such claims can easily be dismissed as a pretext to distract from how he used the Constitution to concentrate his power. Yet this argument was hardly exclusive to Salazar. Whether the corporatist 1933 Constitution in Portugal, social democratic 1934 Constitution in Brazil, or authoritarian 1937 Constitution in Brazil, articles enumerating the economic and social rights marked a new type of constitutionalism that expanded the responsibilities of government toward citizens, and focused "democracy" on economic and social questions.

Portugal's Constitution decreed "a unitary and corporatist republic."[116] Beyond the Corporatist Chamber, its section on economic and social rights is what really gave the Estado Novo its corporatist form and function. As one Portuguese official put it, Portugal was embracing economic and social rights to move "beyond closed concepts of individualism."[117]

The earliest drafts the 1933 Portuguese Constitution expansively enumerated economic and social rights. Across all drafts, it was asserted that "the state will promote the formation and development of a national corporatist economy, with the aim that its agents do not enter into any competition with each other ... and that they collaborate jointly as members of the same collective body."[118] While the first draft was vague on social rights, by mid-February 1932, a new draft included a section dedicated to "the economic and social order," which itemized the new obligations of the state. Words like *development, progress,* and *organization* imbued this section with promises for the state's increased role in national and colonial economies. It designated corporations to maintain social peace between labor and capital and to function as institutions for social insurance and welfare. The national economy itself became the object of state responsibilities, which included "establishing equilibrium" between "labor and capital" as well as between the interests of the "metropole and colonies"; "guaranteeing the lowest price and highest salary with the highest fair profits"; and "promoting the development and settlement of all national territories," including to "control emigration."[119]

Unchanged across all drafts was the declaration that the state had "the right and the obligation to coordinate and regulate aspects of economic and social life."[120] From the start to finish of the constitution-writing process, several articles proclaimed the importance of government interventions to establish equilibrium between labor and capital, populations, and professions. But the mention of "equilibrium" between "metropole and colonies" was removed, for example, from the final draft. So was any mention of *trabalhadores*, or workers.[121] The charter certainly discussed labor, but largely in terms of harmony between labor and capital. Where initially early drafts of the constitution asserted the state's obligation to promote the moral and material well-being of the working classes, women, and children, these specific references were replaced with vague promises of social harmony.[122] Workers may have been omitted for the straightforward objective of minimizing any explicit discussion of class conflict—a socialist paradigm—in favor of social harmony, a buzzword for corporatist ideologues.

With only the constitutional drafts themselves to work with, it is hard to say conclusively why Salazar winnowed down this section on economic and social rights. In part, it seems these edits were concessions to more conservative, integralist factions who found early drafts of the "Economic and Social Order" section excessive. On a February 1932 draft, for instance, law professors Fezes Vital and Nobre de Melo returned it to Salazar's desk with extensive edits and (unsigned) annotations in the margins denouncing the "exaggeration of the state's interventionism in the definition of its economic functions." The constitution had become too "democratic" and "not decentralized enough."[123] These changes can also be understood as concessions to more moderate factions, comprising industrialists, commercial exporters, and military generals, who valued the state's capacity to modernize the nation over political idealism.[124] Early drafts targeted not only labor but capital too, imposing conditions in which private property might be subordinated to national economic imperatives. Thus some of these changes were the result of protests from those concerned with the potential fallout from leading financial and commercial sectors over the state's "exaggerated" role.[125] It seemed safer to keep some things vague or eliminate them altogether so as not to risk alienating key groups. The Constitution's economic orientation remained pronounced, but was tailored to placate fears that too *many* rights had been granted.

With the inclusion of economic and social provisions, the exclusion of civil and political rights became all the more glaring. All the drafts included a section on civil liberties, albeit with different titles. Early drafts referred to "citizens, individually and socially considered"—an attempt to shift the focus from what Theotónio Pereira criticized in "prior political constitutions predicated on the egocentrism of citizens."[126] The final draft settled on "of citizens." It outlined fundamental rights, including property and due process, but it fell short of guaranteeing freedom of expression and assembly or habeas corpus. Moreover, this section asserted that these rights were no longer absolute or inviolable. By the final draft, the individual liberties enumerated in Portugal's

FIGURE 2.2. Poster *Autoridade, ordem e justiça social* circulating prior to the constitutional plebiscite in Portugal (1933). The woman is holding a plaque with "authority, order, and social justice" written in bold red letters. The poster calls on the public to "vote for the new Constitution." Image courtesy of the Biblioteca Nacional de Portugal.

Constitution were so whittled down that jurist and military officer José Martinho Simões remarked, "[It] does not contain a single fundamental guarantee."[127] This comment was intended as praise; he even offered some suggestions to obscure this absence of rights.

In May 1932, the government published a draft of the Constitution so that the public could discuss it ahead of the plebiscite in March 1933. Historians largely doubt the plebiscite's electoral integrity given the small number of

FIGURE 2.3. Poster *Nós queremos um Estado forte!* circulating
prior to the constitutional plebiscite in Portugal (1933). The slogan
"we want a strong state" surrounds a woman holding a child.
The poster calls on the public to "vote for the new Constitution."
Image courtesy of the Biblioteca Nacional de Portugal.

voters and that over 90 percent of them "approved" the Constitution. Even so,
the plebiscite did make the Constitution a public event. Posters conveyed a
clear message: the Constitution brought social justice (figure 2.2), a strong
government (figure 2.3), public order, and economic prosperity (figures 2.4
and 2.5). For Goan jurist Cunha Gonçalves, the Constitution did not signal
the end of democracy but instead merely the eclipse of parliamentary or representative democracy.[128] This propaganda attempted to distance Salazar's

FIGURE 2.4. Poster *Se sois pela ordem votai a nova Constituição* circulating prior to the constitutional plebiscite in Portugal (1933). The poster asks, "Portuguese! Do you want disorder and indiscipline, or do you want discipline and order?" It answers, "If you are in favor of order, vote for the new Constitution!" Image courtesy of the Biblioteca Nacional de Portugal.

FIGURE 2.5. Poster *Cidadãos votai a nova Constituição* circulating prior to the constitutional plebiscite in Portugal (1933). The poster urges, "Citizens, vote for the new Constitution." It includes two drawings to depict the choice before citizens: political chaos and economic hardships (on the left) versus economic and financial stability, represented by wheat and gold deposits at the Banco de Portugal (on the right). Image courtesy of the Biblioteca Nacional de Portugal.

Constitution from dictatorship—a category attached to prior coups, or problematically, the Soviet dictatorship of the proletariat.

In 1934, Brazilian delegates to the constitutional convention found inspiration in Portugal's example. They too emphasized that the 1891 Constitution, which scarcely mentioned the economy, was a "political constitution," following in the "revolutionary cycle" beginning with the US Constitution. That model was now outdated. They intended to "draft a political and social constitution for Brazil."[129]

Scholars continue to debate the content and practice of social rights proclaimed by dictatorships. Brazil's 1934 and 1937 Constitutions, for example, codified labor rights, including the eight-hour workday, yearly vacations, a minimum wage, and the right to bring labor grievances to a special labor tribunal.[130] Yet these social and economic rights were not equally or universally enjoyed by all citizens, and therefore some historians argue that they are perhaps better understood as "privileges" or "patronage" that Vargas "bestowed" on popular classes to generate loyalty and legitimacy rather than as rights. While this top-down notion of citizenship in Brazil does not account for how different social groups maneuvered with and within this new legal architecture, it does offer a starting point for thinking about other innovations introduced with Brazil's two 1930s' Constitutions.[131] Brazilian jurists codified social rights not as individual entitlements but rather as tools for defusing social conflict to support industrialization and economic recovery. This trend becomes especially apparent when we look beyond the labor question to see how else Vargas's team used these legal moves to formally assert the state's prime role in coordinating national economic development.

In December 1933, Brazil's National Constitutional Assembly debated how to design state powers to respond to economic crisis. With its agricultural sector still reeling from the Depression, the question itself was an assault against Brazil's oligarchic, federalist, and liberal First Republic that supported agroexport sectors, but seemed ill-equipped to deal with the economic challenges of the 1930s. A Ceará delegate called for a coordinated government response to combat droughts in the northeast, for example. He turned the economic troubles of one of Brazil's poorest regions into an issue of utmost national importance by elaborating moral, humanitarian, and economic arguments to make droughts a constitutional issue.

Ceará's deputies looked beyond Brazil to make their case for a constitution that tended to economic and social rights, connecting their efforts to Weimar Germany, Republican Spain, and Estado Novo Portugal. Drought prevention connected to broader transformations in the modern state; governments could no longer content themselves with protections for individual rights and property, but had to secure the economic and social well-being of their citizens. For the Ceará delegate, labor rights were incomplete without enumerating other state powers to address economic challenges: "How can we guarantee [labor] rights to northeastern Brazilians without doing any work there against the effects of the droughts?" These were the "new trends in constitutional law," argued the delegate, citing jurist Mirkine-Guetzévitch to assert that "we should not be afraid of the new."[132]

As Brazilian delegates looked abroad for inspiration, Portugal's Constitution seemed especially relevant. Many constitutional drafts circulated between Brazil and Portugal, and with them ideas about the expansion of state powers in economic life. The Ceará delegate cited an early draft of Portugal's 1933 Constitution, quoting Article 29: "The economic organization of the nation is an integral part of its political organization." He continued, "[It] aims to realize the maximum amount of production and wealth that is socially useful in order to establish collective life that supports a strong state and justice between citizens."[133] Portugal codified this economic orientation so "of course," the Ceará delegate concluded, "[these rights] will also appear in the one that we are working on now."[134]

The final draft of the 1934 Constitution introduced bold provisions for economic and social citizenship—though not as bold as the first Itamaraty draft discarded as too radical. It struck a balance between delegates calling for the state to protect labor and stimulate economic production and those who cautioned that too much government interference might, in the words of Paulista industrialist Roberto Simonsen, a deputy to the constitutional assembly, limit the "creative stimulous of progress."[135] The final draft codified labor rights and social welfare, announcing the future creation of the Justiça do Trabalho, or labor courts, to adjudicate grievances between employers and employees. It also enumerated guarantees specific to agricultural labor, including the right to claim abandoned land productively used for at least ten years. Furthermore, it emboldened state powers to intervene in economic production and banking by sanctioning the nationalization of strategic resources, specifically if "essential to the economic or military defense of the nation." With a touch of economic nationalism, it included an article for the nationalization of bank deposits and limits on foreign-owned corporations in Brazil. The final draft tried to discipline capital as well as labor by codifying state powers to limit private property and regulate competition. It even incorporated demands from Ceará and other drought-stricken regions by enshrining the "consequences of droughts in northern states" as the "permanent responsibility of the federal government."[136]

Economic and social rights are one of the dominant (and debated) legacies of the Vargas era.[137] On paper, Brazil's new laws were some of the most progressive in the world and even utopian. As historian Brodwyn Fischer suggests, the aspirational quality of these Constitutions was perfectly consistent with Brazilian lawmaking and tendencies across the civil law world, whereby law was "meant to be a beacon rather than a reflection of reality."[138]

For Brazilian jurists, the Constitution was more than an aspirational blueprint on how to change social conditions: Brazil's interwar constitutions were most original and forward-looking in their economic provisions. The 1937 Constitution was even bolder than the 1934 one in how it expanded state powers to transform the national economy, following in the tradition of Portugal's 1933 Constitution by decreeing a corporatist and nondemocratic government. Brazilian jurists defended dictatorship as an updated form of democracy precisely by emphasizing that the corporatist system would mold private interests in service of the public good. By writing and rewriting constitutions, Brazilian jurists codified economic and social rights as essential to Vargas-style democracy, while also affirming economic order and social harmony to be the government's foremost responsibility.

Brazil's Estado Novo coup was a constitutional event, but one that transpired secretly, without the election of a constitutional assembly. Instead, just nine jurists worked alongside Vargas to pen the document. Justice Minister Campos was its primary author.[139] Considered one of the chief architects of Brazil's Estado Novo, Campos overhauled Brazil's educational, legal, and constitutional frameworks in the 1930s. Born in 1891, Campos hailed from Belo Horizonte and a prominent family with deep roots in the political life of Minas Gerais.[140] As a law student in the 1910s, he was already a critic of liberal democracy.[141] His position matured into a theoretical and practical defense of concentrating power in the executive branch, which inspired the legal documents he wrote, not just in 1937, but decades later in support of the 1964 military dictatorship.[142] In his youth, he practiced law in Belo Horizonte, and in the 1920s, rose quickly in the ranks of local politics. Following the 1930 Revolution, he held positions within the recently created Ministry of Education and Public Health and participated in the National Constitutional Assembly. He advocated for better public administration, championing efforts to build a modern centralized state. In this spirit, he pushed for more technocratic approaches to government and education reforms to train experts. Campos advocated for a corporatist state too, but did not theorize corporatism as a system of labor relations where social harmony depended on state-sponsored professional associations for employers and employees.[143] Rather, he supported class organization and professional representation as a way of coordinating national economic production.[144]

Although written by a closed circle of legal advisers, the 1937 Constitution was still a vehicle for settling ongoing conflicts between political factions. Months before the November coup, Campos shared his draft with Plínio Salgado, leader of the AIB, Brazil's homegrown fascist party. Vargas was trying to forge an alliance with integralists. In fact, it was an integralist member of the Brazilian Army who had planted the fabricated Plano Cohen that outlined a Communist plot to overthrow the government. When Army Chief of Staff Góis Monteiro, a longtime Vargas supporter, "discovered" this plot in September 1937, Vargas had what he needed to declare a state of emergency in preparation for his coup. In this context, the 1937 Constitution became a bargaining chip in negotiations with integralist leaders. Days before the Plano Cohen made news headlines, Campos visited Salgado to ask his opinion on the Constitution—and for his support. Salgado did not think that a new constitution was "necessary," suggesting that the 1934 Constitution be amended to replace "universal suffrage with the corporatist vote, giving greater reach to the state with regard to powers to interfere in the economic-financial rhythm." Still, the integralist leader found the Constitution good enough—for now. It did not embrace the integralist doctrine in its "totality" but instead made considerable progress toward the "corporatist organization of the country." In Salgado's view, this "Constitution offers a first step toward organic democracy, as we had dreamed, and is nothing like Fascist or Nazi regimes."[145] Salgado's comment that this Constitution distinguished Brazil from Europe's dictatorships is significant. Behind-the-scenes conversations provide a partial answer to the "why write a constitution?" question: to shore up support across political movements and make Brazil look less autocratic.

The 1937 Constitution was not just a power play, however; it made clear its ambitions to transform the national economy. Its architects argued that economic renewal required a new constitutional regime—one not weighed down by petty political rivalries or sluggish legislative processes. This push for economic development found institutional expression with the Conselho de Economia Nacional (National Economic Council). Under the 1937 Constitution, the lower house of Congress was indirectly elected by municipal suffrage, a gesture to organic corporatist models, and the upper house with ten delegates was appointed directly by the president. The National Economic Council became the third legislative branch, comprised of representatives from five primary sectors (industry, agriculture, commerce, transportation, and banking), elected by professional associations and labor syndicates as well as "persons qualified due to their special expertise." The National Economic Council was responsible for "promoting the corporatist organization of the national economy."[146] Júlio Barata, chief editor of *A Batalha* and future labor minister during the 1964 military dictatorship, wrote in December 1937 that "the Conselho de Economia Nacional will be our Câmara Corporativa"—a reference to its Portuguese counterpart. In his words, "This organ will promote the corporatist organization of the national economy and will undertake surveys on conditions of labor, agriculture, industry . . . to coordinate and improve Brazil's productive capacity."[147] The 1937 Constitution absorbed foreign legal examples to mold its nondemocratic vision for Brazil's economic future.

Vargas's 1937 Constitution unambiguously gave the president near-absolute powers. For Vargas's jurists, however, the authoritarian qualities of the Constitution were not undemocratic.[148] Rather, Campos boldly declared that "the new Constitution is profoundly democratic" for how it represented the needs of the *povo*, or the people. Rather than have citizens express their interests through the vote, the Estado Novo Constitution put the president "in direct contact with the povo."[149] If, as some scholars contend, populism can evolve into an authoritarian form of democracy, this Constitution gave legal logic to this contention by affirming a direct, inviolable bond between leader and people, and granting the president "supreme powers" to enact the (supposed) will of the people.[150]

And in a corporatist society, the povo's interests were understood in economic terms. After all, this was the idea behind new government institutions for professional and labor representation. The emphasis on economic interests, moreover, proved useful for sidestepping representative democracy. Once established, "corporations" would constitute the "democratic structure of the state," as Themístocles Brandão Cavalcanti, founder of the Clube Três de Outubro and member of the Itamaraty Commission, explained in the preface to his 1938 translation of French law professor Roger Bonnard's *Syndicalismo, corporativismo e estado corporativo*. "Nobody today will fetishize the old formulas for direct representation," he observed, because with "corporatist or syndical representation, the individual is considered as a unit, integrated into their economic or social group." Corporatists promised "a more technical organization of the state, more administrative than purely political, so that public services can be oriented toward the common good." To those insisting that liberal democracy was slow and corrupt, corporatism offered a "program for depoliticizing the state."[151] Such bold aspirations in Brazil's 1937 Constitution amounted not just to a reformulation of the powers of government but a reorganization of society as well.

Many of the corporatist ambitions outlined in the 1937 Constitution, though, would have to wait. This Constitution was a blueprint for the future and only partially promulgated in November 1937, with its full implementation pending a national plebiscite, tentatively scheduled to take place six years later. Meanwhile, the legislative branch remained dissolved, freeing Vargas to rule by decree, and appoint judges, ministers, and technocrats as he saw fit. Nevertheless, this does not make the 1937 Constitution irrelevant or meaningless. It boldly proclaimed a New State that put the economy front and center. In doing so, it argued that political and civil rights needed to be curtailed for the sake of economic order and even justice.

Brazil's two 1930s' Constitutions differed markedly in their ideological orientation and fundamental views of government. The 1937 Constitution discarded the civil and political rights that the 1934 Constitution had upheld as essential to any democratic system. The 1937 Constitution outlined individual rights and freedoms, but these were conditional on national security and eventually suspended. Even more than Portugal's 1933 Constitution, Brazil's 1937 Estado Novo Constitution was boldly authoritarian and undemocratic, even as Vargas and his jurists contorted the word *democracy* to make it seem less so.

Rather than see universal suffrage as the only vehicle for democracy, Campos asserted that democracy should be understood as "the right to productive activities, the right to work, the right to a reasonable standard of living, the right to protections against the accidents and misfortunes of life."[152] Such rights talk, even in dictatorial contexts, shaped how citizens voiced grievances and petitioned for rights.[153]

This new economic order went beyond labor rights or even citizens' welfare. Order became an economic right, which legitimized new government efforts to control and discipline private economic activities in support of national interests above petty individual greed. This became the essence of interwar efforts to use corporatism to rebrand dictatorship as an elevated form of democracy, or what some Brazilian jurists took to calling "authoritarian democracy" or "corporatist authoritarian democracy."[154] Vargas would take this neologism a step further: he called his dictatorship an "economic democracy."[155]

Vargas's and Salazar's path from liberal democracy to authoritarian democracy required undoing certain constitutional assumptions inherited from the nineteenth century and classic liberal tradition. It also required expanding the state's administrative powers over the economy. In Brazil as in Portugal, the executive branch, occupied by dictators, exercised these new powers by creating ministries, tribunals, and technocratic councils closely connected to the executive.

In the 1930s, both Vargas and Salazar defined social and economic rights in opposition to civil and political rights. Their approach to citizenship defied the model that T. H. Marshall put forth to describe the Anglo-American experience in which citizenship expands sequentially from civil to political to social rights.[156] Brazilian and Portuguese scholars have debated the consequences of inverting this sequence. Without political and civil rights to hold government accountable, Brazilian historian José Murilo de Carvalho concludes that this inverted evolution made citizenship in Brazil "passive" and incomplete.[157] While early scholarship on Estado Novo dictatorships interpreted social rights in authoritarian contexts in terms of political opportunism or the co-optation of working classes by a corporatist state, historians now emphasize how labor movements seized on new social rights and struggled for their realization.[158] Others have highlighted the inequalities and exclusions built into this system, or how it favored the interests of capital over labor.[159] It stands to reason that to analyze new constitutionalism in either Brazil or Portugal by looking at law as written misses how law actually shaped citizens' lives, in both intended and unintended ways.[160] Yet to look again at the corporatist logic that inspired drafters requires that we pay attention to how efforts to codify social and economic citizenship were part and parcel of a broader intellectual, legal, and technical project to formalize dictatorship.

These debates in the South Atlantic would continue to reverberate in the postwar period in the wake of decolonization, as newly independent nations set out to draft constitutions. An increasingly global literature on the rise of international legal regimes to preserve human rights has explored this tension between guarantees for individual liberties versus economic and social rights.[161] Already in 1930s Brazil and Portugal, however, debates over whether civil and political rights had to be sacrificed for the development of a national economy were shaping the meanings of and possibilities for democracy.

By putting the corporatist idealism of key jurists front and center to explain the content of interwar authoritarian constitutions, this chapter thus also suggests new ways of thinking about why constitutions get written. In this case, evaluating and looking at constitutions exclusively through the paradigm of citizenship or rights might obscure other bold ambitions that animate political revolutions. Indeed, these constitutions put the spotlight on ambitions to transform economic life. And the process of constitution writing became a form of debate rather than the end product of a debate.

———

In Brazil and Portugal, dictators wrote constitutions, and the constitutions proved to be handy tools for curtailing civil rights and political representation. But there is more to this story, as this chapter has described. On both sides of the Atlantic, Vargas and Salazar wrote and rewrote constitutions as part of a contentious struggle not only to dismantle liberal democracy but also to replace it with something new. The economy became the object of new corporatist systems, while the economic challenges at stake demanded—and legitimized— bold expansions in dictatorial powers. Technocratic ambitions shaped government not only on paper but also via numerous new institutions and government agencies for economic planning. Growing bureaucracies would become essential to the lived experience of corporatism as citizens navigated a maze of new laws, paperwork, and government agencies in order to work, produce, and trade. As we will see, citizens made claims according to codified social and economic rights, including the right to fair prices, and sometimes even achieved justice.

"Dictatorship" is neither self-evident nor uniform, and counterintuitively, a dictator's legal choices expose how they exercise authority. Corporatist constitutions reconceptualized freedoms associated with liberal democracy as corrupt and decadent. These arguments fed debates, which extend to the present day, about the incompatibility of democracy in certain places, and the imperative to (sometimes) put order and discipline above liberty and equality. Recovering the legal logic of dictatorships thus also helps us to understand how and why these arguments persist.

PART II

3

Corporatist Economics
and the Third Path

WITH THE 1933 Constitution, Portugal became the first nation to formally decree a corporatist state, but corporatism was an international movement. In addition to Brazil, Italy, Argentina, Austria, and to some extent Mexico and Cuba experimented with corporatist modes of governance.[1] With all of these experiments, Romanian economist Mihail Manoilescu declared, "The twentieth century will be the century of corporatism, just as the nineteenth century was that of liberalism."[2]

In the 1920s and 1930s, corporatism became a popular economic experiment precisely because it promised a "third path" between free market capitalism and state-controlled command economies. Corporatist ideologues seized on this language of "third ways" or "third currents" to promote their program.[3] Focusing on political calculations, most historians argue that corporatism was a cynical bargain. Catholic conservative groups, industrialists, and landowners supported corporatist dictatorships because they emboldened state powers to discipline labor for the sake of social peace and private property.[4] Fearful of Bolshevism, many across Europe and Latin America supported measures to mobilize secret police, censorship, and special tribunals to surveil and silence organized labor and left-wing political groups. Kurt Weyland has recently contended that fears of communism strengthened conservative factions, emboldening their critiques of liberal democracy and embrace of fascism.[5] But after self-proclaimed corporatist dictatorships purged communists and suppressed labor activism, they needed to develop their own programs of national renewal.

This chapter develops two main arguments. First, corporatism was an inherently transnational enterprise, no less than socialism and liberalism.[6] Intellectuals, jurists, economists, and public officials in Brazil, Portugal, Italy, Romania, and France who wrote about corporatism traveled to other places experimenting with this system. They wrote essays and books about corporatism, and organized academic conferences to facilitate the exchange of corporatist ideas and policies. Universities in southern Europe and Latin America became important sites for the production (and not just the passive reception) of corporatist ideas. Corporatist ideologues, moreover, were not just intellectuals relegated to universities; they also held key government positions where they had to negotiate between idealism and economic realities. With shared language, history, Catholic traditions, and legal culture, these exchanges were especially dynamic between Brazil and Portugal, two nations that both gave the name Estado Novo to their corporatist dictatorships. Economists and intellectuals in Brazil and Portugal celebrated corporatism as modern and progressive in transnational exchanges, but they were also united by the preoccupation that crept into so many of their economic writings that corporatism was in fact their only option for economic transformation on account of their nation's cultural and racial heritage.

This chapter recovers corporatists' forgotten ideas and inspiration—aspirations and anxieties—and the transnational exchanges that defined them. It takes the intellectual history of the Great Depression to overlooked places on the margins of global capitalism. Corporatist third paths emerged from the same economic debates that inspired the New Deal and rise of Keynesianism in the 1930s, but even so the policies and principles executed in Brazil and Portugal have largely been sidelined in English-language interwar histories of economic recovery and state building.[7] This is unfortunate because the transnational framework is as necessary for corporatism as it is for histories of liberalism, republicanism, socialism, fascism, and other political movements.[8] This transnational exercise does not reveal a primary origins story for corporatism, a unified definition, or even a singular political model. Instead, the individuals featured in this chapter were nodes in a global web of ideas and arguments that jointly legitimized the rise of corporatism, even if they did not always agree on what corporatism really offered.

Second, this chapter argues against those who see corporatism as little more than a synonym for fascism or stunted form of capitalism. Rather, corporatist debates over how markets should function produced a genuinely new economic system with real-world consequences. Corporatist economists were certainly united in their hostility to socialism, but it was their shared distrust of liberal doctrine that ultimately shaped the political economy of corporatism. Corporatists tried to disprove classical economic theory, pointing to all the ways in which free exchange and open trade had failed to produce stability and prosperity.[9] Intellectuals in Brazil, Portugal, or Italy insisted that their corporatist model was not a compromise between two broken systems but instead a unique solution adapted to how the economy really works.

Nevertheless, corporatism was perpetually compared with other systems. The first of these was fascism. The rise of corporatism as a new economic system cannot be divorced from its Italian influence along with the expansive intellectual networks that connected Fascist Italy to dictatorships in Latin America and Iberian Europe.[10] To defend corporatism, its proponents had to find ways to distinguish it from fascism, which led them to reinforce the technical and economic solutions offered by corporatism, and in contrast, insist that fascism was a totalitarian political system.

At times, it seems that corporatist theorists had more to say about the failures of the free market than they did about the "third path" they proposed. That corporatist solutions and answers were sometimes vague and imprecise, however, is no reason to discard this exercise. Rather, it indicates how contested and important the corporatist question was—and remains.

Broken Models

The Great Depression triggered a global economic crisis as well as an intellectual one. For Brazilian Catholic intellectual Tristão de Ataíde, the crisis exposed the "bankruptcy of economics as a natural science."[11] For many Brazilians, the Great Depression shattered confidence in the "clarity, simplicity, and logic" of nineteenth-century political economy models in which open markets allowed prices, wages, and interest rates to automatically rebalance supply to demand. Corporatist texts almost invariably began with long, frequently digressive critiques of British and French economists such as Adam Smith, David Ricardo, and Jean-Baptiste Say. One technocrat working in Brazil's newly created Ministry of Labor observed that it had become "impossible to reconcile classical theories and principles with the real evolution of economic events."[12] Corporatist economics grew and then developed further out of transnational efforts to explain the errors of classical economic models.

Debates unfolded worldwide about the shortcomings of classical political economy.[13] In 1924, English economist John Maynard Keynes delivered his now-famous lecture "The End of Laissez-Faire" at the University of Oxford. The laissez-faire logic that "individuals acting independently for their own advantage will produce the greatest aggregate of wealth" increasingly seemed based on a series of flawed assumptions that in turn encouraged inefficient, unproductive, and unequal distributions of wealth.[14] Even so, Keynes was optimistic about the possibilities of reforming rather than overturning the capitalist system. Following the 1929 crash, however, it became increasingly difficult to defend the liberal order. In the 1930s, historian Angus Burgin reminds us, "even a limited defense of the market mechanism was seen by some as symbolic of a deeply reactionary worldview."[15]

The 1929 crisis was not the first global crisis, but this was precisely the problem. In 1930, São Paulo industrialist Roberto Simonsen organized a series of conferences at the Centro das Indústrias do Estado de São Paulo, a private

association of industrialists created in 1928, to study the causes and consequences of the Depression, and figure out how to avoid future crises.[16] Born
in 1889 in the port city of Santos (São Paulo), Simonsen studied civil engineering and then worked in the construction and ceramics industries, quickly becoming a leading voice in public and political debates over Brazil's economic
future. Following World War I, he represented Brazil at international conferences in Paris and Washington, DC that convened leading industrialists worldwide. Simonsen's formal education was more technical than academic, and he
was largely self-taught in political economy. He read canonical economic texts
by Smith and Say through a distinctly Brazilian lens. In the 1930s and 1940s,
he published some of the most important works of Brazilian political economy
and economic history. Simonsen also occupied several key bureaucratic postings, advocating for labor training programs and protectionist policies to promote Brazil's industrialization.[17] According to Portuguese economist Moses
Bensabat Amzalak, Simonsen "devoted" himself intellectually and politically
to "the development of his country."[18] While he wavered in his support of
Getúlio Vargas's regime and policies, he ultimately supported corporatist forms
of state intervention, even if he rarely explicitly used the label *corporatism* in
his writings, partly because of its European (namely fascist) associations.
Nonetheless, Simonsen's worldview was quintessentially corporatist as he argued
that it was the responsibility of *estadistas*, or state officials, to discipline labor and
production for the sake of *paz social*, or social peace.[19]

Well versed in the writings of nineteenth-century economists, Simonsen
understood that some might dismiss the Depression as a transitory event, in-
trinsic to the business cycle. Like many of his contemporaries, though, Simonsen was no longer as sanguine about Say's assessment that industrial freedom
would be enough to avoid economic crisis, retorting, "We do not lack industrial
freedom, and the crises have not ceased to exist."[20] Economic crises brought
social hardships and political instability, and Simonsen insisted that they should
instead be avoided by implementing the right policies, technology, and scientific
know-how. Barbara Weinstein has shown that Simonsen, as an industrialist, was
eager to import the latest technology and labor training strategies, as evident
with his early embrace of Taylorism. Likewise, he believed that it should be
possible to apply his technical expertise to fix economic crises.[21]

While many economists writing during the crisis looked to major centers of
industrial production such as the United States, Great Britain, or Germany, Simonsen turned to Brazil. Britain and Brazil experienced the same crisis very
differently because in Brazil, he argued, *superprodução*, or overproduction, affected agricultural commodity sectors, notably coffee. Brazilian economists
came to understand that they could not rely solely on the writings of British, US,
and French economists to explain the crisis and its consequences. Simonsen

started leaning on the contributions of economists in other corners of the global periphery, and one early source of inspiration came from Romania.

Mihail Manoilescu, Romanian economist and politician, convincingly explained why the Great Depression differently impacted industrial and agrarian nations. Born in 1891 to a modest though well-educated and politically active family, Manoilescu studied engineering in Bucharest and then went to work in government during World War I. After the war, he designed government policies to promote the country's industrial development. By 1931, he had headed several ministries and the National Bank, although his political career also suffered due to conflicts with high-ranking officials. Despite political controversies at home, Manoilescu built his reputation abroad as a leading voice on the causes of underdevelopment. In 1932, he attended a Fascist-sponsored Corporatist Congress in Italy and was invited to Rome to personally discuss the event with Mussolini.[22] Beyond extractivism and colonialism, Manoilescu argued that "inequity created by international exchange" was a form of "invisible exploitation."[23] Manoilescu's 1929 *Théorie du protectionnisme et de l'échange international*, translated into English, Italian, and Portuguese, outlined the consequences of unequal trade relations for agrarian societies. This and other economic writings circulated widely in southern Europe and South America in the 1930s and 1940s, informing, for example, how Argentinean economist Raúl Prebisch formalized his center-periphery model.[24] While western European and US economists discredited many of Manoilescu's assumptions and conclusions, his writings became a "bridge," Joseph Love argues, for the circulation of ideas between "underdeveloped" parts of Europe and Latin America.[25] António de Oliveira Salazar had copies of Manoilescu's books in his personal library and even met with the Romanian economist when he visited Lisbon in 1936.[26] Manoilescu was especially popular in Brazil, where industrialist Simonsen was one of the first to embrace his writings. It was in Brazil that his works were translated into Portuguese, including Brazilian journalist Antônio José Azevedo Amaral's canonical translation of *Le siècle du corporatisme* in 1938. Yet the first of these translations was of Manoilescu's writings on protectionism and international trade, with the Portuguese edition of *Théorie du protectionnisme et de l'échange international* commissioned by the Centro das Indústrias do Estado de São Paulo, under Simonsen's leadership, in 1931.

Manoilescu contended that the global economy was stratified according to "countries that export industrial produce and import raw materials" and those that import "industrial produce" and export raw materials.[27] He debunked Ricardo's theory of comparative advantage, which optimistically asserted that rich and poor nations alike benefited from trade. The Brazilian translation of Manoilescu's text summarized it bluntly: "The Ricardian theory of comparative advantage is false."[28] The problem with classical trade models, according to Manoilescu and other economists, was that agrarian commodity prices fell far more precipitously than industrial prices in the 1920s. The puzzle was to explain why industrial prices did not follow suit given the expansion of industrial production beyond North America and northern Europe. Swedish economist Gustav Cassel offered a hypothesis that influenced Manoilescu's writings not only on protectionism but on corporatism too: the monopolistic tendencies of industrialists and strength of trade unions in highly industrialized countries.[29] After the Great Depression, this gap between classical economic theory and reality became painfully evident for the Romanian economist: "History teaches us, at least along the last century, that wealth has been the destiny of industrial countries, and poverty the lot of agricultural countries."[30] Manoilescu's writings on unequal exchange fashioned the frustrations expressed by so many in Brazil and Portugal into a theoretical critique of free trade and other tenets of the laissez-faire order. The logical conclusion was that agrarian nations needed to protect their domestic markets from foreign competition so as to save commodity sectors from collapse and stimulate industrialization. But tariffs alone could not create conditions for underdeveloped countries to industrialize: they would also need to organize major industries and labor in order to limit internal competition. The corporatist state was the way to do this.

The broken price mechanism became both a topic in this transnational discourse that revealed the shortcomings of classical economic models and the theoretical anchor for the new political economy (see chapter 4). That price became the regulatory mechanism for this new corporatist system was in some ways the most direct translation of group interests. These measures, however, were increasingly backed up by economists and other intellectuals working transnationally to debunk classical economic models along with their emphasis on automatic adjustment mechanisms to return the economy to equilibrium.

In other words, the need to stabilize prices, especially for agricultural producers, drove many of the early efforts to organize commodity sectors in corporatist fashion. "The collapse of agricultural prices," a Portuguese economist later summarized, "is always more intense than that for industrial products."[31] Moreover, the problem of price collapse was not limited to the commodity sector. Brazil and Portugal, like many other countries, experienced general price deflation immediately following the 1929 crash: in Brazil, prices fell 9 percent in 1930 and 4 percent in 1931, and in Portugal, prices fell 5 percent in 1930 and 11 percent in 1931.[32] For this cohort of economists, existing models could not explain why this was so. Simonsen, in one of his earliest essays on the consequences of the Great Depression in Brazil, emphasized that US economist Irving Fisher's quantity theory of money (in rudimentary terms, general price levels [P] fluctuate according to the stock of money [M], velocity of money in circulation [V], and total amount of goods and services transacted [T], or $P = MV/T$) failed to explain steep price fluctuations.[33] Considered by many to be one of the foremost economic minds of the twentieth century, Fisher built his mathematical model in conversation with economic debates stretching back to John Locke and David Hume.[34] According to Fisher, changes in price levels were caused by changes to the money supply, and so it followed that to stabilize price levels, central banks should adjust monetary policy accordingly. Simonsen disagreed. Tinkering with monetary policy was insufficient for Brazil, where the money supply and its velocity were diminishing and slowing too quickly. Falling coffee prices were the beginning of a spiraling deflationary crisis—one not easily explained by formulas promising quick returns to "equilibrium."[35]

Classical and neoclassical models assumed that problems of overproduction would quickly be resolved in the short run by lower prices that would stimulate demand for goods. Trade imbalances, too, would automatically adjust by the same logic. Recent economic crises defied these theories of equilibrium. Following World War I, price levels trended at extremes, with inflationary cycles documented in Germany, Portugal, and France, and deflation accompanying Great Britain's return to the gold standard in 1925. In the real world, equilibrium was not guaranteed; countries might erect trade tariffs to protect domestic markets, or a myriad of other frictions slowed or distorted automatic adjustments theorized in classical models.[36]

Economists, intellectuals, and jurists in southern Europe and Latin America, well trained in classical political economy, were equipped to challenge some of its core assumptions. In June 1931, for instance, Marcello Caetano, then in his early twenties, stood before a committee of law professors at the University of Lisbon to defend his doctoral dissertation.[37] In Portugal, economics was still a field primarily taught in law schools, and Caetano followed in this tradition to specialize in political economy.[38] His dissertation, "A depreciação da moeda depois da guerra," explained Portugal's financial crises following World War I, building on the work of then finance minister Salazar, whose 1916 dissertation on the gold standard had highlighted Portugal's dependency on remittances from Brazil.[39] Caetano critiqued Fisher's quantity theory of money as inaccurate or woefully incomplete at best. Instead, Caetano turned to statistics to "clarify or confirm the truth," and give his economic research "a cold and serene objectivity." Based on empirical evidence, he concluded that fluctuations to price levels in 1920s' Portugal were "irregular and capricious," and far more volatile than shifts in the money supply. Fisher's formula did not explain the Portuguese case. He turned to the work of Keynes as well as French economist Albert Aftalion to elaborate possible alternative explanations: changes to the public's purchasing power or psychological factors, such as anxieties over future economic performance, could influence individual behavior.[40] Caetano's account underscored how past events and future expectations were critical to explaining price fluctuations.

Caetano's approach departed from classical political economy and put him at odds with the faculty chairs. His dissertation committee chair stated bluntly that "his work is that of a journalist and not that of a scientist presenting his work at a university. . . . [T]his analysis is what one presents to economists at a coffeehouse."[41] Fortunately for Caetano, his political career was on the rise. He was already well-known in Lisbon's intellectual and political ranks for his impassioned newspaper columns and as part of Salazar's inner circle.[42] Notwithstanding protests from faculty, Caetano received his doctorate and would apply his critique of old formulas to his work in government.

Caetano's critique of classical economic theory quickly morphed into a sharp position: markets could not be trusted to self-correct. He expanded this conclusion in the essays, newspaper articles, and books he wrote over the next decades as he became Portugal's foremost corporatist theorist. Caetano's writings on corporatism migrated to Brazil. His 1934 *O sistema corporativo*, for example, found its way to the library of Brazilian jurist Oliveira Vianna, who used this text to inform his own thinking while working at the Ministry of Labor.[43] Caetano quickly ascended the ranks of the Estado Novo, serving as Salazar's secretary during ad hoc meetings for the 1933 Constitution; as head of the Mocidade Portuguesa, the regime's youth organization; and as minister of the colonies in the 1940s. Through these postings, he traveled to Brazil several times, thus putting him in contact with Vargas's parallel corporatist experiment.

Caetano illustrates the fluid movement between Portuguese universities and new government ministries. He enjoyed so much influence in Brazil partly because he was respected as both an intellectual and government official. This was a defining feature of Portugal's Estado Novo. Salazar pulled from university ranks and industry practitioners with academic expertise in new fields to fill his cabinets and oversee the corporatist experiment.[44] After all, corporatism was simultaneously being theorized while put into practice.

Salazar appointed leading academics and industry experts to top cabinet positions such as the subsecretary of state for corporations and social security, responsible for creating corporatist institutions, and at the Ministry of Commerce and Industry, responsible for how the grémio system regulated prices and production. The individuals appointed to these offices wrote some of the first textbooks on corporatist economics while on the job. In 1935, for instance, preeminent Portuguese economist and theorist of corporatism João Pinto da Costa Leite, also known as João Lumbrales, published *A doutrina corporativa em Portugal* while serving as subsecretary of state for corporations and social security, a position he held from 1935 to 1936. The person most closely associated with Portugal's corporatist revolution was Pedro Theotónio Pereira, who served as both subsecretary of state for corporations and social security and the minister of industry and commerce in the 1930s. Salazar relied on Theotónio Pereira in these early years to design Portugal's corporatist system, but the two men also fiercely disagreed on the progress of this experiment. Salazar was a pragmatist, putting political expediency above ideological commitments.[45] Theotónio Pereira was an idealist as well as technocrat. In 1937, he published *A batalha do future*, a book of compiled conference presentations on the status of Portugal's corporatist revolution underway. He summarized the progress made to reorganize Portuguese society according to corporatist doctrine and legislation, detailing all the different organisms—from grémios to casas do povo and social security institutions—that now regulated economic life. Corporatism, he admitted, remained an incomplete system, lacking uniformity and coherence in its implementation. This was the *batalha* (battle) ahead.

Neither Capitalist nor Fascist: Transnational Networks and Corporatism

Ideas about corporatism did not merely circulate among university professors and government bureaucrats. They also infiltrated and were conveyed by popular culture. One of the unlikely places that Brazilians learned about the corporatist revolution unfolding in Portugal was in the glossy pages of *O Cruzeiro*, Brazil's leading illustrated weekly magazine, founded in 1928. This was a lifestyle magazine, featuring fashion, appliances, and celebrity news with limited discussions of politics or economics. But after Vargas's 1937 coup, its May issues became unofficial propaganda for Portugal's Estado Novo in honor of Portugal's 1926 Revolution. The cover of the May 1938 issue, for example, was draped in red and green, the colors of the Portuguese flag, and featured a woman balancing a basket of produce on her head, echoing the key elements of Salazarismo by commemorating a hardworking agrarian society (figure 3.1). That *O Cruzeiro* celebrated Portugal's Estado Novo was not unusual per se. Founder Carlos Malheiro Dias, a Portuguese publicist, had gone to Brazil in exile after the fall of Portugal's monarchy in 1910. In Rio de Janeiro, he quickly assumed a prominent place in carioca literary circles. Like other Brazilian newspapers of the day, most of its issues had a section dedicated to news from Portugal. But commemorative issues for the 1926 Revolution conveyed more than cultural nostalgia for Brazil's former imperial power. They featured full-length reports on Salazar, newly inaugurated social housing, and the rights afforded to the working classes, which reportedly organized "without clamor or menace."[46] *O Cruzeiro* made a point of detailing the new laws and institutions

FIGURE 3.1. Cover for *O Cruzeiro: Revista Semanal Illustrada* (May 1938) in commemoration of Portugal's May 28 revolution. Image courtesy of Arquivo O Cruzeiro / EM / D. A. Press.

of Portugal's corporatist revolution, thereby diffusing them across the Atlantic. Parts of the 1933 Portuguese Constitution were reprinted to defend an experiment in which the state, as one journalist described, was "content with its role as the supreme coordinator and regulator of economic and social activities." Portugal's Estado Novo promised to do away with "parasitic exploitation" in order to guarantee "the highest price and salary compatible with the just re-muneration of the other factors of production."[47] Receptivity to the Portu-guese example was a political strategy, as Vargas's supporters hoped to show that benevolent dictatorship was possible and even preferable to liberal gov-ernance.[48] Portugal's Estado Novo also functioned as propaganda for Brazil's own experiment with corporatism.[49]

O Cruzeiro introduced Brazilian readers to corporatist institutions. It fea-tured Portuguese casas do povo and *casas dos pescadores* created to resuscitate "old traditions." The magazine's reporters described how these organs ensured that agrarian workers and fishers "during painful crises . . . will not lack means, nor will they be without bread."[50] A "guarantee of bread" and its fair price became so salient in Brazil because it responded to market insecurities acutely felt in both countries.[51] The most effective propaganda for Portugal's Estado Novo, however, was subtler: advertisements for Portuguese products—olive oil, codfish, and wine—now organized according to the corporatist mode of production (figure 3.2). The May 1937 issue, for example, ran an ad for Portu-guese codfish that depicted an image of fishing boats superimposed with con-gratulatory text about the accomplishments of the Grémio dos Armadores de Navios de Pesca do Bacalhau (figure 3.3).[52] The message was clear: state-regulated producer associations guaranteed safe products for consumers along with fair market conditions and social insurance for fishers. The ad, of course, omitted the ongoing strike in Portugal as fishers protested how corporatist collective contracts limited how fishing boats recruited workers—a labor dis-pute also censored in the Portuguese press.[53] Instead, *O Cruzeiro* celebrated financial stability, economic growth, and social harmony, with Salazar molding "a nation that is, each day, more civilized and progressive." These idyllic depic-tions belied the corruption as well as hardships for those excluded from or opposed to the corporatist system, but in the pages of *O Cruzeiro*, "Portugal was living, in essence, its golden age."[54]

Conversations between Luso-Brazilian thinkers and ideologues unfolded in the footnotes and on the margins of books too. For instance, in Brazil, Oliveira Vianna's personal library held copies of books by several Portuguese jurists—books underlined and annotated in the margins. Prominent Portu-guese economists traveled to Rio de Janeiro and São Paulo to give public talks on the corporatist economy, and Caetano wrote newspaper editorials on Brazil for Portuguese audiences. Salazar's library held several books by Brazilian economists such as A. Lima de Campos and Valdemar Falcão, not to mention by Francisco Campos and Vargas.[55] Their shared language facilitated this cir-culation of books, as economists and jurists on both sides of the Atlantic sought a new economic theory.

Corporatist ideas were debated and refined in this transnational space, both in closed meetings between intellectuals, technocrats, and officials, and the

FIGURE 3.2. Advertisement printed in *O Cruzeiro: Revista Semanal Illustrada* (May 1938) for the Junta Nacional do Azeite e do Grémio dos Exportadores de Azeites. The two-page spread outlines the rights and protections of Portugal's corporatist system. Image courtesy of Arquivo O Cruzeiro / EM / D. A. Press.

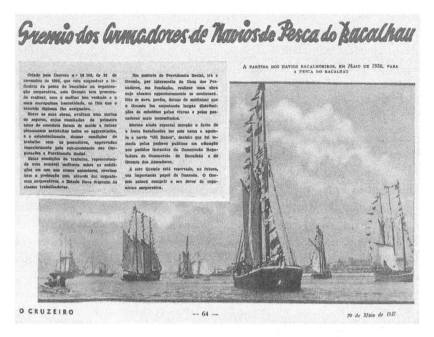

FIGURE 3.3. Advertisement printed in *O Cruzeiro: Revista Semanal Illustrada* (May 1937) for the Grémio dos Armadores de Navios de Pesca do Bacalhau. Image courtesy of Arquivo O Cruzeiro / EM / D. A. Press.

public sphere through magazines, books, essays, and conferences. Much has nonetheless been lost from these conversations. Many of these meetings and conferences were ceremonial, with vague speeches preoccupied with diplomatic niceties. Personal correspondence for many key figures is lost to the archives, or consists of formal and largely superficial exchanges. Many, it seems, were reluctant to keep a precise accounting of their political or economic convictions. While serving as ambassador in Washington, DC, Oswaldo Aranha remarked that his counterparts in the United States did not seem to hesitate to leave paper trails of their thoughts, opinions, and dissent toward government policies. "They do and confirm everything by letters," he explained, "there is nothing here that is not written down."[56] The absence of corresponding documentation was a sign of the political climate in Brazil as much as in Portugal, where dictatorships used censorship and secret police to intimidate or silence opposition as well as discipline even the most loyal supporters.

Liberal voices, to be sure, did not entirely vanish from these transnational conversations to theorize a third path. In Brazil more so than in Portugal, liberal economists remained vocal in public debates over Vargas's reforms and even occupied important government postings. As much as this book recovers the transnational circulation of corporatist intellectuals, moreover, not all foreign visitors to Brazil in these years were corporatists. But even those skeptical of the corporatist model could not trivialize or ignore it. In 1935, a group of French professors traveled to Rio de Janeiro to inaugurate a new university, and one year later French economist Gaston Leduc of the University of Caen in Normandy arrived in Rio de Janeiro to teach in the newly minted economics department.[57] Leduc had begun his career in France within the Finance Ministry in the 1920s before moving to Aix-en-Provence to study economics. He is known for his work in development economics in the post-1945 period; Leduc was one of the first to study colonial economies on their own terms, and not only in relation to the metropole.[58] While in Brazil, Leduc was a frequent contributor to the monthly review *O Observador Econômico e Financeiro*. In July 1936, he penned an article titled "Reflexões sobre a idéa corporativa" (Reflections on the corporatist ideal). Leduc was in no way a corporatist. In fact, he would remain exceptionally loyal to liberal economic models throughout his career.[59] Still, during his time in Brazil, Leduc could not avoid commenting on the corporatist ideas that so many of his colleagues embraced.

Leduc had ambivalent views on corporatism. "Because of its very diversity," he asserted, "corporatist ideas appear to be as rich in possibility as they are in uncertainties." He differentiated between two corporatist camps. The first, of which he was most skeptical, defended corporatism with vague and abstract notions of a new social order and harmony between labor and capital. This model was heir to the medieval guild order, which Leduc dismissed outright as ridiculous for the modern world. The second camp required attention, though, given that it introduced concrete tools by which governments increasingly intervened in economic and social questions. This camp especially elevated corporatism as a new economic system. This vision was shared by those who "no longer had confidence in the functioning of the price mechanism to ensure the stability necessary for the harmonious development of commercial life." He concluded that if nothing else, corporatist doctrine "responds unquestionably to a fundamental necessity of the current times: organization."[60] And while corporatism was hardly everywhere, Leduc seemed resigned to the fact that "the tendency toward economic interventionism is today universal. I believe that the era of laissez-faire is definitively closed, if it ever existed in practice."[61]

As Leduc noted, corporatism was hardly the only strategy that mobilized the state as the primary agent to fix economic problems. Was it just a set of reforms or a distinct economic system—something radically new? Was corporatism *actually* a departure from the capitalist mode of production or instead a capitalist variation?

These were contentious questions for corporatist enthusiasts and critics alike. Some, particularly those in conservative and integralist circles, insisted that corporatism offered a radically new economy. "Nothing of hybrids," one Portuguese publicist exclaimed, "corporatism has its own economy."[62] Others were less adamant on this point, depicting corporatism as part of a wider set of strategies to fix capitalism. Azevedo Amaral, for example, saw corporatism everywhere as he attempted to legitimize Vargas's authoritarian tactics. Likewise, Oliveira Vianna wrote about corporatism in contexts as diverse as New Zealand and the US New Deal.[63] This second group gained momentum in the 1930s.

Some saw corporatism, then, as more an attempt to save capitalism from itself, as a third path that was not so much a brand-new economic system but rather an urgent fix for a broken model. To be sure, many corporatist theorists did end up, in their own ways, penning quite enthusiastic endorsements of the capitalist world order even shortly after its dramatic collapse. Portuguese economist José Joaquim Teixeira Ribeiro, for one, embraced this reformist spirit to argue that corporatism "fits perfectly with the concept of capitalism." It invited private initiative and protected private property, maintaining profit as the objective of economic production, but not, he qualified, "unlimited profits." Instead, in the corporatist system, profit had to conform to "the social good," and—to quote the closing salutation used by Portuguese officials in letters—"*a bem da nação*," or "the good of the nation."[64] Portuguese Goan jurist Luís da Cunha Gonçalves likewise argued that the key was not to abandon capitalism but rather abandon *liberal* capitalism and reject the false promises of socialism:

> The corporatist system aims, only, to eliminate the defects of individualist capitalism or socialism. For this reason, one cannot proclaim a *corporatist economy* because corporatism is not an economic system radically distinct from capitalism as they both share essential ingredients: capital, employers, wages, currency, prices, [and] individual and collective property.[65]

It was no accident that Cunha Gonçalves opted not to include labor in this list of economic variables given that he envisioned corporatism precisely as a system for discipling labor in the cause of increasing national economic production. As corporatism was put into practice, many of its proponents abandoned some—though not all—of their earlier moral arguments, which had been indexed to Catholic social teachings. While social peace remained essential to corporatist doctrine in Brazil and Portugal, academic efforts to turn corporatism into formal economic theory increasingly focused on capital—and not labor. Those keen to define corporatism according to its economic and technocratic elements zeroed in on production in order to explain that corporatism did not attempt to topple capitalism but instead to improve it. Azevedo Amaral even went so far as to call corporatism a type of "*néo-capitalism*."

Corporatism had to confront capitalism—whether and how to distinguish itself as unique from it—but it also had to confront fascism. Corporatism and fascism are not interchangeable ideologies, but the two became deeply entangled. Some corporatists embraced the Italian example that quick economic transformation required strong, statist intervention, while others insisted that their system should not be confused with Mussolini's tyrannical mode of governance. Even for those trying to neutralize corporatism by way of economic theory, the Italian model was inescapable. Italy's corporatist experiment was furthest along, which made it an unavoidable reference point for new laws and institutions. Economics as a discipline was also more established in Italian than in Brazilian and Portuguese universities.[66] Luso-Brazilian intellectuals relied heavily on Italian economists and jurists, who traveled to Brazil and Portugal to give talks, and whose writings were translated into Portuguese.

Corporatism and Italian writings on fascism were both obsessively anti-individual, and this argument was effortlessly transposed into economics. Italian jurist Alfredo Rocco explained in his 1926 essay, "The Political Doctrine of Fascism," that the problem with liberalism was its concern with the rights and "happiness" of individuals. He criticized liberals for wrongly assuming that it was most "profitable to entrust to individual initiative the task of economic development." Rocco summarized Fascist doctrine as "individuals for society," not "society for the individual."[67] Arguments against individualism were mobilized as much to dismantle political democracy as classical political economy. Italian economists aligned with the Fascist Party spoke of organization, discipline, and control. Statistician and demographer Corrado Gini, best known for the Gini coefficient as a measure of income inequality, became one of many who tried to bring scientific coherence to fascist economic programs. His work on demography, in particular, influenced Mussolini, who construed Italy's stagnating population growth, especially because of out-migration, as a key factor in civilizational decline. Gini's findings inspired the regime's pronatalist policies as well as imperial ambitions to absorb out-migration.[68] During his visit to the United States in 1926, Gini made the case for fascism as a model for the "intervention of public authority in economic life," pointing to how such "interventions" ranged from protectionist policies to resolving "conflicts between capital and labor." A "central controlling power," he argued, was necessary for "the subordination of particular interests to those of the nation." Gini turned "limitations" on the "liberties of the individual" into something "necessary," "efficient," and even "revolutionary."[69]

Thanks in part to Mussolini's fascist diplomacy, Italian writings on corporatism circulated far and wide, setting the terms for early debates about this new economic system. The Fascist Party's cultural and diplomatic missions trumpeted the regime's accomplishments abroad and built alliances with other illiberal movements. Italian intellectuals and their books traveled to Brazil, Portugal, or Argentina, among other places. According to Oliveira Vianna, the Boffoni Bookstore in Rio de Janeiro became a "mecca" for those interested in "Mussolini's corporatism." Books written by Italian jurists and economists flew off the shelves, slaking a "thirst for knowledge of the scholars of the new doctrine."[70] In Portugal, the University of Coimbra boasted an expanding library collection on Italy's political economy thanks to the Instituto de Estudos Italianos. In Lisbon, the Instituto de Cultura Italiana, directed by Italian writer and journalist Aldo Bizzarri, published translations of Italian works as well as essays written by Portuguese students of Italian corporatism.[71] In November 1937, Italian economist and politician Bruno Biagi traveled to Lisbon, where he addressed his Portuguese colleagues at the Instituto Superior de Ciências Económicas e Financeiras (figure 3.4) and was honored with a one-on-one visit with Salazar.[72]

Books, doctoral dissertations, and conferences connected the corporatist experiments and theorists of Brazil, Portugal, and Italy. These ideas flowed in multiple directions. Italian economists, for example, traveled to Brazil and Portugal. In October 1933, Italian economist Gino Arias concluded a three-stop tour of Latin America that featured a series of conferences on corporatism. His first stop was in Buenos Aires before speaking in São Paulo at the Escola Livre de Sociologia e Política, founded in 1933 to train social scientists to design policies that could resolve social conflicts over wages or prices without them spilling into the streets or the political arena.[73] Arias then delivered three lectures in Rio de Janeiro at the Liga da Defesa Nacional, a civic association created by conservative intellectuals in 1916. Arias's lectures, organized by the Instituto Italo-Brasileiro de Alta Cultura, explored the corporatist economy in theory and practice. Free and open to the public, the lecture series targeted jurists, economists, and university students with its "scientific illustration of the new direction."[74]

Brazilian and Portuguese intellectuals also traveled to Italy and advanced this transnational flow of economic ideas. In 1938, agronomist Francisco Tavares de Almeida was appointed by the Portuguese minister of agriculture to a multiyear mission to study the corporatist organization of Italy's agricultural sector. This mission began in December 1938, but was cut short after only eighteen months by the outbreak of World War II in Europe. While the agronomist had hoped to survey corporatist institutions across Italy, he could only visit three provinces: Lazio, Tuscany, and Emilia-Romagna. In 1941, he published his findings in *A organização sindical-corporativa da agricultura italiana*, an exhaustive study of the many state and parastate organs created in the 1920s and 1930s to organize agricultural workers into syndicates and producers into associations. His discussion made it clear that a mammoth bureaucracy had inserted the state into nearly every economic transaction. Almeida outlined the benefits he saw

FIGURE 3.4. Professor Bruno Biagi, Italian jurist and politician, speaking on corporatism at the Instituto Superior de Ciências Económicas e Financeiras in Lisbon (November 1937). Image courtesy of the Arquivo Nacional Torre do Tombo. Collection Empresa Pública do Jornal *O Século*, Álbuns Gerais no. 47, doc. PT/TT/EPJS/SF/001-001/0047/2412L.

to this new organizational architecture: the national consortia and corporations that represented producers negotiated with the state on behalf of its members in matters that ranged from increasing the amount of land under cultivation for a given commodity to securing seeds, fertilizer, and other inputs. Almeida claimed to be "strictly objective" in reporting the facts of Italy's economic performance, but he outright disqualified or dismissed individuals who spoke out against the corporatist system, reducing their complaints to a "Latin" tendency to criticize.[75] He praised Italy's economic successes by painstakingly describing the bureaucracy that oversaw labor and price controls. This bureaucracy was corporatism at work to transform economic life. By defining corporatism in solely economic terms, Almeida attempted to distance it from Mussolini's fascist demagogy.

As much as economists and technocrats in Brazil and Portugal were excited about the Italian example, the realities of fascist rule eventually tempered that enthusiasm. As the gains of Italy's Battle for Wheat and other campaigns became difficult to sustain, and enthusiasm dwindled for its corporatist economic program at home, Mussolini shifted focus to imperial renewal, beginning with the brutal invasion of Ethiopia in 1935.[76] Fascist doctrine, after all, required action first and foremost. Italy's aggression was a turning point at home and abroad.[77] It provoked sanctions from the League of Nations and growing criticism in the international press.[78]

For contemporaries, totalitarianism was an extreme version of statism, in which the state tried to control every dimension of life, including in the economic sphere. Yet Italian ambitions for total control were too extreme, even for hardliners in Brazil and Portugal supporting dictatorship. For Brazilian and Portuguese intellectuals, Italy's Fascist government was not just attempting to subordinate personal liberties to national interests but also trying to quash them entirely—a proposition too reminiscent of Bolshevism or Nazism. For Vargas and Salazar, legitimacy depended on a show of moderation and a softer style of dictatorship.

Vargas and Salazar understood that to stay in power and maintain strategic alliances with major global powers, including Great Britain and the United States, they needed to dodge comparisons with Mussolini, Hitler, or Stalin. They depicted their corporatist dictatorships as authoritarian, but not totalitarian: the corporatist state exercised power over economic and social life, yet did not obliterate private property or individual initiative. Corporatist intellectuals redoubled their efforts to distinguish fascism and corporatism precisely by emphasizing that corporatism was an economic program to distract from or absolve the political purges and repressive measures sanctioned by Vargas and Salazar. These arguments were not necessarily convincing. As one US journalist cynically noted, Vargas's efforts to have his regime "clothed in the guise of a corporative regime" was not in and of itself an assurance.[79]

Across the Portuguese-speaking Atlantic, then, the task was to show that corporatism offered a solution with fascist traits, but one comfortably distant from it. Portugal's Estado Novo might have increased state powers over the economy with its expanding bureaucracy, "but it is not totalitarian in its totalitarianism," one Portuguese academic wrote.[80] Azevedo Amaral echoed this logic, insisting that Brazilian corporatism was a third path that offered as much an antidote to fascism as to communism.[81] Another Brazilian economist celebrated Brazil as an illustration of moderation to avoid extremes, with the "Estado Novo equidistant from both liberalism and totalitarianism."[82]

As Fascist Italy lost its luster, Vargas tried to present his Estado Novo as something democratic. Brazilian intellectuals and officials started looking to the United States, a key market for Brazilian goods and rising global power. One Brazilian economist even celebrated Vargas's corporatist-style governance as part of an "advance of 'new deals.'"[83] By "new deals," this economist did not just mean the US example but the global rise of state-directed economies too. To some, these comparisons were a matter of pride and mark of universal convergence toward statist models that loosely bore similar corporatist elements.

The New Deal was hardly coherent in terms of its ideological or policy orientation, and this eclecticism resembled Vargas's own approach. It quickly became a point of reference for other nations experimenting with state-led recovery, but President Franklin D. Roosevelt's government itself also borrowed from parallel experiments elsewhere.[84] New Deal programs, like corporatist ones, grew out of the failures of privately run cooperatives or associations to control competition, labor costs, and prices in the 1920s. After 1929, these groups turned to the regulatory powers of the federal government to impose the economic order that they had not been able to independently enforce.[85] The National Industrial Recovery Act became one of the legislative pillars of the New Deal's recovery program for how it envisioned a collaboration between business, government, and labor in order to limit ruinous competition, establishing sector-specific "codes of fair competition" that determined minimum wages and pricing.[86] It was certainly akin to how corporatist associations in Portugal or Italy worked to regulate competition as well as set wage and price controls by industry. The same can be said about the Agricultural Adjustment Act, which addressed agricultural overproduction by establishing voluntary agreements with producers to control supply. This strategy was similar to Brazilian efforts to prop up commodity prices with national institutes created for coffee and sugar. The Agricultural Adjustment Act, which historian Sarah Milov calls a "New Deal experiment in corporatist planning," offered producers of wheat, corn, tobacco, and other staple commodities benefit payments to take land out of cultivation. The immediate goal was to raise commodity prices and thereby farmers' incomes.[87] In the 1930s, Roosevelt's critics seized on these similarities to systems elsewhere, even discrediting the New Deal by labeling it *fascist.*[88]

It might seem contradictory that the same Brazilian intellectuals who celebrated the illiberal Estado Novo also worked so hard to show that corporatism as an economic system was compatible with liberal democracy. Take, for example, Brazilian readings of the National Industrial Recovery Act, which created the National Recovery Administration to limit competition by issuing self-enforcing industry codes. Like corporatist bargaining in Portugal or Italy, administration codes set minimum wages and prices.[89] In 1938, Oliveira Vianna was working in the Ministry of Labor as a juridical consultant. In his legal opinions and essays that defended his policy choices, he often cited Portuguese, French, and Italian jurisprudence. But he increasingly looked to US law, often celebrating in his writings the progressive legal realists who held that law should respond to social problems. In particular, he drew inspiration from US Supreme Court justice Louis Brandeis. In 1938, Oliveira Vianna published a series of essays on corporatist law, famously using the New Deal to defend the new labor tribunals and national institutes regulating commodity production in Brazil. Brandeis was crucial to his argument, and Oliveira Vianna even called the US justice a "liberal corporatist."[90] He cited Brandeis extensively to argue that corporatism as an economic and labor system could be stretched to fit authoritarian and liberal contexts alike. Yet the Brazilian jurist's assessment of the New Deal—whether unconsciously or strategically—overlooked that the US Supreme Court had declared parts of the National Industrial Recovery Act, namely the industrial codes, unconstitutional in 1935 for improperly limiting interstate competition and delegating Congress's powers to the executive branch.

Setting aside these specific policies, for some in Brazil, the New Deal showed that even countries that had benefited from open markets and free competition were now turning to economic planning to correct the consequent social conflicts and inefficient concentration of wealth.[91] Conservative intellectual Azevedo Amaral celebrated the New Deal as "the most audacious and complete experiment in planning until now attempted within the configurations of the capitalist regime."[92] While reporting on Roosevelt's reelection campaign in 1936, Aranha, Brazilian ambassador to the United States, affirmed that the New Deal was "an 'economic plan,' and nothing more, looking to direct and correct the evils of the liberal economic order."[93] Living in Washington, DC, Aranha witnessed firsthand conflicts over the New Deal, from protests within the business community to the Republican Party's platform and the Supreme Court's overturning of some of its programs. Brazilian admirers of the US New Deal understood that its economic program undercut long-standing liberal traditions.[94] In many respects, it was easier for Brazilian officials to overlook how many New Dealers remained committed liberals, in part because they seemed less relevant to their own experiment. Of greater concern to Brazilians were socialist tendencies in New Deal circles. Aranha was blatantly anticommunist, and this ideology often took the form of antisemitism in his reports from Washington.[95] It was still better to be a fascist or even a liberal than to be a communist.

Meanwhile, some in Brazil, particularly those who viewed Vargas's economic program as excessively interventionist, used the New Deal's "serious setbacks" to critique corporatism at home.[96] In Brazil, liberal economist Eugênio Gudin would become one of the most vocal opponents to *dirigismo* over the next fifty years.[97] He worked in government postings in the Finance Ministry under Vargas in the 1930s, but also for future governments of both liberal and developmentalist varieties. Gudin criticized New Deal programs because it seemed impossible for any government to dictate general rules that could address the particular needs of each industry.[98] He condemned the New Deal to criticize similar policies in Brazil without directly attacking Vargas. After all, Brazilian public officials were keenly aware of the surveillance and censorship under the watchful eye of police.

As the Italian Fascist model fell out of favor following Mussolini's invasion of Ethiopia, Portugal's Estado Novo rose to global attention as the corporatist model to follow. Louis Báudin, French law professor at the University of Paris, dedicated an entire chapter in his *Le corporatisme* to the Portuguese experience, explaining that Portugal "has become an oasis of security and stability in a shaken Europe." To many foreign observers, the corporatist system was at the heart of Portugal's success, but as Báudin emphasized, in ways "profoundly different from the Italian experience."[99] Such positive reviews had partly to do with the success of Salazar's austerity program, which balanced Portugal's budget for ten consecutive years. In just a few years, Salazar had managed not only to achieve budget surpluses but to stem inflation and stabilize the escudo too. Propaganda minister António Ferro boasted at home and abroad about the relative stability of Portugal's economy. Foreign journalists commended, often uncritically, this financial restructuring. By 1936, it was not unusual to see praise for Portugal's finances in the international press, and Salazar's methods especially caught the attention of economists in Brazil. Portugal, one Brazilian politician noted, illustrates "the merits of a dictatorship that repaired its finances and restored its credit."[100] Even liberal economist Gudin could not help but applaud "Professor" Salazar as "a clear, logical, and scientific spirit."[101]

With rising extremism worldwide, Catholic intellectuals in France and across Latin America also looked to Salazar's Estado Novo as an example of a moderate and traditional dictatorship. Salazar emphasized the church and family as the pillars of Portuguese society. He supported a conservative approach to modernization—one that maintained agriculture as the basis of economic life. Portugal, unlike its Spanish neighbor, had managed to avoid bloody descent into civil war.

This too became a mark of success in the eyes of Salazar's sympathizers, especially in Latin America, where elites worried about intensified class conflict and the red scare. Some conservative groups were certainly drawn to Generalísimo Francisco Franco's Catholic crusade against communists and other leftist subversives in Spain.[102] But for others in Latin America, Salazarismo was a less disruptive path. Observed one Peruvian journalist, "Portuguese fascism is sweeter than the political systems of Italy and Germany, and not just in terms of race or climate ... but also in terms of the character of its leader." Salazar's foreign admirers did not overlook that he was a dictator but also celebrated his example as a softer type of authoritarianism with a "modest and industrious dictator."[103]

For others in Latin America, Portugal was an inspiration because it was predominantly agrarian, offering an example to other underdeveloped societies on the margins of global capitalism. Anxieties over backwardness and underdevelopment were a conduit for corporatist economic ideas, but where some saw corporatism as a path for development, others inverted this formula, turning backwardness into the reason why corporatism was the only option for countries like Brazil or Portugal. For many, the Portuguese model was relevant because it demonstrated what a relatively poor nation could do. "If we want to cite an example of what we can accomplish with sound fiscal order and a rational organization of agricultural production," one Brazilian journalist explained, "we should remember the work of Minister Salazar in Portugal."[104] The line between the celebration of and resignation to the corporatist path, however, was quite thin in some cases.

Making the Case for "Why Corporatism" in Portuguese

Across the Portuguese-speaking world, economists and intellectuals designed their corporatist third path to improve on other economic systems that involved either too little or too much state interference in market life. They defended corporatism as modern and progressive in transnational settings, but they could not escape their own preoccupations over why it was a necessary path on account of their national endowments. Race, culture, and history were inescapably implicated in the exchange of corporatist ideas between Brazil and Portugal in particular, and the distinctions between economic systems. Some argued that lacking the cultural or racial preconditions for capitalist development, the new corporatist state was the only institution capable of organizing productive forces in order to transform either Brazil's or Portugal's economy.

Oliveira Vianna had famously made his case for corporatism in Brazil on account of the lack of an "associationalist spirit" among Brazilians—the prerequisite for the autonomous (that is, not statist) organization of society according to economic and social interests. Báudin echoed this logic, noting that the Portuguese were "reluctant to organize themselves" and were a "Latin" people, inclined to act more according to feelings than to reason, evident in their "gentle, peaceful, quite carefree, and even fatalistic nature" due to "Arab influences."[105] These kinds of culturalist and racist modes of analysis prevailed in 1930s' accounts of why corporatism proved such a popular strategy across southern Europe and Latin America, and continued to mark scholarship for decades as social scientists in the 1970s and 1980s took for granted sociocultural explanations for authoritarian models.[106]

In Brazil more than in Portugal, economic anxieties were connected to racial explanations of national backwardness, although such assertions were rarely explicit. To some, Brazil's racial formation explained why corporatism could not work. In 1938, for instance, Simonsen argued against basing Brazil's corporatist experiment on Italian or Portuguese examples because Brazil had a more racially and ethnically heterogeneous society than those European countries, making class cohesion impossible. For Simonsen, the Italian or Portuguese model could never work because it was not possible to organize such a diverse population according to economic interests.[107]

Given these and other differences in demography and economy, Brazilian intellectuals who supported Salazar's Estado Novo had to stretch the historical ties between the two countries and minimize their divergences. With public celebrations of Luso-Brazilian civilization, peppered with references to shared blood, culture, and *raça*, it is all the more striking to note the silences around Brazil as one of the world's most multiracial and multiethnic societies.[108] These omissions are especially notable because of how Brazilian anxieties over backwardness were embedded in racialist explanations, even if such contentions were rarely explicit.[109] In the 1930s, Vargas era propaganda increasingly celebrated Brazil's centuries-long process of racial miscegenation and assimilation, eventually bundled into the myth of racial democracy.[110] At the same time, racist arguments about the country's underdevelopment persisted.[111]

Corporatists like Oliveira Vianna or Azevedo Amaral in particular continued to advocate for whitening strategies, even as they also tried to affiliate economic development and multiracialism.[112] These intellectual projects were not contradictory so much as strategically mobilized. Brazilian public officials and intellectuals often interrupted their economic writings with racist digressions.[113] Oliveira Vianna, for example, was well-known for his practical endorsement of whitening immigration policies. In the Ministry of Labor, Oliveira Vianna lamented in one of his legal opinions that because Brazilian immigration laws did not discriminate by ethnic group, they could not legally prevent the immigration of Chinese workers to Brazil. He explained his opposition to Asian workers in Brazil was on account of their alleged "*infusibilidade*."[114] Oliveira Vianna worried that too much racial or ethnic diversity in Brazil would further stunt the development of an associationalist spirit defined according to economic interests. He never explicitly attributed Brazil's delayed development to its racial formation, but it is not hard to draw this conclusion. Other Brazilian officials bluntly put forward this argument. "What we need in Brazil," Aranha spelled out in unambiguous terms, "is more white people, more whites and always whites, and nothing of other races."[115] Similarly, Azevedo Amaral peppered his analysis of corporatism with discussions of immigration and also supported whitening schemes. He worried about "racial mixing in Brazil." Much like Oliveira Vianna, he added that the "Portuguese were, obviously, the best immigrants [Brazil] could receive."[116] The corporatist stress on diffusing class tension, some have maintained, was a way to avoid talking about race explicitly. At the same time, Brazilian intellectuals could not disentangle their preoccupations about their country's racial and cultural formation from its economic development.

By the mid-1930s, owing to racialized arguments about the connections between countries and the interest in distinguishing corporatism from other systems, Portuguese started outpacing Italian as the main language for the production of corporatist ideas and the bond grew closer between Brazil and Portugal. Translations of corporatist texts into Portuguese by Brazilian and Portuguese intellectuals, originally written in French and Italian, were essential to the transnational circulation of new economic ideas and policies that drew the two countries closer together. These translations were not mere reproductions; rather, they constituted original intellectual productions, evident in how the prefaces and annotations that accompanied these texts allowed their translators to discuss local problems and policies. Several of these translators worked in government, responsible for economic problem-solving in their countries. Local issues shaped their economic analysis, embedded in discussions of how a similar program could look so different in different parts of the world. Yet when multiple countries use the same language, such parochial aims scaled to an international context. A paradox emerged that is essential (albeit not unique) to the history of corporatism: corporatist ideas circulated transnationally to support an orientation that was necessarily *national* and *nationalist*.

In writing histories of how ideas circulate beyond national borders, scholars often focus on retracing networks of people and institutions versus translations. But translations also offered opportunities to adapt foreign ideas to local contexts. This is especially important for Brazil, which did not produce many original monographs on corporatism, but did produce several iconic translations. As regards translation, historians have recently dispensed with "borrowing" diffusion models, which tend to overstate the movement of ideas and institutions from a European center to a non-European periphery.[117] Histories such as James Sanders's work on liberalism in Latin America, or Chris Bayly's work on liberalism in colonial India have emphasized intellectual diffusion by mutual and reciprocal influence. In this framework, the "foreign" acquires new meanings and practices through local application.[118]

Much of this scholarship, however, has focused on liberalism more than extremist or national texts in the 1930s. Applying these new approaches to corporatist theorists in the 1930s, we see that both Brazil and Portugal considered borrowing to be problematic, or at least borrowing from places too dissimilar from their own. Oliveira Vianna in Brazil and Caetano in Portugal, as mentioned earlier, critiqued liberalism as a fundamental social mismatch to their societies.

Then again, corporatism itself could also be called an "imported" ideology inextricably tied as it is in the twentieth century to French and Italian writings, and translations of these works could be construed as a movement of ideas from a European center to peripheral spaces in southern Europe and Latin America. And yet corporatism was not considered alien or misplaced. Instead, throughout the 1930s, many Brazilian and Portuguese intellectuals and political officials exerted themselves to stress deep corporatist roots and traditions. They endorsed corporatism precisely because of its continuities with Roman, medieval, and colonial institutions. In Portugal, for example, Caetano frequently identified the Casa dos Vinte e Quatro, a medieval administrative organ in Lisbon comprised of representatives from various corporations and guilds to govern the city, as the origins of modern corporatism.[119] Some in Brazil pointed to colonial institutions or the incomplete revolution started by positivist military generals in the late nineteenth century. Corporatists insisted that their program was native, all the while arguing that its universal implementation—across Europe and the Americas—made this system new, progressive, and modern. In this way, the program was distinctively national and transnational simultaneously.

In 1934, Portuguese agronomist António Perez Durão published his authorized translation of Italian philosopher Ugo Spirito's *I fondamenti della economia corporativa*, first published in Italy in 1932.[120] Trained in law and philosophy, Spirito was a professor at the University of Rome, and helped to shape Italy's economic policies in the 1920s and early 1930s. Spirito was widely influential in Portugal even before this translation. Famously, he had proposed *homo corporativus* as an alternative to the egotistical and antisocial tendencies of *homo economicus*.[121] Teixeira Ribeiro, a keen reader of Spirito's works, explained that "corporatist man" would be motivated by the "spirit of cooperation and sociability," not by profit alone.[122] That Spirito saw in corporatism a project to remake social relations by regulating market exchange is what made him such a visionary in the eyes of Brazilian and Portuguese intellectuals. Above all, Spirito had two aims: first, to "overcome" the logic and assumptions of classical economic theory in order to clarify, as a second objective, that the corporatist economy was something distinct from capitalism and socialism.[123]

Durão's translation was significant because of its timing, published as Portugal was preparing for the national plebiscite to ratify the 1933 Constitution. We know little of how Durão came to translate this work or to what extent he had contact with Spirito. Durão was not a leading figure in corporatist intellectual circles in Portugal and published little. He was an agronomist whose work focused on how new technological innovations might increase production in the olive oil and dairy sectors. Nonetheless, Durão called his translation a work of "propaganda."[124] His aim was to inspire Portuguese readers with a new corporatist ethos that put national interests above individual pursuits. To use a foreign text as propaganda for a new constitution, a document that would define national values, is not contradictory per se. During the age of revolutions and rise of nineteenth-century liberalism, foreign texts and constitutions inspired nationalist movements across the Atlantic. But liberalism had, and has, long been associated with an internationalist ethos, and this was not the case with corporatism. With corporatism, nationalist commitments had to be conjugated with its international inspirations. Durão packaged his translation of a key Italian work into a celebration of how Portugal's Constitution was putting corporatist principles into action.

While translations situated corporatism in a transnational context, they did not always strictly endorse the translated material. In Brazil, Azevedo Amaral and jurist Themístocles Brandão Cavalcanti engaged in two translation projects that illustrate how Brazilian intellectuals used foreign texts to distance corporatism from fascism, and even to assert it as a new form of democracy. Azevedo Amaral translated Manoilescu's *Le siècle du corporatisme*, first published in French in 1934. José Olympio Editora, one of Brazil's most prestigious publishers, asked him to translate this book, which appeared as *O século do corporativismo* in 1938.

Azevedo Amaral began his preface unusually: by disagreeing with the author. "Translators are often assumed to be in solidarity with the ideas expounded on in the books [they translate]," he begins, but in this case, he wanted to outline all the ways in which he was not. While he was in "intellectual harmony" with much of what Manoilescu had to say, he could not "endorse the author in his way of looking at the relationship between fascism and corporatism."[125] Manoilescu at times criticized totalitarian regimes, but he was also an opportunist who did not hesitate to align with Romania's fascist movement or Nazi Germany.[126] For Azevedo Amaral, in the ideal corporatist state, labor and professional organizations constituted the cellular units of society; these units were vertically integrated to the state, but they retained a degree of autonomy too. Corporate organs would not control individual decision-making but instead function as intermediary agents between collective interests and national imperatives. In Azevedo Amaral's view, Manoilescu failed to fully contend with how Italian Fascism inverted—rather than elevated—this corporatist model by turning corporations into "more or less bureaucratic instruments of an engrossing and omnipotent state."[127]

Trained in medicine, Azevedo Amaral spent much of his career as a journalist, starting at the *Correio da Manhã*, and then editing the monthly magazines *Diretrizes* and *Novas Diretrizes*, which featured essays promoting corporatism, fascism, and integralism. As a journalist, he spent time in London in the 1910s, thus influencing his thinking on industrialization and economic development for postcolonial nations like Brazil.[128] In the 1930s, he shifted to books, writing some of the most important political and economic texts on the Vargas era: *O Brasil na crise atual* (1934), *A aventura política do Brasil* (1935), *O estado autoritário e a realidade nacional* (1938), and *Getúlio Vargas: estadista* (1941). Azevedo Amaral was not a bureaucrat and never worked in Vargas's administration. He contributed instead to public debates about corporatism, and like others of this generation, insisted that it offered a new economic system while recognizing that its novelty inhered in its reinvention of old traditions as well.

Azevedo Amaral's translations alongside these other works were something original: an intellectual effort to define corporatism outside fascism. Azevedo Amaral took the question of authoritarian versus totalitarian in Manoilescu's book and made it central to his own work, *O estado autoritário e a realidade nacional*. While not trained as an economist, his engagement with corporatism was first and foremost as an economic system. He devotes little attention to labor—not even to labor control. Between Manoilescu and Azevedo Amaral, corporatism offered a strategy for economic development; it was a way to transition from an agroexport model to an industrialized, modernized economy.

Across his works, Azevedo Amaral defended the idea of an authoritarian state as a vehicle for economic development, bringing distinctly Brazilian anxieties about backwardness to his endorsement of corporatism. He even asserted corporatism as a type of "democracia autoritária."[129] In his view, Brazil's Estado Novo presented an ideal model for authoritarian democracy. It created a strong state whose primary function was to guarantee social peace and economic progress, but not necessarily individual freedoms. Some intellectual historians see Azevedo Amaral's efforts as a calculated attempt to distance corporatism from fascism in name only. But both his original works and translated texts deserve attention precisely because this idea of "authoritarian democracy" proved so compelling in Brazil. Vargas, after all, returned to power just a few years after the end of World War II, and the economic model that these books proclaimed become the strategy by which Brazil industrialized thereafter.

If Azevedo Amaral used translation to draft a typology for authoritarianism in order to save Brazilian corporatism from fascism, others took this project further to argue for the democratic possibilities that underlay corporatism. One of the most interesting, albeit forgotten, translations in these years belonged to Cavalcanti. His only writings on economic topics happened to be his unique translation of Roger Bonnard's *Syndicalisme, corporatisme et état corporatif*, first published in Paris in 1937. Cavalcanti worked quickly; his translation appeared in Brazilian bookstores the following year. It is unclear how Cavalcanti arrived at Bonnard's work or if the two were in contact. Cavalcanti had studied in Paris as an adolescent, but his résumé shows no other obvious ties to France. What makes this translation exceptional is how Cavalcanti dialogued with Bonnard in a section called "Notes for the Brazilian Edition." In the footnotes, Cavalcanti expanded on Bonnard's analysis to make it more relevant to Brazil, earning praise for the "originality" of his translation. The president of Brazil's Supreme Court, for example, congratulated him on "turning that monograph into a Brazilian book," particularly with its notes and detailed introduction on "our corporatist system as outlined in the current Brazilian Constitution."[130]

Cavalcanti was deeply involved in the politically convulsive 1920s and 1930s. His political activism began in the 1920s, when he used his legal training to defend young tenentes accused of treason, brandishing writs of habeas corpus to get them released. He joined the 1930 Revolution, taking up arms in Minas Gerais and supporting Vargas once in power. Nominated to the first subcommission for the 1934 Constitution, he championed corporatist institutions and professional suffrage. Following the 1964 coup, he collaborated on the 1967 Constitution and served as minister to Brazil's Supreme Court from 1967 to 1969, during the *anos de chumbo* (lead years), the most repressive phase of the military dictatorship.[131] But in 1938, Cavalcanti became director to a newly created economics department (the Faculdade de Ciências Econômicas e Administrativas) in Rio de Janeiro.[132] This economics department was by no means corporatist. In fact, liberal economist Gudin was one of its first full professors. But it was also no coincidence that this department was created shortly after the 1937 coup. It stood in service of "national economic reconstruction," bringing together academics, experts, and industry leaders to "cooperate in finding solutions to the great economic and administrative problems that arise from the new constitutional order."[133]

Cavalcanti arrived at economics through this interest in administrative law. Bonnard and Cavalcanti each understood the *corporation* as a unit for organizing private interests according to economic sector and activity. Cavalcanti analyzed corporatism as an "administrative, economic, and political" system.[134] He concentrated on the conselhos técnicos and *institutos nationais* created to oversee key sectors, like sugar and coffee. Cavalcanti asserted that creating conditions for labor to organize was not itself the goal but rather a means to national development that created conditions for social peace. In his view, the subordination of labor to developmentalist ambitions was not the corruption of the corporatist ideal but instead its very theoretical framework.

Cavalcanti defended corporatism first and foremost as a technical solution that in theory, might conform to many different regimes as a "solution for both democratic and authoritarian states."[135] Bonnard's logic, moreover, influenced Cavalcanti's political goal: neutralize arguments that corporatism was a fascist, repressive, violent solution by focusing on regulation and administration. Translation became essential to making the argument, far more in Brazil than in Portugal, that corporatism was democratic yet still illiberal by making authoritarianism a mechanism for development and social peace.

To assert what a corporatist economy could offer, these translators outlined what corporatism was *not*. Across all three texts, corporatism was defined in opposition to a liberal capitalist market economy. Political arguments became entangled with this project: corporatism was a negative space that was *not* fascist and *not* totalitarian. It might seem paradoxical that intellectuals in Brazil and Portugal distanced themselves from Italy's dictatorship by putting an original spin on texts from Italy—and other locations. But this proved to be a powerful tactic.

The 1930s, however, were a time for action as well as debate. As intellectual projects to define the corporatist third path intersected with the political urgency of fixing economic problems, the meaning of corporatism evolved. Spirito, Manoilescu, and Bonnard emphasized new powers and responsibilities for the state, and their translators highlighted this focus in widely read and cited texts. Azevedo Amaral's translation in fact became a canonical text in Brazilian debates. With these translations, a technocratic vision of corporatism triumphed in which a strong state regulated and disciplined economic life, sidelining the Catholic, organic idealism evident in early writings as well as the totalizing control in fascist models.

The Corporatist State

Following the 1937 coup, Vargas called his regime the Estado Novo—the same name that Salazar had picked for Portugal in 1933. While Vargas and his team never explained the regime's choice, they were certainly aware of events in Portugal. Just before the coup, Brazil's Ministry of Labor organized a commercial mission to Portugal. João Maria de Lacerda, a technocrat working for the Ministry of Labor, traveled to Lisbon, where he met with pivotal figures of the Portuguese Estado Novo, including Theotónio Pereira. Conversations in Lisbon followed Lacerda back to Rio de Janeiro, where the following year he welcomed Portuguese statespersons eager to see Brazil's own corporatist revolution in action.[136]

Inspired by these exchanges, Lacerda was the keynote speaker at an event organized by the Federação das Associações Comerciais in Rio de Janeiro on "Brasil e o corporativismo." Lacerda addressed an auditorium filled with representatives from industrial and commercial sectors curious about his trip. He presented Portugal as an important model that "was feasible in Brazil too." Lacerda's defenses of corporatism were rhetorically familiar: the clash between liberalism and communism, and the ways in which Brazil was "spiritually prepared" to carve out its own third path. He also highlighted the inequalities of the global economy, observing: "There are countries that possess great reserves and poor countries."[137] Few could deny that both Brazil and Portugal were poor countries. Corporatism made sense for both precisely because of the widening gap between rich and poor nations, and between industrialized and agrarian societies.

As Estado Novo suggests, the state itself became the primary agent and object of these experiments. Proponents of corporatism insisted that the problem with classical economic theory was that it treated the state as exogenous to market forces. For some Portuguese economists, the problem was that the state had not been incorporated into the assumptions underlying classical economic theory. With this in mind, Manoilescu underscored that what corporatism offered was "a profound revolution . . . in the concept of the state," while Spirito argued that this distinguished corporatism from a liberal capitalist economy where the state functioned almost as a nebulous "imaginary" entity.[138]

Corporatism became a project to transform the state into the primary actor in economic life. Corporatism was not laissez-faire or fascism, as discussed— and it was not direct state control over production, as with the Soviet model. Given the anticommunism at the core of the Estado Novo ideology (both in Brazil and Portugal), this latter point was crucial. The corporation, Báudin summarized, reconciled antagonistic forces—"public versus private" and "capital versus labor"—by fusing together the "individual and the state from an economic point of view."[139] Spirito even went so far as to affirm that the corporatist state would "elevate every *citizen* to the rank of civil servant."[140] If the goal in liberal models was to keep public and private spheres separate, the corporatist goal was to fuse them.

Yet economists, jurists, and technocrats did not all agree about the emphasis on the state. Some in Brazil and Portugal protested the statist inflection, insisting that corporatism was the reinvention of medieval institutions grounded in autonomous professional, municipal, and religious institutions.[141] Catholic voices did not entirely fade in the 1930s, nor did the political and symbolic power of the Catholic Church.[142] Oliveira Vianna, for instance, envisioned that the Catholic Church could address the needs of groups that could not be integrated into the state's corporatist system, as he drafted a legal opinion for the Ministry of Labor that supported the church's custodianship over Indigenous communities.[143] At the same time, the appeal of corporatism was precisely that it could accommodate a patchwork of state, parastate, and nonstate agencies to discipline social relations—but always in ways that upheld the existing social order.

Rather than a failure of implementation, the incomplete statist reach was by design. Corporatist intellectuals were trying to distance their New States from totalitarian states in Italy, Germany, or Soviet Russia.[144] For this reason, many tried to pitch corporatism as "an equilibrium" between "anarchy produced by

competition" and the "excesses of statism." They worried that the rush to centralize economic planning might lead to what Cavalcanti referred to as "the
absorption of this whole mechanism by a bureaucratic apparatus."[145]

To counter such critiques launched by liberals and others opposed to these
dictatorships, proponents of corporatism in Brazil and Portugal insisted that
their system created channels by which organized interests could petition the
state. In some ways, their vision came to fruition as workers, agricultural producers, warehousers, and other professions in both Brazil and Portugal petitioned their governments to organize their own sindicatos throughout the
1930s.[146] For Cavalcanti, these channels inspired him to invent additional categories like "organized democracy" to defend why a strong "interventionist
state in the economic sphere" was necessary for social peace and economic
progress, the deliverables in this new democracy.[147]

Some rebutted concerns that corporatism would spawn a bureaucratic behemoth by emphasizing discipline, not direct control, as a formula for economic
planning. By this they meant that government did not directly control production but instead organized producers in order to eliminate competition so as to
influence, regulate, and legislate economic behavior. For Azevedo Amaral in
Brazil, corporatism offered more an "equilibrium economy," which he defined
as a "type of dirigismo econômico compatible with maintaining a considerable
degree of freedoms for private initiatives."[148] Explained João Pinto da Costa Leite
(Lumbrales), Portuguese subsecretary for corporations and social security in the
mid-1930s, "Corporatist reforms are not, despite how they sometimes appear, a
form of statism. . . . They are a process for limiting competition . . . and a form by
which to organize at the national level some major branches of production and
external trade in order to condition these according to the interests of the nation."[149] Corporatist institutions were semiautonomous locally, but connected
to various ministries and conselhos técnicos where industry representatives and
technocrats advised policy. For corporatist regimes, the state did not decide
what industrialists or agriculturalists produced but instead set incentives for certain outcomes in the interest of the national economy.

Corporatists attempted to recentralize power in the executive branch and
this required building an administrative state with powers to intervene in
economic life. According to their corporatist ideals, they designed this administrative state by sector, profession, and class interests, and not according
to geographic or regional units. This model especially resonated in Brazil, with
its constant, postindependence conflicts between centralism and federalism.

Historians of Brazil have long debated the extent to which Vargas broke the
decentralized and hyperfederalized structure of the First Republic—in which
power resided in regional oligarchs connected to the export economy—in
order to centralize power in a strong executive branch. Some argue that the

Estado Novo simply formalized the ways in which prior governments had been controlled by and subordinate to regional commodity interests.[150] Corporatism helps explain the logic. One goal in Brazil, as in Portugal and Italy, was to centralize and strengthen the federal government, but in ways that recognized the need for a decentralized management of the economy according to sector. In many ways, Vargas's corporatist state, as historians have argued, repackaged regional sector power into economic sector power. As Campos explained following the 1937 coup, the corporatist organization of the economy was itself an act of "economic decentralization" because the state did not directly control production but rather "devolved to each sector powers to organize and govern itself."[151] Oliveira Vianna saw this as a global trend, explaining in *Problemas de direito corporativo* that corporatism offered "functional decentralization" of the state's activities instead of "territorial decentralization."[152]

———

Out of the transnational intellectual conversations that connected Brazil, Portugal, Italy, Romania, and other countries, the state became the ultimate coordinator in national economic life. Throughout the 1930s and 1940s, new state agencies were created to regulate wages, working conditions, prices, and production, some of which will be explored in the chapters to come. Historians and social scientists have rightly pointed out that this system was not quite implemented anywhere in its pure form. The fact that corporatism was only partially implemented has led some to conclude that it was simply window dressing for dictatorships. Such conclusions, however, overlook the new and original ways in which corporatist theory conceptualized the state as an agent to fix economic problems. The chapters that follow will highlight how corporatist ideas were put into action, and how corporatism fundamentally altered economic life, not despite its incomplete realization, but in part, because of it.

4

Just Price and Production

IN JULY 1936, an economist working for Banco do Brasil published a special report on Brazil's current economic problems.[1] Given the lingering consequences of the Great Depression, Brazil's government had created a slew of new emergency agencies at a breathtaking pace. Disruptions to global trade in 1929 devastated both agroexport sectors and the supply of goods for the internal market. Brazil's federal and state governments had intervened during past crises to support coffee or rubber. But the current crisis extended beyond a single sector or region.

In this context, economists, jurists, and other intellectuals were making a strong case to replace nineteenth-century economic models with corporatist formulas, insisting that the free market could not be counted on to self-adjust and self-regulate, but it was not immediately clear how theory translated into policy. This chapter traces early efforts to navigate this experiment, following these debates through various government ministries and across national borders.

Brazil's experimental, ad hoc, and erratic approach to economic planning in the 1930s was hardly exceptional.[2] With the volume and diversity of programs tested in the 1930s, a quest to find ideological consistency would obscure the reactive nature of state intervention; conversely, to see the experiment as only ad hoc would obscure the labyrinthine architecture of Brazil's new economic system—a system designed for policy minutiae. This bureaucracy left an impressive paper trail, with legislation, internal correspondence, legal opinions, and official reports documenting bold plans to transform economic life, alongside protests and petitions from farmers, merchants, and industrialists whose businesses were directly affected by these plans. The seeds for the developmentalist feats of the 1950s were planted in the 1930s, thanks to this experimentation, and were not limited to the state promotion of industrialization but extended into commodity sectors as well.[3]

As this chapter shows, price became one of the primary sites where corporatist policy and theory intersected. Bureaucrats, economists, and intellectuals designed and implemented corporatist solutions to organize markets in order to secure *preços justos*, or just prices, for producers and consumers alike. The concept of a just price was not invented by or unique to corporatist contexts in the interwar period. In the late nineteenth and early twentieth centuries, social movements and organized labor created campaigns and held protests for government actions to respond to the rising cost of living.[4] In the 1930s, broad political consensus emerged across Europe and Latin America for the government regulation of essential goods and ordinary consumption. Left-leaning Popular Front governments in Chile, Spain, and France turned price into a core component of social citizenship.[5] Even in the United States, with its deeply entrenched liberal traditions, New Deal programs also guaranteed farmers remunerative prices and even intervened in pricing for essential consumer goods.[6] Because of their ubiquity, price controls have not been central to studies on corporatism, and it has seemed a stretch to tie these policies to a specific ideology. Yet the near universality of price controls as an interwar government "best practice" does not mean that these interventions had no grounding in economic theory or political philosophy. To the contrary, state interventions into the marketplace had to be rationalized and implemented locally, according to national traditions and ambitions. In Brazil as much as in Portugal and Italy, the corporatist framework was essential to how a just price was both theorized and implemented.

This chapter is an intellectual history of economic policymaking as viewed through the lens of Brazil's new federal commissions—one that highlights how midlevel technocrats drew inspiration from ongoing corporatist experiments in Portugal and Italy. The Portuguese corporatist experiment was far more theoretically consistent than Brazil's, albeit far from universal or uniform, and is presented as a counterpoint rather than a direct comparison. Across both cases, this chapter recovers the intellectual and technical ambitions of midlevel technocrats appointed to fix the pressing problems of price and production, and considers how the state started to act on the economy. Certainly, not all Vargas era economic planning was directly tethered to the corporatist ideal, but in these early years the circulation of people and policies between Brazil and southern Europe influenced the creation of new corporatist-like agencies to regulate commodity prices and production. This chapter looks at different scales of activity from local to transnational, beginning with state-led efforts to measure and monitor economic activities, highlighting attempts to improve and centralize the collection of national statistics and industry surveys, and then considers the policy experimentation that followed.

Measuring the Cost of Living

Following the 1930 Revolution, economic historians estimate that overall price levels in Brazil fell by 9 percent in 1930 and 4 percent in 1931 (figure 4.1). Much of this downward trend in prices was linked to falling prices for export commodities that caused a slowdown across industries. By the mid-1930s, however, domestic food and fuel prices were slowly on the rise in part because of shortages due to falling imports after 1929. Brazil was not alone in grappling with price volatility, which was quickly becoming a global concern.[7]

By 1936, Artur de Sousa Costa, Brazil's finance minister from 1934 to 1945, with a few interruptions to his tenure, put inflation at the top of his list of challenges facing Brazil's economy.[8] Based on the available longitudinal data on price levels in Rio de Janeiro, the trends for the capital city were quite stark: foodstuff prices had dropped by 16 percent between 1929 and 1933, but then jumped by 40 percent between 1933 and 1937.[9] Rising prices were as much a social as an economic concern for public officials. One government economist feared that inflation would "alarm classes with lower purchasing power" and called on the "public powers to act."[10] As worrisome as inflation appeared in Rio de Janeiro, Brazilian officials did not have nationwide data on price levels to work with, nor could they pinpoint the root cause of rising prices.

The Finance Ministry stepped in to try to fill this gap by organizing its own survey on the cost of living, although Brazilian economists pointed to their government's lack of economic expertise or statistical tools, which made it difficult to measure and analyze conditions.[11] The rush by governments to develop statistical tools was an international as well as national phenomenon.[12] For example, the League of Nations published statistical bulletins on public health, education, finance, and economics in these years.[13] Its Economic and Financial Section was the world's first intergovernmental organization for economic cooperation and collaboration.[14] With this kind of multinational data, national governments were better equipped to compare their performance vis-à-vis other nations and identify domestic challenges.[15]

In Brazil, the creation of a national statistics bureau became a complicated negotiation between different institutions, individuals, and ideas. As things stood, each ministry or agency was responsible for its own data collection; surveys available to policymakers were scattered and unstandardized. Without a more organized approach to data collection, corporatist jurist and government minister Francisco Campos argued that Brazil would not be able to produce the sorts of "eminently scientific studies" required for national unification and development.[16]

Campos, who started his career with Getúlio Vargas's government in the recently created Ministry of Education and Public Health from 1930 to 1932

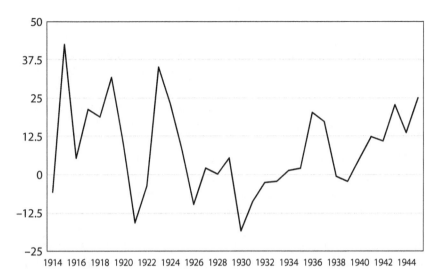

FIGURE 4.1. Inflation in Brazil, 1914–45. *Source:* Inflation rates calculated by author using price index in Annibal Villanova Villela and Wilson Suzigan, *Política do governo e crescimento da economia brasileira, 1889–1945* (Rio de Janeiro: IPEA/INPES, 1973), table VII. Note that for this period, this data largely represents the cost of living in Rio de Janeiro. Villela and Suzigan use data from multiple volumes of the *Anuário Estatístico do Brasil* as well as recent studies by other scholars to approximate a nationwide cost of living index, but even so, much of the raw data is based on Rio de Janeiro.

before serving in the Ministry of Justice and Internal Affairs, became a fierce advocate for better statistics. A deeply influential figure, Campos's illiberal position and skepticism toward representative democracy would be as central to his vision for educational reforms as to the 1937 Constitution that he drafted to codify Brazil's corporatist dictatorship. But before he turned to the task of constitutional reform, he set his sights on narrower objectives. Campos criticized the First Republic for its haphazard and fractured approach to statistics collection—a "regrettable departure," Campos maintained, from efforts under Dom Pedro II, the reigning monarch from 1831 to 1889, to invest in economic surveys to guide Brazil's progress. It is true that Vargas's government was not the first to tackle statistics. Brazil's imperial government created the General Directory of Statistics in 1871 to centralize data on economic output and demographic changes. During the First Republic, the target shifted as census takers became increasingly preoccupied with the nation's racial and ethnic composition as proxy indicators for Brazil's potential to advance in the ranks of nations.[17] Campos, however, denigrated republican efforts by focusing on and celebrating imperial progress. He missed no opportunity to criticize the First Republic generally, and its approach to statistics was no exception. In this regard, Campos was like other Vargas era officials who reductively caricatured past governments to serve their political agendas while overlooking imperial and republican continuities.[18] Political scientist Timothy Mitchell has contended that the national economy only become an object of study in the 1930s.[19] This observation tracks with developments in Brazil, but additional context is necessary. In Brazil, officials increasingly framed their economic recovery efforts in national terms in part because of the impact of the Great Depression and in part because of Vargas era propaganda, which sought to differentiate Vargas's regime from the First Republic, typecast as a loose federation of competing regional economies. Better statistics became a necessary first step in national integration.

In 1934, Vargas's provisional government decreed the National Institute of Statistics, a permanent organ responsible for centralizing data from government ministries and private organizations alike.[20] It would undergo several modifications, an example of the relentless rearrangement of government agencies during the Vargas era. In January 1938, a presidential decree morphed this organ into its present-day form, the Instituto Brasileiro de Geografia e Estatística (IBGE), or Brazilian Institute of Geography and Statistics.[21]

The IBGE was a turning point in the government's capacity to study and manage the economy in order to concentrate power and mold the nation's future. Many of the technocrats working within these new agencies were well aware of their technical limitations and the limits to the data they collected. Brazilian bureaucrats experimented with different ways of visualizing the numbers. Charts, tables, and graphs were increasingly included in internal government reports as well as published in books and specialized trade journals. Brazilian officials utilized this data to diagnose economic problems. As one government statistician summarized in 1937, "To organize an economic plan presupposes the existence of statistics as current and complete as possible."[22]

Brazilian officials cited and circulated the 1936 cost of living chart for Rio de Janeiro to highlight one especially worrisome problem: rising prices. They were also well aware that it only documented trends for Rio de Janeiro.[23] Government bureaucrats consistently complained about the absence of national surveys on the cost of living and lack of price indexes of a "scientific" quality.[24] Only in the 1930s would the federal government start investing in regular efforts to measure national economic activity, looking beyond the capital to capture nationwide trends. The initial task would fall to regional governments to collect data and report to the central agency.[25] In 1938, the IBGE started publishing data on prices beyond Rio de Janeiro, with prices on twenty different foods (where available) for state capitals across the country.[26]

Price data alone was not enough, of course, to explain the causes or even consequences of the rising cost of living. Economists, statisticians, and others working closely with Brazil's new statistical agencies charted the movement of other related indicators, and zeroed in on the structural features of Brazil's economy, namely the proportion of foodstuffs to raw materials produced. And this data revealed a concerning paradox. As much as the price for food was rising alarmingly in major cities, the rate of Brazil's agricultural and livestock production for domestic markets was also on the rise. Were the rising prices "deliberate," or due to "speculative" or greedy commercial behavior?[27] Brazilian officials would seize on the latter explanation to draft new laws to tackle inflation by criminalizing price gouging and other market offenses (see chapter 5). Still, alongside this suspicion that individual greed was to blame for inflation, another explanation fit comfortably: Brazil's output of raw materials to feed national industries or for export was quickly outpacing foodstuff production. Brazilian officials and economists did not have much longitudinal data to work with, and instead based their conclusions on trends since the 1929 crash. Still, they published charts, tables, graphs and ratios to argue that the rising cost of food in major cities was due to dislocations caused by the rising demand for raw materials for national industries: wages for agricultural workers had risen as labor was diverted from food production to more lucrative sectors, while transportation costs remained high. A number of officials grew concerned not just with output but with prices for wholesalers and retailers too. They would use this data and their preliminary conclusions to build new federal agencies and regulatory measures to reorganize national production and guarantee price stability in the 1930s.

Concerns over prices were connected to a larger intellectual project: efforts to build state-directed economic models that could mitigate the volatility of laissez-faire capitalism in recent years, in which the precipitous rise and fall of supply and demand had meant ruin and unrest for Brazilian producers and workers. The production of statistics, ideas, and institutions was all intertwined.

Just Price in Theory and Practice

A growing cohort of Brazilian bureaucrats experimented with a myriad of new agencies to try to tackle rising prices. These officials acknowledged the national and international scale of problems that made it difficult for Brazil to secure feasibly priced food and raw materials to feed both its public and industries. Yet many of their earliest interventions were limited in geographic scope, with economic planning first taking shape in Rio de Janeiro. In August 1936, for example, Decree No. 1.007 declared that the price of "goods of primary necessity" in Rio de Janeiro would be regulated by a commission subordinated to the Ministry of Agriculture.[28] The Comissão Reguladora do Tabelamento, or Regulatory Commission on Price Controls, attempted to guarantee affordable foodstuffs for the city by issuing price maximums for consumer staples.[29] It responded to the acute crisis of food supply and rising cost of living within the national capital, which officials attributed to poor transportation networks and restrictions on food imports. While Brazil's government repealed this commission a few years later in response to accusations against it of corruption and fraud, it nonetheless established an important precedent for how the state should intervene to address the cost-of-living crisis. Commissions like this one would multiply in the years to come to regulate day-to-day market transactions in and beyond Rio de Janeiro.[30]

Soon after the Comissão Reguladora do Tabelamento's creation, petitions from agricultural producers as well as urban consumers trickled into the Ministry of Agriculture. Each of these groups expressed a different position on what was necessary to stabilize prices. For example, the São Paulo–based Cooperativa Agrícola de Cotia, at the time the largest farming cooperative in Brazil, saw poor infrastructure as the root cause of the high prices. It sent Vargas a telegram requesting that the commission focus on controlling exorbitant transportation costs to move foodstuff from this small municipality to the nation's capital.[31]

Brazilian officials working for this quickly expanding bureaucracy created many channels for suggestions and deliberation, but concrete actions were harder to execute. Self-fashioned técnicos justified the regulatory powers of new agencies with exhaustive data and by making reference to similar policies in other countries.[32] Too often, however, officials in one agency deferred their responsibility to another institution, resulting in patchy responses and frustration among those petitioning government. Government bureaucrats, statisticians, and economists also had to contend with the divergent interests of different social groups. Where some producers lobbied for increased government support, quickly acquiring the language of economic planning to make their appeals, other groups protested all the new rules and red tape that accompanied planning. As bureaucrats adjusted to their new responsibilities, economic challenges mounted—and became politically urgent.

For the Frente Nacional Democratica de São Paulo, government programs like the Comissão Reguladora do Tabelamento did too little to tame rising prices.[33] Created in São Paulo in August 1937, the Frente brought together several antifascist political groups, including the Brazilian Communist Party, to advocate for a broadly democratic platform in opposition to the integralist movement.[34] In its political manifesto, the Frente called for "the public powers of the city, state, and nation . . . to [adopt] measures immediately to lower the cost of living and resolve the shortages suffocating the Brazilian people."[35] That the Frente targeted the rising cost of living shows how much this issue had become a matter of social justice. It fused its demands for more government action to curb the rising cost of living to its opposition to Vargas. Blanc de Freitas, president of the Comissão Reguladora do Tabelamento, responded directly and extensively to the Frente's petition for greater government intervention in the price of goods, outlining all the reasons why he could, in fact, do little. Freitas explained that the agency he oversaw was rather effective at studying "the market for staple goods." Its powers over the internal market were nevertheless limited. Its mandate was largely for the national capital, and even there it faced significant hurdles. It had tools to estimate wholesale prices, based on the price of primary materials, fees, taxes, transportation, insurance, and a small profit of 3 to 10 percent. Yet according to Freitas, these estimates were but one diagnostic indicator. The rising costs of living in urban centers did not have a singular cause. Instead, one needed to understand how costs increased at each step of the supply chain, from producer to consumer. But the Comissão Reguladora do Tabelamento simply did not have the power or resources to intervene in each of these steps: "It can do little or nothing to lower the cost of living so long as it only works with [estimates] for the normal conditions that impact the price of goods."

To explain the limitations of this price-regulating organ, Freitas used the example of beef jerky which as a preserved food, was transported and consumed across Brazil. In exhaustive detail, he itemized all the intermediary costs that producers incurred from the cattle ranch to the local market, and the onerous taxes and fees paid at each step of the process. In the case of Minas Gerais, producers still had to pay a state export tax, even though such taxes had been declared unconstitutional with the 1934 Constitution. The export tax, he alleged, not only remained in place but even increased twofold in just a few years. If new government agencies were to have any impact at all in this "struggle for lowering the cost of living," federal powers to regulate these complex marketplaces needed to expand. For Freitas, the problem of inflation rested with intermediaries along with their spiraling and unchecked costs. The way to establish a "true equilibrium between the price paid by the consumer and the amount received by the producer" was to fix the amount paid to intermediaries, and include wholesale prices on receipts given to retailers. Such a plan, though, required more survey data on Brazil's internal market—to better forecast unknowable "disruptions"—and an expansion of the federal government, with the creation of more agencies and employment of more experts to coordinate across sectors and states.[36]

How could producers and consumers both be suffering from prices at once too low and too high? This paradox is evident with a glimpse into public opinion in 1930s' Brazil: magazine advertisements, letters to the editor at newspapers, and lyrics to popular samba songs, all of which reveal how popular classes struggled with the rising prices for essential goods. And with producers suffering as well, the failure of the price mechanism, or how supply and demand interact to set prices, became the object of theoretical debates. By the mid-1930s, segments of civil society called for the government to guarantee goods of "primary necessity" at preços justos (fair prices), or prices reflecting the real "costs of production."[37]

This question of how prices work was debated by top government officials and economists, but also across social groups and in the public sphere. Leading government officials as well as ordinary consumers increasingly blamed "intermediaries" for why both producers and consumers suffered from seemingly neutral laws of supply and demand. To some, greed and profiteering distorted the market mechanism, allowing bankers, warehousers, merchants, or importers to profit at the expense of producers and consumers. To others, the structure of Brazil's internal market posed problems in terms of how demand for raw materials was diverting labor and resources away from food production.

Whatever the causes, corporatist theory was well positioned to fill in the gaps of older economic models. The state would organize producers and establish the rules by which goods circulated within and beyond Brazil. Price ceilings would become the key means by which government agencies could intervene and influence producer decisions without assuming direct control. Other nations in the 1930s experimented with price ceilings, but unique corporatist critiques of the market's ability to self-regulate and self-adjust are crucial to understanding how price became the target of many policy interventions, as much in Brazil as in other corporatist contexts such as Portugal.

It is tempting to draw analogies between corporatist price controls and earlier precedents—perhaps E. P. Thompson's discussion of the early modern "moral economy" of the crowd, the examples of cooperatives in the nineteenth and early twentieth centuries, or contemporaneous experiments with price controls worldwide in the 1930s.[38] Yet in Vargas era Brazil and Salazarist Portugal, the theorization, institutionalization, and even criminalization around price controls concerned not just the obligations of a paternalist state to protect public welfare or survival of a specific sector but also the role of the state as the ultimate arbiter between different groups in society. Increasingly, prices were discussed not just in terms of clearing the supply of goods to a market but in terms of social peace between competing economic groups too. Uniquely, vis-à-vis earlier and contemporaneous experiments, corporatists framed price as a variable that mediates group interests. This definition of price became central to corporatist economic theory and the policies drafted in Brazil as well as in other countries.

Prominent economists such as Roberto Simonsen in Brazil and Marcello Caetano in Portugal penned highly theoretical and academic critiques of the price mechanism in classical economic models, or economic theories that asserted supply and demand as primary mechanisms for determining value (see chapter 3). These critiques in turn seeped into policy papers, bureaucratic memos, and elsewhere. Many of the most famous of these corporatist theoreticians also worked in government postings. Individuals like Francisco José de Oliveira Vianna and Campos in Brazil, or Caetano and João Pinto da Costa Leite (Lumbrales) in Portugal, were responsible for translating ideas into action. In addition to top ministers and intellectuals, many midlevel bureaucrats and industry representatives contributed their analyses, sometimes in unsigned papers and memos—and their work makes it possible to write an intellectual history of policymaking and state making.

In Brazil, the newly created Ministry of Labor was at the forefront of revolutionary efforts to remake the economy. It was also a hotbed of corporatist thinking. Alongside and beyond its work regulating labor relations, this ministry became a factory for new intellectual and technical approaches to increased state involvement in economic life. Its monthly *Boletim do Ministério do Trabalho, Indústria e Comércio* became an important site for improvised economic theory and policymaking. On the matter of explaining inflation, the first step for Labor Ministry technocrats was to discredit classical economic formulas, which no longer held.[39]

Discussion next moved beyond vague and abstract critiques of liberalism and individualism to a rigorous and theoretical focus on their model's better explanation of how economic variables adjusted after economic shocks.[40] Corporatist theorists emphasized price as a constant negotiation between producers and consumers—a variable essential to satisfying key economic interests for the sake of internal market stability. In the corporatist idiom, price—alongside wages—was nothing less than a fulcrum for maintaining social peace.

One of the clearest examples of how price was becoming the focus of new theory, policy, and law involves a legal decision that Oliveira Vianna issued for the Ministry of Labor in 1934. Two matters were at stake: first, whether a sindicato comprised of pharmacists in Rio de Janeiro, legally recognized by the aforementioned ministry, could deny membership to a pharmacist in that city; and second, whether a given firm could boycott the sindicato's decreed price increase for goods in its sector. On the first question, the law was straightforward: No, an individual or firm could not be denied membership in a sindicato since Brazil's corporatist system strictly prohibited multiple sindicatos in a given sector.[41] The second question was of grave importance for Brazil's nascent corporatist system: What was the place of individual rights, here understood in terms of an individual firm's ability to freely choose what price to charge for goods and services, in a syndicalist-corporatist society?[42] For Oliveira Vianna, the sindicato was absolutely right to impose a price increase for its member firms. Specifically, sindicatos representing liberal professions and the employer class had "as one of its major obligations the responsibility to regulate prices and control merchandise for its sector." As Oliveira Vianna summarized it, coordinating "the professional activities of its members and the regulation of price and production is today, looking at corporatist-syndicalist theory, a right absolutely recognized for professional associations." Notably, he added that this regulatory function granted to professional associations was not to be shared by sindicatos representing labor. Fierce in his anticommunism and hostility toward labor activism, he emphasized that "*sindicatos patronais* [employer associations], in contrast with *sindicatos de operários* [workers' unions], which exist for class conflict, have as their primary function precisely this coordinating and controlling task in terms of regulating markets according to its members' interests." Oliveira Vianna cited French, US, and Italian jurisprudence as he branched out beyond the limitations of Brazilian law (he issued this decision prior to the 1934 Constitution) to make his case not just for why "the group is increasingly elevated above the individual" but also for why individual rights, including free exchange, should not be exercised in ways detrimental to the "general interest."[43] Price was more than a reflection of supply and demand; it was a variable negotiated according to individual, group, and national interests.

In a corporatist society, there was an ideal price, salary, and profit commensurate with minimum individual sacrifice for the maximum social gain, and this distinguished how prices were set in free competition contexts. Government officials were not only coming to this conclusion in Brazil but also in Italy, Portugal, and other corporatist contexts. Italian economists, for example, debated the *prezzo justo* or *prezzo corporativo* in their writings on corporatism, which circulated across Europe and Latin America. In 1938, Portuguese agronomist Francisco Tavares de Almeida traveled to Italy to observe its ongoing corporatist experiment (see chapter 3). He reported on how government agencies worked alongside producer associations to guarantee fair prices. In the beet sugar industry, for example, state agencies negotiated between beet producers and industrial buyers in the canned fruits industry, with the ultimate aim of making canned fruit "accessible to more humble classes." Almeida summarized the Italian system by observing that "fixing prices is one of the most important functions attributed to corporations, which are called on to guide and regulate, on a permanent basis, the costs of production in order to create a fair equilibrium between cost and price, and make possible the maximum distributive justice."[44]

This logic was taking hold in Salazarist Portugal as well in the writings of jurists and economists but also in practice, as corporatist organisms exercised more and more controls over pricing decisions in key sectors. "Price in a corporatist economy no longer results from the debate between sellers and buyers excited by their particular interests," explained José Joaquim Teixeira Ribeiro.

"Rather," he added, "it was determined via interactions between persons who operate with a different psychology: the consciousness of public interest." He continued, "It falls to the science of economics to define these values in order to impart on individuals a psychology that is not based in minimum effort for greatest individual return but instead that of minimum sacrifice for maximum social benefit."[45]

As far as consumers were concerned, corporatist theory was vague, more so than in discussions on pricing in the US New Deal or Chile. Some corporatist theorists tried, awkwardly, to fit consumers into their models. In his iconic *O século do corporativismo*, for instance, Mihail Manoilescu briefly discussed consumers as a corrective force to counterbalance the interests of producers and "capitalist enterprises." In his view, consumers in "liberal economic regimes" constituted an "amorphous and disorganized mass." Yet "in a corporatist economy," he contended "consumers of any good are always organized and mobilized for resistance" in part because consumers can easily target which groups to blame for rising prices. In this way, consumers themselves were a type of "sindicato, capable of evaluating their needs and meeting them."[46] He did not elaborate further on his vague notion of consumers as a collective group or explain how this could work in practice. Instead, Manoilescu worried about prices from the perspective of industrialists and agricultural producers, or how to ensure fair remuneration and market entry—an approach that reflected the economic challenges facing predominantly agrarian economies. Fair price, initially at least, was tightly linked to producer interests.

In the years to come, however, corporatist economists attempted to fold consumer interests into their model, especially those trying to advance corporatism as a more just alternative to liberal capitalism. For example, Brazilian economist Felix Contreiras Rodrigues, a disciple of French economist and champion of the cooperative movement Charles Gide, published his doctoral dissertation on corporatist price in 1942, making an economic argument for corporatism by asserting that its price-setting mechanism was essential for social peace. He argued that "no one should be without bread or clothing because this would be harmful to social welfare," which is why the state needed to guarantee prices "at a level accessible to all consumers." He connected the concept of just prices to long-standing Brazilian traditions, but in his view, something shifted in 1930 as the state took greater responsibilities over social welfare. He no longer theorized the market as an aggregate of individual actors but rather an ensemble of collective groups, each with distinct interests: "The justo preço is a distributive formula for collective well-being, and not just for the exclusive well-being of the consumer."[47] Neither consumer nor producer interests could be ignored. This book was widely read, selling out with its first publication in 1942 and going to a second printing in 1951.

In government reports and academic writings, corporatist theorists moved beyond the vague language of social peace by cracking open classical economic theories on how supply and demand *should* determine prices. They pushed convincingly to redefine price instead as a mechanism for disciplining private interests for the public good in order to achieve relative stability in economic life. Government technocrats would take charge of efforts to regulate pricing for goods countrywide, but would do so by consulting with representatives for critical industries in order to rein in the unscrupulous economic behavior that distorted supply and demand for personal gain. Those advocating for this new system rather optimistically predicted that it would lead to "the disappearance of economic crises."[48] Where or how to begin, though, was far less clear.

Price and Production in Portugal

While Brazil and Portugal's economies are quite different in size, structure, and orientation toward export-led growth, Portugal faced similar concerns about rising price levels, especially for food and essential goods, by the mid-1930s. Portugal is an important counterpoint to Brazil partly because its corporatist structure was more consistent with theory and partly because there were fewer competing economic models in Portugal. Therefore it is far easier in the Portuguese case to see how a new notion of corporatist price became integral to the regulation of daily economic life by public institutions.

The consensus among Portuguese historians is that the 1933 constitutional guarantee for fair prices quickly denigrated to a system of monopolistic pricing in which the large landowners, owners of warehouses and silos, and manufacturers of agrarian and industrial outputs represented by grémios were favored over consumers.[49] António de Oliveira Salazar's corporatist utopia and promises of Catholic social justice benefited the few protected by the new system of professional organizations, and left many others—including farmers, fishers, and workers—with depressed wages and higher prices. Within this assessment, the grémio system appears as a mechanism by which Salazar traded economic favors for political support and to maintain power.[50] It was a system rife with corruption and demagogy, behind a facade of technocracy. These conclusions, however, overlook the substance and novelty of corporatist approaches to pricing. They underestimate the unprecedented degree to which the state created or appropriated corporatist organs to recondition how individuals and firms produced as well as consumed goods.

As is so often the case with policymaking in times of crisis, the corporatist solutions implemented in Portugal in the early 1930s were designed to grapple with the recent crisis, namely how the agriculture and fishing sectors suffered bankruptcy and collapse in the 1920s. According to the architects of the Estado

Novo, both foreign competitors (with their dumping schemes) and exploitative national intermediaries had hijacked Portugal's key sectors, sacrificing national producers and consumers alike. Lumbrales recalled the "pathological and abnormal nadir" of prices by the end of the 1920s.[51] Foreign competition had driven national producers out of the market, resulting in a sharp decline in domestic output. Portuguese historians have largely confirmed this assessment for industries like wine or codfish.[52] This context explains why Salazar's promise of social peace was about a harmonious equipoise between the interests of labor and capital as well as guarantees for fair prices for both consumers and producers. Only by stabilizing the internal market could recovery and growth begin.

Salazar and his coterie of economists and agronomists thus saw price guarantees for national producers, in the late 1920s and early 1930s, as the pivotal mechanism by which to stimulate agrarian development. In the short run, the strategy worked. Domestic rice production increased by 252 percent from the early 1920s to the mid-1930s, olive oil output rose by 40 percent from 1925 to 1936, and wheat harvests grew by 171 percent from 1926 to 1935.[53]

Portugal's economic program was coated with a moralizing claim about how corporatism would solve reckless profit-seeking behavior. As Lumbrales explained at a lecture delivered at the University of Coimbra in 1938, grémios and their federations were the only way to "safeguard fair profit . . . , but also guarantee the stable and balanced production [of goods], with dependable prices according to the purchasing power of those involved in the production cycle."[54] In his assessment, the government's actions over the economy were not statist for the sake of control but rather consisted of efforts "to limit competition in order to promote its organic and constructive [properties] by way of curbing and correcting for monopolistic tendencies."[55]

Of course, not all would agree with this utopian assessment of how grémios regulated markets for the greater good. Scholars and opponents of the regime alike discredited corporatist organs for their monopolistic or exploitative power over the economy. Although official regime propaganda celebrated how labor and capital had equal weight in negotiations with the state, in practice the grémios' central function in the national economy was to create an immutable hierarchy of class function and political power that unapologetically buttressed the interests of employers above laborers, or large landowners above rural workers.[56]

That the corporatist scale tilted in favor of grémios was a worrisome dynamic from the start for Pedro Theotónio Pereira, chief architect of Portuguese corporatism. In 1934, in his capacity as subsecretary of state for corporations and social insurance, he fretted that the proliferation of state and parastate institutions, without adequate regulation or economic expertise, would simply turn grémios into "trusts hated by public opinion or transformed into a sort of new commercial association, useless for any constructive action and only adept at making petitions in a whiny tone."[57]

That a formalized system of rights guarantees took time to emerge in Portugal was a frustration that Theotónio Pereira lamented deeply in his blunt assessments on the partial evolution of corporatism. He complained, for instance, that the "corporatist organization comprises only labor syndicates and casas do povo," as employers, industrialists, and large landowners seemed reluctant to collaborate.[58] He felt his efforts to steer Portugal's new social security ministry were squandered. He frequently complained to Salazar, "I work alone on this project and on dangerous territory. I have no ability to act, nor to make others comply with the new laws, not even the ability to ask for your intervention, because weeks go by without being able to catch your ear."[59] Exasperated, he pleaded repeatedly to be allowed to resign.

Among his chief concerns, Theotónio Pereira worried that corporatist organs would degenerate into trusts, cartels, or monopolies—institutions vilified for how they had devastated the small producer and hiked prices in the 1920s. Even worse, corporatist institutions might squander the public's trust and get perceived as little more than class alliances, with each entity clamoring that the state meet its own particular needs. This problem of whether corporatism served the public or private echoed in Brazil.[60] Its relevance across the Atlantic is a testament to how political and economic elites of both nations attempted an alternative to capitalism and communism, yet scarcely considered how opportunities for corruption, defection, or negligence would arise in a system where the state created regulations for all aspects of the economy, with few formal checks and balances.

The other critique launched against the Estado Novo's corporatist organization, by contemporaries and scholars alike, related to its partial implementation and patchiness.[61] Obligatory labor organizations structured some sectors, while others were voluntary ones; regulatory commissions supervised certain industries, while others were left to the vagaries of the free market. Salazar's rhetoric might have been bold in its call for a fully integrated corporatist order, but in practice, the evolution of this system proceeded slowly and cautiously. This was, in part, by design. Corporatism, political scientist Philippe Schmitter would later reflect, only stood a chance if implemented "piece-by-piece, sector-by-sector, level-by-level."[62]

The sluggish pace of corporatist evolution also frustrated some producers. Indeed, citizen petitions from around the nation called for their industry or firm to be incorporated into the corporatist scaffolding of rights and protections. In April 1938, for example, soap makers in Lisbon pleaded with Theotónio Pereira, then serving as minister of commerce and industry, for permission to form a grémio. Alfredo da Silva, the group's spokesperson, drew on the spirit of corporatist justice when he expressed dismay that market disorder threatened their livelihood. Explained Silva, "[With] soap sold at less than its cost [of production], we can scarcely retrieve the costs of raw materials." This ruinous price violated the rights guaranteed under the 1933 Constitution. The language of corporatism suffused his final entreaty: "The creation of a soap makers grémio—in which everyone has their rights and their obligations—is indispensable and urgent in order to put an end to the insubordination that we see practiced [in the industry], and that is the most utter negation of the spirit of the Estado Novo."[63] Despite the soap makers' most earnest pleas, their petition was deflected and ignored.

This was not the only petition that soap manufacturers sent to the Ministry of Commerce and Industry in the late 1930s. The ministry was adamant and inflexible: no grémio would be recognized. The reason, it seemed, was that one of the largest manufacturers of soap in Portugal refused to participate. This was one of many instances in which power and influence over the corporatist structure tilted in favor of larger business interests and sacrificed small-scale producers.[64] Officials in the Ministry of Commerce and Industry found an intermediary solution. In place of a grémio, the soap industry was to be regulated by the Comissão Reguladora das Oleaginosas e Óleos Vegetais (Regulatory Commission for Oilseeds and Vegetable Oils), created in November 1939.[65]

This case illuminates how citizens petitioned for a slice of the corporatist pie as well as the slow pace of the so-called revolution. The example also introduces another set of institutions: regulatory commissions. Another cog in Portugal's corporatist system, these regulatory commissions oversaw *parts* of the production process for the wheat, rice, coal, oilseeds and vegetable oils, metals, pharmaceutical, and chemical industries. The Portuguese government created about twenty regulatory commissions in the 1930s to indirectly administer these industries. For Theotónio Pereira, opting for regulatory commissions in place of grémios was not a betrayal of corporatist ideals; rather, these commissions were provisional "precorporatist" organisms that would create the conditions for the deeper institutionalization of the corporatist project. Ironically, these regulatory commissions would survive the Estado Novo's collapse in 1974, continuing the task of economic planning to the present.[66]

The Portuguese economy in the 1930s, then, was organized by a burgeoning set of *grémios obrigatórios* (mandatory grémios, largely for export sectors), *grémios facultativos* (voluntary associations for firms), *grémios da lavoura* (farmers' associations), *sindicatos nacionais* (national labor unions), and *casas do povo* and *casas dos pescadores* (welfare and social security institutions for farmers and fishers, respectively). These professional organisms formed the base of the social and economic pyramid. The second level was comprised of umbrella class federations and unions—*federações* and *uniões*—that grouped together the local-level labor associations for each sector and in turn played a heavy hand in regulation. This tier overlaid regional landscapes with functional representation. Unions and federations were either created by the state (for key sectors) or voluntarily convened, but always subjected to government approval and oversight. At the tip of the pyramid were *corporações* (corporations), which lumped together federações and uniões according to broadly defined industries: agriculture, fishing, commerce, transportation, and so on. Yet the government only inaugurated the first corporation in 1956. In the interim, three alternative organizations functioned as provisional corporations after 1936: *comissões reguladoras, institutos*, and *juntas*. With these regulatory commissions, appointed state officials exercised administrative powers over a given sector, including to set prices, inspect production methods and product quality, grant subsidies, provide technical assistance, and intervene in the purchase, sale, and warehouse of goods.[67] Taken together, the institutions were "organisms of economic coordination."[68]

In short, the Portuguese economy was coordinated by a myriad of parallel or intersecting corporatist or precorporatist institutions, overseen by several ministries. As difficult as it is for researchers today to piece together how these economic bodies functioned, given multiple archives and voluminous paper trails, it was equally confusing for those who lived under this system, as each of these branches had its own regulatory police and mode of enforcement.

This corporatist regulatory system centered on price controls also extended to the colonies. During the 1930s, to counteract the country's geopolitical vulnerabilities, Estado Novo officials worked tirelessly to resuscitate Portugal's imperial reputation. In 1934, the popular slogan *Portugal não é país pequeno* (Portugal is not a small country) appeared on a map in which Portugal and its colonies filled in much of western Europe (figure 4.2). Propaganda and slogans were not sufficient, though. Portuguese officials, agronomists, economists, and business agents set out to implement a new program, as the early twentieth-century idiom of civilizing mission gave way to that of economic development. Essential to its imperialist ideology, the Estado Novo regime sponsored programs to increase Portuguese settlements in the colonies, offering farmers free passage, housing, and land to encourage their migration to Angola and Mozambique.[69] The white settler population of Angola increased 50 percent between 1930 and 1940—a trend that intensified after the 1945 period, but never reached official targets.[70] While historians generally agree that the Estado Novo's project to turn European farmers into the bedrock of colonial commodity production was suffused with setbacks and inconsistencies, the corporatist organisms created in the 1930s nonetheless established the institutional architecture for colonial trade.

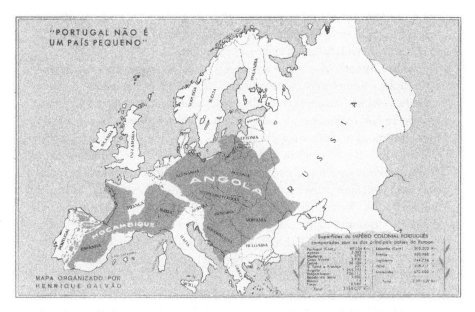

FIGURE 4.2. Map *Portugal não é um país pequeno* (Portugal is not a small country) by Portuguese army officer Henrique Galvão (1934). Displayed at the I Exposição Colonial Portuguesa (First Portuguese Colonial Exhibition) in Porto. First published in Henrique Galvão, *No rumo do império* (Porto: Litografia Nacional, 1934). Image courtesy of Cornell University PJ Mode Collection of Persuasive Cartography.

Portugal's corporatist system was neomercantilist in that it offered a model for imperial preference and protectionism in order to tighten commercial ties between the metropole and colonies.[71] Mercantilist logic holds that when a nation must import food or raw materials, it is better to import from its colonies than from another country.

In Salazarist Portugal as in Vichy France and elsewhere, governments abandoned indirect rule and tried to minimize the role of private concessionaires. Historian Frederick Cooper locates the origins of the developmentalist state in these interwar projects to transform colonial economies in order to supply metropolitan markets.[72] Imperial bureaucrats embraced corporatist planning to safeguard colonial markets from foreign competition, guaranteeing raw materials to Portuguese industrialists and consumers. The same individuals who theorized corporatism also worked in colonial administration. This was true for Luís da Cunha Gonçalves, who served in several civil servant and advisory positions in Mozambique and Goa. Caetano, moreover, became minister of the colonies in 1944. As Caetano asserted, "The corporatist system is not a new label for old vices of bureaucracy."[73] Instead, the corporatist state insisted on order and discipline—a discipline imposed via the "coordination of metropolitan interests and colonial production."[74]

Estado Novo officials created several corporatist and paracorporatist institutions in the colonies to regulate economic life. Much of Portugal's signature corporatist legislation applied equally to the colonies, including the 1933 Estatuto do Trabalho Nacional, or Labor Charter, which outlined the role of grémios, sindicatos, and other regulatory organs. In this spirit, the Ministry of the Colonies recognized grémios and sindicatos to represent colonial workers, producers, and exporters. These programs, which focused on colonial exports such as coffee, cotton, or vegetable oils, were concentrated in Angola, the largest and wealthiest Portuguese colony, and (to a lesser extent) Mozambique. As corporatist institutions, their initial function was to "cultivate a corporatist consciousness and develop a sense of solidarity" among those employed in a given sector.[75] The ultimate aim of these corporatist bodies was to stimulate the production of raw materials and foodstuffs to supply the Portuguese market.[76]

Portugal had started its corporatist experiment with wheat, and so this commodity also became the focus of early campaigns in the colonies. In 1933, Decree Law No. 22.981 created the Grémio do Milho Colonial Português. Headquartered in Lisbon, the grémio had branches in the colonies to represent colonial corn exporters and metropolitan consignees. When founded, it had twenty-six members, largely based in Angola. The grémio's primary task was not to "accumulate profits"—corn was too "poor" an industry according to one official—but rather to encourage corn production by guaranteeing "a just price" to producers.[77] Imperial bureaucrats created this grémio to respond to the "numerous complaints" that corn merchants had sent to the government over the years. While corn is not often considered an important colonial staple, corn exports gradually increased in the 1920s and 1930s. By 1940, corn had become Angola's second most valuable export after diamonds.[78]

By the late 1930s, the Ministry of the Colonies looked for ways to have more direct control over colonial production, and in 1937, created the Junta de Exportacão dos Cereais das Colonias, a regulatory commission responsible for all grain exports from the colonies. For some, the junta threatened the grémio's autonomy by divesting it of regulatory powers, and conflict erupted between these two agencies. This was not just a matter of red tape but instead a bigger crisis in which the meaning of corporatism would shift. For colonial corn exporters, the junta amounted to a government takeover of their business, as they decried that "the corporatist organization had usurped their natural rights."[79] They called the junta a bureaucratic behemoth, without the agility or responsiveness to deal with deteriorating market conditions. But those working for the government-appointed junta retorted that the grémio was never one in the pure, organic sense. In their view, the grémio was a commercial association concerned with profits and private gain just like concessionaires and firms, without concern for Portugal's development.

Portuguese imperial bureaucrats also set out to reorganize coffee and sugar sectors according to this corporatist logic, along with dried fish, cotton, and vegetable oils. In 1937, for example, the Ministry of the Colonies created the Comissão Reguladora do Comércio de Algodão em Rama (Cotton Regulatory Commission) to coordinate the colonial cotton supply to metropolitan textiles and shortly thereafter the Junta de Exportação do Algodão Colonial, a government-appointed board representing cotton exporters. Regulatory commissions like these operated in Portugal and the colonies, integrating all agents in the supply chain for textiles, soaps, and other industrial end products into a single agency. Practically speaking, regulatory commissions issued licenses to metropolitical importers, which all belonged to a state-approved grémio.[80] The government established control over the purchase and distribution of raw materials with corporatist organs, thereby exercising control over metropolitan industries.

The motivation driving the creation of new regulatory commissions was straightforward: imperial officials needed to encourage colonial growers to produce more goods. With cotton, for instance, Portugal's textile industry had nearly quadrupled between 1900 and 1924, but colonial cotton production could not keep pace with the rising demand of metropolitan industrialists. Portuguese firms had to purchase cotton on the global market, which only worsened the country's balance of payments deficit.[81] Once Salazar took control of the Ministry of the Colonies, cotton became one of the first sectors subjected to corporatist experimentation, primarily in Mozambique, partly for the financial stakes and partly because it was a raw material that the colonies could in fact supply. In the early 1930s, imperial officials experimented with several different programs to stimulate cotton production, including efforts to encourage Portuguese rural workers to migrate to Mozambique. Despite modest gains in cotton production, the supply did not meet the demand of Portugal's textile industry. Salazar opted for a corporatist strategy after 1937 with the creation of the junta. The junta had five members, each appointed by the minister of the colonies, to represent the textile industry, shipping interests, and colonial producers. It designed and executed several programs to stimulate production, including the hire of local inspectors and agronomists to identify new production zones, set the timeline for planting and harvests, and especially, fixed the prices for farmers and export firms alike. As historian Allen Isaacman notes, the junta "became the vehicle through which an economically rational and highly repressive system of production and marketing was to supersede the chaotic arrangements of previous years."[82]

In practical terms, the government's primary mechanism for regulating supply and production was price. In cotton, for example, the regulatory commission allotted cotton quotas to importers at fixed prices—a policy that complemented bans on the purchase of foreign cotton until all colonial cotton was placed with a metropolitan buyer. Protectionist policies to tighten commercial links between Portugal and its colonies could only work if the government rigorously enforced price controls and quotas too. Regulatory commissions and grémios issued price controls to mitigate the volatility in global commodity prices in the 1930s and 1940s, but it is important not to overstate the successes of this economic planning.

Imperial officials designed this corporatist architecture to service the interests of metropolitan importers and industries. With only export sectors afforded corporatist representation, many Portuguese settlers were excluded from rights and protections codified into law. In practice, firms often refused to pay minimum salaries or create social insurance institutions.[83] Native African populations, those laboring in harsh conditions to cultivate commodity exports, were explicitly excluded from membership in any corporatist associations. According to the 1937 Decree Law No. 27.552, which outlined Portugal's corporatist system in the colonies, the "political, civil, criminal, economic, and labor status" of Indigenous workers "continue[d] to be governed by the special laws in place."[84] More than exclusionary, this corporatist system would become the catalyst for new forms of legalized forced labor across the Portuguese colonies in order to coerce African farmers into growing colonial staples.[85] Effectively, Portugal's corporatist system hardened and legalized the social and racial hierarchies of colonial life.

By the late 1930s, Portuguese officials had largely abandoned their initial emphasis on an organic and associationalist system in which voluntary associations regulated their own sectors to spearhead a technocratic project in which the state used corporatist organs to regulate the production and distribution of goods. This shift was as evident in Portugal as across its empire. Many scholars, however, point to the "tentacular control" that Portugal's state extended over most industries with this expanding bureaucracy as evidence that corporatism was mere rhetoric.[86] But to evaluate the progress of corporatism according to the decentralized vision of some of its earliest proponents fails to take into account how Portuguese officials continually updated their thinking on how this system should work. This is especially evident when we examine a central objective for corporatist dictatorships: price as an instrument for social peace and economic stability. Portuguese officials argued for statist control over grémios and other corporatist organs because they concluded that only the state could take into account all collective interests to achieve a truly fair price.

Price and Production in Brazil

In Brazil, the project to organize agriculture according to this corporatist structure was enthusiastically supported in some circles, but proved far more challenging to implement than in Portugal. This was precisely the task that Arthur
Eugênio Torres Filho of the Conselho Federal de Comércio Exterior (Federal
Council for Foreign Trade, or CFCE) took on in April 1935 when he adminis-
tered a qualitative and quantitative survey across Brazil to gauge national economic activity. It began with the problem of price. Its first and second questions
were, "What factors contributed to price oscillations?" and "What are the types
of price oscillations seen in your local markets?" For Torres Filho, poor transportation and limited coordination between producer and consumer markets
were to blame for rising prices. "The instability of prices for agricultural products," he lamented, represented "one of the most serious barriers to our commercial expansion."[87] The notion that the federal government would intervene
in the economy was no longer controversial, but the elements of that intervention were still undetermined. Price ceilings and price controls would become
one of the primary solutions implemented in Brazil to address price instability,
and one of the most pervasive forms of economic planning in Brazil.

The CFCE was the most important *conselho técnico*, or advisory council,
created during the Vargas presidency, and its survey of economic activity was
the first step in tackling price controls.[88] Historian John Wirth describes this
advisory organ as the "personal instrument" of Vargas.[89] Vargas handpicked
its members, chosen from the Ministries of Foreign Relations, Finance, Agriculture, and Labor. In corporatist fashion, its members also included industry
representatives, appointed by professional associations, and several técnicos.
Rather than an example of Vargas's arbitrary powers, the CFCE might instead
be construed as a technocratic push to bypass the legislative branch as the
locus of economic policymaking. It forged direct channels between the private
sector and government.[90] Several Brazilian historians note that CFCE powers
increased over the years to constitute a centralizing organ for economic coordination.[91] Its mode of centralization, however, also preserved the influence
of key sectors over federal policy by formalizing their role in a new bureaucracy. In these ways, the CFCE mirrored the corporatist chambers of Salazar's
Portugal or Mussolini's Italy.

To foreign observers, the CFCE was largely responsible for Brazil's balance
of trade.[92] Yet its abundance of committees, institutes, and commissions regulated more than exports; they also tried to increase the production of goods
for the internal market. Efforts to build an internal consumer market for national goods, writes economic historian Rosemary Thorp, were essential
elements of economic nationalism in Brazil, even before import substitution

industrialization dominated after 1945. Brazil's economic recovery after 1929 depended on both continued protections for export sectors and new efforts to diversify domestic industries.[93] In the 1930s and 1940s, the CFCE was at the center of these economic policy decisions in Brazil.[94] Its deliberative nature makes it difficult to determine its direct influence on government economic interventions. But its research orientation distinguished the CFCE as a groundbreaking institution insofar as it centralized the study and collection of data on economic affairs. For 1930s' Brazil, the CFCE archive makes possible research into how midlevel bureaucrats, jurists, intellectuals, and politicians thought about the economy and their capacity to transform it.

Ideology shaped the types of plans and policies debated, but not systematically. Bold economic ambitions were often tempered by the tedium of policymaking within Brazil's growing bureaucracy. As is typical of policymaking in times of crisis, there was too much to fix and too many different policies tossed around for intellectual consistency. Brazil desperately required banking and infrastructure reforms to expand credit and improve transportation. These proposals echoed earlier efforts by positivist engineers in the late nineteenth and early twentieth centuries, but other economic proposals were informed by the rise of a corporatist worldview among an influential group of bureaucrats.[95] This trend is especially apparent in proposals to reorganize agricultural production, as much for export as for domestic consumption. Torres Filho did not always discuss his policy proposals explicitly in the corporatist idiom, but he consistently positioned the federal government as the necessary arbitrator between various sectors in order to promote regional specialization. Both Campos and Oliveira Vianna theorized corporatism as a paradoxical model of what Oliveira Vianna called a "regime that is at once centralizing and decentralizing."[96] Torres Filho outlined some of the practical implications of this approach: the regional specialization of agricultural production in order to satisfy domestic consumption. For Brazil to forge its path forward, as Torres Filho explained, it needed to "trade within our own borders."[97]

Torres Filho is one of the many forgotten Vargas era bureaucrats, with no memoir, biography, or historical study to provide perspective on his work for the CFCE. Born in 1889 in the state of Rio de Janeiro, he was the son of planters whose economic and social status was in decline. His best option was to move from the countryside to the city. In 1910, he graduated with an engineering degree from the Escola Superior de Agricultura Luiz de Queiroz in São Paulo and then worked in the Ministry of Agriculture, Industry, and Commerce from 1921 to 1931.[98] By 1929, Torres Filho was trying to impress on his superiors how World War I had crystallized new responsibilities for the federal government. Looking to reforms across the Atlantic, in Portugal and Italy, to increase domestic food production, he emphasized that without conscious efforts to modernize agriculture, Brazil would inevitably be "subjected to the vicissitudes of a serious crisis."[99] Following the Ministry of Agriculture, he was voted vice president (1931–44) of the Sociedade Nacional de Agricultura (National Agricultural Society) and then its president (1945–46).[100] Thanks to his position with the National Agricultural Society, Vargas appointed Torres Filho to the CFCE in 1934 to represent agriculture interests. In this capacity, he drafted legislation as well as advised on matters related to agricultural production, food prices, and national development.[101] He pushed for the organization of agricultural production into state-regulated cooperatives and recognized the central role of the federal state in establishing equilibrium between various economic interests.[102] He was a partisan of *estadismo*, or statism, and embraced elements of the corporatist model, even advocating for agrarian policies inspired by Mussolini's Italy and Salazar's Portugal. Torres Filho championed the expansion of corporatist institutions to rural areas and even proposed legislation to organize agrarian labor into grémios, as in the Portuguese model.

Like others of Torres Filho's generation, his statist-leaning proposals stemmed from a profound disenchantment with the liberal and federalist First Republic. Nostalgia for the Brazilian Empire was palpable in his assessment of how national unity and economic stability had disintegrated since 1889. On the eve of the 1930 Revolution, Torres Filho detailed the "shocks to the economic order during the [First] Republic, of which the abolition of slavery was the most severe, with its consequences still felt today." For Torres Filho, the failure of Republican promises of "order and progress" rested partly with the "lack of economic programs to promote the welfare of different social classes."[103] His concern for the social question was largely to find ways to avoid or neutralize class conflict. He devoted far more attention to agrarian modernization and often argued that Brazil's "new economy" could not emerge from the breakdown of the First Republic if focused only on the labor question. In his view, social peace depended on the production of consumer staples—and price.

A champion of growth from within, Torres Filho engaged arguments and policies circulating globally, with a particular interest in Italy, Portugal, and France. His CFCE reports treated corporatism in technical and economic terms in an attempt to shield his policy solutions from polarizing ideological contexts. Beyond his bureaucratic postings, he nonetheless was intellectually invested in charting alternatives to liberalism. Torres Filho penned a handful of opinion pieces for Brazilian periodicals in which he combined his statist economic vision with moral discourses on how corporatism could remake modern society and rebuild nations. He published his ideological musings in *Hierarchia*, the short-lived monthly review on politics and economics with an outwardly anticommunist and antiliberal bent, founded by Lourival Fontes, future director of the Departamento de Imprensa e Propaganda (Department of Press and Propaganda) under Vargas. In its brief circulation, *Hierarchia* had a notably Catholic, nationalist, and corporatist flair. In 1932, Torres Filho contributed the essay "Mussolini e a Nova Italia," assessing Italy's economic organization with a focus on its agricultural development. His well-researched synthesis concluded that "without the calm and disciplined environment like that which Mussolini created with the establishment of Fascism, it would not be possible to achieve the economic equilibrium seen in Italy today."[104]

The term *equilíbrio*, or equilibrium, was ubiquitous in the 1930s. It encapsulated the goal of so many technocrats, economists, and intellectuals searching for solutions to the disruptions of the previous twenty years, from price volatility to social unrest and class conflict. Brazil, they argued, suffered general economic disequilibrium, evident in its weak internal consumer markets, the difficulties and high costs of moving goods from one region to another, and the lack of cooperation across classes and economic interests. Their concept of equilibrium, in other words, stretched beyond Keynesian concerns about aggregate demand and employment. Those who supported the corporatist model idealized balance, harmony, and equilibrium as they described how workers should interact with their employers, or how producers should advocate for their sector to government. The creation of commodity agencies to regulate coffee or wheat production were not just economic instruments that would set prices or quotas but also political organs that would represent producers and labor vis-à-vis the state. For Valdemar Falcão (figure 4.3), labor minister from 1937 to 1941, only a corporatist system could guarantee both representation and discipline, with a formula for state intervention that avoided both the "excesses of the fascist regime" and "defects of the Soviet system" in order "to create a state of harmony and equilibrium between all productive forces and labor forces."[105]

Price was neither the only variable where different groups staked their interests nor the only fulcrum for social peace. Nevertheless, in the eyes of key theorists such as Campos or Oliveira Vianna, it was politically easier to discuss prices than wages.

Those in Brazil who argued for price as an essential variable in corporatist social peace did so through unlikely intellectual channels. Gide became one of the most commonly cited foreign economists. Torres Filho, for example, used Gide to contend that prices—rather than wages—distinguished corporatism from socialism; the former saw "the consumer and not the salaried worker as the victim." It followed, as Torres Filho quoted Gide, that "the goal should be to abolish profit and all other factors that increase the cost of production, or in other words, the establishment of a just price."[106] One can assume that Torres Filho, who remained firmly committed to protections for private property, did not actually support calls to abolish profit but rather wanted to limit unjust profits. Whatever the case, borrowed concepts frequently did not align perfectly with the borrower's position. Writing thirty years after Gide, Brazilian officials like Torres Filho hybridized the French economist's model with other

FIGURE 4.3. (*right to left*) Labor Minister Waldemar Falcão and Justice Minister Francisco Campos at the Ministério do Trabalho Indústria e Comércio (November 1937). Both ministers spearheaded efforts to codify corporatist ideas into law during the Estado Novo. Image courtesy of the Centro de Pesquisa e Documentação de História Contempoânea do Brasil, Fundação Getúlio Vargas.

state-centric models in order to defend a new project for Brazil's agrarian sector. His corporatist vision and Gide's cooperative movement were at ideological odds in many ways, with the former emphasizing hierarchical and state-imposed modes of coordination, while the latter stressed autonomous and self-governing approaches. But Torres Filho united these systems because all "civilized nations" were working to reconcile "individual initiatives" with the "superior interests of the nation."[107] He incorporated the French economist's model on how to harmonize the interests of consumers and producers into his own frameworks, and especially appreciated that Gide put price at the core of economic debates.[108]

The transnational circulation of ideas from many places—New Deal programs or Scandinavian cooperatives—seeped into even the most tedious bureaucratic reports. Yet examples from Italy or Portugal held a privileged place for Brazilian technocrats. By the mid-1930s, southern European corporatist experiments offered more than theoretical critiques of liberal and laissez-faire models. Portugal as much as Italy offered tangible illustrations of how to reorganize agriculture according to a corporatist mode of production.

In 1936, for example, Torres Filho was tasked with addressing the problem of rising flour prices in Brazil. In 1935, Brazil had only 145,000 hectares of land under wheat cultivation, largely in the southern states—fewer than in 1929. Domestic producers could only meet 20 percent of the domestic consumption, and by 1937 wheat imports accounted for 13 percent of Brazilian imports.[109] The drive to increase wheat production was part of a broader push for economic self-sufficiency in Brazil. Officials hoped to design a wheat campaign that could reduce the country's dependency on imports. For Oswaldo Aranha, ambassador to the United States, Brazil's persistent balance of payments problem threatened to turn the country into an "economic vassal with the [corresponding] political humiliations." Brazil's challenge was its dependency on petroleum and wheat imports, but the ambassador was optimistic that it could produce a "substitute" for oil, and "could and should produce" more wheat.[110]

The economic problems posed by Brazil's dependency on wheat imports also spawned social problems: rising prices for this essential food staple were eroding the purchasing power of wages. On top of the dependency on foreign markets, the price of flour continued to rise. While the price of flour fell by 8 percent between 1929 and 1933, it was on the rise again. In Rio de Janeiro, flour prices increased by 26 percent in 1936 and 17 percent in 1937.[111] In order to support growing industrial centers in São Paulo, Minas Gerais, or Rio de Janeiro, food prices had to be kept moderate so that workers would not demand higher wages. Concerns about rising prices for wheat flour also aggravated anxieties among Brazilian social scientists and technocrats about the diets of popular classes in this multiracial and multiethnic society.[112] Debates over which commodity staples were necessary to feed Brazilians were sometimes entangled with racist discourses about the superiority of wheat to other staples like manioc, with the former associated with European diets, and the latter with Afro-Brazilian and Indigenous diets. For Agamenon Magalhães, labor minister from 1934 to 1937, the problem of high bread prices was not only an economic one; it was necessary to increase "the national consumption of this product [bread from wheat flour], in a nation like ours, still undergoing its racial formation, where bread is not yet, but needs to become, a staple of popular diets, and for that reason, made accessible to the poorer classes."[113]

Brazilian officials blamed exorbitant flour prices on merchants and other intermediaries.[114] In Brazil, only a few merchants could import wheat. Mills, in turn, formed a vertical monopoly with wheat importers, which kept the price of flour artificially high. In Torres Filho's view, merchants and millers were pernicious intermediaries between producers and consumers. His assessment on Brazil's wheat problem was one shared by many of his peers. Many of the proposals that circulated in these years were steeped in an antitrust logic that motivated much of the ire against the free market.

The wheat campaigns of Portugal and Italy provided a blueprint for how to deal with intermediaries. Torres Filho proposed the creation of what he called an Instituto Federal do Trigo (National Wheat Institute) to organize wheat production "in accordance with legislation adopted in other countries, like Portugal and Italy."[115] Millers would be required to include a fixed proportion of national wheat in flour and be responsible for distributing flour to end users (largely bakers) proportionate to the needs of that region. Others within the CFCE agreed, even as they debated the finer points for years to come. CFCE delegate João Maria de Lacerda, a representative for the Ministry of Labor, echoed this call for a national wheat institute, and also modeled his proposal on Italy and Portugal's wheat campaigns. Lacerda's proposal called for propaganda efforts to encourage more producers to cultivate wheat as well as government support for machinery and mills. It included several corporatist elements, namely the creation of state-supported farmers syndicates and producer associations dedicated to wheat cultivation.[116]

Across proposals, Brazilian bureaucrats debated different ways to organize and vertically integrate producers into a federal agency. Ultimately, however, President Vargas could freely appoint the agronomists and government representatives heading these organs, which also created spaces for clientelism and political favor to shape economic planning, even as Brazil's technocrats aspired to root this out. During debates over Brazil's Wheat Campaign, for example, one of Vargas's brothers wrote to him to recommend an agronomist from Rio Grande do Sul to sit on the wheat institute's directory board, arguing for this candidate's professional qualifications, but also mentioning that he had "helped us in '30 and '32"—a reference to the political revolts that had solidified Vargas's grasp on power. They should "not forget him."[117]

The question of whether and how to create a national institute to organize wheat production was also eagerly debated in the public sphere, with proposals circulating in the press. Those in favor of a national wheat institute celebrated the successes of Italy's and Portugal's programs, emphasizing that corporatist strategies to organize millers and producers would keep foreign agents out and thereby protect domestic producers from ruinous competition. Key to this type of federal intervention in the wheat market was that the government would guarantee producers a prenegotiated "remunerative price" for the good, thereby encouraging more cultivation and ensuring the economic well-being of this group.[118] Political consensus around the organization and scope of such a national institute proved difficult to secure, however, given the ideological polarization in Brazil under the short-lived 1934 Constitution. But parts of Lacerda and Torres Filho's proposal did make their way into law. Brazil's plan to lower "unjustifiable" high bread prices included the creation of a special commission to break the grasp of powerful trusts over wheat imports, implement lower tariffs, and mandate that all flour milled in Brazil include a fixed proportion of national wheat.[119] In support of this policy's strict enforcement, Labor Minister Falcão later noted, "Bread does not become more expensive only because of the actions of bakers but also because of the rates charged by the millers, as we have seen here in Rio de Janeiro and elsewhere."[120]

Brazilian officials recognized the international and national dimensions to the food supply problem, but their ire was squarely directed at the intermediary firms they blamed for profiting from crisis. As president of the recently created Comissão Central de Compras (Central Purchases Commission), Otto Schilling was responsible for purchasing goods for the federal government. As the government created new agencies to oversee health and social services, and invested more in infrastructure and public works, it increased its purchases of raw materials.[121] Wheat was one of the goods this agency purchased in bulk to store in its warehouses. In Schilling's economic worldview, profit and greed were the engines behind the interruptions to global supply chains that triggered the rise and fall of prices. To hold private agents accountable, the government needed to do more. For Schilling, in order to "effectively combat the economic dictatorship imposed by the cartels, trust, and monopolies—the 'deformations of capitalism that work against the popular classes, small producers, merchants, and consumers'—the federal state needed to intervene to regulate the parasitic mills that operated near Brazil's ports and worked in cahoots with wheat importers." Such tirades against the workings of capitalism echoed arguments elaborated by economic thinkers across the ideological spectrum, from those still faithful to liberal models to those writing communist pamphlets and citing Karl Marx or J. A. Hobson. But for Schilling, these injustices would be rectified with mills that belonged to a "corporatist system tightly controlled by a federal department" that would take charge "in the calculation and fixing of prices."[122] Corporatism was touted as a way to tame the corrosive distortions of the market on prices.

By November 1937, when Vargas inaugurated his Estado Novo, Brazil's federal bureaucracy looked very different than in 1930. New ministries and agencies now had formal powers to intervene in pricing or mandate membership in a sindicato to work in a particular trade. Brazilian officials increasingly saw price as the key variable for solving economic challenges. With the cost of living rising, they experimented with price controls as a straightforward enough way to address challenges facing agricultural producers and urban consumers alike. Their proposals drew inspiration from corporatist transformations underway in other parts of the world. From offices in Rio de Janeiro, they would attempt to manage supply chains nationwide in order to guarantee social harmony between farmers and workers, employers and employees, and producers and consumers.

Amid this urgency for transformative action, some sectors were totally transformed while others, despite bold promises, changed more on paper than in

practice. In some ways, the 1937 coup that established Vargas's corporatist dictatorship did not radically alter the economic program underway. Rather, his
usurpation of democratic institutions made it easier to centralize economic
decision-making in the executive branch, thereby making possible the deepening of government involvement in economic life. Many of the more radical
ideas outlined in the 1937 Constitution were never realized, nor did the corporatist model it prescribed get implemented according to the ideal. But just as
the 1930 Revolution galvanized decree laws and new institutions to jump-start
economic development, the 1937 coup unleashed new energy to deepen what
Vargas had started in 1930.

Immediately following the 1937 coup, a vocal group of CFCE delegates
pushed to overhaul national commodity institutes to more closely mirror the
corporatist spirit of the 1937 Constitution. Lacerda, for example, called to reorganize the Instituto do Açúcar e do Álcool (Institute of Sugar and Alcohol) to
be more corporatist.[123] As both a Labor Ministry civil servant and CFCE delegate, Lacerda was leading Brazil's corporatist transformation. While more of
a middling bureaucrat than a visionary thinker, he provided rare insights into
how new economic ideas infiltrated policymaking. In 1938, alongside another
Labor Ministry official, he published *O Estado Novo: Democracia e corporatismo*, a book celebrating corporatism as the only viable path for the "economic
transformation" underway in Brazil.[124] Beyond the generalizations that
marked so much of the intellectual production on corporatism in these years,
Lacerda and his coauthor Eloy de Moura leveraged their technical experience
to defend the corporatist model. In 1930s' Brazil, as in other parts of the world,
theory and policy were being designed in tandem.

Debates over the corporatist structure of commodity production were both
national and transnational. Some of the technocrats who most fiercely supported corporatism spent some time in Europe and wrote about their visits
to Italy or Portugal, offering rare glimpses into how big ideas made their way into
government policy. Lacerda was one of the many Brazilian statespeople to
travel to Portugal in the interwar decades as part of the intellectual and political
networks that bound the two Estado Novos. On the eve of the 1937 coup,
Lacerda went to Lisbon, representing the Ministry of Labor, to promote closer
commercial and intellectual ties between the two countries. There, he delivered a speech that affirmed how both nations were united in a "great battle for
the future," no doubt a reference to a book recently published by the chief
architect of Portuguese corporatism: Theotónio Pereira's *A batalha do futuro:
Organização corporativa*.[125]

In April 1938, informed by these exchanges, Lacerda set out to reform the
sugar industry in ways strikingly similar to the Portuguese corporatist system.
He proposed an organ governed by representatives of all parts of the supply

chain, elected by their respective professional associations and labor sindicatos, which in turn represented landowners, owners of sugar mills and distilleries, sugarcane planters, and other rural workers employed in the industry. The institute would be responsible for collective contracts between these groups.[126] More important, it would "guarantee an internal equilibrium between annual harvests and the consumption of sugar" as well as "promote the manufacture of alcohol," especially for fuel.[127] Brazilian officials worried about the country's dependence on petroleum imports, which is why this state-led effort to increase sugar production became essential to a bigger push for economic self-sufficiency. In contrast with state-led efforts to stabilize coffee production and prices, sugar and its by-products were destined for the internal market, not external markets as was the case with coffee. In other words, the Instituto do Açúcar e do Álcool was not export oriented.

Reforms in 1938 and subsequent years increased federal oversight of the sugar industry, with the Instituto do Açúcar e do Álcool granted a monopoly on exports alongside greater powers to regulate commercial relations between *usineiros* (sugar mill owners) and cane farmers.[128] The institute became responsible for labor disputes and the fulcrum for negotiations between usineiros and workers was not only wages, but also prices. This institute exercised price controls to encourage sugar production in new production zones and stabilize sugar prices for ethanol manufacturers.[129] The prices set by the institute were also essential to the material and social well-being of cane farmers, which consequently turned prices into an arena of social conflict and labor activism for decades to come.[130]

After the 1937 coup, many more institutos were created for other sectors as well, including the Instituto Nacional de Carnes for the meat industry, Instituto Nacional do Mate for yerba maté (used to make the popular maté infusion drink), and Instituto Nacional do Sal for salt. The design differed according to the sector, yet all of these national institutes combined policies to stabilize producer prices in order to encourage production. Price control was the core driver and unifying element across how the national institutes functioned, and how they put corporatist theory into practice. While some of the national institutes managed commodities destined for export markets, they were by and large focused on increasing the production of essential goods for domestic consumers, especially after the outbreak of World War II in 1939. The Instituto Nacional de Carnes, for example, had to figure out how to feed a growing and industrializing nation.[131] One CFCE delegate even proposed quotas on meat destined for export markets so that the "needs of the internal market" could be satisfied first.[132] This marked a dramatic shift in economic orientation. Before 1930, the chief concern for economic elites was how Brazilian beef could compete with Argentinean beef on the international market. Brazilian officials now argued that meeting domestic consumption needs was the urgent precondition for economic growth.

The matter of price was invariably a key rationale for the national institutes as an instrument that could incentivize greater production and ensure social peace. "The first test for our corporatist organization," boasted the president of the Instituto Nacional do Mate, "was to ensure an equilibrium between production and consumption so as to stabilize prices."[133] The Instituto Nacional do Mate, created in 1938, coordinated between the various producer cooperatives that cultivated yerba maté in southern Brazil. The growth of cooperatives was another consequence of Brazil's drive to increase agricultural production in the 1930s—a trend folded into its corporatist makeover. The earliest legislation to regulate agricultural cooperatives dated to 1903, but Vargas's provisional government replaced this law with Decree No. 22.239 in 1932 to limit the autonomy that cooperatives enjoyed. After the 1937 coup, Brazil's government increased its regulation of cooperatives, but so did the regulatory powers that cooperatives could exercise over their sector. The pace at which producers formed and joined cooperatives for agriculture, fishing, and animal husbandry accelerated through the 1930s. According to the Ministry of Agriculture, Brazil had 172 registered cooperatives in 1930—a number that increased to 744 cooperatives by 1938, and 1,574 cooperatives by 1942.[134] São Paulo had the largest number, followed by Rio Grande do Sul.[135] Following the Estado Novo's corporatist logic, the Instituto Nacional do Mate, for instance, oversaw the *agremiação*, or organization, of growers into cooperatives so that individual behaviors aligned with national economic objectives. In theory, this organ exercised control over local producers via licensing and pricing schemes. Most maté was produced for local consumption, but those maté firms that wanted to export had to furnish *guias de exportação*, or export licenses. Similar controls were introduced for domestic consumption. Venders needed *guias de livre transito*, or free trade licenses, to sell locally.[136] Licensing schemes became a mechanism for state control over local production. Directives handed down by commodity institutes to producers were enforced via the punitive application of the law, with fines or revoked licenses for repeat offenders. Producers protested restrictions to their trade even as they benefited from some of the protections afforded.

Despite bold promises for economic equilibrium and market fairness, small producers and consumers denounced commodity institutes from the start. In the case of the Instituto Nacional do Mate, for example, producer cooperatives from Brazil's southern states complained of how it acted with impunity with its market controls. In one telegram from Porto Alegre, the capital of Rio Grande do Sul, an aggrieved citizen described how inspectors "protected by old caudillismo" confiscated maté from venders, only to forcibly sell it back to them at the official rate so that they could go about their commerce.[137] Consumers also complained, citing incidents in which they purchased maté not dried in the traditional manner or sold at egregious prices. Grievances against the Instituto Nacional do Mate reveal the corporatist ambitions—and abuses—that marked this moment of state building in Brazil.

Accounts of fraud, corruption, and abuses launched against the Instituto Nacional do Mate matched those raised by popular classes against the other commodity consortia. Complaints from consumers and small producers articulated demands for market justice. Some called for the state to not just protect the interests of national producers but also defend the *economia popular*, literally the people's savings or people's pocketbook—a category that Vargas turned into promises to defend consumers against unscrupulous market behavior. State-led efforts to transform the national economy created new spaces for people to petition for fair prices too, and protest the economic hardships they faced as producers, rural workers, or consumers.

———

One of the most important legacies of the Vargas era was the transformation from economic regionalism to economic nationalism. For decades, if not centuries, Brazil's economy had been highly decentralized, segmented according to regional export sectors: coffee from São Paulo, cattle from Minas Gerais, sugar from Pernambuco, and rubber from the Amazon.[138] In the 1930s, a rising cohort of bureaucrats—trained in law, finance, economics, and statistics—set their sights on the development of a *national* economy. As much as Vargas celebrated the rise of a powerful, centralized government, his regime's approach also permitted the continuation of Brazilian regionalism by designing state programs around commodity *autarquias*. Scholars, ranging from Fernando Henrique Cardoso to Barbara Weinstein, have argued that regionalism actually deepened with the rise of economic nationalism after 1930.[139] The corporatist redesign of commodity production partly explains how.

In the 1930s, Brazil inaugurated new economic commissions and agencies to transform its national economy as the provision of goods for the internal market increasingly became an urgent matter of national security.[140] Campaigns for economic self-sufficiency were not limited to petroleum or steel, even if these sectors featured prominently in nationalist Vargas era propaganda. Self-sufficiency required increasing wheat, sugar, and maté production too. It depended on stabilizing prices and ensuring that producers and consumers each had fair access. Self-sufficiency necessitated better measurements and maps about Brazil's economic activity. These were the objectives of early efforts at economic planning in Brazil. Brazilian economists, social scientists, and intellectuals—in conversation with those in other countries—worked to create a new administrative state that could develop the national economy.

Many of the plans discussed in this chapter remained incomplete or were never quite implemented. This was as much the case in Brazil as in Portugal. It is sometimes hard to follow in the archive or statistical yearbooks whether this new bureaucracy did much good to stabilize prices or increase production. But 1930s' experiments planted the seeds for Brazil's and Portugal's bigger and bolder pushes for economic development and sovereignty after 1945.[141] The plans and programs of the 1930s were not failures; they established an institutional and intellectual logic that would shape Brazil's and Portugal's bureaucracies for decades to come. Rather than evaluate the laws and agencies of the 1930s purely in terms of output, this chapter has treated these initiatives as the basis for writing an intellectual history of the state. Beyond well-known figures such as Theotónio Pereira, Oliveira Vianna, or Campos, midlevel bureaucrats were on the front lines of efforts to increase the state's role in economic life and legitimize these incursions into market relations. Corporatist ideas and institutions from other countries offered a template for government efforts to organize producers and discipline supply.

On both sides of the South Atlantic, economists and technocrats increasingly saw fair prices as essential for social peace and economic equilibrium. They expanded on the new theories of price circulating within and beyond their countries that critiqued neoclassical economic models. The next chapter focuses on Brazil to examine how price controls and other market regulations proliferated in the late 1930s and early 1940s in "defense of the popular economy" as the economic theories elaborated in these years were fused with a new legal infrastructure to intervene in everyday market transactions, targeting those who violated corporatist tenets of fair competition and just price.

5

Popular and Political Economy

ON AUGUST 11, 1944, Emanuel Rebouças Maia went to his neighborhood grocery store to purchase some essentials: a kilogram each of black beans, flour, rice, and lard, and five hundred grams of salt. A local police agent doing a routine inspection for potential economic crimes interrupted the transaction. The police officer arrested the grocer, Martinho Romão da Rocha, for allegedly selling goods to a customer at prices that exceeded the official price table. The grocer pleaded innocent, explaining that his hired hand was responsible for customer sales, but the young employee had little experience and knew nothing of price tables. In fact, the grocer insisted that what the police interpreted as a plot to hide his crime—taking the receipt and scribbling in lower prices—was actually his attempt to correct the error.[1] That he did so at the very moment the police entered the shop was an unfortunate coincidence. His explanation did not convince the police agents, who proceeded with the arrest.

A hasty investigation followed. The police collected eyewitness testimonies, gathered evidence in the form of invoices, and confiscated the goods. Much of this investigation, however, rested on the testimony of a handful of police agents. Days later, the case was transferred to the Tribunal de Segurança Nacional (National Security Tribunal, or NST), a special military tribunal first created in 1936 for political trials. The defense team put forth a convincing case, pointing to problems with the police investigation. To begin with, the grocer accused of violating the price tables did not handle the transaction. And no crime had actually transpired; the police had interrupted the purchase of goods to make the arrest. As the defense attorney smugly asserted in his written opinion, the police very well could have waited for money to change hands.[2]

The judge was convinced by the defense attorney's logic and acquitted Rocha based on these reasons, but also because he appeared to be an "honest" man.[3] As in ordinary criminal proceedings, historians of Brazil have shown, judgments about a defendant's character and social standing mattered for verdicts.[4] The judge's decision was not binding, as acquittals were automatically appealed by a plenary session of the remaining judges. A few weeks later, the other five NST judges freed Rocha of all charges.[5] The grocer could go back to his shop in Botafogo and resume business.

This economic trial was one of hundreds following president turned dictator Vargas' ratification of Decree Law No. 869 in November 1938—a law designed to protect the economia popular against speculation, injurious competition, usury, price gouging, and other economic crimes.[6] In Portuguese, *economia popular* literally translates to "the people's savings," but its meaning evolved through the 1930s and 1940s to signify, as mentioned earlier, the "people's pocketbook," or any sort of buying, selling, borrowing, or lending that might impact the economic well-being of the popular classes. This law departed dramatically from how business was done in Rio de Janeiro because it called into question the notion of free and self-adjusting markets in which price or interest rates were set by market conditions, namely supply and demand. This chapter explores how Decree Law No. 869 turned the price of everyday goods—like bread or butter—into the focus of government efforts to transform economic norms and expectations in Brazil.

It is impossible to know whether this grocer's account was truthful, or whether he was indeed trying to swindle customers into paying more than what was legally permitted for essential goods. Whatever the case, it illustrates how Decree Law No. 869 subjected all sorts of everyday market transactions to public scrutiny and state action. More important, it highlights police agents' overzealous and occasionally impetuous surveillance of the market as well as their arbitrary powers.[7] That the police served as the investigative arm of the special tribunal (and decided which transgressions deserved the NST's attention) made both retailers and consumers uneasy. What Brazilian anthropologist Roberto Kant de Lima has termed the "hierarchical and inquisitorial" approach taken in Brazilian police investigations is not specific to the Estado Novo, but the corporatist zeal for state-led economic planning and skepticism of unfettered individual interests were.[8] Public campaigns against market speculators introduced skepticism into even the most basic of market transactions, while the uncertainty of standing before a tribunal of such ill repute created a climate of mistrust. More so, despite the bold promises of social harmony and economic justice, these new economic laws and institutions were not easy to navigate; consumers, retailers, and firms faced a new set of hasty, confusing, and frequently indeterminate rules for doing business.

Justice Minister Francisco Campos emphasized Decree Law No. 869 as the "first doctrinal incursion of the Estado Novo into the domain of the public economy."[9] Once and for all it disrupted the "laissez-faire, laissez-passer" order. Brazil's corporatist jurists and policymakers tried to turn the popular economy into a sphere of everyday buying and selling organized according to fair prices and just competition rather than the "free market." The making of the popular economy was as much a legal project as it was an economic one, as Estado Novo jurists had to reimagine the function and scope of law. Where the liberal legal state saw law as a tool for the enforcement of private property and contracts, the corporatist state saw law as a tool for disciplining economic interests in order to support national development. Brazil's jurists debated these new legal ideas at length and often in dialogue with legal arguments unfolding in other parts of the world. Even in authoritarian contexts, law and legal arguments were central to how and why the state acted as it did.

The economia popular in Brazil has a convoluted and complex history. It inherited its institutions from a violent political process—one marked by Vargas's usurpation of power with the coup and constitution that decreed the authoritarian Estado Novo. From 1938 to 1945, crimes committed against the popular economy were adjudicated by the NST, although the court was originally created for summary trials of political dissidents. Historians have largely focused on these political trials, which targeted liberals, communists, and organized labor. The NST engaged first in a "red phase" targeting communists and then a "green phase" targeting integralists, a Far Right fascist movement.[10] But in 1938, once political purges subsided, the NST was repurposed for economic crimes. From 1936 to 1945, over nineteen thousand individuals were indicted for national security crimes, including economic crimes. About eleven thousand stood trial, with the others dismissed or remitted to another court. Of those sentenced, the NST acquitted nearly eight thousand and found over three thousand guilty.[11] Official court statistics do not offer a breakdown of trials and sentencing by type of crime, but a review of case file suggests that about 60 percent of the NST trials after 1940 were for economic trials.[12] With NST denunciations largely originating in Rio de Janeiro and São Paulo, thousands of individuals like Rocha the grocer faced crimes of usury, price gouging, hoarding, fraud, cartelization, unfair competition, or other practices threatening the people's pocketbook. Despite this volume, historians tend to dismiss economic crimes as a dictator's disguise of a corrupt political court into an organ of social justice.[13] This conclusion, however, overlooks the political, ideological, and economic consequences of having a special military tribunal that decided market fairness. Little has been written on how (or why) the NST became the venue for economic crimes and antitrust proceedings.[14] This chapter explores the confluence of two tendencies in Brazil's Estado Novo: an authoritarian legalism that overhauled civil rights and legal procedures as well as emboldened state ambitions to regulate market life.

This chapter focuses on the NST and its procedures to show how it became part of broader government efforts to tame the rising cost of living and redress economic hardships. It then explores popular economy trials to show how individual citizens, firms, and organized professional interests navigated new rules of doing business in Vargas era Brazil. Examining these trials, I argue that corporatism was an experiment to not only harmonize the interests of labor and capital but also balance the rights of consumers and producers. This focus on market rather than class relations—the more common stress in studies of corporatism—is deliberate. The Estado Novo's emphasis on basic needs and economic stability was a strategy to submerge class struggle with an alternative language for membership in society. The focus on consumer protections and market fairness anticipated the rise of a new model of citizenship in the post-war era—one in which notions of economic justice included a decent standard of living and the satisfaction of basic needs.[15] Already in the 1930s, the Estado Novo used the popular economy to make good on commitments to economic order and progress, but in ways that subordinated economic rights to national development interests.

The Constitution and the Popular Economy

Obscured in the history of Vargas's new constitution in 1937 is the extent to which laws and institutions created for political repression were repurposed to deal with the economic challenges of the late 1930s and early 1940s. The legal history of the economia popular begins with the Lei de Segurança Nacional (National Security Law), which President Vargas pushed through Congress in April 1935.[16] Implemented to counter alleged communist plots to overthrow the government, the law outlined crimes against the social and political order, including actions that incited "class warfare," and all but suspended constitutional guarantees for civil liberties. The communist scare undergirding these legal measures for surveillance and repression, in Brazil at least, combined fact and fiction. Its immediate motivation was the formation in March 1935 of the Aliança Nacional Libertadora, a popular front that united democrats, organized workers, socialists, leftist intellectuals, and communists. In the months that followed, the law's claims over national security were further emboldened by the Brazilian Communist Party's mobilization in the northeastern cities of Natal and Recife, where members murdered senior military officers. This revolt, swiftly crushed by police and the army, convinced Congress to declare a state of siege in late 1935, which it renewed four times in 1936.[17]

Vargas and his legal team worked hastily to build a juridical apparatus that could quickly process crimes against national security in an effort to give state repression a veneer of legitimacy. The NST was inaugurated in 1936 as a special tribunal subordinated to the military courts system.[18] It comprised five judges, both civilian and military, handpicked by Vargas.[19] Between September 1936 and December 1937, during the heyday of Vargas's purge of political opponents, an estimated 1,420 persons were indicted by this court and thousands more tortured by federal police agents during interrogations.[20] These detentions and summary trials of the mid-1930s were the most repressive phase of Vargas's rule.

Tactics to vilify leftist dissidents were integral to how Vargas legitimized his self-coup to create the Estado Novo. To recall, on November 10, 1937, Vargas suspended Congress and seized power with a newly drafted constitution in hand—one that allowed him to rule by decree until 1945. Vargas had so effectively laid the groundwork across the country for his authoritarian and corporatist vision that he only needed to replace two recalcitrant state governors, both in the northeast. Integralist leader Plínio Salgado initially collaborated in the coup, united against a shared communist enemy. Weeks later, though, Vargas issued a decree banning all political parties, including the AIB, which led Salgado to go into exile in Portugal for eight years.[21] The NST was now tasked with stamping out this right-wing movement.

This political story of how public enemies were created, processed, and inculpated for the nation's ills is inseparable from the Estado Novo story. The NST's history has been tied to Vargas's political and personal vendettas; for critics, both then and now, this tribunal did not constitute the rule of law but rather the arbitrary exercise of power by a despotic government.[22] That may be so, but the NST was neither accidental nor reactive. It may have begun as an organ to neutralize political opponents, but it was eventually transformed— by way of meticulous legal theory, constitutional renewal, and debate—into one that redefined economic life. Beyond communists, the NST targeted grocers, merchants, bakers, and bankers.

The Estado Novo coup was not only a political event but a constitutional one too. The 1937 Constitution was the most original and prospective with regard to the state's role in the organization, control, and development of the national economy. Indeed, while the outward justification of the coup might have been threats of "communist infiltration" and class warfare, Vargas made it quite clear that his ambitions were bolder.[23]

In the spirit of confronting all the crises and obstacles to national development, the 1937 Constitution codified "special protections" for the economia popular. Earlier mentions of this concept narrowly focused on efforts to increase national savings, especially household savings. Following the Great Depression, Brazil struggled with the global credit squeeze.[24] Bureaucrats, industrialists, and economists applied the macroeconomic accounting that national savings equals investments to harness popular savings for development projects. Economia popular even made its way into the short-lived 1934 Constitution, which outlined government commitments to "promote the development of economia popular" in articles related to expanding credit markets, nationalizing banks, and banning usury.[25] Drafters linked legal protections for popular finances to industrialization. As Paulista economist and industrialist Roberto Simonsen voted during debates over the 1934 Constitution, special protections for popular economic transactions were essential to "the development and enrichment of the country."[26] The 1937 Constitution took these ambitions further and expanded the concept beyond savings to encompass the economic activities of "honest" people vulnerable to exploitation. It targeted ruinous competition and other price manipulations. Articles 122 and 141 of the Constitution even put "crimes committed against the popular economy" on equal footing with acts against the "security and integrity of the state," appointing the same exceptional tribunal used against political enemies to regulate market behavior.[27]

In November 1938, one year after his constitutional putsch, Vargas issued a bold federal decree to transform everyday economic transactions into matters of national security. Decree Law No. 869 defined crimes against the popular economy. The legislation itemized economic crimes, including hoarding or destruction of goods of primary necessity with the intent to artificially raise prices; abandoning the production, cultivation, or manufacture of goods (or distortions to supply); forming monopolies or trusts with the intent to raise profits or promote unfair competition; selling of goods below production costs to monopolize the market; providing false information or advertisement; selling fraudulent products or false reporting on the weight of goods; charging usurious interest rates; defying official price tables; and so on.[28] Written by President Vargas and Justice Minister Campos, the law gave legal force to Articles 122, 141, and 142 of the 1937 Constitution, which had established that crimes of economic "chicanery" were considered as dangerous to the nation's well-being as political sedition.[29] In this way, the law was "revolutionary," observed Campos, because it turned crimes of price gouging and unfair competition into national security matters.[30]

It is unsurprising that legal efforts to recondition basic market transactions came in the wake of a coup legitimized by exaggerating communist plots against the government. Vargas and his advisers feared class warfare, and thus tried to detach debates over social rights from class to emphasize national economic growth instead, above individual or group interests.[31] As much as Vargas cultivated a more direct and personalist relationship with workers, he and his closest advisers were also careful not to cede ideological ground to leftist movements.[32]

Conveniently, Decree Law No. 869 offered a legal solution for neutralizing both exploitative capitalist behavior and communist class warfare. It paralleled Vargas's approach to the social question in other arenas. For example, Vargas decreed labor legislation and courts, departing from how prior governments had treated labor conflicts as a *caso de polícia*, or police matter (although to be sure, force and coercion remained tactics used against labor, despite new legal channels expanding social citizenship).[33] Vargas's Estado Novo not only channeled labor conflicts into the state on terms established in recent labor legislation and with the creation of a labor courts system; these legal tools also generated a normative legal language for discussing hardships and grievances according to corporatist notions of social peace and collaboration.[34] The legal recognition of protections for the popular economy was part of this process. Vargas understood that economic instability could trigger unrest, with inflation a dangerous political liability. In the early twentieth century, police responded to protests against the rising cost of living with violence, but Vargas deployed a different strategy in the 1930s: Decree Law No. 869 would channel popular economic grievances into the courtroom rather than onto the streets.[35]

Decree Law No. 869, however, was not just a political stunt. It responded to real and pressing economic problems facing Brazil.[36] By 1938, inflation joined credit scarcity as an economic problem and the recently created IBGE, Brazil's statistics bureau, started keeping meticulous track of prices across Brazil (see chapter 4). Daily newspapers reported on the "misery of workers" working for "hunger wages" that could scarcely keep up with the price of bread. Textile workers in Santo Aleixo, just north of the city of Rio de Janeiro, embarked on a thirty-kilometer protest against the price of basic goods.[37] Both in the popular imagination and actions taken by government officials, rising prices were explained as a problem caused by greedy intermediaries. Technocrats certainly understood the structural causes at play as they proposed policies to increase domestic food production, fix transportation bottlenecks, and ease credit. But they also sanctioned Decree Law No. 869 for its swift, satisfying actions against bankers, merchants, and other intermediaries who took advantage of market asymmetries.

With this decree, prices or interest charged to consumers or borrowers were subjected to review by regulatory commissions, police agents, and judges. While little scholarship exists on popular economy crimes, trial proceedings, newspaper coverage, and police ledgers all suggest that the law targeted financiers and street venders alike, with thousands of arrests made in the late 1930s and early 1940s over the price of butter or interest rate on a loan. The penalty for such crimes often combined a six-month to two-year prison sentence with fines of two thousand mil réis to ten thousand mil réis, or between US$120 and $600 (1939 dollars)—a meaningfully punitive amount.[38] In trials on usury and excessive profits, judges could increase fines if the guilty party was of a higher socioeconomic status than the victim, or if the victim was an industrial or agricultural worker. Campos designed NST sentencing guidelines in accordance with the paternalist logic at the core of his corporatist worldview, bestowing economic protections in ways that reinforced a fixed social hierarchy.

Law and Economics

Legal architects of the Estado Novo championed Decree Law No. 869 as a model of how law should be used as a tool for economic development and social harmony. It and similar decrees were inspired by critiques of the liberal and laissez-faire economic order. Legal reforms were thus tethered to debates over corporatist economics (see chapters 3–4), especially in terms of what constituted just price or fair competition. Indeed the decree's author, Justice Minister Campos, argued that price should be determined according to real economic factors—understood as interest rates, wages, prices of primary products, taxes, transportation, or the general costs of production—and not market forces. This economic model reflected a world in which the price set between producers and consumers should "raise the general well-being of the people."[39] Notably absent from Campos's analysis was any mention of the clearing function of price as a value at which the demand for goods or services equaled its supply; he rejected classical economic theories on the grounds that they encouraged speculative or monopolistic behavior. Subtly, Campos and other Estado Novo jurists defended this notion of price as a value that balanced the interests of consumers and producers, deeply committed to corporatist ideas of social harmony via the top-down management of economic life.

As a foremost architect of the Estado Novo, Campos coauthored countless decree laws and collaborated on the 1940 Penal Code (still in place today) in addition to his work on the 1937 Constitution.[40] He supported jurisprudence that elevated public law above private law and an economic outlook that placed the nation's progress above concerns for individual liberties.[41] Rather than focus on labor relations, what ultimately drove Campos's vision of corporatism was the ambition to build an "efficient government machine" so that the state could rationally organize economic life.[42]

For Campos, corporatism was the necessary antidote for the ruinous competition and profit-seeking egoism of capitalism. As he summarized it, "Under corporatist organization, economic power has a legal expression: it does not need to negotiate or bribe, and does not use loopholes, or look for circuitous or furtive means to achieve its goals." Only an "independent, authoritarian, and just state" could secure economic progress.[43] He emphasized technical councils, government experts, and the statist management of economic life. This orientation shaped his legal solutions for the problems of market competition and economic justice.

Campos and other jurists looked eclectically to business practices alongside academic monographs and legal journals to defend and justify the policing of everyday market transactions with both erudite and commonsense arguments.[44] For jurist Roberto Lyra, law professor in Rio de Janeiro and (another) author of Brazil's 1940 penal code, the nineteenth-century stress on legal protections for private property and private contracts was outdated and counterproductive. Decree Law No. 869 established new mechanisms for the pursuit of "social justice."[45] In *A paisagem legal do Estado Novo*, for example, Gil Duarte, a lawyer from Pernambuco, defended the legal architecture of corporatism in Brazil. "For hundreds of years," he wrote, "profit was always at the whims of merchants who ... sold goods at whatever price they chose, for the sake of increasing their own gain."[46]

Some might charge these jurists with authoritarian doublespeak, as they attempted to present the repeal of individual freedoms and property rights as a new type of justice, bestowed by an allegedly benevolent dictator. But Estado Novo jurists maintained that they lived in exceptional times, which necessitated that the government exercise unprecedented powers over the lives of citizens. The 1930s and 1940s, asserted Lyra, no longer permitted the "romanticism" of "economic freedom ... [as] a path toward just prices."[47]

Laws of supply and demand were nimbly contorted to fit a corporatist worldview. For Nelson Hungria, a leading jurist and the author of a widely cited commentary on the 1940 penal code, the laissez-faire, laissez-passer formula of capitalism, combined with the First Republic's absentee state, had abandoned individuals to their "pure caprice" and let reign the "laws of the jungle."[48] The Great Depression was a transformative moment in modern economic history for Hungria because the collapse of international markets further aggravated the price instability of the 1920s and destabilized domestic economies around the globe. In his view, the crisis could not only be blamed on anonymous market forces; "capitalist agents" commandeered the economy by using "stratagems and gimmicks" to "artificially promote the abandonment of crops and plant closures, control the supply of products, and hoard production for the sole purpose of causing famine and raising prices."[49] Campos echoed this jaundiced notion of capitalism as a system of "free competition" for the sake of "an endless race for purely individual objectives."[50] The solution was Decree Law No. 869. As Lyra argued with no apparent irony, it would "coercively ensure an honest environment and respect for general well-being."[51]

Labor Ministry official Francisco José de Oliveira Vianna drew together the legal writings of jurists in the United States, France, Italy, and Portugal to make the point that fair pricing was impossible if left to individual buyer and seller discretion. In essays published in Brazil's leading newspaper *Jornal do Commércio*—and later republished in 1938 as *Problemas de direito corporativo*—he deployed new theories of sociological jurisprudence to contend that price, like other economic variables, was constituted in a broader social context, departing from the liberal logic that price was a contractual value agreed to by the parties.[52] Specifically, Oliveira Vianna looked to French jurist Emmanuel Lévy to argue that the price of goods at a market was in fact a collective contract. Lévy's jurisprudential contributions have largely been forgotten, yet in the early twentieth century he stood uniquely at the cross section of two schools of legal philosophy: *socialisme juridique*, or the legal defense of socialism, and the ballooning field of sociology of law. Despite his personal anticommunist zeal, Oliveira Vianna was drawn to Lévy's works on legal sociology, largely overlooking the French jurist's ambivalent political writings.[53] He found in Lévy a critique of legal orthodoxy and especially a rebuttal to the will theory of contract law, which asserts that a judge cannot question the fairness of a contract so long as both parties have voluntarily agreed to it.[54]

Oliveira Vianna mobilized French jurisprudence to argue against the liberal legal state and its protections for decentralized, competitive, and self-executing markets. In *Les fondements du droit* (1935), for example, Lévy recounted a trip to a market to purchase butter in order to illustrate that even in this simple exchange between grocer and customer, price was not a matter of "individual contracts, not even of those made in good faith."[55] Instead, it was the product of a collective contract, and one that absorbed the beliefs and interests of all parties. Oliveira Vianna paraphrased Lévy's legal rationale so that it mirrored his own corporatist response to the social question. "In truth, this small, one-sided trade, this individual contract of buying and selling, did not constitute a free debate between the two contracting parties in order to stipulate the price, as is assumed in the classical theory of contracts," observed Oliveira Vianna. "Rather, that price had already been fixed in advanced by an invisible agreement forged by the collectivity," he added, "an accord with which the two contracting parties must abide."[56] The price of butter, in other words, should reflect "the common and collective interests of local groups, or all the producers and consumers of said commodity."[57] Decree Law No. 869 gave legal heft to this definition of price, and now the state needed a forum or means to enforce it.

National Security Tribunal

Vargas's Estado Novo turned to an unlikely institution to discipline economic behavior: the NST. This military tribunal was chosen because of the "quickness of its procedures."[58] Lyra, for example, argued that economic crimes required a special tribunal because of the obvious pitfalls of the ordinary judicial system: "Speculators and architects of 'schemes' had an open field in which to undertake their dubious activities as they enjoyed the assurance that their behaviors were difficult to prove [in courts of law] given how the chicanery of lawyers and inherent equivocations of the legal formalism of ordinary courts would, in practice, guarantee their impunity."[59] Estado Novo jurists were disappointed with the liberal state along with its overstated concerns for the rights of individuals and due process, which they discredited with the catchall "chicanery." They were now free to design a different type of legal system.

The NST was also chosen for economic crimes because Estado Novo jurists wanted to keep it active, even as political trials dwindled. With reforms in 1938, the NST became a permanent organ for three types of crimes: those committed against the "existence, security, and integrity of the state"; transgressions against the "structure of institutions"; and crimes against the "popular economy."[60] It retained structural vestiges of its origins in the military courts system, but was now comprised of six judges (all freely appointed by Vargas) with two civilian judges, a military judge, an army official, a navy official, and a lawyer of "remarkable" competence.[61] Cases brought before NST judges were subjected to summary decisions to avoid the "likelihood of chicanery and delay" that might arise from granting the accused time to form an adequate defense as well as to resolve the tremendous backlog caused by the purge of communists and integralists.[62] The NST had a murky relationship with the ordinary judiciary system, evident in how its president, Frederico de Barros Barreto, nominated in 1936 to head the special tribunal, was also appointed by Vargas to Brazil's Supreme Federal Court (Supremo Tribunal Federal) in 1939. Historian Emília Viotti da Costa has accordingly emphasized how Vargas not only created new legal institutions but also conditioned the independence of preexisting ones.[63]

In matters related to the popular economy, a case often began with a complaint or denunciation to a local police precinct, which if merited, would be investigated by the police, frequently by the Departamento de Ordem Política e Social (Department of Political and Social Order, or DOPS), Vargas's "political police" force, along with any relevant economic regulatory agencies. Economic denunciations also arose out of routine inspections of businesses, performed by regulatory agencies or DOPS. Following a police investigation, the case was transferred to the NST. On the trial date, attorneys for the defense and prosecution each had thirty minutes to present their case before the judge issued a decision. This timeline was not strictly observed, but proceedings were nevertheless typically swift. Speedy judgments were deliberate; Campos and other jurists believed that too many "juridical formalities" slowed down or tempered sentences.[64] Procedural rules disadvantaged the defense, especially the fact that all acquittals were automatically appealed, yet convictions were appealed only if the defendant motioned to do so. Witness testimonies were presented in written form and not subjected to cross-examination. Moreover, hearings were held in public, which turned economic trials into a spectacle at times.[65]

The NST was adept in its multitasking toggle between economic trials and political trials. Its docket filled with economic crimes, but Vargas's campaign against political dissidents never quite evaporated. The NST continued to try communists alleged to be mounting offensives in the Amazon or integralists mobilized in São Paulo, with sentences far stiffer than those reserved for economic crimes.[66] This special tribunal also continued to hear—or as was more often the case, refused to hear—habeas corpus petitions by which political prisoners appealed their unlawful detentions. Still, its shift to the economic sphere was what increasingly garnered headlines in newspapers and legitimized the institution, at least partially.

Some of the most thorough assessments of the NST were penned by foreign observers in Brazil. In the early 1940s, for example, Karl Loewenstein, a professor of political science and jurisprudence at Amherst College, embarked on an academic mission to Brazil, supported by the Guggenheim Foundation. He intended to report back to US readers on law and constitutionalism under authoritarian regimes in South America. As a Jewish German–born scholar of constitutional law who was exiled to the United States after Hitler took power, Loewenstein did not disguise his disapproval of Vargas's heavy-handed rule, legal manipulations, or disregard for civil liberties. Nonetheless, he couched his assessment of laws in defense of the popular economy in a progressive language that highlighted their "decidedly social character," and their assault "against tangible excesses of predatory capitalism and against the misuse of superior economic power against the weak." Loewenstein commended Vargas and his government's efforts "to put a brake on [the] 'rugged' individualism of the liberal period."[67]

For Loewenstein and the "informants" who aided his research, this activism in the realm of everyday economic transactions was "praiseworthy," yet the NST less so. He dedicated a chapter in *Brazil under Vargas* (1942) to the special tribunal, calling it one of the Estado Novo's "most interesting and most discussed institutions." Loewenstein was well aware of the criticisms launched against the court, considered by many an illustration of the nonobservance of the rule of law by authoritarian regimes and even likened to the *Volksgerichtshof* in Nazi Germany. But to him, the structure of the court was transparent enough. Furthermore, judges could not create new crimes, and their convictions were restricted to the penalties outlined by law—a practice that separated Vargas's Brazil from Hitler's Germany or Mussolini's Italy.[68] Loewenstein noted objectionable features such as unstandardized evidentiary rules, inadequate protections for the accused, and how the presumption of innocence did not apply. These shortcomings, however, were not sufficient for him to dismiss the court outright, as he did not see it as exceptional, vindictive, or arbitrary. Rather, it functioned according to the Estado Novo's laws and statutes.

Loewenstein's assessment of the NST turned somewhat more favorable when it came to the popular economy, which constituted a vast proportion of the special tribunal's docket after 1939.[69] Like many in Brazil, he was initially optimistic that the NST could shield the popular economy from speculation and corporate malfeasance alike, as judges and prosecutors fashioned themselves as crusaders against predatory capitalism. Within the first few months of Decree Law No. 869's implementation, 197 sentences were imposed in the state of São Paulo alone.[70] Grocers and street venders stood trial for price gouging and slighting the weight of goods sold to consumers, but so did bank directors and captains of industry.[71]

One of the earliest trials related to the popular economy was that of small-time banker Appolonio Pinto de Carvalho, accused in January 1939 of lending money at usurious interest rates to soldiers of state militias in São Paulo. Found guilty, he was sentenced to seven months in prison and a hefty fine.[72] He was not alone. In July 1939, for example, the directors of the Caixa Rural e Operária da Parahyba stood trial for defrauding their clients—rural workers who deposited their money in this bank—by charging usurious interest rates.[73] The defendants hired many lawyers but to no avail: the caixa's president and managing director were both sentenced to two years in prison, in addition to a sizable fine, and the bank itself soon went bankrupt. Journalists in Rio de Janeiro exclaimed that this conviction was the first of its kind in Brazil: a *bacharel* (a term applied to those with an academic degree to connote high social standing) and senior officer of the Banco do Brazil sent to prison for swindling rural workers.[74] The severity of the sentences seemed proof enough that the NST was serving its duty to economic justice admirably. José Maria Mac Dowell da Costa, lead prospector to the court, boasted that the law would "greatly benefit the people [o povo], with the loan sharks who violate it prosecuted and convicted."[75] His boastful assessment, though, was premature. The economic shock of World War II jolted the NST into a different kind of institution. In Brazil, the policing of the popular economy became more oriented to the urgency of everyday market crises of inflation and food shortages rather than the machinations of big capitalism.

The NST turned criminal law into a tool for economic justice. But what constituted justice in corporatist Brazil did not overlay neatly on ideas of justice in liberal democratic societies. This does not mean that the NST was a sham, however. Instead, it needs to be contextualized as the by-product of new legal arguments for regulating economic life. Estado Novo jurists rejected the classical legal thought of the nineteenth century—primarily invested in individual rights, the enforcement of contracts, and protections for private property—as they focused on the social and economic sphere. Well before the heyday of developmentalism in the 1950s and 1960s, these jurists insisted on the triumph of public law over private law, and public welfare over individual liberties. In Brazil, law was consciously designed as a tool by which the state intervened in economic affairs. This trend, as Lyra insisted, was "as often present in surviving democracies as in various totalitarian models."[76]

Indeed, jurists working for Vargas's government read widely on French sociological jurisprudence and US legal realism to understand how courtrooms could serve as sites for the state to regulate citizens' economic behavior.[77] For legal scholar Duncan Kennedy, corporatism was one of many offshoots of this new legal philosophy, giving law an increasingly social orientation during the first half of the twentieth century. Lawyers, legal scholars, and judges expanded the function of law beyond the enforcement of private property so that it could be used to achieve social goals, even in instances where this required intervention in market relations.[78] Legal innovations in Brazil were not outliers but rather were part of a global transformation in legal norms and expectations after the Great Depression.

Economic Trials

Businesses—big and small—had to learn quickly how to navigate Brazil's new legal landscape, as Decree Law No. 869 forced firms to justify their actions according to the public good. In August 1938, for example, months before the decree went into effect, four coffee firms in Belo Horizonte (Minas Gerais) signed a *convênio*, or agreement. They agreed to charge the same price for coffee, effectively increasing the retail price by restricting the supply with fixed quotas on how much coffee each firm sold per month. The firms designed this agreement to eliminate ruinous competition "contrary to public interest."[79] When the decree went into effect, José Segundo da Rocha, one of the signatories, pulled out from the convênio, calling it a crime against the economia popular. The other firms disagreed and brought a civil suit against Rocha for breach of contract. Rocha, in turn, denounced his former partners to the NST, positioning himself as a crusader for justice by "defending the people's pocketbook against these greedy hoarders."[80]

This case bounced between Minas Gerais civil courts and the NST in Rio de Janeiro. Both sides defended their claims through the 1937 Constitution, as these firms contended with conflicting ideas of economic freedom and how best to serve the public economic order. It is possible, of course, that these lawsuits and denunciations were actually motivated by feuds between Rocha and his competitors, or a strategy to undercut competition and increase market share. Yet there is no mention of such vendettas or motives in the case file. And regardless of any personal interests, all parties had to articulate and defend their economic behavior according to the Estado Novo's new norms and rules.

During the civil suit, for instance, one lawyer defended the convênio by insisting that the firms acted in the spirit of Brazil's corporatist economy, with its organizing actions analogous to the Departamento Nacional de Café or Instituto de Açúcar e do Álcool, federal organs created in the early 1930s to organize coffee and sugar producers, respectively. The legal imposition of this corporatist ethos, however, did not immediately submerge old economic formulas.

This lawyer covered all bases as he leveraged liberal economic theory too, citing Austrian economist Friedrich Hayek to defend a merchant's right to freely
enter into private contracts.[81] Another lawyer—defending the convênio before the NST—cited Italian and US jurisprudence to defend this cartel-like
arrangement.

This trial even featured one of Brazil's most famous lawyers, Heráclito Fontoura Sobral Pinto, well-known for his outspoken criticism of Vargas and
handling of high-profile trials like that of Communist Party leader Luís Carlos
Prestes.[82] Sobral Pinto opted for pragmatic rather than ideological arguments,
presenting data on local coffee prices to show that the convênio fixed prices in
accordance with rising production costs. The firms, he concluded, enjoyed
"reasonable" profits of 9 percent, pointing to precedents that "maximum profits of 30 percent were reasonable."[83]

The coffee convênio tested the Estado Novo's efforts to refashion market
relations according to its corporatist ethos. With nearly all economic trials,
Decree Law No. 869 asserted that merchants were no longer at liberty to
charge whatever prices they wanted. In terms of what constituted a fair price,
jurists mobilized economic and legal theory in order to legitimize the state's
intervention into private business transactions (see chapter 4).[84] Popular
economy laws were designed ultimately to transform the nature of commerce
and production across Brazil.

Bold ambitions for the transformative potential of the decree often fell short
in practice, though. The coffee trial—like so many other economic trials—hinged
on more formulaic interpretations of the law; NST judges concluded that
because the firms signed the convênio prior to Decree Law No. 869 and suspended it during the investigation, no illegal transactions had taken place. It took
two years to reach this decision. It was not until March 1941 that NST judges
acquitted the coffee merchants, without any comment about fair prices.

Acquittals were quite common in popular economy trials, with (approximately) two-thirds of the defendants either absolved or transferred to ordinary
courts between 1941 and 1945. This was the case partly because denunciations
were frequently based on hearsay and flimsy evidence, but also because NST
judges were reluctant—or perhaps ill-equipped—to weigh in on theoretical
questions of fair profits or pricing. As much as Brazil's jurists tried to use law to
design a new economic system, the process would be long and incomplete.

High acquittal rates, however, should not distract from the consequences
of using this special tribunal in market life. Standing trial was no small thing.
Trials were costly; lengthy investigations could lead to business closures, repu-
tational damage, and steep lawyer fees, not to mention the unease of standing
before an infamous tribunal with limited oversight and unchecked scope. For
Loewenstein, the NST's economic trials came to epitomize Vargas's "split

personality," oscillating between "legality" and "arbitrariness."[85] Loewenstein used the "dual state" framework, coined by German Jewish lawyer Ernst Fraenkel for Nazi Germany, to explain that authoritarian regimes govern in two modes: one maintains the rational legal system essential to capitalism while another uses extrajudicial violence to eliminate opposition.[86] For Loewenstein, Brazil was an "elusive" case that did not fit the mold of European Fascist dictatorships precisely because the Estado Novo's disregard for the rule of law was not "sufficient in quantity and quality to stamp the regime as a whole as arbitrary." To him, the regime did "not touch the common man in his daily doings; his life goes on as before."[87] But if nothing else, NST trials debunk that claim.

Protests and Petitions

Once Decree Law No. 869 went into effect, a slew of petitions and denunciations reached Campos at the Ministry of Justice from those who sought clarification on how the new law would impact their businesses. In January 1939, for example, a lawyer in Rio de Janeiro petitioned the Ministry of Justice to ask whether his client, a merchant, could sell goods at a price below the "official tables," adding that this client still planned to "earn profits" and their aim was only to "increase their sales volume, without any intent, therefore, to eliminate competition."[88] Almost immediately, the new norms of Decree Law No. 869 had seeped into the business vocabulary of merchants as they tried to defend their profits against public scrutiny.

A few months later, Joaquim Rodrigues de Almeida and Manoel José Andrade, coffee transporters from the port city of Santos in the state of São Paulo, petitioned Campos to denounce owners of transportation vehicles and wholesale coffee venders. These coffee transporters complained that collusion between those businesses compromised their livelihood and thus constituted a crime against the popular economy.[89] In this case, Decree Law No. 869 was the source of rights and protections for the average citizen, organized against monopolies that threatened their livelihoods.[90]

For others in Brazil, Decree Law No. 869 was a petty and vindictive law only perfunctorily connected to the pursuit of market fairness. Indeed, the mazelike growth of state bureaucracies also created more opportunities for individuals or groups to get ensnared by these very rights and guarantees. Of course, the controversy over popular economy laws hewed to social position and economic interests as much as ideological proclivities. If the aim of corporatism was to create a society organized according to professional and economic interests—one that balanced the interests of labor and capital, or producer and consumer—the question of who decided "fair value" was as contentious as ever. Under the decree, appointed judges decided the hierarchy of group interests—a highly contested approach. The NST's incursions into the economic sphere inspired debate not only about the rule of law under the Estado Novo but the limits of state powers over economic life too.

Sobral Pinto was among the first to protest the NST's impunity over the popular economy. Over the course of his career, Sobral Pinto served as the defense attorney for scores of litigants brought to the NST, earning the reputation of a civil rights crusader who even defended many clients pro bono. Sobral Pinto epitomized his times. A devout Catholic, he was skeptical of liberalism and its emphasis on individual freedoms. On the other hand, he was deeply critical of Vargas and the way his intellectual allies flocked to the seemingly vague promises of the third path. Despite his protests against Vargas, Sobral Pinto enjoyed personal and professional relationships with many prominent Estado Novo jurists, including Campos, and received several nominations for public appointments. In 1936, for example, Campos nominated Sobral Pinto for an NST seat, which he declined in protest of the court's indifference to due process in favor of legal expediency.[91]

The case of grocer Augusto Pereira made Sobral Pinto famous, and caused him to break ties with friends and colleagues sympathetic to the Estado Novo. In May 1942, Pereira was denounced in Rio de Janeiro by a customer for price gouging on his produce, and three price commission inspectors immediately investigated. Charges were brought against Pereira, and his case was transferred to the NST. Sobral Pinto took the case because he suspected that it was motivated not by economic justice but instead by a petty vendetta between the grocer and NST president Barros Barreto. It seemed that Barros Barreto was a longtime customer accustomed to deferring payments. Moreover, it turned out that Barreto's military orderly had made the initial police complaint. Sobral Pinto's case hinged on this coincidence, and the fact that the orderly's salary was too small to afford such lavish purchases of fruits and vegetables. The strategy failed. Pereira was sentenced to three and a half months in prison and a hefty fine in a decision praised in national newspapers for the NST's noble actions against the "sharks" menacing the popular economy.[92] For Sobral Pinto, however, this trial was a farce. These events stoked his conviction that the NST was an "anarchist" or "Bolshevist" institution—an ironic allegation given the political cases previously tried by this court—on account of how it closed businesses, confiscated goods, and otherwise undermined property rights with few checks on its powers.[93]

Sobral Pinto also defended wealthy bankers and members of the employer class who did not take lightly to new restrictions on their profit margins. He defended financial brokers accused of usury, bankers charged with speculative behavior, and wholesale retailers denounced for price fixing. Sobral Pinto opposed Decree Law No. 869 because he believed, forthrightly, that the law was nothing but a front for petty vendettas, state policing, and the vindictive nature of the rule of law under the Estado Novo. He made these claims in NST chambers and the pages of Brazil's leading newspapers, with his weekly column "Pelos domínios do direito" ("For the rule of law") in the *Jornal do Commércio*.

Sobral Pinto's column exposed many internal contradictions to corporatism. He did not protest that the state should regulate economic life but instead questioned Vargas's tactics. In 1941, for instance, bakers in Recife and Olinda, in northeastern Pernambuco, organized an association in defense of their professional interests, which included an agreement to coordinate prices for their customers. These bakers were accused of price collusion and unfair competition. This case came before the NST, which declared their actions a crime against the popular economy. Sobral Pinto used one of his weekly columns to defend the bakers' association and its regulatory actions over the economy: it was not the judiciary that should determine economic fairness but rather producers and professionals organized on behalf of their collective interests.[94] The bakers were merely exercising their corporatist rights to do so.

The real question was whether professional associations could unilaterally fix prices without the state's sanction. Professional organs were endowed with public powers to regulate their economic sector, and this was one of the central distinctions between corporatism and the laissez-faire order. Yet this model depended on the state's recognition of labor and professional associations along with approval of their actions.[95] NST judges found Recife's bakers guilty of misusing their powers to regulate price and sacrificing their consumers' interests for the sake of personal gain. Sobral Pinto saw this ruling as a grave misstep, with "no logic, no direction, and no constructive purpose."[96] On July 19, 1941, he dedicated his *Jornal do Commércio* column to the controversies at the heart of the popular economy. As he saw it, professional associations could only promote economic order if they had powers to establish prices and expel members who failed to observe the rules of fair trade.[97] As in corporatist Portugal, professional associations should work as "admirable instruments" in defense of both class interests and the nation's economic well-being.[98]

While these events might seem contrary to the Estado Novo's ethos, for Campos, as noted earlier, the true revolutionary potential of corporatism was the state's rational and aggressive management of economic life. Campos and other jurists agreed on the importance of professional and class associations to regulate competition, but disagreed on the methods. Which professional associations should have regulatory powers over the economy, and what hierarchy should organize economic interests? For corporatist jurists, professional representative organs were but the lowest rung on a ladder of state institutions, with ultimate authority residing in the executive branch as well as the judges, ministers, and technocrats appointed by the president.

Although the NST had authority, using it to adjudicate market fairness raised lots of questions—and protests. A necessary condition for a crime against the popular economy was that it was committed knowingly as well as with the intent to deceive and reap excess profit. How would judges distinguish between prices "artificially elevated" and "normal" prices? In certain cases, a judge was free to determine what constituted a "just price" based on "ears and experts" presented as testimony as well as their personal conviction, while in other cases judges ruled according price tables fixed by state commissions along with any markups permitted for miscellaneous costs of production or transportation.[99] If judges lacked expertise in economic matters, how could they recognize speculation?

Opposition to popular economy laws was especially fierce in the industrial state of São Paulo. The Paulistas channeled their protests to the federal government via São Paulo's own corporatist-like chamber: Conselho de Expansão Económica do Estado de São Paulo (São Paulo State Council for Economic Expansion). Created on December 24, 1938, by the São Paulo *interventor federal*, or the governor appointed by Vargas, the council was one of many advisory bodies created in the 1930s for state-directed economic development.[100] During the height of Brazil's corporatist experiment, from 1938 to 1942, this organ supported Paulista commercial and industrial interests, and was responsible for debate and research on economic policies.[101] The detailed minutes of its biweekly meetings prolifically document how industrial, political, and economic elites envisioned the state's role in regulating economic production and internal markets. Simonsen was one of its members.

In January 1939, the chamber's members rallied against Decree Law No. 869. Their protests concerned a recent petition sent by three of São Paulo's largest commercial and industrial employer associations to Campos calling for the repeal of several articles of the legislation. They defended the cartels and trusts vilified by the new law as essential tools by which producers and merchants coordinated prices. These actions staved off liquidation for small and large businesses alike, they argued, and thus "were in some instances even more beneficial to the [national] community because they avoided the dangerous oscillations that result from ruinous price wars." The Paulista position did not deny the abuses committed by *some* monopolies—those that unfairly acquired market share for the sake of future price hikes and personal gain. The state should certainly "avoid and suppress such abuses."[102] But Paulista industrial and commercial leaders wondered why this task should fall to military officials and appointed judges.

For Paulista industrialists, it seemed reckless to use "violent weapons—like heavy fines and prison sentences—in the sphere of economic activities, where everything is unstable, delicate, and precarious." The market required a gentler touch: "No domain of human action lends itself less to such rigid rules."[103] Paulistas proposed instead a special commission, comprised of people with expertise and experience in industry and commerce, to interpret and enforce Decree Law No. 869. This was actually a rather corporatist solution—one that envisioned trained technocrats working alongside industry experts. It also cited examples from France, Germany, and the United States to argue for how industry experts and technocrats should steer market transactions.

This Paulista petition found its way to the CFCE in Rio de Janeiro (see chapter 4), where federal technocrats saw matters differently.[104] Decree Law No. 869, they argued, was no different from laws in place across Europe and North America in which price collusion was deemed "harmful to society" and prohibited outright. Collusion was not a solution for market volatility but instead its fundamental cause. This position was not a strike against free enterprise; rather, it was intended to curb how capital "made use of violent and criminal methods in order eliminate competition" to attain "fabulous profit margins" in which resellers and other intermediaries exploited both consumers and producers. The law targeted only those with malicious intent. As for the authority of the special tribunal over such economic transactions, its jurisdiction stemmed directly from the 1937 Constitution, which placed the national economy "under the direct protection of the state itself," and conferred on the state powers to "coordinate and control, in the economic domain, the factors of production, whenever there is need for its intervention for the public's good."[105]

It is difficult to track the Paulista petition beyond this debate. Indeed, Estado Novo's bloated bureaucracy produced so much paperwork that it is sometimes difficult to follow any single paper trail, or definitively determine if a particular matter was resolved, dismissed, or merely forgotten. In this instance, pleas to repeal parts of Decree Law No. 869 were not heeded. Yet subsequent revisions to the law would address Paulista concerns over whether military officers and appointed judges were equipped to evaluate economic fairness.[106]

Populist Politics and the Popular Economy

Although economic debates have been the focus of the chapter thus far, it would be a mistake to concentrate only on economics and ignore the political motivations behind Decree Law No. 869. Highly publicized economic trials hinged on a populist "us" versus "them" understanding of the economy, as Vargas and Campos mobilized exceptional legal tools to manufacture economic villains to take the blame for major economic problems. The NST trials—with their reliance on popular participation, quick proceedings, and corruptible rules—turned popular economy laws into a weapon for Vargas to wield against political enemies (real and imagined) or for daily political grandstanding.

The fate of Paul Deleuze, a French banker of Jewish heritage, illustrates this. Deleuze was an ideal scapegoat for financial capitalism and an easy target for Vargas's villainization. In 1916, the financier started doing business in Brazil, amassing millions as well as a reputation for being a dishonest businessperson. One journalist called him the "most notable swindler ever to be recorded in any criminal registry worldwide."[107] For two decades Deleuze had evaded lawsuits of financial malfeasance, hiding behind complex multinational corporations.[108] The Estado Novo changed this. Arrested in December 1938, Deleuze was charged under Decree Law No. 869 for fraud, bribery, collusion, and "defaming" Brazil with negative financial assessments.[109] The public assault against Deleuze bore subtle yet consistent marks of nativism and antisemitism. In contrast to Argentina or Europe, historian Jeffrey Lesser notes, popular and official antisemitism was not as rampant in Brazil. Still, influential intellectuals and political officials certainly mobilized stereotypes of Jews, and in the 1930s these stereotypes centered on negative associations with communists and capitalists.[110] The NST—created first to target communists and then capitalists—institutionalized such antisemitic tropes, although this was more evident in political trials (especially those targeting communists) than economic ones.

This case took an unexpected turn when Deleuze committed suicide. With no child or spouse, his nephew in France came forward as heir. For Vargas, it was inconceivable to export such wealth. With no legal means in French or Brazilian law to disinherit the nephew, Vargas decreed a law to "disinherit under specified conditions *all* nephews."[111] Even Deleuze's harshest critics denounced this asset forfeiture.[112] In seizing Deleuze's property, Vargas enriched federal coffers to finance state-sponsored development. Yet this served political ambitions as well; Deleuze owned the newspaper *A Noite*, which once seized, became a government mouthpiece.[113]

Deleuze illustrates the fusion of popular economic laws with authoritarianism, but additionally, how Vargas flouted the liberal logic that legal protections for private property were prerequisites for development.[114] Police and prosecutors harassed industrialists and confiscated property, as the Estado Novo belied the expectation that *most* dictatorships will shield the economy—namely economic elites and foreign capital—from the arbitrary practices used against political enemies.[115]

Initially, Decree Law No. 869 was designed to target "capitalists" like Deleuze or special interests like the Belo Horizonte coffee cartel. But it quickly became apparent that this law was not really doing the work of antitrust legislation as its application expanded in unexpected ways. Financial crimes never completely disappeared from the NST's docket, but white-collar crimes represented only a fraction of its cases. Instead, the NST's caseload began to fill up with trials about the everyday buying and selling of goods.

What made Decree Law No. 869 "popular"—or "populist"—was not just that it depended on a Manichaean conception of an economy with villains (speculators) and victims (the people) but that this law's enforcement depended on citizen's denunciations too. Justice, moreover, was performed publicly as the NST trials were open to the public. The ease—and frequency—of the denunciations might well have been intentional as a sort of safety valve so that popular classes could voice their frustrations. Economic trials empowered citizens to seek justice for real economic grievances while also allowing the Estado Novo to publicize its actions in service of nation and citizen.

As the roster of popular economy denunciations expanded, the target villains increasingly became small-scale commercial establishments in urban centers such as wholesale traders, produce venders, and owners of dry goods shops, called *armazéns de secos e molhados*. In the major cities of Rio de Janeiro and São Paulo, these establishments were often run by immigrants—Italian, Syrian Lebanese, and especially Portuguese. Far from wealthy, these *comerciantes* nonetheless exercised a lot of power in local market settings. During hard economic times, they were frequently (rightly or wrongly) targets of public outrage for ostensibly profiting from overcharging or hoodwinking consumers.[116] In this setting and others, economic grievances cannot be isolated from their wider social and political context, or disaggregated from the class, racial, or ethnic tensions that fueled popular economic denunciations.[117]

In 1939, for example, an (anonymous) denunciation reached DOPS offices in São Paulo, relating an elaborate scheme orchestrated between workers at São Paulo Tramway, Light and Power Company, the Canadian utility company in operation since 1899, and several nearby commercial establishments. These workers were members of the Sociedade Beneficente dos Empregados da Light and Power, a benevolent society for employees that, among other benefits, offered its members vouchers to purchase merchandise at subsidized prices. These vouchers became the basis of an elaborate speculative scheme. Some Light and Power employees (allegedly) used their vouchers to buy merchandise that they then resold to nearby commercial establishments, namely armazéns de secos e molhados. Those accused of participating in this scheme were charged with violating Decree Law No. 869. The NST prosecutor alleged that this amounted to a crime of usury because the commercial establishments exchanged cash for goods at a value less than what the workers originally paid with their vouchers. The retailers, in turn, allegedly "illegally resold" the merchandise at "advantageous prices, earning excessive profits."[118] A police investigation coordinated across several commercial establishments documented large quantities of olive oil, rice, manioc flour, cigarettes, sugar, soap, and other items bought and sold under this scheme. To give a sense of the scale, police confiscated nearly 130 kilograms of olive oil alone during the investigation.

In testimonies provided by Light and Power employees, the workers admitted to participating in this scheme over several months or even years, defending their actions because they needed cash to support their families and pay rent.[119] The workers, moreover, said they had been exploited time and again in this scheme but had no recourse. All parties understood the economic question at stake: whether the buyers had acquired excessive profits from this arrangement, with the comerciantes insisting that their profits were reasonable—2 to 3 percent—while the workers claimed the profit margins were 15 or 20 percent.[120] Several of the defendants, in turn, presented themselves as victims. Carolino Augusto, a Brazilian working for his father's armazém, argued that he himself "was poor" and with "those small purchases he could save some extra money to help take care of his family."[121] As the lawyer for another defendant, the Portuguese owner of an armazém, explained, "He has a small shop, and he lives by his honest labor, to support his family," adding that "the true speculators against the people—the loan sharks—are out there, living freely and without disruption."[122] Several defendants echoed these assertions, leveraging Estado Novo trabalhismo rhetoric to affirm that they were honest and industrious workers.[123]

After this lengthy investigation, eight individuals—seven men and one woman—faced a single trial before the NST. None of them were physically present at their trial; their lawyers presented testimonies and evidence in writing. None of the defendants denied participating in the voucher-for-cash scheme, but collectively insisted that none obtained "excessive profits." None of the parties clarified how they measured profits or what would constitute "excessive profits," but they—or their lawyers—used Decree Law No. 869's ambiguity about this to their advantage. After a yearlong investigation and scores of testimonies, all eight individuals were acquitted on the grounds of insufficient evidence of excessive profits.[124] Without knowing who made the initial complaint, it is impossible to know whether the investigation was motivated by the actual economic abuse endured by workers or simply a vendetta.

These examples would make it easy enough to dismiss Decree Law No. 869 as a farce, but that would ignore the wider context of the trials. Certainly, the ease of popular economy denunciations created plenty of opportunities for people to "consume justice," to borrow from historian Daniel Smail's study of fourteenth-century France, in which people used the courtroom purely to satisfy personal feuds and vendettas.[125] For others, popular economy denunciations might have been an opportunity to simply air complaints, without any expectation of judicial recourse.[126] Such personal appropriations of legal institutions can occur in any court, but some of the NST's shambolic features made it especially ripe for such opportunities. Setting aside this reductive conclusion, however, other things can be learned from the economic trials.

Even if motivated by vendettas, litigants had to make their claims according to the corporatist vocabulary that informed the system.

In this respect, popular economy trials provide a surprising glimpse into Brazil's economic transformation in the 1930s and 1940s. The Estado Novo's illiberal corporatist experiment asserted the state's authority over economic life by mobilizing a new language of economic justice and social peace. As E. P. Thompson argued in his study of England's eighteenth-century moral economy, grievances had to be articulated according to both a popular and political consensus as to "what were legitimate and what were illegitimate practices."[127] With the NST, not all grievances were *truly* economic in nature, but people learned quickly how to contort personal conflicts into the Estado Novo mold.[128]

Furthermore, with Decree Law No. 869, the courtroom became another venue for the airing of everyday economic conflicts, grievances, and hardships. Following Vargas's 1937 coup, the NST transformed from an organ of political tyranny to one promising economic justice for the *pequenos*, or "little ones."[129] With the NST, the ease of citizen denunciations—combined with overzealous policing—was meant as a tool that popular classes could wield against powerful special interests. Ironically, though, the economically weak were most vulnerable because it was so easy to make a complaint and have it prosecuted to the extreme. Already in 1938, one journalist had predicted that "punishment from this special tribunal . . . will fall on the humble and unprotected backs" of "smalltime retailers and producers."[130] This prophesy would come to fruition as economic trials proliferated with the onset of World War II.

————

Tristão de Ataíde, the nom de plume of Catholic nationalist (and integralist sympathizer) Alceu Amoroso Lima, wrote in 1945 that the previous fifteen years were a period of "illegality."[131] What he likely meant was that the rule of law was suspended during Vargas's rule, and most scholars and a good number of contemporaries would agree with him. Yet this conclusion is not quite right. It is not that government agents exercised arbitrary and unchecked powers; rather, laws were rewritten according to the corporatist, centralizing, and developmentalist ambitions guiding the Estado Novo. Understanding this period of authoritarian legalism or even authoritarian hyperlegalism is critical because this proliferation of laws shaped how citizens encountered the state in their everyday economic lives.

At the same time, the extent to which the economia popular became a sphere of legal intervention in Brazil reveals the rising cost of living and general sense of economic instability in urban centers. In other words, incidents of price gouging or misreported weights were not epiphenomenal events but instead symptoms of an economic crisis that required the Brazilian government to think about the interactions of urban and rural markets for food on local, regional, and national scales. Vargas responded to these economic challenges with programs to stimulate domestic food production, as discussed in the previous chapter, but he also understood the importance of immediate relief in both symbolic and practical terms.

The next chapter turns to World War II, which aggravated these economic challenges, particularly for the most vulnerable populations. New (and old) state institutions were mobilized to limit market uncertainty and increase production. Brazil's internal market was no longer seen as an aggregation of private contracts, nor something neutral, automatic, and self-regulating. It had become a sphere of government action and economic justice. The legal history of the popular economy is entangled with that of how the Estado Novo attempted to increase the state's capacity to transform the national economy as well as its limitations.

PART III

6

Wartime Economics

ON AUGUST 22, 1942, Brazil declared war on Germany and Italy. The South American nation's shift from neutrality to belligerence was a response to relentless acts of Axis aggression against commerce and civilians, not to mention pressure from the Allied powers to join the war. For months, German submarines attacked Brazilian vessels as they crossed the Atlantic Ocean. Hundreds of Brazilians lost their lives, while disruptions to trade caused food shortages, fuel scarcity, and rising prices. In March 1942, when a German U-boat torpedoed the Brazilian SS *Cairu*, riots erupted in Rio de Janeiro and across the country, targeting German businesses.[1] Brazil's formal declaration of war still took months of cajoling, as the United States extended cultural exchange missions and cushy incentives in the form of trade agreements, foreign direct investment, and the construction of military bases in the northeast.[2] Brazil's role in World War II was slight but pivotal. Its geographic position provided transport support for US soldiers crossing the South Atlantic.[3] It also proved invaluable on the diplomatic front as Brazilian officials played a decisive role in convincing another stalwart neutral nation—Portugal—to make strategic concessions to the Allied powers.

Across the Atlantic, Portugal found itself in a distinct yet comparable position to Brazil. Much like Vargas's initial stance, Salazar stubbornly insisted on Portugal's neutrality during the six-year conflict, asserting its right to trade with all belligerent powers. Neutrality, however, did not shield Portugal from the consequences of war, which this small, impoverished nation endured most acutely in the economic sphere. Prices for essential good skyrocketed, trade disruptions strained supply chains, and contraband networks pulled domestic goods to more lucrative markets in neighboring Spain. Its colonies in Asia and Africa were targets of Axis imperial ambitions. Portugal might have remained neutral during the war, but it was hardly a bystander. Salazar's dogmatic stance (eventually following tedious diplomatic negotiations) softened on two critical matters: an embargo on the sale of wolframite, a strategic ore in weapons manufacturing, to Axis powers and permission for the Allied powers to use the mid-Atlantic Azores Islands as a naval base.[4] Lisbon, moreover, became a transit point between war and genocide in Europe and relative tranquility in the Americas, overfilling with refugees looking for safe passage across the Atlantic. Between 1939 and 1945, historians estimate that fifty to a hundred thousand refugees moved through Portugal.[5] Lisbon became a city of espionage and profiteering too. British, US, and German spies kept close tabs on events on the ground, while various contrabandists sought opportunities for profit.[6]

World War II was a turning point for Estado Novo dictatorships in Brazil and Portugal. The war forced diplomatic realignments, while blockades brought economic dislocations to the emergent corporatist systems and threatened the sovereignty and stability of these regimes. Vargas and Salazar were dictators, and proudly so. But World War II was a struggle between democracy and dictatorship. The Axis powers were responsible for fifty to eighty million casualties worldwide by the war's end. Unsurprisingly, Vargas and Salazar would try to distance themselves from the label "fascist," claiming—at home and abroad—to be soft or benevolent dictatorships, in contrast to Mussolini and Hitler. They argued that corporatism was *not* fascist, and just an economic and social program.

This chapter explores what happened to corporatism during World War II. It considers intellectual efforts to save corporatism from fascism and the acceleration of the corporatist economic project during the war. In both Brazil and Portugal, officials responded to wartime crisis by increasing statist intervention in the economy as regulatory commissions, planning boards, and corporatist bodies mobilized to increase the production of essential goods. In corporatist fashion, producers were expected to work with—or according to—government-decreed production targets and price controls. These corporatist experiments with planning and controls, however, largely failed to withstand wartime disruptions. Producers navigated a labyrinth of new rules and institutions designed to increase output, even as merchants found ways to evade controls. Contraband markets sprung up for essential goods from bread to cement. High inflation became a pressing concern for government officials and everyday hardship for consumers. As the economic crises compounded, so did political and intellectual crises. Could corporatism really be untangled from fascism or comparisons to Mussolini's Italy? Brazilian and Portuguese officials defended corporatist experiments against accusations of totalitarianism in part by drawing closer to one another. Despite disruptions to transatlantic travel, these countries invested resources to strengthen the intellectual connections between their two Estado Novo regimes. Economic and legal ideas were often embedded in culturalist, racist, and civilizational discourses to defend corporatism as a uniquely Luso-Brazilian project for national and imperial renewal. Both nations leveraged their shared heritage to simultaneously distance their corporatist project from Anglo-American capitalist materialism and fascist aggression.

Despite efforts to harness this shared heritage, this chapter shows that Brazil and Portugal were evolving along different tracks. The two Estado Novo regimes diverged further during World War II. This is evident in how corporatist theory and practice started to unravel in both countries. In Portugal, wartime economic strategies remained tethered to corporatist logic, while in Brazil, wartime planning was far more eclectic and ad hoc as policy experimentation became less preoccupied with ideology. This chapter unfolds in three parts. The first part considers Portugal's deepening experiment with corporatism during the war, even in the face of shortages and contraband across its empire. The second part explores how Brazilian and Portuguese officials deepened intellectual and political exchanges as each country considered the future of corporatism in light of wartime challenges. Last, the chapter shifts to Brazil, where corporatism becomes less ideologically rigid even as Brazilian officials expanded economic planning during the war.

War in Portugal: The Search for Corporatist Control

In July 1943, Gracinda Ludovica, a forty-seven-year-old woman from a small village in the Algarve region, was detained for selling bread to the public at a 75 percent markup above the official price. In doing so, she stood in defiance of Decree Law No. 29.964 for participating in an "illegal trade" and "speculation on the sale of bread."[7] Decreed October 1939, this law intended to "defend the national economy against disorder."[8] Its thirty articles targeted economic crimes like hoarding merchandise, defying price controls, noncompliance with corporatist membership rules, and other practices that raised prices above values fixed by law. Portuguese officials anticipated that the war would destabilize the domestic economy. This decree was one of many issued to deter individuals from price gouging, hoarding, and other behaviors that aggravated the cost of living. Price controls on essential goods became Portugal's response to wartime inflation, which reached 22 percent in 1942, but this led many to hoard goods, thereby leading to scarcity as contraband markets and smuggling routes proliferated.

Portugal's government responded to wartime disruptions by increasing regulations over market life in ways that reinforced the country's corporatist organization. Grémio membership and compliance with corporatist rules became more important, even as the war exposed the limits to and incompleteness of this system. Those excluded by choice or circumstance from grémios looked for their own ways to survive. Ludovica's trial is an example of corporatism in practice—how citizens navigated, evaded, resisted, or suffered the consequences of corporatist rules. Portuguese officials tried to undercut the "free market," imposing discipline on individual profit-seeking motives. But discipline required enforcement, starting with bread prices.

Even as a neutral country, Portugal could not avoid the economic consequences of war.[9] Overall, Portugal's economic performance was not dire (figure 6.1), but macroeconomic variables do not account for everyday hardships as residents faced inflation and scarcity, booms and busts. After September 1939, naval blockades reduced maritime traffic, making it increasingly difficult for Portugal to import fertilizers and machinery. Domestic food production fell during the war as poor harvests made a bad situation worse.[10] The Battle of the Atlantic disrupted trade between Portugal and other parts of the world, including its colonies. It became harder to offset domestic shortages with imports. Food became scarce and expensive. In 1943, for example, the domestic production of wheat only covered four months of national consumption, with imports hard to secure. Similar scarcities impacted other essential goods, especially codfish and sugar. The Ministry of the Economy, created in 1940 by fusing the Ministry of Agriculture and the Ministry of Commerce and Industry, aggressively imposed controls and rationing. It required that all warehousers and large-scale retailers of essential goods (codfish, rice, sugar, potatoes, and so on) join a centralizing grémio, the Grémio dos Armazenistas de Mercearia, which in turn became responsible for negotiating alongside other regulatory agencies the import of basic necessities and overseeing their distribution across the country. This grémio was essential to government efforts to issue price controls and rationing across Portugal to stabilize the domestic food supply. It also became the target of public ire; citizens complained of corruption and denounced those connected to the grémio for profiting from black market transactions while so many went hungry.[11] By 1944, Lisbon residents, in a city overwhelmed by refugees, were allotted only four hundred grams of rice, four hundred grams of codfish, one kilogram of sugar, and five hundred grams of potatoes per month.[12]

With the outbreak of war, the corporatist system predicated on market discipline started to unravel. In early September 1939, Portuguese and colonial merchants, importers, wholesale vendors, and producers braced themselves for disruptions. Thousands of telegrams circulated between firms across Portugal and its empire as well as to trading partners in Brazil, France, and England. Wholesalers complained about how prices for raw materials had spiked by anywhere from 15 to 150 percent overnight. Some firms opted to suspend all business transactions while they awaited instructions on "new prices," even as others sent instructions to their agents that they could "sell only without guarantees on prices or date of delivery."[13] Speculative buying and selling began at once—not to mention hoarding—especially for strategic materials. This frenzy impacted all sectors, from cotton to cereals, coal to

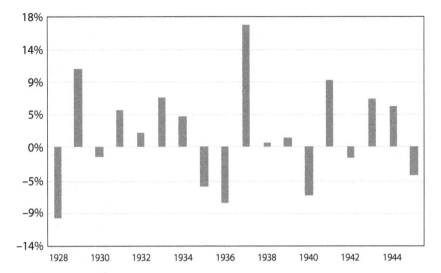

FIGURE 6.1. Portugal's real GDP growth, 1928–45. *Source:* GDP growth rate calculated by author using data in Angus Maddison, *The World Economy: Historical Statistics* (Paris: OECD Publishing, 2003), table 1b.

codfish. Firms reported that it was impossible to procure codfish or that beans seemingly disappeared overnight across the country. Wholesale buyers and vendors quibbled over exorbitant prices for essential goods. As one firm in northern Portugal gasped, "Your prices are unacceptable. Such prices are no longer relevant."[14] Whatever economic logic had functioned in the past no longer applied.

Despite Salazar's emphasis on self-sufficiency, Portugal could not escape the tailspin of global market forces as laws of supply and demand once again dictated firm behavior and individual decision-making. The corporatist ethos elevating national interests above self-interested profit motives vanished. Economic disruptions and opportunism were hardly unique to Portugal, but what is surprising is that many in Portugal decided to "suspend sales and wait for the new price table," as one Porto firm told its associates. A cynical reading might conclude that they were hoarding, holding out for higher future prices. No doubt, some were. But other firms remained committed to the top-down market discipline imposed in recent years. They petitioned recently created regulatory commissions and denounced competitors behaving "contrary to corporatist principles." Some even trusted that the "new order," in the words of one manufacturer of motor oils, would be reestablished in due course.[15]

By early October, Portugal's government responded to "disturbances to the national economy" with a series of decree laws and ordinances to reimpose order on the internal market.[16] These measures included price controls and antihoarding ordinances. During the war, thousands of memos, ordinances, and mandates were sent from the Ministry of the Interior or Ministry of the Economy to municipal governments and local grémios across the country in attempts to stem inflationary pressures and the scarcity of essential goods. Such efforts hardly worked. Black markets proliferated for nearly every commodity as shortages became more acute and price differentials widened between official and contraband sales. By 1943, olive oil was 229 percent more expensive on the black market than its legal price of 7$30 escudos per liter.[17] Consumers accused vendors of deliberately hoarding high-quality goods to clandestinely sell at exorbitant prices. Fish vendors allegedly off-loaded their inferior stock to consumers at the legally permitted prices while "reserving their best merchandise for the black market."[18] Salaries could not keep pace as consumers often had no choice but to resort to illegal trades to feed their families.

That wartime economic disruptions give rise to clandestine markets, speculative pricing, and profiteering is not unique or exceptional to either World War II or Portugal. Economic theories do not easily survive wartime dislocations, so we might expect the corporatist commitment to weaken. Wartime expediency led many interwar governments to abandon corporatist theory for more immediate and direct forms of state control over the economy.[19] In Portugal, however, the war only accelerated the corporatist makeover of the economy, spawning new government agencies and corporatist organisms responsible for the national economy.

This process was as evident at the highest levels of government as it was in everyday economic life. Many voluntary corporatist organs became obligatory, while new ones were created.[20] In 1942, Salazar boasted that the number of corporatist associations had increased by nearly 40 percent since the war, with 176 voluntary grémios for commerce and industry, 183 grémios da lavoura, and 440 sindicatos across the country. By Salazar's accounting, in 1942 alone, 28,767 rural workers and 7,581 fishers had signed collective contracts, while salaries had increased by as much as 25 percent since 1940.[21] Even regions without formal corporatist institutions experienced this growth in associational life: 227,542 Portuguese citizens were enrolled in over 400 casas do povo, social security institutions for agricultural workers, by 1942.[22] The Junta Central das Casas do Povo, a federal union of all rural associations, provided 2,322 disabled farmers with pensions in 1942 (doubling the 1941 figure).[23] By 1945, the government sponsored 563 casas do povo to distribute health care and social benefits to its over 270,000 members in rural areas.[24] In a country where 53 percent of the active population, or 1.5 million people, was employed in the agricultural and fishing sectors, only a fraction of the population had access to this welfare system. Still, official statistics compiled in the *Anuário*

Estatístico meticulously documented the progression of Portugal's corporatist revolution, and public officials—with the help of the propaganda ministry—broadcasted these numbers at home and abroad to celebrate Salazar's accomplishments.

Most Portuguese citizens were not yet incorporated into the corporatist system, though. In small but growing industrial centers in Lisbon or Porto, some workers who did not belong to a sindicato protested their exclusion from the rights and benefits guaranteed with membership. Across agricultural sectors, many farmers and rural workers remained without grémio membership, which meant that they were excluded from accessing markets for their goods or left without price protections.[25] Even workers inside the system complained that their collective contracts did not keep pace with rising prices.

This incomplete progress is partly what got Ludovica in trouble. In 1929, the cereal sector was the first put under corporatist organization in Portugal (see chapter 1). Corporatist organs had a dual function, responsible for the social well-being of members but also for making sure that members complied with market controls. Grémios, in other words, represented the private interests of members while also functioning as public agencies to regulate local production. Grémios for millers and bakers were responsible for ensuring that members abided by price controls and quotas. Ludovica did not belong to a grémio. She was caught conducting an illegal trade—running a clandestine and unregistered bakery out of her house—by an inspector working for the Grémio dos Industriais de Panificação de Faro, the Faro bread guild.[26] For bread, wine, or olive oil, grémios were sometimes responsible for routine inspections.[27] Ludovica allegedly violated Decree Law No. 29.964 by selling bread to the public at 2$54 escudos per kilogram, when the legal price was 1$90 escudos.

Ludovica might have sold bread at unjust rates to her neighbors, but she was also the casualty of an economic system that prevented free entry into the bread-making industry. Without grémio membership, she resorted to clandestine markets. Ludovica defended her participation in the informal economy, here branded the "free market," out of dire necessity and indicated that she only sold bread to the public "in moments when she found herself more distressed."[28] The inspector had little interest in her justification, confiscating her loaves and transferring her case to a special military tribunal.

In Portugal, a special tribunal within the military court system—the Tribunal Militar Especial Económico—became responsible for enforcing market controls. Active from 1942 to 1945, it processed nearly four thousand economic trials, frequently trying multiple defendants at once.[29] Trials dealt with exportable wartime commodities like wolframite or sardines, and industrial inputs such as steel. Sometimes trials targeted large *armazenistas*—warehousers—attempting to hoard supply. Big businesses, however, constituted only a sliver of the tribunal's docket. Rather, thousands of farmers, bakers, and winemakers stood trial—and received prison sentences—for violating price controls. In this way, Ludovica's trial resembles hundreds of popular economy trials in Brazil.

Ludovica was not present at her trial in Lisbon. Instead, her lawyer submitted a written opinion to the military tribunal. Ludovica's lawyer did not deny the charges but rather defended her actions by stressing the poverty and hardships she faced. Ludovica was "extremely poor and had young children at a tender age." If it were not for her informal and occasional bread business, she would not have the means to support her family. The tribunal had little sympathy for her "sad and precarious situation," however.[30] She was found guilty, and sentenced to a significant fine of 1.200$00 escudos and ten days in prison.[31] Not all trials before this special tribunal resulted in guilty sentences, yet judges often applied the most literal interpretations of economic laws in order to coerce compliance.

In Portugal, the Tribunal Militar Especial Económico evolved out of prior national security emergencies in which special military tribunals were created to root out perceived internal enemies.[32] In the early 1930s, special military tribunals sentenced trade unionists, communists, integralists, and others suspected of political extremism.[33] For example, the Tribunal Militar Especial Político, which operated from 1933 to 1945, functioned as the juridical arm of the secret police to provide quick summary judgments for political dissidents. Portugal adapted this framework to deal with wartime economic emergency, with officials arguing that ordinary courts were too slow or inconvenient to respond to the economic emergency.[34] Speculators—rather than communists or trade unionists—now threatened the social peace. Price and production controls were already a feature of Portugal's corporatist system throughout the 1930s, with grémios and administrative agencies responsible for routine inspections of commercial establishments and handing out fines. With the war, police and special military brigades exercised powers over more and more regulatory matters. In 1942, for instance, Faro's government responded to the urgent problem of the city's meat supply by appointing the police to handle routine inspections to repress "unscrupulous abuses committed by merchants."[35] By deploying police and military to enforce market controls, Salazar turned economic planning from an administrative to a criminal matter.

Price controls were also implemented in Vichy France, Nazi Germany, Fascist Italy, and even the United States, where the Emergency Price Control Act of 1942 broke political opposition to government intervention.[36] While in the United States, penalties for price ceiling violations were small—fines or revoked licenses—in other belligerent contexts, criminal prosecution became common. This pattern tracks with how war necessitates (or legitimizes) states of emergency and other interruptions to legal normalcy.[37] Wartime shifts in state-market relations, though, cannot be explained entirely as emergency responses. In each country, wartime planning had to be retrofitted to preexisting ideological and institutional frameworks.

For example, in 1940, Marshal Philippe Pétain established an authoritarian government in unoccupied France, implementing corporatist institutions to regulate the economy.[38] The Vichy regime folded wartime controls into its corporatist paradigm, disavowing the free market in favor of greater state intervention "to protect the nation against exploitation for private profit."[39] Pétain in France—like Vargas in Brazil and Salazar in Portugal—relied on already established moral language to justify the state's "vigilant control of consumption and prices" in the name of "greater justice in the distribution of goods."[40]

Nazi Germany is perhaps most scrutinized by historians hoping to understand economic planning under dictatorship. It never formally embraced corporatism, and Salazar did not cite Nazi examples due to his personal unease about Hitler's plans for Portugal and its colonies. Still, parallels existed. Until the mid-1930s, private cartels under government supervision and the *Reichsnährstand* (Reich Food Estate), with its semicorporatist structure, regulated food production and price fixing.[41] Harsh policing forced farmers and small businesses into compliance.[42] During the war, this system derailed and black markets proliferated.[43] One US observer noted that nearly four thousand Berlin shopkeepers were found guilty of price control violations in March 1941 alone.[44] Yet Nazi Germany stood apart from corporatist cases as it transformed from a state-directed to a state-controlled economy for wartime planning.[45] Given the catastrophic consequences, Nazi Germany remains a necessary case for understanding how dictatorships seized control, but it also overshadows the tactics—and consequences—of other dictatorships.

For Salazar's dictatorship, market controls extended a decade-long process to expand state capacity over the market, through corporatist logic, in order to subordinate private profits to national interests. The Tribunal Militar Especial Económico is a case study in the centrality of law in how authoritarian regimes attempt to remake economic life. In theory, this tribunal protected public well-being from private greed. In practice, Ludovica's trial offers another illustration of the uneven and hierarchical distribution of justice. Ironically, since she pleaded poverty and hardship, Ludovica's "illegal" bread was donated to a local charity after her arrest—a routine practice with confiscated goods. Ludovica suffered not only because she could not participate in this trade but because corporatist membership excluded her from certain social security protections too. Members of casas do povo, for example, were often given higher bread rations.[46] And while the 1933 Constitution might have promised social protections like a family salary as a fundamental right, charity remained the only way many could access relief from economic hardship.[47]

Without doubt, it was more politically expedient to scapegoat Ludovica and thousands like her than to do nothing, or worse, admit that corporatist controls were useless for wartime crisis. Government technocrats responded to spiraling economic crises by blaming greed and profiteering. Because officials blamed inflation on individual behavior rather than on structural factors, they turned price controls into an even more important tool of legitimacy as wartime economic challenges distorted and dismantled the carefully erected corporatist institutions of the 1930s.

The economic challenges that Portugal faced during World War II also strained the relationship between metropole and colonies. Salazar worried that one belligerent power or another would take control of Angola, Portugal's wealthiest colony and the "jewel coveted by foreigners."[48] These concerns intensified in 1942, when Japanese forces invaded East Timor. Portugal's imperial sovereignty in Africa remained intact during the war, but its perceived weaknesses led some foreign powers to speculate on how its colonial possessions might be put to better uses. World War II was a moment of reckoning for corporatism in both contexts.

Within weeks after the war began, corporatist price controls in the colonies unraveled due to speculative trading. As mentioned earlier, corn was one of the first colonial commodities subjected to corporatist reorganization (see chapter 4). Starting in 1939, exports started to decline and were cut in half by 1943. The corn sector in particular faced several problems. Much of the agricultural production in Angola fell to native African workers, who labored in harsh conditions and were paid a fraction of what European settlers earned. Corporatist promises of fair prices applied only to white farmers. Even as corn prices skyrocketed during the war, African workers received less and less. Corporatist scaffolding in the colonies had added intermediaries, taxes, insurance, transportation, and warehousing, and these expenses eroded the prices paid to African workers. The exploitative and abusive dynamics of Portuguese colonization are well documented, with forced labor a continued practice.[49] For a kilogram of corn, most African producers earned $20 escudos, with a retail price that was ten times higher. This ratio worsened during the war, just as the cost of living spiked. Imperial bureaucrats protested this exploitation for reasons of profits rather than human rights. With such dismal conditions, African workers found strategies to turn to more lucrative commodities, or as one imperial bureaucrat noted, "Those who could, [would] break free [and] run away."[50] Despite a decade of economic theory that emphasized corporatism as a moral economy, the colonial problem could only be articulated in terms of incentives and coercion.

Even with—or perhaps because of—all the oversight in corporatism, officials reduced economic problems to their simplest parts. Global supply chain disruptions turned into smaller debates over prices, fees, and taxes. A web of rules such as those that had snared Ludovica extended to the colonies, although to a far lesser extent. In Luanda, for example, bakeries formed a cartel to set prices. The Ministry of the Colonies and Ministry of the Economy produced successive reports on flour and bread, committed to making this sector more efficient so that "profits [would] be fair."[51] Intermediaries became scapegoats for corporatist failings. In 1942, the governor-general of Angola attacked the "expensive . . . corporatist machine, with thousands of contos pulled from the national economy, as producers and consumers suffer, while intermediaries profit."[52] The failures of corporatism in the colonies mirrored those in the metropole.

In October 1939, Lisbon's soap makers complained to Salazar about the skyrocketing prices on global markets for the vegetable oils used to make soap. They had recently sent the *Mirandela* vessel to Angola to acquire two thousand tons of oils, yet could not even purchase a thousand tons.[53] Fifteen kilograms of coconuts—a common soap input—had cost sixteen escudos in early September, but the price had jumped 60 percent by mid-December.[54] The same occurred for palm oils, fish oils, and other raw ingredients. Coconut growers in northern Angola had easy access to buyers in the Belgian Congo (the present-day Democratic Republic of the Congo). For Portuguese soap makers, the only alternative source was São Tomé. "On that island," however, "the dearth of workers was great." Without a "good price" for the coconuts, one imperial civil servant noted that it was impossible to increase its production because "everyone works in cacao [plantations]," the island's primary export. He cynically suggested that "only in hospitals, when the *serviçais* were in convalescence," was any labor diverted to peel coconuts.[55] The category *serviçais* often referred to Angolan workers contracted to work in São Tomé. It first appeared after the abolition of slavery in the late nineteenth century to describe new conditions of bonded or semibonded labor in the Portuguese colonies.[56]

The neomercantilist impetus behind corporatism aimed to turn the colonies profitable for the metropole (see chapter 4). During the war, though, contraband and smuggling ran rampant within Portugal's colonies and along imperial borders. In northern Angola especially, colonial producers and merchants could access lucrative markets in belligerent powers' colonies, with goods eventually making their way to Europe. Contraband led to acute shortages in raw goods, angering Portuguese importers and manufacturers.[57]

Lisbon soap makers, like many Portuguese manufacturers, took their complaints directly to Salazar. Citing rumor, statistics, and other sources, they asked for protections from foreign merchants who took advantage of porous imperial borders to profit unlawfully from Portugal's imperial wealth. The Estado Novo's ability to enforce market controls seemed weak in comparison to global market forces. "If we cannot pay that [higher] price," one soap maker explained, "the coconut, given its geographic position, will either stay on the palm trees, or if harvested, will find its way to foreign competitors, where they pay properly."[58]

In theory, the corporatist system guaranteed a fair price to both colonial producers and Portuguese buyers of vegetable oils. But economic controls also contributed to the system's undoing because in practice, price controls generated scarcity. Merchants knew they could fetch higher prices in neighboring regions. This was not a closed, autarkic system. For Lisbon's soap makers, contraband vegetable oil was the inevitable consequence of too many controls. High costs and scarce supplies of raw materials were problems because a regulatory commission controlled domestic soap prices. To prevent further ruin, one Lisbon firm petitioned Salazar to increase official prices from thirty escudos a box to eighty escudos—calculations based on production costs plus a "fair profit" of 10 percent to manufacturers. With a piercing critique of this corporatist ethos, the soap maker insisted that "manufactured products have to be sold at a price that covers the cost of raw materials and not at fantasy prices."[59]

Harsh critiques of the system in place should not be mistaken for calls to abandon controls and protections altogether. Portuguese merchants and manufacturers continued to advocate for their interests within the corporatist framework, without (any discernible) nostalgia for free and self-correcting markets.

Contraband markets became a site of resistance against corporatist controls and the ambitions of economic planners in Lisbon. Those excluded from corporatist protections, like Ludovica, engaged in illegal market activities as a survival strategy. For others, contraband trade was motivated by opportunism. Some merchants and producers continued to enjoy their monopoly privileges and still found ways to profit extravagantly from black market offsprings of the formal system. Some Portuguese soap makers, for example, participated in contraband markets of their own invention. Frustrated by the official prices for their product, they sent caravans of contraband soap to the Spanish border. During the Spanish Civil War, as agricultural production came to a standstill with the fighting and land occupations, Spanish merchants had turned to the Portuguese contraband trade, particularly for soap, meat, coffee, sugar, and rice.[60] Illegal trade intensified during World War II. Police patrolling the Luso-Spanish border reported acute scarcities of soap in rural villages and urban areas, while boxes of soap were confiscated from raids on warehouses and trucks along the borders, abandoned by smugglers.[61]

From Spain via smuggling routes, goods traveled during the war to belligerent powers throughout Europe. Contraband business largely originated with firms in Porto and Lisbon, which took advantage of Portugal's porous borders and border residents' willingness to participate in this lucrative trade. Local residents—of all genders and ages—faced grave risks to haul goods on foot or mules. Contraband was an important economic activity for impoverished rural border villages. Much of the agricultural production in these villages had remained outside formal corporatist control, largely for home consumption or local markets. Limited state capacity meant that the contraband trade could flourish here, although the rise of illegal activities in these remote regions attracted more inspectors and police surveillance too.

Contraband networks along the Portuguese-Spanish border were not created by Estado Novo controls.[62] Rather, these networks were a by-product of the nation-building process that imposed seemingly artificial boundaries on regional economies. This process had accelerated in the late eighteenth century, punctuated by moments when these national governments intensified their efforts to demarcate national territories and differences.[63] The 1930s and 1940s marked another turning point in this process. War—first the Spanish Civil War and then World War II—increased the importance of border policing. By the late 1930s, Salazar had created new police forces and military brigades to specifically target "crimes against the national economy."[64] Even the Polícia de Vigilância e Defesa do Estado was tapped. As Salazar's secret police force, it was responsible for national security, infamous for its surveillance, torture, and arrest of political dissidents and labor activists. Known as the Polícia Internacional e de Defesa do Estado after 1945, the Polícia de Vigilância e Defesa do Estado was responsible for border patrol and any internal security issues. Contraband fell in its jurisdiction.

In many cases, contraband goods confiscated on the border were traced back to firms in Lisbon or Porto.[65] In September 1941, for example, inspectors in the northern city Chaves, close to the Spanish border, apprehended 2,190 kilograms of coffee in a warehouse destined for Spain and beyond. Coffee, likely originating either in Africa or Brazil, was one of the most important commodities to cross the Luso-Spanish border.[66] That same week, in Guarda, brigade inspectors happened on 152,120 kilograms of highly deteriorated coffee in a single warehouse. The owner of this particular warehouse was rumored to operate out of the port cities Figueira da Foz and Lisbon, as the agent concluded that this coffee as well as the beans, sugar, and cacao were part of a re-exportation scheme to Spain.[67]

The prosecution of individuals such as Ludovica seems comical in comparison to the big business contraband networks developing across Portugal and its empire. By 1943, Estado Novo officials in Lisbon were well aware of these asymmetries. Deputies to the National Assembly accused large firms of being black markets rogues. They benefited from corporatist and monopolist protections, yet still pursued illegal activities. Deputies fumed over anecdotes that some retailers even sent customers who entered their empty shops to black markets to purchase goods. In villages and cities across Portugal, affirmed one National Assembly deputy in April 1943, "local authorities themselves were the first to break official ordinances, and in that way, generated, with legal protections, the black market."[68] Portugal's elaborate system of controls may indeed have depended on contraband markets as a safety valve for popular classes and powerful interests alike.

The mobilization of secret police and military tribunals to deal with economic emergency was thus significant for another reason. Historians have probed how the Salazarist regime curtailed civil liberties through overzealous surveillance and censorship.[69] Yet for the average citizen in this impoverished and largely rural nation, it was perhaps in the economic rather than political sphere that most people encountered draconian aspects of dictatorship. That the police regulated everyday commerce shows the extent to which the economy had become a national emergency, thereby greatly expanding police powers to search businesses, seize property and merchandise, and suspend trade, often without due process.

By the same token, contraband during the war was not just about economics; it also constituted an act of everyday resistance by rural populations against the state.[70] This resistance, although not explicitly political, illustrates how popular classes undermined and defied a brutally repressive dictatorship.[71] Ministry of the Economy officials complained that their inspections were often blocked or diverted by local residents, who prevented them from entering train stations or catching sight of illegal activities.[72] Inspectors, too, saw the actions of local populations as forms of dissent, reporting back to Lisbon on how "the passive resistance on the part of local residents continues, which greatly impairs the work of the brigades."[73]

Despite the corruption, scarcity, and poverty evident during the war, Portuguese officials remained committed to the corporatist path as the only solution to market lawlessness. They turned to a convenient scapegoat in order to explain wartime hardships: capitalist greed had corrupted the corporatist system. Ludovica's trial shows how national economic problems were individualized in this way. Corporatism was celebrated as an antidote to the individualistic ethos of the free market. Portuguese officials sidestepped questions of why the corporatist framework had faltered during the war by blaming inflation and scarcity on the "few hundred individuals ... concentrated in border towns without any known occupation and entirely dedicated to the illegal export of goods."[74] Contraband markets became proof that the *homo corportivus* had not yet vanquished the *homo economicus*.

Corporatist Conversations across the Atlantic: Transnational National Projects

In August 1941, a special delegation of Portuguese officials arrived in Rio de Janeiro to negotiate a new cultural agreement. The thirteen-day mission was a huge event: government ministries, academic centers, and immigrant associations across Brazil organized banquets and parades to honor Portuguese dignitaries, while Vargas held formal audiences with the delegation.[75] António Ferro called these events a celebration of Luso-Brazilian civilization as "one race, two nations, one world."[76] It may seem a frivolous event in wartime, but deeper issues were at play here. There is a tendency to see globalism or internationalism as more compatible with liberal, democratic projects, yet for Brazilian and Portuguese officials, appeals to a Luso-Brazilian world were also attempts to situate their political experiment in a global context—one polarized at the time into democracy versus totalitarianism, capitalism versus communism, or modern versus backward.[77]

The two Estado Novos attempted to reinvent their dictatorships as instruments for progress, and corporatism was key to this project. As Marcello Caetano emphasized during his 1941 visit to Brazil, "Corporatist law is enjoying, at this moment, its dramatic golden age."[78] Caetano, serving as director of the Mocidade Portuguesa (Portuguese Youth), was one of the youngest members of Portugal's delegation to Brazil. As noted earlier, his name was already familiar in Brazilian legal circles as a leading corporatist.[79] During his stay in Rio de Janeiro, Caetano dined with Vargas and met with several top ministers. Valdemar Falcão, former labor minister recently appointed to Brazil's Supreme Federal Court, called Caetano "a perennial source of constructive energy, dedicated to the innovative work of corporatist organization and [Portugal's] administrative rejuvenation."[80]

To commemorate Caetano's visit to Rio de Janeiro, Brazilian officials organized a conference on "exchanges in legal culture between Portugal and Brazil," hosted by the Instituto da Ordem dos Advogados, a lawyers' association. The highly publicized event convened leading experts in corporatist law, and they used this as an opportunity to celebrate Brazil's recent achievements, especially the 1937 Constitution. For Falcão, corporatism was a shared Luso-Brazilian project, obliquely suggesting intellectual "collaboration" between Brazilian and Portuguese jurists in writing these constitutions. His speech, reprinted in newspapers and academic journals, stressed corporatism as a modern political system that was rejuvenating the nation with the "spirit of discipline and order."[81]

In addition, Falcão and others in attendance drew on the notion of a shared Luso-Brazilian race to get their message across. Metaphors of blood and body made the ties between these two nations seem primal and organic. "Portugal feels in Brazil the smooth synchronism of just one and the same heart," Caetano explained, "beating at the impulse of the same blood that flows in the veins of and tones the stiff muscles of the Brazilian people, the direct result of that colonizing mission that was planted here nearly four and a half centuries ago."[82] Corporeal language was not at all exceptional for the 1930s and 1940s, as nations worldwide legitimized their political projects through racial arguments and blood purity.[83] Similarly, with these meetings, Brazilian and Portuguese officials mobilized civilizational discourses to manufacture a unified Luso-Brazilian project as the wellspring of past greatness and future prosperity. In an age of virulent nationalism, the Vargas and Salazar dictatorships invented this transnational Luso-Brazilian identity in order to embolden their national projects.

The push for closer ties between Brazil and Portugal became a project in historical revisionism. For too long, these societies had been cast as failures, in contrast to the North Atlantic, or what contemporaries stylized as Anglo-Saxon civilization. By elevating Luso-Brazilian civilization, Brazilian and Portuguese officials debunked arguments that these societies were culturally or racially inferior to nations in North America and northern Europe. In Brazil specifically, nineteenth-century scientists and politicians had worried that it was a degenerated nation owing to its racial composition and tropical climate. To be sure, Brazilians never wholesale accepted the eugenic conclusions of their northern European counterparts or their emphasis on racial purity, and yet their preoccupation with whiteness consistently shaped their political and economic visions for national progress.[84] By the 1930s, however, celebrations of Brazil as a nation shaped by racial miscegenation became official state ideology. Brazilian sociologist Gilberto Freyre was crucial to this intellectual transformation. His 1933 *Casa Grande e Senzala* described Brazil's evolution as a nation forged through the mixing of Indigenous, African, and Portuguese peoples, reinterpreting this heterogeneity not as the source of its backwardness but instead its strength. Freyre celebrated racial heterogeneity all the while casting the Portuguese in a triumphant role.[85] His theory of *luso-tropicalismo*, elaborated over several decades, insisted that the Portuguese made better colonizers than other Europeans because they were more suited to life in the tropics.[86] Freyre's writings silenced the violence, rape, and enslavement essential to Portuguese colonialism, euphemizing this process as a "biological and social experiment."[87]

Freyre's efforts to celebrate Brazil's ties to Portugal intensified during World War II, in part because of official government efforts to defend Luso-Brazilian civilization as a viable and progressive political agent. In June 1940, for example, Freyre delivered a speech at the Gabinete Português de Leitura de Pernambuco in Recife calling for "the rehabilitation of the figure—maligned for so long—of the Portuguese colonizer in Brazil; . . . to restore Luso-Brazilian culture, threatened today, more than you think, by the agents of ethnocentric imperialism, interested in discrediting us as a race—one that they qualify as 'mestiço,' 'inept,' or 'corrupt'—that they disdain as inferior to their own."[88] Freyre's writings were readily absorbed and disseminated in Portugal, and he became one of the fiercest proponents of Salazar's efforts to rehabilitate Portugal's imperial project.[89] Freyre fashioned himself a supporter of democratic politics, which sometimes put him politically at odds with Vargas. But his critiques of dictatorship at home did not deter him from praising Salazar. Freyre even accepted Salazar's invitation to participate in an official mission, organized by the Ministry of the Colonies, to Angola, Mozambique, and Goa in the 1950s.[90]

While anti-Portuguese sentiments had been quite fierce in some commercial and political circles in Brazil throughout the nineteenth century, by the 1930s and 1940s not all in Brazil looked to or even cared about Portugal. The Luso-Brazilian project was one largely supported by conservatives, particularly those committed to the authoritarian, nationalist, Catholic, and corporatist path that both nations were taking. Still, some Brazilians worried that closer ties between Brazil and Portugal would draw Brazil deeper into a European sphere of influence dominated by dictators. With heightened censorship during World War II, public criticism of Vargas's diplomacy was frequently vague and muted. But private correspondence and editorials intercepted and censored by Brazilian authorities reveal how some worried about how much time Portuguese propaganda minister Ferro was spending in Brazil and other parts of Latin America to "spread *iberismo* in opposition to pan-Americanism," because it might well be a path to fascism and totalitarianism: "It seems that not only Salazar but also Franco and even possibly Hitler might well follow."[91] For those in Brazil who supported a return to democracy, closer ties with Portugal amounted to a defense of dictatorship. They recognized Brazil's potential as a large and growing nation, with wealth in natural resources and the capacity for rapid economic transformation. For this reason, many liberal and left-leaning intellectuals had little interest in the reinvention of a colonial past. Some preferred to look to the United States. Closer commercial, financial, and political ties with the United States were already a boost to infrastructure and industrialization projects. Growing diplomatic and economic ties between Brazil and the United States during the war, historian Jessica Graham argues, also helped both nations bolster their democratic images through radio programming, music, and literature. Where Brazil's conservative corporatist intellectuals celebrated shared blood and history with Portugal to make dictatorship seem progressive, liberal, communist, and antifascist intellectuals looked instead to the United States, putting race and racism at the center of their democratic project.[92]

Notwithstanding these detractors, those in Brazil who looked to Portugal did not do so out of nostalgia but rather as a means to defend their worldview and delineate a leading role for Brazil in international affairs. For some within Vargas's government, moreover, Portugal's colonies were becoming more of a draw than the country itself, as they saw Portugal as a stepping stone to stronger commercial relations in Africa and Asia. Within the CFCE, Brazilian officials strategized on how to introduce Brazilian products in Portuguese Africa.[93] During World War II, Brazilian firms attempted to seize on disruption to normal trade relations to increase exports of textiles and other light manufactured goods to Portuguese colonies, especially to Angola.[94]

For their part, Portuguese intellectuals put empire at the heart of their project to claim Brazil as the "país mais-que-irmão de Além-Atlântico," or a sister nation across the Atlantic.[95] In Portugal's Estado Novo propaganda, Brazil served as a bridge between past and future imperial glory. The most prominent example was the 1940 Exposição do Mundo Português, a centennial celebration of the foundation of the Portuguese nation in 1140 and restoration of its sovereignty from Spain in 1640. This was Portugal's response to the 1937 Exposition Internationale des Arts et Techniques das la Vie Moderne in Paris, or the 1939 San Francisco Golden Gate International Exposition.[96] Ferro attempted to shape international public opinion by showcasing Portugal's imperial past alongside recent feats of the Estado Novo.[97] Brazil was the only nation honored with its own pavilion.[98] Oswaldo Aranha saw Portugal's gesture to include Brazil as a coparticipant as an expression of the "union of two nations in defense of the race and civilization they represent, and of the ideas and sentiments they share in common."[99]

In this spirit, the propaganda ministry of each country established satellite offices in the other. This meant that Brazil's Departamento de Imprensa e Propaganda had an office in Lisbon and Portugal's Secretariado da Propaganda Nacional opened one in Rio de Janeiro, making it easier to publish and circulate news between them. Ferro and his Brazilian counterpart, Lourival Fontes (figure 6.2), even cocreated and coedited the transatlantic magazine *Atlântico: Revista luso-brasileira* thanks to this agreement. For Fontes, "What Brazil seeks to discover in Portugal is not just its past but also its present and its future."[100]

To be sure, Brazil hardly needed to strengthen its ties with Portugal, thereby making these intellectual efforts all the more significant. Brazil by the 1940s had already outstripped its former colonial power in many respects. It was the most populous nation in South America, boasting the continent's second-largest economy.[101] Still, Brazilian political and economic elites were aware of the importance of retaining ties to Portugal as a commercial hub for its goods. In 1942, Brazilian ambassador to Portugal João Neves da Fontoura argued that Brazil could improve its global standing through its relationship with Portugal:

FIGURE 6.2. (*left to right*) Lourival Fontes, director of Brazil's Departamento de Imprensa e Propaganda, Getúlio Vargas, and António Ferro, Portuguese director of the Secretariado da Propaganda Nacional, meeting to sign a cultural agreement in Catete Palace, Rio de Janeiro (1941). Image courtesy of the Centro de Pesquisa e Documentação de História Contempoânea do Brasil, Fundação Getúlio Vargas.

"Portugal is our entry point, the neutral intermediary for the expansion of our moral and political influence over the Latin European world. France will come out of the war weakened, divided, and impoverished. Italy will be in utter ruins. And Franco looks like a confused cockroach after the fall of Mussolini."[102] With Brazil as the world's largest Catholic nation, it could become a new center of cultural and political influence across the Atlantic. As Fontoura explained, "I still firmly believe that Brazil will have a global, and not just continental, projection in the future, especially if it positions itself as the advocate for *latinidade*."[103]

As Brazilian intellectuals observed a shifting world order, they did not want the uniqueness of their model forgotten in the violent conflict between totalitarian models and liberal stalwarts. Many attributed Brazil's economic successes in these years to the ways that Vargas had fiercely "substituted economic liberalism for the [state-]directed economy."[104] Even if Vargas rarely evoked corporatism explicitly, and even if the war spawned more and different kinds of economic planning, beyond corporatism, he consistently affirmed his economic vision as a third path between "abusive and unjust classical capitalism" and the seductive yet dangerous promises of "revolutionary Marxism."[105] To many corporatist ideologues, Brazil's third path was deeply indebted to its colonial antecedents. Vargas's genius was that he managed to "restore us using the authoritarian and corporatist traditions of the Portuguese Crown."[106] In past and present form, for Vargas's opponents as much as for his fiercest supporters, the Portuguese connection was inseparable from ongoing efforts to establish a third path between total liberty and total control in the economic sphere.

This improvised political theory might have been just a smoke screen to detract from Salazar and Vargas's suppression of civil and political rights. But to dismiss such arguments would be to overlook intellectual projects to make some dictatorships seem palatable and even necessary. Salazar enjoyed popularity abroad, especially in Catholic countries. He drew on his academic credentials and ascetic lifestyle to build his reputation as more professor than strongman. Salazar himself proved to be a great argument for how corporatism was not fascist because fascism required a bombastic cult of personality to rally the masses. In contrast, many Catholic intellectuals emphasized, Salazar was a "scholar, almost a recluse" and "bachelor," with his reputation mired by "neither romance, nor scandal, nor uproar."[107] Salazar himself often sidestepped the question of democracy altogether, sometimes accepting the category *dictator* because the dichotomy of democracy or dictatorship did not leave room for his regime.[108]

Vargas similarly dodged labels and comparisons, but in his own way. Where Salazar used convoluted arguments to avoid directly responding to the question of dictatorship, Vargas seemed to make light of the matter. "The president mocks democracies," one Chilean diplomat remarked after meeting with Vargas in 1940.[109] Vargas's "mockery" of democracy often stemmed from his insistence that his regime was not a dictatorship but rather a truer form of democracy than found in liberal contexts. Vargas's replies to questions about democracy were frequently as strategic as they were noncommittal.

In the early 1940s, opposition against Vargas nonetheless mounted, in part because liberal and left-wing groups felt emboldened by the horrific actions of European dictatorships to protest dictatorship at home. Repression, closures, and censorship followed, becoming more routine. In October 1941, for example, when law students in São Paulo marched against Vargas, the university's director closed the school for six days.[110] Newspapers reported on the protests, but left the details vague. This was typical. Dissent was often glossed over or censored in newspapers to conceal growing opposition to Vargas. Instead, rumors of dissent circulated at in-person meetings as well as in letters within and beyond Brazil vulnerable to police interception.

Vargas's regime responded to opposition groups with censorship and force. But he also tried to neutralize opposition groups by emphasizing the democratic potential of corporatism. To appease student protests, Vargas promised not elections, for instance, but instead to finally convene the corporatist chamber promised in the 1937 Constitution.[111]

Vargas always insisted that corporatism was not fascism but rather democracy designed according to Brazilian necessities. He and his team engaged in a delicate balancing act with corporatism as a transnational ideal and nationalist project that was original, autonomous, and responsive to Brazil's unique social as well as racial formation. As one minister asserted, Brazil had a "particular physiognomy in its corporatism" because "fortunately, we did not want to establish [here] an improvised corporatist organization that was foreign to our national reality."[112] Brazil's Estado Novo, after all, was a deeply nationalist regime, embracing protectionism, canceling foreign debt, curbing immigration, nationalizing strategic resources, and turning foreign bankers and business agents into capitalist villains. Brazilian intellectuals seized on corporatist ideas and laws circulating globally, while insisting that their program was organic and original. In 1943, Oliveira Vianna contended that this corporatist system was "planned, executed, and finalized with Brazil always in mind."[113] But the meaning and practice of corporatism was hardly finalized. During the war, Brazilian officials continued experimenting with this corporatist system as they also engaged in new forms of economic planning to tackle production shortages and price control, as the next section discusses.

War in Brazil: Planning beyond Corporatism

As the war began and throughout the early 1940s, the crisis of wartime inflation hijacked the intellectual ambitions of Brazilian jurists and technocrats to define corporatism as a third path, and redefine profits and prices according to corporatist ideals of social peace. The big ideas and laws tested during the 1930s were now fully mobilized to deal with another economic crisis, while many new strategies were implemented too. In the process, as we will see, Brazil's corporatist experiment lost some of its ideological coherence, but also—and perhaps counterintuitively—quickly expanded in scope.

For prices specifically, a cohort of technocrats seized on the war to emphasize the importance of thinking of price in a corporatist logic. In September 1939, just weeks after the outbreak of war in Europe, rice exporting firm Ries & Cia from Rio Grande do Sul sent a telegram to its commercial buyer in Recife announcing a price increase of two thousand réis per fifty-kilogram bag of rice. This telegram was intercepted by DOPS agents, Vargas's police for social and political surveillance, which had raided both business offices to confiscate communication and business records. Police scrutinized these documents in order to ascertain whether the price increase was fair or an act of speculation.

Prosecutors in Rio de Janeiro charged Ries & Cia under Decree Law No. 869 (see chapter 5) for price speculation. Months later, the NST heard the trial. Over lengthy proceedings, Ries & Cia defended its pricing by compiling price data for competing export firms along with costs for the raw materials and transportation. The price of rice, it insisted, was "controlled" by the Instituto do Arroz do Rio Grande do Sul, the corporatist organ representing large-scale rice producers in the region, and responsible for coordinating producers and purchasing excess stocks to stabilize prices. The Ries & Cia partners repeatedly argued that their wholesale prices were "just prices in accordance with market conditions"— namely laws of supply and demand—but also asserted their loyalty to Vargas and his moral economy.[114] The firm's lawyers quoted Justice Minister Francisco Campos, explaining Ries & Cia's business contracts in terms of the regime's corporatist philosophy, and promising that this firm was neither a "financial tycoon" nor "capitalist enterprise."[115] Ries & Cia became the first of many firms caught in the maelstrom of another economic emergency, triggered by war.

During the six-year war, Brazil's economy sputtered along. Its national output generally expanded but not without disruptions (figure 6.3). Inflation crept upward and reached 25 percent in 1945.[116] Brazil's trade statistics captured the economic volatility: exports fell by 17 percent, but the nominal value of exports increased by nearly 120 percent because of the spike in commodity prices.[117] Economic performance varied greatly by sector, as some experienced a boon (like the 30 percent increase in rubber exports between 1939 and 1943) while others did not. Iron mining, for example, was highly inconsistent, with sharp upticks and downturns. Moreover, certain commodity outputs dropped precipitously, as with the 30 percent decline in yerba maté output between 1939 and 1943.[118] The IBGE, Brazil's statistics agency, compiled exhaustive statistics on the wartime economy to document the uncertain pace of development.

Brazil's Estado Novo scrambled to prepare the nation for the economic consequences of a global war. Despite the country's initial neutrality, government officials anticipated that trade blockades would make food imports more precarious and expensive, and worldwide demand for raw materials would trigger price hikes. Vargas turned to Decree Law No. 869 to protect the popular economy and reinforce the state's control over the national economy, targeting pharmacies, urban retailers, and wholesale distributors to discourage them from profiteering from the war.[119] Journalists reported on how judges sentenced market vendors to six months in prison for selling beef at a price above the official table, and denunciations flooded police precincts over markups on basic provisions.[120]

Brazil's government created many, often overlapping institutes, commissions, and commodity boards after 1939 to defend or mobilize the domestic market. For the rice sector in southern Brazil, it officially recognized the

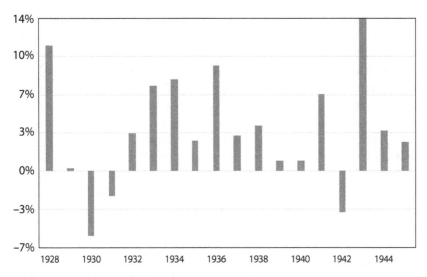

FIGURE 6.3. Brazil's real GDP growth, 1928–45. *Source:* GDP growth rate calculated by author using data in Angus Maddison, *The World Economy: Historical Statistics* (Paris: OECD Publishing, 2003), table 4b.

Instituto do Arroz do Rio Grande do Sul as an *autarquia pública*, or autonomous public organ, in 1940. First created in the 1920s as a cartel representing the state's rice producers, this organ had slowly transformed into a public entity during the 1930s in corporatist spirit (see chapter 1). In 1940, this transformation became official as the institute now exercised regulatory powers over the sector, including powers to establish an equilibrium between production and consumption.[121] Together, this mix of old and new strategies reflected Vargas's highest ambition: state direction (but not control) of national production and consumption. Ultimately, all of this state making depended on Vargas's decree laws, revealing the extent to which executive power controlled the administrative state.

Alongside this mobilization of preexisting laws and institutions, Vargas created new state agencies to regulate the economy in response to the war. In late September 1939, just weeks after the Nazi invasion of Poland, Vargas decreed the Comissão de Defesa da Economia Nacional (Commission for National Economic Defense). The commission's immediate task was to shield the economy from wartime hardships, especially disruptions to industrial, fuel, and food imports. Its concrete actions become difficult to precisely describe given the Estado Novo's bureaucratic labyrinth. Historians often focus on the Comissão de Defesa da Economia Nacional's early role in Brazil's efforts to control imports—a policy that would expand into import substitution industrialization after the war.[122] It helped, for instance, manufacturing industries secure necessary imports such as sodium hydroxide, a chemical base used in the manufacture of textiles, paper, soap, and other goods.[123] It worked alongside the Comissão do Abastecimento (Food Supply Commission), also created in September 1939, to oversee the supply and circulation of foodstuff and raw materials across Brazil. This commission was the successor to the Comissão Reguladora do Tabelamento (see chapter 4), expanding state powers to fix price controls and regulate commerce beyond Rio de Janeiro in order to deal with the cost-of-living crisis during the war. With these organs, Brazil's technocrats defended greater state intervention by reinforcing the prevailing economic logic: global disturbances compromised "the freely functioning mechanisms of the market."[124]

In August 1942, Brazil's government joined the Allied effort by declaring war on Nazi Germany and Fascist Italy. Just days later, Vargas used powers granted by the 1937 Constitution to declare a state of siege.[125] The war turned all aspects of the economy into urgent matters for state planning, from heavy industry to the types of flour in bread making. Public officials also looked for ways to mobilize civilians in the war effort.[126] A fundamental question underscored these debates: Should the government adapt peacetime institutions to wartime needs or create new institutions?[127] The answer for Brazil was to combine both strategies.

A new organ epitomized how Vargas's approach to economic planning built on prior practices: the Coordenação da Mobilização Econômica (Coordination for Economic Mobilization, or CME). Vargas decreed the CME in September 1942 to replace the Comissão de Defesa da Economia Nacional. This "super-ministry," as it was called, was headquartered in Rio de Janeiro, with regional offices nationwide. The CME had an advisory board comprised initially of Fontoura, a gaucho politician who had played a decisive role during the 1930 Revolution before breaking with Vargas's provisional dictatorship to support the 1932 Constitutionalist Movement in São Paulo and whose tenure was brief because he was soon after appointed ambassador to Portugal; Paulista industrialist Roberto Simonsen; João Daudt d'Oliveira, president of the Associação Comercial do Rio de Janeiro; and Rio industrialist Euvaldo Lodi, with the latter two going on to represent Brazil at the Bretton Woods Conference in New Hampshire.[128] In corporatist fashion, both government technocrats and industry leaders directed the CME. Labor was conspicuously missing from this superministry, consistent with how corporatist institutional practices skewed in favor of capital. The CME set out to coordinate between all state and parastate agencies—both old and new—in order to increase national production and establish price stability.[129] One of the CME's more infamous initiatives was a special agency, supported by US financing, that displaced fifty thousand workers to the Amazon to extract rubber.[130] State-coordinated projects to extract raw materials for wartime industry—steel, rubber, or petrol—offer especially vivid examples of early state-led development.

The CME targeted inflation and food shortages too. Starting in 1941, the federal government started limiting export licenses for cassava flour, lard, tomato paste, bananas, oranges, and coffee, even though the last of these commodities saw its price on the global market spike. But these efforts did little to improve the domestic food supply, and Brazil's entry into the war made matters worse. Some CME officials pushed for the total "centralization of production and distribution of goods of primary necessity," yet others rejected such a radical approach on account of the government's limited enforcement resources.[131] For the state to directly control production also fell outside the institutional architecture built over the past years by leading corporatist intellectuals like Oliveira Vianna or midlevel technocrats working for the Ministry of Labor or CFCE.

As the food crisis in Brazil intensified during the war, particularly in major cities, the government experimented with new programs to increase domestic production. Scores of new agricultural colonies were established in the rural environs of major cities like Rio de Janeiro and São Paulo. In the early 1940s, for example, the CME, alongside the Ministry of Agriculture, sponsored agricultural cooperatives on the outskirts of the national capital to feed the growing number of industrial workers. The government tried to incentivize rural workers to move to new production zones by providing housing and land, machinery, seeds, and fertilizers as well as health facilities, schools, and other welfare provisions. Officials celebrated early successes as statistics and images of foods produced locally circulated in Brazilian newspapers.[132]

Brazil's growing but still inchoate corporatist system was mobilized during the war to support federal efforts to expand domestic food production. A layering of federal agencies, producer associations, and local government bodies conditioned agricultural production in these years. For instance, the Sindicato dos Lavradores do Distrito Federal, first established (following Ministry of Labor recognition) in December 1932 to represent agricultural laborers from Campo Grande on the outskirts of Rio de Janeiro, promised to fulfill its obligations as an organized class in service of national interests. The sindicato echoed Vargas's anti-laissez-faire rhetoric and promised to rein in the profit-seeking motivations of individual workers. Its members committed to selling goods in accordance with CME priorities and price controls, promising not to divert their energies to "other more lucrative activities."[133]

At the same time that the Estado Novo mobilized agricultural cooperatives and sindicatos to increase food production, Vargas and other top officials softened their political efforts to fully incorporate agriculture into Brazil's corporatist labor laws and institutions. Excluding agriculture from Brazil's growing corporatist pyramid rested on practical, not theoretical, arguments. For some officials, those employed in agricultural production were not easily categorized in the binary of labor or capital. For others, the exclusion of rural workers had to do with shifting priorities. In 1940, 63 percent of the economically active population was employed in the primary sector, representing a moderate decline from the 68 percent reported in 1920. At the same time, between 1930 and 1945, Brazilian agriculture grew at 2.1 percent per annum, while industry grew at 6.2 percent per annum. On account of this growth, industry increased its share of Brazil's economic output from 20 percent in 1929 to 29 percent in 1945, while agriculture decreased its share from 37 to 28 percent in this same period.[134] Brazil's corporatist system adapted to the needs of a quickly industrializing society.[135]

Across Brazil, those employed in agriculture continued to advocate for inclusion in new social security and economic decrees.[136] In 1944, for example, the Sindicato dos Lavradores do Distrito Federal petitioned the Ministry of Labor to be eligible for the labor protections guaranteed in new legislation. Even as this collective worked with the CME to ensure its members abided by production quotas and price tables, the Ministry of Labor denied the petition because the new legislation did not apply to "professional activities related to agriculture and livestock."[137] Instead, government officials responded as they had done over the past ten years: by creating special commissions and soliciting reports. Bureaucratic obfuscation became a strategy for deferring political action. In 1944, the Comissão de Sindicalização Rural was installed to advocate for giving "rural workers the same legal recognition and benefits that industrial workers already enjoy."[138] Francisco Malta Cardoso, a representative from São Paulo, called to amend the 1937 Constitution to expand corporatist protections to agricultural sindicatos. He advocated for rural sindicatos that included members from both *empregadores* (employers) and *empregados* (employees)—both waged rural labor and propertied individuals. He even quoted Salazar to defend his proposal as similar to Portugal's grémios and casas do povo.[139]

Cardoso might have remained enthusiastic about the corporatist ideal that was still expanding in Portugal, but many Brazilian officials were less concerned with the ideological or institutional completeness of Brazil's corporatist system. Conservative corporatist ideologues like Campos, Falcão, and Oliveira Vianna resigned from their public offices in the early 1940s because they faced opposition to their efforts to expand Brazil's corporatist system. Oliveira Vianna, for instance, resigned from the Ministry of Labor in protest at how industrialists had hijacked corporatist legislation in order to prevent the disbanding of the Federação das Indústrias do Estado de São Paulo (Federation of Industries of the State of São Paulo) and similar professional associations that represented employer interests across several sectors.[140] These debates, however, were about more than representation for labor and producer classes vis-à-vis the state. At stake were different models of government intervention over economic decision-making and different visions of how to transform Brazil into what Simonsen hoped could become "a sufficiently developed economy."[141]

In sum, with World War II, Vargas's government seized on economic emergency to embolden public powers over private markets. New agencies like the CME introduced many stopgap measures to address economic shortages and bottlenecks, but they were building on a decade-long corporatist project. While support for the corporatist project might have dwindled in some corners of Brazil's bureaucracy, the corporatist logic of how the state should intervene for the sake of social peace and economic equilibrium proved harder to erase. The government's efforts at wartime price control offer one of the clearest illustrations of how corporatist ideas survived by getting folded into new forms of state intervention.

By the time Brazil joined the war in August 1942, fears that war would bring inflation and food scarcity were more than confirmed, especially for the national capital. Inflation in 1941 stood at 10.2 percent and jumped to 16.3 percent in 1942, creeping to 25 percent by 1945. Price levels in Brazil increased by 121 percent during the six-year conflict.[142] The Estado Novo tried to use its burgeoning bureaucracy to counteract the rising cost of living that threatened the social peace promised by the corporatist order.

In January 1943, the CME tackled the problem of rising prices. It issued monthly price tables for Rio de Janeiro in the *Diário Oficial*, stipulating maximum prices for basic goods such as cassava, tomatoes, milk, bread, bananas, soap, and salt.[143] The CME (typically) only intervened directly in Rio de Janeiro, facing an acute cost of living crisis.[144] At the same time, it created a web of institutions extending beyond the nation's capital: Comissões Estaduais de Preços, or state price commissions, and Comissões Municipais de Preços, for major municipalities and their surrounding "economic zones."[145] Government technocrats based their "fixing of a fair price" on "concrete experiences"—or economic data—to account for local conditions and the need for "elasticity."[146] Experts staffed these price commissions, as did labor and industry leaders, representing their professional interests. CME efforts at price control would constitute a daily interaction between consumers and government economic planning as well as lay the institutional foundation for postwar efforts to limit inflation.[147]

In Brazil as in Portugal, wartime efforts to control inflation did not begin with the war. Rather, the CME inherited the corporatist economic theory and institutional logic that had been installed throughout the 1930s to cement notions of a just price. Determining just price was not easy, particularly in wartime. "The setting of fair prices cannot be left to magic," one journalist exhorted; "it depends on lengthy processes, during which many experiments will fail."[148] With this in mind, government bureaucrats implemented several initiatives to collect data on the cost of living. In 1942, the Ministry of Labor organized a nationwide survey to study inflation and collect data on monthly salaries in various professions as well as the price of different foods, clothing, types of fuel, leisure activities, and housing.[149] After September 1942, moreover, all industrial and commercial businesses in state capitals were legally required to report stocks of merchandise, sales, and employment data as part of the IBGE's Inquéritos Econômicos para a Defesa Nacional, or economic surveys for national defense.[150] Surveys like these were part of a global revolution in national accounting—a drive to measure and quantify economic life—and not unique to Brazil. The economy, as Timothy Mitchell has argued, became a national statistical object in the 1930s.[151] More than a technocratic project, this rush to carry out economic surveys filtered into popular economic life in the form of price tables. Popular classes also became surveyors themselves—to denounce those who ignored market controls.

Donas de casa (housewives) became essential to the establishment and enforcement of price controls. They were responsible for stretching household budgets in inflationary times, and as such were often the direct victims of price gouging and other economic crimes.[152] Donas de casa formed neighborhood economic watch groups, responsible for observing retailers' compliance with, or not, price tables and gathering denunciations against violators. Women acted as market vigilantes on the "internal front," watchful against "saboteurs."[153] This was not an entirely informal enforcement mechanism: women worked alongside federal agencies to advise on fair prices for essential goods and train housewives to economize spending.[154] In January 1943, for example, the CEM superministry created its first sub-Comissão Feminina de Preços in Rio de Janeiro. The ten-woman subcommittee supervised housewives "in the work of defending the interests of the household and public economy."[155] Participation in these new technocratic organs and neighborhood groups created new public roles for women in the Estado Novo.[156] Economic citizenship was undeniably gendered, with women as consumers and caretakers.[157] Despite their visibility, however, women had limited public authority. Officials questioned women's capacity to understand the policies they enforced; as one journalist jeered, housewives were ill-equipped to "understand frequent price variations."[158] Brazil's paternalistic, corporatist state bestowed rights and responsibilities on women in ways that formalized—rather than overturned— the existing social order.

Many women's denunciations landed on the NST's docket. Decree Law No. 869 (see chapter 5) was originally designed to target bankers, merchants, and industrialists for usurious lending or price collusion, but with the outbreak of World War II seemingly any economic transaction potentially threatened the national well-being. Decree Law No. 869 thus became a primary enforcement mechanism for wartime controls. With this appropriation of a prewar decree to a wartime emergency, Vargas and Campos repositioned the NST to hold firms and individuals accountable for the torrent of new ordinances and market controls. NST judges could punish anyone found in violation of CME ordinances with up to three years in prison and a fine. The CME depended on inspectors and police agents to ensure compliance, and also called on the "people" to "exercise vigilance against all saboteurs of the war effort."[159]

Economic trials increased in 1943, with price control violations the most frequent offense.[160] Zozimo Venancio Avila de Lima, a Portuguese butcher in Rio de Janeiro, was one such target, arrested for allegedly overcharging for a kilogram of meat after a CME inspector approached a woman exiting his shop to ask her how much she had paid for groceries. These sorts of informal surveys occurred regularly in major cities, as everyday transactions were scrutinized and vilified. After a swift trial, the NST found the butcher guilty, sentencing him to one month in prison and a fine.[161] Hundreds of similar cases appeared on the NST docket.

Several dynamics explain why price controls became the target of police power. Certainly, inflationary pressures squeezed household purchasing power. Popular economy denunciations were easy, and hence consumers used the NST to voice economic hardships and sometimes even feel the satisfaction of holding greedy grocers accountable. Vargas recognized the importance of such a safety valve to hedge against popular protests.

But as everyday buying and selling increasingly became the target of NST trials during the war, several contradictions started to emerge. Vargas had decreed popular economy laws to assert the state's primacy over private interests by means of extremely public—and populist—appeals to the economic well-being of ordinary citizens. The regime claimed to protect the people from big capitalism, even if by design, economic policy was incredibly technocratic and opaque. As much as Vargas celebrated the national scope of his economic program, the NST largely heard cases originating in São Paulo, Minas Gerais, and Rio de Janeiro, revealing the limited reach of the Estado Novo's capacity to enforce new economic norms beyond the industrializing urban centers.

Moreover, scholars have largely dismissed popular economy trials as "ridiculous" because the crimes were so petty, such as price markups on flour or the sale of rationed steak.[162] But small-scale denunciations were an unforeseen social dynamic in the corporatist system and not by institutional design.

In wartime, Brazil's government rapidly expanded powers over economic life, often in draconian and arbitrary ways that it legitimized under the cover of wartime emergency. Ironically, attempts at expanded, all-encompassing, large-scale economic planning allowed citizens to turn the courtroom into a small-scale, everyday outlet for economic and social tensions. In other words, the NST's social function evolved beyond its technocratic design as popular classes used it to redress local economic grievances and (sometimes) settle personal vendettas, exposing the limits of state capacity, even in authoritarian contexts.

To enforce price controls, state agencies depended on citizen participation and vigilance, which inevitably, if unintentionally, fostered opportunities for people to use the NST to resolve conflicts beyond the purely economic.[163] For example, in July 1944, in rural Pirajú (São Paulo), Francisco Alves da Silva denounced retailer Herminio Bérgami for selling salt at double its legal price. Some witnesses rallied to his defense, claiming he was a poor, vulnerable rural worker, hoodwinked by an unscrupulous grocer. Others testified that the victim, nicknamed Chico Preto (Chico is a common nickname for Francisco and *preto* is Portuguese for Black), was a scam artist, vagrant, and indolent gambler.[164] Trial proceedings for economic crimes were often silent on the race of any party involved—a trend consistent with legal proceedings in ordinary criminal proceedings. Even so, racialized descriptors or other categories of social rank sometimes appeared in witness testimonies, frequently to impugn an individual's work ethic, honesty, and credibility.[165] Because popular economy trials often relied on hearsay and gossip presented in witness testimonies, such prejudices certainly swayed the verdict. For this trial, witnesses disqualified Silva's denunciation by making oblique references to his appearance and social standing in order to allege that a local landowner had paid off the rural worker to denounce the grocer because of some feud. Reading across conflicting witness testimonies, this trial was not about the price of salt but rather local rivalries and racial tensions that now were transliterated into the language of price controls and market fairness. The NST judges acquitted Bérgami on account of "fragile evidence" and the "suspicious accusation."[166] Acquittal rates were quite high in the NST in part because NST judges recognized that vendettas and feuds motivated many denunciations.[167] In NST trials over the price of rice or salt, many different economic (and noneconomic) forces conditioned how people mobilized the Estado Novo's new institutions and laws.

Across Brazil, the public looked at all these agencies and special commissions created to tackle the problem of food supply and the rising cost of living with increasing skepticism, in part because of their draconian and confusing enforcement, and in part because they did not work to reduce the cost of living. Samba musicians used irony and hyperbole to convey citizens' exasperation with the government's response.[168] In 1943, Wilson Batista and Haroldo Lobo offered the samba "Não é economia (Alô padeiro)":

Alô, padeiro, bom dia	*Hello, baker, good morning*
De amanhã em diante	*Starting tomorrow*
eu vou suspender o pão.	*I won't be coming to buy bread anymore.*
Eu explico a razão:	*I'll explain why:*
não é economia.	*I'm not being frugal.*
É que aqui em casa	*It's that, here at home*
eu agora estou sozinho,	*I'm now all alone,*
aquela morena	*that girl*
já não me faz companhia.	*no longer keeps me company.*

Protests, petitions, and complaints proliferated in newspapers, government reports, and private conversations. Vargas had not delivered on the economic justice and equilibrium promised. News of Brazil's troubles traveled abroad, with reports arriving on Salazar's desk in Portugal about the food supply crisis in Rio de Janeiro, highlighting how Brazilian government agencies "failed to meet the food needs of that city."[169] To the contrary, the quick pace of rules and regulations only seemed to add to wartime chaos.

People also got frustrated with all the surveys and economic monitoring, not only the informal inspections, but the formal *inqueritos*, or questionnaires, that producers, wholesalers, and retailers were obliged to fill out. Bureaucratic efforts to measure the supplies of essential goods and keep track of prices were tools for wartime economic management. We see traces of this sort of planning at work in NST case files. In one NST trial, a commercial farmer from rural São Paulo was accused of insulting Brazil's government when during a survey, he (allegedly) uttered under his breath, "Getúlio Vargas wants to know everything, but he offers little to me or to my farm."[170] A case like this is, on the one hand, an example of the sort of gossip and hearsay that animated some NST trials. But context matters: in the midst of ongoing crisis, people gossiped about the economy. The NST trials offer a partial glimpse of how producers, workers, and consumers faced scrutiny and suspicion in their everyday economic transactions, and the frustration that some felt precisely because these controls were not actually fixing economic problems.

Economies worldwide grappled with similar problems of food supply and price speculation, but feelings on the ground in Rio de Janeiro were that this crisis was of a different magnitude. In January 1944, the daily newspaper *Diário Carioca* reported that the price of basic utilities had risen more in the Brazilian capital than in London or New York, while staple foods had entirely disappeared from the market and fruit was only accessible for "millionaires."[171] Medical professionals and anthropologists in Rio de Janeiro debated the social and medical consequences of food shortages.[172] Brazil's incipient middle class was a group defined by its purchasing power, which was now threatened by a problem as basic as the provision of cassava.

For some, the failure of price tables and other efforts to control production and consumption seemed so obvious that it was difficult to recall why such a massive bureaucracy for this purpose had been implemented in the first place. As one carioca journalist concluded,

> Global experience has shown that price tables without rationing leads to the disappearance of products [in the legal market] and formation of black markets. Rationing without price tables causes prices to skyrocket, making essential goods inaccessible to the poorest segment of the population. The only solution is to produce. And no one will plant corn, beans, or potatoes if you can plant something else that will earn a higher profit margin. [173]

And in this fashion, the idiom of the free market had returned. To many, incentives, not discipline or professional solidarity, once again became the most efficient way to allocate resources in order to meet the needs and wants of a society.

Even technocrats working at the CME superministry were coming to terms with their limitations and ineffectiveness. Within the CME, Jorge Felippe Kafuri headed the Setor Preços (Price Division) overseeing price controls. Before his appointment, he was a professor of political economy, statistics, and finance at a preeminent engineering polytechnic in Rio de Janeiro. He ultimately became one of the fiercest critics of price controls as he admitted that no amount of planning could circumvent the laws of supply and demand—a conclusion he presented to the CME director following a trip to the United States. It was impossible for Brazil to address the underlying economic problems by only focusing on the "symptoms," which in this case were rising prices. Despite all the inspections and penalties for price control violations, prices continued to rise. Instead, Kafuri argued that the only way to fix inflation was to "establish some sort of balance between prices for agricultural goods and prices for industrial goods, and to the extent possible, between rural salaries and industrial salaries" in order to increase "the purchasing power of the masses."[174] Kafuri's economic theory was rudimentary, but he explained inflation as a consequence of Brazil's underdevelopment, especially the asymmetries between agricultural and industrial sectors. Price was a mechanism for balancing group and regional interests, as corporatist economists had theorized. But Brazil's economic problems could not be so easily resolved by concentrating only on negotiations between these groups. Narrow economic definitions of social peace had revealed structural constraints on Brazil's economic development.[175] Kafuri resigned from the Price Division after a few months, but accepted a new position, also within the CME, with the Setor Planejamento (Planning Division).

But the failures of price controls could not erase their promises. This is evident in an NST trial in September 1943, when a Portuguese immigrant working for an agricultural cooperative in Campo Grande on the outskirts of Rio de Janeiro denounced the directors of the cooperative for paying him less than two cruzeiros for every box of oranges, even though the legal price was seven cruzeiros. The cooperative oversaw orange cultivation and had recently been founded as part of a government drive to increase food production to feed the nation's capital during the war. The case file suggests that there was more to this trial than the price of oranges as it seems the Portuguese farmer, like many other plaintiffs, might have been motivated by a personal feud. Still, he articulated his claims in terms of his "right" to the price fixed by law, making appeals to "public justice" and "protections for the popular economy."[176]

Another story can also be gleaned from these accounts of frustration and failure. NST trials about salt in Pirajú, rice in Rio Grande do Sul, or oranges in Rio de Janeiro captured the phenomenal centralization—as well as the reach—of Brazil's new legal and economic institutions. The price of these goods was no longer considered a private contract between buyer and seller; these transactions were now subjected to a forceful constitution, presidential decrees, statisticians, price tables, police, consumer complaints, and a strident tribunal. Furthermore, neither the fact that cases like these were sometimes facades for private conflicts nor that acquittals were common deterred people from denouncing their bankers, grocers, or pharmacists. When he visited Brazil during the war, German political scientist Karl Loewenstein remarked that the NST had become "a bogeyman [used] by the 'little fellow' against the economic sharks."[177] Loewenstein was correct to conclude that Decree Law No. 869 and other similar laws hardly deterred greedy, speculative, or profiteering behavior. He also understood, however, that a law's impact cannot only be measured in terms of its enforcement. Vargas's commitments to fair prices and state intervention on behalf of the "little fellow" acquired unexpected dimensions as popular classes increasingly looked to their government, its laws, and tribunals to address social as well as economic hardships. That laws and controls did not function in practice as on paper is hardly surprising, nor is it a satisfying conclusion. Rather, the failures and frustrations with planning are a starting point for understanding what in this experiment survived the war, and why.

Economists, journalists, state officials, consumers, merchants, and producers across Brazil thus had to reconcile unrelenting market laws with the lessons learned from their experiments with planning. Vargas gradually extinguished the CME's powers by late 1944, and called on the CFCE to brainstorm new institutions to guide Brazil's transition back to economic normalcy and, critically, encourage its industrial future. In 1945, he inaugurated two new institutions for the task: the Conselho Nacional de Política Industrial e Comercial, headed by Simonsen, and the Comissão do Planejamento Econômico, piloted by liberal economist Eugênio Gudin. The two men held radically divergent views of the state's role in economic life—views that erupted into an acrimonious debate. Simonsen embraced corporatism in practice (even if not always in name), and supported expanding both formal and informal channels for industry and state to collaborate. Gudin was not, as some of his critics insist, totally against state intervention. Rather, he advocated for more limited and episodic forms of intervention, largely to deal with financial crises. He criticized the type of planning Vargas had implemented, calling the Estado Novo a "totalitarian regime of state capitalism."[178]

Gudin was vicious in his attack of Simonsen, discrediting the industrialist's proposal as vague and baseless. He disparaged how over the past fifteen years, so many people had accepted the concept of planning at face value as a panacea for all economic troubles, regardless of the actual plans in question. Gudin scorned Simonsen for his alignment with those who "see the 'plan' [as] a solution for all economic problems, a kind of magic that resolves everything, a mystique of planning that left us with the failed American New Deal, the corporatist economies of Italy and Portugal, and the five-year plan of Russia. I do not share this faith."[179] Gudin cited Austrian economist Friedrich Hayek's recently published *The Road to Serfdom* (1944) to empower his position that state economic planning planted the seeds for dictatorship and political repression. The Brazilian economist combined examples from the Soviet Union and United States to make a case for the return to laissez-faire. He was not arguing into a void. Gudin's rejection of planning had transnational dimensions. Thanks in part to his role in Brazil's delegation to the Bretton Woods Conference in July 1944, Gudin had connected with a growing cohort of neoliberals. He would strengthen these ties in the postwar decades, even participating in a Mont Pelerin Society meeting in Princeton, New Jersey, in 1958.[180] Gudin's economic ideas were not produced in universities, nor relegated to the theoretical realm.[181] With Gudin as with Simonsen, economic ideas were being produced through policymaking and debated through the rigmarole of state making. At stake, moreover, was not just planning versus *not* planning. Instead, Vargas deliberately summoned these two economists to debate the issue as he weighed his political options for Brazil at the end of World War II. As much as the war had exposed the limits of corporatist planning, many in Brazil were not yet ready to give up on the experiment entirely.

World War II proved to be a disaster for the economic interventions introduced with corporatism in the 1930s. But at the same time, it made permanent the state's responsibility to deal with economic crisis. In both Brazil and Portugal, inflation soared, food shortages intensified, and black markets proliferated. While such wartime economic challenges are well documented, they are largely treated as the backdrop to economic histories that emphasize how the war jump-started state-directed industrialization. In Brazil especially, the rise of state-owned companies for strategic resources like the steel plant in Volta Redonda takes center stage in histories of state-led development.[182] Industrialization thus becomes the triumphant outcome to the economic crises of the 1930s and 1940s. But the rise of economic planning was hardly triumphant. Indeed, many in Brazil and Portugal recognized that controls did not necessarily equate to planning, blaming the crisis precisely on the "lack of a defined plan."[183] Many blamed corporatism with its complex—if inchoate—system of controls for how consumers and producers alike were suffering at the hands of black markets, runaway inflation, and food scarcity. The economic puzzle of World War II in Brazil and Portugal therefore becomes not how corporatist institutions were mobilized to ignite state-led development at this critical juncture but instead how this idea survived into the postwar period, despite all of its failures.

This chapter has underscored the transformative powers of failure, showing how corporatist experiments mobilized various strategies—to varying degrees of efficacy—for state intervention over the economy. The next chapter charts how these experiments—through trial and error, but also ideological repurposing—ultimately morphed into something that endured well into the postwar period. My emphasis here on failure is partly to reframe long-standing debates about corporatism as scholars tend to cast it as window dressing for dictators, or focus on its incomplete realization and corruption. To put it simply, the puzzle is *not* why corporatism failed but rather how ideas and institutions endured despite all the ways that the war undermined corporatist experiments. After all, both Vargas and Salazar outlasted the war, even with the global wave of redemocratization in 1945. Corporatism, too, survived. It never quite shed its association with fascism, but its practices and institutions ultimately became normalized as part of the state's architecture. While corporatism is not the only way to explain how these dictators shape-shifted to survive the war, its endurance—and even recurrence—across the twentieth century offers a compelling example of how political projects sometimes survive through defeat.

7

Corporatism to Planning

IN 1945, the word *corporatism* was deleted from Brazil's 1937 Constitution. Corporatism had gone out of fashion in the 1940s when many intellectuals and political leaders distanced themselves from this illiberal political and economic project, irreparably tainted by its associations with Fascism, Nazism, and the horrors of authoritarianism. Its honeycomb of institutions and laws, however, remained intact. This chapter follows the eclipse—but not erasure—of Brazil's corporatist Estado Novo as Vargas's authoritarian regime collapsed with the global democratic wave that followed the war. It connects this process to parallel events in Salazarist Portugal. The fall of many dictatorships at the close of the war sounded the death knell for corporatism as a potentially modernizing and even progressive form of political economy. But corporatism hardly disappeared, neither in name nor practice. Instead, its institutions and ideas evolved and contorted to fit a postwar context. Even before the war's end, Brazilian public officials had started rebranding corporatism with a more neutral language of state intervention in the economy as it became more common to talk in terms of economic planning.

In the postwar period, corporatist theorists tried to camouflage their project in a world polarized between capitalism and communism. The rise of the United States and Soviet Union as global hegemons is a well-studied and debated consequence of World War II.[1] In the early 1940s, though, a world divided between the United States and Soviet Union was not predestined, nor was it evident that either polity would hold so much cultural and financial leverage. To understand Brazil or Portugal's economic trajectory in the postwar period, the familiar Cold War binary between communism and capitalism falls short. Vargas and Salazar had already put into motion top-down, state-led programs for national self-sufficiency and development following the Great Depression, guided partly by corporatist principles. If corporatism was to survive the war, it would need to be folded into new ideological trends.

The chapter begins with the eclipse of corporatist ideals in the early 1940s through a series of legal as well as institutional debates following the clash between corporatist ideas, key corporate interests, and political expediency. Debates over corporatist law, legislation, and policy were also fierce and destabilizing debates over how to structure the relationship between state and market to assert a hierarchy for economic development.

While pockets of resistance to Vargas and Salazar were present throughout their tenures in power, opposition grew during World War II. Students and workers organized protests against dictatorship and the failed promises for social justice. It became increasingly difficult for the propaganda ministries of both Estado Novo regimes to twist authoritarianism into something progressive as the horrors of war and genocide in Europe made all too real the consequences of illiberal governance. Corporatism as ideology and policy got caught in the crosshairs of growing opposition to dictatorship as regimes struggled to separate the economic system from its political origins. As the war came to a close, these tensions even vibrated within the inner circles and advisory chambers of Vargas and Salazar. In Portugal, the National Assembly investigated the corruption of corporatist institutions during the war and how best to salvage the program. In Brazil, opposition to the Estado Novo's corporatist vision grew in public protests, how organized interests pushed to maintain their autonomy, and the special commissions created to plan the country's economic future. Liberal voices were never totally excluded from economic debates, but the failings of dirigisme in many parts of the world energized this source of opposition to Vargas's rule. The military and opposition forces led Vargas to self-imposed exile in 1945. Many in Brazil formally turned away from the corporatist program as ideas came up against shifting alliances and brute political power.

Still, the question of the state's role in economic life did not disappear in the postwar period. Nor did the entanglement of corporatism in politics deter prominent government officials and intellectuals from trying to rebrand corporatism—and to a certain extent they succeeded. The state's role in the economy, in fact, took on new urgency as war-torn Europe and postcolonial nations also searched for new (or old) formulas for development, modernization, and industrialization. This chapter explores some of the ways in which corporatist ideas and institutions endured past 1945. Where in the 1930s, the national governments of Brazil and Portugal embraced corporatist strategies for economic stability and recovery, these ideas had to be repurposed in the postwar era to serve the long-run challenges of development. Key to the survival of corporatism, as the first two sections examine, is how Brazilian and Portuguese jurists, officials, and economists debated the successes and failures of this system in order to figure out what parts of this interwar experiment could be folded into the rise of Keynesianism and other forms of the mixed economy.

While Estado Novo dictatorships in Brazil and Portugal were quite distinct from one another at the start, they diverged even more after the war. As the final section shows, in Portugal, Salazar's regime remained committed to corporatism throughout the postwar period in law and rhetoric, even as its corporatist experiment got folded into bolder programs for economic planning and development. For Brazil, its interwar corporatist experiment opened up new forms of technocracy that survived well into the twentieth century, evident in the rise of economic planning and other forms of state intervention in economic life. While it is impossible to know what Brazil's developmentalist state might have looked like without its corporatist precursor, a few legacies of its interwar experiment are evident: the state's role in balancing organized interests, a skepticism toward free market mechanisms, a focus on food and raw material production to supply the internal market and support industrialization, an insistence on the government's role in enforcing just prices for producers and consumers alike, and a preference for technocratic rather than political approaches to policymaking. Despite divergences, in both Brazil and Portugal, corporatist institutions and laws persisted in and shaped postwar development approaches.

Reinventing Corporatist Politics in Brazil

Vargas understood how unsavory dictatorships had become. On November 10, 1943, the sixth anniversary of the 1937 Constitution and the deadline for the constitutional plebiscite, he vowed to the nation that civil liberties and democratic politics would be fully restored at the war's end. Enthusiasm for this promise fulminated in the streets and press, as the Estado Novo's censorship machine could not keep pace with popular support for redemocratization. Antitotalitarian and antifascist marches were organized in cities across the country, as university students, organized labor, and other sectors of civil society chanted prodemocracy slogans. Vargas recognized the importance of these popular mobilizations. He even endorsed a successor, Minister of War Eurico Gaspar Dutra—something he had refused to do in 1937.

By 1944, Vargas shrewdly understood that the postwar order would be guided by democratic and liberal regimes.[2] He prepared for another swing of the ideological pendulum, increasingly shredding his authoritarian pronouncements during the war by summoning "democratic principles."[3] Vargas engineered this political transformation by celebrating his labor legislation and social programs as evidence of his advocacy and work for the poor and working classes. He would become known as *pai dos pobres*—father of the poor—a category that only started to circulate toward the end of his tenure in power in 1945. Initially, his detractors dubbed Vargas pai dos pobres ironically, or as a criticism of either his increasingly populist discourse or the obvious gap between his discourse and practice. Scholars have long debated the sincerity or duplicity of Vargas's opportunistic embrace of populist ideas and policies.[4] Yet these shifts were not just political stratagem; they reflected evolving intellectual paradigms worldwide.

As these tensions unfolded, Vargas appointed Alexandre Marcondes Filho, a lawyer from São Paulo, to serve as both labor minister (1941–45) and justice minister (1943–45). Marcondes Filho arrived relatively late to Vargas's camp. Born in São Paulo, he studied law at the Faculdade de Direito de São Paulo, and then engaged in local and state politics in the 1920s. Like many Paulistas, he participated in the Revolução Constitutionalista (Constitutionalist Movement) in 1932 to protest Vargas's provisional government and his program to centralize federal powers at the expense of regional interests. And like other prominent Paulistas, he eventually reversed his original opposition to Vargas following the 1937 coup, realizing the potential of working with and within the Estado Novo to ensure that Brazil's new legal, social, and economic program protected the Paulistas' regional interests.[5] As labor minister, he launched a period of especially close collaboration between São Paulo industrialists and the federal government, thus in turn shaping social policy. Marcondes Filho, for example, ultimately became responsible for Vargas's signature labor law, the Consolidação das Leis do Trabalho, decreed on May Day 1943.[6] This charter, which many have qualified for its inspiration in the fascist Italian Carta del Lavoro, was more progressive and encompassing than any other labor legislation in place at the time.[7] It was celebrated, as historian John French notes, as one of the most advanced systems of labor rights and social security in the world.[8]

At the same time, an emphasis on economic development became central to how Brazil's legal team attempted to refashion its authoritarian system into something democratic after the war. This argument was intimately connected to the corporatist structure of Brazil's Estado Novo, even as the word *corporatism* appeared less frequently in debates over the nation's constitutional future. In 1944, Marcondes Filho delivered a speech on the 1937 Constitution and its corporatist institutions. He backtracked on the political significance of the Conselho de Economia Nacional (National Economic Council), to be composed of industry representatives and modeled on Portugal's Câmara Corporativa (see chapter 2). Marcondes Filho insisted that Brazil's corporatist chamber would only function as a technical or administrative organ, without lawmaking powers. Corporatism, he assured his audience, was an economic system, not a political one. As Marcondes Filho summarized it, "I have already explained that the Brazilian state is *semicorporatist*. While the Conselho de Economia Nacional will collaborate directly and efficiently with the government, it will not constitute an organ of political power, nor an internal or integral part of our National

Parliament."[9] As global ideological winds shifted during the war, Estado Novo officials made their case for their regime's compatibility rather than dissonance with liberal democratic arrangements. *Corporatism* was now a word tainted by its association with fascist dictatorships, and the catastrophic toll of "authoritarian democracy" could no longer be sidestepped or spun as something progressive.

In February 1945, Vargas and his legal team called for another round of constitutional reforms—the third in fifteen years. The 1937 Constitution, as mentioned earlier, was only partially in effect because Vargas had never convened the plebiscite to ratify it. For this reason, the fact that Brazilian jurists continued to edit the Constitution is curious. Rather than dismiss Marcondes Filho's gesture as hollow legalism or a political distraction, this round of reform was an ideological reckoning.[10] The word *corporatism* was removed from the 1937 charter. Article 61, which outlined the National Economic Council as the organ of the corporatist revolution, remained intact. This organ was still responsible for establishing "norms relative to the state's support for professional associations, labor syndicates, or institutes."[11] The only substantial change to the article was that the word *corporatism* was deleted here. The team of legal advisers explained that they needed to alter the National Economic Council's features in order to eliminate talk of efforts to "promote the corporatist organization of the national economy."[12] The 1937 Constitution, as Marcondes Filho explained, "reflected the contingencies of the moment in which it was decreed," breaking with "traditional institutions as much in the political realm as in the economic and social realm."[13] He now tried to dial back some of these breaks.[14]

Brazilian jurists pushed through additional constitutional changes. Constitutional Law No. 9, for example, scaled back the powers of the president and reaffirmed the importance of Congress, now to be elected by direct suffrage. But the question of corporatism remained controversial, despite these edits and deletions. One adamant critic of Vargas's Estado Novo accused those rewriting the Constitution of "philofascism," protesting that the "reforms" merely put "corporatism in disguise" and that Vargas remained "stubborn in maintaining, in South America, the fascist system." The revisions, Vargas's opponents ridiculed, were more pretext than commitment: the task was to "give the impression of having extinguished the corporatist-fascist system, which remains fully in place, albeit disguised by the replacement of the word *corporatism*."[15] Did Vargas and his team really think that this shift in vocabulary was sufficient to stake out legitimacy in the new postwar order? To stay in power? Following the end of the Estado Novo in 1945, the word *corporatist* or *corporation* was similarly deleted or replaced from other fundamental Vargas era laws, even as their content remained largely intact.

In Brazil, then, a paradox emerged: corporatism as an idea lost favor as it suffered legal, institutional, and political defeats, but corporatism in practice remained intact, surviving into the postwar period.

Fall and Survival of Dictatorship

As World War II approached its end, dictatorships had collapsed globally, and to some these events promised a new wave of democracy. The transition from World War II to the Cold War, however, would prove more complicated: democracy and social democracy suffered losses in the United States, and promises to decolonize also did not deliver in many parts of the world as armed conflict became a necessary path for many. In Latin America, a "democratic spring" and more inclusive politics nonetheless emerged, albeit briefly, with the end of dictatorships across the region. This was an important context for Brazil, where government officials and the public at large debated the consequences of the war's end for the Estado Novo.

Vargas became increasingly emphatic in his pronouncements for social justice and economic development, vowing to reduce the cost of living and expand welfare services. By May 1945, a new mass movement emerged in Brazil: Queremismo, after the slogan "Queremos Vargas," or "We want Vargas." This outpouring of popular support apparently convinced Vargas that he was still viable as a leader. In October 1945, with elections on the horizon, Vargas surprised the military establishment by appointing his brother Benjamin Vargas to the position of chief of police in Rio de Janeiro. The move agitated military leaders and regime insiders, who saw this nomination as a sign that Vargas planned to keep himself in power. Dutra and General Góis Monteiro, a former ally as well as someone rather sympathetic to corporatism and dictatorial politics, presented Vargas with an ultimatum: resign or be removed from office.[16]

On October 29, 1945, Vargas went into exile in his home state of Rio Grande do Sul. After fifteen years of power in the hands of one man, Vargas exited the presidential Catete Palace. This was not quite a victory for democratic mobilization, but nor should Vargas's political fall be reduced to a military power play—a narrative that tends to situate 1945 as preamble to the 1964 military coup. Rather, the changing global intellectual and political climate forged this chain of events. With the 1929 crisis, it was easy enough for dictators to argue that authority—not liberty—was necessary for economic recovery and development. But fifteen years later, as Karl Loewenstein observed during his visit to Brazil, it seemed that "in the end there is no conclusive evidence that authoritarian governments are better promoters of progress although they have fewer restraints in removing obstacles." Or more precisely, he added, "At any rate they are more capable of advertising what they have accomplished or are out to accomplish."[17]

In Brazil, this ideological and political recalibration came once again in the form of a new constitution. In this case, a popularly elected Constitutional Assembly drafted Brazil's fifth constitution (its third in fifteen years), ratified in September 1946. That this constitution was written so quickly was a testament to the new postwar consensus in Brazil. This Constitutional Assembly reinstated individual freedoms and moderated the powers of the president, but still affirmed the state's role in ensuring social rights and economic development.

In 1946, one constitutional drafter even evoked Keynes as the visionary who had normalized the "directed economy" by throwing "a última pá de cal" on classical economic models (or giving the final blow to).[18] That these drafters looked to Keynes is telling for two reasons. First, they skipped over—and even erased—the Portuguese, French, and Italian writings on corporatism that had shaped the rise of the mixed economy in Brazil. Keynes was hardly the economist of reference during the Estado Novo; in fact, his *The General Theory of Employment, Interest and Money* was only translated into Portuguese in 1964. With the falling popularity of corporatist economic models, Brazilian economic planning got retrofitted into a Keynesian idiom and folded back into an Anglo-American intellectual framework.[19] Keynes's entry into Brazilian debates, moreover, is largely linked to liberal economist Eugênio Gudin, who was a critic of Keynes. In other words, 1930s' corporatist debates are forgotten in the transfer of Keynesianism and origins of developmentalist thought in Brazil. The postwar celebration of Keynes served to erase not only corporatism but also Brazil's intellectual ties to Portuguese and Italian dictatorships.[20]

Growing interest in Keynes among Brazilian economists and political leaders is key for a second reason. In the postwar decades, Anglo-American economists managed to incorporate Keynes into their classical economic models to assert that Keynesianism worked with—not against—liberal capitalist development. In other parts of the North Atlantic and Europe, as Peter Hall has shown, Keynesianism was in distinct ways incorporated into many different economic models too.[21] And likewise, from the 1940s to the 1980s, some of the most iconic debates in Brazilian political economy were reperceived through the Keynesian lens. Both the developmentalist and liberal camps in Brazil used Keynes to defend their program. Too often, however, Brazilian historians of economic ideas begin this discussion in 1945—a gesture that obscures not only the origins of economic planning in Brazil but its motivations as well. For example, Brazilian liberal economist Otávio Gouveia de Bulhões— who like Gudin, worked in the Finance Ministry and related commissions in the 1930s, and would become finance minister during the military dictatorship from 1964 to 1967—later remarked that following the 1930 Revolution, Brazil's tenentes "were Keynesians before Keynes." With this pithy statement, Bulhões emphasized how Vargas's government understood that deficit spending was the only option for Brazil to bounce back from the Great Depression but downplayed other forms of state intervention tested in the 1930s. Bulhões, to be sure, even supported some limited forms of state involvement in the market, namely in moments of acute economic and financial crisis, or even to safeguard strategic resources. For instance, he supported Brazil's state-owned steel mill. In this way, Bulhões was less radical than Gudin in his opposition to state planning. Rather, Bulhões argued that the key question revolved around which kinds of strategies to implement. Much like the corporatists who held sway in the 1930s, he understood that strategies that worked in the United States could not work in Brazil. For him, Keynesianism always seemed like a misfit to Brazil because "Keynes cured the Depression, and that was not our problem. Our problem is development."[22]

Even as the word *corporatism* largely disappeared from Brazilian economic debates and legislative acts in the 1940s and 1950s, its institutions remained largely intact. Take, for example, the 1943 Consolidação das Leis do Trabalho. In January 1946, Decree Law No. 8.740 introduced several amendments to the Consolidação das Leis do Trabalho, revising its language to align it more closely to rising democratic sentiments. *Corporatist* was deleted from several articles, yet with little impact on the function or spirit of this legislation. Brazilian scholars often note the authoritarian and even repressive dynamics of the Consolidação das Leis do Trabalho as well as its disciplining engagement with the working classes—a legacy that cannot be divorced from its corporatist origins. Labor was never totally disciplined, many would add, as workers attempted both within and outside the corporatist legal scaffolding to advance their interests and rights.[23] Other corporatist institutions also survived, including many conselhos técnicos created in the 1930s, even if they were renamed in the postwar period. Scholars of Brazilian corporatism frequently note these legacies (or relics) of Estado Novo laws, contending with their persistence and status as targets of liberal or neoliberal debate.[24] Moreover, Brazil's corporatist experiment survived in more subtle ways through its critiques of laissez-faire capitalism and how it pushed the state to the forefront of economic debates.

Survival of Corporatism: Portuguese Counterpoint

The history of the fall and survival of corporatism in Brazil is also a history of the fall and survival of dictatorship. Portugal's trajectory is a counterpoint to Brazil. While Vargas fell in 1945, temporarily at least, Salazar survived the war and so did his Estado Novo. For contemporaries observing events in real time, Salazar's grasp on power actually appeared weaker than Vargas's or other dictators. Brazilian ambassador to Portugal João Neves da Fontoura witnessed the fallout from Lisbon as popular protests over food scarcity erupted, as did pressures from the Allied powers for Salazar to concede the use of the Azores.[25] By mid-1943, Fontoura described to Vargas how the "dominant preoccupation" palpable across the city was whether they could count on the "survival of the Portuguese regime."[26] The survival—and indeed entrenchment—of Salazar's corporatist system in Portugal is puzzling precisely because it was so robustly attacked by the war's end.

Salazar's government was as threatened by internal discontent as by global events. Seizing on growing instability, underground socialist and communist groups mounted an offensive in the public sphere, organizing congresses and publishing pamphlets critical of the Salazarist regime and the lack of social and economic progress. During the war, the Portuguese Communist Party also supported industrial workers in organizing strikes, largely concentrated in the Lisbon region, to protest for higher salaries and better conditions, with some of this general strike activity spreading to rural areas.[27] In response to growing tensions, Salazar intensified his recourse to secret police and censorship, making it difficult, but not impossible, for opposition groups to organize.[28] Novels, pamphlets, and translations of foreign texts did circulate, but underground. Public protests were few, but workers dissented against the corporatist system in other ways. Evidence of Salazar's weakening grasp on power existed beyond these pockets of organized dissent. Even some of Salazar's most loyal supporters pointed to the disappointments and hardships of the previous fifteen years. Persistent poverty was perhaps among the biggest indictments of the Estado Novo. The infant mortality rate in Portugal had dropped by 35 percent between 1930 and 1950, but was still more than three times the rate in England.[29] Despite mounting evidence of the failures of this corporatist experiment, Portugal's Estado Novo managed to not only survive World War II but also endure until 1974.

World War II had sent Portugal—to a greater extent than Brazil—into an economic tailspin. As much as the Estado Novo tried to anticipate, control, and manage the chaos of contraband markets, food scarcity, and inflation with new commissions and task forces, ordinary citizens endured hardship and uncertainty. Given wartime pressures, questions and critiques regarding the future of economic planning were articulated in legislative chambers, advisory councils, and letters from citizens to their government. Some lamented, reluctantly, that the laws of supply and demand were not so easily dodged, while others were even nostalgic for days of the laissez-faire order. One forthright critic penned in their anonymous letter that "it is not a secret for anyone, Mr. President, that the corporatist organization has not yielded the result that Your Excellency aspired to when you adopted this program and had it put into action."[30]

As in Brazil, Portuguese economists and statespeople after the war asked pointed questions about the very nature of a state-directed economy. They debated whether, possibly, the corporatist organization of the economy might have been the cause of the crises and disequilibriums suffered during the war and its aftermath. Following the war, it took several years for Portugal to return to economic normalcy.[31] In 1947, a special parliamentary commission—the Comissão Parliamentar de Inquérito aos Elementos da Organização Corporativa—convened to investigate charges of corruption and malfeasance against corporatist organs. This massive survey collected qualitative and quantitative data on nearly every sector of the Portuguese economy, such as the codfish, cork, and wine industries. Representative political organs do not function in authoritarian contexts as they do in democratic contexts; nonetheless, they were spaces for (managed) dissent and key constituents to petition or complain.[32] Assembly deputies in charge of the investigation collected statistics on production and prices, debriefed directors of grémios and regulatory commissions, and amassed letters and petitions from citizens who had complained of corruption, speculation, and fraud during the war.

For one Estado Novo official, the task at hand was that "we need to be able to explain whether the scarcity was *because of* the corporatist organization, or if what we were missing was the true corporatist organization of the economy." This question was not taken lightly. One deputy blamed the grémios for Portugal's economic instability during the war. Grémios representing owners of warehouses and retail shops had allegedly taken advantage of consumers during the war, deliberately committing fraud by tampering with the quality or price of goods (see chapter 6). National Assembly deputies decried shortages of rice, codfish, flour, sugar, and potatoes as the "fault of the grémios!" These grémios were also blamed because "prices [were] so high for the consumer and low for the producer."[33] In some cases, grémio members were accused of participating in black markets. In the eyes of those called on to investigate the grémio system, corruption was the inevitable consequence of granting so many public powers to professional associations that represented private interests. Grémios were "integrated into a system of *economia dirigida* [directed economy], and not just as organism[s] of a purely corporatist mold."[34] As the Estado Novo expanded the powers of grémios and regulatory commissions, it failed to implement checks and balances on how these organs exercised public authority over the economy. Historians of the Portuguese Estado Novo often center on Salazar to explain how power influenced action, but the grémio system constituted its own nodes of power and influence.[35] The severity of the complaints and criticisms against grémios and regulatory commissions put the Estado Novo at a crossroads: whether to deepen its commitment to corporatism or let it go to consider alternatives.

Where planning and organization only five years earlier would have been couched in the idiom of progress, it was now discredited as tyrannical, oppressive, and retrograde. "In each of these corporatist organisms," one anonymous citizen decried, "there exists a despotic dictator, without head or tail, that is hostile, infuriating and antieconomic." More so, the expansive bureaucracy erected in these years—ministries, special commissions, and councils—was from the perspective of consumers and merchants, headed by "half a dozen boys, some old and some young, but all childishly irresponsible."[36] It was not just the grémio system that was under attack but also faith in government itself. These sentiments were shared by members of the public who submitted *queixas*, or complaints, against the shortages, red tape, and rising prices. The Estado Novo's tendency for planning, regulation, and control had given way to skepticism. Even those most loyal to the corporatist third path recognized the need to revisit the theory on which their model was built.

Despite growing opposition to the state-directed economy, some leading intellectual and political figures redoubled their commitment to corporatism. In Portugal, the future of economic intervention was never quite as Manichaean as the clash between Gudin and Simonsen in Brazil (see chapter 6). Those loyal to the Estado Novo regime did not reject corporatism as a theory or aspiration, even as they recognized its shortcomings. They vowed to return to the idealism of the early 1930s. Rehabilitating corporatism required a new public campaign, and so Portugal's propaganda ministry, renamed the Secretariado Nacional de Informação, published pamphlets, books, and posters to defend this "in-between doctrine." This printed material translated high economic theory into a popular vernacular to explain the benefits of corporatism to the workers, shopkeepers, and producers affected by its rules. One such pamphlet, *Pequena história das doutrinas económicas*, published by the Secretariado Nacional de Informação for its Biblioteca do Trabalhador (Workers' Library) series, offered an overview of major economic doctrines, starting with mercantilism and ending with corporatism. It attempted to separate corporatism from totalitarian models that embraced corporatism in name only as a "facade" for "hostile" forms of "statism" and even "collectivism." Its primary talking points were not so different from those of key theorists like José Joaquim Teixeira Ribeiro or Marcello Caetano: corporatism offered a model for the "coordination" and "control" of private economic activities in ways that protected private property and the "regime of capitalist firms." Corporatism was positioned between liberalism and socialism; it was a form of the mixed economy that rehabilitated medieval legal protections for "just prices" and "just salaries" to guarantee a "decent" standard of living for workers. This experiment did not fail during the war. Rather, Estado Novo supporters asserted that the war demonstrated just how urgent it was to continue building this "system based in the principle of organizing all productive economic forces."[37]

Many of these talking points were consistent with 1930s' propaganda, but subtle differences also reveal how Estado Novo officials tried to rebrand corporatism as something compatible with the emerging postwar order. Alongside a discussion of social peace, Salazar's propaganda team adopted new political vocabularies, namely an emphasis on human rights and personal liberty. The individual was certainly not celebrated as the agent of political or economic transformation, but nor was the individual explicitly denigrated. Corporatism now promised a way to "safeguard the fundamental rights of people" with the "ultimate" aim of achieving "human liberty and dignity."[38]

Public efforts at rebranding were often shallow, however, with limited reach. In a country where only 45 percent of the population could read and write in 1945, one of the highest illiteracy rates in western Europe, the many books and pamphlets published on corporatist theory had a limited audience beyond the small pockets of the urban middle classes.[39] Rehabilitating the Salazarist economic project largely remained an academic and technocratic exercise.

This intellectual project was spearheaded by the economists, jurists, and social scientists who created new academic institutions to bring corporatism into the postwar period. In 1949, the University of Lisbon inaugurated the Gabinete de Estudos Corporativos under the leadership of José Pires Cardoso to fortify the next phase of this experiment with social scientific research. Pires Cardoso studied law at the University of Lisbon before going to the Instituto Superior de Ciências Económicas e Financeiras to earn a doctorate in 1941. Like other leading corporatist theorists, he was a university professor teaching law and economics, and enjoyed prominent postings within the Estado Novo, including a brief stint as minister of the interior and a long career as a deputy to the Câmara Corporativa.[40] Pires Cardoso is recognized as one of the most brilliant corporatist theorists, often credited for the concept's adaptation to postwar contexts. He worried about the "setbacks" that corporatism faced on account of wartime disruptions in terms of both its place in the "world of ideas" and its concrete accomplishments. Teaching on corporatism at the Instituto Superior de Ciências Económicas e Financeiras, he pushed beyond interwar doctrine. He limited his discussion of Catholic social teachings, or even the ills of liberalism and laissez-faire capitalism, and voiced skepticism toward, or at least ambivalence about, the relevance of labor and capital as categories for organizing modern economic relations.[41] He remained true to older idealistic paradigms of a "corporatist mentality" that valued solidarity between groups above individual interests, while also insisting on a more scientific and institutional approach—one guided by doctors, engineers, agronomists, and professors.[42] To be sure, 1930s' corporatists had already embraced technocratic forms of governance. But Pires Cardoso made this turn explicit, defining corporatism in terms of its institutional framework erected over previous decades to regulate economic behavior. His focus was less the grémio and other forms of representation, and more the *empresa*, or firm, emphasizing the need for scientific management in labor relations and producer decisions. But these efforts to modernize corporatist theory also revealed its limitations. Portugal's corporatist system had been erected to organize its predominantly agrarian economy: Would it serve the country's push to industrialize?

As much as some Portuguese economists remained faithful to the corporatist third path, others explored the emerging and growing fields of welfare as well as development economics to conjugate corporatism with industrial development.[43] Portuguese economist António Jorge da Motta Veiga would become one of Salazar's closest economic advisers in the postwar period, even serving in the Council of Ministers, from which he coordinated Portugal's development plans in the 1960s. Motta Veiga never abandoned the corporatist paradigm, but he understood the importance of adapting it to postwar development challenges. While completing his doctorate in political economy at the University of Lisbon Law School, he insisted that "corporatist economics surpasses but does not disown classical economics." He made this argument while still citing Italian fascist economists, but added works by English economists Keynes and Joan Robinson to his footnotes. Throughout the 1930s, corporatist economists insisted that their model was better equipped to respond to real-world problems because "the direct intervention of the state is accepted as necessary to eliminate errors," with "errors" connoting the classical economic dependence on self-interest and individual decision-making.[44] By the 1940s, the idea that government played a role in regulating market forces was hardly new, even if it was still polemical.

This is not to say that corporatism became or was Keynesian. For Motta Veiga and others in Portugal, Keynes's *The General Theory of Employment, Interest and Money* was "still incomplete because the actions of the state do not form part of the theory of economic equilibrium as a necessary and fundamental premise."[45] In Keynes's model, the market remained the primary mechanism for maintaining economic equilibrium. If anything, Keynes made more concrete the shortcomings of an economic model in which individual choices conditioned the allocation of goods and services. Some Portuguese economists opted to read Keynes's moderate or sometimes vacillating assessment of government planning as an endorsement for Salazar's program. But Keynes did not endorse the types of planning at the core of the corporatist experiment—price controls, state-managed labor relations, and production quotas. Portuguese economists recognized this divergence, and continued to defend their model as better attuned to real-world economic crises and social hardships, remaining committed especially to their definition of price as a social value, not to be exclusively defined by supply and demand.

In the 1950s, the corporatist ideal of how to increase state control over economic decision-making had started to loosen. Economic planning was now guided by many different ideas, examples, and policies. Corporatist economic theory fell by the wayside, in part because these attempts to synthesize corporatism and the Keynesian-neoclassical consensus largely failed. Historian Carlos Bastein has argued that even the fiercest proponents of corporatism had to come to terms with the fact that all economies seemed to obey the same laws. By the late 1950s, economics as a discipline had become somewhat detached from the corporatist experiment. New research institutes like the Centro de Estudos Económicos of the Instituto Nacional de Esatística focused more on macroeconomic questions such as economic growth.[46] Others saw corporatism as a system borne out of medieval revivalism and Catholic social doctrine, invested in maintaining agriculture as the economic foundation of Portuguese society and upholding traditional social relations.[47] Departing from the idealism of the 1930s, public officials in Portugal increasingly framed corporatism as a social security system and less as an economic model. Corporatism, in other words, was not a distinct economic system that would build a new citizen, the *homo corporativus*; it was a set of strategies that could be combined and mixed almost à la carte.

Declining interest in corporatist economics as theory, though, unfolded even as corporatist economic controls, regulations, and institutions all remained in place. For some sectors, corporatism not only survived but also expanded in postwar Portugal. In fact, corporatism only obtained its full, institutional expression in August 1956 with legislation that finally created national corporations that grouped together all the local grémios and sindicatos by sector.

Pires Cardoso once called Portugal the "courageous *casa da guarda*," or guardhouse, of corporatism, "indifferent to all international hostility," and "intransigent and indifferent to internal and external attacks."[48] In part, he was right. Even as most of western Europe and the Americas embraced democracy after 1945, Salazar's dictatorship did not stop serving as a model for this third path. For a small but important faction of Brazilian officials—many of whom stayed in their prominent postings or would return to power with the 1964 military dictatorship—Salazar offered a positive example of dictatorship: durable, stable, austere, and prudent. Salazar was a "notable economist" who was able to restore financial stability to Portugal without external loans. "A country headed for bankruptcy was saved by the realistic genius of a simple patriot," one Brazilian woman proclaimed. In part, Salazar's earlier successes with austerity helped him to rebrand his image in the postwar period. Supporters of Salazar also claimed that his dictatorship was less violent than others in Europe. One Brazilian rhetorically asked, "In Portugal, they never recorded the same heinous crimes committed in Fascist Italy, Nazi Germany, and Communist Russia. Don't Portuguese concentration camps look quite a bit like our classic prisons on Ilha Grande and Fernando Noronha?"[49] Brazilian journalist Assis Chateaubriand even praised Salazar's regime in 1951 as a "democracia autoritária," or "authoritarian democracy."[50] This concept of democracy as "authority not liberty" professed by Oliveira Vianna and others in the 1930s survived into the postwar period as it was mirrored in Portugal's Estado Novo. Indeed, Catholic, conservative, corporatist factions in Brazil—and beyond— continued to see the Salazarist model as an alternative to the materialist excesses of liberal capitalism and rising specter of Soviet collectivism.

New models of corporatism emerged in this context as well. Franco in Spain embraced corporatism to rebuild the nation's economy following a violent civil war. Corporatism was also given new expression in nominally democratic contexts. In France, for example, corporatist ideas survived among Catholic, conservative circles.[51] French conservative intellectuals, moreover, maintained their interest in the Portuguese experiment as economist François Perroux corresponded with many in Portugal. In Mexico, corporatism found its expression in the leftist politics of Lázaro Cárdenas, which survived in the postwar period. The corporatist organizations that Cárdenas created to deliver on promises of social welfare and agrarian reform also made it possible for him and subsequent presidents to further centralize political power in the executive branch to such an extent that scholars tend to see one-party rule under the Partido Revolucionario Institucional as one of the most effective forms of authoritarianism in twentieth-century Latin America.[52] Portuguese economists took an interest in Mexico's corporatist governance, especially its efforts to increase agricultural production. Works by Mexican sociologists and economists made their way to the library of the Gabinete de Estudos Corporativos, and leading Portuguese social scientists cited Mexican essays and legislation.[53] Argentina became the next corporatist context to watch, with Juan Perón as president.[54] In 1947, newspapers around the world asked, "Is Salazar the Portuguese Perón, or is Perón the Argentinean Salazar?"[55]

Journalists, intellectuals, and social scientists gathered at academic conferences worldwide throughout the 1950s and 1960s questioned if corporatism was still a "viable" third path—and the answer was "yes" in both old and new ways.[56] Portugal had become a leading example of how.[57]

As much as corporatism remained the guiding ideology of Portugal's Estado Novo, the regime's chief intellectuals had to make room for new ideas and paradigms. The shift away from corporatism—or perhaps the expansion away from it—coincided with the shift from an agrarian to industrial vision of modernization and development. Here, Portuguese economists started borrowing from their Brazilian and Latin American counterparts.[58] Even more than before, "underdevelopment" became formalized as an explanation for Portugal's economic problems. Joseph Love, for instance, has followed the circulation of structuralist ideas from Latin America to Portugal. The Gabinete de Estudos Corporativos became one site where these debates unfolded.[59] In fact, as Love has argued, Portuguese economists were far more open than their Spanish neighbors to calling their nation "underdeveloped," with Portuguese economists embracing works by Brazilian economist Celso Furtado on techniques of economic planning necessary for overcoming structural challenges. Furtado's structuralist development theories were enthusiastically received in Portugal, not only on account of the shared language, but because of the tradition established over previous decades for the circulation of books and ideas between the two countries. Portuguese economist Alfredo de Sousa, for example, incorporated Furtado's ideas into his analysis of Portugal's economic stagnation and even coauthored a piece with Furtado.[60] Jointly, they emphasized structural themes like the need to push industrialization, move excess agricultural labor to industry, and deal with balance of payments problems to support the importation of capital goods and technology. They were also united in how they explained price instability in terms of disarticulations in internal and global markets between producers of raw materials and industrial producers, building on earlier corporatist critiques of classical economic price theories.[61] As Europe started building a regional economic bloc, Portugal remained more connected to Latin America in its economic models and intellectual circuits.

Plans and Planning in Postwar Brazil and Portugal

From modernization theory and W. W. Rostow's stages of economic growth to import substitution industrialization or the dependency analysis developed by economists at the United Nations Economic Commission for Latin America and the Caribbean (Comisión Económica para América Latina y el Caribe in Spanish, or CEPAL), theories abounded on how to explain—and ultimately fix—why some nations were poorer than others.[62] Underdevelopment became urgent for newly independent postcolonial nations in Africa or Asia as well as the poorer pockets of Latin America and southern and Eastern Europe. A growing cohort of economists and technocrats working for national governments across these regions tried to chart a new course.[63] Development became an intellectual and technical problem—one increasingly managed by international organizations such as the United Nations or World Bank along with major global powers. The problem of how poorer nations could launch development was also a geopolitical issue: the United States and Soviet Union each offered different paths to modernization—one capitalist and the other communist.[64] These international networks that increasingly shaped postwar economic policy did not eclipse the nation, though. In one way or another, national governments—and their growing state capacity—were at the center of all of these programs. The mixed economy still took different forms in different places, in part because of its diverse origins, but seemed securely installed.[65]

For Portugal as much as for Brazil, corporatist strategies to organize national production in the 1930s and 1940s became the substrate to which postwar development strategies adhered. Even though this generation of corporatists nimbly endorsed state intervention while also insisting that their program would not lead to total state control of the economy, in reality corporatist governments intervened in matters of national production via price controls, state-managed labor relations, licensing requirements, import/export controls, and other forms of direct and indirect control. All of these policies required building an increasingly unwieldy bureaucracy, sometimes draconian in its enforcement, and sometimes merely frustrating and ineffective. Scholars have come to a similar conclusion concerning bureaucracy. Portuguese historian Nuno Luís Madureira observed that for the Salazarist regime, the "ideal of a 'self-managed economy'" had turned into a "reality of the bureaucratically managed economy."[66]

To critics, corporatism had become a system of too many controls and too much red tape—but to others this bureaucracy was a starting point for the rise of economic planning in the postwar period. Portugal, like other nations, embarked on a series of five-year development plans in the 1950s and 1960s. Economist Motta Veiga, who took a central role in designing the III Plano de Fomento (Development Plan) (1968–73), defined development planning simply and straightforwardly as a "program of action" that combined "joint participation" between the state and private sectors.[67] In his view, Portugal was not following other countries but in fact had been an early trendsetter, tracing the intellectual and technical origins of Portugal's development plans to a 1935 government program for economic reconstruction. He conveniently sidestepped Soviet antecedents. Even as Portuguese economists increasingly used benchmarks, graphs, statistics, and mathematical formulas to talk about economic development, the language of corporatism persisted as well. The nation remained the object of ambitious economic planning. The corporatist framework to harness collective interests for national interests nestled comfortably into this new development paradigm. "A development plan is, above all, an affirmation of the collective will," explained economist José de Sousa Mendes, "in the sense that the entire nation must actively and consciously participate in building its own future."[68]

In 1953, Portugal launched the first of its eventual four five-year plans to modernize Portuguese agriculture, improve infrastructure, accelerate manufacturing, promote heavy industries, and create conditions for general economic growth. Development plans were implemented equally in Portugal and across its colonies.[69] The goal was to transform the composition of Portugal's economy by stimulating rapid industrialization, or as one economist put it, "Get out of the backward state we find ourselves in."[70]

By 1960, at the start of the second Plano, 44 percent of Portugal's active population was still engaged in agriculture and fishing, with 29 percent in industrial activities. According to data compiled by the Banco de Portugal, however, the primary sector only accounted for 22 percent of the national output, with industry and construction accounting for 36 percent.[71] Economists cited these numbers as arguments for why Portugal's government needed to coordinate a major initiative for industrialization. The gap between labor input and productive output provided evidence not only of the inefficiency of Portuguese agriculture but also its consequences; the low purchasing power of the "masses," one economist noted, meant that "the consumer market remained very limited."[72] The standard of living was quite low across Portugal too, but especially in rural areas. Poverty and underemployment in rural areas became a major driver for both documented and undocumented emigration from Portugal to destinations such as Brazil, France, and the United States from the 1950s to the 1970s.[73] Capital was another limiting factor for Portugal's economic transformation. The government provided a major source of credit for all Planos, covering about 25 percent of the expenditures. Portugal inaugurated its Banco de Fomento Nacional, or National Development Bank, in 1958 to facilitate lending. Breaking from some of the autarkic conditions of the 1930s, the Planos also invited foreign investment, albeit still on a limited and controlled basis. While the first Plano was largely financed internally, external borrowing amounted to 25 percent of the second Plano's projected expenditures.[74]

With the Planos, Portugal liberalized some economic sectors, although corporatist rules and controls remained intact.[75] Corporatist institutions got folded into development plans, albeit sometimes in awkward ways that revealed underlying ideological tensions. Government officials were careful to distance their Planos from those of socialist countries by showing how their planning techniques worked to support and even "perfect" the market as the primary mechanism for allocating goods and services—not to truncate it. Portuguese economists put considerations of economic justice or social peace largely beyond the scope of these two-thousand-page programs in which labor was discussed in terms of employment rates and prices in terms of inflation. But *corporações*, or the different types of corporatist organs representing producers, merchants, or industrialists and other economic groups, were not forgotten in the development plans. These organs were pitched as agents of the "private sector," key to coordination between the public and private. For economist Motta Veiga, the way in which corporatist organs facilitated the participation of the private sector in meeting development targets was the "crowning achievement" of Portugal's development plans. To leverage corporatist entities as an illustration of how "private initiative" took a "leading role in guiding national economic progress" departed from the expressly illiberal and anticapitalist orientation of the Estado Novo's earlier position.[76] Portuguese officials now tried to make corporatism synonymous with public-private collaboration, showcasing how its third path was compatible with other forms of the *capitalist* mixed economy emerging across Europe and the Americas.

Even as corporatism in ideological and theoretical terms was no longer fore-grounded in debates about Portuguese development, corporatist organisms were still the cellular unit for sector organization. Economic planning and pro-grams for development were funneled through the corporatist state and its many ancillary institutions. Corporatist organisms remained essential units of Portugal's growing administrative state: they were still entities with regula-tory powers over production, commerce, and labor. These organisms were primary units in postwar Planos de Fomento and still absorbed government expenditures. Moreover, even as some economists embraced more quantita-tive metrics for progress, others recycled corporatist rhetoric, as the Salazarist regime continued to position itself as an agent for social peace and economic stability, guaranteeing equipoise between producers and consumers. Econo-mist Luís Maria Teixeira Pinto exclaimed in 1965 at the headquarters for the Federação dos Grémios da Lavoura de Entre Douro e Minho, "We are all to be congratulated because everything worked—the services worked, beyond what was expected, the corporations worked, the cooperatives worked."[77]

In reality, Portugal's corporatist system was unraveling. Agricultural produc-ers resented the grémio system, protesting its price controls, red tape, and obligatory contributions. The strains were evident in the ongoing vigilance of Portugal's police forces toward popular agitation against the corporatist sys-tem; they resorted to arresting workers and farmers who protested. In 1971, for example, agricultural workers who were "obligatorily registered" in the local grémio da lavoura in Viseu refused to pay the "coercive" dues owed.[78] Women were rumored to be at the forefront of efforts to evade payment and prevent the confiscation of goods as punishment, goading public authorities when they came around to collect dues.[79] The issue fell to Portugal's Tribunal de Trabalho, or Labor Tribunal, which issued arrest warrants for those who refused to pay their dues. Public officials worried that their protest could spill over into the nearby regions and warned local landowners of the potential for social unrest.[80]

In the 1960s and early 1970s, popular opposition against corporatist con-trols grew as poverty persisted, and the promises of social peace and economic justice remained unfulfilled. Like Salazar, his successor, Caetano, who as-sumed power in 1968, boasted of his accomplishments as a prudent professor turned dictator, but the legacy of their combined forty-plus-year dictatorship in promoting Portugal's economic development is hardly clear or straightfor-ward. Portugal's GDP per capita increased nearly fivefold between 1928, the

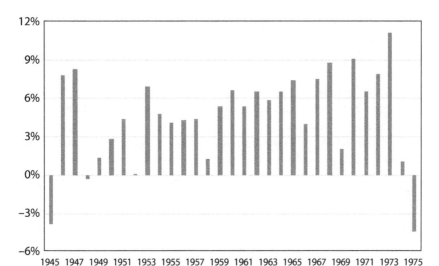

FIGURE 7.1. Portugal's real GDP growth, 1945–75. *Source:* GDP growth rate calculated by author using data in Angus Maddison, *The World Economy: Historical Statistics* (Paris: OECD Publishing, 2003), table 1b.

year Salazar entered the Finance Ministry, and 1974. While the country did not achieve the high growth rates associated with economic "miracles" in other parts of the world, its economy did grow at a consistent and strong pace in the postwar decades (figure 7.1). Portugal even closed some of the gap between its economic performance and that of its European neighbors. In 1928, for instance, Portugal's GDP per capita was only 20 percent of the United Kingdom's, but this value climbed to 60 percent by 1974.[81] Economic historians have long debated Portugal's "particularly good economic performance" from the 1930s up to the Estado Novo's collapse in 1974. Some scholars attribute its economic growth to internal factors, namely the economic stability generated by balanced budgets and low inflation combined with corporatist reforms to protect domestic markets, organize producers, control wages and prices, and regulate supply chains. Others argue that market controls actually inhibited higher levels of growth.[82] Furthermore, according to many economic and human development indicators, Portugal remained the poorest country in western Europe. In a way, Salazar's commitment to corporatism proved limiting. The corporatist system functioned to keep both prices and wages low, in both rural and urban areas. This strategy might have appeased industrialists and large landowners by keeping inflation low and labor costs cheap, but compressing wages also hampered the growth of a domestic market that could support industrialization. With wages so low, Portuguese workers looked elsewhere, thereby triggering severe labor shortages.[83] High levels of emigration—first to Brazil and then France—were driven by economic hardships in rural areas and limited opportunities in major cities. Emigration became a necessary safety valve in the postwar period for the Estado Novo regime, while remittances back home cushioned the balance of payments. By 1970, the value of emigrant remittances equaled that of 52 percent of exports and 8 percent of the country's total output.[84]

But these safety valves would not hold. In the 1960s, the Estado Novo launched a series of violent colonial wars to hold onto overseas territories in Asia and Africa. It imposed widely unpopular obligatory military service. As colonial wars dominated government spending, inflation ticked upward. Political opposition mounted against continued political repression, even as Salazar's successor, Caetano, attempted reform. The Portuguese Estado Novo collapsed on April 25, 1974, with the Carnation Revolution, a bloodless coup led by military officers that quickly unfolded into a popular uprising for democracy.[85] Caetano went into exile in Brazil, where he found refuge with many old friends and interlocutors, some of whom were recently appointed to prominent postings in the military dictatorship installed in 1964. In Rio de Janeiro, Caetano continued writing about corporatism as well as the legal and economic experiments he had supported for over four decades.

The postwar history of corporatism is that of a set of ideas pushed up against economic realities and political contingencies. In part, corporatism was able to penetrate so deep into Portugal's political and economic institutions because it circulated globally in the 1930s. A generation of jurists, intellectuals, and economists were deeply convinced that corporatism would work to fix national problems and jump-start development, and they took inspiration from how their counterparts in other parts of the world were trying to do the same thing. Many corporatist theorists had served as technocrats within government—not merely relegated to universities or think tanks—and so their ideas were constantly being put into laws and policy, and indeed action. As with any political experiment, the collusion between ideas and interests proved delicate and ephemeral. Some embraced the corporatist third path as politically expedient to advance their economic interests or above all stay in power—until it was not.

Plans and planning were even more dramatic in Brazil from the 1940s onward. President Eurico Gaspar Dutra, president from 1946 to 1951, had a liberal orientation in both practice and ideology. He tackled the grave problems of postwar economic adjustment, and his government's liberal approach—after fifteen years of active government intervention, support, and subsidies—was not well received by crucial sectors of Brazil's economy. To appease key industrial and agricultural groups, he launched the SALTE Plan in 1947 with great fanfare, although it only amounted to the bundling of preexisting projects in health, food, transportation, and energy sectors. Dutra's departure from liberal campaign promises with his less than laissez-faire SALTE plan, however, requires context.[86] While liberal economists in Brazil such as Gudin would remain fiercely opposed to government planning, worldwide it seemed that planning was no longer quite as controversial, or tainted by prior associations with fascist or Soviet economics.[87] At the end of World War II, the US-financed Marshall Plan in Europe had heralded planning for postwar recovery and development, and national governments in other parts of the world followed. As early as 1947, the United Nations Department of Economic Affairs produced a list of dozens of state agencies involved in economic planning and development in Latin American countries.[88] While some economic historians of Brazil emphasize the incoherence or contradictions in how postwar governments oscillated between liberal and state developmentalist economic ideas to highlight the intellectual battles between the orthodox and heterodox camps, these decades were also defined by a remarkable degree of institutional continuity.[89] Corporatist institutions such as the Instituto Nacional do Mate, Instituto do Açúcar e do Álcool, and many other commodity agencies created in the 1930s were included on the United Nations' list for Brazil, as was the CFCE.[90] As in Portugal, corporatist entities created in the 1930s were repurposed for new postwar planning in Brazil.

While the end to the war had triggered regime change in Brazil, much of the Estado Novo endured. Vargas himself returned to power in 1951, now as a popularly elected populist president. Vargas had started plotting his return to power from the minute he left it in 1945, working to build political and popular support during his exile in Rio Grande do Sul, and even brokering a détente with the Brazilian Communist Party to better access the labor base.[91] He campaigned on his legacy as he criticized Dutra's economic policies, especially his lax support for Brazil's industrial sectors and excessive austerity policies. Vargas's candidacy was supported by major industrial interests. Euvaldo Lodi, now president of the Confederação Nacional da Indústria, was a major financial contributor to his campaign.[92] The governors and economic elites of Brazil's most powerful states supported him too. As much as Vargas understood the importance of maintaining the support of leading industrialists and landowners, he leaned into his populist messaging as well, promising to improve the standard of living for the poor and working classes.

Vargas campaigned on long-term goals like industrialization and modernization along with the amelioration of hardships, such as inflation, endured by the poor and working classes.[93] Geraldo Pereira's 1951 samba celebrated Vargas's election:

> Seu Presidente,
> Sua Excelência mostrou que é de fato
> Agora tudo vai ficar barato
> Agora o pobre já pode comer

> Mr. President,
> Your Excellency has shown that it's true
> Now everything will be cheaper
> Now the poor will be able to eat

During Vargas's second presidency, industrial workers in particular mobilized against the constantly rising prices of food staples in major cities. Wages had failed to keep pace with inflation. In a democratic context framed by new political parties competing for influence and power, the labor constituency could not be ignored. The Ministry of Labor tried to absorb workers protests into its architecture in corporatist style. But workers did not just petition for higher wages or fair arbitration.[94] Historian Rafael Ioris shows that workers in Rio de Janeiro and São Paulo repeatedly argued that food production and distribution should be placed under stricter public supervision by enhancing the role of state officials and eliminating foreign agents. Workers demanded annual adjustments on wages, indexed to inflation, along with price controls on essential goods. In addition, workers petitioned for their sindicatos to be involved in setting price freezes and controls.[95]

Workers' demands for price controls in the postwar period are not exclusive to Brazil or even corporatist contexts as a similar pattern is evident in the United States and Chile.[96] Nevertheless, the call for price controls in Brazil shows how labor shaped Brazil's developmentalist ideology by turning corporatist definitions of just price in the 1930s into a collective struggle for economic justice.

Vargas understood that he could not ignore popular appeals. In 1951, he promised crowds at the Maracanã soccer stadium to "before anything else, curb the cost of living, establishing a *justo preço* for essential foodstuff." Critically, he added, "the doors of the presidency of the republic are open to all of your advice, criticisms, and complaints."[97]

Legislation on the popular economy and other efforts to discipline the free market in the 1930s had altered popular and political language for talking about the economy and had rewired popular expectations of market fairness. In the late 1940s, Dutra's liberal government had eliminated most price controls on essential goods. Some Brazilians welcomed this return to the so-called free market given how retailers and grocers generally and increasingly ignored the price controls. As skeptical as some consumers were of government efforts to tame inflation, mocking the price tables that remained affixed to retail establishments, others asked in earnest whether inflation would not in fact be far worse without controls (figures 7.2 and 7.3). This debate would mark consumer politics in Brazil for decades to come as Vargas's postwar populist government returned to the laws and policies first tested in the 1930s to deal with inflation.

Brazil underwent massive transformations during postwar decades with industrialization, urbanization, and the growth of a middle-class consumer society. Brazil's automobile sector along with state-owned steel and oil companies flourished.[98] Its economy grew at impressive rates (figure 7.4), but inflation persisted as a nagging obstacle to midcentury growth (figure 7.5). Throughout this transformation, popular economy laws—and consumer denunciations— remained a safety valve to ameliorate the impacts on everyday life of fast-paced development.

Economic denunciations remained an outlet for popular classes to voice grievances, although the NST was dismantled in 1945 and denunciations were now heard in ordinary courts.[99] Through the late 1940s and into the 1950s, a large number of individuals continued to be arrested and tried for economic crimes.[100] These trials also remained a vehicle for settling feuds and even ill-fated romances. In 1958, for example, a woman was denounced by her former lover for selling codfish outside the rules set by the Comissão Federal de Abastecimento e Preços, an organ created in 1951 to regulate the distribution of essential goods, with powers to fix prices or buy and sell directly. The Comissão Federal de Abastecimento e Preços was the successor to Estado Novo commissions such as the Comissão Reguladora do Tabelamento or similar organs under the Comissão de Mobilização Econômica (see chapters 4 and 6). O Cruzeiro humorously concluded that this ill-fated love did not follow the tragic ending of William Shakespeare's Romeo and Juliet but instead "ended with an investigation by the popular economy police."[101] It is hard to say whether an actual infraction took place or if the jilted lover merely acted out of spite. In either case, concepts like fair price survived not only in law but also in the popular imagination, notwithstanding their failures.

Although they persisted, price controls or other legislative legacies from the corporatist Estado Novo hardly offer a story of government's triumph over economic problems. The Estado Novo fractured and reduced concerns such as inflation, scarce credit, or food shortages to their simplest parts. Paradoxically, the anti-individualist spirit behind price controls individualized economic problems by scapegoating grocers, bakers, and butchers. Popular economy laws did not fix inflation or other structural problems partly because they did not address the root causes. Still, the realization of this did not stop subsequent

FIGURE 7.2. "Seis preços para os mesmos tomates," or "Six different prices for the same tomatoes." Printed in *O Cruzeiro: Revista Semanal Illustrada* (September 1946). The article documents continued price speculation, black market sales, and other ways that retailers in Rio de Janeiro failed to observe official price tables to the detriment of the popular economy. Image courtesy of Arquivo O Cruzeiro / EM / D. A. Press.

governments, whether democratic or dictatorial, from using criminal law to target economic issues. In fact, Brazil's military dictatorship installed in 1964 again used military tribunals against civilians, largely for political repression and (sometimes) economic crimes.[102] Certainly, this practice of subjecting prices to legal oversight and police enforcement has a long history in Brazil. The rise of liberalism and free trade ideology in the nineteenth century might have inspired Brazilian officials to repeal colonial era price controls, but the notion of a just price survived in part because the poor and working classes demanded government actions to tame the rising cost of living.[103] Vargas might not have invented the concept of a just price, but he did reintroduce the legal codification of this economic right. Once the right to a fair price became a constitutional promise, it was not easy to dismantle, even if price controls and their criminal enforcement hardly worked. This makes Vargas era

SUSPENSÃO DO TABELAMENTO

O Sr. Augusto de Souza, de Belo Horizonte, envia-nos uma interessante carta, e termina perguntando: "Poderá Vossa Senhoria explicar-me se a propalada extinção do tabelamento, beneficiará a população?

FIGURE 7.3. Political cartoon "Quem dá mais?" or "Who will pay more?" in *O Cruzeiro: Revista Semanal Illustrada* (November 1946). The cartoon accompanied a letter to the editor in which a reader asked whether the end of price controls would improve conditions for the public or worsen inflation in Brazil. Image courtesy of Arquivo O Cruzeiro / EM / D. A. Press.

laws to defend the popular economy important for another reason: they reveal a pattern of precarious solutions to long-run challenges like inflation. Moreover, they demonstrate that in mid-twentieth-century Brazil, fair price was a concept not only debated by law professors and technocrats but litigated daily in courtrooms, markets, and households too.

Vargas also returned to the agricultural and industrial policies that he had implemented during his prior fifteen-year tenure, but adjusted them to the new international order. His messaging amplified the 1930s' ethos with a more bombastic take of economic nationalism epitomized by his iconic *o petróleo é nosso* (the oil is ours) campaign that surrounded the creation of Brazil's state-owned oil company, Petrobras, in 1953. The seeds for Petrobras were first planted with articles on subsoil wealth in the 1934 and 1937 Constitutions along with the creation of the Conselho Nacional do Petróleo in 1938. In addition, Vargas reinforced his messaging on the central role of the state as an agent of economic development. Although agriculture was still a pillar of Vargas's political economy, industrialization without a doubt became the primary focus.

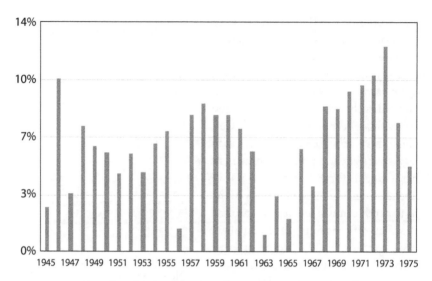

FIGURE 7.4. Brazil's real GDP growth, 1945–75. *Source:* GDP growth rate calculated by author using data in Angus Maddison, *The World Economy: Historical Statistics* (Paris: OECD Publishing, 2003), table 4b.

FIGURE 7.5. Inflation in Brazil, 1945–75. *Source:* Francisco Vidal Luna and Herbert S. Klein, *The Economic and Social History of Brazil since 1889* (New York: Cambridge University Press, 2014), table A.3.

Vargas's industrialization program in the 1950s reaffirmed his commitment to a *caminho do meio,* or "path down the middle," adapting the third path language to new contexts. Vargas defended the role of the state in economic development while also looking to strengthen the private sector. He emphasized the need to build a "new technical bureaucracy as a modernizing agent," as historian Maria Antonieta P. Leopoldi describes it.[104] Brazil's industrial class would play an active role in making industrial policy as well. The sorts of high-stakes and controversial debates that had pitted Estado Novo ideologues like Oliveira Vianna against industrialists in the 1930s and 1940s receded into the background. The industrial bourgeoise and its corporatist associations were on board to play a key role during the second Vargas era as industrialization took off. Industrial associations like the Federação das Indústrias do Estado de São Paulo also pushed for a say in the internal structure of the state and its agencies.[105] Brazil's government, accordingly, absorbed—in corporatist fashion—industrial leadership to work in its agencies, just as had happened in the 1930s. In July 1951, the Comissão de Desenvolvimento Industrial (Commission for Industrial Development) became the planning arm of the Ministry of Finance in order to support industrialization, bringing together representatives from various government ministries with representatives chosen by industrialists. This organ had a deliberate "neocorporatist character," Leopoldi explains, repurposing strategies developed in the 1930s.[106] Protectionist policies had both private and public support, as did efforts to promote energy independence and self-sufficiency in food production. These organs were now situated in a democratic context, coexisting with Congress and political parties. But special commissions played an elevated role, bypassing legislative organs in key areas of economic policy.[107] Once again, corporatism became a bridge to technocracy.

Vargas's approach to economic development, in other words, mirrored that of the 1930s with the creation of many new special commissions, staffed with técnicos with specialized training.[108] But it was also meaningfully different. In the Cold War context, for example, Brazil forged closer ties to the United States. It benefited from new international organizations as well, receiving loans from the World Bank, which furnished US$104 million in credit between 1951 and 1954.[109] The Banco Nacional de Desenvolvimento Econômico e Social (National Bank for Economic and Social Development), Brazil's development bank created in 1952, benefited from international loans to finance major infrastructure projects, especially electrification. In contrast with how Brazil's 1930s' experiment had to navigate global credit scarcity and protectionism, economic planning and development in the postwar period was an international endeavor, even as economic nationalism remained an essential counterpart to populist political rhetoric and economic strategy.

The promised corporatist equilibrium between sectors and social peace started to crack during Vargas's presidency. In 1953, the end of the Korean War triggered a global recession, and the drop in commodity prices particularly impacted Brazil. Domestically, inflation inched upward and workers increasingly protested their depreciating wages. In 1953, workers turned against Vargas, organizing work stoppages and strikes. Vargas responded in early 1954 by doubling the minimum wage, hoping to keep the support of this base. Industrialists and investors were angry, thereby triggering a rupture between industrial associations and the government.[110] As Vargas's hold over this delicate corporatist triangle of interests eroded, a series of political and corruption scandals erupted. Opposition camps seized on his weakness. Members of the armed forces plotted to force Vargas's resignation, and many in the public suspected a coup was inevitable. Vargas preempted it. On August 15, 1954, he took his own life, leaving a note that positioned his suicide as his final and ultimate sacrifice to the Brazilian people, while putting the blame on foreign and domestic enemies.[111]

After a few politically tumultuous years, Juscelino Kubitschek, from Minas Gerais, became president, attempting to build on Vargas's development legacy. Economic planning became both metaphor and policy. Kubitschek's economic ambitions were bolder than those of Vargas. He famously called for "Fifty Years in Five," or fifty years of modernization in just five. This accelerated growth was organized around the Plano de Metas, or Plan of Goals, which focused on energy, food, industry, education, and transport in order to modernize and diversify Brazil's economy. The Plano de Metas was not an exercise in total economic planning. It targeted key sectors of Brazil's economy so that the state could facilitate overcoming bottlenecks, especially in infrastructure, that limited the growth of the internal market. Moreover, Kubitschek's policies were layered on top of the conciliatory politics of Vargas's corporatist system, in which planning became an instrument in minimizing and reconciling economic and political tensions—a way of bureaucratizing social conflicts into planning metrics.[112] With these goals in mind, Kubitschek opened Brazil to foreign capital, accelerating the growth of new industries like the automobile and household appliances.[113] To crown these achievements, he moved Brazil's capital to the interior of the country, inaugurating the planned city of Brasília with its impressive modernist architecture. With this, economic planning had become a concrete reality. Bold ambitions, however, were realized at steep costs. Brazil's debt increased by one billion US dollars between 1956 and 1960, while annual inflation rates reached 31 percent by 1960.[114] Kubitschek's government was also plagued by accusations of corruption, which further eroded public confidence. He might have met his planning targets, but planning had created new economic problems and not completely resolved the old ones.

During Kubitschek's time in office, a new intellectual tool kit started to take hold, in Brazil and across Latin America. His push for industrialization was underpinned by CEPAL's analysis of deteriorating terms of trade and its interpretation of Brazil's persistent balance of payments problems.[115] Historian Joseph Love has argued that the writings of Latin American economists like Raúl Prebisch on structuralism—the seeds of dependency theory—had their origins in Romanian corporatist economist Mihail Manoilescu's writings on protectionism in the 1920s and 1930s (see chapter 3).[116] Manoilescu's writings had exposed the ways in which "agricultural countries 'are poor and stay poor.'"[117]

Yet Love never fully clarified how or why Manoilescu's writings appealed so broadly in southern Europe and Latin America, or the intellectual circuits by which his early writings inspired structuralist thought. Corporatism is the missing but necessary bridge from Manoilescu's writings in Romania to the founding of CEPAL in Latin America. Corporatist ideas circulated from Europe to Latin America, and back from Latin America to Europe, reformulated in the idiom of developmentalism.

In Brazil, on March 31, 1964, the armed forces organized a military coup to overthrow President João Goulart, installing a twenty-one-year military dictatorship. It is not unusual for histories of the Vargas era to end with this coup, as many scholars look to the 1930s and 1940s to explain how the military gained and sustained power—as a corporate entity and political player—and how it worked behind the scenes during the Vargas years to influence political and economic decisions. The 1964 coup thus becomes not an aberration but rather part of a pattern in which the military intervened in moments of social and economic turmoil as the agent appointed to restore order and protect the interests of capital.[118]

But the military was not the only authoritarian praxis in Brazil, neither during the Vargas era nor in the subsequent decades. This was something that economists and social scientists writing in the 1960s and 1970s understood as they tried to explain the proliferation of military coups in Latin America. Argentinean political scientist Guillermo O'Donnell underscored the corporatist roots of the rise of what he called "bureaucratic authoritarianism." As he contended, "'Corporatism' should be understood as a set of structures which link society with the state." This need not be an authoritarian mode of governance, as indeed many similar models exist in democratic contexts. For O'Donnell, though, corporatism might start as a set of formal institutions through which private interests are represented vis-à-vis the state, but the corporatist logic is also to limit representative channels, or "put an end to 'excessive' or 'premature' demands for political and economic participation by the popular sector."[119] This limiting logic is precisely what, decades prior, had motivated Oliveira Vianna's definition of *authoritarian democracy* as "democracy based on authority and not liberty."[120] Corporatism offers a system of hierarchy, exclusion, authority, and order. And because by definition, corporatism privileges functional—or economic—representation, its political rationale becomes its economic rationale too. This helps to explain why corporatism was touted in the 1930s and again in the 1960s as the only possible fix for economic crises—whether short-run financial crises or long-run crises of underdevelopment.

———

This chapter has told a connected history of the survival and failure—or failure and survival—of corporatism in and between Brazil and Portugal. In the case of Brazil, many laws and institutions survived the Vargas era, with names slightly altered or text edited after the taint of fascism and genocide during World War II to remove any mention of *corporatism*. Even as corporatism as an ideal faltered, a corporatist logic survived into the postwar years as governments in Brazil and Portugal looked for new ways to strategize economic development by incorporating private interests—whether labor, industry, or agriculture—into the architecture of the state. This formula proved especially well suited to the postwar problems of underdevelopment in southern Europe and Latin America as the rise of economic planning solidified the mixed economy in its many different forms.

One of the places where corporatist ideas and institutions survived into the postwar period was in efforts to regulate prices and access to food for internal markets. Historians of Brazil have largely focused on how the Vargas period is essential for the origins of state-directed industrialization in terms of both policies to support industrialists and organize them through the state. But there is another origin story here in terms of all the state's efforts to organize the internal market, increase food production, and regulate prices in the context of workers' protests. These postwar efforts built on debates over just price in the 1930s and corporatist critiques of laissez-faire capitalism.

Rather than conclude that corporatism failed because its practice diverged too much from its ideal type, this economic system created an institutional architecture for postwar development schemes. The aim in this chapter has not been to explain the success or failure of corporatist dictatorships but instead how corporatist ideas, fashioned by ideologues and technocrats, mutated into postwar iterations of development. The illiberal logic at the core of interwar corporatist models also persisted. In Brazil much as in Portugal, postwar jurists and intellectuals attempted to show all the ways in which corporatism was compatible with democratic values, all the while continuing to defend authoritarian forms of government as essential for economic order and progress. Their skepticism of both political and economic liberalism would, through the course of the twentieth century, mutate again and again into new economic arguments in support of dictatorship.

Conclusion

IN 1949, Saint Lucian economist Arthur Lewis called the period between the First and Second World Wars "an age of dislocation and an age of experiment" for the global economy.[1] Global wars and economic crisis had altered the world along with its ideological coordinates, and nations started experimenting with building strong, centralized, and activist states. Lewis based his analysis on the experiences of industrialized nations in North America and northern Europe, but his conceptualization of the mid-twentieth century as a time of trial, experiment, and reaction is all the more compelling when we look southward to Latin America and southern Europe.

This book makes a case for the importance of incorporating the corporatist third path into twentieth-century global economic histories—a history often bifurcated via a Cold War lens that pits communism against capitalism. Corporatism offers an alternative genealogy for the rise of state-led development. In the aftermath of World War II, the globe reeled over the astounding human casualties, mass displacement, and physical destruction caused by the six-year conflict. One of the starkest legacies of this aftermath was the east/ west polarization in Europe that came to divide the world into "communist" and "capitalist" blocs.[2] The Cold War made many interwar experiments seem like irrelevant relics, or worse, failures, but this book has recovered one of those overlooked projects so as to resuscitate the search for third paths between the laissez-faire order and collectivist or command economies. Across ideological and political divides, twentieth-century governments worldwide experimented with new market regulations, protectionist policies, and social welfare provisions in order to accelerate economic growth and improve social well-being. To fully understand the intellectual and institutional creativity that informed the rise of state-directed development, we have to draw corporatism into the conversation. Corporatist experiments mattered not only because they happened but because they fundamentally redesigned the architecture of state-market relations in Brazil and Portugal, and in many other countries too.

A Third Path also argues more generally for looking beyond regionalism when we think about global exchange and influence. In the interwar decades, the Luso-Brazilian corridor was vibrant with intellectual and political exchange. Its relevance to midcentury economic experimentation has been silenced given the tendency among social scientists to organize the globe into continental and regional categories that are themselves products of Cold War geopolitics. In the United States, for example, anxieties over the spread of communism led governmental and nongovernmental agencies to sponsor area studies programs in universities and within the federal government to produce regional experts who could advance foreign policy goals.[3] Thus the postwar order was not only polarized according to two divergent economic camps but increasingly organized according to geographic regions as well.

The shrinking relevance of the South Atlantic as a space for political and cultural exchange was a casualty of these postwar intellectual and geopolitical shifts. Portugal was initially outside Europe's new regional framework, holding firm to its isolationism, save for its pivotal relationship with Brazil. Salazar was notoriously skeptical of the United States, spurning its brash capitalist spirit and wary of its imperialist ambitions. By 1950, however, Salazar agreed to Marshall Plan aid, despite his initial rejection of the funds. Between North Atlantic Treaty Organization membership and the Marshall Plan, Portugal shifted away from its Atlantic orientation, which according to historian Fernanda Rollo, had long been marked by the fierce defense of its empire and close ties with Brazil.[4]

Latin America, too, launched its own initiatives for regional economic and political cooperation. Most famous among these was CEPAL, founded in 1948 to promote the industrialization of Latin American economies. While European recovery initiatives tended to emphasize the importance of open trade between member nations, CEPAL economists were concerned about the damaging terms of trade for nations on the global periphery, or agrarian producers. Even the intellectual origins of this regional organization, however, was partially shaped by the transnational networks that had given rise to interwar corporatist experiments. To recall, bundled with his writings on international exchange, Manoilescu's works on corporatism circulated from Europe to Latin America, casting a wide network of corporatist thinkers that connected Argentina and Brazil to Portugal and Italy.[5] This network is forgotten in most postwar histories of developmentalism. Thus as Portugal drew closer to Europe, Brazil drew closer to Argentina, Chile, and Mexico, becoming a regional superpower as economists from these nations constituted a Latin American space for thinking about and acting on economic problems.[6] Luso-Brazilian connections become less relevant in a world increasingly governed by regional economic unions or international institutions such as the United Nations or World Bank.

At the same time, the importance of Luso-Brazilian cultural and political ambitions did not evaporate, nor did the networks explored in this book disintegrate with the fall of Vargas or even Salazar. Brazil's government, for example, worked to forge closer ties with Portuguese-speaking Africa on commercial and diplomatic fronts. As historian Jerry Dávila has expertly shown, Brazil became an essential player during the continent's decolonization struggles as it positioned itself to become a world power. Brazilian diplomats turned *luso-tropicalismo*, a term, as noted earlier, that Brazilian sociologist Gilberto Freyre coined to celebrate the Portuguese as uniquely adept colonizers on account of their adaptability to tropical climates and affinity for relations with other races, into the point of departure for new political and economic ties to Angola and other African nations. As Brazilian intellectuals and diplomats started looking to Africa, a right-wing military dictatorship seized power in 1964. Ties between Brazil and Portugal remained strong during Brazil's twenty-plus-year military dictatorship, as conservative jurists and political officials continued to look to Portugal to defend their authoritarian projects. Brazil's military government remained "sentimentally bound" to Portugal, Dávila argues, even as Portugal launched a violent military campaign to quash anticolonial movements, and Brazilian officials started emphasizing Brazil's racial and historical ties to African countries in order to assert its place as an industrializing leader among developing or "third world" countries.[7] The third path that had drawn Brazil and Portugal together in the 1930s gave way to new third world possibilities in the 1960s, but it did not lose relevance. Just how strong the political and intellectual networks between Brazil and Portugal remained is perhaps best encapsulated in the fact that Marcello Caetano took his exile in Rio de Janeiro after the 1974 Carnation Revolution. He would write and publish his memoir *Minhas memórias de Salazar* in Rio de Janeiro as he continued to also reaffirm his corporatist vision to Brazilian audiences even as it was being dismantled in Portugal.

Historians of the nineteenth century have stressed the continuity of financial and commercial ties between postindependence Brazil and the Portuguese Empire, especially in terms of the slave trade.[8] But little is written about the persistence of intellectual, financial, economic, or diplomatic ties into the twentieth century. This is a shame because, as this book has outlined, these ties were instrumental in the rise of dictatorships across the century. Such ties were also important in other ways, though. Consider, for instance, the various channels of immigration that continue to bind these two nations—rural migration from Portugal to Brazil in the 1950s and 1960s, Brazilian economic immigration to Portugal in the 1980s and 1990s during its hyperinflationary crises, the emigration of Portuguese, especially young professionals, to Brazil during the euro crisis, and recent movements of middle-class Brazilians to Portugal amid

Brazil's current uncertain political and economic climate. The corporatist connections between interwar Estado Novo regimes thus offers a context for thinking transregionally about events throughout the twentieth century. It shows one of the many ways in which two nations formally bound by empire remain connected, even if that connection is perpetually changing, and the balance between these two powers shifting.

Corporatist experiments also mattered because they shaped the rise of state-led development as much in Brazil as in Portugal. The first part of this legacy has to do with the logic and institutions by which the state intervened in markets. Much of the scholarship on developmentalism begins in 1945, cementing a tendency (even if not explicit) to conflate developmentalism with the revival of liberal democracy in the postwar period. This narrative has been challenged by Frederick Cooper and others writing about the origins of developmentalist policies in empire.[9] Historians of Latin America, moreover, have long argued that governments responded to the 1929 crisis with various new forms of state intervention in the economy, but the logic of such interventions is often assumed to be reactive to crisis, and not necessarily grounded in a particular set of ideas or ideologies. Hence developmentalism, a set of strategies, ideals, and rational planning, remains a story of postwar decades. In stretching the origins of this process back to the interwar decades, we see that the vision proclaimed by corporatist ideologues in the 1930s and 1940s shaped how Brazil's and Portugal's governments (and other ones) attempted to transform their nations, in ways insistent on maintaining social peace, political authority, and a deeply hierarchical society.

One unexpected way in which corporatist jurists and economists designed new states to secure social peace was by focusing their efforts on price. They deployed erudite arguments and formal models in order to debunk the assumptions of classical political economy, and redefine concepts of *fair price* or *just competition* in terms of how to mediate between different group interests for the sake of social peace and national development. Brazilian and Portuguese economists fused technical debates over the price mechanism to sweeping critiques of laissez-faire capitalism. This was not a purely intellectual project. To set and enforce price controls, officials in both countries experimented with new forms of government intervention in market transactions, mobilizing corporatist producer associations, new government agencies, and ordinary citizens to enforce price controls. In both Brazil and Portugal, Estado Novo dictators branded those who defied price controls or hoarded goods as speculators and capitalist rouges, mobilizing military tribunals and police campaigns to enforce increasingly byzantine market regulations. Vargas's and Salazar's dictatorships were hardly the first or only governments to experiment with price controls in the 1930s and 1940s; many interwar governments tackled the problem of price during these decades of protracted economic instability and unpredictability. Still, the corporatist logic that informed price controls in Brazil and Portugal shaped not only interwar practices but also long-run institutional experiments for price stability. Brazil and Portugal specifically not only faced major global economic crises, including two world wars and the Great Depression, but also the enduring problem of underdevelopment. Brazilian and Portuguese officials did not experiment with price controls as stopgap or emergency solutions; they understood price as the variable determining how much wheat a farmer grows, how much food a worker can buy, and how much coffee a country will export. Corporatist economists and jurists seized on social and political conflicts over prices in order to build their New States—in which the state functioned as the arbiter between different groups and interests for the sake of national development. Their experiments in state making, however, generated new conflicts over economic fairness and how people understand price.

As government officials and the public at large confronted the failures of and frustrations with specific state-led strategies at price control, they also had to continuously reckon with the bigger question of whether free markets or government planning worked better to allocate resources as well as ensure that a society has its needs and wants met. That Vargas and Salazar made appeals to economic justice or tried to rebrand their dictatorships as authoritarian democracies should not be dismissed as a failure or farce. Rather, conflict over prices became but one arena in which intellectuals and bureaucrats hashed out their vision of economic justice—where justice remained a fiercely contested concept. To assert the importance of price in corporatist state making across the twentieth century is not a conclusion but rather an avenue for future research into the unexpected ways in which dictatorships shape popular expectations of economic progress—and enduring debates over economic justice and the responsibilities of government.[10]

In addition, the history of corporatism is tied to another phase of development in Latin America during the brutal military dictatorships that took hold in the 1960s and 1970s. Instead of looking to interwar dictatorships to understand the connections between development and dictatorship, Latin American social scientists writing in the 1960s and 1970s focused on the problems (or exhaustion) of populist politics to explain the succession of military coups across the region. Sociologists Fernando Henrique Cardoso and Enzo Faletto dedicated the final chapter of their famous *Dependency and Development in Latin America* to this problem: How did populism and developmentalism give way to a wave of "authoritarian-corporatist regime[s]"? Brazil was a prime example after the 1964 coup, when military generals usurped political control to govern as a "technobureaucratic corporation."[11] Still, their argument that populism generated corporatism obscures the origins of each. Indeed, scholars have rehabilitated the study of populism in part to explain the resurgence of populist rhetoric and practices across the ideological spectrum in recent years. But just as midcentury populism has its legacies and afterlives, so too does the corporatist legal and economic project from which populist political move- ments emerged. Populist leaders in twentieth-century Latin America did not rely on rhetoric alone; leaders like Vargas in Brazil (or Perón in Argentina and Cárdenas in Mexico, for that matter) cultivated a personalist, even mythical, connection to the people precisely because they commanded and became closely identified with a growing state bureaucracy that allocated rights, privi- leges, and protections defined in corporate and collective terms, and not as individual claims.[12] Certainly, some of these leaders came to power through democratic processes, and yet the technocratic nature of corporatist gover- nance enabled the concentration of political power in a strong executive branch and thereby the proliferation of new forms of authoritarianism.[13] In other words, if we ignore corporatism, we also ignore the legal and economic tools that dictators used to seize and maintain power.

There is in fact another legacy of corporatism as well, or at least another way in which the corporatist logic survived. In Brazil as in Portugal, its propo- nents idealized corporatism as a solution for the ills of both political and eco- nomic liberalism. The authoritarian dimensions of corporatism were essential to its intellectual rationale and how it turned into a political reality. It is not just that dictators opted for corporatism as their economic system of choice but rather that they saw corporatism as an opportunity to rebrand their dicta- torships as some new type of democracy—an authoritarian or economic de- mocracy. Certainly the category *authoritarian democracy* can be dismissed outright as an oxymoron or doublespeak. Yet this category also became politi- cally expedient, especially as dictators asserted that democracy should not be defined according to "liberty" but instead "authority," "discipline," and "order." The economy became the object of such arguments and the rationale behind the corporatist system. This is another legacy of corporatism.

Corporatist institutions were not totally effaced with the collapse of these military regimes either, as these institutions penetrated deep, and contoured how the state and market continue to interact, and state and citizen as well. Corporatism, in the words of one Brazilian scholar, offers "a true miracle of durability, serving, practically intact, democracies and dictatorships alike."[14] It even survived beyond neoliberal reforms in the 1990s. In fact, in 1994, amid a wave of enthusiasm for neoliberalism, president-elect Fernando Henrique Cardoso addressed Brazil's Senate and felt compelled to affirm that he would, once and for all, close the Vargas era. He only partially fulfilled his promise.[15] In other words, the legal and economic institutions inaugurated with the in- terwar corporatist experiment persisted throughout nearly a century of Brazil's oscillation between democracy and dictatorship.

Beyond specific labor legislation, consumer protection laws, sindicatos, or federal commissions that can trace their origins to Vargas's 1930s' experiment, what has ultimately survived in Brazil is the ambition shared by many to carve out a development path on its own terms. The promise of this third path is no longer called *corporatist*, but Brazil has remained committed to an economic system that views with skepticism the rules and expectations emanating from the United States and other liberal or neoliberal contexts. In recent decades, new political and popular movements have emerged to attempt their own third paths, such as the pink tide movements in Brazil and across Latin America that called for programs to expand social justice, while emphasizing gradual and pragmatic approaches to reform in ways that would not disavow or disrupt capitalist visions of progress. Such movements might not share ideological or policy affinities with corporatist dictatorships, but they struggle with a similar problem: to design new economic systems that fundamentally alter how governments regulate property, profits, or prices, yet without totally breaking with the assumptions that underpin global capitalism.[16]

Corporatism therefore also reminds us that there is no singular development model, nor singular variety of capitalism. It offers one example of the mixed economy that triumphed in the mid-twentieth century as the state took on an enlarged role in economic and social life. This history is especially relevant today. For anyone who supports deepening government welfare protections or greater regulations over how goods are produced and profits distributed, the history of corporatism offers important lessons in how utopian visions for economic transformation are put into action and the consequences of limiting who participates in shaping this process. In the past few decades, debates over whether governments or markets are more efficient at addressing the needs and wants of a society have been as fierce as ever, as new financial, economic, and public health crises expose once again that markets do not always self-adjust, and certainly not in equitable ways. Past corporatist experiments might not offer practical or desirable solutions for current crises, yet they do remind us that alternatives are possible.

NOTES

All translations are the author's unless otherwise noted. All titles and quotations in Portuguese, French, Italian, and Spanish retain the original spelling and grammar, which accounts for different spellings in Brazilian and Portuguese sources. Names have in some instances been updated to account for the most common spelling.

Introduction

1. "Continua recebendo homenagens a embaixada especial portuguesa," *Correio da Manhã* (August 12, 1941).

2. Schmitter, "Still the Century of Corporatism?," 86.

3. On Vargas, see Levine, *Father of the Poor?*; Dávila, "Myth and Memory"; Skidmore, *Politics in Brazil.* For overviews of the many ways in which Vargas's tenure in power transformed Brazilian politics, culture, and economy, see the edited volumes Hentschke, *Vargas and Brazil*; Pandolfi, *Repensando o Estado Novo.*

4. Schmitter, "Still the Century of Corporatism?," 87–88; Love, *Crafting the Third World*, 11–12.

5. Deutsch, *Las Derechas*, 7.

6. On how corporatism relates to Catholic social thought, see Pollard, "Corporatism and Political Catholicism." A vast literature exists on corporatism as a system of labor relations, especially for Brazil. See, for example, Werneck Vianna, *Liberalismo e sindicato no Brasil; Gomes, Burguesia e trabalho*; French, "The Origin of Corporatist State Intervention in Brazilian Industrial Relations." Early debates on the topic focused on the ways in which conservative classes turned to corporatism to address rising social unrest and labor activism in the early twentieth century. See Maier, *Recasting Bourgeois Europe*, chap. 1.

7. While they do not explicitly discuss corporatism, Aldo Musacchio and Lazzarini credit Vargas for turning the state into an active agent in organizing economic production. Musacchio and Lazzarini, *Reinventing State Capitalism*, chap. 4. Political scientist Atul Kohli emphasizes the importance of the corporatist structures created to control labor to explain the rise of state-directed industrialization in places like Brazil. See Kohli, *State-Directed Development*. For Argentina, see Brennan and Rougier, *The Politics of National Capitalism*, chap. 1. For the United States, scholars do not often evoke the concept of corporatism, but debates over regulatory capture highlight the formal and informal channels through which organized interests can influence the regulatory policies for their own industry. See Novak, "A Revisionist History of Regulatory Capture."

8. Hobsbawm, *The Age of Extremes*, 4.

9. This history of corporatism is not a comparative one but instead in line with how historian Tore Olsson describes his study of agrarian reform in the United States and Mexico as "not a

comparative history but rather a history of comparisons, a study of interactions and exchanges."
Olsson, *Agrarian Crossings*, 4.

10. Over the past fifteen to twenty years, historians have increasingly examined the movement of people, goods, and ideas across national boundaries to critique the nation as the natural
as well as inevitable vessel for economic, political, social, or legal evolution. Rodgers, *Atlantic
Crossings*; Rodgers, "Bearing Tales." Federico Finchelstein offers a southward gaze to how ideas
and ideologies traveled in the interwar decades to demonstrate how fascism circulated transnationally. Finchelstein, *Transatlantic Fascism*. On interwar connections between France and Brazil
that ran parallel to those examined in this book between Portugal and Brazil, see Merkel, *Terms
of Exchange*. These works are influential for their transnational focus, but also for how they offer
innovative approaches to the history of ideas by showcasing a history of people thinking about
social problems across national borders. Other useful frameworks for the transnational approach include Briggs, McCormick, and Way, "Transnationalism"; Seigel, "Beyond Compare";
Werner and Zimmermann, "Beyond Comparison."

11. On the survival and importance of Luso-Brazilian political collaborations in shaping new
imperial orders in the nineteenth century, see Paquette, *Imperial Portugal in the Age of Atlantic
Revolutions*.

12. Much of the recent innovative work on corporatism has been presented in a series of
edited volumes, including Martinho and Pinto, *O Corporativismo em português*; Pinto and Martinho, *A vaga corporativa corporativismo e ditaduras na Europa e na América latina*; Pinto, *Latin
American Dictatorships in the Era of Fascism*; Pinto and Finchelstein, *Authoritarianism and
Corporatism in Europe and Latin America*.

13. See, for example, Link, *Forging Global Fordism*; Offner, *Sorting Out the Mixed Economy*;
Thornton, *Revolution in Development*.

14. Bockman, *Markets in the Name of Socialism*.

15. Canning, "The Corporation in the Political Thought of the Italian Jurists of the Thirteenth
and Fourteenth Centuries"; Klein, "Corporatism."

16. For the Portuguese Empire and Brazil specifically, see Schwartz, *Sovereignty and Society
of Colonial Brazil*; Schwartz, "Magistracy and Society in Colonial Brazil."

17. For the Spanish Empire, historian Tamar Herzog emphasizes the importance of horizon-
tal ties within legally demarcated communities alongside the vertical ties between distinct
groups, professions, and communities and the sovereign. See Herzog, *Defining Nations*. On legal
pluralism in the Spanish Empire and how Indigenous communities were incorporated into this
system in corporate terms—and how this conflicted with later liberal experiments in the nineteenth century, see Echeverri, "Sovereignty Has Lost Its Rights." For a legal definition of *fueros*
in the Spanish Empire, see Owensby, "The Theater of Conscience in the 'Living Law' of the
Indies," 128–29. On the legacies or vestiges of this legal system into the nineteenth century, see
Chiaramonte, "The 'Ancient Constitution' after Independence."

18. Curiously, during the dictatorship of Francisco Franco, Spanish jurists adopted the term
fuero in discussions of corporatist legislation. Notably, the labor charter issued by the Francoist
regime to outline labor rights and protections in 1938 was called the Fuero del Trabajo. See, for
example, Gutiérrez-Solana, "Democracia, totalitarismo y corporativismo."

19. On liberalism in postindependence Brazil, see, for example, Costa, *The Brazilian Empire*,
chap. 3. On how new economic and legal priorities were inscribed in law across the region, see

Adelman, "Liberalism and Constitutionalism in Latin America in the 19th Century"; Gargarella, "Towards a Typology of Latin American Constitutionalism."

20. In Brazil, one key question that animated conservatives, beyond slavery, was their defense of greater political and territorial centralization in how Brazil was governed. See Carvalho, "Federalismo e centralização no Império brasileiro." In Portugal, conservative and counterrevolutionary political movements also emerged following Brazil's independence to protest the so-called importation of liberal ideas. See Paquette, *Imperial Portugal in the Age of Atlantic Revolutions*, chap. 4. For an overview of the rise of conservatism in Latin America following independence, as conservative groups had their own legal project to preserve the Catholic, corporate, and colonial institutions that had for centuries upheld the existing social order, see Gargarella, *The Legal Foundations of Inequality*, chap. 2.

21. Russian economic historian Alexander Gerschenkron would describe Saint-Simon's vision for "his society of the future [to be] some kind of corporate state in which the 'leaders of industry' would exercise major political functions." Gerschenkron, "Economic Backwardness in Historical Perspective," 23. See also Maier, *In Search of Stability*, 32.

22. Positivists opposed liberalism, but they were not reactionary, and did not support a return to monarchical or hereditary rule. On the influence of positivism on Vargas in Brazil, see Fonseca, *Vargas*, 52–58.

23. Brazilian historians such as Luiz Werneck Vianna have traced the origins of modern authoritarianism back to a positivist influence on the Brazilian conservative elite in the late nineteenth century. Werneck Vianna, "Americanistas e Iberistas." See also Vieira, *Autoritarismo e corporativismo no Brasil*; Abreu, Martins, and Munareto, *Designing the Future*.

24. On how positivist ideas influenced military engineers and their modernization projects, see Diacon, *Stringing Together a Nation*.

25. Solari, "The Corporative Third Way in Social Catholicism."

26. Historian Giuliana Chamedes does not discuss corporatism as part of Catholic social thought, but her work highlights the importance of thinking in transnational terms to understand the rise of illiberal political projects. Chamedes, *A Twentieth-Century Crusade*. See also Chappel, "The Catholic Origins of Totalitarianism Theory in Interwar Europe."

27. That corporatist dictatorships were able to usurp power by seizing on growing fears of communism is an argument central to many political histories of the interwar decades. See, for example, Weyland, *Assault on Democracy*.

28. On liberalism as a misplaced idea in Brazil, see Schwarz, *Misplaced Ideas*.

29. Curiously, corporatists tended to portray liberalism as an Anglo-American invention, with some discussion also of French influences. Historian Helena Rosenblatt has recently argued that this tendency to see liberalism as an Anglo-American invention was a consequence of Cold War politics, as she argues for the importance of French and German debates in shaping the trajectory of liberalism. Rosenblatt, *The Lost History of Liberalism*.

30. Over the past few decades, historians have endeavored to write new histories of liberalism, both to expose its internal contradictions—like how a doctrine based on individual freedom was proselytized alongside the expansion of slavery and empire—and stress how local actors creatively reinvented, selectively implemented, or strategically blended liberal doctrine to fit local problems and agendas. See Sartori, *Liberalism in Empire*; Bayly, *Recovering Liberties*; Benton, "Constitutions and Empires." On popular liberalism in Latin America, see Sanders,

"Citizens of a Free People"; Thomson, "Popular Aspects of Liberalism in Mexico"; Adelman, "Liberalism and Constitutionalism in Latin America in the 19th Century."

31. For an initial definition of fascism, see Paxton, "The Five Stages of Fascism." The question of whether corporatism is fascism under a different guise is far more pronounced in the historiography on Salazarist Portugal than Vargas era Brazil. See, for example, Cruz, "Notas para uma caracterização política do salazarismo." For a recent synthesis on this debate, see Pinto, *Salazar's Dictatorship and European Fascism.*

32. On Mexico's 1917 Constitution, see Suarez-Potts, *The Making of Law.* See also Semo, "El cardenismo revisado."

33. Political scientist Philippe Schmitter emphasizes the non-Iberial and non–Latin American origins of modern corporatism in order to argue against the ways in which social scientists in the 1970s tended to explain the rise of corporatism in these regions as a consequence of specific cultural endowments. This argument, however, overlooks the creativity and collaboration unfolding in and between countries like Brazil and Portugal to shape corporatism. Schmitter, "Still the Century of Corporatism?," 90.

34. A point emphasized in Moyn and Sartori, "Approaches to Global Intellectual History."

35. In other words, sociological and racial ideas were often bundled with economic and legal ideas. On bundling and transnational circulation, see Rodgers, "Bearing Tales."

36. Imperial nostalgia, to be sure, is not exclusive to corporatist ideologues as it also influenced other economic programs in the interwar period, as Quinn Slobodian, for example, notes that the neoliberals in his study likewise wanted to restore a different set of recently vanquished empires. Slobodian, *Globalists.*

37. Villela and Suzigan, *Política do governo e crescimento da economia brasileira,* 255.

38. On early forms of state intervention, see Topik, *The Political Economy of the Brazilian State.* For an overview of industrialization and market diversification trends during the First Republic, see Luna and Klein, *The Economic and Social History of Brazil since 1889,* chap. 1.

39. On this shift from emergency state intervention to a permanent role for the state in the economy, see Fonseca, *Vargas,* chaps. 4–5. See also Werneck Vianna, *Liberalismo e sindicato no Brasil,* 213.

40. There is a vast literature on Vargas era labor laws and the extent to which they marked a departure from how prior governments had addressed the social question. Scholars have debated the political and ideological forces shaping Vargas era legislation, especially in terms of the influence of industrialists in shaping policy. See Werneck Vianna, *Liberalismo e sindicato no Brasil;* Gomes, *Burguesia e trabalho.* For sociolegal approaches and how workers exercised legal activism to maneuver within this bureaucracy, see French, *Drowning in Laws.* On the exclusions and gaps in this labor and welfare system, see Fischer, *A Poverty of Rights.*

41. For a case study, see Dinius, *Brazil's Steel City.*

42. Diniz, "Engenharia institucional e políticas públicas."

43. For one of the earliest studies of Portugal's corporatist system, including its institutional evolution and key legislation, see Lucena, *A evolução do sistema corporation português.*

44. Valério, *Estatísticas históricas portuguesas,* 37, 178–79.

45. On nineteenth-century imperial projects, see Alexandre, *Velo Brasil, novas Áfricas.*

46. Cleminson, *Catholicism, Race and Empire,* 31.

47. Fischer, Grinberg, and Mattos, "Law, Silence, and Racialized Inequalities in the History of Afro-Brazil."

48. On scientific racism in late nineteenth-century Brazil, including Brazilian responses to European racial theories, see Schwarcz, *The Spectacle of the Races*; Stepan, *The Hour of Eugenics*; Loveman, "The Race to Progress."

49. Skidmore, *Black into White*; Lesser, *Negotiating National Identity*; Seyferth, "Construindo a nação."

50. Loveman, "The Race to Progress," 437.

51. Directoria Geral de Estatística, *Recenseamento do Brazil: Realizado em 1 de Setembro de 1920*, 4:lxi.

52. "Estudos brasileiros no estrangeiro (em sessão de 26 de Dezembro de 1941)," in Carneiro, *Na academia*, 178–79.

53. On this point, see also Cardoso, "The Originality of a Copy."

54. Fischer, *A Poverty of Rights*, 117; Merryman and Pérez-Perdomo, *The Civil Law Tradition*.

55. Costa, *Origens do corporativismo brasileiro*.

56. Gargarella, *Latin American Constitutionalism*, 1.

57. Barros, *Constitutionalism and Dictatorship*, 1.

58. Meng, *Constraining Dictatorship*.

59. Barbosa, *História constitucional brasileira*, 52–77.

60. For a comparison between Brazil's 1937 Constitution and the Italian Carta del Lavoro, see French, *Drowning in Laws*, 15.

61. Abreu and Rosenfield, "Conservadorismo, autoritarismo e legitimação política do Estado Novo."

62. On this antiliberal doctrine, see Werneck Vianna, *Liberalismo e sindicato no Brasil*, 211–15.

63. Kennedy, "Three Globalizations of Law and Legal Thought."

64. This approach benefits from, and builds on, recent histories of economic thought focused on individual thinkers or intellectual networks. The book is indebted to many recent contributions to the history of economic ideas, namely to situate economic ideas in their political and social contexts. See Rothschild, *Economic Sentiments*; Burgin, *The Great Persuasion*.

65. Scholarship on the rise of technocracy and cult of expertise identifies the 1930s as a key turning point, even as the focus of these studies is on the postwar period. See Babb, *Managing Mexico*; Young, *Transforming Sudan*; Mitchell, "Fixing the Economy."

66. On the role of powerful industrialists in shaping the state's approach to labor relations and other economic questions, see Diniz, *Empresário, Estado e capitalismo no Brasil*; Gomes, *Burguesia e trabalho*; and Weinstein, *For Social Peace*.

67. Of course, as Gilbert M. Joseph and Daniel Nugent note, "The state is not a *thing*, an object the one can point to." Alongside writing a political and intellectual history of the state in Brazil and Portugal, this book reveals some of the everyday ways in which these new states shaped popular economic behavior, and vice versa. Joseph and Nugent, "Popular Culture and State Formation in Revolutionary Mexico," 19.

68. On parallel experiments in other parts of the world, see Nord, *France's New Deal*; Rodgers, *Atlantic Crossings*; Patel, *The New Deal*; Link, *Forging Global Fordism*.

69. The "center" and "periphery" framework is closely associated with the writings of Argentinean Raúl Prebisch, who is influenced by Romanian corporatist theorist Mihail Manoilescu, as Joseph Love argues. Love, *Crafting the Third World*; Love, "Structuralism and Dependency in Peripheral Europe."

70. On parallel transnational conversations between the United States and Mexico about agricultural development, see Olsson, *Agrarian Crossings*.

71. On the interwar and postwar project to center the meaning of citizenship on price in other political contexts, see, for Chile, Frens-String, *Hungry for Revolution*. For the United States, see Jacobs, *Pocketbook Politics*. For the United States in particular, Laura Phillips Sawyer has recently argued that the question of fair pricing became essential to the building of its administrative state in the early part of the twentieth century. During the Great Depression, a model of state capitalism in which businesses had to comply with pricing rules issued by new administrative agencies was briefly tested, before being declared unconstitutional, but this corporatist legacy would be imprinted into subsequent legislation. Sawyer, *American Fair Trade*.

72. The question of backwardness and underdevelopment—or how the so-called periphery fell behind—has framed much of the economic history of Latin America and southern Europe for decades, if not centuries. Recently, historians have moved away from explaining underdevelopment to take this problem as the object of histories of economic ideas. See Love, *Crafting the Third World*; Gootenberg, *Imagining Development*. See also Fajardo, *The World That Latin America Created*.

73. Wiarda, "Corporatism and Development in the Iberic-Latin World," 6.

74. Wirth, *The Politics of Brazilian Development 1930–1954*, 4.

75. Corporatism also becomes important for thinking about authoritarianism beyond formal dictatorships, as in the case of Mexico. In fact, Mexican historians continue to debate the extent to which Cárdenismo gave way to a purely corporatist mode of governance on account of the continued importance of one-party rule under the Partido Nacional Revolucionario (later the Partido Revolucionario Institucional). Cárdenas oversaw the creation of national sindicatos and agrarian leagues that facilitated the organization of society along vocational and sectoral lines. These institutions functioned as the social base for the deepening of one-party rule and the concentration of political power in a highly centralized bureaucracy governed by a powerful executive branch. Semo, "El cardenismo revisado," 219–22. Historian Gladys I. McCormick, moreover, has emphasized the violent tactics for social control exercised in the countryside as essential to the authoritarian nature of Mexico's corporatist mode of governance, starting in the 1930s and especially in the postwar decades. See McCormick, *The Logic of Compromise in Mexico*. On Mexico's "strange dictatorship," see Gillingham, *Unrevolutionary Mexico*.

76. On corporatism and delayed dependent development, see Malloy, "Authoritarianism and Corporatism in Latin America," 5–8; Schmitter, "Still the Century of Corporatism?," 105–8. In explaining the rise of bureaucratic-authoritarianism in the 1960s and 1960s as a consequence of dependent capitalist development, political scientist David Collier notes how this trend might in fact be the "restoration" of corporatist authoritarian modes of governments dating to the 1930s. Collier, "Introduction," 7. While not formally a dictatorship, these debates were also relevant to Mexico. See Hamilton, *The Limits of State Autonomy*.

77. There are countless economic works on "lateness" and industrialization, from Alexander Gerschenkron's focus on "late industrializers" like Russia and Germany, or the "late, late industrializers" that Albert Hirschman discusses. See Love, *Crafting the Third World*, 9.

78. Schmitter, "The 'Portugalization' of Brazil?," 179. Schmitter's emphasis on the bureaucratic rather than personalist aspects of Salazar's rule in Portugal was in dialogue with Guillermo O'Donnell's work on bureaucratic authoritarianism. See O'Donnell, *Modernization and Bureaucratic-Authoritarianism*.

79. Schmitter, *Corporatism and Public Policy in Authoritarian Portugal*, 8.

80. Social scientists at the University of São Paulo rejected the hagiographic narratives put forth by Vargas's supporters and instead asserted that the Estado Novo was an "estado de compromisso" because the fall of regional oligarchs connected to agroexport sectors was not met with the rise of an independent industrial class that could guide a capitalist transformation. See Fausto, *A revolução de 1930*; Weffort, *O populism na política brasileira*.

81. Diniz achieved a middle ground between interpretations that privileged a protagonist bourgeoisie and those that emphasized the weakness of the industrialist class. She mapped the articulations between this rising class and the state, and analyzed how employer associations maneuvered within the Estado Novo's corporatist apparatus. See Diniz, *Empresário, Estado e capitalismo no Brasil*. Weinstein shows how industrialists from Brazil's wealthiest region of São Paulo shaped new labor legislation, and collaborated in public-private ventures to train workers and rationalize production. See Weinstein, *For Social Peace in Brazil*.

82. Cooper, "Writing the History of Development."

83. Historians acknowledge the importance of the 1930s, but often treat it as background to the feats of developmentalist states in the post-1945 period. See Ioris, *Transforming Brazil*; Dinius, *Brazil's Steel City*; Thornton, *Revolution in Development*.

Chapter 1: Crisis

1. Torgal, "Duas 'Repúblicas' portuguesas no Brasil em 1922."

2. On Brazilian modernism, see Miceli, *Nacional estrangeiro*; Schwartz, *Vanguarda e cosmopolitismo na década de 20*; Gouveia, *The Triumph of Brazilian Modernism*.

3. Raimundo, *António Ferro*, chap. 9. On Carvalho and his ties to Brazilian modernism, see Botelho, *O Brasil e os dias*.

4. António Ferro, "Nós," *Klaxon* 3 (July 1922): 1–2.

5. Even before his visit in 1922, Ferro had encouraged closer ties between Brazilian and Portuguese artists. See Torgal, "O modernismo português na formação do Estado Novo de Salazar," 1099.

6. Castro, *António Ferro*; Raimundo, *António Ferro*.

7. On Ferro's Luso-Brazilian project, see Ribeiro, "Um intelectual orgânico no Estado Novo de Salazar." See also Williams, *Culture Wars in Brazil*, 230–51.

8. António Ferro, "Plano duma campanha de lusitanidade em toda a América, em especial no Brasil," 1940, Arquivo Nacional Torre do Tombo, Lisbon (hereafter ANTT), Arquivo Oliveira Salazar, AOS/PC-12E.

9. On the crisis of democratic governance, see Mazower, *Dark Continent*, 3–40; Hobsbawm, *The Age of Extremes*, 109–29.

10. Ferro, *Viagem à volta das ditaduras*, 39, 170.

11. While crises arguments are not sufficient to explain major political and economic reforms, a growing number of social scientists have analyzed the role of crises with greater theoretical and empirical specificity. See, for example, Weyland, *The Politics of Market Reform in Fragile Democracies*.

12. In Brazil, antiliberal thought is influenced by proslavery arguments, concerns about excessive territorial decentralization, and in the late nineteenth century, rising positivism. See Carvalho, "Federalismo e centralização no Império brasileiro." In Portugal, counterrevolutionary and

Catholic influences shaped antiliberalism in the century prior to Salazar's Estado Novo. See Leal, "Nacionalismo e antiliberalismo em Portugal."

13. The category *backwardness* is used because it offers the closest translation of categories used by Brazilian and Portuguese intellectuals in interwar decades, alongside concepts such as *poor* and *disorganized*. Backwardness was widely used by economists beyond these countries prior to 1945 to describe a country's lack or lesser degree of industrialization. On its usage after 1945, see Alexander Gerschenkron's case for backwardness for its temporal dimensions over categories like *underdevelopment*. Gerschenkron, "Economic Backwardness in Historical Perspective."

14. While there is some variation in these statistics, scholars agree that the impact of epidemics and malnutrition on Portugal's population was severe and disproportionate. Correia, "The Veterans' Movement and First World War Memory in Portugal (1918–33)," 534; Sobral and Lima, "A epidemia da pneumónica em Portugal no seu tempo histórico," 51; Mata and Valério, *História económica de Portugal*, 181.

15. Valério, *Estatísticas históricas portuguesas*, 636.

16. This monetary easing owed not only to official emissions by the Banco de Portugal but also to local administrative organs that printed illegal banknotes. Mata and Valério, *História económica de Portugal*, 182; Valério, *A moeda em Portugal*, 24.

17. Correia, "Celebrating Victory on a Day of Defeat."

18. Gregor, *Italian Fascism and Developmental Dictatorship*, 282.

19. Strachan, *The First World War in Africa*, 161.

20. Portugal did have a seat on the League of Nation's Permanent Mandates Commission, comprised largely of representatives from imperial powers to address pressing questions of empire. Historian Susan Pedersen in fact calls Portugal's member an "unblushing advocate of forced labor for African men." While Portugal was part of conversations on how to economically transform colonial territories, the country did not have a leading role, and the state of its own empire was often criticized. Pedersen, *The Guardians*, 2, 61–64.

21. There is an extensive literature on coffee production in Brazil, including but not limited to the rise of regional oligarchies, infrastructure development and early industrialization, the expansion of slavery during the nineteenth century, flows of immigrant labor, and emerging commercial and cultural ties between Brazil and consumer markets. See Stein, *Vassouras*; Love, *São Paulo in the Brazilian Federation*; Topik, *The Political Economy of the Brazilian State*; Topik, "Coffee"; Summerhill, *Order against Progress*; Mauricio, *Coffee and Transformation in São Paulo*; Saba, *American Mirror*, esp. chap 4.

22. Dean, "The Brazilian Economy," 700.

23. *Anúario Estatístico do Brasil: Ano I (1908–1912)*, xxxvi–xxxix, 126.

24. Dean, "The Brazilian Economy," 700.

25. On the problems of food supply in Brazil, especially for the nineteenth century, see Aguiar, *Abastecimento*.

26. Dean, "The Brazilian Economy," 691.

27. Meade, "Living Worse and Costing More," 262.

28. Cost-of-living protests are often folded into studies of class-based collective action in Brazil, revealing how the price and supply of essential goods was an early focus of poor and working-class efforts to organize for government action in pursuit of a higher standard of living. See Meade, *"Civilizing" Rio*.

29. Graham, *Feeding the City*, chap. 10.

30. Albert, *South America and the First World War*, 265.

31. Meade, "Living Worse and Costing More," 244.

32. On the *Revista do Brasil*, see Luca, *A Revista do Brazil*.

33. Gomes, *A invenção do trabalhismo*, 123–24.

34. Roio, "A gênese do Partido Comunista."

35. Dulles, *Anarchists and Communists in Brazil*, 334–39.

36. Wirth, "Tenentismo in the Brazilian Revolution of 1930," 165.

37. On the different strands and influences of Brazilian modernism, see Miceli, *Intelectuais e classe dirigente no Brasil*; Miceli, *Nacional estrangeiro*; Schwartz, *Vanguarda e cosmopolitismo na década de 20*.

38. Bertonha, *Plínio Salgado*, 54–86. On Plínio Salgado in Italy, see also, Gonçalves, "Transnational Fascism."

39. Like other fascist movements, the AIB reinforced patriarchal social norms while also mobilizing women. See Deutsch, "Spartan Mothers."

40. It linked Brazil and Portugal in particular. See Bertonha, "Plínio Salgado, o integralismo brasileiro e as suas relações com Portugal."

41. On Maurras and the Action Française, see Dard, *Charles Maurras*; Sternhell, *Ni droite ni gauche*, 75–80, 115–21.

42. Plínio Salgado, *A Offensiva* 1 (1934), 1.

43. Bertonha, "Plínio Salgado, o integralismo brasileiro e as suas relações com Portugal," 77.

44. Raimundo, *António Ferro*.

45. Ferro, *Viagem à volta das ditaduras*, 171.

46. Certainly, not all Portuguese modernists shared Ferro's enthusiasm for Mussolini. Some Portuguese journalists and intellectuals penned essays in opposition to fascism. See Barreto, "Mussolini é um louco," 231.

47. Ferro, *Viagem à volta das ditaduras*, 171.

48. Zamagni, *The Economic History of Italy*, 210–38.

49. Tannenbaum, *The Fascist Experience*, 3.

50. Gregor, *Italian Fascism and Developmental Dictatorship*, 97. For key works on fascist theory and practice in Italy, see also Grazia, *The Culture of Consent*; Grazia, *How Fascism Ruled Women*; Finchelstein, *Transatlantic Fascism*; Ben-Ghiat, *Fascist Modernities*.

51. On the difficulties in defining fascism, see Paxton, "The Five Stages of Fascism."

52. Ferro, *Viagem à volta das ditaduras*, 69, 70, 71.

53. See, for example, Bosworth, *Mussolini's Italy*, xxii; Villari, *The Fascist Experiment*, vi.

54. Ferro, *Viagem à volta das ditaduras*, 71.

55. Ferro, *Viagem à volta das ditaduras*, 75.

56. Pinto, "A queda da Primeira República."

57. On political conflicts prior to and during the war, see Valente, "Revoluções."

58. Castro, *António Ferro*, 46, 79; Torgal, "O modernismo português na formação do Estado Novo de Salazar," 1098.

59. António Ferro, "Sinfonia heróica," *O Jornal* (December 5, 1919), reprinted in Castro, *António Ferro*, 244.

60. Meneses, "Sidónio Pais, the Portuguese 'New Republic' and the Challenge to Liberalism in Southern Europe." See also Pinto, "Corporatism and 'Organic' Representation in European Dictatorships."

61. Meneses, "Sidónio Pais, the Portuguese 'New Republic' and the Challenge to Liberalism in Southern Europe," 112, 121.

62. Rocha and Labaredas, *Os trabalhadores rurais do Alentejo e o sidonismo*; Sá, "Projectos de reforma agrária na I República," 602.

63. Jerónimo, *Livros brancos, almas negras*, chap. 5.

64. Ross, *Seventy Years of It*.

65. Mantero, "A mão-de-obra indígena nas colónias africanas," 1.

66. "Na Itália, entrevista com o actual Ministro de Portugal em Roma," *Jornal de Comércio e das Colónias* (February 15, 1927).

67. Ferro, *Viagem à volta das ditaduras*, 166.

68. On Portugal's imperial crises in the 1920s and the different projects for renewal debated, see Alexandre, "Ideologia, economia e política."

69. Quoted in António de Oliveira Salazar, "Acerca do futuro estatuto constitucional," interview, 1932, ANTT, AOS/CO/PC-1B.

70. Mazower, *Dark Continent*, 19.

71. Ferro, *Viagem à volta das ditaduras*, 337, 294.

72. There is a wealth of literature on how nationalist movements are not incompatible with transnational or international movements. To the contrary, international connections not only strengthen nationalist movements but also help to define nations and national identities. See, for example, Seigel, *Uneven Encounters*; Sluga, *Internationalism in the Age of Nationalism*.

73. Pinto, *O Brasil actual (Duas conferências)*, 20.

74. On anti-Portuguese protests immediately following independence, see Paquette, "In the Shadow of Independence."

75. On the continued importance of ties between France and Brazil, see Merkel, *Terms of Exchange*.

76. Ribeiro, "Um intelectual orgânico no Estado Novo de Salazar," 48.

77. *A Universidade de Coimbra e o Brasil*, 78.

78. For Brazil, the 1904 Revolta da Vacina epitomizes the violent and racist tactics underpinning reform efforts. See Benchimol, "Reforma urbana e revolta da vacina na cidade do Rio de Janeiro"; Needell, "The Revolta Contra Vacina of 1904."

79. There is a vast literature on how eugenics and scientific racism influenced geopolitics, international relations, and imperialism. See, for example, Lake, *Drawing the Global Colour Line*; Kramer, "Empires, Exceptions, and Anglo-Saxons."

80. Initially published anonymously, this essay was later attributed to Oliveira Vianna. Directoria Geral de Estatística, *Recenseamento do Brasil*, vol. 1. See also Loveman, "The Race to Progress," 463. Oliveira Vianna used demographic statistics and other data as evidence for his scientific propositions, as he insisted on the objectivity of his analysis not only in his whitening theory and its racist prescriptions for Brazil's future but also his analysis of regional differences within Brazil. On Oliveira Vianna as a sociologist, see Bresciani, *O charme da ciência e a sedução da objetividade*.

81. Like other Brazilian sociologists and anthropologists of his generation, Oliveira Vianna did not embrace strictly biological explanations for Brazil's development but emphasized climatic, political, and geographic factors as well. This is consistent with the influence of neo-Lamarckism in Brazil. See Stepan, *The Hour of Eugenics*.

82. Historian Ângela de Castro Gomes once noted that Oliveira Vianna was "the last of the saquaremas," the nineteenth-century political party of landed elites. Gomes, "A práxis corporativa de Oliveira Vianna," 57.

83. Needell, "History, Race and the State in the Thought of Oliveira Viana," 4–8.

84. Oliveira Vianna's analysis built on the writings of positivist Alberto Torres. See Brasil Junior, "Oliveira Vianna e os dilemas da ação coletiva no Brasil."

85. Sociologist João Batista de Vasconcelos Torres, quoted in Vieira, Oliveira Vianna e o estado corporativo, 28.

86. Bresciani, O charme da ciência e a sedução da objetividade, 33, 355.

87. Oliveira Vianna draws on these points in nearly all of his writings, and especially in Oliveira Vianna, O idealismo da constituição (1927). On patronage and personal loyalty in nineteenth-century Brazilian politics, see Graham, Patronage and Politics in Nineteenth-Century Brazil.

88. On how Oliveira Vianna embraced corporatism as a modern and updated equivalent to monarchy, see Needell, "History, Race and the State in the Thought of Oliveira Viana." Beyond corporatist contexts, Quinn Slobodian similarly notes that neoliberals wanted to restore a recently vanquished imperial order. Slobodian, Globalists.

89. Santos, Ordem burguesa e liberalismo político, 93–117. For a more recent synthesis, see Gentile, "Uma apropriação criativa."

90. Quoted in Schwarz, Misplaced Ideas, x–xi. This translation is taken from John Gledson's introduction.

91. Oliveira Vianna, O idealismo da constituição (1927), 83.

92. Brazilian literary critic Roberto Schwarz explored this question of how maladjusted liberalism was to Brazilian realities—an assertion ultimately spun into an inescapable paradox in which (any) foreign ideas in Latin America had to be "reconstructed on the basis of local contradictions." Quoted in Palti, "The Problem of 'Misplaced Ideas' Revisited," 156.

93. Oliveira Vianna, O idealismo da constituição (1927), 140.

94. Quoted in "Estudos brasileiros e conciência de realidades," A Offensiva 1, no. 25 (November 1934), 2.

95. António de Oliveira Salazar, "Ditadura adminstrativa e revolução política," May 28, 1930, reprinted in Salazar, Discursos, 64.

96. Meneses, Salazar.

97. Historians continue to debate the influence of Catholicism on Salazar's politics. He joined Catholic political organizations at Coimbra, but his writings were largely secular in subject and orientation. He does, however, take Rerum Novarum as a point of reference for his discussion of the social question. See, for example, Alexandre, O roubo das almas, 15–21. Moreover, once prime minister, Salazar was not generous in conceding special rights or privileges to the Catholic Church, maintaining a separation of church and state. See Carvalho, A concordata de Salazar.

98. While Salazar and others of this generation leaned on culturalist and racist discourses, eugenics had limited influence in Portugal. See Cleminson, Catholicism, Race and Empire.

99. Alexandre, O roubo das almas, 20–21.

100. Salazar, "A democracia e a Igreja," 217.

101. Braga, Intensificação econômica no Brasil, 12, 14.

102. On Portugal's performance, see, for example, Reis, "A industrialização num país de desenvolvimento lento e tardio."

103. Lains, *Os progressos do atraso*, 41; Lains, "Growth in a Protected Environment."

104. Silva and Amaral, "A economia portuguesa na I República," 291–92. Data from Maddison, *The World Economy*, 58–68.

105. Maddison, *The World Economy*, 142–43.

106. Almeida, *Brasil errado*, 48.

107. On Prebisch and his early discussion of the terms of trade while working for Argentina's Central Bank during the Great Depression, see Fajardo, *The World That Latin America Created*, 36. See also Prebisch and Cabañas, "El desarrollo económico de la América Latina y algunos de sus principales problemas," 361.

108. According to Joseph Love, Prebisch first used his "center-periphery" terminology in 1944. Love, *Crafting the Third World*, 128.

109. Amzalak, *A indústria da pesca de bacalhau e a sua intensificação em Portugal*, 7.

110. Pinto, *O problema monetário no Brasil*, 4.

111. Cabreira called for increasing domestic agricultural production, but not of wheat. He resigned himself to Portugal's dependency on wheat imports, which is noteworthy because wheat is where corporatist economic planning began. See Nunes, "Tomás Cabreira."

112. Cabreira, *A defesa económica de Portugal*, 42, 7.

113. Pinto, *O problema monetário no Brasil*, 4.

114. José Maria Whitaker, "Soluções práticas tendentes a resolver deficiências do Brasil," September 1927, Centro de Pesquisa e Documentação de História Contempoânea do Brasil, Fundação Getúlio Vargas, Rio de Janeiro (hereafter CPDOC), Arquivo José Maria Whitaker, JMW 30.11.17.

115. Temin and Toniolo, *The World Economy between the Wars*, 28.

116. Wartime governments experimented with different strategies to oversee equitable prices and distribution, often propelled to action by popular demands. In 1916, the German government, for example, inaugurated the War Food Office to control food distribution after several months of organized popular demands. Davis, *Home Fires Burning*, chap. 6.

117. Maier, *Recasting Bourgeois Europe*, 11.

118. On Argentina and the Radical Civic Union's promises to defend the social and economic well-being of popular classes against the political establishment, see Elena, *Dignifying Argentina*, 45. On citizens' expectations for government to protect against inflation and speculation, see Trentmann, *Empire of Things*, 278.

119. Bosworth, *Mussolini's Italy*, 124.

120. It is not unusual for dictators to come to power without any sort of economic program. See, for example, how the Chicago Boys came to influence Augusto Pinochet's neoliberal economic program for Chile. See Valdes, *Pinochet's Economists*.

121. On Mussolini's austerity program, see Mattei, *The Capital Order*. See also Gregor, *Italian Fascism and Developmental Dictatorship*, 142.

122. Mussolini, *My Autobiography*, 241.

123. For a brief biography of Stefani, see Coco, "Italian Advisors in Nationalist China," 953–57.

124. Segreto, "Giuseppe Volpi," 912–19.

125. Romano, *Giuseppe Volpi et l'Italie moderne*, 242.

126. Bosworth, *Mussolini's Italy*, 225.

127. Gregor, *Italian Fascism and Developmental Dictatorship*, 145; Cohen, "Fascism and Agriculture in Italy," 73.

128. On how plant geneticists participated in 1920s' wheat campaigns in Italy as well as in Portugal, see Saraiva, *Fascist Pigs*.

129. Saraiva, "Fascist Labscapes," 462–63, 475.

130. Schmidt, "The Italian 'Battle of Wheat.'"

131. Mattei, *The Capital Order*, 240.

132. Gregor, *Italian Fascism and Developmental Dictatorship*, 146.

133. Mattei, *The Capital Order*, 242.

134. Gregor, *Italian Fascism and Developmental Dictatorship*, 146. See also Schmidt, "The Italian 'Battle of Wheat,'" 650.

135. Gregor, *Italian Fascism and Developmental Dictatorship*, 155–61.

136. Saraiva, *Fascist Pigs*, 22–23.

137. Quoted in Fanno, *Introduzione allo studio della teoria economica del corporativismo*, cover.

138. For the skeptical assessment of one US engineer, see, for example, Wright, "Capital and Labor under Fascism in Italy."

139. On how Mussolini's advisers and diplomats circulated to influence the policies and politics of other countries, see Coco, "Italian Advisors in Nationalist China." See also Finchelstein, *Transatlantic Fascism*. On the Italian influence on the US New Deal, see Patel, *The New Deal*, esp. 67–69.

140. Pasetti, "The Fascist Labour Charter and Its Transnational Spread." For Brazil, see French, *Drowning in Laws*, 15.

141. Mussolini, quoted in "A reorganização económica italiana os projectos de saneamento financeiro francês," *Diário dos Açores* (July 7, 1926), retrieved from ANTT, Ministério do Interior DGAPC, pt. 1148.

142. Historians continue to debate the finer points of how the financial crisis contributed to the 1926 military coup, with some scholars emphasizing Portugal's recovery by 1925. Yet it is hard to deny that conservative groups turned the economy into one of many examples of how liberal governance had failed the country. Silva and Amaral, "A economia portuguesa na I República"; Pinto, "A queda da Primeira República."

143. On economic liberalism in nineteenth-century Portugal, see Mata, "Economic Ideas and Policies in Nineteenth-Century Portugal."

144. Valério, *Estatísticas históricas portuguesas*, 636, 737.

145. Mata and Valério, *História económica de Portugal*, 185–86.

146. Diniz, "Crise cambial portuguesa."

147. Salazar, *A reorganização financeira*.

148. Some scholars emphasize banking and monetary reforms implemented prior to Salazar taking office. See Mata and Valério, "Monetary Stability, Fiscal Discipline and Economic Performance."

149. This argument is elaborated in Capotescu, Sanchez-Sibony, and Teixeira, "Austerity without Neoliberals."

150. Not all sectors of Portugal's economy were in favor of Salazar's financial restructuring since some industrialists worried that austerity might limit the purchasing power of the domestic market. Salazar worked to assuage these concerns and bring industrialists into his coalition. On Salazar's austerity program, see Telo, "A obra financeira de Salazar," 790–93.

151. "À margem das leis: Conselho de Economia Nacional," Newspaper clipping (source unknown), April 1927, retrieved from ANTT, Ministério do Interior DGAPC nt. 704, pt. 128.

152. Decreto Nº13.457, *Diário do Govêrno* (April 12, 1927).

153. Pais et al., "Elementos para a história do fascismo nos campos," 415.

154. Decreto Nº17.252, *Diário do Govêrno* (August 21, 1929).

155. Pais et al., "Elementos para a história do fascismo nos campos."

156. Costa, *As cooperativas e a economia social.*

157. Portugal's Wheat Campaign not only has parallels in Fascist Italy but also with agrarian reforms and agricultural policies in liberal capitalist economies. The key difference is that the national government in Italy and Portugal inaugurated and set the terms of the wheat campaigns. On the rise of cooperative farming movements in the United States and Europe in the 1920s, see Rodgers, *Atlantic Crossings,* 318–43. See also Phillips, *This Land, This Nation,* 36–47.

158. Lucena, "Salazar, a 'fórmula' da agricultura portuguesa e a intervenção estatal no sector primário."

159. Freire, Ferreira, and Rodrigues, "Corporativismo e Estado Novo."

160. Garrido, *Queremos uma economia nova!,* 61.

161. On the gap between the promise and reality of the corporatist system, see Lucena, "Salazar, a 'fórmula' da agricultura portuguesa e a intervenção estatal no sector primário."

162. Rosas, *O Estado Novo nos anos trinta,* 165; Amaral, "Política e economia," 468.

163. Gonçalves, *O Estado Novo e a Assembléa Nacional,* 14.

164. There are several biographies of Vargas, all of which emphasize how he was shaped by *gaúcho* politics, conflicts, and culture. See, for example, Levine, *Father of the Poor?,* 13–18.

165. On how positivist ideology influenced republican gaúcho politics, see Hentschke, *Positivismo ao estilo gaúcho.*

166. Fonseca, *Vargas,* 50.

167. Fonseca, *Vargas,* 36–40.

168. On coffee valorization, see Topik, *The Political Economy of the Brazilian State,* chap. 3.

169. Bak, "Cartels, Cooperatives, and Corporatism," 261.

170. Fonseca, *RS,* 69; Fonseca, *Vargas,* 39.

171. Bak situates the rice cartel in the context of rising cooperative movements in the region in the 1920s to respond to the postwar economic slump. Bak, "Some Antecedents of Corporatism," 314–15.

172. Government interventions to support the coffee sector, in particular, are key examples. See Topik, "Coffee"; Topik, *The Political Economy of the Brazilian State.*

173. On Vargas's antiliberal thinking and how it shaped early state interventions in Rio Grande do Sul, see Bak, "Cartels, Cooperatives, and Corporatism," 257–66.

174. Feinstein, Temin, and Toniolo, *The World Economy between the World Wars,* 94–95.

175. Almeida, *Brasil errado,* 30.

176. Quoted in Tota, "Cultura, política e modernidade em Noel Rosa," 47.

177. Gordon-Ashworth, "Agricultural Commodity Control under Vargas in Brazil," 91–92; Fausto, *A Revolução de 1930*, 334.

178. Almeida, *Brasil errado*, 33.

179. Villela and Suzigan, *Government Policy and the Economic Growth of Brazil*, 137–39; Maddison, *The World Economy*, 133.

180. "Reactive" policies meaning currency depreciations, abandoning the gold standard, purchase and destruction of excess coffee, and suspension of debt servicing. Díaz-Alejandro, "Latin America in the 1930s," 209.

181. Historians reject the *outorga* thesis for assuming passivity among the working classes in relation to the making of a new social contract. See Gomes, *Burguesia e trabalho*. For a historiographical overview, see French, "The Origin of Corporatist State Intervention in Brazilian Industrial Relations."

182. Manuel Lopes Barros to Getúlio Vargas, April 16, 1931, CPDOC, Arquivo José Maria Whitaker, JMW 30.11.05/4.

183. Arthur d'Oliveira Guita to Getúlio Vargas, n.d., CPDOC, Arquivo José Maria Whitaker, JMW 30.11.05/4.

184. Report from Porto University Engineering School, March 21, 1931, ANTT, Ministério do Comércio e Indústria, Direcção do Comércio e Indústria, caixa 60.

185. "Portugal," *Jornal do Comércio* (November 11, 1932). See also Maddison, *The World Economy*, 56; Lains, "Growth in a Protected Environment," 151.

186. Inocêncio Camacho Rodrigues (governor of Banco de Portugal), memorandum, April 1, 1931, ANTT, Ministério do Comércio e Indústria, Direcção do Comércio e Indústria, caixa 60.

187. Patriarca, *A questão social no salazarismo*, 56.

188. Camacho Rodrigues, memorandum.

189. António F. Domingues de Freitas (Centro Comercial do Porto), February 3, 1931, ANTT, Ministério do Comércio e Indústria, Direcção do Comércio e Indústria, caixa 60.

190. Report from Porto University Engineering School, March 21, 1931, ANTT, Ministério do Comércio e Indústria, Direcção do Comércio e Indústria, caixa 60.

191. António Oliveira Salazar, "Princípios fundamentais da revolução política," July 30, 1930, reprinted in Salazar, *Discursos*.

192. Patriarca, "A institucionalização corporativa."

193. Decreto Nº20.342, Art. 2, *Diário do Govêrno* (September 1931).

194. Preface by Tristão de Ataíde, in Melo, *Ritmo Novo*, 41–44.

195. Preface by Tristão de Ataíde, in Melo, *Ritmo Novo*, 61–62, 66–67.

Chapter 2: Experiments in Corporatist Constitutions

1. "Falando à nação: o discurso hontem pronunciado pelo presidente Getúlio Vargas no palácio Guanabara," *Correio da Manhã* (November 11, 1937).

2. On the communist revolt in 1935, see Pinheiro, *Estratégias da ilusão*.

3. Transcript of telephone conversation between Sousa Costa, Luís Aranha, and Oswaldo Aranha, November 16, 1937, CPDOC, Arquivo Getúlio Vargas, GV c 1937.11.16/3.

4. This debate extends back centuries, at least to Thomas Hobbes. On whether constitutions written by dictators can be self-binding, see Fraenkel, *The Dual State*; Barros, *Constitutionalism and Dictatorship*, 16–17.

5. On constitutions as a site of political negotiation and claims making, see De, *A People's Constitution*; Cooper, *Citizenship between Empire and Nation*, esp. chap. 2; Hulsebosch, *Constituting Empire*; Adelman, "Liberalism and Constitutionalism in Latin America in the 19th Century."

6. "Falando à nação."

7. In many ways, corporatist jurists set out to codify the social, racial, and economic inequalities that had been protected by and even generated through Brazilian law and legal institutions since the colonial period. There is a vast literature on these issues that centers on how slavery was upheld and sustained by law as well as Brazil's administrative state, which in turn upheld and sustained racial and social inequalities. See Chalhoub, *A força da escravidão*; Grinberg, *O fiador dos brasileiros*; Fischer, Grinberg, and Mattos, "Law, Silence, and Racialized Inequalities in the History of Afro-Brazil"; Mattos, *Escravidão e cidadania no Brasil monárquico*.

8. Mazower, *Dark Continent*, 5–11.

9. For Austria, see Botz, "'Corporatist State' and Enhanced Authoritarian Dictatorship."

10. Mussolini in Italy or Franco in Spain, for example, preferred piecemeal decree laws that over many years amounted to stitched together de facto constitutions. Reale, "The Italian Constitution under Fascism"; Giménez Martínez, "El Fuero del Trabajo."

11. On constitutions as politics in Latin America, see González-Jácome, "From Abusive Constitutionalism to a Multilayered Understanding of Constitutionalism."

12. This trend in codifying the state's role in social and economic life was a global one, starting in the 1920s, but it takes on different forms in different parts of the world. See Kennedy, "Three Globalizations of Law and Legal Thought." Statism in constitutional form is not, however, universal. As legal scholars David Law and Mila Versteeg document, contemporary constitutions can often be categorized as either "statist" or "libertarian." Law and Versteeg, "The Evolution and Ideology of Global Constitutionalism."

13. Oliveira Vianna, *O idealismo da constituição* (1927), 64.

14. Alcides Bezerra, December 18, 1934, quoted in *Annaes da Assembléa Nacional Constituinte 1933/1934, Vol. 2*, 386.

15. How global and imperial contexts molded modern constitutions was first explored in Palmer's classic work on eighteenth-century revolutions. Palmer, *The Age of the Democratic Revolution*. More recent contributions foreground how founding constitutional documents traveled beyond the nation-state. See Armitage, *The Declaration of Independence*; Bilder, *The Transatlantic Constitution*; Billias, *American Constitutionalism Heard Round the World, 1776–1989*. On the nation-state as a narrow framework in writing legal history, with an emphasis on the imperial turn, see also Benton, "Constitutions and Empires," 178.

16. Brazil and Portugal not only share legal traditions on account of past imperial connections, but even postindependence the two countries borrowed from each other's constitutions. For example, the 1826 Portuguese Constitution was inspired by the Brazilian 1824 Constitution. See Paquette, "The Brazilian Origins of the 1826 Portuguese Constitution."

17. Salazar had this book in his private library. See ANTT, Arquivo Oliveira Salazar, AOS/J-1. See also Araújo, *A lei de Salazar*, 111.

18. Mirkine-Guetzévitch, *Les nouvelles tendances du droit constitutionnel*, 85.

19. Moyn, "The Secret History of Constitutional Dignity," 42–43.

20. Mazower, *Dark Continent*, 5–11.

21. Mexico's 1917 Constitution also strengthened the powers of the executive branch while limiting the lawmaking powers of the legislature, as would become another trend in interwar constitutionalism. On this point, see Hamilton, "Mexico: The Limits of State Autonomy," 85. On how articles in Mexico's Constitution pertaining to workers' rights built on prior decades of labor activism, social legislation, and legal innovation, see Suarez-Potts, *The Making of Law*, esp. chap. 5.

22. On how Latin America's liberal tradition differs from an Anglo-American one, see Grandin, "The Liberal Traditions in the Americas."

23. Bolivia's 1938 Constitution was drafted via a constitutional assembly that included worker representation. See Gotkowitz, *A Revolution for Our Rights*, chap. 4. While no new constitution was promulgated in Colombia, constitutional reforms in 1936, especially agrarian reform Law 200, addressed the social question. See LeGrand, "Acquisition and Social Conflict on the Colombian Frontier"; Tirado Mejía and Velásquez, *La reforma constitucional de 1936*. Samuel Moyn, in turn, inserts Ireland's 1937 constitutional commitment to the "dignity" of the human person into a genealogy of human rights indebted to Catholic thought on the social question. Moyn, "The Secret History of Constitutional Dignity"; Moyn, *Christian Human Rights*.

24. For Brazil, see Santos, *Cidadania e justiça*.

25. Alcides Bezerra, quoted in *Annaes da Assembléa Nacional Constituinte 1933/1934, Vol. 2*, 384–85.

26. Mirkine-Guetzévitch, *As novas tendências do direito constitucional*.

27. Mirkine-Guetzévitch, *Les constituitions de l'Europe nouvelle*, 12.

28. Werneck Vianna, "Introdução"; Werneck Vianna, *Ensaios sobre política, direito e sociedade*, 47–49.

29. Santos, *Cidadania e justiça*. See also Fortes, "O Estado Novo e os trabalhadores."

30. Mirkine-Guetzévitch, *Les constituitions de l'Europe nouvelle*, 14.

31. The University of Coimbra, in particular, had been responsible for training Brazilian lawyers not only in the colonial period but also throughout the nineteenth century. This influence was still evident in the early twentieth century. See Mendes and Reis, "Entre a formação humanista e a tecnicista."

32. On the importance of these civilizational categories, see Kramer, "Empires, Exceptions, and Anglo-Saxons." Specific to Latin American and Iberian contexts, political scientist Howard Wiarda was one of the earliest to theorize the cultural dimensions that generated different varieties of capitalism, albeit in essentialized and deterministic ways. Wiarda, "Corporatism and Development in the Iberic-Latin World."

33. Cunha Gonçalves, quoted in Silva, *Os trabalhadores portugueses e o estado corporativo*.

34. Ferreira, "Prof. Luiz da Cunha Gonçalves."

35. Nunes, Cardoso, and Porto, "Elementos para a história do ensino universitário de economia e finanças."

36. Burbank and Cooper, *Empires in World History*, 9.

37. There is a vast and growing literature interrogating the ways in which liberalism and imperialism were mutually sustained throughout the nineteenth and twentieth centuries. See Sartori, *Liberalism in Empire*; Kramer, "Imperial Openings."

38. Burbank and Cooper, *Empires in World History*, 5.

39. Cunha Gonçalves, quoted in Silva, *Os trabalhadores portugueses e o estado corporativo*.

40. Cunha Gonçalves, *Da compra e venda no direito comercial português*.

41. Cunha Gonçalves, *Da compra e venda no direito comercial brasileiro*, 11–12.

42. On the civilizational underpinnings of international law beyond the Luso-Brazilian world, see Coates, *Legalist Empire*.

43. Unpublished interview with António de Oliveira Salazar, "Acerca do futuro estatuto constitucional," 1932, ANTT, Arquivo Oliveira Salazar, AOS/CO/PC-1B.

44. Valdemar Falcão, scribbled comments in preparation for a speech at the National Constitutional Assembly, April 9, 1934, CPDOC, Arquivo Valdemar Falcão, VF Falcão pi VCR 34.04.09.

45. Bresciani, *O charme da ciência e a sedução da objetividade*.

46. Original in italics. Oliveira Vianna, *O idealismo da constituição* (1927), 21–22, 48.

47. Pedro Theotónio Pereira, "6º Aniversário do movimento nacional de 28 de Maio de 1926," May 28, 1932, ANTT, Arquivo Oliveira Salazar, AOS/CO/PC-5.

48. Perhaps odd but not unique. On this tension in Vladimir Lenin's views on law and revolution, see Burbank, "Lenin and the Law in Revolutionary Russia."

49. P. Vitor C. de Almeida to Oswaldo Aranha, August 19, 1931, CPDOC, Arquivo Oswaldo Aranha, OA cp 1931.08.04/10.

50. Abilis Gomes Carneiro to Oswaldo Aranha, August 4, 1931, CPDOC, Arquivo Oswaldo Aranha, OA cp 1931.08.04/10.

51. Guaracy Silveira (Missões da Igreja Metodista do Brasil e Portugal) to Getúlio Vargas, July 17, 1931, CPDOC, Arquivo Oswaldo Aranha, OA cp 1931.08.04/10.

52. João Cabanas to Getúlio Vargas, August 4, 1931, CPDOC, Arquivo Oswaldo Aranha, OA cp 1931.08.04/10.

53. Sanglard, "Luiz Carpenter."

54. Carpenter, "O projecto da Nova Constituição política e a entidade território," 58.

55. On corporatism as an updated form of empire in Oliveira Vianna's imaginary, see Needell, "History, Race and the State in the Thought of Oliveira Viana."

56. Oliveira Vianna, *Problemas de direito corporativo*, 49.

57. Corporatism, in other words, preserved and potentially deepened official silence about racial matters in Brazilian laws and legal institutions apparent across Brazil's history. On institutional silences and racial inequalities, see Mattos, *Escravidão e cidadania no Brasil monárquico*; Chalhoub, *A força da escravidão*; Fischer, Grinberg, and Mattos, "Law, Silence, and Racialized Inequalities in the History of Afro-Brazil."

58. *Constituição política da República Portuguesa* (1916), Art. 67.

59. Alexandre and Proença, *A questão colonial no Parlamento*, 20–51; Lains, *Os progressos do atraso*, 223–45.

60. Amzalak, *O néo-mercantilismo*, 9.

61. Filomeno da Câmara, "Prefácio," in Ferro, *Viagem à volta das ditaduras*, 7–52.

62. Castelo, *Passagens para África*, 363. See also Meneses, *Salazar*, 96–97.

63. Araújo, *A lei de Salazar*, 22. On Quirino de Jesus's position in debates over how to overhaul Portugal's imperial administration, see Leal, "Quirino Avelino de Jesus, um católico 'pragmático,'" 385–86.

64. Jesus, *Nacionalismo português*, 188.

65. Acto Colonial, Art. 45, *Diário do Govêrno* (July 8, 1930); Castelo, *Passagens para África*, 63.

66. Cooper, "Modernizing Bureaucrats, Backward Africans, and the Development Concept"; Burbank and Cooper, *Empires in World History*, 287.

67. Acto Colonial, Art. 2, *Diário do Govêrno* (July 8, 1930). On Portugal's "civilizing" mission, see Jerónimo, *Livros brancos, almas negras*.

68. Bender, *Angola under the Portuguese*; Isaacman, *Cotton Is the Mother of Poverty*; Kagan Guthrie, *Bound for Work*.

69. Caetano, *História breve das constituições portuguesas*, 124–25.

70. Gonçalves, *O estado corporativo e a política do império no direito constitucional português*, 55.

71. "Uma reunião no Ministério do Interior para tratar da futura organização política e administrativa," *Diário de Lisboa* (July 24, 1930).

72. "A reforma da constituição portuguesa," *Correio da Manhã* (Rio de Janeiro, July 24, 1930).

73. Araújo, *A lei de Salazar*.

74. Pimentel, *Memórias do capitão*.

75. Patriarca, *A questão social no salazarismo*.

76. Pedro Theotónio Pereira to António de Oliveira Salazar, March 3, 1931, ANTT, Arquivo Oliveira Salazar, AOS/CP-213.

77. Martins, *Pedro Theotónio Pereira*, 13–49, 150–85, 264.

78. On this commission, the Conselho Político Nacional, see Araújo, *A lei de Salazar*, 191–93.

79. Caetano, *Minhas memórias de Salazar*, 44.

80. Araújo, *A lei de Salazar*, 20–21.

81. Pinto, "O império do professor."

82. Araújo, *A lei de Salazar*, 166.

83. Caetano, *Minhas memórias de Salazar*, 44.

84. On the 1932 Constitutionalist Movement, see Weinstein, *The Color of Modernity*; Moraes, *1932*.

85. Levi Fernandes Carneiro to Getúlio Vargas, October 5, 1932, Rio de Janeiro, CPDOC, Arquivo Getúlio Vargas, GV c 1932.10.05/1.

86. Azevedo, *Elaborando a constituição nacional*, xii–xviii.

87. On sham constitutionalism, see Law and Versteeg, "Sham Constitutions."

88. *Constituição política da República Portuguesa* (1933), Art. 106.

89. Political scientist Anne Meng has recently made a case for the importance of formal (including constitutional) constraints on the exercise of power in dictatorships, with a focus on sub-Saharan Africa. Meng, *Constraining Dictatorship*.

90. "Constituição política—Trabalhos preparatórios projeto de constituição," 1932, ANTT, Arquivo Oliveira Salazar, AOS/CO/PC-5B.

91. Theotónio Pereira, "6º Aniversário do movimento nacional de 28 de Maio de 1926."

92. Unpublished interview with António de Oliveira Salazar, "Acerca do futuro estatuto constitucional," 1932.

93. "Projeto da Constituição, I edição impressa," ANTT, Arquivo Oliveira Salazar, AOS/CO/PC-5B.

94. Catholic associations like the Ação Social Católica also lost their centrality. See Santos, *A segunda separação*; Rezola, *O sindicalismo católico no Estado Novo*.

95. Araújo, *A lei de Salazar*, 74.

96. "Constituição política—Trabalhos preparatórios projeto de constituição."

97. "Constituição política—Trabalhos preparatórios projeto de constituição."

98. Cardoso and Ferreira, "A Câmara Corporativa (1935–1974) e as políticas públicas no Estado Novo"; Ferreira, "A Câmara Corporativa no Estado Novo."

99. Preface by Walter Costa Pinto, quoted in Azevedo, *Elaborando a constituição nacional*, xv.

100. Levi Fernandes Carneiro to Getúlio Vargas, October 5, 1932, Rio de Janeiro, CPDOC, Arquivo Getúlio Vargas, GVc1932.10.05/1.

101. Francisco José de Oliveira Vianna to Afrânio Melo Franco, 1932–33, Casa Oliveira Vianna, Niterói (hereafter COV), OVN-CA-0031.01.

102. Schmitt, *Légalité et légitimité*, 44, retrieved from COV, 320.1.5355L.

103. Francisco José de Oliveira Vianna marginalia in his copy of Schmitt, *Légalité et légitimité*, 44, retrieved from COV, 320.1.5355L.

104. Charles Merriam's *New Aspects of Politics* (1925), quoted in Oliveira Vianna, *Problemas de política objetiva*, 172–73.

105. Quoted in Azevedo, *Elaborando a constituição nacional*, 90.

106. Oliveira Vianna, *Problemas de política objetiva*, 190–91.

107. For an overview of technical councils in Brazilian corporatist thought, see Abreu, "Sindicalismo e corporativismo no Brasil," 108–10; Diniz, "Engenharia institucional e políticas públicas"; Diniz, *Empresário, Estado e capitalismo no Brasil*.

108. Gomes, "A representação de classes na constituinte de 1934."

109. Caetano, *Direito constitucional*, 560. On the Poder Moderador, see Carvalho, "Federalismo e centralização no Império brasileiro."

110. *Constituição da República dos Estados Unidos do Brasil*, Art. 90.

111. This trend is also apparent in other Latin American countries, as with the *científicos* under Porfirio Díaz. See Hale, *The Transformation of Liberalism in Late Nineteenth-Century Mexico*.

112. Teixeira, "Making a Brazilian New Deal."

113. António de Oliveira Salazar, notes on the constitution, December 9, 1931, ANTT, Arquivo Oliveira Salazar, AOS/CO/PC-5.

114. Caetano, *Direito constitucional*, 560.

115. Unpublished interview with António de Oliveira Salazar, "Acerca do futuro estatuto constitucional," 1932.

116. *Constituição política da República Portuguesa* (1933), Art 5.

117. Theotónio Pereira, "6º Aniversário do movimento nacional de 28 de Maio de 1926."

118. See, for example, Art. 87 in one of the earliest drafts, "Projeto da Constituição, I edição impressa."

119. This enumeration of government responsibilities would make its way to the final draft, except for mention of the "metropole and colonies." "Constituição política—Trabalhos preparatórios projeto de constituição."

120. *Constituição Política da República Portuguesa* (1933), Art 31.

121. The only mention of workers in the 1933 Constitution was in the Acto Colonial in reference to Indigenous workers.

122. See, for example, Art. 87 in early drafts, "Projeto da Constituição, I edição impressa."

123. "Constituição política—Trabalhos preparatórios projeto de constituição."

124. Araújo, *A lei de Salazar*, 166–68.

125. Comments [by unidentified person] on February 1932 draft, "Constituição Política—Trabalhos preparatórios projeto de constituição."

126. Theotónio Pereira, "6º Aniversário do movimento nacional de 28 de Maio de 1926."

127. José Martinho Simões, "Comentários e propostas de alterações," July 5, 1932, ANTT, Arquivo Oliveira Salazar, AOS/CO/PC-5A.

128. Cunha Gonçalves, "Causas e efeitos do corporativismo português."

129. José Carlos, March 10, 1934, *Annaes da Assembléa Nacional Constituinte 1933/1934, Vol. 11*, 47.

130. To compare social and economic rights between these two constitutions, see Werneck Vianna, *Liberalismo e sindicato no Brasil*, 219–21.

131. Labor and social historians continue to push back against this top-down understanding of social citizenship in Brazil, either emphasizing the activism of the working classes or reframing the question of citizenship from the perspective of those excluded from this system. See Gomes, *Burguesia e trabalho*; Fortes, "*Revendo a legalização dos sindicatos*"; Fischer, *A Poverty of Rights*; French, *Drowning in Laws*.

132. Alcides Bezerra, "As sêcas na futura constituição," December 18, 1934, *Annaes da Assembléa Nacional Constituinte 1933/1934, Vol. 2*, 384, 385.

133. *Constituição Política da República Portuguesa* (1933), Art. 29, quoted in Bezerra, "As sêcas na futura constituição," 385.

134. Bezerra, "As sêcas na future constituição," 385.

135. As historian Barbara Weinstein shows, Simonsen himself wavered between these two positions as he articulated his position on what Brazil needed to achieve social peace and economic progress. Simonsen quoted in Weinstein, *For Social Peace*, 79–80.

136. *Constituição da República dos Estados Unidos do Brasil (1934)*, Arts. 117 and 177.

137. Dávila, "Myth and Memory."

138. Fischer, *A Poverty of Rights*, 117. In terms of the civil law tradition, the utopian aspirations of lawmaking are especially pronounced in the French tradition, particularly compared to the German historical tradition. See Merryman and Pérez-Perdomo, *The Civil Law Tradition*, 27–33. See also Herzog, *A Short History of European Law*, 207–16.

139. A first draft of the 1937 Constitution is held at the Coleção Francisco Campos at the Biblioteca da Procuradoria Geral do Estado in Rio de Janeiro.

140. Malin, "Campos, Francisco."

141. Santos, "Francisco Campos e os fundamentos do constitucionalismo antiliberal no Brasil," 286.

142. Campos wrote Institutional Act No. 1, the first legal decree that followed the 1964 military coup. See Skidmore, *Politics in Brazil*, 19–20.

143. Santos, "Francisco Campos e os fundamentos do constitucionalismo antiliberal no Brasil," 305.

144. Campos, "Directrizes do estado nacional," 45–46.

145. Plinio Salgado to Getúlio Vargas, January 28, 1938, CPDOC, Arquivo Getúlio Vargas, GVc1938.01.28/3.

146. *Constituição dos Estados Unidos do Brasil (de 10 de Novembro de 1937)*, Art. 57, 61.

147. Júlio Barata, "Regime corporativo," *A Batalha*, December 14, 1937, 1. For a biography, see "Barata, Júlio de Carvalho," 182.

148. On the different and shifting meanings of democracy in 1930s' Brazil, see Graham, *Shifting the Meaning of Democracy*.

149. Campos, "Entrevista do Doutor Francisco Campos, Ministro da Justiça, ao 'Correio da Manhã,'" 16, 14.

150. Finchelstein and Urbinati, "On Populism and Democracy"; Campos, "Entrevista do Doutor Francisco Campos, Ministro da Justiça, ao 'Correio da Manhã,'" 19.

151. Cavalcanti, "Prefácio," xv–xvi, xix.

152. Campos, "Entrevista do Doutor Francisco Campos, Ministro da Justiça, ao 'Correio da Manhã,'" 17.

153. On the practical and political importance of rights talk for building a new social and economic order in another authoritarian context, the Soviet Union, see Nathans, "Soviet Rights-Talk in the Post-Stalin Era."

154. Cesarino Junior, *Direito corporativo e direito do trabalho (soluções práticas)*, 6.

155. Quoted in Alexandre Marcondes Filho, "A Constituição de 1937 e a solução corporativa" (1944–45), CPDOC, Arquivo Alexandre Marcondes Filho, AMF pi 44/45.00.00/2.

156. For Marshall, this order was sequential, and could not be reorganized or inverted. This narrative for the evolution of rights, however, is incomplete even for liberal Anglo-American experiences. Marshall, "Citizenship and Social Class."

157. Carvalho, *Cidadania no Brasil*, 125–26.

158. French, *Drowning in Laws*; Fortes, "*O Estado Novo e os trabalhadores*."

159. Fischer, *A Poverty of Rights*.

160. A point emphasized in French, "The Origin of Corporatist State Intervention in Brazilian Industrial Relations."

161. Burke, "Some Rights Are More Equal than Others"; Burke, "From Individual Rights to National Development."

Chapter 3: Corporatist Economics and the Third Path

1. In Argentina, General José Félix Uriburu staged a military coup in 1930. As president, he tried to implement a corporate system to reverse the legacies of the French Revolution. See Finchelstein, *The Ideological Origins of the Dirty War*, 17–20. Directly inspired by Salazar's Constitution, Austrian chancellor Engelbert Dollfuss pushed his corporatist constitution through Parliament in April 1934. While short-lived, Austria's corporatist experiment gave political form to Catholic social encyclicals in an attempt to stave off both Nazi aggression and communist opposition at home. See Chappel, "The Catholic Origins of Totalitarianism Theory in Interwar Europe." Corporatist ideas also inspired Fulgencio Batista's 1933 revolution in Cuba and Lázaro Cárdenas in Mexico. See Whitney, *State and Revolution in Cuba*; Hamilton, *The Limits of State Autonomy*. In fact, during Cárdenas's presidential campaign in 1934, he framed his platform in terms of what historian Ilán Semo calls the "tercera vía" or "third path" between outdated formulas of classical liberalism and the Soviet experiment in Russia. Cárdenas, quoted in Semo, "El cardenismo revisado," 198.

2. Manoilescu, *O século do corporativismo*, ix. See also "O Brasil e o corporativismo: A conferencia de hotem na Federação das Associações Commerciaes," *Correio da Manhã* (April 21, 1938).

3. In 1933, Marcello Caetano, then a young law professor at the University of Lisbon, called corporatism the "third current," one cutting in between "doctrines commonly called Bolshevik" and the "bankruptcy of classical democracy and evils of individualism." Marcello Caetano,

"Corporativismo," *Jornal do Comércio e das Colónias* (February 16, 1933). French economist Maurice Byé echoed this logic, calling corporatism a "third regime" that was "fundamentally different from liberalism and socialism." Byé, "Capitalisme, socialisme, économie corporative, économie dirigée," 1209.

4. On France, Germany, and Italy, see Maier, *Recasting Bourgeois Europe*.

5. Weyland, *Assault on Democracy*.

6. Historians of liberalism and socialism have produced excellent transnational and global histories of these ideologies, perhaps in part because these ideologies (in different ways) were universal and international in their orientation. On liberalism or neoliberalism, see Sanders, *The Vanguard of the Atlantic World*; Slobodian, *Globalists*. On socialism, see Friedman, *Ripe for Revolution*.

7. On North Atlantic exchanges, see Rodgers, *Atlantic Crossings*; Patel, *The New Deal*.

8. Fascism, for example, has recently been the subject of new global and transnational approaches. See Finchelstein, *Transatlantic Fascism*; Link, *Forging Global Fordism*.

9. See, for example, Love, *Crafting the Third World*.

10. On fascist connections between Germany, Italy, and Portugal, see Saraiva, *Fascist Pigs*. For Brazil, the Italian influence on labor laws has been especially well studied. See Silva, "The Brazilian and Italian Labor Courts."

11. Tristão de Ataíde, "Posição da economia," *Hierarchia* 1 (1931): 33.

12. "Pensamento econômico," 201, 202.

13. Corporatist economists broadly critiqued classical and neoclassical economics. By classical economics, they referred to the first efforts in the late eighteenth and nineteenth centuries to describe economic transactions within a liberal or free market framework, largely based in and building on works by Smith, Say, and Ricardo along with Thomas Malthus and John Stuart Mill. For intellectual histories on the rise of and debates surrounding classical economic ideas, see, for example, Rothschild, *Economic Sentiments*; Todd, *L'identité économique de la France*. Neoclassical economics is more difficult to define given its diversity. Roughly, neoclassical economics emerged in the late nineteenth century, following what economists call the "marginal revolution" in which economics became more mathematical and focused on how marginal utility, as opposed to total utility, determined the value of goods and services. Economists in this tradition include William Jevons, Carl Menger, Vilfredo Pareto, and Léon Walras. On the marginal revolution, especially its Austrian school, see Wasserman, *The Marginal Revolutionaries*. See also Yonay, *The Struggle over the Soul of Economics*, chap. 2.

14. Keynes, *The End of Laissez-Faire*, 32.

15. Burgin, *The Great Persuasion*, 46.

16. In 1931, the Centro das Indústrias do Estado de São Paulo became the Federação das Indústrias do Estado de São Paulo (Federation of Industries of the State of São Paulo) in order to gain recognition by the Ministry of Labor.

17. For a professional and intellectual biography of Simonsen, see Weinstein, *For Social Peace in Brazil*, 13–27.

18. Amzalak, *Economistas brasileiros*, 5.

19. Simonsen, *As crises no Brasil, Outubro de 1930*, 9.

20. Simonsen, *As crises no Brasil, Outubro de 1930*, 8. In his argument that capitalism is inherently crisis-ridden, Simonsen did not engage or cite Karl Marx, dialoguing largely with classical political economists.

21. On how Simonsen engaged discourses of technical competence and expertise to expand his authority over both workers and government officials, see Weinstein, "The Discourse of Technical Competence." See also Weinstein, *For Social Peace in Brazil*.

22. Love, *Crafting the Third World*, 75–76.

23. Manoilescu, *L'équilibre économique européen*, 4, 13.

24. On Prebisch's center-periphery model in post-1945 Latin America, see Fajardo, *The World That Latin America Created*.

25. Love, *Crafting the Third World*, 11, 91–92, 97.

26. Inventory of Salazar's personal library, ANTT, Arquivo Oliveira Salazar, AOS/J-1; Love, *Crafting the Third World*, 77.

27. Manoilescu, *L'équilibre économique européen*, 5.

28. Manoilescu, *Theoria do proteccionismo e da permuta internacional*, 349.

29. In other words, during economic downturns, industrial prices were "stickier" than agricultural ones because of the power of organized labor compared to its unorganized counterpart in agrarian countries. See Love, *Crafting the Third World*, 79.

30. Manoilescu, *L'équilibre économique européen*, 7.

31. Seabra, *A industrialização dos países agrícolas*.

32. For Brazil, data is available for price levels in Rio de Janeiro. See *Anuário Estatístico do Brasil: Ano IV, 1938*, 331. For Portugal, see Valério, *Estatísticas históricas portuguesas*, 637.

33. Simonsen, *Crisis, Finances and Industry*, 28.

34. See Dimand, "Irving Fisher and Modern Macroeconomics," 442. Fisher also recognized the severity of deflation following the 1929 crash and offered his own explanation in terms of debt and deflation in which distressed sales to meet debt payments drove prices even further. See Levy, *Ages of American Capitalism*. Fisher published his debt-deflation argument in 1933, and this is perhaps why Brazilian and Portuguese economists largely critiqued his simplified quantity theory of money. On Fisher and the US economics profession, see Yonay, *The Struggle over the Soul of Economics*, 45.

35. Simonsen, *Crisis, Finances and Industry*, 28.

36. This argument, for example, was elaborated by Brazilian Labor Ministry officials. See "Pensamento econômico," 204.

37. "Na Faculdade de Direito começou hoje um doutoramento," *Diário de Lisboa* (March 12, 1931).

38. Bastien, "The Advent of Modern Economics in Portugal."

39. Salazar, *O ágio do ouro, sua natureza e suas causas*.

40. Caetano, *A depreciação da moeda depois da guerra*, preface, 360–61, 167–78.

41. "Sobre economia politica: Na Faculdade de Direito iniciaram-se hoje as provas do concurso para o doutoramento," *República* (June 12, 1931). Article reprinted in Castilho, *Marcelo Caetano*, 92.

42. Caetano was introduced to Salazar by Theotónio Pereira and soon after given a job in the Ministry of Finance. See Martinho, *Marcello Caetano and the Portuguese "New State,"* 45.

43. Caetano, *O sistema corporativo*. Retrieved from COV, 331.8.C128S.

44. Pinto, "O império do professor."

45. Martins, *Pedro Theotónio Pereira*, 269.

46. Gastão Bettencourt, "Portugal sob o Estado Novo," *O Cruzeiro* (May 28, 1938), 29–31.

47. Campos da Fonseca, "Constituição portuguesa," *O Cruzeiro* (May 29, 1937), 24.

48. Even as censorship intensified following Vargas's 1937 coup, targeting communist and socialist publications, but also German and Italian ones celebrating Hitler or Mussolini, high-profile Brazilian magazines and newspapers were able to run propaganda for Salazar's Estado Novo without interruption.

49. "Colónias portuguesas no Brasil: Manifestações de apoio ao governo português," memorandum, 1937, Arquivo Histórico-Diplomático do Ministério dos Negócios Estrangeiros, Lisbon (hereafter MNE), P3, A11, M376.

50. "Portugal, terra de pescadores," *O Cruzeiro* (May 28, 1938), 38–39.

51. Gastão Bettencourt, "28 de Maio," *O Cruzeiro* (May 29, 1937), 28–29.

52. On the corporatist reoroganization of the codfish sector, see Garrido, *O Estado Novo e a campanha do bacalhau.*

53. Garrido, "Os bacalhoeiros em revolta."

54. Cezar Coutinho, "Uma nova luz," *O Cruzeiro* (May 29, 1937), 23.

55. Inventory of Salazar's personal library, AOS/J-2/M0012.

56. Oswaldo Aranha to Eugênio Gudin, April 9, 1935, CPDOC, Arquivo Eugênio Gudin, EUG 35.03.22.

57. On teaching economics in Brazil, see Loureiro, "Economistas e elites dirigentes no Brasil." Much of this literature is focused on the post-1945 period, but it identifies the 1930s as a turning point for creating new schools and programs. Note that Leduc was not part of the French academic mission discussed in Merkel, *Terms of Exchange.*

58. See Guitton, "Gaston Leduc." His doctoral dissertation, "La théorie de prix de monopole" (1927), focused on the monopolistic theory of price, and students in France used this work as a reference for years to come. See Bonnefous, "Allocution prononcée par Édouard Bonnefous," 3.

59. Gaston attended, for example, meetings of the Mont Pelerin Society, which advocated for neoliberal policies. See Guitton, "Gaston Leduc."

60. Gaston G. B. Leduc, "Reflexões sobre a idéa corporativa," *O Observador Econômico e Financeiro* (July 1936), 46–47.

61. "Economia, moeda, valorização e commercio: o que nos disse o professor Gaston Leduc," *Correio da Manhã* (August 18, 1936).

62. Sousa [pseud. Miguel Sidónio], "Diálogos fáceis sobre a económia corporativa, moral e humana," 33.

63. Teixeira, "Making a Brazilian New Deal."

64. Teixeira Ribeiro, *Lições de direito corporativo,* 117.

65. Cunha Gonçalves, *Princípios de direito corporativo,* 46–47.

66. In both Brazil and Portugal, political economy was still largely taught in law schools, though the 1930s would bring institutional experiments to both countries to establish economics departments. Loureiro, "Economistas e elites dirigentes no Brasil"; Bastien, "The Advent of Modern Economics in Portugal."

67. Rocco, "The Political Doctrine of Fascism," 396, 403–4, 402.

68. Gregor, *Italian Fascism and Developmental Dictatorship,* 270–81.

69. Gini, "The Scientific Basis of Fascism," 107–8, 99, 111.

70. Quoted in Silva, "The Brazilian and Italian Labor Courts," 407. See also Oliveira Vianna, "Razões da originalidade do sistema sindical brasileiro," 278–79.

71. "Obras recebidas na redacção da 'Biblos,'" 662.

72. For Salazar's calendar, I am grateful to Portuguese historian Rita Almeida de Carvalho for access to the database that she created based on Salazar's diary.

73. Weinstein, *For Social Peace*, 73–74.

74. "Instituto Ítalo-Brasileiro de Alta Cultura: As próximas conferências do professor Gino Arias sobre o corporativismo italiano," *Correio da Manhã* (October 11, 1933); "Instituto Ítalo-Brasileiro de Alta Cultura: As conferências do professor Gino Arias sobre a economia corporativa," *Correio da Manhã* (October 14, 1933).

75. Almeida, *A organização sindical-corporativa da agricultura italiana*, 5, 7.

76. Grand, "Mussolini's Follies."

77. On the hardships of war-related austerity, see Grazia, *How Fascism Ruled Women*, chap. 4.

78. Pedersen, *The Guardians*, chap. 11.

79. "Is It Fascism," *Evening Star* (likely December 1937), newspaper article sent to Getúlio Vargas, CPDOC, Arquivo Getúlio Vargas, GVc1937.12.07.

80. "O Estatuto do Trabalho Nacional e as casas do povo pelo Dr. Leite de Sampaio," 6.

81. Azevedo Amaral, *O Estado autoritário e a realidade nacional*, 216.

82. Rodrigues, *Conceitos de valor e preço*, 19.

83. A. de Lima Campos (Banco do Brasil), "O atual problema econômico brasileiro (na órbita nacional e na órbita internacional)," July 1936, Arquivo Nacional do Brasil, Rio de Janeiro (hereafter AN-RJ), Fundo Conselho de Economia Nacional, lata 177.

84. It combined lessons learned from Progressive era reforms with programs modeled on Fascist Italy's corporatist experiment. See Rodgers, *Atlantic Crossings*; Brinkley, *The End of Reform*; Patel, *The New Deal*.

85. There is a vast literature on this point. For perspectives that particularly resonate with Brazil's own experiment, see Gordon, *New Deals*.

86. Jacobs, *Pocketbook Politics*, 107–8. See also Sawyer, *American Fair Trade*, chap. 6.

87. Milov, *The Cigarette*, 48–53. US New Dealers would insist, nonetheless, on the differences between the Agricultural Adjustment Act and corporatism, see Balogh, *The Associational State: American Governance in the Twentieth Century*, 148.

88. Schivelbusch, *Three New Deals*; Vaudagna, "The New Deal and Corporativism in Italy"; Milov, *The Cigarette*, 49.

89. Jacobs, *Pocketbook Politics*, 109.

90. Oliveira Vianna elaborated this argument in essays that appeared in both legal journals and newspapers. See, for example, "Brandeis e o seu americanismo," *Correio da Manhã* (March 21, 1939); Oliveira Vianna, "O individuo e o grupo," *Correio da Manhã Correio* (March 28, 1939). Both these essays had previously been published in law review *Revista Forense*. See also Teixeira, "Making a Brazilian New Deal."

91. Oswaldo Aranha to Getúlio Vargas, September 24, 1935, CPDOC, Arquivo Getúlio Vargas, GVc1935.09.24.

92. Azevedo Amaral, *O Estado autoritário e a realidade nacional*, 267.

93. Oswaldo Aranha to Getúlio Vargas, September 24, 1935, CPDOC, Arquivo Getúlio Vargas, GVc1936.06.30/2.

94. Mário de Pimentel Brandão to Getúlio Vargas, December 23, 1938, CPDOC, Arquivo Getúlio Vargas, GVc1938.12.23.

95. Oswaldo Aranha to Getúlio Vargas, September 24, 1935, CPDOC, Arquivo Getúlio Vargas, GVc1937.05.19.

96. Oswaldo Aranha to Eugênio Gudin, April 9, 1935, CPDOC, Arquivo Eugênio Gudin, EUG 35.03.22.

97. Historian Ricardo Bielschowsky refers to Gudin as not only a liberal but also the theoretical leader of neoliberals in Brazil. Bielschowsky, "Ideologia e desenvolvimento," 76–79.

98. Eugênio Gudin, "Sem Rumo," *O Jornal* (November 14, 1934), retrieved from CPDOC, Arquivo Eugênio Gudin, EUG 35.03.22.

99. Báudin, *Le corporatisme*, 88, 109.

100. José Augusto, "A democracia e as finanças públicas," *O Observador Econômico e Financeiro* (December 1936), 20.

101. Gudin, "Sem rumo."

102. Weld, "The Spanish Civil War and the Construction of a Reactionary Historical Consciousness in Augusto Pinochet's Chile."

103. Interview with António de Oliveira Salazar in Peruvian newspaper *El Comércio*, May 21, 1938, retrieved from ANTT, Arquivo Oliveira Salazar, AOS/CO/PC-1B.

104. Valetim F. Bouças, "Notas editoriais," *O Observador Econômico e Financeiro* (July 1936), 6.

105. Báudin, *Le corporatisme*, 106.

106. Some social scientists emphasized how corporatism fit with Catholic, patriarchal, and absolutist tendencies in Iberian and Latin American culture. See, for example, Wiarda, "Corporatism and Development in the Iberic-Latin World." Such arguments were already politically charged in 1930s and used even by those who endorsed corporatism.

107. Roberto Simonsen, November 29, 1938. Speech reprinted in *Ata da sétima sessão ordinária do Conselho de Expansão Econômica do Estado de São Paulo*, Arquivo Público do Estado de São Paulo, São Paulo (hereafter APESP), Conselho de Expansão Econômica do Estado de São Paulo, Livros de Atas e Decretos, caixa 1.

108. Corporatist ideologue Azevedo Amaral edited the weekly periodical *Diretrizes* where this sort of language often appeared to discuss Salazar and Portugal's Estado Novo.

109. This silencing of race in official policy discussions in Brazil is consistent with longstanding practices in law and bureaucratic proceedings. See Fischer, Grinberg, and Mattos, "Law, Silence, and Racialized Inequalities in the History of Afro-Brazil."

110. Despite public and academic celebrations of multiracialism, Brazilian intellectual efforts to celebrate miscegenation continued to reify preexisting racist hierarchies by the erasure or euphemized denigration of non-European influences. See Skidmore, *Black into White*; Skidmore, "Raízes de Gilberto Freyre"; Borges, "Review Essay"; Williams, *Culture Wars in Brazil*.

111. On racial discourses and underdevelopment in Brazil, see Weinstein, *The Color of Modernity*; Weinstein, "Developing Inequality."

112. For an overview of the racial typologies explained in Oliveira Vianna and Azevedo Amaral's works particularly as they pertain to immigration, see Abreu, Martins, and Munareto, *Embracing the Past, Designing the Future*, 50–62.

113. Scholars of Brazil have documented how racist sociological writings continued to shape public health, social welfare, and education projects in the 1930s. See, for example Otovo, *Progressive Mothers, Better Babies*.

114. Oliveira Vianna, legal opinion for Ministry of Labor on Chinese immigration to Brazil, n.d., COV, caixa 6, parecer No. 2.286.

115. Oswaldo Aranha to Eugênio Gudin, July 23, 1935, CPDOC, Arquivo Eugênio Gudin, EUG 35.03.22.

116. Azevedo Amaral, *O Estado autoritário e a realidade nacional*, 262.

117. Palti, "The Problem of 'Misplaced Ideas' Revisited." On "misplaced" ideas in Brazil, see Schwarz, *Misplaced Ideas*.

118. Sanders, *The Vanguard of the Atlantic World*; Bayly, *Recovering Liberties*.

119. Marcello Caetano, "Panorama corporativo português," *Jornal do Comércio e das Colónias* (February 20, 1933).

120. Preface by António Perez Durão, in Spirito, *Princípios fundamentais de economia corporativa*, xi.

121. Spirito critiques the *homo economicus* at length in Spirito, *Princípios fundamentais de economic corporativa*, esp. 251–60. On intellectual efforts to define the *homo corporativus*, see Bastien and Cardoso, "From Homo Economicus to Homo Corporativus." Corporatist efforts to celebrate a New Man parallel debates in socialist contexts over social organization, although these parallels were rarely acknowledged. And as political scientist Jan Feldman notes, the concept of a New Man is also not distinct to socialist contexts. Feldman, "New Thinking about the 'New Man.'"

122. Teixeira Ribeiro, *Lições de direito corporativo*, 96–97.

123. Spirito, *Princípios fundamentais de economia corporativa*, i.

124. Preface by António Perez Durão, in Spirito, *Princípios fundamentais de economia corporativa*, ix.

125. Preface by Azevedo Amaral, in Manoilescu, *O século do corporativismo*, v, vi.

126. Love, *Crafting the Third World*, 98.

127. Preface by Azevedo Amaral, in Manoilescu, *O século do corporativismo*, vi.

128. Gomes, "Azevedo Amaral e *O século do corporativismo*," 188.

129. Azevedo Amaral, *O estado autoritário e a realidade nacional*, 310. See also Gomes, "Azevedo Amaral e *O século do corporativismo*," 189.

130. Letter to Themístocles Brandão Cavalcanti, August 4, 1938, CPDOC, Arquivo Themístocles Brandão Cavalcanti, TBCc1938.04.18

131. "Cavalcanti, Temístocles."

132. Loureiro, "Economistas e elites dirigentes no Brasil," 55.

133. "Faculdade de Ciências Econômicas e Administrativas do Rio de Janeiro," *A Noite* (March 2, 1939).

134. Cavalcanti, "Prefácio," viii.

135. Cavalcanti, "Prefácio," v.

136. "Relatório da Missão Comercial ao Brasil," 1938, ANTT, Ministério do Comércio e Indústria, caixa 2.

137. Quoted in "O Brasil e o corporativismo: a conferencia de hotem na Federação das Associações Commerciaes," *Correio da Manhã* (April 21, 1938).

138. Manoilescu, *O século do corporativismo*, v; Spirito, *Princípios fundamentais de economia corporativa*, 165.

139. Báudin, *Le corporatisme*, 15.

140. Spirito, *Princípios fundamentais de economia corporativa*, 167.

141. Lima Neto, *O Ribatejo e a sua influência no desenvolvimento do municipalismo e do corporatismo em Portugal*; Cruz, "O integralismo lusitano nas origens do salazarismo"; Reale, *O Estado Moderno*.

142. Catholic charities continued to fill gaps left by the welfare state. See, for example, Otovo, *Progressive Mothers, Better Babies*, chap. 5.

143. Oliveira Vianna, legal opinion, n.d., COV, caixa 6, parecer No. 2133.

144. The origins of planning predate the rise of corporatist dictatorships, with the USSR an early pioneer. See Temin, "Soviet and Nazi Economic Planning in the 1930s."

145. Cavalcanti, "Prefácio," xiii.

146. See the hundreds of petitions sent to the Brazilian Ministry of Labor to recognize sindicatos and cooperatives in the Arquivo Nacional do Brasil, Brasília (hereafter AN-B), Fundo Ministério do Trabalho, Indústria e Comércio.

147. Cavalcanti, "Prefácio," viii, xiii.

148. Azevedo Amaral, *O estado autoritário e a realidade nacional*, 223.

149. Leite (Lumbrales), *Professor e homem de Estado*.

150. Weinstein, "Racializing Regional Difference"; Abreu, "Elites políticas regionais."

151. Campos, "Entrevista do Doutor Francisco Campos, Ministro da Justiça, ao 'Correio da Manhã,'" 22.

152. Oliveira Vianna, *Problemas de direito corporativo*, 48.

Chapter 4: Just Price and Production

1. A. de Lima Campos (Banco do Brasil), "O atual problema econômico brasileiro (na órbita nacional e na órbita internacional)," July 1936, AN-RJ, Fundo Conselho de Economia Nacional, lata 177.

2. For other contexts, see Nord, *France's New Deal*; Tooze, *The Wages of Destruction*. On agrarian development projects in these years, see Olsson, *Agrarian Crossings*.

3. The economic history of the 1930s is often cast in terms of efforts to industrialize, taking for granted the transition from an agrarian to industrial economy. See Wirth, *The Politics of Brazilian Development 1930–1954*; Cano, "Crise de 1929, soberania na política econômica e industrialização"; Fonseca, *Vargas*. Archival documents on the state's management of the economy, though, reveal the persistence of questions of how to organize the agrarian sector, not only for export commodities, but for basic provisions.

4. Meade, "Living Worse and Costing More." See also Stapleford, *The Cost of Living in America*.

5. On Chile, see Frens-String, *Hungry for Revolution*.

6. Milov, *The Cigarette*, 48–53; Sawyer, *American Fair Trade*.

7. "A alta mundial dos preços de productos básicos," *O Observador Econômico e Financeiro* (August 1936), 40. Globally, rising concerns about inflation were by no means homogeneous given macroeconomic variations and the different consequences of the Great Depression across countries. See *World Economic Survey: Fifth Year, 1935–36*, 75–101; *World Economic Survey: Sixth Year, 1936–37*, 85; *World Economic Survey: Seventh Year, 1937–38*, 77.

8. Sousa Costa's report is discussed in Valentim F. Bouças, "Notas editorials," *O Observador Econômico e Financeiro* (July 1936), 6.

9. *Anuário Estatístico do Brasil: Ano IV, 1938*, 331.

10. "A alta dos preços e a estatística da produção," 10.

11. "O custo da vida no Brasil: Os cálculos por família padrão," *O Observador Econômico e Financeiro* (February 1936), 38.

12. On the increased efforts to collect and mobilize statistics during the interwar decades, see Tooze, *Statistics and the German State*; Stapleford, *The Cost of Living in America*; Desrosières, "The History of Statistics as a Genre."

13. Nichols, "The Statistical Work of the League of Nations"; Ward, *Quantifying the World*, 36–48, 79.

14. It was also known as the Princeton Group after moving from Geneva to Princeton University during World War II. As the League of Nation's largest technical organ, it was responsible for producing reliable statistics as well as offering policy recommendations on a wide range of economic and financial questions to advise member and nonmember nations. See Ekbladh, "Exile Economics," 2; Clavin and Wessels, "Transnationalism and the League of Nations," 478–81. See also Clavin, *Securing the World Economy*.

15. Efforts to collect and quantify data on the nation did not originate in the interwar period, as countless initiatives of this sort marked the history of nineteenth-century nation building. But the 1920s and 1930s did bring an internationalization of such efforts. See Desrosières, "The History of Statistics as a Genre." See also Coyle, *GDP*, 8–17.

16. Francisco Campos to José Maria Whitaker, 1930–31, CPDOC, Arquivo José Maria Whitaker, JMW-30.11.05/4.

17. Loveman, "The Race to Progress."

18. See, for example, "A alta dos preços e a estatística da produção."

19. Mitchell, "Fixing the Economy."

20. Decreto Nº24.609 de 6 de Julho de 1934, printed in *Boletim do Ministério de Trabalho Comércio e Indústria* 1 (September 1934).

21. Decreto Lei Nº218 de 26 de Janeiro de 1938: Muda o nome do Instituto Nacional de Estatística e o do Conselho Brasileiro de Geografia, *Diário Oficial da União* (February 1, 1938).

22. Resolução Nº15 de 30 de Dezembro de 1936, *Resoluções da Assembléa Geral do Conselho Nacional de Estatística*, 1:62.

23. The government statistical yearbook published prior to 1930, the *Anuário Estatístico do Brasil* for 1908–12, included data on prices for essential commodities in the city of Rio de Janeiro, but lacked pricing data for other cities and regions.

24. Xavier, "O problema do custo da vida," 25.

25. Resolução Nº7 de 30 de Dezembro de 1936, *Resoluções da Assembléa Geral do Conselho Nacional de Estatística*, 1:23.

26. *Anuário Estatístico do Brasil: Ano IV, 1938*, 331–39.

27. "A alta dos preços e a estatística da produção."

28. Decreto Nº1.007 de 4 de Agosto de 1936: Cria a Commissão Reguladora de Tabelamento dos gêneros de primeira necessidade, *Diário Oficial da União* (August 8, 1936).

29. Pereira, "Política agrícola brasileira e a pequena produção familiar," 300; Mueller, *Das oligarquias agrárias ao predomínio urbano-industrial*.

30. On the CRT and related administrative efforts, see Wahrlich, *Reforma administrativa na era de Vargas*, 216; Júnior, *Direito social brasileiro*, 195; Linhares and Silva, *História política do abastecimento*, 102.

31. Lupercio Araujo, Cooperativa Agrícola de Cotia to Getúlio Vargas, n.d., AN-RJ, Fundo Conselho de Economia Nacional, lata 260.

32. Historians often see the 1930s as a turning point for how experts feature in modern polities, although focus on the significance for the post-1945 period. See Mitchell, *Rule of Experts Egypt, Techno-Politics, Modernity*; Babb, *Managing Mexico*.

33. President of Frente Nacional Democrática to Getúlio Vargas, August 20, 1937, AN-RJ, Fundo Conselho de Economia Nacional, lata 260.

34. Dulles, *The São Paulo Law School and the Anti-Vargas Resistance*, 36.

35. Frente Nacional Democracia to Getúlio Vargas, August 20, 1937, AN-RJ, Fundo Conselho de Economia Nacional, lata 260.

36. Blanc de Freitas, "Barateamento do custo da vida," October 1, 1937, AN-RJ, Fundo Conselho de Economia Nacional, lata 260.

37. "Clamando no deserto . . . ," *Correio da Manhã* (March 3, 1936).

38. On the moral economy and paternalism, see Thompson, "The Moral Economy of the English Crowd in the Eighteenth Century." See also Graham, *Feeding the City*.

39. "Pensamento econômico," 202.

40. On the general shift away from economic orthodoxy in 1930s' Brazil, see Bastos and Gomes, "Ortodoxia e heterodoxia econômica antes e durante a Era Vargas"; Fonseca, *Vargas*, 172–202.

41. The *sindicato único* principle—the Ministry of Labor will recognize one sindicato for a given profession in a designated region—was what distinguishes corporatism in Brazil from pluralist systems. Werneck Vianna, *Liberalismo e sindicato no Brasil*, 223–27.

42. Beyond labor and capital, liberal professions, merchants, and small-scale firms also formed sindicatos in 1930s' Brazil. See Vannucchi, "Advogados e corporativismo de classe média no Brasil pós-1930."

43. Oliveira Vianna, "O indivíduo e o syndicato," 114–15, 117.

44. Almeida, *A organização sindical-corporativa da agricultura italiana*, 95.

45. Teixeira Ribeiro, *Lições de direito corporativo*, 97–98.

46. Manoilescu, *O século do corporativismo*, 219–23.

47. Rodrigues, *Conceitos de valor e preço*, 460, 461.

48. Manoilescu, *O século do corporativismo*, 223.

49. Madureira, "O Estado, o patronato e a indústria portuguesa," 791.

50. Rosas, *O Estado Novo nos anos trinta*, 269–74.

51. Leite (Lumbrales), *A doutrina corporativa em Portugal*, 164.

52. Freire, *Produzir e beber*; Garrido, *O Estado Novo e a campanha do bacalhau*.

53. Rosas, *O Estado Novo nos anos trinta*, 165–72.

54. Leite (Lumbrales), *A doutrina corporativa em Portugal*, 135–36.

55. Leite (Lumbrales), *Professor e homem de Estado*, 10.

56. Madureira, "O Estado, o patronato e a indústria portuguesa"; Freire, *Produzir e beber*; Confraria, "Política industrial do Estado Novo"; Lucena, "Salazar, a 'fórmula' da agricultura portuguesa e a intervenção estatal no sector primário."

57. Pedro Theotónio Pereira, "Sobre alguns aspectos urgentes da vida corporativa nacional: Grémios, Instituto Nacional de Trabalho, desemprego, Conselho Corporativo," ANTT, Arquivo Oliveira Salazar, AOS/CO/PC-10A.

58. Pedro Theotónio Pereira to António de Oliveira Salazar, February 12, 1934, ANTT, Arquivo Oliveira Salazar, AOS/CP-213.

59. Pedro Theotónio Pereira to António de Oliveira Salazar, April 25, 1934, ANTT, Arquivo Oliveira Salazar, AOS/CP-213.

60. Focusing on industrialists and labor policies, historian Barbara Weinstein elaborates on this critique of Vargas era public-private collaborations. Weinstein, *For Social Peace.*

61. Rosas, *O Estado Novo nos anos trinta*, 269–74.

62. Schmitter, *Corporatism and Public Policy in Authoritarian Portugal*, 11.

63. Alfredo da Silva to António de Oliveira Salazar, April 8, 1938, ANTT, Arquivo Oliveira Salazar, AOS/CO/EC-16.

64. Gabinete do Ministro, Conselho Técnico Corporativo do Comércio e da Indústria, March 1, 1939, ANTT, Secretaria-Geral da Presidência do Conselho de Ministros, Gabinete do Presidente, caixa 12, proc. 15/6 Nº1.

65. Decreto Nº30.021, *Diário do Govêrno* (November 3, 1939).

66. Garrido, *Queremos uma economia nova!*, 113–21.

67. Freire, Ferreira, and Rodrigues, "Corporativismo e Estado Novo," 17–18.

68. Andrade, "Prefácio," vii.

69. Galvão, *O povoamento europeu nas colónias portuguesas.*

70. Castelo, *Passagens para África*, 97; Bender, *Angola under the Portuguese*, 101.

71. Imperial reformers embraced corporatism as part of this developmentalist push not only in Salazarist Portugal but also in places such as France's empire under the Vichy regime. See Jennings, *Vichy in the Tropics.*

72. Cooper, "Modernizing Bureaucrats, Backward Africans, and the Development Concept"; Cooper, "Writing the History of Development."

73. Marcello Caetano, "Espírito corporativo," May 12, 1939, newspaper editorial clipping retrieved from ANTT, Arquivo Marcello Caetano, AMC caixa 1.

74. Junta de Exportação dos Cereais das Colónias, "Relatório," 1947, ANTT, Arquivo Oliveira Salazar, AOS/CO/PC-17C.

75. "Projecto de decreto para creação da Junta de Exportação de Peixe," July 1938, Arquivo Histórico Ultramarino, Lisbon (hereafter AHU), DG Economia, Repartição Administrativa, 1932–1951, vol. 123, caixa 14.

76. Conselho Técnico Coprorativo do Comérico e da Indústria, "Relatório," November 1938, ANTT, Secretaria-Geral da Presidência do Conselho de Ministros, Gabinete do Presidente, caixa 35, proc. 330/17 Nº4.

77. Junta de Exportação dos Cereais das Colónias, "Relatório."

78. Vieira, *Angola.*

79. Junta de Exportação dos Cereais das Colónias, "Relatório."

80. Pitcher, *Politics in the Portuguese Empire*, 101–5.

81. Isaacman, *Cotton Is the Mother of Poverty*, 29.

82. Historian Allen Isaacman documents the grueling labor conditions and surveillance endured by African farmers, especially women. Isaacman, *Cotton Is the Mother of Poverty*, 35.

83. Chefe da Repartição dos Serviços Económicos Direcção Geral do Fomento Colonial, "Relatório," November 3, 1945, AHU, DG Economia, Repartição Administrativa, 1932–1951, vol. 123, caixa 14.

84. Decreto Lei Nº27.552, Art. 2, *Diário do Govêrno* (March 3, 1937).

85. Specifically, a 1942 decree reintroduced forced labor. On how new legalized forms of forced labor were introduced in order to coerce women in particular into cotton cultivation, see Kagan Guthrie, *Bound for Work*, 69–72.

86. Pitcher, *Politics in the Portuguese Empire*, 101.

87. Arthur Eugênio Torres Filho, "O alargamento do mercado interno," April 8, 1935, AN-RJ, Fundo Conselho de Economia Nacional, lata 188.

88. Motoyama, "1930–1964," 269.

89. Wirth, *The Politics of Brazilian Development 1930–1954*, 18.

90. The Estado Novo's institutional innovations are often interpreted as new structures by which economic elites could exercise political power. Nathaniel Leff, for example, argues that despite efforts to modernize, the relations between private enterprise and the state in Brazil remained subordinated to personal relationships rather than according to organized interest groups. Fernando Henrique Cardoso, in turn, uses the term *anéis* (rings) to describe the relationship between the state and private interests. Leff, *Economic Policy-Making and Development in Brazil*; Cardoso, *Autoritarismo e democratização*. This question of how effective corporatism was in creating institutions for collective bargaining and cooperative relations between industry and the state is a staple in studies of Latin American political sociology and political economy. See Schneider, *Business Politics and the State in Twentieth-Century Latin America*; Schmitter, *Interest Conflict and Political Change in Brazil*. On the other hand, Maria Antonieta Leopoldi is not quite so dismissive of how such corporatist legislative chambers facilitated the organization of collective groups and successful negotiations between private and public interests for the sake of national development. Leopoldi, *Política e interesses*.

91. Draibe, *Rumos e metamorfoses*, 115.

92. Wirth accordingly translates the CFCE as "Foreign Trade Council," and largely focuses on its role in managing exports and foreign cooperation. Trade, though, was only one of the CFCE's responsibilities. Wirth, *The Politics of Brazilian Development 1930–1954*, 27.

93. Thorp, "A Reappraisal of the Origins of Import-Substituting Industrialization."

94. The CFCE was only replaced with the Conselho Nacional de Economia in 1949. The Conselho Nacional de Economia was dismantled by the military dictatorship in 1967 and another centralized economic organ created in its place. See Ioris, *Transforming Brazil*, 169–70, 183. See also Diniz, *Empresário, Estado e capitalismo no Brasil*, chap. 6.

95. On the emergence of this class of técnicos and their importance for Brazil, see Leff, *Economic Policy-Making and Development in Brazil*, 132–53. On positivist-influenced projects for economic development, see Diacon, *Stringing Together a Nation*.

96. Oliveira Vianna, *Problemas de direito corporativo*, 50.

97. Torres Filho, "O alargamento do mercado interno."

98. Sonia Regina de Mendonça, *Agronomia e poder no Brasil*, 31.

99. Torres Filho, *Relatório apresentado ao Dr. Geminiano Lyra Castro por Arthur Torres, Filho*, 5.

100. Labor Minister Agamemnon Magalhães to Getúlio Vargas, "Exposição de motivos assinada pelo Ministro do Trabalho, Indústria e Comércio," July 1, 1936, AN-RJ, Gabinete Civil da Presidência da Republica, Congresso Nacional 1936, Lata 81; Poliano, *A Sociedade Nacional de Agricultura, resumo histórico*, 139.

101. The National Agricultural Society was founded in 1897 in Rio de Janeiro, following the abolition of slavery. In the 1920s and 1930s, it was deeply involved in various modernization

campaigns for agriculture. See Belleza, *Evolução do Ministério da Agricultura*, 12; Poliano, *A Sociedade Nacional de Agricultura, resumo histórico*, 24.

102. The *cooperativismo* that Torres Filho supported was an agrarian model of corporatism, and he frequently used the terms *corporatismo* and *cooperativismo* interchangeably. The cooperatives he advocated for would be organized by the state, marking a stark difference with the cooperative movements of the early twentieth century. See Welch, *The Seed Was Planted*, 78–83. On the cooperative moment in Brazil, see Mendonça, *A política de cooperativização agrícola do estado brasileiro*.

103. Torres Filho, *Relatório apresentado ao Dr. Geminiano Lyra Castro por Arthur Torres, Filho*, 5–6.

104. Arthur Torres Filho, "Mussolini e a nova Itália," *Hierarchia* 5 (March–April 1932), 160.

105. Valdemar Falcão, "A representação de classes resume um objetivo natural da democracia integral," 1933, CPDOC, Arquivo Valdemar Falcão, VCR 33.00.00.

106. Charles Gide's *História das doutrinas econômicas* (recently translated into Portuguese), quoted in Arthur Torres Filho, "Justificação de voto," July 3, 1938, AN-RJ, Fundo Conselho de Economia Nacional, lata 253, proc. 771.

107. Torres Filho, "Justificação de voto."

108. Gide, *Principes d'économie politique*. See also Garnsey, "Charles Gide," 293.

109. "O problema da producção do trigo," *O Observador Econômico e Financeiro* (March 1936), 47; *Anuário Estatístico do Brasil: Ano IV, 1938*, 178, 324–29.

110. Oswaldo Aranha to Getúlio Vargas, July 1, 1935, CPDOC, Arquivo Getúlio Vargas, GVc1935.07.01.

111. *Anuário Estatístico do Brasil: Ano IV, 1938*, 331.

112. On nutrition politics in Brazil, see Brinkmann, "Leite e modernidade." On malnutrition during the Vargas era, see Crocitti, "Vargas Era Social Policies."

113. Agamenon Magalhães quoted in Torres Filho, "Justificação de voto."

114. Müller, "Cotrijuí," 100–103.

115. "Exposição de motivos assinada pelo Ministro do Trabalho, Indústria e Comércio," July 1, 1936, AN-RJ, Gabinete Civil da Presidência da República, Congresso Nacional 1936, Lata 81.

116. "O problema da produção do trigo," *O Observador Econômico e Financeiro* (March 1936), 47.

117. Protásio Dornelles Vargas to Getúlio Vargas, April 27, 1937, CPDOC, Arquivo Getúlio Vargas, GVc1937.04/27/7.

118. "A criação do Conselho Nacional de Trigo," *Jornal do Brasil* (February 13, 1936).

119. CFCE Report, "Cultura e moagem de trigo no Brasil," May 2, 1938, AN-RJ, Fundo Conselho de Economia Nacional, lata 249, proc. 744.

120. Valdemar Falcão, "Consulta sobre matéria ventilada em parecer referente ao moinho fluminense," June 30, 1939, CPDOC, Arquivo Valdemar Falcão, VF37.11.12.

121. *Relatório apresentado pela Comissão Central de Compras do Governo Federal em Março de 1935*.

122. Otto Schilling to J. A. Barbosa Carneiro (CFCE president), February 24, 1938, AN-RJ, Fundo Conselho de Economia Nacional, lata 249, proc. 744.

123. João Maria de Lacerda, "Reorganização do Instituto do Açúcar e do Álcool dentro do sistema corporativo," April 5, 1938, AN-RJ, Fundo Conselho de Economia Nacional, lata 249, proc. 752.

124. Lacerda and Moura, *O Estado Novo: Democracia e corporatismo, a posição do Brasil*, 28–29, 33.

125. "As relações comerciais luso-brasileiras," *Diário de Notícias* (October 16, 1937). See also Pereira, *A batalha do futuro*.

126. On the Instituto do Açúcar e do Álcool, see Carli, *História contemporânea do açúcar no Brasil*; Szmrecsányi, *O planejamento da agroindústria canavieira do Brasil*.

127. Lacerda, "Reorganização do Instituto do Açúcar e do Álcool dentro do sistema corporativo."

128. Szmrecsányi, *O planejamento da agroindústria canavieira do Brasil*, 196–201.

129. Guimarães, "O Instituto do Açúcar e do Álcool e a indústria do álcool-motor no primeiro governo vargas."

130. In 1938, Decreto Lei N⁰ 505 extended to workers in sugar and alcohol factories the same labor protections conferred on industrial workers in other sectors—rights later formalized in the 1941 Estatuto da Lavoura Canavieira. Historians have emphasized that this legislation regulating sugarcane farmers and sugar mill workers blurred the boundaries between industrial and rural labor, offering a singular example of how Vargas era labor legislation extended to rural labor. Given the vertical ties between sugar mill owners and the Instituto do Açúcar e do Álcool, however, sugar mill owners were often privileged in labor disputes over workers. On how sugar workers nonetheless seized on these rights and mobilized to access better working conditions, wages, and prices, see McGillivray and Rogers, "Real Labor Movements, Imagined Revolutions."

131. Joaquim Eulálio (CFCE) to Getúlio Vargas, January 17, 1942, AN-RJ, Fundo Conselho de Economia Nacional, lata 274, proc. 1.023.

132. "Trata da conveniência de o Governo Federal regular o fornecimento de carnes e derivados ao consumo nacional," May 28, 1942, AN-RJ, Conselho de Economia Nacional, lata 274, proc. 1.023.

133. "As cooperativas hervateiras e o Instituto Nacional do Mate," July 15, 1940, AN-RJ, Fundo Conselho de Economia Nacional, lata 80, proc. 1.064.

134. Mendonça, *A política de cooperativização agrícola do estado brasileiro*, 77. See also, "Cooperativismo e economia," *O Observador Econômico e Financeiro* (June 1942), 24.

135. "O cooperativismo no Rio Grande do Sul," *O Observador Econômico e Financeiro* (September 1939), 101.

136. Euvaldo Lodi to Getúlio Vargas, July 24, 1940, AN-RJ, Fundo Conselho de Economia Nacional, lata 80, proc. 1.064.

137. João Amado to Odalgiro Corrêa, August 27, 1939, AN-RJ, Fundo Conselho de Economia Nacional, lata 80, proc. 1.064.

138. Economic histories of the First Republic (1889–1930) are largely written through the lens of Brazil's three most powerful regions on account of the administrative decentralization following the fall of the monarchy: São Paulo, Minas Gerais, and Rio Grande do Sul. See Love, *São Paulo in the Brazilian Federation*; Love, *Rio Grande do Sul and Brazilian Regionalism*; Wirth, *Minas Gerais in the Brazilian Federation*. For a review of this literature and how Brazil's trend toward regional autonomy in these decades relates to the seemingly reverse trend toward greater centralization and nation-state building in other parts of the Americas and in Europe and Asia, see Weinstein, "Brazilian Regionalism."

139. See, for example, Weinstein, "Racializing Regional Difference."

140. Diniz, *Empresário, Estado e capitalismo no Brasil*, chap. 6; Diniz, "Engenharia institucional e políticas públicas"; Fonseca, "Instituições e política econômica," 173–77.

141. For post-1945 continuities in wheat-producing experiments, see, for example, Müller, "Cotrijuí."

Chapter 5: Popular and Political Economy

1. Polícia Civil do Distrito Federal, "Auto de apresentação e apreensão," August 11, 1944, AN-RJ, Fundo Tribunal de Segurança Nacional, C8.0.APL.1917, proc. 5.288.

2. "Defesa prévia," September 1944, AN-RJ, Fundo Tribunal de Segurança Nacional, C8.0.APL.1917, proc. 5.288.

3. Pedro Borges da Silva, Ministro do Tribunal de Segurança Nacional, "Sentença," September 11, 1944, AN-RJ, Fundo Tribunal de Segurança Nacional, C8.0.APL.1917, proc. 5.288.

4. Fischer, "Quase Pretos de Tão Pobres?"; Caulfield, *In Defense of Honor*.

5. Tribunal de Segurnaça Nacional, "Confirma-se a sentença apelada . . . ," October 3, 1944, AN-RJ, Fundo Tribunal de Segurança Nacional, C8.0.APL.1917, proc. 5.288.

6. Decreto-Lei Nº869 de 18 de Novembro de 1938: Define os crimes contra a economia popular sua guarda e seu emprego, *Diário Oficial da União* (November 21, 1938).

7. These policing tactics were not new to the Vargas period nor specific to economic crimes. On the broad and discretionary powers exercised by Rio de Janeiro police in the nineteenth century as a mechanism for social control that targeted enslaved persons and people of color, see Chazkel, "Toward a History of Rights in the City at Night."

8. For Kant de Lima, the inquisitorial nature of police investigations is one of the defining characteristics of Brazil's legal system. He explains this feature both in terms of the colonial legal traditions and civil law tradition, in which codes are elaborated by a closed circle of jurists and legal experts, and not subjected to judge-made interpretation to account for context or precedent as in the common law tradition. These currents enshrined a hierarchical legal system. Kant de Lima, "Bureaucratic Rationality in Brazil and in the United States," 161.

9. Campos, "A lei de proteção à economia popular," 174.

10. Campos, *Repressão judicial no Estado Novo*; Oliveira and Siqueira, "Pequeno ensaio sobre a injustiça."

11. *Tribunal de Segurança Nacional: Relatório dos trabalhos realizados em 1944 apresentado em sessão de 30 de Janeiro de 1945 pelo Presidente Ministro Frederico de Barros Barreto*, 7.

12. Estimates are based on the author's calculations using summaries of trial judgments published in *Jurisprudência: Tribunal de Segurança Nacional*, a quarterly government publication in the 1940s, and annual volumes of *Tribunal de Segurança Nacional: Relatório dos trabalhos realizados*, years 1938–45.

13. Campos, *Repressão judicial no Estado Novo*, 99; Dulles, *Sobral Pinto*, 89.

14. On economic crimes in the postwar period, see Silva, "Justiça e ditadura militar no Brasil." See also Pimentel, "Vida e morte do Tribunal do Juri de economia popular."

15. Scholarship on economic citizenship in Latin America has largely focused on the post-1945 period, but historians have noted the origins of these debates in the 1930s, especially in terms of cost of living and food struggles. See Elena, *Dignifying Argentina*; Frens-String, *Hungry for Revolution*; Adair, *In Search of the Lost Decade*. For Brazil, scholars point to Decree Law

No. 869 as the legal origins for consumer protection laws and antitrust laws. See Cabral, "Autoritarismo e gênese antitruste."

16. Lei N° 38 de 4 de Abril de 1935: Define crimes contra a ordem política e social, *Diário Oficial da União* (June 28, 1935).

17. Skidmore, *Politics in Brazil*, 20–24.

18. Debates over the creation of the NST transpired within the Chamber of Deputies and Brazilian press in 1935. See Covello, *A lei de segurança*.

19. Lei N° 244 de 11 de Setembro de 1936: Institue, como orgão da Justiça Militar, o Tribunal de Segurança Nacional, *Diário Oficial da União* (September 12, 1936).

20. Among those tortured and/or convicted by the NST were economist Caio Prado Júnior and novelist Graciliano Ramos. Ramos immortalized the torture he withstood as part of Vargas's communist purge in his memoirs *Memórias do Cárcere*, published posthumously in 1953. Most famous among these cases was that of Luís Carlos Prestes, leader of Brazil's Communist Party. His Jewish German wife, Olga Benario, was deported to Germany, where in 1942, she died in a concentration camp. See Oliveira and Siqueira, "Pequeno ensaio sobre a injustiça," 115–16; Campos, *Repressão judicial no Estado Novo*.

21. On Salgado's exile in Portugal, see Bertonha, "Plínio Salgado, o integralismo brasileiro e as suas relações com Portugal"; Gonçalves, "Plínio Salgado e integralismo."

22. On the rule of law (and lack thereof) in authoritarian contexts, see Raz, "Rule of Law and Its Virtue"; Pereira, "An Ugly Democracy?"; Pereira, *Political (In)Justice*.

23. Preamble to *Constituição dos Estados Unidos do Brasil (de 10 de Novembro de 1937)*.

24. Marcondes, "Malogro da fortuna." For an overview of economic conditions in Brazil in the 1930s, see Leff, *Underdevelopment and Development in Brazil*; Silva, "A era Vargas e a economia."

25. *Constituição da República dos Estados Unidos do Brasil*, Art. 117.

26. "Justificação," December 15, 1933, *Annaes da Assembléa Nacional Constituinte 1933/1934*, Vol. 4, 166–67.

27. *Constituição dos Estados Unidos do Brasil (de 10 de Novembro de 1937)*, Arts. 122 and 141.

28. Decreto-Lei N°869 de 18 de Novembro de 1938, Define os crimes contra a economia popular sua guarda e seu emprego, *Diário Oficial da União* (November 21, 1938).

29. Francisco Campos, "Um mandamento expresso da Constituição," *A Noite* (November 28, 1938), reprinted in Lyra, *Crimes contra a economia popular*, 83.

30. Campos, "A lei de proteção à economia popular," 589.

31. Barbosa, "Os sindicatos corporativistas no Brasil entre os anos de 1934 e 1939."

32. On the rise of *trabalhismo*, or laborism, ideology, see Gomes, *A invenção do trabalhismo*.

33. On coercion and control, see Dinius, "Defending Ordem against Progresso."

34. At the same time, historians such as John French and others emphasize that these new legal channels created spaces for legal activism among workers and the emergence of a legal consciousness about the new rights decreed. On the labor courts in Brazil, see French, *Drowning in Laws*. See also Fortes, "O Estado Novo e os trabalhadores."

35. On how prior governments responded to popular and working-class mobilizations against the rising cost of living, see Meade, "Living Worse and Costing More."

36. On other government efforts to tackle malnutrition and high food prices during the Vargas era, see Crocitti, "Vargas Era Social Policies."

37. "Como vive a populacão de Santo Aleixo," *A Manhã* (May 23, 1935).

38. The figures use the 1939 exchange rate of 16$645 mil-réis per US dollar. See Gordon-Ashworth, "Agricultural Commodity Control under Vargas in Brazil," 105, appendix II. Note that the mil-réis was replaced by the cruzeiro in 1943 and the exchange rate became Cr$16.57 per US dollar.

39. Campos, "A lei de proteção à economia popular," 175.

40. Medici, *Código penal.*

41. Santos, "Francisco Campos e os fundamentos do constitucionalismo antiliberal no Brasil."

42. Campos, "Directrizes do estado nacional," 63.

43. Campos, "Directrizes do estado nacional," 64.

44. Campos, "A lei de proteção à economia popular," 175.

45. Lyra, *Crimes contra a economia popular*, 91.

46. Duarte, *A paisagem legal do Estado Novo*, 119; "*A paisagem legal do Estado Novo*: Entregue às livrarias o novo livro do sr. Gil Duarte," *O Imparcial* (March 4, 1941).

47. Lyra, *Crimes contra a economia popular*, 94.

48. Hungria, *Dos crimes contra a economia popular*, 6. On how racial and class prejudices influenced Hungria's approach to criminology and criminal law, see Fischer, "Quase Pretos de Tão Pobres?," 45–48.

49. Hungria, *Dos crimes contra a economia popular*, 6–7.

50. Quoted in Hungria, *Dos crimes contra a economia popular*, 8.

51. Lyra, *Crimes contra a economia popular*, 96.

52. On legal debates regarding the freedom of contract in the United States, see Horwitz, *The Transformation of American Law*, chap. 2.

53. Cotterrell, "Emmanuel Lévy and Legal Studies," 133. On Lévy's socialist jurisprudence, see Lévy, *La vision socialiste du droit.*

54. While the will theory is often discussed in common law contexts, it also has civil law parallels and remains a controversial assumption. See Kennedy, "From the Will Theory to the Principle of Private Autonomy."

55. Lévy, *Les fondements du droit*, 35.

56. Oliveira Vianna, *Problemas de direito corporativo*, 138, paraphrasing Lévy, *Les fondements du droit*, 34.

57. Oliveira Vianna, *Problemas de direito corporativo*, 137–38.

58. Francisco Campos, quoted in Hungria, *Dos crimes contra a economia popular*, 196.

59. Lyra, *Crimes contra a economia popular*, 84.

60. Art. 4, Decreto-Lei Nº 88 de 20 de Dezembro de 1937: Modifica a Lei Nº 244 de 11 de Setembro de 1936 que instituiu o Tribunal de Segurança Nacional, *Diário Oficial da União* (December 24, 1937).

61. Art. 2, Decreto-Lei Nº 88.

62. Francisco Campos, "Um mandamento expresso da constituição," *A Noite* (November 28, 1938), reprinted in Lyra, *Crimes contra a economia popular*, 89.

63. In 1960, Barros Barreto was appointed president of Brazil's Supreme Federal Court. Like many other Estado Novo jurists, he enjoyed a lengthy legal career. See Costa, *O Supremo Tribunal Federal e a construção da cidadania*, 74, 143.

64. Dulles, *Sobral Pinto*, 89.

65. Loewenstein, *Brazil under Vargas*, 216.

66. Campos, *Repressão judicial no Estado Novo*.

67. Loewenstein, *Brazil under Vargas*, 153.

68. Loewenstein, *Brazil under Vargas*, 212, 218–19.

69. Loewenstein, *Brazil under Vargas*, 154.

70. "A applicação, em São Paulo da Lei de Economia Popular," *Correio da Manhã* (June 22, 1939).

71. "A primeira decisão sobre a Lei de Economia Popular," *Correio da Manhã* (January 5, 1939).

72. "A primeira applicação da Lei de Economia Popular," *Correio da Manhã* (January 25, 1939).

73. "Infractores da Lei da Economia Popular: Denunciados ao Tribunal de Segurança os directores da Caixa Operária de Parahyba," *Correio da Manhã* (March 6, 1939); "Infractores da Lei da Economia Popular," *Correio da Manhã* (July 5, 1939).

74. "A directoria da Caixa Operária da Parahyba perante o Tribunal de Segurança," *Correio da Manhã* (August 18, 1939).

75. "As violações da Lei de Economia Popular: O procurador do Tribunal de Segurança em São Paulo," *Correio da Manhã* (August 25, 1939).

76. Lyra, *Crimes contra a economia popular*, 91.

77. See especially Oliveira Vianna, *Problemas de direito corporativo*. This argument is further elaborated in Teixeira, "Making a Brazilian New Deal."

78. Kennedy, "Three Globalizations of Law and Legal Thought," 41–42.

79. Lawyer Fabio O. Penna, "Um trust de café na capital" (legal brief), November 14, 1939, AN-RJ, Fundo Tribunal de Segurança Nacional, C8.0.APL.665, proc. 1.363.

80. José Segundo da Rocha to Procurador do Tribunal de Segurança Nacional, July 1, 1940, AN-RJ, Fundo Tribunal de Segurança Nacional, C8.0.APL.665, proc. 1.363.

81. Penna, "Um trust de café na capital."

82. Dulles, *Sobral Pinto*, 52–65.

83. Heráclito F. Sobral Pinto to Coronel Augusto Maynard Gomes, Juiz do Tribunal de Segurança Nacional, February 7, 1941, AN-RJ, Fundo Tribunal de Segurança Nacional, C8.0.APL.665, proc. 1.363.

84. Recall, for example, Rodrigues, *Conceitos de valor e preço*, 461.

85. Loewenstein, *Brazil under Vargas*, 325.

86. Fraenkel explained the dual state in terms of the "normative state" and "prerogative state." While Jewish, he was permitted to practice law during the early years of Nazi Germany, and his 1941 *The Dual State* is based on firsthand observations as an attorney at the Berlin Court of Appeals from 1933 to 1938. After 1938, he had to escape into exile. Fraenkel, *The Dual State*, xxiii.

87. Loewenstein, *Brazil under Vargas*, 328.

88. Ministry of Justice civil servant to Francisco Campos, with João Rego's letter attached, January 24, 1939, AN-RJ, Fundo Ministério da Justiça e Negócios Interiores, caixa 373, proc. 825.

89. Denuncia contra um convenio de transportadores de café, 1939, AN-RJ, Fundo Ministério da Justiça e Negócios Interiores, caixa 373, proc. 1213/29.

90. The NST economic trials reveal one of the many ways in which the Estado Novo's corporatist experiment created new channels through which citizens could petition their

government to make appeals to justice, express hardship and frustration, or perhaps a bit of both, with a touch of irony. On the culture of petitioning during the Vargas era, often to Vargas personally, see Fischer, *A Poverty of Rights*, 91–92.

91. Dulles, *The São Paulo Law School and the Anti-Vargas Resistance*, 117, 33–50.

92. Dulles, *The São Paulo Law School and the Anti-Vargas Resistance*, 121–23.

93. Quoted in Dulles, *The São Paulo Law School and the Anti-Vargas Resistance*, 116.

94. H. Sobral Pinto, "O sindicato em face da lei da economia popular," *Jornal do Commércio* (July 19, 1941).

95. Santos, *Cidadania e justiça*; Werneck Vianna, *Liberalismo e sindicato no Brasil*.

96. Quoted in Dulles, *Sobral Pinto*, 114.

97. Similar conflicts unfolded in the United States, as early twentieth-century private efforts to organize industry pricing standards get absorbed into an emergent regulatory state during the New Deal. See Sawyer, *American Fair Trade*.

98. H. Sobral Pinto, "O sindicato em face da lei da economia popular."

99. Lyra, *Crimes contra a economia popular*, 148–49.

100. Decreto Nº 9.860 de 24 de Dezembro de 1938: Cria a Secretaria Geral do Conselho de Expansão Econômica do Estado de S. Paulo, *Diário Oficial do Estado de São Paulo—E.U. do Brasil* (December 25, 1938).

101. Vanda Maria Ribeiro Costa discusses how the Conselho de Expansão Econômica do Estado de São Paulo functioned as a forum for state-led development, but how it also became an instrument that business interests could use for personal gain. Costa, *A armadilha do Leviatã*, 160. It is important to note as well that in the case of São Paulo, the creation of these new political institutions coincided with a shift in the ruling class as a new class of self-fashioned experts and industrialists replaced landed oligarchies and rural political bosses. For a quantitative overview, see Condato, "A formação do campo político profissional no Brasil."

102. Petition from the Associação Comercial de São Paulo, Federação das Indústrias do Estado de São Paulo, and Federação Comercial do Estado de São Paulo to Justice Minister Francisco Campos, presented at the Conselho de Expansão Econômica do Estado de São Paulo, March 7, 1939, APESP, Secretaria do Governo, Conselho de Expansão Econômica do Estado de São Paulo, Livro de Atas e Decretos, vol. 2, caixa I, ordem 9397.

103. Petition from the Associação Comercial de São Paulo, Federação das Indústrias do Estado de São Paulo, and Federação Comercial do Estado de São Paulo to Justice Minister Francisco Campos, presented at the Conselho de Expansão Econômica do Estado de São Paulo, December 22, 1938, APESP, Secretaria do Governo, Conselho de Expansão Econômica do Estado de São Paulo, caixa VII, ordem 9403.

104. Conselho de Expansão Econômica do Estado de São Paulo, Parecer Nº32, February 28, 1939, AN-RJ, Fundo Conselho de Economia Nacional, lata 269, proc. 996.

105. CFCE deputy Joaquim Costa Mello, September 26, 1939, AN-RJ, Fundo Conselho de Economia Nacional, Lata 269, proc. 996.

106. In October 1939, Decree Law No. 1.716 acknowledged the importance of investigations carried out by economic regulatory bodies. For the NST, these sorts of technical reports were now on an equal footing with police investigations. Decreto-Lei Nº 1.716 de 28 de Outubro de 1939: Dispõe sobre a configuração e o julgamento dos crimes contra a economia popular, *Diário Oficial da União* (October 31, 1939).

107. Silva Gordo, *O caso da Northern*, 10.

108. "A 'São Paulo Northern Railroad Co.' e suas actividades no Brasil," *O Jornal* (December 16, 1938).

109. "O caso Paul Deleuse," *Jornal do Commércio* (April 23, 1939).

110. Lesser, *Welcoming the Undesirables*, 2–3.

111. Loewenstein, *Brazil under Vargas*, 323.

112. "A fortuna de Deleuze," *O Jornal* (November 16, 1939).

113. Loewenstein, *Brazil under Vargas*, 322.

114. On institutions and development, see North and Weingast, "Constitutions and Commitment." On institution making and development in Latin America, see Summerhill, *Inglorious Revolution*; Sikkink, *Ideas and Institutions*; Adelman, *Republic of Capital*.

115. Authoritarian regimes often claim legitimacy by promising economic growth and development, with reliable courts and the rule of law conceded (for the market) as necessary prerequisites to support growth, foreign direct investment, or international trade. Political scientists have pointed to this trend in Latin American dictatorships in the 1960s to the 1980s, even though in practice such guarantees were not absolute. See Pereira, "An Ugly Democracy?"; Moustafa, "Law and Courts in Authoritarian Regimes"; O'Donnell, *Modernization and Bureaucratic-Authoritarianism*.

116. On police control over street sellers of foods and other basic provisions during the First Republic, with attention to the place of immigrants in urban markets, see Acerbi, *Street Occupations*.

117. For the early twentieth century, historian Sidney Chalhoub uses criminal proceedings to examine social tensions in Brazil's postabolition society, illuminating the many ways in which the working classes endured social exclusion and various forms of insecurity in the face of a sometimes arbitrary public power. Chalhoub, *Trabalho, lar e botequim*.

118. "Classificação do delito," November 4, 1939, AN-RJ, Fundo Tribunal de Segurança Nacional, C8.0.APL.0425, proc. 861.

119. São Paulo Departamento de Ordem Política e Social, "Termo de declarações," September 27, 1939, AN-RJ, Fundo Tribunal de Segurança Nacional, C8.0.APL.0425, proc. 861.

120. São Paulo Departamento de Ordem Política e Social, "Testemunhas," October 9, 1939, AN-RJ, Fundo Tribunal de Segurança Nacional, C8.0.APL.0425, proc. 861.

121. "Mandado," December 2, 1939, AN-RJ, Fundo Tribunal de Segurança Nacional, C8.0.APL.0425, proc. 861.

122. "Mandado," December 11, 1939, AN-RJ, Fundo Tribunal de Segurança Nacional, C8.0.APL.0425, proc. 861.

123. Gomes, *A invenção do trabalhismo*.

124. Pedro Borges da Silva, Juiz do Tribunal de Segurança Nacional, 23 February 1940, Fundo Tribunal de Segurança Nacional, C8.0.APL.0425, proc. 861.

125. Smail, *The Consumption of Justice*.

126. Historian Amy Chazkel similarly asks if popular denunciations might have been an opportunity for airing complaints as so often they resulted in juridical "dead ends." Chazkel, *Laws of Chance*, 239.

127. Thompson, "The Moral Economy of the English Crowd in the Eighteenth Century," 79.

128. Historians have reached similar conclusions about how people petitioned Estado Novo institutions in other arenas, especially in labor issues. See Fischer, *A Poverty of Rights*; French, *Drowning in Laws*.

129. Lyra, *Crimes contra a economia popular*, 84.

130. "Economia Popular," *O Observador Econômico e Financeiro* (December 1938): 100.

131. Alceu Amoroso Lima in *O Jornal* (March 25, 1945), quoted in Dulles, *Sobral Pinto*, ix.

Chapter 6: Wartime Economics

1. Lochery, *Brazil*, 138.

2. For a social and political history of the US bases, especially in terms of labor relations, see Herman, *Cooperating with the Colossus*.

3. Lochery, *Brazil*, 176.

4. Telo, *Os Açores e o controlo do Atlântico*.

5. On the question of Portugal's role in the Holocaust, Irene Pimentel and Cláudia Ninhos have published several works on the Estado Novo's relationship to Nazi Germany as well as the antisemitic sentiments of some Portuguese statespeople. Their work largely focuses on how Lisbon became a secure port for refugees looking to escape Nazi persecution. Pimentel and Ninhos, *Salazar, Portugal e o Holocausto*. See also Pimentel, *Judeus em Portugal durante a II Guerra Mundial*; Pimentel and Ninhos, "Portugal, Jewish Refugees, and the Holocaust."

6. On espionage activity in wartime Lisbon, see Pimentel, *Espiões em Portugal durante a II Guerra mundial*. See also Peiss, *Information Hunters*.

7. Instituto Nacional do Pão, "Auto de notícia," July 7, 1943, AHM, Tribunal Militar Especial Económico, proc. 1098/43S, livro 6, folhas 99v.

8. Decreto-lei Nº29.964, *Diário do Govêrno* (October 10, 1939).

9. For a comprehensive overview of the economic crisis in Portugal during the war, see Rosas, *Portugal entre a paz e a guerra*.

10. Lains, "Growth in a Protected Environment," 149–52, statistical appendix, table A1 on output and production.

11. Rosas, *Portugal entre a paz e a guerra*, 135–36, 282–83.

12. Reports on rationing differ but generally approximate these values. The values listed here are taken from Rosas, *Portugal entre a paz e a guerra*, 287. See also "A vida em Lisboa durante a Guerra," *Política* 2, no. 1 (September 1944).

13. Telegram from Águeda (Aveiro District), September 1939, ANTT, Secretaria-Geral da Presidência do Conselho de Ministros, Gabinete do Presidente, SGPCM/GPC caixa 20, proc. 232/10, Nº 9.

14. Telegram Lamego to Castelo Branco, September 1939, ANTT, Secretaria-Geral da Presidência do Conselho de Ministros, Gabinete do Presidente, SGPCM/GPC caixa 20, proc. 232/10, Nº 9.

15. Telegram Porto to Lisbon, September 14, 1939, ANTT, Secretaria-Geral da Presidência do Conselho de Ministros, Gabinete do Presidente, SGPCM/GPC caixa 20, procº 232/10, Nº 9.

16. Minister of Interior to António de Oliveira Salazar, September 27, 1939, ANTT, Secretaria-Geral da Presidência do Conselho de Ministros, Gabinete do Presidente, SGPCM/GPC caixa 20, proc. 232/10, Nº 9.

17. Rosas, *Portugal entre a paz e a guerra*, 303.

18. Comissão de Inquérito aos Elementos da Organização Corporativa, "Relatório sobre peixe fresco," 1947, ANTT, Arquivo Oliveira Salazar, AOS/CO/PC-17B, pt.1.

19. As historian Adam Tooze describes for Nazi Germany, early efforts at corporatist-like experiments gave way to a total war-planning machine. Tooze, *The Wages of Destruction*.

20. Garrido, *Queremos uma economia nova!*, 118–22.

21. António de Oliveira Salazar to labor sindicato leaders, July 14, 1942, ANTT, Arquivo Oliveira Salazar, AOS/CO/PC/10B.

22. "Casas do povo resumo," July 1942, ANTT, Arquivo Oliveira Salazar, AOS/CO/PC/10B.

23. "Resumo das receitas e despesas das casas do povo," 1941–42, ANTT, Arquivo Oliveira Salazar, AOS/CO/PC-10B.

24. *Anuário Estatístico-1945*, 93.

25. Workers also continued to protest the dismantling of autonomous labor unions as police surveillance did not subside. Labor militancy continued in rural areas too, especially in southern Portugal, a region defined by the latifundial system and waged labor.

26. Instituto Nacional do Pão, "Auto de notícia," July 7, 1943.

27. A summary gleaned from the hundreds of case files consulted within the Archive of the Inspecção Geral dos Serviços de Fiscalização dos Géneros Alimentícios at the ANTT.

28. Lawyer [signature illegible] to Presidente do Tribunal Military Especial de Lisboa, n.d., AHM, Tribunal Military Especial Económico, proc. 1098/43S, livro 6, folhas 99v.

29. See the catalog for Tribunal Militar Especial Económico at AHM.

30. Lawyer [signature illegible] to Presidente do Tribunal Military Especial de Lisboa, n.d.,

31. Tribunal Militar Especial Secção de Lisboa, "Acta da audiência de julgamento," August 15, 1944, AHM, Tribunal Military Especial Económico, proc. 1098/43S, livro 6, folhas 99v.

32. Decreto Nº18.640, *Diário do Govêrno* (July 19, 1930).

33. Serrão, *História de Portugal*, 13:88; Rosas and Pimentel, *Tribunais políticos*, 16.

34. Tribunal Militar Especial president Coronel Joaquim Inacio de Barcelos Junior to António de Oliveira Salazar, January 7, 1946, ANTT, Secretaria-Geral da Presidência do Conselho de Ministros, Gabinete do Presidente, SGPCP/GPC, proc. 932/71, Nº 4.

35. Governo Civil de Faro to Direcção Geral de Administração Política e Civil, Ministério do Interior, April 30, 1942, ANTT, Arquivo Ministério do Interior, DGAPC, Lv89-A, proc Z-4/11, mç 1155.

36. On France, see Mouré, "Food Rationing and the Black Market in France." For the United States, see Hart-Landsberg, "Popular Mobilization and Progressive Policy Making"; Jacobs, *Pocketbook Politics*, chap. 5; Jacobs, "How about Some Meat?"

37. Even in liberal contexts such as the United States, World War I and especially World War II marked a turning poin. See Atanassow and Katznelson, "Negotiating the Rule of Law," 52–53. As Rohit De explains for late colonial India, draconian criminal laws were introduced to enforce economic controls because "regulating the economy was no longer viewed as the domain of the private." De, "Commodities Must Be Controlled," 292.

38. On Vichy and corporatism, see Le Crom, *Syndicats, nous voilà!*

39. Mouré, "Marcel Aymé and the Moral Economy of Penury in Occupied France," 714.

40. Pétain, quoted in Mouré, "Marcel Aymé and the Moral Economy of Penury in Occupied France," 714.

41. Saraiva, *Fascist Pigs*, 82–83. On the price commission, see Ernest Martin, *Price Control in Nazi Germany*.

42. Tooze, *The Wages of Destruction*, 192–94.

43. Zierenberg, *Berlin's Black Market*.

44. Ernest Martin, *Price Control in Nazi Germany*, 15.

45. On the shift from state directed to state controlled, see Tooze, *The Wages of Destruction*; James, "Banks and Business Politics in Nazi Germany"; Link, *Forging Global Fordism*.

46. Historian Fernando Rosas suggests that preferential treatment for members of casas do povo was not official policy but instead a well-established practice by those administering rations; he notes how one official defended this practice by calling out the skepticism and selfish interests of anyone who refused to join corporatist organs. Rosas, *Portugal entre a paz e a guerra*, 278–79.

47. The continued reliance on charity (often Catholic charities) to fill in the gaps of the welfare state is another parallel between Portugal's corporatist system and that in Brazil. On Brazil, charity, and Vargas era social security, see Fischer, *A Poverty of Rights*, 136–42; Otovo, *Progressive Mothers, Better Babies*, chap. 5.

48. Gonçalves, *O Estado Novo e a Assembléa Nacional*, 20.

49. Formally abolished in 1928, forced labor nonetheless persisted, including under new legal measures. See Kagan Guthrie, *Bound for Work*; Bender, *Angola under the Portuguese*.

50. Junta de Exportação dos Cereais das Colónias, "Relatório," 1947, ANTT, Arquivo Oliveira Salazar, AOS/CO/PC-17C.

51. Vieira, *Angola*, 211.

52. Junta de Exportação dos Cereais das Colónias, "Relatório."

53. "Memorial," October 12, 1939, ANTT, Secretaria-Geral da Presidência do Conselho de Ministros, Gabinete do Presidente, caixa 31, proc. 250/15, Nº 8.

54. Alfredo da Silva (Companhia União Fabril) to José Lourenço Vasco de Carvalho (soap consortium representative), October 10, 1939, ANTT, Secretaria-Geral da Presidência do Conselho de Ministros, Gabinete do Presidente, caixa 31, proc. 250/15, Nº 8.

55. "Memorial," October 12, 1939, ANTT, Secretaria-Geral da Presidência do Conselho de Ministros, Gabinete do Presidente, caixa 31, proc. 250/15, Nº 8.

56. Neto, "De escravos a 'serviçais,' de 'serviçais' a 'contratados.'"

57. Contraband was, of course, not new to corporatist imperial pacts. Indeed, there is an expanding historiography on contraband and mercantilist systems. See, for example, Kwass, *Contraband*.

58. Alfredo da Silva to José Lourenço Vasco de Carvalho, October 7, 1939, ANTT, Secretaria-Geral da Presidência do Conselho de Ministros, Gabinete do Presidente, caixa 31, proc. 250/15, Nº 8.

59. Alfredo da Silva to José Lourenço Vasco de Carvalho, October 11, 1939, ANTT, Secretaria-Geral da Presidência do Conselho de Ministros, Gabinete do Presidente, caixa 31, proc. 250/15, Nº 8.

60. Godinho, "Desde a idade de seis anos, fui muito contrabandista," 41. Political refugees also crossed this porous border to flee the Francoist regime, which in all likelihood, was far more troubling for Salazar and his secret police given the regime's ardent anticommunism. See Lanero Táboas, Míguez Macho, and Gallardo, "La 'raia' galaico-portuguesa en tiempos convulsos," 62–63. On the Spanish Civil War, see Seidman, *The Victorious Counterrevolution*.

61. Ministério da Economia, Inspecção Geral das Indústrias e Comércio Agrícolas, "Mapa da actuação das brigadas para repressão de exportação ilegítima de mercadorias," September 14–20,

1941, ANTT, Secretaria-Geral da Presidência do Conselho de Ministros, Gabinete do Presidente, caixa 62, proc. Nº 2.

62. Contraband networks adapted to changing economic times and specific commodity demands. This long history of contraband along the *raia*, or border, was punctuated according to the *tempo dos ovos, tempo da farinha, tempo do minério, tempo do café, tempo do gado,* and so on. Each commodity required a particular organizational structure for warehousing, transportation, and distribution, inspiring new tactics. See Lanero Táboas, Míguez Macho, and Gallardo, "La 'raia' galaico-portuguesa en tiempos convulsos," 19.

63. On the making and consequences of this process of defining territorial borders between Spain and Portugal, see Herzog, *Frontiers of Possession.*

64. Ministério da Economia, Inspecção Geral das Indústrias e Comércio Agrícolas, "Repressão do comércio ilegítimo de mercadorias: Estatutos dos relatórios semanais," November 30–December 6, 1941, ANTT, Secretaria-Geral da Presidência do Conselho de Ministros, Gabinete do Presidente, caixa 62, proc. 10.

65. Lanero Táboas, Míguez Macho, and Gallardo, "La 'raia' galaico-portuguesa en tiempos convulsos," 72.

66. Coffee was the third most frequent contraband commodity, after textiles and foodstuffs. Godinho, "Desde a idade de seis anos, fui muito contrabandista," 102–3.

67. Ministério da Economia, Inspecção Geral das Indústrias e Comércio Agrícolas, "Repressão do comércio ilegítimo de mercadorias," September 7–13, 1941, ANTT, Secretaria-Geral da Presidência do Conselho de Ministros, Gabinete do Presidente, caixa 62, proc. 1.

68. Clemente Fernandes, April 9, 1943, *Diário das Sessões da Assembleia Nacional,* III Legislatura, Sessão Legislativa 1, no. 4 (April 9, 1943), 425.

69. Rosas and Pimentel, *Tribunais políticos.*

70. There is a vast literature on "everyday forms of resistance" in peasant communities. For some initial theoretical considerations, see Scott, *Weapons of the Weak.* Building on this, for a review essay on how everyday forms of resistance can shape not only community consciousness and popular culture but also the very process of state formation, see Joseph and Nugent, "Popular Culture and State Formation in Revolutionary Mexico."

71. Godinho, "Desde a idade de seis anos, fui muito contrabandista."

72. "Repressão do comércio ilegítimo de mercadorias," September 7–13, 1941.

73. Ministério da Economia, Inspecção Geral das Indústrias e Comercio Agrícolas, "Mapa da actuação das brigadas para repressão de exportação ilegítima de mercadorias," December 14–20 1941, ANTT, Secretaria-Geral da Presidência do Conselho de Ministros, Gabinete do Presidente, caixa 62, proc. Nº 12.

74. "Mapa da actuação das brigadas para repressão de exportação ilegítima de mercadorias," December 14–20, 1941.

75. Program for welcome event for Brazil's Missão Especial, July 1941, ANTT, Arquivo Oliveira Salazar, AOS/CO/PC22A.

76. Ferro, "Algumas palavras de António Ferro," i.

77. To be sure, globalism or transnationalism has never been an inherently or exclusively liberal democratic project, but corporatism seems, at first, harder to reconcile with globalism on account of the emphasis on national self-sufficiency and renewal. On how internationalism and nationalism were in fact constructed *in tandem* along the twentieth century, see Sluga,

Internationalism in the Age of Nationalism. On undemocratic global visions of the liberal variety, see Slobodian, *Globalists.*

78. Quoted in "Continua recebendo homenagens a embaixada especial portuguesa," *Correio da Manhã* (August 12, 1941).

79. Espínola, "Discurso do Presidente do Supremo Tribunal Federal."

80. Falcão, "O corporativismo e o regime político brasileiro," 231.

81. Falcão, "O corporativismo e o regime político brasileiro," 231, 234.

82. Caetano, "Intercâmbio da cultura jurídica de Portugal e do Brasil," 230.

83. See, for example, Kiernan, *Blood and Soil.*

84. See, for example, Weinstein, *The Color of Modernity.*

85. There is a vast literature on Freyre and his writings. For intellectual biographies, see Burke and Pallares-Burke, *Gilberto Freyre*; Skidmore, "Raízes de Gilberto Freyre."

86. Several prominent Brazilian intellectuals and officials became invested in this project to rebrand Portugal's image as a "good colonizer" in the 1930s. Freyre is perhaps the best known in this camp, but Lusophilia, as historian Daryle Williams notes, also became part of Vargas's propaganda efforts to celebrate national renewal. Williams, *Culture Wars in Brazil,* 227–29. For a recent collection of essays that explores the global power and influence of Freyre's concept of luso-tropicalism, see Anderson, Roque, and Santos, *Luso-Tropicalism and Its Discontents.*

87. Freyre, *Uma cultura ameaçada,* 50.

88. The speech also circulated in print, with the first edition quickly selling out, and subsequent editions in Spanish and English. See Freyre, *Uma cultura ameaçada,* 5.

89. Léonard, "Salazarisme et lusotropicalisme, histoire d'une appropriation"; Castelo, *"O modo português de estar no mundo."* See also Castelo, "Gilberto Freyre's View of Miscegenation and Its Circulation in the Portuguese Empire, 1930s–1960s."

90. Burke and Pallares-Burke, *Gilberto Freyre,* 119.

91. Jane Braga to Sherry Mangan (letter intercepted by Brazilian authorities), August 22, 1941, CPDOC, Arquivo Getúlio Vargas, GV confid 1941.08.22/2.

92. Graham, *Shifting the Meaning of Democracy.*

93. Conselho Federal de Comércio Exterior, "Ofícios," April 17, 1936, Itamaraty Archive, Rio de Janeiro.

94. Conselho Federal de Comércio Exterior, "Ofícios," July 18, 1940, Itamaraty Archive, Rio de Janeiro.

95. Letter to António de Oliveira Salazar from [unknown], February 24, 1938, ANTT, Arquivo Oliveira Salazar, AOS/CO/PC-22.

96. On the various diplomatic and political uses of international expositions, see the collection of essays in Leerssen and Storm, *World Fairs and the Global Moulding of National Identities.*

97. António Ferro, "Relatório sobre as projectadas comemorações de 1939–1940," February 24, 1938, ANTT, Arquivo Oliveira Salazar, AOS/CO/PC-22.

98. Cayolla, *Pavilhão da colonização na exposição do mundo português,* 5.

99. Oswaldo Aranha to General Francisco José Pinto, April 12, 1940, CPDOC, Arquivo Oswaldo Aranha, OA cp 1940.04.12.

100. Fontes, "Unidade espiritual por Lourival Fontes," 1.

101. For economic comparisons, see Maddison, *The World Economy.*

102. João Neves da Fontoura to Getúlio Vargas, August 5, 1943, CPDOC, Arquivo Oswaldo Aranha, OA cp 1943.01.29.

103. João Neves da Fontoura to Oswaldo Aranha, October 21, 1943, CPDOC, Arquivo Oswaldo Aranha, OA cp 1943.01.29.

104. Letter forwarded to Getúlio Vargas, January 20, 1940, CPDOC, Arquivo Getúlio Vargas, GV c 1941.01.20.

105. Report on Vargas's speech, Delegacia Especial de Segurança Política e Social, June 12, 1940, CPDOC, Arquivo Getúlio Vargas, GV c 1940.06.11.

106. A. V. Dindsey to "Times" Magazine (letter intercepted by Brazilian authorities), June 1941, CPDOC, Arquivo Getúlio Vargas, GV confid 1941.07.26.

107. Patterson, "Salazar, the Inspirer of Portugal's New State," 249.

108. Unpublished interview with António de Oliveira Salazar, April 18, 1937, ANTT, Arquivo Oliveira Salazar, AOS/CO/PC-18.

109. Chilean diplomat to Oswaldo Aranha, August 2, 1940, CPDOC, Arquivo Getúlio Vargas, GV c 1940.06.22/3.

110. "Fechada a Faculdade de Direito de São Paulo," *Correio da Manhã* (October 1, 1941); "Universidade de S. Paulo," *Correio Paulistano* (October 4, 1941).

111. Plínio Salgado (exiled in Lisbon), (letter intercepted by Brazilian authorities), October 4, 1941, CPDOC, Arquivo Getúlio Vargas, GV confid 1941.10.04/1.

112. Falcão, "O corporativismo e o regime político brasileiro," 232.

113. Oliveira Vianna, *Problemas de direito sindical*, xiii–xiv.

114. Procurador Eduardo Jara, "Classificação do delito," June 20, 1940, AN-RJ, Fundo Tribunal de Segurança Nacional, C8.0.APL.0713, proc. 1.069.

115. Lawyer for Otto Ries and Genuino Ferreira da Silva, written statement to the NST, June 18, 1940, AN-RJ, Fundo Tribunal de Segurança Nacional, C8.0.APL.0713, proc. 1.069.

116. Calculated by the author from data in Villela and Suzigan, *Política do governo e crescimento da economia brasileira, 1889-1945*, table VII.

117. *Anúario Estatístico do Brasil: Ano VI 1941–1945*, 246.

118. Calculated from data in *Anúario Estatístico do Brasil: Ano VI 1941–1945*, 53–55.

119. "Contra a alta dos gêneros," *Correio da Manhã* (September 10, 1939).

120. "Os julgamentos hontem realizados no tribunal de segurança," *Correio da Manhã* (January 4, 1940).

121. Costa and Netto, "O Instituto Rio Grandense do Arroz."

122. Corsi, "Política externa, projeto nacional e política econômica ao final do Estado Novo," 81.

123. "Indústria da soda cáustica no Brasil: Outra resolução do Conselho Federal de Comercio Exterior aprovada pelo Presidente da República," *O Dia* (July 17, 1943).

124. Decreto-Lei Nº 1.641 de 29 de Setembro de 1939: Dispõe sobre a criação o funcionamento da Comissão de Defesa da Economia Nacional," *Diário Oficial da União* (October 2, 1939)

125. Decreto Nº 10.358 de 1 de Setembro de 1942: Declara o estado de guerra em todo o território nacional, *Diário Oficial da União* (September 1, 1942).

126. CFCE deputy Gileno de Carli, September 14, 1942, AN-RJ, Fundo Conselho de Economia Nacional, lata 85, proc. 1.234.

127. "Plano de mobilização economica," CFCE memorandum, September 9, 1942, AN-RJ, Fundo Conselho de Economia Nacional, lata 85, proc. 1.234.

128. Decreto-Lei Nº 4,750 de 28 September 1942: Mobiliza os recursos econômicos do Brasil, e dá outras providências, retrieved from AN-RJ, Fundo Conselho de Economia Nacional, lata

85, proc. 1.234-V3. On João Neves da Fontoura and his enthusiastic support for the Constitutionalist Movement, see Weinstein, *The Color of Modernity*, 104, 154. He would, like many others aligned with the Paulista rebellion, later work closely with Vargas and take on several key positions in the Estado Novo.

129. Draibe, *Rumos e metamorfoses*, 111.

130. On labor migration to the Amazon during World War II, see Garfield, "The Environment of Wartime Migration."

131. "O abastecimento do D. Federal," *O Observador Econômico e Financeiro* (July 1943), 49, 58.

132. "Distrito Federal: Produção do núcleo Santa Cruz," *O Observador Econômico e Financeiro* (June 1944), 133.

133. President of Sindicato dos Lavradores do Distrito Federal to Minister of Labor, February 2, 1944, AN-B, Fundo Ministério do Trabalho, Indústria e Comércio, Reconhecimento Sindical, caixa 1, proc. 7524.

134. Luna and Klein, *The Economic and Social History of Brazil since 1889*, 115, 106.

135. Labor sindicatos were concentrated in industrializing southeastern regions to not only organize workers' interests but also serve as a tool by which the government could control labor to increase industrial production. See Wolfe, *Working Women, Working Men*; French, *The Brazilian Workers' ABC*.

136. Historian Cliff Welch explores, for example, how rural workers in São Paulo seized on new institutions and legislation, as limited as they might have been, to mobilize for their political inclusion and better social and economic conditions. Welch, *The Seed Was Planted*.

137. Art. 58 Decreto-Lei Nº 1.402 de 5 de Julho de 1939: Regula a associação em sindicato, *Diário Oficial da União* (July 1939). Rural workers were also excluded from or progressively marginalized within labor and welfare systems in other countries too. In the United States, agriculture workers were excluded from New Deal welfare protections to appease southern Democrats, who wanted to uphold the Jim Crow regime. See Katznelson, *Fear Itself*, chap. 5. In Mexico, industrialism overshadowed agriculture in the 1930s and 1940s. See Gauss, *Made in Mexico*.

138. "Instalou-se, ontem, a Comissão de Sindicalização Rural," *Gazeta de Notícias* (September 30, 1944).

139. Cardozo, *Sindicatos rurais na federação*, 75, 85.

140. According to Oliveira Vianna and other corporatists, each professional association should only represent a single industry, and there should only be one legally recognized association for each region. For industrialists, especially powerful Paulista business leaders, this corporatist approach required that they disband their preexisting professional associations. On Oliveira Vianna's resignation, see Costa, *Origens do corporativismo brasileiro*, 41–65.

141. Simonsen, *Ensaios sociais, políticos e econômicos*, 113.

142. Calculated from data in Maddison, *The Political Economy of Poverty, Equity, and Growth*, 215.

143. Setor Preços: Resolução Nº 52, Gabinete do Coordenador da Mobilização Econômica, April 30, 1943, AN-RJ, Fundo Concelho de Economia Nacional, lata 288, proc. 1.167.

144. Setor preços: homologação, *Diário Oficial* (January 25, 1943), retrieved from AN-RJ, Fundo Concelho de Economia Nacional, lata 288, proc. 1.167.

145. Instruções Nº 3, *Diário Oficial* (April 22,1943), retrieved from AN-RJ, Fundo Concelho de Economia Nacional, lata 288, proc. 1.167.

146. "O abastecimento do D. Federal," 51.

147. The interwar origins of postwar price control policy in Brazil is often acknowledged by scholars but rarely explored. See Mata, "Controles de preços na economia brasileira."

148. "O abastecimento do D. Federal," 51.

149. Labor Minister Alexandre Marcondes Filho to Getúlio Vargas, March 4, 1942, AN-RJ, Fundo Concelho de Economia Nacional, lata 288, proc. 1,167.

150. *Anúario Estatístico do Brasil: Ano VI 1941–1945*, 302–5.

151. Mitchell, "Fixing the Economy."

152. On women and World War II price controls, see Jacobs, "How about Some Meat?"

153. "O abastecimento do D. Federal," 51.

154. "As donas de casa na Comissão de Preços," *A Noite* (January 21, 1943).

155. "A mulher brasileira na defesa da economia popular," *A Noite* (January 23, 1943).

156. For Chile during these years, women also pushed for greater state intervention to guarantee access to essential foods at fair prices, albeit in a political context defined by the Popular Front in which it was socialist groups advocating for national price controls. See Frens-String, *Hungry for Revolution*, 48–53.

157. Hardly any scholarship exists on women's subcommittees in Brazil. That the practice of economic citizenship was gendered in Brazil, however, fits into a broader story of gendered citizenship in Latin America. See Alvarez, *Engendering Democracy in Brazil*; Rosemblatt, *Gendered Compromises*.

158. "O abastecimento do D. Federal," 51.

159. "O abastecimento do D. Federal," 51.

160. While the number of trials in 1943 surpassed the total number of trials for the 1937–39 period, the peak of political purges, the number of individuals indicted in 1943 still did not surpass the number of individuals indicted in 1938, the year that recorded the largest number of political trials, given how many defendants were tried per political trial. *Tribunal de Segurança Nacional: Relatório dos trabalhos realizados durante o ano de 1938 apresentado em sessão de 30 de Janeiro de 1939 pelo Presidente Desembargador Frederico de Barros Barreto; Tribunal de Segurança Nacional: Relatório dos trabalhos realizados em 1943 apresentado em sessão de 28 de Janeiro de 1944 pelo Presidente Ministro Frederico de Barros Barreto*.

161. *Jurisprudência: Tribunal de Segurança Nacional*, proc. 3.172, 14:29–30.

162. Campos, *Repressão judicial no Estado Novo*, 116.

163. Historian Sueann Caulfield notes that one of the goals of nineteenth-century liberal legal reformers had been to update the inherited colonial legal system such as the Philippine Ordinances along with the ways in which they had authorized the use of law to satisfy private vengeance and patriarchal privileges. New nineteenth- and twentieth-century codes, however, continued to uphold the concepts of morality and honor that in turn had upheld those privileges. Caulfield, *In Defense of Honor*, chap. 1.

164. On how lawsuits over insults and dishonoring words can reveal the moral and cultural codes that people used to define social inclusion and exclusion, see Gotkowitz, "Trading Insults."

165. Fischer, "Quase Pretos de Tão Pobres?"

166. Processo-crime de Hermínio Bérgami, Rio de Janeiro, August 8, 1944, AN-RJ, Fundo Tribunal de Segurança Nacional, C8.0.APL.1941, proc. 5.184.

167. NST judges would sometimes, but not always, note in their judgments if they suspected that a denunciation was motivated by personal feuds.

168. On how samba became a marker of Brazilian national identity in the 1930s, see McCann, *Hello, Hello Brazil*; Hertzman, *Making Samba*.

169. "Relatório: O Brasil na guerra," July 4, 1944, ANTT, Arquivo Oliveira Salazar, AOS/CO/NE-2A1.

170. *Jurisprudência: Tribunal de Segurança Nacional*, proc. 1.415, 1:21–23.

171. "O problema da carestia: A vida pela hora da morte," *Diário Carioca* (January 19, 1944).

172. "Conferência pública sobre alimentação," *Diário Carioca* (January 1, 1944).

173. "Abastecimento, preços e crise de hospedagem," *O Observador Econômico e Financeiro* (June 1944): 72.

174. Jorge Felippe Kafuri to João Alberto, 1943, reprinted in "Nova etapa na mobilização econômica," *Gazeta de Notícias* (July 23, 1943).

175. A few decades later, Brazilian economists formalized this idea into a structural explanation of inflation that underpinned emerging theories of underdevelopment and dependency.

176. Processo-crime de João Ferreira Guimarães e Guilmar Gomes Ferreira, Rio de Janeiro, July 31, 1944, AN-RJ, Fundo Tribunal de Segurança Nacional, C8.0.APL.1915, proc. 4.365.

177. Loewenstein, *Brazil under Vargas*, 230.

178. Eugênio Gudin, "Rumos da política econômica," reprinted in Simonsen and Gudin, *A controvérsia do planejamento na economia brasileira*, 55.

179. Gudin, quoted in Simonsen and Gudin, *A controvérsia do planejamento na economia brasileira*, 54.

180. Brazilian political scientist Camila Rocha shows how the translation of Hayek's *The Road to Serfdom* in 1946 into Portuguese was motivated by the rise of a liberal Catholic movement in Brazil as she finds early promarket writings in Catholic journals. In other words, as much as Catholicism underpinned the rise of corporatism in the 1930s, conservative Catholic elites were hardly all corporatist, and also found ways to unite Catholicism to their promarket ideology in the 1940s and 1950s. Rocha, *Menos Marx, mais Mises*, 36–39.

181. Bielschowsky, *Pensamento econômico brasileiro*, 7. While some neoliberals in North America or Europe like Hayek or Frank Knight were products of and tied to university settings, neoliberal thought was also produced outside universities. The Mont Pelerine Society, for example, included businesspeople, journalists, and so on. See Burgin, *The Great Persuasion*; Slobodian, *Globalists*.

182. Dinius, *Brazil's Steel City*.

183. Junta de Exportação dos Cereais das Colónias, "Relatório."

Chapter 7: Corporatism to Planning

1. Young, "The Age of Global Power"; Geyer and Bright, "World History in a Global Age"; Eckes and Zeiler, *Globalization and the American Century*; Westad, *The Global Cold War*.

2. Levine, *Father of the Poor?*, 69–74.

3. Alexandre Marcondes Filho to Getúlio Vargas, 1944–45, CPDOC, Arquivo Alexandre Marcondes Filho, AMF43.00.00/2pi.

4. Levine, *Father of the Poor?*; Dávila, "Myth and Memory"; Fonseca, "O mito do populismo econômico de Vargas"; Hentschke, *Vargas and Brazil*.

5. Codato, "Elites e instituições no Brasil," 215.

6. On how the Federação das Indústrias do Estado de São Paulo influenced labor policy with Marcondes Filho in the Ministry of Labor, see Weinstein, *For Social Peace*, 100–105.

7. On debates surrounding the Italian influence on the Consolidação das Leis do Trabalho, see French, *Drowning in Laws*, 4, 14–16. On Italian influences more broadly in Brazilian labor laws, see Silva, "The Brazilian and Italian Labor Courts."

8. French, *Drowning in Laws*, 1.

9. Alexandre Marcondes Filho, "A constituição de 1937 e a solução corporativa," 1944–45, CPDOC, Arquivo Alexandre Marcondes Filho, AMFpi44/45.00.00/2.

10. On Marcondes Filho's political and ideological evolution in his growing support of Vargas, see Codato, "Elites e instituições no Brasil," 215–17.

11. Lei Nº 9 de 9 Fevereiro de 1945: Altera a Constituição Federal de 1937, in Porto, *Constituições Brasileiras: 1937*, 105.

12. Anonymous, "Em que consistiram as alterações a carta de 1937," March 1945, CPDOC, VMF45/03/00/2.

13. Alexandre Marcondes Filho to Getúlio Vargas.

14. Historian Robert Levine notes that Marcondes Filho was a former Integralist, but above all rather "cynical" in his approach to lawmaking as minister of labor. Indeed, beyond his emphasis on social peace based loosely on Catholic principles, little of his prior allegiances are apparent in his 1940s' speeches. Levine, *Father of the Poor?*, 53.

15. Anonymous, "Em que consistiram as alterações a carta de 1937."

16. Skidmore, *Politics in Brazil*, 48–53.

17. Loewenstein, *Brazil under Vargas*, 330.

18. Daniel Faraco (Partido Social Democrático, Rio Grande do Sul), 16 May 1946, *Anais da Assembléia Constituinte 1946*, 203–4.

19. This tendency is still evident in histories of Brazil's economic development, which insert the developmentalist ideology that crystallized after the 1950s in terms of a Keynesian paradigm. See Bielschowsky, *Pensamento econômico brasileiro*, 733.

20. After the fall of the Vichy regime in France, corporatist economists like François Perroux repackaged their corporatist ideas of government intervention in their support for Keynesianism. See Cohen, "Du corporatisme au Keynésianisme."

21. For an overview of the spread of Keynesianism, see Hall, *The Political Power of Economic Ideas*.

22. Bulhões, *Depoimento*, 23, 31.

23. French, *Drowning in Laws*.

24. Hall, "Corporativismo e Fascismo."

25. Rosas, *Portugal entre a paz e a guerra*, 412–16.

26. João Neves da Fontoura to Getúlio Vargas, August 5, 1943, CPDOC, Arquivo Oswaldo Aranha, OAcp1943.01.29.

27. Rosas, *Portugal entre a paz e a guerra*, 373–415.

28. Madeira, Farinha, and Pimentel, *Vítimas de Salazar*.

29. Valério, *Estatísticas históricas portuguesas*, 480. Portugal reported an infant mortality rate of 94.1 per 1,000 live births in 1950, whereas England and Wales reported a rate of 29.9 for that year. *International Comparison of Perinatal and Infant Mortality*, 23

30. Anonymous letter, March 9, 1941, ANTT, Arquivo Oliveira Salazar, AOS/CO/PC-10A.

31. Rosas, *Portugal entre a paz e a guerra*, 18.

32. Portuguese historians have recently demonstrated the ways in which parliamentary investigations are crucial to understanding how economic and political conflict was absorbed into

Estado Novo institutions. See Cardoso and Ferreira, "A Câmara Corporativa (1935–1974) e as políticas públicas no Estado Novo."

33. Deputy Albano de Magalhães, *Diário das Sessões da Assembleia Nacional* (April 1, 1943), 361.

34. Comissão Parlamentar de Inquerito aos Elementos da Organização Corporativa, "Relatório: Grémio dos Armazenistas de Mercearia," January 1947, ANTT, Arquivo Oliveira Salazar, AOS/CO/PC-17B.

35. Echoing this point, see Madureira, "O Estado, o patronato e a indústria portuguesa"; Garrido, *Queremos uma economia nova!*, 120–26.

36. Anonymous letter, March 9, 1941.

37. *Pequena história das doutrinas económicas*, 55, 58–59, 62, 69.

38. *Pequena história das doutrinas económicas*, 70.

39. Valério, *Estatísticas históricas portuguesas*, 747.

40. Nunes, "Histórias, uma história e a história," 12–16.

41. José Pires Cardoso, "Prefácio," in Nunes, *Situação e problemas do corporativismo*, 11, 14–17.

42. Bastien, "O Instituto Superior de Ciências Económicas e Financeiras e o corporativismo."

43. On the post-1945 push for industrialization in Salazarist Portugal, see Brito, *Industrialização portuguesa no pós-guerra*; Rosas, *Salazarismo e foment económico*; Mata and Valério, *História económica de Portugal*, 200–231.

44. Veiga, *A economia corporativa e o problema dos preços*, 94, 82.

45. Veiga, *A economia corporativa e o problema dos preços*, 83.

46. Bastien, "The Advent of Modern Economics in Portugal."

47. Martinez, "Sentido económico do corporativismo," 15–16.

48. José Pires Cardoso, "Prefácio," in Nunes, *Situação e problemas do corporativismo*, 12–13.

49. Helena da Cunha, "Salazar," 1945 or 1946, CPDOC, VLC pi Cunha, H. 1945/1946.00.00.

50. Assis Chateaubriand, "O espírito europeu das duas democracias portuguesas," speech published in several Brazilian newspapers, retrieved from ANTT, Arquivo Oliveira Salazar, AOS/CO/NE-2A1.

51. Nord, *France's New Deal*; Dard, "Le corporatisme entre traditionalistes et modernisateurs."

52. On Mexico and corporatism, see Hamilton, *The Limits of State Autonomy*; Semo, "El cardenismo revisado." On how these institutional practices generated new practices of authoritarianism, see McCormick, *The Logic of Compromise in Mexico*.

53. Biblioteca Gabinete de Estudos Corporativos, Library Catalog, Instituto de Ciências Sociais, Lisbon.

54. In Argentina, Perón similarly oversaw the building of a new political system in which organized labor, business, and agriculture interests worked with and within government bureaucracies to influence economic policy and pressure the executive branch. See Brennan and Rougier, *The Politics of National Capitalism*.

55. "Es Salazar el Perón portugués, o Perón el Salazar argentino?," newspaper clipping, May 21, 1947, ANTT, Arquivo Oliveira Salazar, AOS/CO/PC-27.

56. Asked and answered in Martinez, "Sentido económico do corporativismo," 15–16.

57. The continued relevance of Portuguese corporatism, in particular, would lead social scientists in the 1970s to look to the Estado Novo to understand the rise of new authoritarian regimes across Latin America. Schmitter, "The 'Portugalization' of Brazil?"

58. Love, "Structuralism and Dependency in Peripheral Europe."

59. Moura, "Estagnação e crescimento da economia portuguesa."

60. Sousa, "O desenvolvimento económico e social português"; Love, "Structuralism and Dependency in Peripheral Europe," 136.

61. On the structuralist explanation for inflation, see Fajardo, *The World That Latin America Created*, chap. 3; see also Bielschowsky, *Pensamento econômico brasileiro*.

62. On modernization theory and the intellectual history of postwar development thinking, see Isaac, "The Human Sciences in Cold War America"; Gilman, *Mandarins of the Future*; Latham, "Ideology, Social Science, and Destiny." On CEPAL, see Love, "CEPAL as Idea Factory for Latin American Development"; Fajardo, *The World That Latin America Created*.

63. There is a vast literature on the rise of trained experts and government officials dedicated to overseeing the process of national development. For some recent contributions, see Ioris, *Transforming Brazil*; Thornton, *Revolution in Development*; Young, *Transforming Sudan*; Tignor, *W. Arthur Lewis and the Birth of Development Economics*.

64. Gilman, *Mandarins of the Future*; Latham, "Ideology, Social Science, and Destiny"; Rostow, *The Stages of Economic Growth*; Mazower, *Governing the World*; Staples, *The Birth of Development*; Friedman, *Shadow Cold War*; Field, *From Development to Dictatorship*.

65. On the connected rise of the mixed economy in the United States and Colombia, see Offner, *Sorting Out the Mixed Economy*.

66. Madureira, "Cartelization and Corporatism," 95.

67. Veiga, *Draft of the Third Development Plan for 1968–1973*, 6.

68. Sousa Mendes, "Administração e desenvolvimento," 458.

69. *Plano de fomento da metrópole e do ultramar* (draft), 1953–58, ANTT, Arquivo Oliveira Salazar, AOS/CO/EC-5.

70. Dores, *O desenvolvimento da economia portuguesa e o plano para 1959–1964*, 12.

71. Valério, *Estatísticas históricas portuguesas*. See also Lains, *Os progressos do atraso*.

72. Dores, *O desenvolvimento da economia portuguesa e o plano para 1959–1964*, 10.

73. Baganha, "As correntes emigratórias portuguesas no século XX e o seu impacto na economia nacional."

74. *As finanças e a política de fomento*.

75. Brito, *Industrialização portuguesa no pós-guerra*; Carvalho, "Aspectos da repartição do rendimento em Portugal"; Rosas, *Salazarismo e fomento económico*.

76. Veiga, *Linhas gerais do III Plano de Fomento*, 8, 23, 24.

77. Teixeira Pinto, *Aspectos da política económica portuguesa (1963–1964)*, 309.

78. Direcção-Geral de Segurança, Delegação de Coimbra, "Agitação popular, no conselho de Viseu, pela obrigatoriedade do pagamento de taxas ao grémio da lavoura," September 28, 1971, ANTT, Arquivo Polícia Internacional e de Defesa do Estado PIDE/DGS Inspecção Geral dos Serviços de Fiscalização dos Géneros Alimentícios, NT1144, proc.CI(1)-2, pasta 14.

79. Direcção-Geral de Segurança, Delegação de Coimbra, "Descontentamento entre os sócios dos grémios da lavoura," July 9, 1971, ANTT, Arquivo Polícia Internacional e de Defesa do Estado PIDE/DGS Inspecção Geral dos Serviços de Fiscalização dos Géneros Alimentícios, NT1144, proc. CI(1)-2, pasta 14.

80. Direcção-Geral de Segurança, Delegação de Coimbra, "Reacção ao pagamento de quotas aos grémios da lavoura, November 17, 1971, ANTT, Arquivo Polícia Internacional e de Defesa do Estado PIDE/DGS Inspecção Geral dos Serviços de Fiscalização dos Géneros Alimentícios, NT1144, proc. CI(1)-2, pasta 14.

81. Maddison, *The World Economy*, 64–69.

82. Lains, "Catching up to the European Core," 370.

83. Teixeira Pinto, *Aspectos da política económica portuguesa (1963–1964)*, 310–11.

84. Baganha, "As correntes emigratórias portuguesas no século XX e o seu impacto na economia nacional," 978. See also Leeds, "Industrialização e emigração em Portugal."

85. Maxwell, *The Making of Portuguese Democracy*.

86. The SALTE Plan, to be sure, was not really approved until 1950, and then Vargas returned to power with his own planning goals. Bielschowsky, *Pensamento econômico brasileiro*, 371.

87. Bastos, "Desenvolvimento incoerente?"

88. Love, "CEPAL as Idea Factory for Latin American Development," 32.

89. Bastos and Gomes, "Ortodoxia e heterodoxia econômica antes e durante a Era Vargas"; Bastos, "Desenvolvimento incoerente?"; Bielschowsky, *Pensamento econômico brasileiro*.

90. United Nations, *Economic Development in Selected Countries*, 62–74.

91. Levine, *Father of the Poor?*, 76–81.

92. Leopoldi, "O difícil caminho do meio," 164.

93. Levine, *Father of the Poor?*, 82; Dávila, "Myth and Memory."

94. According to historian Joel Wolfe, when Paulista workers went on strike in March 1953, they concentrated their demands on price controls to deal with the rising cost of living. Wolfe, *Working Women, Working Men*, 176–88. To be sure, debates over price controls also arose within and between different labor groups in the late 1940s and early 1950s. See, for example, French, *The Brazilian Workers' ABC* 167–79, 250.

95. Ioris, "Fifty Years in Five," 279–80, 272–73.

96. In the United States, price controls endured after World War II and became a huge area of conflict as one of the Congress of Industrial Organization's (CIO) main demands in the postwar strike wave was the extension of price controls. For the United States, however, price controls were largely removed in 1946 in a government policy shift that historian Nelson Lichtenstein explains in terms of how this type of corporatist planning failed because it was opposed by the CIO itself. See Lichtenstein, *Labor's War at Home*, 220–23.

97. José Amádio, "Getúlio no Maracanã," *O Cruzeiro* (March 10, 1951), 88.

98. Wolfe, *Autos and Progress*; Woodard, *Brazil's Revolution in Commerce*.

99. Pimentel, "Vida e morte do Tribunal do Juri de economia popular."

100. See, for example, "Mapas de detidos, 1946–49," Arquivo Público do Estado de Rio de Janeiro (APERJ), Fundo Delegacia Especial de Segurança Política e Social, DPS, notação 38.005 and 38.014. Newspapers also continued to report on economic crimes. See, for example, "Na polícia e nas ruas," *Jornal do Brasil* (May 4, 1947).

101. "Conversa com o leitor," *O Cruzeiro* (January 3, 1959).

102. Silva, "Justiça e ditadura militar no Brasil."

103. Graham, *Feeding the City*, 172–90.

104. Leopoldi, "O difícil caminho do meio," 162.

105. Weinstein, *For Social Peace in Brazil*.

106. Leopoldi, "O difícil caminho do meio," 170.

107. Draibe, *Rumos e metamorfoses*.

108. While few scholars deny the importance of Vargas's first government in laying the groundwork for intensive and fast-paced industrialization after 1950, the content of the 1930s and 1940s is

often relegated to preparation for the policies and institutions created during Vargas's second government. See Bielschowsky, "Estratégia de desenvolvimento e as três frentes de expansão no Brasil."

109. Leopoldi, "O difícil caminho do meio," 168.

110. Levine, *Father of the Poor?*, 85.

111. On the symbolic and political interpretations assigned to Vargas's suicide, see Williams and Weinstein, "Vargas Morto."

112. Lafer, *JK e o programa de metas, 1956–1961*, 49–56.

113. Wolfe, *Autos and Progress*, chap. 5.

114. Luna and Klein, *The Economic and Social History of Brazil since 1889*, 363, 369.

115. Love, "CEPAL as Idea Factory for Latin American Development," 35.

116. Love, *Crafting the Third World*.

117. Love, "Structuralism and Dependency in Peripheral Europe," 120.

118. On these questions, see the essays in Abreu and Silveira, *De Vargas aos militares*.

119. O'Donnell, "Corporatism and the Question of the State," 47, 59.

120. Oliveira Vianna, *O idealismo da constituição* (1939), 149.

Conclusion

1. Lewis, *Economic Survey*, 12, cited in Thorp, *Progress, Poverty and Exclusion*, 97.

2. On how postwar development became a process tightly connected to Cold War geopolitics, see Westad, *The Global Cold War*; Cullather, *The Hungry World*; Immerwahr, *Thinking Small*; Sackley, "The Village as Cold War Site."

3. Engerman, "Social Science in the Cold War." On the rise of area studies programs focused on Latin America, see Chilcote, "The Cold War and the Transformation of Latin American Studies in the United States."

4. Rollo, *Portugal e o Plano Marshall*. See also Leitão, "The Reluctant European."

5. Love, "Structuralism and Dependency in Peripheral Europe"; Love, *Crafting the Third World*.

6. Fajardo, *The World That Latin America Created*; Love, "CEPAL as Idea Factory for Latin American Development."

7. Dávila, *Hotel Trópico*, 8.

8. Alexandre, *Velho Brasil, Novas Áfricas*, esp. 65–120; Paquette, *Imperial Portugal in the Age of Atlantic Revolutions*, chaps. 4–5; Ferreira, "Measuring Short- and Long-Term Impacts of Abolitionism in the South Atlantic, 1807–1860s."

9. Cooper, "Modernizing Bureaucrats, Backward Africans, and the Development Concept."

10. See, for example, Adair, *In Search of the Lost Decade*.

11. Cardoso and Faletto, *Dependency and Development in Latin America*, 166–71.

12. Historian Daniel James, for example, emphasizes the corporatist logic that underpinned how Perón built his populist appeal in Argentina. James, *Resistance and Integration*, 17–19.

13. On this political and institutional dynamic in shaping Mexico's "strange" dictatorship, see Gillingham, *Unrevolutionary Mexico*; McCormick, *The Logic of Compromise in Mexico*.

14. Santana, "O making of *da implantação do projeto corporativo no Brasil*," 186.

15. Filho, "A era Vargas."

16. For similar debates in Mexico, especially in the 1980s, see Thornton, *Revolution in Development*, 190–99.

BIBLIOGRAPHY

Archive and Manuscript Collections

Brazil

Arquivo Histórico do Itamaraty, Rio de Janeiro (AHI)
Arquivo Nacional do Brasil, Brasília (AN-B)
    Fundo Ministério do Trabalho, Indústria e Comércio
Arquivo Nacional do Brasil, Rio de Janeiro (AN-RJ)
    Fundo Conselho de Economia Nacional
    Fundo do Tribunal de Segurança Nacional
    Fundo Ministério da Justiça e Negócios Interiores
    Gabinete Civil da Presidência da República
Arquivo Público do Estado do Rio de Janeiro, Rio de Janeiro (APERJ)
    Fundo Delegacia Especial de Segurança Política e Social, Rio de Janeiro
Arquivo Público do Estado de São Paulo (APESP)
    Conselho de Expansão Econômica do Estado de São Paulo
    Secretaria do Governo, Conselho de Expansão Econômica do Estado de São Paulo
Biblioteca da Procuradoria Geral do Estado do Rio de Janeiro, Rio de Janeiro
    Coleção Francisco Campos (CFC)
Casa Oliveira Vianna, Niterói (COV)
Centro de Pesquisa e Documentação de História Contempoânea do Brasil, Fundação
    Getúlio Vargas, Rio de Janeiro (CPDOC)
    Arquivo Alexandre Marcondes Filho
    Arquivo Eugênio Gudin
    Arquivo Getúlio Vargas
    Arquivo José Maria Whitaker
    Arquivo Oswaldo Aranha
    Arquivo Themístocles Brandão Cavalcanti
    Arquivo Valdemar Falcão
    Arquivo Virgílio de Melo Franco

Portugal

Arquivo Histórico-Diplomático do Ministério dos Negócios Estrangeiros, Lisbon (MNE)
Arquivo Histórico Militar, Lisbon (AHM)
    Tribunal Militar Especial

Arquivo Histórico Ultramarino, Lisbon (AHU)
Arquivo Nacional Torre do Tombo, Lisbon (ANTT)
    Arquivo Marcello Caetano
    Arquivo Oliveira Salazar
    Arquivo Polícia Internacional e de Defesa do Estado PIDE/DGS Inspecção Geral dos
        Serviços de Fiscalização dos Géneros Alimentícios
    Empresa Pública do Jornal *O Século*
    Ministério do Comércio e Indústria
    Ministério do Interior
    Secretaria-Geral da Presidência do Conselho de Ministros, Gabinete do Presidente
Instituto de Ciências Sociais, Lisbon
    Biblioteca Gabinete de Estudos Corporativos

Periodicals and Serial Government Publications

Brazil

A Batalha
A Manhã
A Noite
A Offensiva
Atlântico: Revista Luso-Brasileira (a joint publication between Brazil and Portugal)
Boletim do Ministério do Trabalho, Indústria e Comércio
Correio da Manhã
Correio Paulistano
Diário Carioca
Diário Oficial da União
Diário Oficial do Estado de São Paulo—E.U. do Brasil
Diretrizes
Gazeta de Notícias
Hierarchia
Jornal do Brasil
Jornal do Commércio
Jurisprudência: Tribunal de Segurança Nacional
Klaxon
Novas Diretrizes
O Cruzeiro: Revista Semanal Illustrada
O Dia
O Imparcial
O Jornal
O Jornal do Comércio
O Observador Econômico e Financeiro
Política
Revista do Brasil

Portugal

Diário das Sessões da Assembleia Nacional
Diário de Lisboa
Diário de Notícias
Diário do Govêrno
Diário dos Açores
Jornal de Comércio e das Colónias
Jornal do Comércio
República

Printed Primary and Secondary Sources

"A alta dos preços e a estatística da produção." *Revista de Economia e Estatística* 1, no. 2 (October 1936): 9–11.

"A mão-de-obra indígena nas colónias africanas." 2º Congresso Colonial Nacional, 1924

A Universidade de Coimbra e o Brasil: Percurso iconobibliográfico. Coimbra: Imprensa da Universidade de Coimbra, 2012.

Abreu, Luciano Aronne de. "Elites políticas regionais: O caso das interventorias gaúchas." *Revista de Sociologia e Política* 16, no. 30 (2008): 187–97.

———. "Sindicalismo e corporativismo no Brasil: O olhar autoritário de Oliveira Vianna." In *Autoritarismo e cultura política*, edited by Luciano Aronne de Abreu and Rodrigo Patto Sá Motta, 91–121. Porto Alegre: EdiPUCRS, 2013.

Abreu, Luciano Aronne de, Luís Carlos dos Passos Martins, and Geandra Denardi Munareto. *Embracing the Past, Designing the Future: Authoritarianism and Economic Development in Brazil under Getúlio Vargas*. Brighton, UK: Sussex Academic Press, 2020.

Abreu, Luciano Aronne de, and Luis Rosenfield. "Conservadorismo, autoritarismo e legitimação política do Estado Novo: Notas sobre os 'Comentários à Constituição de 1937' de Pontes de Miranda." *Revista Novos Estudos Jurídicos* 24, no. 3 (2019): 736–56.

Abreu, Luciano Aronne de, and Helder Gordim da Silveira, eds. *De Vargas aos militares: Autoritarismo e desenvolvimento econômico no Brasil*. Porto Alegre: EdiPUCRS, 2014.

Acerbi, Patricia. *Street Occupations: Urban Vending in Rio de Janeiro, 1850–1925*. Austin: University of Texas Press, 2017.

Adair, Jennifer. *In Search of the Lost Decade: Everyday Rights in Post-Dictatorship Argentina*. Oakland: University of California Press, 2019.

Adelman, Jeremy. "Liberalism and Constitutionalism in Latin America in the 19th Century." *History Compass* 12, no. 6 (2014): 508–16.

———. *Republic of Capital: Buenos Aires and the Legal Transformation of the Atlantic World*. Stanford, CA: Stanford University Press, 1999.

Aguiar, Pinto de. *Abastecimento: Crises, motins e intervenção*. Rio de Janeiro: Philobiblion, 1985.

Albert, Bill. *South America and the First World War: The Impact of the War on Brazil, Argentina, Peru, and Chile*. Cambridge: Cambridge University Press, 1988.

Alencastro, Luiz Felipe de. *O trato dos viventes: Formação do Brasil no Atlântico Sul, séculos XVI e XVII*. São Paulo: Companhia das Letras, 2000.

Alexandre, Valentim. *Velho Brasil, novas Áfricas: Portugal e o Império (1808–1975)*. Porto: Edições Afrontamento, 2000.

———. "Ideologia, economia e política: A questão colonial na implantação do Estado Novo." *Análise Social* 28, no. 4 (1993): 1117–36.

———. *O roubo das almas: Salazar, a igreja e os totalitarismos (1930–1939)*. Lisbon: Publicações Dom Quixote, 2006.

Almeida, Francisco Tavares de. *A organização sindical-corporativa da agricultura italiana: Relatório de uma missão de estudo*. Lisbon: Ministério da Economia, Serviço Editorial da Repartição de Estudos, Informação e Propaganda, 1941.

Almeida, Martins de. *Brasil errado: Ensaio político sobre os erros do Brasil como paiz*. Rio de Janeiro: Schmidt Editor, 1932.

Alvarez, Sonia E. *Engendering Democracy in Brazil: Women's Movements in Transition Politics*. Princeton, NJ: Princeton University Press, 1990.

Amaral, Luciano. "Política e economia: O Estado Novo, os latifundiários alentejanos e os atecedentes da EPAC." *Análise Social* 31, no. 136–37 (1996): 465–86.

Amzalak, Moses Bensabat. *A indústria da pesca de bacalhau e a sua intensificação em Portugal*. 1º Congresso Económico Nacional reunido no Porto. Lisbon: Museu Comercial de Lisboa, 1921.

———. *Economistas brasileiros: Roberto Cochrane Simonsen*. Coimbra: Coimbra Editora, 1944.

———. *O néo-mercantilismo*. Lisbon: Of. Gráf. do Museu Comercial de Lisboa, 1929.

Anais da Assembléia Constituinte 1946. Vol. 9. Rio de Janeiro: Imprensa Nacional, 1948.

Anderson, Warwick, Ricardo Roque, and Ricardo Ventura Santos, eds. *Luso-Tropicalism and Its Discontents: The Making and Unmaking of Racial Exceptionalism*. New York: Berghahn Books, 2019.

Andrade, M. Rebelo de. "Prefácio." In *Uma série de conferências, realizadas de 19 a 30 Outubro de 1936*, vii. União Nacional, Centro de Estudos Corporativos. Lisbon: União Nacional, 1937.

Annaes da Assembléa Nacional Constituinte 1933/1934, Vol. 2. Ed. fasc. Biblioteca Digital da Câmara dos Deputados. Rio de Janeiro: Imprensa Nacional, 1935.

Annaes da Assembléa Nacional Constituinte 1933/1934, Vol. 4. Ed. fasc. Biblioteca Digital da Câmara dos Deputados. Rio de Janeiro: Imprensa Nacional, 1935.

Annaes da Assembléa Nacional Constituinte 1933/1934, Vol. 11. Ed. fasc. Biblioteca Digital da Câmara dos Deputados. Rio de Janeiro: Imprensa Nacional, 1935.

Anúario Estatístico do Brasil: Ano I (1908–1912). Rio de Janeiro: Typographia da Estatistica, 1917.

Anúario Estatístico do Brasil: Ano IV, 1938. Rio de Janeiro: Instituto Brasileiro de Geografia e Estatística, 1939.

Anúario Estatístico do Brasil: Ano VI 1941–1945. Rio de Janeiro: Serviço Gráfico do Instituto Brasileiro de Geografia e Estatística, 1946.

Anuário Estatístico-1945. Lisbon: Instituto Nacional de Estatística, 1946.

Araújo, António de. *A lei de Salazar: Estudos sobre a Constituição Política de 1933*. Coimbra: Editora Tenacitas, 2007.

Armitage, David. *The Declaration of Independence: A Global History*. Cambridge, MA: Harvard University Press, 2007.

As finanças e a política de fomento: Princípios informadores das propostas de lei e diplomas legais correspondentes, 1956–1961. Lisbon: Imprensa Nacional de Lisboa, 1961.

Atanassow, Ewa, and Ira Katznelson. "Negotiating the Rule of Law: Dilemmas of Security and Liberty Revisited." In *States of Exception in American History*, edited by Gary Gerstle and Joel Isaac, 39–67. Chicago: University of Chicago Press, 2020.

Azevedo, José Affonso Mendonça de. *Elaborando a constituição nacional: Atas da subcomissão elaboradora do anteprojeto 1932/1933*. Ed. facsimile. Brasília: Senado Federal, Secretaria de Documentação e Informação, Subsecretaria de Edições Técnicas, 1933.

Azevedo Amaral, Antônio José. *O estado autoritário e a realidade nacional*. Rio de Janeiro: Livraria José Olympio Editora, 1938.

Babb, Sarah. *Managing Mexico: Economists from Nationalism to Neoliberalism*. Princeton, NJ: Princeton University Press, 2001.

Baganha, Maria Ioannis B. "As correntes emigratórias portuguesas no século XX e o seu impacto na economia nacional." *Análise Social* 29, no. 128 (1994): 959–80.

Bak, Joan Lamaysou. "Cartels, Cooperatives, and Corporatism: Getúlio Vargas in Rio Grande do Sul on the Eve of Brazil's 1930 Revolution." *Hispanic American Historical Review* 63, no. 2 (1983): 255–75.

———. "Some Antecedents of Corporatism: State Economic Intervention and Rural Organization in Brazil. The Case of Rio Grande do Sul, 1890–1937." PhD diss., Yale University, 1977.

Balogh, Brian. *The Associational State: American Governance in the Twentieth Century*. Philadelphia: University of Pennsylvania Press, 2015.

"Barata, Júlio de Carvalho." In *Dicionário histórico-biográfico da Primeira República (1889–1930)*, edited by Alzira Alves de Abreu and Israel Beloch, 1:294. Rio de Janeiro: Editora Forense-Universitária FGV/CPDOC, 1984.

Barbosa, Leonardo Augusto de Andrade. *História constitucional brasileira: Mudança constitucional, autoritarismo e democracia no Brasil pós-1964*. Brasília: Câmara dos Deputados Edições Câmara, 2018.

Barbosa, Pedro Paulo Lima. "Os sindicatos corporativistas no Brasil entre os anos de 1934 e 1939." *Cadernos de História* 9, no. 1 (2014): 202–20.

Barreto, José. "Mussolini é um louco: Uma entrevista desconhecida de Fernando Pessoa com um antifascista italiano." *Pessoa Plural—Revista de Estudos Pessoanos* 1 (2012): 225–52.

Barros, Robert. *Constitutionalism and Dictatorship: Pinochet, the Junta, and the 1980 Constitution*. Cambridge: Cambridge University Press, 2002.

Bastien, Carlos. "The Advent of Modern Economics in Portugal." In *The Development of Economics in Western Europe since 1945*, edited by A. W. Bob Coats, 162–83. London: Routledge Press, 2000.

———. "O Instituto Superior de Ciências Económicas e Financeiras e o corporativismo (1934–1974)." In *Documento de Trabalho / Working Paper No. 46*. Lisbon: Gabinete de História Económica e Social, 2011.

Bastien, Carlos, and José Luís Cardoso. "From Homo Economicus to Homo Corporativus: A Neglected Critique of Neoclassical Economics." *Journal of Socio-Economics* 36, no. 1 (2007): 118–27.

Bastos, Pedro Paulo Zahluth. "Desenvolvimento incoerente? Comentários sobre o projeto do segundo governo Vargas e as idéias econômicas de Horácio Lafer (1948–1952)." *Revista Economia* 6, no. 3 (2005): 191–222.

Bastos, Pedro Paulo Zahluth, and Ângela de Castro Gomes. "Ortodoxia e heterodoxia econômica antes e durante a era Vargas." In *A era Vargas: Desenvolvimentismo, economia sociedade*, edited by Pedro Paulo Zahluth Bastos and Pedro Cezar Dutra Fonseca, 179–218. São Paulo: Editora UNESP, 2011.

Báudin, Louis. *Le corporatisme*. Paris: Librairie Générale de Droit et de Jurisprudence, 1941.

Bayly, Christopher A. *Recovering Liberties: Indian Thought in the Age of Liberalism and Empire*. Cambridge: Cambridge University Press, 2012.

Belleza, Newton. *Evolução do Ministério da Agricultura*. Rio de Janeiro: Ministério da Agricultura Serviço de Informação Agrícola, 1955.

Benchimol, Jaime. "Reforma urbana e revolta da vacina na cidade do Rio de Janeiro." In *O Brasil republicano: O tempo do liberalismo excludente—da proclamação da República à Revolução de 1930*, edited by Jorge Ferreira and Lucilia de Almeida Neves, 231–86. Rio de Janeiro: Civilização Brasileira, 2003.

Bender, Gerald J. *Angola under the Portuguese: The Myth and the Reality*. Berkeley: University of California Press, 1978.

Ben-Ghiat, Ruth. *Fascist Modernities: Italy, 1922–1945*. Berkeley: University of California Press, 2001.

Benton, Lauren. "Constitutions and Empires." *Law and Social Inquiry* 31, no. 1 (2006): 177–98.

Bertonha, João Fábio. *Plínio Salgado: Biografia política (1895–1975)*. São Paulo: Editora da Universidade de São Paulo, 2018.

———. "Plínio Salgado, o integralismo brasileiro e as suas relações com Portugal (1932–1975)." *Análise Social* 46, no. 198 (2011): 65–87.

Bielschowsky, Ricardo. "Estratégia de desenvolvimento e as três frentes de expansão no Brasil: Um desenho conceitual." *Economia e Sociedade* 21 (2012): 729–47.

———. "Ideologia e desenvolvimento: Brasil, 1930–1964." In *50 anos de ciência econômica no Brasil: Pensamento, instituições, depoimentos* edited by Maria Rita Loureiro, 71–103. Petrópolis: Editora Vozes, 1997.

———. *Pensamento econômico brasileiro: O ciclo ideológico do desenvolvimentismo*. Rio de Janeiro: IPEA/INPES, 1988.

Bilder, Mary Sarah. *The Transatlantic Constitution: Colonial Legal Culture and the Empire*. Cambridge, MA: Harvard University Press, 2004.

Billias, George Athan. *American Constitutionalism Heard Round the World, 1776–1989: A Global Perspective*. New York: NYU Press, 2009.

Bockman, Johanna. *Markets in the Name of Socialism: The Left-Wing Origins of Neoliberalism*. Stanford, CA: Stanford University Press, 2011.

Bonnard, Roger. *Syndicalismo, corporativismo e estado corporativo*. Translated by Themístocles Brandão Cavalcanti. Rio de Janeiro: Livraria Editora Freitas Bastos, 1938.

Bonnefous, Édouard. "Allocution prononcée par Édouard Bonnefous Président de l'Académie dans la séance du 11 Juin 1968." In *Académie des Sciences Morales et Politiques: Notice sur la vie et les travaux de Claude Joseph Gignoux (1890–1966) par M. Gaston Leduc*. Paris: Institut de France, 1968.

Borges, Dain. "Review Essay: Brazilian Social Thought of the 1930's." *Luso-Brazilian Review* 31, no. 2 (1994): 137–50.

Bosworth, R.J.B. *Mussolini's Italy: Life under the Dictatorship, 1915–1945*. London: Allen Lane Penguin Books, 2005.

Botelho, André. *O Brasil e os dias: Estado-nação, modernismo e rotina intelectual*. Bauru: EDUSC, 2005.

Botz, Gerhard. "'Corporatist State' and Enhanced Authoritarian Dictatorship: The Austria of Dollfuss and Schuschnigg (1933–38)." In *Corporatism and Fascism: The Corporatist Wave in Europe*, edited by António Costa Pinto, 144–73. London: Routledge Press, 2017.

Braga, Cincinato. *Intensificação econômica no Brasil*. São Paulo: Secção de Obras do "Estado de S. Paulo," 1918.

Brasil Junior, Antonio da Silveira. "Oliveira Vianna e os dilemas da ação coletiva no Brasil." *Perspectivas: Revista de Ciências Sociais* 31 (2007): 65–83.

Brennan, James P., and Marcelo Rougier. *The Politics of National Capitalism: Peronism and the Argentine Bourgeoisie, 1946–1976*. University Park: Pennsylvania State University Press, 2009.

Bresciani, Maria Stella Martins. *O charme da ciência e a sedução da objetividade: Oliveira Vianna entre intérpretes do Brasil*. São Paulo: Editora UNESP, 2005.

Briggs, Laura, Gladys McCormick, and J. T. Way. "Transnationalism: A Category of Analysis." *American Quarterly* 60, no. 3 (2008): 625–48.

Brinkley, Alan. *The End of Reform: New Deal Liberalism in Recession and War*. New York: Alfred A. Knopf, 1995.

Brinkmann, Sören. "Leite e modernidade: Ideologia e políticas de alimentação na era Vargas." *História, Ciências, Saúde-Manguinhos* 21, no. 1 (2014): 1–17.

Brito, José Maria Brandão de. *Industrialização portuguesa no pós-guerra (1948–1965): O condicionamento industrial*. Lisbon: Publicações Dom Quixote, 1989.

Bulhões, Octavio Gouvêa de. *Depoimento*. Rio de Janeiro: Programa de História Oral do CPDOC/FGV, 1990.

Burbank, Jane. "Lenin and the Law in Revolutionary Russia." *Slavic Review* 54, no. 1 (1995): 23–44.

Burbank, Jane, and Frederick Cooper. *Empires in World History: Power and the Politics of Difference*. Princeton, NJ: Princeton University Press, 2010.

Burgin, Angus. *The Great Persuasion: Reinventing Free Markets since the Depression*. Cambridge, MA: Harvard University Press, 2012.

Burke, Peter and Maria Lúcia G. Pallares-Burke. *Gilberto Freyre: Social Theory in the Tropics*. Oxford: Peter Lang, 2008.

Burke, Roland. "Some Rights Are More Equal than Others: The Third World and the Transformation of Economic and Social Rights." *Humanity: An International Journal of Human Rights, Humanitarianism, and Development* 3, no. 3 (2012): 427–48.

———. "From Individual Rights to National Development: The First UN International Conference on Human Rights, Tehran, 1968." *Journal of World History* 19, no. 3 (2008): 275–96.

Byé, Maurice. "Capitalisme, socialisme, économie corporative, économie dirigée." *Revue d'Économie Politique* 49, no. 3 (1935): 1208–10.

Cabral, Mário André Machado. "Autoritarismo e gênese antitruste: Francisco Campos e a imaginação concorrencial no Estado Novo." *História do Direito* 2, no. 3 (2021): 224–243.

Cabreira, Tomás. *A defesa econômica de Portugal*. Lisbon: Imprensa Libanio da Silva, 1917.

Caetano, Marcello. *A depreciação da moeda depois da guerra*. Coimbra: Coimbra Editora, Lda., 1931.

———. *Direito constitucional*. Rio de Janeiro: Forense, 1977.

———. *História breve das constituições portuguesas*. Lisbon: Editorial Verbo, Ltd., 1968.

———. "Intercâmbio da cultura jurídica de Portugal e do Brasil." *O Direito* 73, no. 8 (October 1941): 226–28.

———. *Minhas memórias de Salazar*. Lisbon: Edição Verbo, 1977.

———. *O sistema corporativo*. Lisbon: Oficinas gráficas de O Jornal de comércio e das colónias, 1938.

Campos, Francisco. "A lei de proteção à economia popular: Entrevista do Sr. Ministro da Justiça." *Revista Forense* (December 1938): 174–77.

———. "Directrizes do estado nacional." In *O estado nacional: Sua estrutura, seu conteúdo ideológico*, 33–68. Rio de Janeiro: José Olympio Editora, 1941.

———. "Entrevista do Doutor Francisco Campos, Ministro da Justiça, ao 'Correio da Manhã,' a respeito da Constituição de 10 de Novembro." *Boletim do Ministério do Trabalho, Indústria e Comércio* 40 (December 1937): 2–26.

Campos, Reynaldo Pompeu de. *Repressão judicial no estado Novo: Esquerda e direita no banco dos réus*. Rio de Janeiro: Edições Achiamé, 1982.

Canning, J. P. "The Corporation in the Political Thought of the Italian Jurists of the Thirteenth and Fourteenth Centuries." *History of Political Thought* 1, no. 1 (1980): 9–32.

Cano, Wilson. "Crise de 1929, soberania na política econômica e industrialização." In *A era Vargas: Desenvolvimentismo, economia sociedade*, edited by Pedro Paulo Zahluth Bastos and Pedro Cezar Dutra Fonseca, 121–57. São Paulo: Editora UNESP, 2011.

Capotescu, Cristian, Oscar Sanchez-Sibony, and Melissa Teixeira. "Austerity without Neoliberals: Reappraising the Sinuous History of a Powerful State Technology." *Capitalism: A Journal of History and Economics* 2 (2022): 379–420.

Cardoso, Fernando Henrique. *Autoritarismo e democratização*. São Paulo: Paz e Terra, 1975.

———. "The Originality of a Copy: CEPAL and the Idea of Development." *CEPAL Review* 4 (1977): 7–40.

Cardoso, Fernando Henrique, and Enzo Faletto. *Dependency and Development in Latin America*. Translated by Marjory Mattingly Urquidi. Berkeley: University of California Press, 1979.

Cardoso, José Luís, and Nuno Estêvão Ferreira. "A Câmara Corporativa (1935–1974) e as políticas públicas no Estado Novo." *Ler História* 64 (2013): 31–54.

Cardozo, Francisco Malta. *Sindicatos rurais na federação: Empregados e empregadores na agricultura (Constituição Federal de 10 de Novembro de 1937)*. São Paulo: Imprensa Oficial do Estado, 1941.

Carli, Gileno de. *História contemporânea do açúcar no Brasil*. Rio de Janeiro: Edição do Instituto do Açúcar e do Alcool, 1940.

Carneiro, Levi. *Na academia*. Rio de Janeiro: Editora Civilização Brasileira, 1943.

Carpenter, Luiz F. S. "O projeto da nova constituição política e a entidade território." *Política: Revista de Direito Público, Legislação Social e Economia* 1, no. 1 (January 1934).

Carvalho, José Murilo de. *Cidadania no Brasil: O longo caminho*. 3rd ed. Rio de Janeiro: Civilização Brasileira, 2002.

———. "Federalismo e centralização no Império brasileiro: história e argumento." In *Pontos e bordados: escritos de história e política*, 155–88. Belo Horizonte: Editora UFMG, 1999.

Carvalho, Odete Esteves de. "Aspectos da repartição do rendimento em Portugal: Análise no período dos I e II Planos de Fomento." *Análise Social* 7, no. 27–28 (1969): 584–631.

Carvalho, Rita Almeida de. *A concordata de Salazar*. Lisbon: Temas e Debates, 2013.

Castelo, Cláudia. "Gilberto Freyre's View of Miscegenation and Its Circulation in the Portuguese Empire, 1930s–1960s." In *Luso-Tropicalism and Its Discontents: The Making and Unmaking of Racial Exceptionalism*, edited by Warwick Anderson, Ricardo Roque, and Ricardo Ventura Santos, 23–44. New York: Berghahn Books, 2019.

———. *"O modo português de estar no mundo": O luso-tropicalismo e a ideologia colonial portuguesa, 1933–1961*. Porto: Edições Afrontamento, 2011.

————. *Passagens para África: O povoamento de Angola e Moçambique com naturais da metrópole (1920–1974)*. Lisbon: Edições Afrontamento, 2009.

Castilho, José Manuel Tavares. *Marcelo Caetano: Uma biografia política*. Coimbra: Edições Almedina, 2012.

Castro Leal, Ernesto. *António Ferro: Espaço político e imaginário social (1918–1932)*. Lisbon: Edições Cosmos, 1994.

Caulfield, Sueann. *In Defense of Honor: Sexual Morality, Modernity, and Nation in Early-Twentieth-Century Brazil*. Durham, NC: Duke University Press, 2000.

Cavalcanti, Themístocles Brandão. "Prefácio." In *Syndicalismo, corporativismo e estado corporativo*, by Roger Bonnard, v–xxviii. Rio de Janeiro: Livraria Editora Freitas Bastos, 1938.

"Cavalcanti, Temístocles." In *Dicionário histórico-biográfico da Primeira República (1889–1930)*, edited by Alzira Alves de Abreu and Israel Beloch, 1:754–57. Rio de Janeiro: Editora Forense-Universitária FGV/CPDOC, 1984.

Cayolla, Júlio. *Pavilhão da colonização na exposição do mundo português*. Lisbon: Bertrand Irmãos, 1940.

Cesarino Junior, A. F. *Direito corporativo e direito do trabalho (soluções práticas)*. São Paulo: Livraria Martins, 1940.

Chalhoub, Sidney. *A força da escravidão: Ilegalidade e costume no Brasil escravista*. São Paulo: Companha das Letras, 2012.

————. *Trabalho, lar e botequim: O cotidiano dos trabalhadores no Rio de Janeiro da belle époque*. Campinas: Editora da Unicamp, 2001.

Chamedes, Giuliana. *A Twentieth-Century Crusade: The Vatican's Battle to Remake Christian Europe*. Cambridge, MA: Harvard University Press, 2019.

Chappel, James. "The Catholic Origins of Totalitarianism Theory in Interwar Europe." *Modern Intellectual History* 8, no. 3 (2011): 561–90.

Chase, Helen C. *International Comparison of Perinatal and Infant Mortality: The United States and Six West European Countries*. Washington, DC: US Department of Health, Education, and Welfare, Public Health Service, 1967.

Chazkel, Amy. *Laws of Chance: Brazil's Clandestine Lottery and the Making of Urban Public Life*. Durham, NC: Duke University Press, 2011.

————. "Toward a History of Rights in the City at Night: Making and Breaking the Nightly Curfew in Nineteenth-Century Rio de Janeiro." *Comparative Studies in Society and History* 62, no. 1 (2020): 106–34.

Chiaramonte, José Carlos. "The 'Ancient Constitution' after Independence (1808–1852)." *Hispanic American Historical Review* 90, no. 3 (2010): 455–88.

Chilcote, Ronald H. "The Cold War and the Transformation of Latin American Studies in the United States." In *Latin American Studies and the Cold War*, edited by Ronald H. Chilcote, 33–76. Lanham, MD: Rowman and Littlefield, 2022.

Clavin, Patricia. *Securing the World Economy: The Reinvention of the League of Nations, 1920–1946*. Oxford: Oxford University Press, 2013.

Clavin, Patricia, and Jens-Wilhelm Wessels. "Transnationalism and the League of Nations: Understanding the Work of Its Economic and Financial Organization." *Contemporary European History* 14, no. 4 (2005): 465–92.

Cleminson, Richard. *Catholicism, Race and Empire: Eugenics in Portugal, 1900–1950*. Budapest: Central European University Press, 2014.

Coates, Benjamin Allen. *Legalist Empire: International Law and American Foreign Relations in the Early Twentieth Century*. Oxford: Oxford University Press, 2016.

Coco, Orazio. "Italian Advisors in Nationalist China: The Mission and Work of Alberto de' Stefani, High Commissioner of Chiang Kai-Shek." *International History Review* 43, no. 5 (2021): 951–65.

Codato, Adriano Nervo. "Elites e instituições no Brasil: Uma análise contextual do Estado Novo." PhD diss., Universidade Estadual de Campinas–UNICAMP, 2008.

Cohen, Antonin. "Du corporatisme au Keynésianisme: Continuités pratiques et ruptures symboliques dans le sillage de François Perroux." *Revue Française de Science Politique* 56, no. 4 (2006): 555–92.

Cohen, Jon S. "Fascism and Agriculture in Italy: Policies and Consequences." *Economic History Review* 32, no. 1 (1979): 70–87.

Collier, David. "Introduction." In *The New Authoritarianism in Latin America*, edited by David Collier, 3–16. Princeton, NJ: Princeton University Press, 1980.

Condato, Adriano. "A formação do campo político profissional no Brasil: Uma hipótese a partir do caso de São Paulo." *Revista de Sociologia e Política* 16, no. 30 (2008): 89–105.

Confraria, João. "Política industrial do Estado Novo. A regulação dos oligopólios no curto prazo." *Análise Social* 26, no. 112–13 (1991): 791–803.

Constituição da República dos Estados Unidos do Brasil. Rio de Janeiro: Imprensa Nacional, 1934.

Constituição dos Estados Unidos do Brasil (de 10 de Novembro de 1937). Rio de Janeiro: Imprensa Nacional, 1937.

Constituição política da República Portuguesa. Lisbon: Imprensa Nacional, 1916.

Constituição política da República Portuguesa. Lisbon: Imprensa Nacional, 1933.

Cooper, Frederick. *Citizenship between Empire and Nation: Remaking France and French Africa, 1945–1960*. Princeton, NJ: Princeton University Press, 2014.

———. "Modernizing Bureaucrats, Backward Africans, and the Development Concept." In *International Development and the Social Sciences: Essays on the History and Politics of Knowledge*, edited by Frederick Cooper, 64–92. Berkeley: University of California Press, 1997.

———. "Writing the History of Development." *Journal of Modern European History* 8, no. 1 (2010): 5–23.

Correia, Sílvia. "Celebrating Victory on a Day of Defeat: Commemorating the First World War in Portugal, 1918–1933." *European Review of History: Revue Européenne d'Histoire* 24, no. 1 (2017): 108–30.

Correia, Sílvia Barbosa. "The Veterans' Movement and First World War Memory in Portugal (1918–33): Between the Republic and Dictatorship." *European Review of History: Revue Européenne d'Histoire* 19, no. 4 (2012): 531–51.

Corsi, Francisco Luiz. "Política externa, projeto nacional e política econômica ao final do Estado Novo." *Política & Sociedade* 7, no. 12 (2008): 67–93.

Costa, Achyles Barcelos da, and Carlos G. A. Mielitz Netto. "O Instituto Rio Grandense do Arroz." *Revista Brasileira de Inovação* 11, no. 2 (2012): 467–80.

Costa, Emília Viotti da. *The Brazilian Empire: Myths and Histories*. Chapel Hill: University of North Carolina Press, 2000.

———. *O Supremo Tribunal Federal e a construção da cidadania*. São Paulo: Editora UNESP, 2006.

Costa, Fernando Ferreira da. *As cooperativas e a economia social*. Lisbon: Livros Horizonte, 1985.

Costa, Vanda Maria Ribeiro. *A armadilha do Leviatã: A construção do corporativismo no Brasil.* Rio de Janeiro: Editora UERJ, 1999.

———. *Origens do corporativismo brasileiro.* Rio de Janeiro: CPDOC, 1991.

Cotterrell, Roger. "Emmanuel Lévy and Legal Studies: A View from Abroad." *Droit et Société* 1, no. 56–57 (2004): 131–41.

Covello, Antônio Augusto de. *A lei de segurança: Trabalhos parlamentares.* São Paulo: Revista dos Tribunais, 1935.

Coyle, Diane. *GDP: A Brief but Affectionate History.* Princeton, NJ: Princeton University Press, 2014.

Crocitti, John J. "Vargas Era Social Policies: An Inquiry into Brazilian Malnutrition during the Estado Novo (1937–45)." In *Vargas and Brazil: New Perspectives,* edited by Jens R. Hentschke, 143–71. Basingstoke, UK: Palgrave Macmillan, 2007.

Cruz, Manuel Braga da. "Notas para uma caracterização política do salazarismo." *Análise Social* 18, no. 72/74 (1982): 773–94.

———. "O integralismo lusitano nas origens do salazarismo." *Análise Social* 18, no. 70 (1982): 137–82.

Cullather, Nick. *The Hungry World: America's Cold War Battle against Poverty in Asia.* Cambridge, MA: Harvard University Press, 2010.

Cunha Gonçalves, Luís da. "Causas e efeitos do corporativismo português." *Economia e Finanças* 4 (1936): 109–23.

———. *Da compra e venda no direito comercial brasileiro.* 2nd ed. São Paulo: Max Limonad, 1950.

———. *Da compra e venda no direito comercial português.* 2nd ed. Coimbra: Imprensa da Universidade, 1924.

———. *O Estado Novo e a Assembléa Nacional: Discursos proferidos na propaganda eleitoral.* Lisbon: Ottosgráfica, 1934.

———. *Princípios de direito corporativo.* Lisbon: Instituto Superior de Ciências Económicas e Financeiras, 1935.

Dard, Olivier. *Charles Maurras: Le maître et l'action.* Paris: Armand Colin, 2013.

———. "Le corporatisme entre traditionalistes et modernisateurs: des groupements aux cercles du pouvoir." In *Les expériences corporatives dans l'aire latine,* edited by Didier Musiedlak, 67–102. Bern: Peter Lang, 2010.

Dávila, Jerry. *Hotel Trópico: Brazil and the Challenge of African Decolonization, 1950–1980.* Durham, NC: Duke University Press, 2010.

———. "Myth and Memory: Getúlio Vargas's Long Shadow over Brazilian History." In *Vargas and Brazil: New Perspectives,* edited by Jens R. Hentschke, 257–82. Basingstoke, UK: Palgrave Macmillan, 2007.

Davis, Belinda J. *Home Fires Burning: Food, Politics, and Everyday Life in World War I Berlin.* Chapel Hill: University of North Carolina Press, 2000.

De, Rohit. "'Commodities Must Be Controlled': Economic Crimes and Market Discipline in India (1939–1955)." *International Journal of Law in Context* 10, no. 3 (2014): 277–94.

———. *A People's Constitution: The Everyday Life of Law in the Indian Republic.* Princeton, NJ: Princeton University Press, 2018.

Dean, Warren. "The Brazilian Economy, 1870–1930." In *Cambridge History of Latin America. Volume 5, c. 1870–1930,* edited by Leslie Bethell, 685–724. Cambridge: Cambridge University Press, 1986.

Desrosières, Alain. "The History of Statistics as a Genre: Styles of Writing and Social Uses." *Bulletin de Méthodologie Sociologique* 119 (2013): 8–23.

Deutsch, Sandra McGee. *Las Derechas: The Extreme Right in Argentina, Brazil, and Chile, 1890–1939*. Stanford, CA: Stanford University Press, 1999.

———. "Spartan Mothers: Fascist Women in Brazil in the 1930s." In *Right-Wing Women: From Conservatives to Extremists around the World*, edited by Paola Bacchetta and Margaret Power, 155–67. New York: Routledge, 2002.

Diacon, Todd A. *Stringing Together a Nation: Cândido Mariano da Silva Rondon and the Construction of a Modern Brazil, 1906–1930*. Durham, NC: Duke University Press, 2004.

Díaz-Alejandro, Carlos F. "Latin America in the 1930s." In *Trade, Development and the World Economy: Selected Essays of Carlos F. Díaz-Alejandro*, 185–211. Oxford: Basil Blackwell, Inc., 1988.

Dimand, Robert W. "Irving Fisher and Modern Macroeconomics." *American Economic Review* 87, no. 2 (1997): 442–44.

Dinius, Oliver J. *Brazil's Steel City: Developmentalism, Strategic Power, and Industrial Relations in Volta Redonda, 1941–1964*. Stanford, CA: Stanford University Press, 2011.

———. "Defending Ordem against Progresso: The Brazilian Political Police and Industrial Labor Control." In *Vargas and Brazil: New Perspectives*, edited by Jens R. Hentschke, 176–206. New York: Palgrave Macmillan, 2006.

Diniz, Augusto Alves. "Crise cambial portuguesa: Aspectos e soluções." In *Congresso das Associações Comerciais e Industriais de Portugal: Teses e actas*. Tip. Emp. Diário de Notícias: Lisbon, 1923.

Diniz, Eli. *Empresário, Estado e capitalismo no Brasil: 1930–1945*. Rio de Janeiro: Editora Paz e Terra, 1978.

———. "Engenharia institucional e políticas públicas: Dos conselhos técnicos às câmaras setoriais." In *Repensando o Estado Novo*, edited by Dulce Chaves Pandolfi, 21–38. Rio de Janeiro: Editora Fundação Getúlio Vargas, 1999.

Directoria Geral de Estatística. *Recenseamento do Brazil: Realizado em 1 de setembro de 1920*. Vol. 1. Rio de Janeiro: Typ. de Estatistica, 1922.

———. *Recenseamento do Brazil: Realizado em 1 de setembro de 1920*. Vol. 4, *População*. Rio de Janeiro: Typ. de Estatística, 1926.

Dores, Maria Elsa. *O Desenvolvimento da economia portuguesa e o plano para 1959–1964*. Lisbon: Estudos de Economia Aplicada Associação Industrial Portuguesa, 1959.

Draibe, Sônia. *Rumos e metamorfoses: Um estudo sobre a constituição do Estado e as alternativas da industrialização no Brasil, 1930–1960*. Rio de Janeiro: Paz e Terra, 1985.

Duarte, Gil. *A paisagem legal do Estado Novo*. Rio de Janeiro: Livraria J. Olympio Editora, 1941.

Dulles, John W. F. *Anarchists and Communists in Brazil, 1900–1935*. Austin: University of Texas Press, 1973.

———. *The São Paulo Law School and the Anti-Vargas Resistance (1938–1945)*. Austin: University of Texas Press, 1986.

———. *Sobral Pinto, "The Conscience of Brazil": Leading the Attack against Vargas (1930–1945)*. Austin: University of Texas Press, 2002.

Echeverri, Marcela. "'Sovereignty Has Lost Its Rights': Liberal Experiments and Indigenous Citizenship in New Granada, 1810–1819. In *Justice in a New World: Negotiating Legal*

Intelligibility in British, Iberian, and Indigenous America, edited by Brian P. Owensby and Richard J. Ross, 238–69. New York: New York University Press, 2018.

Eckes, Alfred E., Jr., and Thomas W. Zeiler. *Globalization and the American Century.* Cambridge: Cambridge University Press, 2003.

Ekbladh, David. "Exile Economics: The Transnational Contributions and Limits of the League of Nations' Economic and Financial Section." *New Global Studies* 4, no. 1 (2010): 1–6.

Elena, Eduardo. *Dignifying Argentina: Peronism, Citizenship, and Mass Consumption.* Pittsburgh: University of Pittsburgh Press, 2011.

Engerman, David C. "Social Science in the Cold War." *Isis* 101, no. 2 (2010): 393–400.

Ernest Martin, Doblin. *Price Control in Nazi Germany.* Division of Research, Foreign Information Branch, 1943.

Espínola, Eduardo. "Discurso do Presidente do Supremo Tribunal Federal." *O Direito* 73, no. 8 (October 1941): 228–30.

Fajardo, Margarita. *The World That Latin America Created: The United Nations Economic Commission for Latin America in the Development Era.* Cambridge, MA: Harvard University Press, 2022.

Falcão, Valdemar. "O corporativismo e o regime político brasileiro." *O Direito* 73, no. 8 (October 1941): 230–34.

Fanno, Marco. *Introduzione allo studio della teoria economica del corporativismo.* Padua: Casa Editrice Dott. Antonio Milani, 1936.

Fausto, Boris. *A Revolução de 1930: Historiografia e história.* São Paulo: Editora Brasiliense, 1970.

Feinstein, Charles H., Peter Temin, and Gianni Toniolo. *The World Economy between the World Wars.* Oxford and New York: Oxford University Press, 2008.

Feldman, Jan. "New Thinking about the 'New Man': Developments in Soviet Moral Theory." *Studies in Soviet Thought* 38, no. 2 (1989): 147–63.

Ferreira, Nuno Estêvão Figueiredo Miranda. "A Câmara Corporativa no Estado Novo: Composição, funcionamento e influência." PhD diss., Instituto de Ciências Sociais da Universidade de Lisboa, 2009.

Ferreira, Roquinaldo. "Measuring Short- and Long-Term Impacts of Abolitionism in the South Atlantic, 1807–1860s." In *Networks and Trans-Cultural Exchange: Slave Trading in the South Atlantic, 1590-1867,* edited by David Richardson and Filipa Ribeiro da Silva, 221-37. Leiden: Brill, 2015.

Ferreira, Waldemar Martins. "Prof. Luiz da Cunha Gonçalves." *Revista da Faculdade de Direito, Universidade de São Paulo* 42 (1947): 232–36.

Ferro, António. "Algumas palavras de António Ferro." *Atlântico: Revista Luso-Brasileira* 1, no. 1 (1942).

———. *Viagem à volta das ditaduras.* Lisbon: Emprensa do Diário de Notícias, 1927.

Field, Thomas C. *From Development to Dictatorship: Bolivia and the Alliance for Progress in the Kennedy Era.* Ithaca, NY: Cornell University Press, 2014.

Filho, Hermógenes Saviani. "A era Vargas: Desenvolvimentismo, economia e sociedade." *Economia e Sociedade* 22, no. 3 (2013): 855–60.

Finchelstein, Federico. *The Ideological Origins of the Dirty War: Fascism, Populism, and Dictatorship in Twentieth-Century Argentina.* Oxford: Oxford University Press, 2014.

———. *Transatlantic Fascism: Ideology, Violence, and the Sacred in Argentina and Italy, 1919–1945.* Durham, NC: Duke University Press, 2010.

Finchelstein, Federico and Nadia Urbinati. "On Populism and Democracy." *Populism* 1, no. 1 (2018): 15–37.

Fischer, Brodwyn. *A Poverty of Rights: Citizenship and Inequality in Twentieth-Century Rio de Janeiro*. Stanford, CA: Stanford University Press, 2008.

———. "Quase Pretos de Tão Pobres? Race and Social Discrimination in Rio de Janeiro's Twentieth-Century Criminal Courts." *Latin American Research Review* 39, no. 1 (January 1, 2004): 31–59.

Fischer, Brodwyn, Keila Grinberg, and Hebe Mattos. "Law, Silence, and Racialized Inequalities in the History of Afro-Brazil." In *Afro-Latin American Studies: An Introduction*, edited by Alejandro de la Fuente and George Reid Andrews, 130–76. Cambridge: Cambridge University Press, 2018.

Fonseca, Pedro Cezar Dutra. "Instituições e política econômica: Crise e crescimento do Brasil na Década de 1930." In *A era Vargas: Desenvolvimentismo, economia sociedade*, edited by Pedro Paulo Zahluth Bastos and Pedro Cezar Dutra Fonseca, 159–78. São Paulo: Editora UNESP, 2011.

———. "O mito do populismo econômico de Vargas." *Revista de Economia Política* 31, no. 1 (2011): 56–76.

———. *RS: Economia e conflitos políticos na República Velha*. Porto Alegre: Mercado Aberto, 1983.

———. *Vargas: O capitalismo em construção*. São Paulo: Editora Brasiliense, 1989.

Fontes, Lourival. "Unidade espiritual por Lourival Fontes." *Atlântico: Revista Luso-Brasileira* 1, no. 1 (1942).

Fortes, Alexandre. "O Estado Novo e os trabalhadores: A construção de um corporativismo latino-americano." *Locus: Revista de História* 13, no. 2 (2011): 63–86.

———. "Revendo a legalização dos sindicatos: metalúrgicos de Porto Alegre (1931–1945)." In *Na luta por direitos: Estudos recentes em história social do trabalho*, edited by Alexandre Fortes, 20–49. Campinas: Editora Unicamp, 1999.

Fraenkel, Ernst. *The Dual State: A Contribution to the Theory of Dictatorship*. Translated by Jens Meierhenrich. Oxford: Oxford University Press, 2017.

Freire, Dulce. *Produzir e beber: A questão do vinho no Estado Novo* (1929–1939). Lisbon: Âncora Editora, 2011.

Freire, Dulce, Nuno Estevão Ferreira, and Ana Margarida Rodrigues. "Corporativismo e Estado Novo: Contributo para um roteiro de arquivos das instituições corporativas (1933–1974)." *ICS Estudos e Relatórios*. Lisbon: Instituto de Ciências Sociais da Universidade de Lisboa, 2014.

French, John D. *The Brazilian Workers' ABC: Class Conflict and Alliances in Modern São Paulo*. Chapel Hill: University of North Carolina Press, 1992.

———. *Drowning in Laws: Labor Law and Brazilian Political Culture*. Chapel Hill: University of North Carolina Press, 2004.

———. "The Origin of Corporatist State Intervention in Brazilian Industrial Relations, 1930–1934: A Critique of the Literature." *Luso-Brazilian Review* 28, no. 2 (December 1, 1991): 13–26.

Frens-String, Joshua. *Hungry for Revolution: The Politics of Food and the Making of Modern Chile*. Oakland: University of California Press, 2021.

Freyre, Gilberto. *Casa grande & senzala*. Madrid: Allca XX, 2002.

———. *Uma cultura ameaçada: A luso-brasileira*. 2nd ed. Rio de Janeiro: Departamento Cultural da CEB, 1942.

Friedman, Jeremy. *Ripe for Revolution: Building Socialism in the Third World*. Cambridge, MA: Harvard University Press, 2022.

————. *Shadow Cold War: The Sino-Soviet Competition for the Third World*. Chapel Hill: University of North Carolina Press, 2015.

Furtado, Celso. *A pré-revolução brasileira*. Rio de Janeiro: Editora Fundo de Cultura, 1962.

Galvão, Henrique. *O povoamento europeu nas colónias portuguesas: Primeira conferência económica do império colonial português*. Lisbon: Tip. Cristóvão Augusto Rodrigues, 1936.

Garfield, Seth. "The Environment of Wartime Migration: Labor Transfers from the Brazilian Northeast to the Amazon during World War II." *Journal of Social History* 43, no. 4 (2010): 989–1019.

Gargarella, Roberto. *Latin American Constitutionalism, 1810–2010: The Engine Room of the Constitution*. Oxford: Oxford University Press, 2013.

————. *The Legal Foundations of Inequality: Constitutionalism in the Americas, 1776–1860*. Cambridge: Cambridge University Press, 2010.

————. "Towards a Typology of Latin American Constitutionalism, 1810–60." *Latin American Research Review* 39, no. 2 (2004): 141–53.

Garnsey, Morris E. "Charles Gide." *American Economic Review* 22, no. 4 (1932): 692–93.

Garrido, Álvaro. *O Estado Novo e a campanha do bacalhau*. Rio de Mouro: Círculo de Leitores, 2003.

————. "Os bacalhoeiros em revolta: a 'greve' de 1937." *Análise Social* 37, no. 165 (2003): 1191–211.

————. *Queremos uma economia nova!: Estado Novo e corporativismo*. Lisbon: Temas e Debates, 2016.

Gauss, Susan M. *Made in Mexico: Regions, Nation, and the State in the Rise of Mexican Industrialism, 1920s–1940s*. University Park: Pennsylvania State University Press, 2010.

Gentile, Fabio. "Uma apropriação criativa: Fascismo e corporativismo no pensamento de Oliveira Vianna." In *A vaga corporativa: Corporativismo e ditaduras na Europa e na América Latina*, edited by António Costa Pinto and Francisco Palomanes Martinho, 223–53. Lisbon: Imprensa de Ciências Sociais, 2016.

Gerschenkron, Alexander. "Economic Backwardness in Historical Perspective." In *Economic Backwardness in Historical Perspective: A Book of Essays*, 5–30. New York: Frederick A. Braeger, 1962.

Geyer, Michael, and Charles Bright. "World History in a Global Age." *American Historical Review* 100, no. 4 (1995): 1034–60.

Gide, Charles. *Principes d'économie politique*. 24th ed. Paris: Librairie de la Société du Recueil Sirey, 1923.

Gillingham, Paul. *Unrevolutionary Mexico: The Birth of a Strange Dictatorship*. New Haven, CT: Yale University Press, 2021.

Gilman, Nils. *Mandarins of the Future: Modernization Theory in Cold War America*. Baltimore: Johns Hopkins University Press, 2007.

Giménez Martínez, Miguel Ángel. "El Fuero del Trabajo: La 'constitución social' del franquismo." *Studia Historica* 33 (2015): 219–52.

Gini, Corrado. "The Scientific Basis of Fascism." *Political Science Quarterly* 42, no. 1 (1927): 99–115.

Godinho, Paula. "'Desde a idade de seis anos, fui muito contrabandista': O concelho de Chaves e a comarca de Verín, entre velhos quotidianos e novas modalidades emblematizantes." In

Contrabando na fronteira luso-espanhola: Práticas, memórias e patrimónios, edited by Dulce Freire, Eduarda Rovisco, and Inês Fonseca, 29–56. Lisbon: Edições Nelson de Matos, 2009.

Gomes, Ângela de Castro. *A invenção do trabalhismo.* São Paulo: Vértice, 1988.

———. "A representação de classes na constituinte de 1934." *Revista de Ciência Política* 21, no. 3 (1978): 53–116.

———. "Azevedo Amaral e *O século do corporativismo,* de Michael Manoilesco, no Brasil de Vargas." *Sociologia e Antropologia* 2, no. 4 (2012): 185–209.

———. *Burguesia e trabalho: Política e legislação social no Brasil, 1917–1937.* Rio de Janeiro: Editora Campus Ltda., 1979.

———. "A práxis corporativa de Oliveira Vianna." In *O pensamento de Oliveira Vianna,* edited by Élide Rugai Bastos and João Quartim de Moraes, 43–61. Campinas: Editora Unicamp, 1993.

Gonçalves, Caetano. *O estado corporativo e a política do império no direito constitucional português: Lições proferidas em 7 e 10 de Dezembro de 1934.* Lisbon: Academia das Ciências de Lisboa, 1935.

Gonçalves, Leandro Pereira. "Plínio Salgado e integralismo: Relação franco-luso-italiana." *Lusitania Sacra* 26 (2012): 133–54.

———. "Transnational Fascism: Portugal and the Brazilian Integralism of Plínio Salgado." *Journal of Iberian and Latin American Studies* 29, no. 2 (2023): 273–93.

González-Jácome, Jorge. "From Abusive Constitutionalism to a Multilayered Understanding of Constitutionalism: Lessons from Latin America." *International Journal of Constitutional Law* 15, no. 2 (2017): 447–68.

Gootenberg, Paul. *Imagining Development: Economic Ideas in Peru's "Fictitious Prosperity" of Guano, 1840–1880.* Berkeley: University of California Press, 1993.

Gordon, Colin. *New Deals: Business, Labor, and Politics in America, 1920–1935.* Cambridge: Cambridge University Press, 1994.

Gordon-Ashworth, Fiona. "Agricultural Commodity Control under Vargas in Brazil, 1930–1945." *Journal of Latin American Studies* 12, no. 1 (1980): 87–105.

Gotkowitz, Laura. *A Revolution for Our Rights: Indigenous Struggles for Land and Justice in Bolivia, 1880–1952.* Durham, NC: Duke University Press, 2007.

———. "Trading Insults: Honor, Violence, and the Gendered Culture of Commerce in Cochabamba, Bolivia, 1870s–1950s." *Hispanic American Historical Review* 83, no. 1 (2003): 83–118.

Gouveia, Saulo. *The Triumph of Brazilian Modernism: The Metanarrative of Emancipation and Counter-Narratives.* Chapel Hill: University of North Carolina Press, 2013.

Graham, Jessica Lynn. *Shifting the Meaning of Democracy: Race, Politics, and Culture in the United States and Brazil.* Oakland: University of California Press, 2019.

Graham, Richard. *Feeding the City: From Street Market to Liberal Reform in Salvador, Brazil, 1780–1860.* Austin: University of Texas Press, 2010.

———. *Patronage and Politics in Nineteenth-Century Brazil.* Stanford, CA: Stanford University Press, 1990.

Grand, Alexander de. "Mussolini's Follies: Fascism in Its Imperial and Racist Phase, 1935–1940." *Contemporary European History* 13, no. 2 (2004): 127–47.

Grandin, Greg. "The Liberal Traditions in the Americas: Rights, Sovereignty, and the Origins of Liberal Multilateralism." *American Historical Review* 117, no. 1 (February 1, 2012): 68–91.

Grazia, Victoria de. *The Culture of Consent: Mass Organization of Leisure in Fascist Italy*. Cambridge: Cambridge University Press, 1981.

———. *How Fascism Ruled Women: Italy 1922–1945*. Berkeley: University of California Press, 1992.

Gregor, A. James. *Italian Fascism and Developmental Dictatorship*. Princeton, NJ: Princeton University Press, 2014.

Grinberg, Keila. *O fiador dos brasileiros: Cidadania, escravidão e direito civil no tempo de Antonio Pereira Rebouças*. Rio de Janeiro: Civilização Brasileira, 1994.

Guimarães, Carlos Gabriel. "O Instituto do Açúcar e do Álcool e a indústria do álcool-motor no primeiro governo Vargas (1930–1945)." *História Econômica e História de Empresas* 15, no. 1 (2012): 135–68.

Guitton, Henri. "Gaston Leduc: 1904–1979." *Revue d'Économie Politique* 90, no. 1 (1980): 1–2.

Gutiérrez-Solana, Miguel Fagoaga. "Democracia, totalitarismo y corporativismo." *Cuadernos de Política Social* 19 (1953): 7–34.

Hale, Charles. *The Transformation of Liberalism in Late Nineteenth-Century Mexico*. Princeton, NJ: Princeton University Press, 1989.

Hall, Michael M. "Corporativismo e fascismo: As origens das leis trabalhistas brasileiras." In *Do corporativismo ao neoliberalismo: Estado e trabalhadores no Brasil e na Inglaterra*, edited by Angela Maria Carneiro Araújo, 13–28. São Paulo: Boitempo Editorial, 2002.

Hall, Peter A. *The Political Power of Economic Ideas: Keynesianism across Nations*. Princeton, NJ: Princeton University Press, 1989.

Hamilton, Nora. *The Limits of State Autonomy: Post-Revolutionary Mexico*. Princeton, NJ: Princeton University Press, 1982.

———. "Mexico: The Limits of State Autonomy." *Latin American Perspectives* 2, no. 2 (1975): 81–108.

Hart-Landsberg, Martin. "Popular Mobilization and Progressive Policy Making: Lessons from World War II Price Control Struggles in the United States." *Science and Society* 67, no. 4 (2003–4): 399–428.

Hentschke, Jens. *Positivismo ao estilo gaúcho: A ditadura de Júlio de Castilhos e seu impacto sobre a construção do Estado e da nação no Brasil de Getúlio Vargas*. Porto Alegre: EdiPUCRS, 2015.

———, ed. *Vargas and Brazil: New Perspectives*. New York: Palgrave Macmillan, 2006.

Herman, Rebecca. *Cooperating with the Colossus: A Social and Political History of US Military Bases in World War II Latin America*. New York: Oxford University Press, 2022.

Hertzman, Marc A. *Making Samba: A New History of Race and Music in Brazil*. Durham, NC: Duke University Press, 2013.

Herzog, Tamar. *Defining Nations: Immigrants and Citizens in Early Modern Spain and Spanish America*. New Haven, CT: Yale University Press, 2003.

———. *Frontiers of Possession: Spain and Portugal in Europe and the Americas*. Cambridge, MA: Harvard University Press, 2015.

———. *A Short History of European Law: The Last Two and a Half Millennia*. Cambridge: Cambridge University Press, 2018.

Hobsbawm, Eric. *The Age of Extremes: A History of the World, 1914–1991*. New York: Vintage Books, 1996.

Horwitz, Morton J. *The Transformation of American Law, 1870–1960: The Crisis of Legal Orthodoxy*. New York: Oxford University Press, 1992.

Hulsebosch, Daniel Joseph. *Constituting Empire: New York and the Transformation of Constitutionalism in the Atlantic World, 1664–1830*. Chapel Hill: University of North Carolina Press, 2005.

Hungria, Nelson. *Dos crimes contra a economia popular e das vendas a prestações com reserva de dominio*. Rio de Janeiro: Livraria Jacintho, 1939.

Immerwahr, Daniel. *Thinking Small: The United States and the Lure of Community Development*. Cambridge, MA: Harvard University Press, 2015.

Ioris, Rafael R. "'Fifty Years in Five' and What's in It for Us? Development Promotion, Populism, Industrial Workers and *Carestia* in 1950s Brazil." *Journal of Latin American Studies* 44, no. 2 (2012): 261–84.

———. *Transforming Brazil: A History of National Development in the Postwar Era*. New York: Routledge, 2014.

Isaac, Joel. "The Human Sciences in Cold War America." *The Historical Journal* 50, no. 3 (2007): 725–46.

Isaacman, Allen F. *Cotton Is the Mother of Poverty: Peasants, Work, and Rural Struggle in Colonial Mozambique, 1938–1961*. Portsmouth, NH: Heinemann, 1996.

Jacobs, Meg. "'How about Some Meat?': The Office of Price Administration, Consumption Politics, and State Building from the Bottom Up, 1941–1946." *Journal of American History* 84, no. 3 (1997): 910–41.

———. *Pocketbook Politics: Economic Citizenship in Twentieth-Century America*. Princeton, NJ: Princeton University Press, 2007.

James, Daniel. *Resistance and Integration: Peronism and the Argentine Working Class, 1946–1976*. Cambridge: Cambridge University Press, 1993.

James, Harold. "Banks and Business Politics in Nazi Germany." In *Business and Industry in Nazi Germany*, edited by Francis R. Nicosia and Jonathan Huener, 43–65. New York: Berghahn Book, 2004.

Jennings, Eric T. *Vichy in the Tropics: Pétain's National Revolution in Madagascar, Guadeloupe, and Indochina, 1940–1944*. Stanford, CA: Stanford University Press, 2001.

Jerónimo, Miguel Bandeira. *Livros brancos, almas negras: A "missão civilizadora" do colonialismo português, c. 1870–1930*. Lisbon: Imprensa de Ciências Sociais, 2010.

Jesus, Quirino Avelino de. *Nacionalismo português*. Porto: Empresa Industrial Gráfica do Porto, 1932.

Joseph, Gilbert M. and Nugent, Daniel. "Popular Culture and State Formation in Revolutionary Mexico." In *Everyday Forms of State Formation: Revolution and the Negotiation of Rule in Modern Mexico*, edited by Gilbert M. Joseph and Daniel Nugent, 3–23. Durham, NC: Duke University Press, 1994.

Júnior, Antônio Ferreira Cesarino. *Direito social brasileiro*. Rio de Janeiro: Livraria Freitas Bastos, 1963.

Jurisprudência: Tribunal de Segurança Nacional. Vol. 1. Rio de Janeiro: Imprensa Nacional, 1941.

Jurisprudência: Tribunal de Segurança Nacional. Vol. 14. Rio de Janeiro: Imprensa Nacional, 1943.

Kagan Guthrie, Zachary. *Bound for Work: Labor, Mobility, and Colonial Rule in Central Mozambique, 1940–1965*. Charlottesville: University of Virginia Press, 2018.

Kant de Lima, Roberto. "Bureaucratic Rationality in Brazil and in the United States: Criminal Justice Systems in Comparative Perspective." In *The Brazilian Puzzle: Culture on the Borderlands of the Western World*, edited by David J. Hess and Roberto A. DaMatta, 241–69. New York: Columbia University Press, 1995.

Katznelson, Ira. *Fear Itself: The New Deal and the Origins of Our Time*. New York: Liveright Publishing, 2013.

Kennedy, Duncan. "From the Will Theory to the Principle of Private Autonomy: Lon Fuller's 'Consideration and Form.'" *Columbia Law Review* 100, no. 1 (2000): 94–175.

———. "Three Globalizations of Law and Legal Thought: 1850–2000." In *The New Law and Economic Development: A Critical Appraisal*, edited by David M. Trubek and Alvaro Santos, 19–73. Cambridge: Cambridge University Press, 2006.

Keynes, John Maynard. *The End of Laissez-Faire*. London: Hogarth Press, 1927.

Kiernan, Ben. *Blood and Soil: A World History of Genocide and Extermination from Sparta to Darfur*. New Haven, CT: Yale University Press, 2009.

Klein, Steven. "Corporatism." In *The Cambridge Handbook of Constitutional Theory*, edited by Richard Bellamy and Jeffry King. Cambridge: Cambridge University Press, forthcoming.

Kohli, Atul. *State-Directed Development: Political Power and Industrialization in the Global Periphery*. Cambridge: Cambridge University Press, 2004.

Kramer, Paul A. "Empires, Exceptions, and Anglo-Saxons: Race and Rule between the British and United States Empires, 1880–1910." *Journal of American History* 88, no. 4 (2002): 1315–53.

———. "Imperial Openings: Civilization, Exemption, and the Geopolitics of Mobility in the History of Chinese Exclusion, 1868–1910." *Journal of the Gilded Age and Progressive Era* 14, no. 3 (2015): 317–47.

Kwass, Michael. *Contraband: Louis Mandrin and the Making of a Global Underground*. Cambridge, MA: Harvard University Press, 2014.

Lacerda, João Maria de, and Eloy de Moura. *O Estado Novo: Democracia e corporatismo, a posição do Brasil*. Rio de Janeiro, 1938.

Lafer, Celso. *JK e o programa de metas, 1956–1961: Processo de planejamento e sistema político no Brasil*. Rio de Janeiro: FGV Editora, 2002.

Lains, Pedro. "Catching up to the European Core: Portuguese Economic Growth, 1910–1990." *Explorations in Economic History* 40, no. 4 (2003): 369–86.

———. "Growth in a Protected Environment: Portugal, 1850–1950." *Research in Economic History* 24 (2007): 119–60.

———. *Os progressos do atraso: Uma nova história económica de Portugal, 1842–1992*. Lisbon: Imprensa de Ciências Sociais, 2003.

Lake, Marilyn. *Drawing the Global Colour Line: White Men's Countries and the International Challenge of Racial Equality*. Cambridge: Cambridge University Press, 2008.

Lanero Táboas, Daniel, Antonio Míguez Macho, and Ángel Rodríguez Gallardo. "La 'raia' galaico-portuguesa en tiempos convulsos: Nuevas interpretaciones sobre el control político y la cultura de frontera en las dictaduras ibéricas (1936–1945)." In *Contrabando na fronteira luso-espanhola: Práticas, memórias e patrimónios*, edited by Dulce Freire, Eduarda Rovisco, and Inês Fonseca, 57–87. Lisbon: Edições Nelson de Matos, 2009.

Latham, Michael. "Ideology, Social Science, and Destiny: Modernization and the Kennedy-Era Alliance-for-Progress." *Diplomatic History* 22, no. 2 (1998): 199–229.

Law, David S., and Mila Versteeg. "The Evolution and Ideology of Global Constitutionalism." *California Law Review* 99 (2011): 1163–254.

———. "Sham Constitutions." *California Law Review* 101, no. 4 (2013): 863–952.

Le Crom, Jean-Pierre. *Syndicats, nous voilà!: Vichy et le corporatisme*. Paris: Éditions de l'Atelier, 1995.

Leal, Ernesto Castro. "Nacionalismo e antiliberalismo em Portugal: Uma visão histórico-política (1820–1940)." *História Crítica* 56 (2015): 113–35.

———. "Quirino Avelino de Jesus, um católico 'pragmático': Notas para o estudo crítico da relação existente entre publicismo e política (1894–1926)." *Lusitania Sacra* 6 (1994): 355–89.

Leeds, Elizabeth. "Industrialização e emigração em Portugal: Sintomas inevitáveis de uma doença estrutural." *Análise Social* 29, no. 77–79 (1983): 1045–81.

Leerssen, Joep, and Eric Storm, eds. *World Fairs and the Global Moulding of National Identities: International Exhibitions as Cultural Platforms, 1851–1958*. Leiden: Brill Press, 2022.

Leff, Nathaniel H. *Economic Policy-Making and Development in Brazil, 1947–1964*. New York: John Wiley and Sons, 1968.

———. *Underdevelopment and Development in Brazil*. Vol. 1, *Economic Structure and Change, 1822–1947*. London: Allen and Unwin, 1982.

LeGrand, Catherine. "Labor Acquisition and Social Conflict on the Colombian Frontier, 1850–1936." *Journal of Latin American Studies* 16, no. 1 (1984): 27–49.

Leitão, Nicolau. "The Reluctant European: A Survey of the Literature on Portugal and European Integration, 1947–1974." *E-Journal of Portuguese History* 3, no. 1 (2005): 1–12.

Leite (Lumbrales), João Pinto da Costa. *A doutrina corporativa em Portugal*. Lisbon: Livraria Clássica Editora, 1936.

———. *Professor e homem estado: Conferência realizada na Sala dos Capelos da Universidade de Coimbra no dia 27 de Abril de 1938*. Coimbra: Coimbra Editora, 1938.

Léonard, Yves. "Salazarisme et lusotropicalisme, histoire d'une appropriation." *Lusotopie* (1997): 211–26.

Leopoldi, Maria Antonieta P. "O difícil caminho do meio: Estado, burguesia e industrialização no segundo governo Vargas (1951–54)." In *Vargas e a crise dos anos 50*, edited by Ângela Maria de Castro Gomes, 161–203. Rio de Janeiro: Relume-Dumará, 1994.

———. *Política e interesses: As associações industriais, a política econômica e o Estado na industrialização brasileira*. São Paulo: Paz e Terra, 2000.

Lesser, Jeffrey. *Negotiating National Identity: Immigrants, Minorities, and the Struggle for Ethnicity in Brazil*. Durham, NC: Duke University Press, 1999.

———. *Welcoming the Undesirables: Brazil and the Jewish Question*. Berkeley: University of California Press, 1995.

Levine, Robert M. *Father of the Poor?: Vargas and His Era*. New York: Cambridge University Press, 1998.

Lévy, Emmanuel. *La vision socialiste du droit*. Paris: Marcel Giard, 1926.

———. *Les fondements du droit*. Paris: F. Alcan, 1933.

Levy, Jonathan. *Ages of American Capitalism: A History of the United States*. New York: Random House, 2021.

Lewis, William Arthur. *Economic Survey, 1919–1939*. London: Routledge, 2003.

Lichtenstein, Nelson. *Labor's War at Home: The CIO in World War II*. Philadelphia: Temple University Press, 2003.

Lima Neto, A. *O Ribatejo e a sua influência no desenvolvimento do municipalismo e do corporatismo em Portugal*. Lisbon: Tip. da Gráfica Lisbonense, 1938.

Linhares, Maria Yedda Leite, and Francisco Carlos Teixeira da Silva. *História política do abastecimento (1918–1974)*. Brasília: Biblioteca Nacional de Agricultura-BINAGRI, 1979.

Link, Stefan J. *Forging Global Fordism: Nazi Germany, Soviet Russia, and the Contest over the Industrial Order*. Princeton, NJ: Princeton University Press, 2020.

Lochery, Neill. *Brazil: The Fortunes of War, World War II and the Making of Modern Brazil*. New York: Basic Books, 2014.

Loewenstein, Karl. *Brazil under Vargas*. New York: Macmillan Company, 1942.

Loureiro, Maria Rita. "Economistas e elites dirigentes no Brasil." *Revista Brasileira de Ciências Sociais* 7, no. 20 (1992): 47–65.

Love, Joseph L. "CEPAL as Idea Factory for Latin American Development: Intellectual and Political Influence, 1950–1990." In *State and Nation Making in Latin America and Spain: The Rise and Fall of the Developmental State*, edited by Miguel A. Centeno and Agustin E. Ferraro, 29–50. Cambridge: Cambridge University Press, 2018.

———. *Crafting the Third World: Theorizing Underdevelopment in Rumania and Brazil*. Stanford, CA: Stanford University Press, 1996.

———. *São Paulo in the Brazilian Federation, 1889–1937*. Stanford, CA: Stanford University Press, 1980.

———. *Rio Grande do Sul and Brazilian Regionalism, 1882–1930*. Stanford, CA: Stanford University Press, 1971.

———. "Structuralism and Dependency in Peripheral Europe: Latin American Ideas in Spain and Portugal." *Latin American Research Review* 39, no. 2 (2004): 114–40.

Loveman, Mara. "The Race to Progress: Census Taking and Nation Making in Brazil (1870–1920)." *Hispanic American Historical Review* 89, no. 3 (2009): 435–70.

Luca, Tania Regina de. *A Revista do Brazil: Um diagnóstico para a (n)ação*. São Paulo: Editora UNESP, 1998.

Lucena, Manuel de. *A evolução do sistema corporativo português*. Lisbon: Perspectivas & Realidades, 1976.

———. "Salazar, a 'fórmula' da agricultura portuguesa e a intervenção estatal no sector primário." *Análise Social* 26, no. 110 (1991): 97–206.

Luna, Francisco Vidal, and Herbert S. Klein. *The Economic and Social History of Brazil since 1889*. New York: Cambridge University Press, 2014.

Lyra, Roberto. *Crimes contra a economia popular: Doutrina, legislação e jurisprudência*. Rio de Janeiro: Livraria Jacinto, 1940.

Maddison, Angus. *The World Economy: Historical Statistics*. Paris: OECD Publishing, 2003.

Maddison, Angus. *The Political Economy of Poverty, Equity, and Growth: Brazil and Mexico*. Oxford: Oxford University Press, 1992.

Madeira, João, Luís Farinha, and Irene Flunser Pimentel. *Vítimas de Salazar: Estado Novo e violência política*. Lisbon: A Esfera dos Livros, 2007.

Madureira, Nuno Luís. "Cartelization and Corporatism: Bureaucratic Rule in Authoritarian Portugal, 1926–45." *Journal of Contemporary History* 42, no. 1 (2007): 79–96.

———. "O Estado, o patronato e a indústria portuguesa (1922–1957)." *Análise Social* 32, no. 148 (1998): 777–822.

Maier, Charles S. *Recasting Bourgeois Europe: Stabilization in France, Germany, and Italy in the Decade after World War I*. Princeton, NJ: Princeton University Press, 1975.

———. *In Search of Stability: Explorations in Historical Political Economy*. Cambridge: Cambridge University Press, 1987.

Malin, Mauro, and Marcos Penchel. "Campos, Francisco." In *Dicionário histórico-biográfico da Primeira República (1889–1930)*, edited by Alzira Alves de Abreu and Israel Beloch, 1:571–82. Rio de Janeiro: Editora Forense-Universitária FGV/CPDOC, 1984.

Malloy, James M. "Authoritarianism and Corporatism in Latin America: The Modal Pattern." In *Authoritarianism and Corporatism in Latin America*, edited by James M. Malloy, 3–19. Pittsburgh: University of Pittsburgh Press, 1977.

Manoilescu, Mihail. *L'équilibre économique européen*. Bucarest: Regia M. O., Imprimeria Nationala, 1931.

———. *O século do corporativismo: Doutrina do corporativismo integral e puro*. Translated by Antônio José Azevedo Amaral. Rio de Janeiro: José Olympio Editora, 1938.

———. *Theoria do proteccionismo e da permuta internacional*. Translated and edited by the Centro das Indústrias do Estado de São Paulo. São Paulo: Escolas Profissionaes do Lyceu Coração de Jesus, 1931.

———. *Théorie du protectionnisme et de l'échange international*. Paris: Giard, 1929.

Mantero, Francisco. "A mão-de-obra indígena nas colónias africanas." 2° *Congresso Colonial Nacional* (Lisbon: Sociedade de Geografia, 1924).

Marcondes, Renato Leite. "Malogro da fortuna: Política de créditos, hipotecas e caixas econômicas na década de 1930." *Nova Economia* 25, no. 2 (2016): 261–87.

Marshall, T. H. "Citizenship and Social Class." In *Citizenship and Social Class, and Other Essays*. Cambridge: University of Cambridge Press, 1950.

Martinez, Pedro Soares. "Sentido económico do corporativismo." In *Comunicação apresentada ao Centro de Estudos Politico-Sociais no dia 18 de Maio de 1960*. Lisbon: Centro de Estudos Politico-Sociais, 1960.

Martinho, Francisco Carlos Palomanes. *Marcello Caetano and the Portuguese "New State": A Political Biography*. Brighton, UK: Sussex Academic Press, 2018.

Martinho, Francisco Carlos Palomanes, and António Costa Pinto, eds. *O corporativismo em português: Estado, política e sociedade no salazarismo e no varguismo*. Rio de Janeiro: Civilização Brasileira, 2007.

Martins, Fernando. *Pedro Theotónio Pereira: O outro delfim de Salazar*. Lisbon: Publicações Dom Quixote, 2020.

Mata, Eugénia. "Economic Ideas and Policies in Nineteenth-Century Portugal." *Luso-Brazilian Review* 39, no. 1 (2002): 29–42.

Mata, Eugénia, and Nuno Valério. *História económica de Portugal: Uma perspectiva global*. Lisbon: Editorial Presença, 1993.

———. "Monetary Stability, Fiscal Discipline and Economic Performance: The Experience of Portugal since 1854." In *Currency Convertibility: The Gold Standard and Beyond*, edited by Jorge Braga de Macedo, Barry Eichengreen, and Jaime Reis, 204–27. London: Routledge, 1996.

Mata, Milton da. "Controles de preços na economia brasileira: Aspectos institucionais e resultados." *Pesquisa e Planejamento Econômico* 10, no. 3 (1980): 911–53.

Mattei, Clara E. *The Capital Order: How Economists Invented Austerity and Paved the Way to Fascism*. Chicago: University of Chicago Press, 2022.

Mattos, Hebe. *Escravidão e cidadania no Brasil monárquico*. Rio de Janeiro: Jorge Zahar, 2001.

Mauricio, Font, A. *Coffee and Transformation in São Paulo, Brazil*. Lanham, MD: Lexington Books, 2010.

Maxwell, Kenneth. *The Making of Portuguese Democracy*. Cambridge: Cambridge University Press, 1995.

Mazower, Mark. *Dark Continent: Europe's Twentieth Century*. New York: Vintage, 2000.

———. *Governing the World: The History of an Idea*. London: Allen Lane, 2012.

McCann, Bryan. *Hello, Hello Brazil: Popular Music in the Making of Modern Brazil*. Durham, NC: Duke University Press, 2004.

McGillivray, Gillian, and Thomas D. Rogers. "Real Labor Movements, Imagined Revolutions: The Northeastern Brazilian Sugar Zone through US Eyes, 1955–1964." In *The Entangled Labor Histories of Brazil and the United States*, edited by Fernando Teixeira da Silva, Alexandre Fortes, Thomas D. Rogers, and Gillian McGillivray, 203–38. Lanham, MD: Lexington Books, 2023.

McCormick, Gladys I. *The Logic of Compromise in Mexico: How the Countryside Was Key to the Emergence of Authoritarianism*. Chapel Hill: University of North Carolina Press, 2016.

Meade, Teresa. *"Civilizing" Rio: Reform and Resistance in a Brazilian City, 1889–1930*. University Park: Penn State University Press, 2005.

———. "'Living Worse and Costing More': Resistance and Riot in Rio de Janeiro, 1890–1917." *Journal of Latin American Studies* 21, no. 1–2 (1989): 241–66.

Medici, Fernando Penteado, ed. *Código penal: Decreto-lei Nº2.848 de 7 de dezembro de 1940, acompanhado da exposição de motivos do Exmo. Snr. Dr. Francisco Campos, Ministro da Justiça, e um índice alfabético, analítico e remissivo*. São Paulo: Edição Saraiva, 1941.

Melo, Martinho Nobre de. *Ritmo novo: Palavras de um português ao Brasil*. Rio de Janeiro: Academia das Ciências de Lisboa, 1932.

Mendes, Renat Nureyev, and Jair Teixeira dos Reis. "Entre a formação humanista e a tecnicista: Perspectivas do ensino jurídico e do bacharelismo no Brasil—do auge ao declínio." *Revista da Faculdade de Direito da UERJ* 30 (2016): 297–321.

Mendonça, Sonia Regina de. *Agronomia e poder no Brasil*. Rio de Janeiro: Vício de Leitura, 1998.

———. *A política de cooperativização agrícola do estado brasileiro (1910–1945)*. Niterói: Editora da Universidade Federal Fluminense, 2002.

Meneses, Filipe Ribeiro de. *Salazar: A Political Biography*. New York: Enigma Books, 2009.

———. "Sidónio Pais, the Portuguese 'New Republic' and the Challenge to Liberalism in Southern Europe." *European History Quarterly* 28, no. 1 (1998): 109–30.

Meng, Anne. *Constraining Dictatorship: From Personalized Rule to Institutionalized Regimes*. Cambridge: Cambridge University Press, 2020.

Merkel, Ian. *Terms of Exchange: Brazilian Intellectuals and the French Social Sciences*. Chicago: University of Chicago Press, 2022.

Merryman, John Henry, and Rogelio Pérez-Perdomo. *The Civil Law Tradition: An Introduction to the Legal Systems of Europe and Latin America*. Stanford, CA: Stanford University Press, 2007.

Miceli, Sergio. *Intelectuais e classe dirigente no Brasil (1920–1945)*. São Paulo: DIFEL, 1979.

———. *Nacional estrangeiro: História social e cultural do modernismo artístico em São Paulo*. São Paulo: Companhia das Letras, 2003.

Milov, Sarah. *The Cigarette: A Political History*. Cambridge, MA: Harvard University Press, 2019.

Mirkine-Guetzévitch, Boris. *As novas tendências do direito constitucional*. Translated by Candido Motta Filho. São Paulo: Companhia Editora Nacional, 1933.

———. *Les constituitions de l'Europe nouvelle*. Paris: Librairie Delagrave, 1928.

———. *Les nouvelles tendances du droit constitutionnel*. Paris: M. Giard, 1931.

Mitchell, Timothy. "Fixing the Economy." *Cultural Studies* 12, no. 1 (1998): 82–101.

Mitchell, Timothy. *Rule of Experts Egypt, Techno-Politics, Modernity*. Berkeley: University of California Press, 2002.

Moraes, Francisco Quartim de. *1932: A história invertida*. São Paulo: Fundação Mauricio Grabois, 2018.

Motoyama, Shozo. "1930–1964: Período desenvolvimentista." In *Prelúdio para uma história: Ciência e tecnologia no Brasil*, edited by Shozo Motoyama, 249–316. São Paulo: Editora da Universidade de São Paulo, 2004.

Moura, Francisco Pereira de. "Estagnação e crescimento da economia portuguesa." *Revista do Gabinete de Estudos Corporativos* 7, no. 26 (1956).

Mouré, Kenneth. "Food Rationing and the Black Market in France (1940–1944)." *French History* 24, no. 2 (2010): 262–82.

———. "Marcel Aymé and the Moral Economy of Penury in Occupied France." *French Historical Studies* 34, no. 4 (2011): 713–43.

Moustafa, Tamir. "Law and Courts in Authoritarian Regimes." *Annual Review of Law and Social Science* 10, no. 1 (2014): 281–99.

Moyn, Samuel. *Christian Human Rights*. Philadelphia: University of Pennsylvania Press, 2015.

———. "The Secret History of Constitutional Dignity." *Yale Human Rights and Development Journal* 17, no. 1 (2014): 39–73.

Moyn, Samuel, and Andrew Sartori. "Approaches to Global Intellectual History." In *Global Intellectual History*, edited by Samuel Moyn and Andrew Sartori, 3–30. New York: Columbia University Press, 2013.

Mueller, Charles Curt. *Das oligarquias agrárias ao predomínio urbano-industrial: Um estudo do processo de formação de políticas agrícolas no Brasil*. Rio de Janeiro: IPEA/INPES, 1983.

Müller, Geraldo. "Cotrijuí: Tentativa de criação de um conglomerado de capital nacional." In *Cooperativas agrícolas e capitalismo no Brasil*, edited by Maria Rita Garcia Loureiro, 97–131. São Paulo: Cortez Editora, 1981.

Musacchio, Aldo, and Sergio G. Lazzarini. *Reinventing State Capitalism: Leviathan in Business, Brazil and Beyond*. Cambridge, MA: Harvard University Press, 2014.

Mussolini, Benito. *My Autobiography*. New York: C. Scribner's Sons, 1936.

Nathans, Benjamin. "Soviet Rights-Talk in the Post-Stalin Era." In *Human Rights in the Twentieth Century*, edited by Stefan-Ludwig Hoffman, 166–90. New York: Cambridge University Press, 2011.

Needell, Jeffrey D. "History, Race and the State in the Thought of Oliveira Viana." *Hispanic American Historical Review* 75, no. 1 (1995): 1–30.

———. "The Revolta Contra Vacina of 1904: The Revolt against 'Modernization' in Belle-Époque Rio de Janeiro." *Hispanic American Historical Review* 67, no. 2 (1987): 233–69.

Neto, Maria da Conceição. "De escravos a 'serviçais,' de 'serviçais' a 'contratados': Omissões, perceções e equívocos na história do trabalho africano na Angola colonial." *Cadernos de Estudos Africanos* 33 (2017): 107–29.

Nichols, Charles K. "The Statistical Work of the League of Nations in Economic, Financial and Related Fields." *Journal of the American Statistical Association* 37, no. 219 (1942): 336–42.

Nord, Philip. *France's New Deal: From the Thirties to the Postwar Era*. Princeton, NJ: Princeton University Press, 2012.

North, Douglass C., and Barry R. Weingast. "Constitutions and Commitment: The Evolution of Institutions Governing Public Choice in Seventeenth-Century England." *Journal of Economic History* 49, no. 4 (1989): 803–32.

Novak, William J. "A Revisionist History of Regulatory Capture." In *Preventing Regulatory Capture: Special Interest Influence and How to Limit It*, edited by Daniel Carpenter and David A. Moss, 25–48. New York: Cambridge University Press, 2014.

Nunes, Adérito Sedas. "Histórias, uma história e a história: Sobre as origens das modernas ciências sociais em Portugal." *Análise Social* 24, no. 100 (1988): 11–55.

———. *Situação e problemas do corporativismo: Princípios corporativos e realidades sociais*. Lisbon: Gabinete de Estudos Corporativos, 1954.

Nunes, Ana Bela. "Tomás Cabreira: um economista político num país de finanças avariadas." *Notas Económicas: Revista da Faculdade de Economia da Universidade de Coimbra* 29 (2009): 8–25.

Nunes, Manuel Jacinto, José Luís Cardoso, and Manuel Lopes Porto. "Elementos para a história do ensino universitário de economia e finanças (1911–1974)." *Boletim de Ciências Económicas* 59 (2016): 329–91.

"O Estatuto do Trabalho Nacional e as casas do povo pelo Dr. Leite de Sampaio." In *União Nacional: Uma série de conferências realizadas 19–30 Outubro 1936*. Lisbon: Centro de Estudos Corporativos, 1937.

"Obras recebidas na Redacção da 'Biblos.'" *Biblos* (January 1939): 559–662.

O'Donnell, Guillermo A. "Corporatism and the Question of the State." In *Authoritarianism and Corporatism in Latin America*, edited by James M. Malloy, 47–87. Pittsburgh: University of Pittsburgh Press, 1977.

———. *Modernization and Bureaucratic-Authoritarianism: Studies in South American Politics*. Berkeley: Institute of International Studies, University of California, 1973.

Offner, Amy C. *Sorting Out the Mixed Economy: The Rise and Fall of Welfare and Developmental States in the Americas*. Princeton, NJ: Princeton University Press, 2019.

Oliveira, Marcelo Andrade Cattoni de, and Gustavo Silveira Siqueira. "Pequeno ensaio sobre a injustiça: Memórias secas de um Tribunal de Segurança Nacional." *Seqüência* 61 (2010): 111–25.

Oliveira Vianna, Francisco José de. *O idealismo da constituição*. Rio de Janeiro: Edição de Terra de Sol, 1927.

———. *O idealismo da constituição*. São Paulo: Companhia Editora Nacional, 1939.

———. "O indivíduo e o syndicato." *Boletim do Ministério do Trabalho, Indústria e Comércio* 11 (July 1935): 112–22.

———. *Problemas de direito corporativo*. Rio de Janeiro: Livraria José Olympio Editora, 1938.

———. *Problemas de direito sindical*. Rio de Janeiro: Editora Max Limonad Ltda., 1943.

———. *Problemas de política objetiva*. 2nd ed. São Paulo: Companhia Editora Nacional, 1947.

———. "Razões da originalidade do sistema sindical brasileiro." In *Ensaios inéditos*. Campinas: Editora da Unicamp, 1991.

Olsson, Tore C. *Agrarian Crossings: Reformers and the Remaking of the US and Mexican Countryside*. Princeton, NJ: Princeton University Press, 2017.

Otovo, Okezi T. *Progressive Mothers, Better Babies: Race, Public Health, and the State in Brazil, 1850–1945*. Austin: University of Texas Press, 2016.

Owensby, Brian P. "The Theater of Conscience in the 'Living Law' of the Indies." In *New Horizons in Spanish Colonial Law: Contributions to Transnational Early Modern Legal History*, edited by Thomas Duve and Heikki Pihlajamäki, 3:125–50. Frankfurt: Max Planck Institute for Legal History, 2015.

Pais, José Machado, Aida Maria Valadas de Lima, José Ferreira Baptista, Maria Fernanda Marques de Jesus, and Maria Margarida Gameiro. "Elementos para a história do fascismo nos campos: A «Campanha do Trigo»: 1928–38 (I)." *Análise Social* 12, no. 46 (1976): 400–474.

Palmer, Robert Roswell. *The Age of the Democratic Revolution: A Political History of Europe and America, 1760–1800.* Princeton, NJ: Princeton University Press, 1959.

Palti, Elías José. "The Problem of 'Misplaced Ideas' Revisited: Beyond the 'History of Ideas' in Latin America." *Journal of the History of Ideas* 67, no. 1 (2006): 149–79.

Pandolfi, Dulce Chaves, ed. *Repensando o Estado Novo.* Rio de Janeiro: Editora FGV, 1999.

Paquette, Gabriel. "The Brazilian Origins of the 1826 Portuguese Constitution." *European History Quarterly* 41, no. 3 (2011): 444–71.

———. *Imperial Portugal in the Age of Atlantic Revolutions: The Luso-Brazilian World, c. 1770–1850.* Cambridge: Cambridge University Press, 2013.

———. "In the Shadow of Independence: Portugal, Brazil, and Their Mutual Influence after the End of Empire (Late 1820s–Early 1840s)." *E-Journal of Portuguese History* 11, no. 2 (2013): 101–19.

Pasetti, Matteo. "The Fascist Labour Charter and Its Transnational Spread." In *Corporatism and Fascism: The Corporatist Wave in Europe,* 60–77. London: Routledge Press, 2017.

Patel, Kiran Klaus. *The New Deal: A Global History.* Princeton, NJ: Princeton University Press, 2016.

Patriarca, Fátima. "A institucionalização corporativa—das associações de classe aos sindicatos nacionais (1933)." *Análise Social* 26, no. 110 (1991): 23–58.

———. *A questão social no salazarismo, 1930–1947.* Lisbon: Imprensa Nacional Casa da Moeda, 1995.

Patterson, Laurence K. "Salazar, the Inspirer of Portugal's New State: The Catholic Corporation Experiment Is Successful." *America* 58, no. 11 (1937): 249–50.

Paxton, Robert O. "The Five Stages of Fascism." *Journal of Modern History* 70, no. 1 (1998): 1–23.

Pedersen, Susan. *The Guardians: The League of Nations and the Crisis of Empire.* Oxford: Oxford University Press, 2015.

Peiss, Kathy. *Information Hunters: When Librarians, Soldiers, and Spies Banded Together in World War II Europe.* New York: Oxford University Press, 2020.

"Pensamento econômico: As concepções novas devem trazer com elas alguma coisa a mais e não apenas uma negação pura e simples e uma crítica ou censura ao liberalismo." *Boletim do Ministério do Trabalho, Indústria e Comércio,* no. 7 (March 1935): 200–210.

Pequena história das doutrinas económicas. Lisbon: Secretariado Nacional da Informação, 1945.

Pereira, Anthony W. *Political (In)Justice: Authoritarianism and the Rule of Law in Brazil, Chile, and Argentina.* Pittsburgh: University of Pittsburgh Press, 2005.

———. "An Ugly Democracy? State Violence and the Rule of Law in Post-Authoritarian Brazil." In *Democratic Brazil: Actors, Institutions, and Processes,* edited by Peter R. Kingstone and Timothy J. Power, 217–35. Pittsburgh: University of Pittsburgh Press, 2000.

Pereira, Márcio Fernandes. "Política agrícola brasileira e a pequena produção familiar: Heranças históricas e seus efeitos no presente." *Revista Brasileira de Gestão e Desenvolvimento Regional* 6, no. 3 (2010): 287–311.

Pereira, Pedro Theotónio. *A batalha do futuro: Organização corporativa*. Lisbon: Livraria Clássica Editora, 1937.

Phillips, Sarah T. *This Land, This Nation: Conservation, Rural America, and the New Deal*. Cambridge: Cambridge University Press, 2007.

Pimentel, Irene Flunser. *Espiões em Portugal durante a II Guerra Mundial: Como o nosso país se tornou local de passagem de agentes ingleses e alemães*. Lisbon: Esfera dos Livros, 2014.

———. *Judeus em Portugal durante a II Guerra Mundial: Em fuga de Hitler e do Holocausto*. Lisbon: Esfera dos Livros, 2006.

Pimentel, Irene Flunser, and Cláudia Ninhos. "Portugal, Jewish Refugees, and the Holocaust." *Dapim: Studies on the Holocaust* 29, no. 2 (2015): 101–13.

———. *Salazar, Portugal e o Holocausto*. Lisbon: Temas e Debates, 2012.

Pimentel, João Sarmento. *Memórias do capitão*. Porto: Editorial Inova, 1974.

Pimentel, Manoel Pedro. "Vida e morte do Tribunal do Juri de economia popular." *Revista da Faculdade de Direito Universidade de São Paulo* 69, no. 2 (1974): 75–86.

Pinheiro, Paulo Sérgio. *Estratégias da ilusão: A revolução mundial e o Brasil, 1922–1935*. São Paulo: Companhia das Letras, 1992.

Pinto, Adolpho Augusto. *O problema monetário no Brasil: Artigos publicados no jornal "O Estado de S. Paulo" em Março de 1919*. São Paulo: Casa Vanorden, 1919.

Pinto, Álvaro. *O Brasil actual (Duas conferências)*. Lisbon, 1935.

Pinto, António Costa. "A queda da Primeira República." In *A Primeira República Portuguesa: Entre o liberalismo e o autoritarismo*, edited by António Costa Pinto and Nuno Severiano Teixeira, 25_44. Lisbon: Edições Colibri, 2000.

———. "Corporatism and 'Organic' Representation in European Dictatorships." In *Corporatism and Fascism: The Corporatist Wave in Europe*, edited by António Costa Pinto, 3–41. New York: Routledge, 2017.

———. *Latin American Dictatorships in the Era of Fascism: The Corporatist Wave*. New York: Routledge Press, 2020.

———. "O império do professor: Salazar e a elite ministerial do Estado Novo (1933–1945)." *Análise Social* 35, no. 157 (2001): 1055–76.

———. *Salazar's Dictatorship and European Fascism: Problems of Interpretation*. New York: Columbia University Press, 1995.

Pinto, António Costa, and Federico Finchelstein, eds. *Authoritarianism and Corporatism in Europe and Latin America: Crossing Borders*. New York: Routledge, 2019.

Pinto, António Costa, and Francisco Carlos Palomanes Martinho, eds. *A vaga corporativa: Corporativismo e ditaduras na Europa e na América Latina*. Lisbon: Imprensa de Ciências Sociais, 2016.

Pitcher, M. Anne. *Politics in the Portuguese Empire: The State, Industry, and Cotton, 1926–1974*. New York: Oxford University Press, 1993.

Poliano, L. Marques. *A Sociedade Nacional de Agricultura: Resumo histórico*. Rio de Janeiro: Gráfica Econômica Ltda, 1942.

Pollard, John. "Corporatism and Political Catholicism: The Impact of Catholic Corporatism in Inter-War Europe." In *Corporatism and Fascism: The Corporatist Wave in Europe*, edited by Antonio Costa Pinto, 42–59. New York: Routledge, 2017.

Porto, Walter Costa. *Constituições Brasileiras: 1937*. 3rd ed. Brasília: Senado Federal: Secretaria Especial de Editoração e Publicações Subsecretaria de Edições Técnicas, 2012.

Prebisch, Raul, and Gustavo Martínez Cabañas. "El desarrollo económico de la América Latina y algunos de sus principales problemas." *El Trimestre Económico* 16, no. 63(3) (1949): 347–431.

Proença, Maria Cândida, and Valentim Alexandre. *A questão colonial no Parlamento*. Lisbon: Publicações Dom Quixote, 2008.

Raimundo, Orlando. *António Ferro: O inventor do salazarismo*. Lisbon: Dom Quixote, 2015.

Raz, Joseph. "Rule of Law and Its Virtue." In *The Authority of Law: Essays on Law and Morality*, edited by Joseph Raz, 210–29. Oxford: Oxford University Press, 1979.

Reale, Egidio. "The Italian Constitution under Fascism." *Foreign Affairs* 18, no. 1 (1939): 153–57.

Reale, Miguel. *O estado moderno: Liberalismo, fascismo, integralismo*. Rio de Janeiro: Livraria J. Olympio, 1934.

Reis, Jaime. "A industrialização num país de desenvolvimento lento e tardio: Portugal, 1870–1913." *Análise Social* 23, no. 96 (1987): 207–27.

Relatório apresentado pela Comissão Central de Compras do Governo Federal em março de 1935. Rio de Janeiro: Ministerio da Fazenda, 1935.

Resoluções da Assembléa Geral do Conselho Nacional de Estatística. Vol. I. Rio de Janeiro: Imprensa Nacional, 1937.

Rezola, Maria Inácia. *O sindicalismo católico no Estado Novo, 1931–1948*. Lisbon: Editorial Estampa, 1999.

Ribeiro, Carla Patrícia Silva. "Um intelectual orgânico no Estado Novo de Salazar: As ideias e os projetos de luso-brasilidade de António Ferro." *Intellèctus* 16, no. 2 (2017): 45–67.

Rocco, Alfredo. "The Political Doctrine of Fascism." *International Conciliation* 11 (October 1926): 393–415.

Rocha, Camila. *Menos Marx, mais Mises: O liberalismo e a nova direita no Brasil*. São Paulo: Todavia, 2021.

Rocha, Francisco Canais, and Maria Rosalina Labaredas. *Os trabalhadores rurais do Alentejo e o sidonismo: Ocupação de terras no Vale de Santiago*. Lisbon: Edições 1 de Outubro, 1982.

Rodgers, Daniel T. *Atlantic Crossings: Social Politics in a Progressive Age*. Cambridge, MA: Belknap Press of Harvard University Press, 1998.

———. "Bearing Tales: Networks and Narratives in Social Policy Transfer." *Journal of Global History* 9, no. 2 (2014): 301–13.

Rodrigues, Felix Contreiras. *Conceitos de valor e preço (fundamentos para uma ordem democrática-corporativa)*. Rio de Janeiro: Gráfica Olímpica Editora, 1951.

Roio, Marcos del. "A gênese do Partido Comunista (1919–29)." In *A formação das tradições (1889–1945)*, edited by Jorge Ferreira and Daniel Aarão Reis, 223–48. Rio de Janeiro: Civilização Brasileira, 2007.

Rollo, Fernanda. *Portugal e o Plano Marshall: Da rejeição à solicitação da ajuda financeira norte-americana (1947–1952)*. Lisbon: Editorial Estampa, 1994.

Romano, Sergio. *Giuseppe Volpi et l'Italie moderne: Finance, industrie et État de l'ère giolittienne à la Deuxième Guerre mondiale*. Rome: École Française de Rome, 1982.

Rosas, Fernando. *O Estado Novo nos anos trinta: Elementos para o estudo da natureza económica e social do salazarismo, 1928–1938*. Lisbon: Editorial Estampa, 1986.

———. *Portugal entre a paz e a guerra, 1939–1945*. Lisbon: Editorial Estampa, 1990.

———. *Salazarismo e fomento económico (1928–1948)*. Lisbon: Editorial Notícias, 2000.

Rosas, Fernando, and Irene Flunser Pimentel, eds. *Tribunais políticos: Tribunais militares especiais e tribunais plenários durante a ditadura e o Estado Novo*. Lisbon: Temas e Debates, 2009.

Rosemblatt, Karin Alejandra. *Gendered Compromises: Political Cultures and the State in Chile, 1920–1950*. Chapel Hill: University of North Carolina Press, 2000.

Rosenblatt, Helena. *The Lost History of Liberalism: From Ancient Rome to the Twenty-First Century*. Princeton, NJ: Princeton University Press, 2018.

Ross, Edward A. *Seventy Years of It: An Autobiography*. New York: D. Appleton-Century Company, 1936.

Rostow, Walt Whitman. *The Stages of Economic Growth: A Non-Communist Manifesto*. 3rd ed. New York: Cambridge University Press, 1990.

Rothschild, Emma. *Economic Sentiments: Adam Smith, Condorcet, and the Enlightenment*. Cambridge, MA: Harvard University Press, 2002.

Sá, Vítor de. "Projectos de reforma agrária na I República." *Análise Social* 19, no. 77/79 (1983): 591–610.

Saba, Roberto. *American Mirror: The United States and Brazil in the Age of Emancipation*. Princeton, NJ: Princeton University Press, 2021.

Sackley, Nicole. "The Village as Cold War Site: Experts, Development, and the History of Rural Reconstruction." *Journal of Global History* 6 (October 17, 2011): 481–504.

Salazar, António de Oliveira. "A democracia e a Igreja (Conferência no Porto e em Viseu, 1914)." In *Inéditos e dispersos*, vol. 1, *Escritos Político-Sociais e Doutrinários (1908–1928)*, edited by Manuel Braga da Cruz, 199–233. Lisbon: Bertrand Editora, 1997.

———. *A reorganização financeira: Dois anos no Ministério das Finanças, 1928–1930*. Coimbra: Coimbra Editora, 1930.

———. *Discursos, vol. 1 1928–1934*. Coimbra: Coimbra Editora, 1935.

———. *O ágio do ouro, sua natureza e suas causas*. Coimbra: Imprensa da Universidade, 1916.

Sanders, James E. "'Citizens of a Free People': Popular Liberalism and Race in Nineteenth-Century Southwestern Colombia." *Hispanic American Historical Review* 84, no. 2 (2004): 277–313.

———. *The Vanguard of the Atlantic World: Creating Modernity, Nation, and Democracy in Nineteenth-Century Latin America*. Durham, NC: Duke University Press, 2014.

Sanglard, Pedro Elias Erthal. "Luiz Carpenter." *Revista da Associação Brasileira de Pesquisadores de História e Genealogia* 2 (1995): 87–90.

Santana, Marco Aurélio. "O making of da implantação do projeto corporativo no Brasil." *Revista Brasileira de Ciências Sociais* 15, no. 43 (2000): 186–90.

Santos, Paula Borges. *A segunda separação: A política religiosa do Estado Novo, 1933–1974*. Coimbra: Edições Almedina, 2016.

Santos, Rogerio Dultra dos. "Francisco Campos e os fundamentos do constitucionalismo antiliberal no Brasil." *Revista de Ciências Sociais* 50, no. 2 (2007): 281–323.

Santos, Wanderley Guilherme dos. *Cidadania e justiça*. Rio de Janeiro: Campus, 1979.

———. *Ordem burguesa e liberalismo político*. São Paulo: Livraria Duas Cidades, 1978.

Saraiva, Tiago. "Fascist Labscapes: Geneticists, Wheat, and the Landscapes of Fascism in Italy and Portugal." *Historical Studies in the Natural Sciences* 40, no. 4 (2010): 457–98.

———. *Fascist Pigs: Technoscientific Organisms and the History of Fascism*. Cambridge, MA: MIT Press, 2016.

Sartori, Andrew Stephen. *Liberalism in Empire: An Alternative History*. Berkeley: University of California Press, 2014.

Sawyer, Laura Phillips. *American Fair Trade: Proprietary Capitalism, Corporatism, and the "New Competition," 1890–1940*. Cambridge: Cambridge University Press, 2018.

Schivelbusch, Wolfgang. *Three New Deals: Reflections on Roosevelt's America, Mussolini's Italy, and Hitler's Germany, 1933–1939*. Translated by Jefferson Chase. New York: Metropolitan Books, 2006.

Schmidt, Carl T. "The Italian 'Battle of Wheat.'" *Journal of Farm Economics* 18, no. 4 (1936): 645–56.

Schmitt, Carl. *Légalité et légitimité*. Paris: Librairie Générale de Droit et de Jurisprudence, 1936.

Schmitter, Philippe C. *Corporatism and Public Policy in Authoritarian Portugal*. London: Sage Publications, 1975.

———. *Interest Conflict and Political Change in Brazil*. Palo Alto, CA: Stanford University Press, 1971.

———. "The 'Portugalization' of Brazil?" In *Authoritarian Brazil: Origins, Policies, and Future*, edited by Alfred Stepan, 179–232. New Haven, CT: Yale University Press, 1973.

———. "Still the Century of Corporatism?" *Review of Politics* 36, no. 1 (1974): 85–131.

Schneider, Ben Ross. *Business Politics and the State in Twentieth-Century Latin America*. Cambridge: Cambridge University Press, 2004.

Schwarcz, Lilia Moritz. *The Spectacle of the Races: Scientists, Institutions, and the Race Question in Brazil, 1870–1930*. New York: Hill and Wang, 1999.

Schwartz, Jorge. *Vanguarda e cosmopolitismo na década de 20: Oliverio Girondo e Oswald de Andrade*. São Paulo: Editora Perspectiva, 1983.

Schwartz, Stuart B. "Magistracy and Society in Colonial Brazil." *Hispanic American Historical Review* 50, no. 4 (1970): 715–30.

———. *Sovereignty and Society of Colonial Brazil: The High Court of Bahia and Its Judges, 1609–1751*. Berkeley: University of California Press, 1973.

Schwarz, Roberto. *Misplaced Ideas: Essays on Brazilian Culture*. Edited by John Gledson. New York: Verso, 1992.

Scott, James C. *Weapons of the Weak: Everyday Forms of Peasant Resistance*. New Haven, CT: Yale University Press, 1985.

Seabra, Fernando Maria Alberto de. *A industrialização dos países agrícolas: Introdução ao estudo do problema*. Coimbra: Atlântida Livraria Editora, 1945.

Segreto, Luciano. "Giuseppe Volpi: Il grande mediatore tra istituzioni, politica ed economia." *Studi Storici* 61, no. 4 (2020): 905–34.

Seidman, Michael. *The Victorious Counterrevolution: The Nationalist Effort in the Spanish Civil War*. Madison: University of Wisconsin Press, 2011.

Seigel, Micol. "Beyond Compare: Comparative Method after the Transnational Turn." *Radical History Review* 2005, no. 91 (December 21, 2005): 62–90.

———. *Uneven Encounters: Making Race and Nation in Brazil and the United States*. Durham, NC: Duke University Press, 2009.

Semo, Ilán. "El cardenismo revisado: La tercera vía y otras utopías inciertas." *Revista Mexicana de Sociología* 55, no. 2 (1993): 197–223.

Serrão, Joaquim Veríssimo. *História de Portugal*. 18 vols. Lisbon: Editorial Verbo, 1977.

Seyferth, Giralda. "Construindo a nação: Hierarquias raciais e o papel do racismo na política de imigração e colonização." In *Raça, ciência e sociedade*, edited by Marcos Chor Maio and Ricardo Ventura Santos, 41–58. Rio de Janeiro: Editora Fiocruz, 1996.

Sikkink, Kathryn. *Ideas and Institutions: Developmentalism in Brazil and Argentina*. Ithaca, NY: Cornell University Press, 1991.

Silva, Álvaro Ferreira da, and Luciano Amaral. "A economia portuguesa na I República." In *Outubro: A revolução republicana em Portugal (1910–1926)*, edited by Luciano Amaral, 257–98. Lisbon: Edições 70, 2011.

Silva, Ângela Moreira Domingues da. "Justiça e ditadura militar no Brasil: O julgamento dos crimes contra a economia popular." *Diálogos* 18, no. 1 (2014): 51–73.

Silva, Fernando Teixeira da. "The Brazilian and Italian Labor Courts: Comparative Notes." *International Review of Social History* 55, no. 3 (2010): 381–412.

Silva, Mário Matta e. *Os trabalhadores portugueses e o estado corporativo*. Lisbon: Imp. Moderna, 1935.

Silva, Salomão L. Quadros da. "A era Vargas e a economia." In *As instituições brasileiras da era Vargas*, edited by Maria Celina D'Araujo, 137–54. Rio de Janeiro: Ed. UERF and Ed. Fundação Getúlio Vargas, 1999.

Silva Gordo, Adolpho Affonsa da. *O caso da Northern nos devidos eixos: Verdades núas e crúas que ninguem disse mas que foram ditas por mim*. São Paulo: Edição de Obras "O Estado de S. Paulo," 1921.

Simonsen, Roberto C. *As crises no Brasil, Outubro de 1930*. São Paulo: São Paulo Editora, 1930.

———. *Crisis, Finances and Industry*. São Paulo: São Paulo Editora Limitada, 1931.

———. *Ensaios sociais, políticos e econômicos*. Rio de Janeiro: Edição da Federação das Indústrias do Estado de São Paulo, 1943.

Simonsen, Roberto C., and Eugênio Gudin. *A controvérsia do planejamento na economia brasileira: Coletânea da polêmica Simonsen X Gudin desencadeada com as primeiras propostas formais de planejamento da economia brasileira ao final do Estado Novo*. Rio de Janeiro: IPEA/INPES, 1977.

Skidmore, Thomas E. *Black into White: Race and Nationality in Brazilian Thought*. Durham, NC: Duke University Press, 1993.

———. *Politics in Brazil, 1930–1964: An Experiment in Democracy*. New York: Oxford University Press, 1967.

———. "Raízes de Gilberto Freyre." *Journal of Latin American Studies* 34, no. 1 (2002): 1–20.

Slobodian, Quinn. *Globalists: The End of Empire and the Birth of Neoliberalism*. Cambridge, MA: Harvard University Press, 2018.

Sluga, Glenda. *Internationalism in the Age of Nationalism*. Philadelphia: University of Pennsylvania Press, 2013.

Smail, Daniel Lord. *The Consumption of Justice: Emotions, Publicity, and Legal Culture in Marseille, 1264–1423*. Ithaca, NY: Cornell University Press, 2003.

Sobral, José Manuel, and Maria Luísa Lima. "A epidemia da pneumónica em Portugal no seu tempo histórico." *Ler História* 73 (2018): 45–66.

Solari, Stefano. "The Corporative Third Way in Social Catholicism (1830 to 1918)." *European Journal of the History of Economic Thought* 17, no. 1 (2010): 87–113.

Sousa, Alfredo de. "O desenvolvimento económico e social português: reflexão crítica." *Análise Social* 7, no. 27–28 (1969): 393–419.

Sousa, António Ribeiro da Silva e [pseud. Miguel Sidónio]. "Diálogos fáceis sobre a económia corporativa, moral e humana." In *Cadernos Corporativos*. Lisbon: Edição do Sindicato Nacional dos Empregados de Escritórios dos Serviços de Navegação, 1941.

Sousa Mendes, José de. "Administração e desenvolvimento." *Análise Social* 7, no. 27–28 (1969): 447–74.

Spirito, Ugo. *Princípios fundamentais de economia corporativa*. Translated by António Perez Durão. Lisbon: Livraria Clássica Editora, 1934.

Stapleford, Thomas A. *The Cost of Living in America: A Political History of Economic Statistics, 1880–2000*. Cambridge: Cambridge University Press, 2009.

Staples, Amy L. S. *The Birth of Development: How the World Bank, Food and Agriculture Organization, and World Health Organization Have Changed the World, 1945–1965*. Kent, OH: Kent State University Press, 2006.

Stein, Stanley J. *Vassouras: A Brazilian Coffee Country, 1850–1900*. Cambridge, MA: Harvard University Press, 1957.

Stepan, Nancy. *The Hour of Eugenics: Race, Gender, and Nation in Latin America*. Ithaca, NY: Cornell University Press, 1991.

Sternhell, Zeev. *Ni droite ni gauche: L'idéologie fasciste en France*. 2nd ed. Paris: Éditions du Seuil, 1983.

Strachan, Hew. *The First World War in Africa*. Oxford: Oxford University Press, 2004.

Suarez-Potts, William J. *The Making of Law: The Supreme Court and Labor Legislation in Mexico, 1875–1931*. Stanford, CA: Stanford University Press, 2012.

Summerhill, William R. *Inglorious Revolution: Political Institutions, Sovereign Debt, and Financial Underdevelopment in Imperial Brazil*. New Haven, CT: Yale University Press, 2015.

———. *Order against Progress: Government, Foreign Investment, and Railroads in Brazil, 1854–1913*. Stanford, CA: Stanford University Press, 2003.

Szmrecsányi, Tamás. *O planejamento da agroindústria canavieira do Brasil (1930–1975)*. Campinas: Editora Hucitec, 1979.

Tannenbaum, Edward R. *The Fascist Experience: Italian Society and Culture, 1922–1945*. New York: Basic Books, 1972.

Teixeira, Melissa. "Making a Brazilian New Deal: Oliveira Vianna and the Transnational Sources of Brazil's Corporatist Experiment." *Journal of Latin American Studies* 50, no. 3 (2018): 613–41.

Teixeira Pinto, Luís Maria. *Aspectos da política económica portuguesa (1963–1964)*. Lisbon: Imprensa Nacional, 1965.

Teixeira Ribeiro, José Joaquim. *Lições de direito corporativo*. Coimbra: Coimbra Editora, 1938.

Telo, António José. "A obra financeira de Salazar: A 'ditadura financeira' como caminho para a unidade política, 1928–1932." *Análise Social* 29, no. 128 (1994): 779–800.

———. *Os Açores e o controlo do Atlântico, 1898–1948*. Porto: Edições Asa, 1993.

Temin, Peter. "Soviet and Nazi Economic Planning in the 1930s." *Economic History Review* 44, no. 4 (1991): 573–93.

Temin, Peter, and Gianni Toniolo. *The World Economy between the Wars*. Oxford: Oxford University Press, 2008.

Thompson, E. P. "The Moral Economy of the English Crowd in the Eighteenth Century." *Past and Present* 50 (1971): 76–136.

Thomson, Guy. "Popular Aspects of Liberalism in Mexico." *Bulletin of Latin American Research* 10, no. 3 (1991): 265–92.

Thornton, Christy. *Revolution in Development: Mexico and the Governance of the Global Economy.* Oakland: University of California Press, 2021.

Thorp, Rosemary. *Progress, Poverty and Exclusion: Economic History of Latin America in the 20th Century.* Baltimore: Johns Hopkins University Press, 1998.

———. "A Reappraisal of the Origins of Import-Substituting Industrialization, 1930–1950." *Journal of Latin American Studies* 24, no. S1 (1992): 181–95.

Tignor, Robert L. *W. Arthur Lewis and the Birth of Development Economics.* Princeton, NJ: Princeton University Press, 2006.

Tirado Mejía, Alvaro, and Magdala Velásquez. *La reforma constitucional de 1936.* Bogotá: Editorial La Oveja Negra, 1982.

Todd, David. *L'identité économique de la France: Libre-échange et protectionnisme, 1814–1851.* Paris: Bernard Grasset, 2008.

Tooze, Adam. *Statistics and the German State, 1900–1945: The Making of Modern Economic Knowledge.* Cambridge: Cambridge University Press, 2001.

———. *The Wages of Destruction: The Making and Breaking of the Nazi Economy.* New York: Allen Lane, 2006.

Topik, Steven C. "Coffee." In *The Second Conquest of Latin America: Coffee, Henequen, and Oil during the Export Boom, 1850–1930,* edited by Steven C. Topic and Allen Wells, 37–84. Austin: University of Texas Press, 1998.

———. *The Political Economy of the Brazilian State, 1889–1930.* Austin: University of Texas Press, 1987.

Torgal, Luís Reis. "Duas 'Repúblicas' portuguesas no Brasil em 1922: António José de Almeida e António Ferro." In *A experiência da Primeira República no Brasil e em Portugal,* edited by Alda Mourão and Angela de Castro Gomes Gomes, 25–54. Coimbra: Imprensa da Universidade de Coimbra, 2014.

———. "O modernismo português na formação do Estado Novo de Salazar: António Ferro e a Semana de Arte Moderna de São Paulo." In *Estudos em homenagem a Luís António de Oliveira Ramos,* edited by Francisco Ribeiro da Silva, Maria Antonieta Cruz, Jorge Martins Ribeiro, and Helena Osswald, 1087–102. Porto: Faculdade de Letras da Universidade do Porto, 2004.

Torres Filho, Arthur. *Relatório apresentado ao Dr. Geminiano Lyra Castro por Arthur Torres, Filho, anno de 1929.* Rio de Janeiro: Ministério da Agricultura, Indústria e Comércio, 1930.

Tota, Antonio Pedro. "Cultura, política e modernidade em Noel Rosa." *São Paulo em Perspectiva* 15, no. 3 (2001): 45–49.

Trentmann, Frank. *Empire of Things: How We Became a World of Consumers, from the Fifteenth Century to the Twenty-First.* New York: HarperCollins, 2016.

Tribunal de Segurança Nacional: Relatório dos trabalhos realizados durante o ano de 1938 apresentado em sessão de 30 de Janeiro de 1939 pelo Presidente Desembargador Frederico de Barros Barreto. Rio de Janeiro: Imprensa Nacional, 1939.

Tribunal de Segurança Nacional: Relatório dos trabalhos realizados em 1943 apresentado em sessão de 28 de Janeiro de 1944 pelo Presidente Ministro Frederico de Barros Barreto. Rio de Janeiro: Imprensa Nacional, 1944.

Tribunal de Segurança Nacional: Relatório dos trabalhos realizados em 1944 apresentado em sessão de 30 de Janeiro de 1945 pelo Presidente Ministro Frederico de Barros Barreto. Rio de Janeiro: Imprensa Nacional, 1945.

United Nations. *Economic Development in Selected Countries: Plans, Programmes and Agencies.* Lake Success, NY: UN Department of Economic Affairs, 1947.

Valdes, Juan Gabriel. *Pinochet's Economists: The Chicago School in Chile.* New York: Cambridge University Press, 2008.

Valente, Vasco Pulido. "Revoluções: A 'República Velha' (ensaio de interpretação política)." *Análise Social* 27, no. 115 (1992): 7–63.

Valério, Nuno. *A moeda em Portugal, 1913–1947.* Lisbon: Livraria Sá da Costa Editora, 1983.

———, ed. *Estatísticas históricas portuguesas.* Vol. 1. Lisbon: Instituto Nacional de Estatística, 2001.

Vannucchi, Marco Aurélio. "Advogados e corporativismo de classe média no Brasil pós-1930." *Passagens: Revista Internacional de História Política e Cultura Jurídica* 8, no. 3 (2016): 506–25.

Vaudagna, Maurizio. "The New Deal and Corporativism in Italy." *Radical History Review* 4, no. 2–3 (1977): 3–35.

Veiga, António Jorge da Motta. *A economia corporativa e o problema dos preços (ensaio de teoria económica).* Lisbon: Faculdade de Direito da Universidade de Lisboa, 1941.

———. *Draft of the Third Development Plan for 1968–1973.* Lisbon: National Information Office, 1967.

———. *Linhas gerais do III Plano de Fomento.* Entrevista de Fernando Moutinho concedida ao "Diário de Notícias" em 25 de Outubro de 1967. Lisbon: Secretariado Nacional da Informação, 1967.

Vieira, Evaldo Amaro. *Autoritarismo e corporativismo no Brasil (Oliveira Vianna e companhia).* São Paulo: Editora UNESP, 2010.

———. *Oliveira Vianna e o estado corporativo: Um estudo sobre corporativismo e autoritarismo.* São Paulo: Editorial Grijalbo, 1976.

Vieira, Manuel Saraiva. *Angola: Relatório de uma missão de estudo.* Lisbon: Ministério das Colónias, Junta de Exportação dos Cereais das Colónias, 1940.

Villari, Luigi. *The Fascist Experiment.* London: Faber and Gwyer, 1926.

Villela, Annibal Villanova, and Wilson Suzigan. *Government Policy and the Economic Growth of Brazil, 1889–1945.* Rio de Janeiro: Instituto de Planejamento Econômico e Social, 1975.

———. *Política do governo e crescimento da economia brasileira, 1889–1945.* Rio de Janeiro: IPEA/INPES, 1973.

Wahrlich, Beatriz M. de Souza. *Reforma administrativa na era de Vargas.* Rio de Janeiro: Editora da Fundação Getúlio Vargas, 1983.

Ward, Michael. *Quantifying the World: UN Ideas and Statistics.* Bloomington: Indiana University Press, 2004.

Wasserman, Janek. *The Marginal Revolutionaries: How Austrian Economists Fought the War of Ideas.* New Haven, CT: Yale University Press, 2019.

Weffort, Francisco. *O populismo na política brasileira.* Rio de Janeiro: Paz e Terra, 1978.

Weinstein, Barbara. "Brazilian Regionalism." *Latin American Research Review* 17, no. 2 (1982): 262–76.

———. *The Color of Modernity: São Paulo and the Making of Race and Nation in Brazil.* Durham, NC: Duke University Press, 2015.

————. "Developing Inequality." *American Historical Review* 113, no. 1 (2008): 1–18.

————. "The Discourse of Technical Competence: Strategies of Authority and Power in Industrializing Brazil." *Political Power and Social Theory* 12 (1998): 141–79.

————. "Racializing Regional Difference: São Paulo versus Brazil, 1932." In *Race and Nation in Modern Latin America*, edited by Nancy P. Appelbaum, Anne S. Macpherson, and Karin Alejandra Rosemblatt, 237–62. Chapel Hill: University of North Carolina Press, 2003.

————. *For Social Peace in Brazil: Industrialists and the Remaking of the Working Class in São Paulo, 1920–1964*. Chapel Hill: University of North Carolina Press, 1996.

Welch, Cliff. *The Seed Was Planted: The São Paulo Roots of Brazil's Rural Labor Movement, 1924–1964*. University Park: Pennsylvania State University Press, 1999.

Weld, Kirsten. "The Spanish Civil War and the Construction of a Reactionary Historical Consciousness in Augusto Pinochet's Chile." *Hispanic American Historical Review* 98, no. 1 (2018): 77–115.

Werneck Vianna, Luiz. "Americanistas e Iberistas: A polêmica de Oliveira Vianna com Tavares Bastos." *Dados: Revista de Ciências Sociais* 34, no. 2 (1991): 145–89.

————. *Ensaios sobre política, direito e sociedade*. São Paulo: Hucitec, 2015.

————. "Introdução." In *A judicialização da política e das relações sociais no Brasil*, edited by Luiz Werneck Vianna, Maria Alice Rezende de Carvalho, Manuel Palacios Cunha Melo, and Marcelo Baumann Burgos, 15–44. Rio de Janeiro: Revan, 1999.

————. *Liberalismo e sindicato no Brasil*. Rio de Janeiro: Paz e Terra, 1976.

Werner, Michael, and Bénédicte Zimmermann. "Beyond Comparison: Histoire Croisée and the Challenge of Reflexivity." *History and Theory* 45, no. 1 (2006): 30–50.

Westad, Odd Arne. *The Global Cold War: Third World Interventions and the Making of Our Times*. Cambridge: Cambridge University Press, 2007.

Weyland, Kurt. *Assault on Democracy: Communism, Fascism, and Authoritarianism during the Interwar Years*. Cambridge: Cambridge University Press, 2021.

————. *The Politics of Market Reform in Fragile Democracies: Argentina, Brazil, Peru, and Venezuela*. Princeton, NJ: Princeton University Press, 2002.

Whitney, Robert. *State and Revolution in Cuba: Mass Mobilization and Political Change, 1920–1940*. Chapel Hill: University of North Carolina Press, 2001.

Wiarda, Howard. "Corporatism and Development in the Iberic-Latin World: Persistent Strains and New Variations." *Review of Politics* 36, no. 1 (1974): 3–33.

Williams, Daryle. *Culture Wars in Brazil: The First Vargas Regime, 1930–1945*. Durham, NC: Duke University Press, 2001.

Williams, Daryle, and Barbara Weinstein. "Vargas Morto: The Death and Life of a Brazilian Statesman." In *Death, Dismemberment, and Memory: Body Politics in Latin America*, edited by Lyman L. Johnson, 273–316. Albuquerque: University of New Mexico Press, 2004.

Wirth, John D. *Minas Gerais in the Brazilian Federation, 1889–1937*. Stanford, CA: Stanford University Press, 1977.

————. *The Politics of Brazilian Development 1930–1954*. Stanford, CA: Stanford University Press, 1970.

————. "Tenentismo in the Brazilian Revolution of 1930." *Hispanic American Historical Review* 44, no. 2 (1964): 161–79.

Wolfe, Joel. *Autos and Progress: The Brazilian Search for Modernity*. Oxford: Oxford University Press, 2010.

Wolfe, Joel. *Working Women, Working Men: São Paulo and the Rise of Brazil's Industrial Working Class, 1900–1955.* Durham, NC: Duke University Press, 1993.

Woodard, James P. *Brazil's Revolution in Commerce: Creating Consumer Capitalism in the American Century.* Chapel Hill: University of North Carolina Press, 2020.

World Economic Survey: Fifth Year, 1935–36. Geneva: League of Nations, 1936.

World Economic Survey: Seventh Year, 1937–38. Geneva: League of Nations, 1938.

World Economic Survey: Sixth Year, 1936–37. Geneva: League of Nations, 1937.

Wright, Charles Will. "Capital and Labor under Fascism in Italy." *Annals of the American Academy of Political and Social Science* 174 (1934): 166–72.

Xavier, Rafael. "O problema do custo da vida." *Revista de Economia e Estatística* 3, no. 1 (January 1938): 17–32.

Yonay, Yuval P. *The Struggle over the Soul of Economics: Institutionalist and Neoclassical Economists in America between the Wars.* Princeton, NJ: Princeton University Press, 1998.

Young, Alden. *Transforming Sudan: Decolonization, Economic Development, and State Formation.* New York: Cambridge University Press, 2018.

Young, Marilyn. "The Age of Global Power." In *Rethinking American History in a Global Age,* edited by Thomas Bender, 274–94. Berkeley: University of California Press, 2002.

Zamagni, Vera. *The Economic History of Italy, 1860–1990.* Oxford: Clarendon Press, 1993.

Zierenberg, Malte. *Berlin's Black Market: 1939–1950.* New York: Palgrave Macmillan, 2015.

INDEX

Page entries for photographs, posters, cartoons, newspapers, magazines, and maps are noted in italics. Page entries for tables are noted in bold type.

A aventura política do Brasil (Azevedo Amaral), 124

A batalha do future (Pereira), 105

"A depreciação da moeda depois da guerra," 103

A doutrina corporativa em Portugal (Leite), 104

A organização sindical-corporativa da agricultura italiana (Almeida), 113–114

Action Française, 33

Acto Colonial, 69–72

Aftalion, Albert, 103–104

Agricultural Adjustment Act, 116

AIB Ação Integralista Brasileira (Brazilian Integralist Action), 33, 168

Aliança Liberal (Liberal Alliance), 54–55

Aliança Nacional Libertadora, 167

Almeida, Francisco Tavares de, 113–114, 140

Amzalak, Moses Bensabat, 43, 70, 100

Angola, 12, 27, 36–37, 70, 146–148, 200–201, 208, 259

Aranha, Oswaldo, 51, 59, 68, 109, 117, 120, 156, 208

Arias, Gino, 113

Ataíde, Tristão de, 58, 99, 187. *See also* Lima, Alceu Amoroso

Atatürk, Mustafa Kemal, 27, 38

Austro-Hungarian Empire, 9

authoritarianism, 15–16, 19, 40, 118, 124, 240, 255, 262

Azevedo Amaral, Antônio José, 101, 111, 115, 117, 120, 123–124, 126, 128

Banco Nacional de Desenvolvimento Econômico e Social (National Bank for Economic and Social Development), 253

Barro, João de, 54

Barros Barreto, Frederico de, 174, 180

Battaglia del Grano (Battle for Wheat), 46–47

Battaglia per la Lira (Battle for the Lira), 46

Báudin, Louis, 118, 119, 127

Biagi, Bruno, 113, *114*

Bizzarri, Aldo, 113

Bolshevism, 36, 97, 115

Bonnard, Roger, 91, 124–125

Brandeis, Louis, 116–117

Brazil: 1930 Revolution in, 55–56; 1934 Constitution of, 63, 67, 74–75, 78–81, 88; 1937 Constitution of, 60–61, 74–75, 90–91, 168–169, 226, 230–231; authoritarian development in, 18–21; Brazil (map), *xiv*; corporatist structure of economy in, 10–11; Estado Novo of, 89, 165–166, 167–168; 1914–45 inflation in, **133**; 1945–75 inflation in, **252**; Juscelino Kubitschek as president of, 254; military coup of 1964, 251, 255–256, 259, 261–262; modernist movement in, 25, 33; popular support for redemocratization in, 228; population growth in, 10; population whitening strategies in, 13, 39, 120; real GDP growth of, 1928–45, **213**; real GDP growth of, 1945–75, **252**; transformations during postwar decades, 249; Vargas returns to power, 247–248. *See also*

Brazil (*continued*)
  Decree Laws, Brazilian; First Republic
  (Brazil); Great Depression (Brazil);
  NST Tribunal de Segurança Nacional
  (National Security Tribunal); Vargas,
  Getúlio
Bulhões, Otávio Gouveia de, 232–233

Cabreira, Tomás, 43
Caetano, Marcello: 1941 visit to Brazil, 1,
  205–206; defends his doctoral dissertation,
  103–104; as Minister of the Colonies,
  147–148; as secretary to record drafting
  process of 1933 Constitution, 74; as
  successor to Salazar, 2, 244, 246; takes
  exile in Rio de Janeiro after 1974 Carnation
  Revolution, 80, 246, 259; writings
  on corporatism, 71, 121–122, 138–139,
  147–148, 236
Câmara Corporativa (Corporatist Chamber),
  74, 76–78, 229, 237
Campanha do Trigo (Wheat Campaign),
  49–51, 50, 156–157
Campos, Francisco: 1937 Constitution written
  by, 74, 89; as author of Decree Law No. 869,
  165, 169, 170, 171, 183, 219; on capitalism,
  172; with Labor Minister Waldemar Falcao
  at the Ministério do Trabalho Indústria e
  Comércio (November 1937), 155; as Minister
  of Education and Public Health, 132–134;
  as Minister of Justice receiving petitions,
  179, 182, 212, 216; writings on corporatism,
  152, 181
capitalism: corporatism as third path between
  command economies and, 97; corporatism as variety of, 20; inherent greed of, 7;
  laissez-faire capitalism, 40, 135; strategies
  to fix, 111
Cárdenas, Lázaro, 9, 240, 262
Cardoso, Francisco Malta, 216
Carnation Revolution, 246, 259
Carneiro, Levi, 14
Carpenter, Luiz F.S., 69
Carta del Lavoro (Labor Charter), 15, 47,
  49, 229

Casa dos Vinte e Quatro, 122
Casa Grande e Senzala (Freyre), 206
casas do povo, 77, 105, 107, 144–145, 196–197,
  199, 216
Cassel, Gustav, 102
Catholic Church: crusades against communists, 118; first draft of 1933 Constitution
  explicitly Catholic, 76; and groups unable
  to be integrated into corporatist system
  of Portugal, 127; and integralism, 33;
  Portuguese constitution affirming
  separation of state and, 77; and social
  thought, 7; support of corporatist
  dictatorships, 97
Cavalcanti, Themístocles Brandão, 91, 123,
  124–125, 128
Centro das Indústrias do Estado de São Paulo,
  99–101
CEPAL Comisión Económica para América
  Latina y el Caribe (Economic Commission
  for Latin America and the Caribbean),
  241, 254–255, 258
CFCE Conselho Federal de Comércio
  Exterior (Federal Council of Foreign
  Trade), 151–153, 157, 159–160, 183, 208, 215,
  224, 247
Clube Três de Outubro (Third of October
  Club), 78, 91
CME Coordenação da Mobilização
  Econômica (Coordination for Economic
  Mobilization), 214–219, 222–224
codfish, 28, 43, 50, 107
coffee: collapse of price of, 54; as contra-
  band goods, 203; denunciation of coffee
  transporters, 179; economic growth in
  Brazil dependent on, 29; government
  discipline of producers of, 11; restricting
  supply of, 177; valorization program, 52
Comissão de Defesa da Economia Nacional
  (Commission for National Economic
  Defense), 213–214
Comissão do Abastecimento (Food Supply
  Commission), 214
Comissão do Itamaraty (Itamaraty
  Commission), 75, 78–79, 88

Comissão do Planejamento Econômico, 224
Comissão Parliamentar de Inquérito
 aos Elementos da Organização Corpora-
 tiva, 235
Comissão Reguladora do Tabelamento
 (Regulatory Commission on Price
 Controls), 135–137, 214, 249
Comte, Auguste, 6
Conselho da Economia Nacional (National
 Economic Council), 90, 229–230
Conselho Nacional de Política Industrial e
 Comercial, 224
Conselho Superior de Economia Nacional
 (Superior Council for the National
 Economy), 49
Consolidação das Leis do Trabalho, 229, 233
Constitution of Brazil, 1934, 63, 67, 74–75,
 78–81, 88
Constitution of Brazil, 1937: became defining
 document of Vargas's rule, 60–61, 74–75,
 90–91; codified special protections for
 economia popular, 168–169; constitutional
 changes made in 1945 to, 230–231; corporatism deleted in 1945 from, 226
Constitution of Portugal, 1911, 66, 70, 76
Constitution of Portugal, 1933, 69, 72–74,
 75–77, 106
corporatism: associated with Middle Ages,
 5–6; and authoritarian development, 18–21,
 255, 261–262; corporatist constitutions,
 15–16, 59–62, 67–75, 93; corporatist regulatory system in Portuguese colonies,
 146–150; corporatist state, 126–129; defined,
 3–5; and dismantling legal systems
 predicated on individual rights, 64–65;
 as economic system, 17–18, 21, 99–105,
 238–239; expansion of in Portugal, 196;
 and fair pricing, 18, 140–141, 172–173, 248;
 history of, 5–8; as inherently transnational
 enterprise, 97–98; and integralism, 33; as
 law, 14–16, 205, 227, 234–241; as nationalist
 and transnational experiment, 8–14; new
 models of, 240; as political alternative to
 liberalism, 8, 27, 44, 61, 64–65; and positivism, 6–7, 13–14, 51, 52; price controls

become regulatory mechanism for, 102–103,
 138–141, 260–261; reasons for rise in
 Portuguese-speaking world, 8–11, 27–28,
 42–44, 68, 98–99; and relationship to
 fascism, 8, 98–99, 112; resurgence across
 South America in 1960s-1970s, 19, 261–262;
 and Roman law, 5; as social security model,
 12, 50, 196, 216, 239; as structure of Brazil's
 economy, 10–11; as third path, 1, 4, 97; word
 corporatism deleted from 1937 Constitution of Brazil, 226. See also corporatist
 constitutions
corporatist constitutions: 1933 Constitution of
 Portugal, 69, 72–74, 75–77, 106; 1934 Constitution of Brazil, 63, 67, 74–75, 78–81, 88;
 1937 Constitution of Brazil, 60–61, 74–75,
 90–91, 168–169, 226, 230–231; Brazilian
 coup and creation of new constitution, 61;
 and content and practice of social rights
 proclaimed by dictatorships, 87; function
 of social rights in corporatist contexts, 63;
 and imperial design of corporatist model,
 65, 69; post-World War I constitutions, 63;
 used to implement new economic state,
 63. See also corporatism
Correia, António Augusto Mendes, 58
cotton, 29, 149–150
Cunha Gonçalves, Luís da, 51, 65–66, 84, 111, 147

de Saint-Simon, Henri, 6
de' Stefani, Alberto, 45
Decree Laws, Brazilian: No. 8.740, introduction of amendments to Consolidação das
 Leis do Trabalho, 233; No. 19.770, to regulate
 creation of sindicatos, 55; No. 869, to protect
 economia popular, 165, 169–173, 176–180,
 182–187, 219
Decree Laws, Portuguese: No. 17.252,
 established Campanho do Trigo
 (Wheat Campaign), 49; No. 22.981,
 created Grémio do Milho Colonial
 Português, 148; No. 27.552, outlined
 Portugal's corporatist system in colonies,
 150; No. 29.964, outlined economic
 crimes during World War II, 193, 197

Deleuze, Paul, 184

Demolins, Edmond, 41

Departamento Nacional do Café (National Coffee Department), 54

Development Plans (Planos de Fomento), 238, 242–244

Diretrizes (monthly magazine), 123

DOPS Departamento de Ordem Política e Social (Department of Political and Social Order), 174, 185, 211

Durão, António Perez, 122–123

Dutra, Eurico Gaspar, 228, 231, 246–247

Eça de Queiroz, José Maria de, 40

economia popular, *See* economy, popular

economy, popular: and 1937 Constitution, 168–169; and Decree Law No. 869, 165–166, 169, 171, 185; history of in Brazil, 166–167; NST Tribunal de Segurança Nacional (National Security Tribunal), 164–170, 173–187, 249; denunciations and trials in postwar period, 249, 251; petitions and denunciations, 179–183; police procedure in cases related to, 174; public assault against Paul Deleuze, 184; trial of grocer Augusto Pereira, 180; trial of grocer Martinho Romão da Rocha, 164, 166; trial of participants in voucher scheme related to São Paulo Tramway, Light and Power Company, 185–186; trial of retailer Herminio Bérgami, 220; trial related to Belo Horizonte coffee convênio, 178–179; trial of rice exporting firm Ries & Cia, 211–212; trial of Zozimo Venancio Avila de Lima, 219

Emergency Price Control Act of 1942, 198

"End of Laissez-Faire, The" (Keynes), 99

Escola Livre de Sociologia e Política, 113

Estado Novo (Brazil), 89, 165–166

Estado Novo (Portugal), 12–13, 104, 165–166

Ethiopia, 115, 118

Exposição do Mundo Português, 208

Faculdade de Ciências Econômicas e Administrativas, 125

Falcão, Valdemar, 67, 154, 155, 157–158, 205, 216

fascism: and comparisons to corporatism, 8, 98–99, 112; different from corporatism according to Vargas and Salazar, 210, 211; interest of Ferro in, 34, 36; Italian Fascism, 33, 34–36, 47–48; and Portugal, 118; Salgado and Brazilian fascist movement, 33. *See also* Italy; Mussolini, Benito

fazendeiro (landholding class), 39

Ferro, António: as director of Secretariado da Propaganda Nacional, 25–27; interest in Turkey under leadership of Atatürk, 38; with Lourival Fontes and Getúlio Vargas, meeting to sign a cultural agreement in Catete Palace, Rio de Janeiro, 209; and Mussolini, 34–37; for the newspaper *Diário de Notícias* aboard the *Cap Polonio*, standing with journalists representing Portuguese and international newspapers, 35; and Portuguese modernism, 25, 27; Portuguese poet and journalist, 26; spending time in Latin America to spread *iberismo*, 207; *Viagem à volta das ditaduras*, 27, 37, 70; viewed fascism as model to restore greatness to Portugal, 36; visits to Brazil, 25, 205

Fezas Vital, Domingos, 74, 77

First Republic (Brazil): coffee crisis as explanation for fall of, 54; extent to which Vargas broke decentralized and hyperfederalized structure of, 128–129; Francisco Campos' criticisms of, 133–134; laissez-faire logic more myth than reality in, 10; Oliveira Vianna critiques, 40–41; positivist influence offers model for progressive conservatism in, 6; Torres Filho's disenchantment with, 153; Vargas takes power after 1930 Revolution that ends, 2; World War I exposes weaknesses in economic and social foundation of, 29

First Republic (Portugal), 28, 36, 48, 71

First Tenente Revolt, 31–33

Fisher, Irving, 102–103

Fontoura, João Neves da, 208–209, 214, 233–234

Ford, Henry, 57

France: Catholic intellectuals in, 33, 118; corporatist ideas and modes in, 1, 118, 240; emigration from Portugal to, 243, 246; Gaston Leduc's career in, 110; price controls implemented in, 198–199; as source of artistic and intellectual inspiration, 25, 38; Vichy France, 147, 198, 199

Franco, Francisco 19, 63, 118, 209, 240

Freitas, Blanc de, 137

French, John, 229

French Revolution, 6, 8, 33

Freyre, Gilberto, 58, 206–207, 259

fueros, 6

General Theory of Employment, Interest, and Money, The (Keynes), 232, 238

Germany: economic planning under Nazi dictatorship of, 199; interested in Portuguese territories, 37; Nazi Germany, 179, 199, 214, 239; price controls implemented in, 198–199; Weimar Germany, 18, 87

Getúlio Vargas: estadista (Azevedo Amaral), 124

Gini, Corrado, 112

Goulart, João, 255

Great Depression (Brazil), 53–55, 99, 100, 101–102

Great Depression (Portugal), 53, 56–57, 101–102

Grémio dos Armazenistas de Mercearia, 194

grémios/grémios da lavoura, 12, 49–51, 142–145, 148, 196, 244

Gudin, Eugênio, 117, 118, 224, 232

guilds: during French Revolution, 5; during Middle Ages, 8; as origins of modern corporatism, 122

Hayek, Friedrich, 224

Hitler, Adolph, 79

Hume, David, 103

I fondamenti della economia corporativa (Spirito), 122

IBGE Instituto Brasileiro de Geografia e Estatística (Brazilian Institute of Geography and Statistics), 134, 170, 212, 218

industrialization: Brazil transforms with, 249; CEPAL founded to promote, 258; hardships associated with, 6, 15, 16; important role of, 253; as outcome to economic crises of 1930s and 1940s, 225; promotion of Brazilian, 100, 247–248, 251–252, 254; stimulating rapid industrialization in Portugal, 241–242, 243; ties with United States boost, 207

infant mortality rate, 234

inflation: and austerity program of Salazar, 118; in Brazil, 1914–45, 132, **133**, 170, 217, 222; in Brazil, 1945–75, 248–251, **252**; inflationary cycles following World War I, 103; in Italy, 45; price controls as Portugal's response to, 135, 193–200; during World War I, 28–30, 103; during World War II, 193, 212, 217, 222

Instituto de Cultura Italiana, 113

Instituto de Estudos Italianos, 113

Instituto Italo-Brasileiro de Alta Cultura, 113

Instituto Nacional de Carnes, 160

Instituto Nacional do Mate, 160–162

Instituto Superior de Ciências Económicas e Financeiras, 65, 113, 237

Italy: Battaglia del Grano (Battle for Wheat) in, 46–47; experiments with corporatism in, 45, 140; Fascist model in, 47, 118; Fascist Party of, 1, 4, 8, 34–35; government increases state powers over economy of, 46–47; imperial ambitions of, 37, 115, 118; writings and conferences connect corporatist experiments and theorists of Brazil, Portugal, and, 113; writings on corporatism in, 112–113. See also Mussolini, Benito

Jesus, Quirino Avelino de, 62–63, 71, 73–74, 77

Junta Central das Casas do Povo, 196–197

justo preço (just price), 16, 18, 29, 107, 131, 138, 140–143, 162–165, 178, 217–218, 248–251, 260

Kafuri, Jorge Felippe, 222–223
Keynes, John Maynard, 99, 103, 232–233, 238
Keynesianism: 98, 227, 232–233, 238–239
Kubitschek, Juscelino, 254

labor unions (*sindicatos*). See *sindicatos* (labor unions)
Lacerda, João Maria de, 126–127, 157, 159–160
Le Bon, Gustave, 41
Le siècle du corporatisme or *O século do corporativismo* (Manoilescu, trans. Azevedo Amaral), 101, 123, 141
League of Nations: on invasion of Ethiopia, 115; Portugal denied major role in, 29; publishes multinational data, 132; scrutinizes abuses in Portuguese colonies, 37
Leduc, Gaston, 110
Legality and Legitimacy (Schmitt), 79
Lei de Segurança Nacional (National Security Law), 167
Leite (Lumbrales), João Pinto da Costa, 104, 128, 139, 143
Leo XIII (pope), 7
Les fondements du droit (Lévy), 173
Les nouvelles tendances du droit constitutionnel (Mirkine-Guetzévitch), 62
Lévy, Emmanuel, 172–173
liberalism: condemnation of, 40–41; corporatism as political alternative to, 8; decay of nineteenth-century liberalism, 27; fascism as rebuke of, 35–36; as imported ideology, 7
Liga da Defesa Nacional, 113
Lima, Alceu Amoroso (Tristão de Ataíde), 58, 99, 187
Locke, John, 103
Loewenstein, Karl, 175, 178–179, 223, 231
Luís, Washington, 54
Luso-Brazilian cultural exchanges: António Ferro's visit to Brazil in promotion of, 25–26, 205; conferences and meetings in celebration of, 58; continuities following collapse of Estado Novo dictatorships, 259; dissemination of corporatism as part of, 1, 107, 112, 205–207; educational

collaborations between Portugal and Brazil as part of, 38–39; Gilberto Freyre's participation in, 207
Luso-tropicalismo, 206–207, 259

Malheiro Dias, Carlos, 105
Mangabeira, João, 78
Manoilescu, Mihail, 97, 101–102, 123–124, 126–127, 141, 255, 258
Marcondes Filho, Alexandre, 229–230
maté, 11, 51, 160–162, 212, 247
Maurras, Charles, 33
Mello Franco, Afrânio de, 75
Melo, Martinho Nobre de, 58, 74, 77, 82
Melo Cabral, Filomeno da Câmara de, 36, 70
Mercantilism, 70, 236
Ministério do Trabalho, Indústria e Comércio, or Ministry of Labor, Industry, and Commerce (Ministry of Labor), 39, 55, 99, 104, 116, 126, 139, 216, 248
Mirkine-Guetzévitch, Boris, 62–64
Monteiro, Pedro Góis, 78, 89, 231
Mozambique, 12, 29, 65, 146–149, 207
Mussolini, Benito, 9, 34–36, 37, 45, 46, 47, 112, 114–115, 118. See also Italy
"Mussolini e a Nova Italia" (Torres Filho), 153–154

"Não é economia (Alô padeiro)" (Batista and Lobo), 221
National Constitutional Assembly, 75, 79–80
National Industrial Recovery Act, 116, 117
National Recovery Administration, 116
New Deal (United States): as growing influence on Brazil, 10; guarantees farmers remunerative prices, 131; as model for mixed economy, 4, 10, 98, 111, 155; as point of reference for other nations, 11, 115–117; policies to control competition, labor costs, and prices during, 116, 131
Novas Diretrizes (monthly magazine), 123
NST Tribunal de Segurança Nacional (National Security Tribunal), 164–170, 173–187, 212, 219–223, 249

O Brasil na crise atual (Azevedo Amaral), 124
O Cruzeiro (illustrated weekly magazine),
    105–107, 249–251
O estado autoritário e a realidade nacional
    (Azevedo Amaral), 124
O Estado Novo: Democracia e corporatismo
    (Lacerda and Moura), 159
O Observador Econômico e Financeiro
    (monthly magazine), 110
O sistema corporativo (Caetano), 104
O'Donnell, Guillermo, 255
olive oil, 122, 143, 185, 196, 197
Oliveira Vianna, Francisco José de: bio-
    graphical information about, 39–40;
    engagement with foreign corporatist
    models, 80, 104, 107, 111, 113, 172; formation
    of Brazil contrasted to Anglo-Saxon
    development, 40, 58, 67, 119; as influenced
    by positivism, 32; as legal architect of
    Brazil's corporatist system within the
    Ministry of Labor, 39, 127, 139–140, 163,
    215–216; participation in drafting 1934
    Constitution of Brazil, 75, 78–80; popula-
    tion whitening strategies under, 39, 120;
    on problem of using foreign ideologies, 41;
    rejection of individual rights in political
    writings of, 62, 121, 139–140, 240, 255;
    sociological writings on Brazilian devel-
    opment, 39–41, 67, 69, 119; uses New Deal
    to defend corporatism in Brazil, 111, 116–117;
    writings on constitutions, 41, 211; writings
    on corporatism, 129, 139–140, 152, 172–173,
    211, 215–216; writings on price, 139, 154,
    172–173
Ottoman Empire, 9, 27

Pais, Sidónio, 36–37
Pereira, Pedro Theotónio, 67, 72–73, 82, 105,
    126, 143–145, 159, 163
Pétain, Philippe, 199
Pinto, Álvaro, 38
Pires Cardoso, José, 237, 239
Plano Cohen, 89–90
police: dealing with economic emergencies,
    204; Polícia de Vigilância e Defesa do
Estado/Polícia Internacional e de Defesa
    do Estado, 203; procedure in cases related
    to popular economy, 174; Salazar intensifies
    use of, 234; surveillance and censorship
    by, 117, 204; and Tribunal Militar Especial
    Político, 198; used for political purges, 7;
    used in suppressing opposition move-
    ments, 16; used to intimidate or silence
    opposition, 109. *See also* NST Tribunal de
    Segurança Nacional (National Security
    Tribunal)
political cartoons, posters, and advertise-
    ments: Advertisement printed in *O
    Cruzeiro: Revista Semanal Illustrada* (May
    1937) for the Grémio dos Armadores de
    Navios de Pesca do Bacalhau, *109*; Adver-
    tisement printed in *O Cruzeiro: Revista
    Semanal Illustrada* (May 1938) for the Junta
    Nacional do Azeite e do Grémio dos
    Exportadores de Azeites, *108*; Cover for
    O Cruzeiro: Revista Semanal Illustrada
    (May 1938) in commemoration of Portu-
    gal's May 28 revolution, *106*; in *O Cruzeiro*
    (illustrated weekly magazine), 105–107;
    Political cartoon "O açambarcador,"
    or "The hoarder," *31*; Political cartoon
    "O açambarcador dos gêneros," or "The
    hoarder of foodstuff," *32*; Political cartoon
    "Quem dá mais?" or "Who will pay more?"
    in *O Cruzeiro: Revista Semanal Illustrada*,
    251; Poster *Autoridade, ordem e justiça social*
    circulating prior to the constitutional pleb-
    iscite in Portugal, *83*; Poster *Cidadãos votai
    a nova Constituição* circulating prior to the
    constitutional plebiscite in Portugal, *86*;
    Poster *Nós queremos um Estado forte!* cir-
    culating prior to the constitutional plebi-
    scite in Portugal, *84*; Poster *Se sois pela ordem
    votai a nova Constituição* circulating prior to
    the constitutional plebiscite in Portugal,
    85; Posters on public display in Portugal
    for the Campanha Nacional do Trigo, or
    National Wheat Campaign, *50*; "Seis preços
    para os mesmos tomates," or "Six different
    prices for the same tomatoes," *250*

"Political Doctrine of Fascism, The" (Rocco), 112

Populações meridionais do Brasil I (Oliveira Vianna), 39

Populism, 2, 91, 183, 219, 229, 247, 249, 261–262,

Portugal: 1911 Constitution of, 66, 70, 76; 1933 Constitution of, 69, 72–74, 75–77, 106; Acto Colonial of, 70–72; agriculture and industry in, 12, 243; authoritarian development in, 18–21; Carnation Revolution in, 246, 259; connecting corporatist experiments and theorists of Italy, Brazil and, 113; corporatist regulatory system in colonies of, 146–150; corporatist system in, 142–150, 237–238; effects of Great Depression on, 56–57; Empire of, 6, 10, 12–13, 16, 37, 69–72, 146–150, 200–202, 207–208, 259; Estado Novo of, 12–13, 104, 165–166; fascism in, 118; First Republic, 28, 36, 48, 71; grémio and sindicato organization in, 145–146; human rights abuses in colonies of, 37; immigration to Brazil from, 14, 58, 120, 259; imperial ideology in, 6, 12–13, 14; infant mortality rate in, 234; launch of Campanha do Trigo (Wheat Campaign) in, 49–51; Map of, *xv*; Map *Portugal não é um país pequeno* (Portugal is not a small country) by Portuguese army officer Henrique Galvao, *147*; population growth in, 12; real GDP growth of, 1928–45, **195**; real GDP growth of, 1945–75, **245**; Portuguese Communist Party, 234; postwar industrialization in, 242–246; Salazarismo movement in, 27, 105. *See also* Decree Laws, Portuguese; First Republic (Portugal); Great Depression (Portugal); Salazar, António Oliveira

positivism, 6–7, 80, 122, 150

Prebisch, Raúl, 42–43, 101, 255

Prestes, Júlio, 54–55

price mechanism, 138–139

prices (cost of living), 132–135. *See also* inflation; justo preço (just price)

Princípios de direito corporativo (Cunha Gonçalves), 65

Problemas de direito corporativo (Oliveira Vianna), 129, 172–173

Queremismo, 231

Quota novanta (Ninety Quota), 46

racism: antisemitism, 33, 117, 184; fascism and, 8; "natural" hierarchy of races and cultures, 41; racial hierarchy, 13, 14, 39; racial miscegenation and assimilation, 120; racialized theories of degeneracy, 39; racist modes of analysis in 1930s, 119–121; stereotypes of Jews, 184; strategies for whitening of society, 13, 39, 120

Radical Civic Union (Unión Cívica Radical), 45

República Nova (New Republic), 36–37

Rivera, Miguel Primo de, 9, 27, 38, 70

Road to Serfdom, The (Hayek), 224

Rocco, Alfredo, 112

Rodrigues, Felix Contreiras, 141

Roosevelt, Franklin D., 116

Rosa, Noel, 54

Ross, Edward, 37

rubber, 29

Salazar, António Oliveira de: austerity program of, 118; biographical information about, 41; Catholic social thought of, 7, 76, 77, 118, 142; defense of dictatorship of, 15, 210; defining social and economic rights in opposition to civil and political rights, 92–93; dictatorship of, 2; Gilberto Freyre as fierce proponent of imperial project of, 207; on gremio system, 142, 196; as minister of the Colonies, 70, 149; as minister of finance, 48–49, 57, 70; political survival after World War II, 233–241; response to global crisis caused by Great Depression, 57; rise to power of, 48–49; work on drafting 1933 Constitution, 76. *See also*

Decree Laws, Portuguese; Estado Novo (Portugal); Portugal

Salgado, Plínio, 33, 34, 41, 89–90, 168

SALTE Plan, 247

Schilling, Otto, 158

Schmitt, Carl, 79

secret police, *See* police

Simonsen, Roberto: on advisory board of CME Coordenação da Mobilização Econômica (Coordination for Economic Mobilization), 214; career of, 99–101; clash between Eugênio Gudin and, 224, 236; economic writings of, 102–103, 119–120, 138–139; as member of Conselho de Expansão Econômica do Estado de São Paulo (São Paulo State Council for Economic Expansion), 119–120, 182

Sindicato Arrozeiro do Rio Grande do Sul, 52

Sindicato dos Lavradores do Distrito Federal, 215–216

sindicatos (labor unions): of 1930s Portugal as base of social and economic pyramid, 145–146; and Decree No. 19770, 55; Estado Novo mobilizes agricultural cooperatives and sindicatos to increase food production, 215–216; grouping together of all local grémios and sindicatos by sector, 239; and number of corporatist associations increases during war, 196; prior to 1930 Revolution and after Vargas takes power, 11–12; on question of individual firm's ability to freely choose what price to charge for goods and services in syndicalist-corporatist society, 139–140; role of grémios, sindicatos, and other regulatory organs, 148; various types of workers petition their governments to organize their own, 128; workers petition for their sindicatos to be involved in setting price freezes and controls, 248

slavery: abolition of, 6, 153, 201; Brazil as slave society, 13; legacies of, 6, 54, 66–67

soap industry, 144–145, 201

Sobral Pinto, Heráclito Fontoura, 178, 180–181

Sociedade Nacional de Agricultura (National Agricultural Society), 152–153

Sousa Costa, Artur de, 132

Spirito, Ugo, 122

SS *Cairu*, 191

Stalin, Joseph, 26, 115

"Still the Century of Corporatism?" (Schmitter), 2

sugar, 11, 29, 160

Syndicalismo, corporativismo e estado corporativo or *Syndicalisme, corporatisme et état corporatif* (Bonnard, trans. Cavalcanti), 91, 123–126

Teixeira Pinto, Luís Maria, 244

Teixeira Ribeiro, José Joaquim, 111, 122, 140

tenentes, 32, 33, 78, 125, 232

Théorie du protectionnisme et de l'échange international (Manoilescu), 101

Torres, Alberto, 6, 32

Torres Filho, Arthur Eugênio, 151–155

totalitarianism, 115, 192, 205

Tribunal Militar Especial Económico, 197–199

Tribunal Militar Especial Político, 198

Vargas, Benjamin, 231

Vargas, Getúlio: 1930 Revolution in Brazil, 55–56; 1937 Constitution of Brazil, 60–61, 74, 75, 90–91, 169; 1937 coup of, 59, 61, 168; biographical information about, 51; at Catete Palace in Rio de Janeiro addressing the public to decree the 1937 Constitution, 60; consistently affirms economic vision as third path between capitalism and Marxism, 208–209; defense of dictatorship of, 15; defining social and economic rights in opposition to civil and political rights, 92–93; dictatorship of, 2, 15; effect of "red scare" upon government of, 7; as father of the poor, 228; goes into exile, 231; industrialization under government of, 247–254, 256; labor activism under, 10–11; with Lourival Fontes and António Ferro,

Vargas, Getúlio (*continued*)
  meeting to sign a cultural agreement
    in Catete Palace, Rio de Janeiro, *209*;
    Ministry of Labor of, *55, 139, 248*;
    National Constitutional Assembly under,
    75; postwar political transformation by,
    228–229; return to presidency in 1951, *2,
    247–248*; suicide of, *254*. *See also* Brazil;
    Decree Laws, Brazilian; Estado Novo
    (Brazil); NST Tribunal de Segurança
    Nacional (National Security Tribunal)
Veiga, António Jorge da Motta, *238, 242–243*
verde-amarelismo movement, *33*
Viagem à volta das ditaduras (Ferro), *27, 37, 70*
Vichy France, *147, 198, 199*
Victor Emmanuel III, King of Italy, *35*
Volpi, Giuseppe, *45–46*

Weimar Germany, *45, 79*
wheat: becomes first sector reorganized in
    corporatist fashion in Portugal, *45, 49–51,
    143, 145, 148*; Brazilian dependency on
    imports of, *29, 52, 155–158, 162*; grémios
    in Portugal regulate production and
    commerce of, *50*; Mussolini's "Battle for
    Wheat" economic plan, *46–47, 114*;
    Portuguese dependency on imports of, *28*
Wheat Campaign (Campanha do Trigo),
    49–51, 50, 114
Whitaker, José Maria, *44*
wolframite, *191, 197*
World War I: 1917 general strike in Brazil
    during, *29–30*; Brazilian dependency on
    foreign markets during, *28*; disruptions
    to Portugal during, *28–29*; great influenza
    epidemic during, *28*; inflation and food
    scarcity in Brazil during, *30*; inflation and
    food scarcity in Portugal during, *28*;
    League of Nations and peace negotiations

following, *28–29*; political instability of
    Portugal during, *36–37*
World War II: black markets and clandestine
    markets during, *196–197, 199, 204*; Brazil
    declares war on Germany and Italy, *191,
    214*; Comissão de Defesa da Economia
    Nacional (Commission for National
    Economic Defense) used to shield
    Brazilian economy during, *213–214*;
    contraband and smuggling in Portuguese
    empire during, *201, 202–204*; efforts by
    Brazil to control inflation and food scarcity
    during, *217–218, 221–223*; Coordenação
    da Mobilização Econômica (Coordina-
    tion for Economic Mobilization) (CME)
    as economic planning body during,
    214–219, 222–224; political connections
    between Portugal and Brazil during,
    192–193, 208; Portugal's role of neutrality
    and involvement during, *191–192*; Portugal's
    Tribunal Militar Especial Económico
    responsible for enforcing market controls
    during, *197–199*; Portuguese government
    increases regulations over market life
    during, *193–194*; predictions of João
    Neves da Fontoura about Brazil's future
    during, *208–209*; price controls, anti-
    hoarding ordinances, and rationing in
    Portugal during, *194–196*; price controls
    in Portuguese colonies during, *200–201*;
    push for closer ties between Brazil and
    Portugal during, *205–206*; role of *donas
    de casa* (housewives) in Brazil during, *218*;
    roles of Portugal and Brazil in, *191–193*;
    speculators as threat to social peace in
    Portugal during, *198*; trial of Gracinda
    Ludovica during, *193, 197–198, 199–200*;
    trials over price control in Brazil during,
    211–212, 219–221, 223

Printed in the USA
CPSIA information can be obtained
at www.ICGtesting.com
JSHW081752150424
61216JS00016B/91/J

9 780691 191027